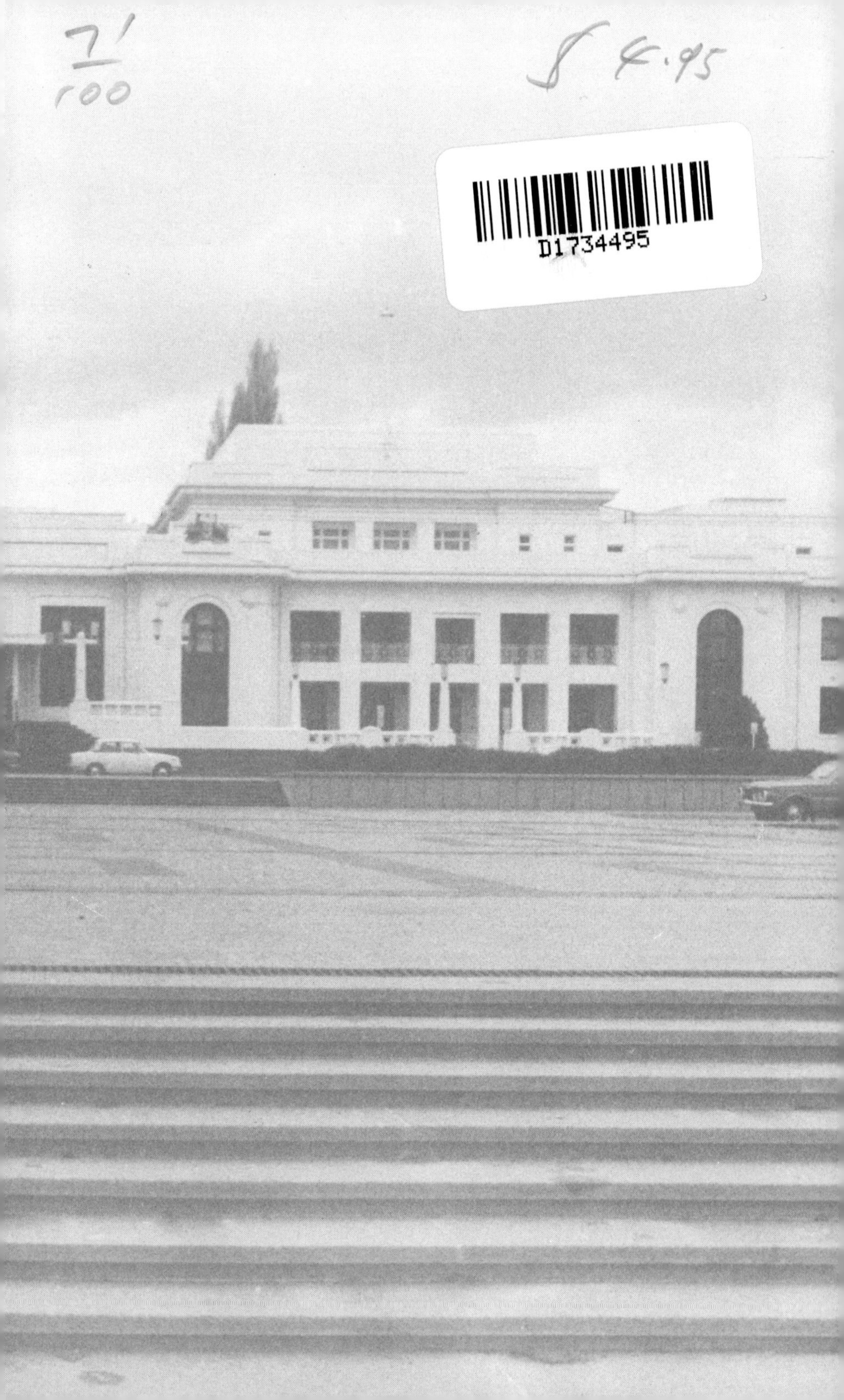

The Gorton Experiment

The
Gorton
Experiment

by
Alan Reid

Shakespeare Head Press
Sydney ━━━━━━━

First published in Australia 1971 by
Shakespeare Head Press, Sydney

Photographs Peter Hardacre

ISBN 0 85558 048 8

Set up in Australia by L. J. Duggan Pty. Ltd. and
printed in Australia by Halstead Press Pty. Ltd.
Registered at the G.P.O. Sydney for transmission
by post as a book.

"The democratic Parliamentary system is the worst in the world, except for every other that man has tried throughout his history."
—*Attributed to Sir Winston Churchill.*

Contents

CHAPTER *1*

TOWARDS midnight on Saturday, October 25, 1969, John Grey Gorton, then 58 and Prime Minister of Australia, entered the main hall of Lyneham High School in Canberra, Australia's capital. The hall was hot, crowded, and noisy. There was the smell of sweat and excitement, and the staccato rattle of voices as men talked incessantly to TV cameras and into microphones and telephones under the steamy heat of TV arc lamps. On a semi-circular board at the end of the hall attendants changed figures, like jerky puppets in a quick action miming play. The hall was temporarily the nerve centre of the general Federal election then taking place. The nation was deciding who should rule Australia federally for the ensuing three years—the Liberal-Country Party coalition which with, first, Sir Robert Menzies, then the late Harold Holt, and, more recently Gorton, as Prime Minister had governed Australia continuously since 1949, or the Australian Labor Party, led by Edward Gough Whitlam, Q.C., then 53, and titular head of a party whose turbulent faction fights had debarred it from serious consideration as an alternative government for longer than a decade.

Gorton was seen immediately he entered the hall. TV cameras switched from the impersonal excitement of the board which was recording the changing drama of the figures to register Gorton's presence. The representatives of the news media transferred their interest from the play unfolding before their eyes in the shape of the Coalition Government's declining fortunes to the principal author of those declining fortunes—the lanky, six foot one inch ex-fighter pilot with the attractively ugly, war-damaged face, who in the comparatively brief period he had occupied the Prime Ministership had provided the nation with a greater measure of unconventionality and controversy of both an official and personal nature than any Prime Minister since the six Australian states federated in 1901 to become a commonwealth.

A bastard by birth,[1] gregarious by habit, distrustful by nature, wilful by temperament, Gorton was Prime Minister by accident. The accident was the disappearance of his predecessor in the Prime Ministership, Harold Holt, when bathing on Sunday,

December 17, 1967, in heavy and treacherous seas off Cheviot Beach, on the Mornington Peninsula, in Victoria, at a time when aspirants for the office of Prime Minister, more powerful in the Liberal Party and more senior and experienced in government than Gorton, were engaged in bitter, divisive, and self-defeating quarrels.[2] But for the unusual circumstances then existing, Gorton would almost certainly have lived out his political life in the comfortable obscurity of the sixty-member Australian Senate,[3] nominally the senior chamber of the two Australian federal legislative assemblies, but inferior in power, prestige, and political importance to the larger 125-strong House of Representatives, whose majority decided what was to be the political complexion of the government of the day and from whose membership the bulk of the Ministry was drawn.

A chain smoker of cigarettes, fond of convivial drinking and the relaxing juvenility of pointless parties,[4] conspicuous for informality but inconspicuous for discretion, Gorton had for an Australian prime minister a novel approach to his office, both as an individual and officially. He was a deliberate experimenter,[5] but indulged in experiments rather than planning them, like a carefree schoolboy mixing chemicals haphazardly for the excitement of seeing what would happen. Unlike his prime ministerial fore-runners, he insisted as an individual upon his right to shift at will from being John Gorton, Prime Minister and holder of the nation's No 1 political office, to being John Gorton, orchardist,[6] free-wheeling "good bloke" and extrovert. In this latter role, he asserted that he was entitled to behave as he pleased without being subjected to criticism or comment. When told by Gorton at a parliamentary party given by Senate Government Leader, Ken Anderson, in March, 1969, that Gorton proposed leaving for an official visit to the United States on the following Saturday, Vincent Gair, leader of the Democratic Labor Party, farewelled Gorton with a trite, usually meaningless Australian adieu. "Good luck," said Gair. "Behave yourself." From this emerged a clash which epitomised the differing beliefs on how a prime minister should approach the "grey" area where a prime minister's public and private lives impinge each on the other. Gorton gave Gair a verbal blast. "John Grey Gorton will bloody well behave precisely as John Grey Gorton bloody well decides he wants to behave," Gorton said. Gair, a squat little man, a former Premier of Queensland, very tough, with an elephant-like memory, put the other side of the coin with brutal candour. "Personally, I couldn't care less if John Grey Gorton jumps into the Yarra and drowns himself," said Gair. "But John Grey Gorton happens also to be Prime Minister of

10

Australia. I do care how John Gorton conducts himself as Prime Minister of Australia."[7]

This problem—the problem of how much of a prime minister's life should be private or can be private in a parliamentary democracy where the news media operates under only legal restraints—is a recurring problem. The problem is not soluble in black and white terms. Public and private lives overlap and it is difficult to disentangle the two. Menzies, as Prime Minister, had solved the problem by giving complete priority to the demands of his high office, reducing the area of his private life to a minimum, and rigidly segregating even that reduced private area from the public arena in which he operated on an almost 24-hour a day basis. Holt, Menzies' successor, had not been quite so successful in achieving a clear cut separation of his public and private lives. Eager and affable, Holt wanted to convey to the Australian electorate that he was a prime minister who was "with it." Photographs of him indulging in the skindiving which he loved and of his decorative, mini-skirted or bikini-clad daughters-in-law appeared frequently in the Australian press, and the "grey" area, in which the Prime Minister's official and private lives coexisted, simultaneously extended. But even in this "grey" area, Holt was circumspect. He always saw that he emerged as Holt, the "with it" Prime Minister, rather than as Holt, private citizen possessed of slightly bohemian tastes and outlook.

Gorton enlarged even further this "grey area." A freewheeling extrovert, who, at the drop of a hat, would climb into swimming trunks, don a surf lifesaver's cap and pull an oar in a surf boat, swill beer or play darts at a workers' club, dance cheek-to-cheek all night with the prettiest girl in the room, Gorton liked to project himself as the prototype of the typical Australian, egalitarian, fond of grog and a party, blunt sometimes to the point of rudeness but goodnaturedly so, liking to loll round a swimming pool in swimming trunks, or appear at the weekend in the national summer dress of shorts and a tail-displaying shirt, informal and "one of the boys." But Gorton resented paying the political price that went with such a projection. Where, more realistic than Gorton, Holt recognised that in projecting his image of the "with it" Prime Minister he was extending the area of his public life, and was prepared to make the necessarily restricting adjustments to make his situation politically viable, Gorton cultivated the "freewheeling" image, believing it to be electorally advantageous, but sought to evade the inevitable consequences by claiming the right to nominate arbitrarily when he was functioning as John Gorton, Prime Minister, and when he was functioning as John Gorton, orchardist and private citizen. His view that how he behaved as John Gorton, private citizen, was no concern of anyone else was not a view shared by all of his Liberal followers. Disagreement arose on when he was functioning as John Gorton, citizen, and when he was functioning as John Gorton, Prime Minister.

Gorton had another characteristic which distinguished him not only from his prime ministerial predecessors but from most Australian politicians. Australian politics are still very much a masculine preserve in which the rare female practitioner's sex is—mainly—deducible only from the accident of her skirts. Any interest in women other than wives is regarded as a political weakness unless the sexual adventurer conducts himself with discretion which usually he does. Gorton's wife, Bettina, Maine-born, possessor of dual Australian-United States citizenship, with a cool, withdrawn manner, attractive, clearcut features, and a studious nature—she had resumed her university studies late in life and collaborated in the work of producing an Indonesian-English dictionary—was Gorton's constant companion, and a person upon whose political advice Gorton called for guidance. But Gorton was unusual for an Australian politician in that he not only liked the company of women and liked talking to them, but was sufficiently uninhibited to parade this liking.[8] When a lone woman was present in a company of men, he gravitated towards her, whatever her age or degree of attractiveness, as though drawn irresistibly. This predilection for the company of women had already caused him public embarrassment[9] and was to some degree responsible for his government's reduced electoral popularity. It was to cause him further embarrassment in the weeks ahead, when what was claimed to be his preference for female rather than male advice was to be advanced as the reason for some of his political decisions.[10]

As well as the Gorton personal style which had given the election campaign that was culminating on that election night its uniqueness as far as Australian politics were concerned, Gorton's political approach had come under criticism and was also to receive some of the blame in the weeks ahead for the heavily reduced votes for government candidates, particularly Liberal Party candidates,[11] then being recorded, with Australia wide uniformity, on the Lyneham School Hall tallyboard.

Gorton had a concept of the power and role of a prime minister which differed from that held by the two Liberal Prime Ministers, Menzies and Holt, who had occupied the prime ministerial seat prior to Gorton's advent and during eighteen of the Liberal-CP coalition's twenty years in power. Holt, in many ways a humble

12

man, observed the conventions of the cabinet system of government as developed in Australia. He viewed himself as the chairman of a committee, the first among equals, vested with the responsibility of giving leadership but where the consensus of cabinet opinion was clearly against him the instrument and executor of the majority decision. More arrogant and probably, after seventeen unbroken years in the Prime Ministerial chair, more assured of the infallibility of his judgment, Menzies has been described as considering himself as the first among inferiors. But shrewd, sagacious, and balanced, a man who had learned from such reverses as his wartime deposition from the Prime Ministership by his own party in 1941, Menzies was not only sensitively aware of how power operated within the Australian democratic parliamentary system, but had a respect for the institutions wherein he served, such as Parliament and the Cabinet. He knew that as Prime Minister he had great power but did not possess a power monopoly and that even the power he exercised, federally, as Prime Minister was shared by Cabinet and potentially and ultimately by the rank and file of his Liberal parliamentary supporters and had to be exercised with discretion and judgment if he were to avoid party turmoil and electoral rebuffs.

Menzies and Holt also acknowledged other power points and the need to operate within the framework of restraint upon prime ministerial power which these power points provided. There was the Parliament itself. Their sense of history enabled them to recognise the Parliament's reserve, if seldom used, power to chastise, discipline, or depose a recalcitrant prime minister. They had the wariness to pay the tribute of lip service to its lofty status as the supreme legislative body and in this way keep quiescent at least the government section over which they presided. There were the six Australian states, with their Premiers operating from a base embedded firmly in the Australian Constitution. There was the Liberal Party organisation, whence the Liberal Parliamentary Party derived the routine electoral assistance which Menzies and Holt knew was essential at election time to keep the Liberal-CP coalition in office. There was the Democratic Labor Party, an invaluable electoral ally to the Liberals since it had hived off from the ALP in 1954/55 to turn from that day onwards into the ALP's most effective and hostile political antagonist. There were the commonwealth and state bureaucracies, employers' associations, the churches, the trade union movement, and a host of other groupings, as well as the Liberals' formal opposition, the ALP, then out of office in all six states as well as federally, but as its history had repeatedly demonstrated possessed of enormous resilience and capable of producing even in opposition a social atmosphere that no government, however well entrenched, could ignore without risking significant electoral reverses. Menzies and Holt were prepared to use, cooperate with, outmanoeuvre, or frustrate these power points, but, with the single exception of the ALP, the formal opposition, they did not oppose them frontally or capriciously unless the need to do so was politically imperative.

Gorton's approach was cruder but not unrealistic. He regarded only two power points as vital. One was the Liberal Parliamentary Party which had elevated him to the prime ministership. The other was the general electorate. If he maintained his position within these power points he considered he did not have to worry unduly, if at all, about any others. Of the two he viewed the general electorate as by far the more important. Provided he could extract mass support from the general electorate he could (a) preserve the Liberal Parliamentary Party as the major grouping within the Liberal-Country Party coalition, (b) secure the return of the Liberal-CP coalition government because of his hold upon the general electorate and (c) ensure the continuance of his predominance within the Liberal Parliamentary Party and his position as Prime Minister.

While he had undisputed control of these two power points, Gorton could afford to ignore the criticisms that he disregarded the parliament,[12] rejected the traditional system of cabinet government, regarded the premiers as mere irritants, antagonised the Democratic Labor Party, alienated the upper echelons of the Commonwealth Public Service, treated representations and complaints from employers' associations with casual disdain, did nothing to counter the mounting restiveness in the trade union movement, and discarded as wishful thinking the ALP's claims to be regarded as a potential alternative government. He proceeded to concentrate upon the two power points he not only regarded as vital, but in the case of the Liberal Parliamentary Party room he had already described it publicly as "the centre of government."

In seeking to control the general electorate, Gorton was both less hypocritical and—unconsciously—more cynical than either Menzies or Holt. Political leaders, even those with integrity and high morality, are often prone to identify the national interest with the moves they make to secure electoral loyalty. Menzies and Holt were no exceptions.[13] When they took steps to ingratiate themselves with the mass of voters they invariably pleaded the good of the nation. But, professionally equipped for the role of leaders in a democratic community, they fitted their manoeuvres into a philosophical framework which gave their actions at least the appearance

14

of consistency. Gorton substituted ad hoc reactions for careful planning, and, as a consequence, produced a public impression of rudderless vacillation, extraordinary in a man with Gorton's seeming firmness of mind.

Gorton's personal freewheeling and ad hoc policy approaches in his twenty-two months as Prime Minister had not impaired his supremacy in the Liberal Parliamentary Party, though they created difficulties for him, difficulties which included a public and sustained attack upon his personal and official behaviour by a former follower and Liberal, Edward St John, QC, who then held in the House of Representatives the Liberal stronghold of Warringah in the well-to-do area of Sydney's North Shore.

Gorton maintained his supremacy within the Liberal Parliamentary Party in three ways. He skilfully and progressively provided for the removal from the Parliament of potential rivals, including the then Minister for External Affairs, Paul Hasluck, who had been his major formal rival for the prime ministership after Holt's disappearance, and the then Defence Minister Allen Fairhall, an intellectually timid man, who, though he had a respectful and admiring following in both the Liberal Parliamentary Party and the Liberal organisation, dithered endlessly and ineffectively like a political Hamlet on the cliff edge of self assertion. He made bold use of the patronage and promise of patronage that his office of Prime Minister enabled him to dispense to convert to his support men who had previously had bonds of friendship with potential rivals[14] whom he could not, for one reason or another, eliminate immediately. Finally, he enlisted the services of a Liberal Parliamentary group which operated under the guise of a dining club and the quaint title of "The Mushroom Club"[15] and shrewdly converted it into a faction dedicated to his interest and the prospects of advancement.[16]

Though the degree to which they were used differed with the individual using them, employment of such techniques within a Parliamentary party was not novel. Menzies resorted to patronage and the services of a faction when he was Prime Minister in the pre-war and early war years. But removed from the prime ministership by the vote of his own Party in 1941, he benefited from adversity and his ensuing years in the political wilderness of opposition. He was a wiser, shrewder man when he was returned to office as Liberal leader in 1949 after Chifley's ALP government was defeated at the polls. He chose his political friends and allies in preference to buying them, recognising that the individuals he could buy could be bought back by higher bidders. He had learned also that when a leader creates and depends upon the support of a faction within a parliamentary party other factions form in self defence, with the result that the leader's survival then depends on his personal agility rather than upon the solid base of general party support. The older Menzies cultivated friends but did not seek to group them into a faction.

While his use of patronage to buttress his position was age old, Gorton as befitted a political product of the age of electronics, had quite an original concept of how to acquire and retain the loyalty of the mass electorate. While he adopted the traditional method of reserving what he viewed as electoral douceurs for election year and preferably the period immediately before the voters exercised their franchise, Gorton relied to a degree, unprecedented in Australian political history and virtually to the exclusion of other publicity media, upon his ability to attract votes on TV.

Probably influenced by successful, gratifying experiences in the post-Holt leadership struggle, Gorton believed that he could engage and hold the electorate's majority loyalty by an application of the low-key TV demagogery he had used skilfully as an indirect pressure to secure the vote of Liberal parliamentarians after Holt's disappearance. Gorton had then set out, deliberately, to give on the TV screens to which the drama of his bid for prime minister-ship gave him extensive access, the impression of a fairly ordinary, decent Australian, modest, egalitarian, with a sense of humor, intelligence, and the capacity to make decisions. He judged that the content, or what he said, was not important so long as he made no gross mistakes, and that it would be the impression that would count. His judgment seemed vindicated by the outcome. He convinced both the public and a decisive number of his parliamentary colleagues, who undoubtedly were influenced by the favorable reaction to the Gorton TV personality[17] that he, rather than Hasluck, Leslie Bury, then Labour Minister, or Billy Snedden, then Immigration Minister, who all competed against him in the ballot for Liberal Party leadership on Tuesday, January 9, 1968, had the qualities to make an able and electorally appealing Australian prime minister.

Gorton's belief in the efficacy of TV demagogery in the intimate and casual style he had made his hallmark was not fully tested in the campaign which had culminated in the results being posted on the tallyboard of the Lyneham School Hall on that night of October 25, 1969.

For some reason, possibly an overconfidence that made him reject the warning of TV professionals that the technique which had served him so well in the leadership struggle would not be

16

nearly so effective in the different context of an election campaign, possibly because the St John charges and the events that followed them had shaken him more than he publicly acknowledged, Gorton's TV virtuosity had failed him during the seventeen days he had formally campaigned for support from the general electorate. In front of TV cameras, he had not communicated successfully. His policy speech, which he had made to the cameras in the presence of a hand-picked Liberal audience whose reactions had been funereal, had been stilted, dreary and uninspiring, and, as a consequence, the inferior nature and the imperfectly thought-through nature of some of the policy speech contents, had acquired an importance that might in other circumstances have been lacking.[18] His subsequent TV appearances, though often stage-managed and deliberately contrived to place him in a position where he could appear as the omniscient master of all situations and subjects, had been similarly depressing. His once laconic, direct speech degenerated damagingly into long, convoluted utterances, incomprehensible and wandering.[19]

It is possible that the influences of the divergent power points within the Australian community which Gorton had either ignored or antagonised would have had their effect upon the mass general electorate whatever Gorton's TV brilliance.[20] With Gorton fumbling, obscure and rattled,[21] these influences obtruded into the election campaign to a degree that neither Gorton nor the more sycophantic of his admiring followers had anticipated. By the time Gorton arrived at the Lyneham Hall, he, or more accurately the electorally vulnerable of his parliamentary followers, had already started to pay a high price for what was unmistakably a breakdown in the Gorton experiment in a new kind of Australian politics. Though all the traditional domestic criteria—the full employment, urban affluence, booming development and obvious prosperity from which only a scattered and electorally ineffective minority was debarred—pointed towards the government of the day being returned with relative ease, the massive majority of thirty-eight in the then 124-strong House of Representatives achieved by the Holt-led Liberal-CP coalition in the 1966 general elections was eroding like wet mud down a steep hillside. It was clear that the ALP would have at least seventeen more seats in the new 125-strong House of Representatives, bringing the ALP's minimum strength to fifty-nine in the chamber whose majority would decide what was to be the political hue of the new government. Though prospects favored the government in the handful of seats—seven—which would decide the overall result, it was obvious that the votes would be close and the government could not be

17

finally assured of the size of its majority until virtually 'he last votes were in and counted.

Gorton, in common with nearly 5,000,000 of his fellow Australians, had cast his vote earlier that day. He had voted in Higgins, the conservative, largely middle-class Melbourne electorate, which he had inherited from Holt, along with the big House of Representatives' majority and the prime ministership. He had then flown back by VIP plane to await at the Lodge, official residence of the Prime Minister in Canberra, the outcome of the poll. Accompanying him throughout the day was his wife, Bettina.

The Gortons were joined at the Lodge by the Federal President of the Liberal Party, Mr J. E. ("Jock") Pagan[22] and his elegant wife, Marjorie, Mr Tony Eggleton, the highly professional and discreet press secretary who had served previous Prime Ministers Menzies and Holt and was now loyally struggling to present attractively to the Australian electorate the figure of a much less conventional occupant of Australia's highest political office, and Miss Ainsley Gotto, young, petite, and vivaciously energetic, who as secretary to former Government Whip, Mr Dudley Erwin, had participated in the involved Byzantine manoeuvring which had raised Gorton to the prime ministership, and who, now Gorton's private secretary and the arbiter on many occasions on who should get access to the Prime Minister, was shortly to be accused publicly by the same Erwin of playing the part of female Svengali to Gorton's male Trilby in the delicate exercise of cabinet making. Also present during the night were Joanna, the Gortons' daughter, who worked as a computer engineer in Canberra, and Mrs Ruth Mussen, an old family friend of the Gortons, non-political but loyal.

Shortly after 8.15, the first figures started to come in at the Lyneham High School hall, about four miles distant from the Lodge, and were repeated on the Lodge TV sets. Technicians had installed a direct telephone line from the Lodge to Mr Bede Hartcher, Federal Director of the Liberal Party and its electoral expert. Hartcher was in the Lyneham school hall, surrounded by assistants who directed his attention to facets that he might in the flurry overlook. But Gorton phoned Hartcher only a few times that night. He preferred to rely upon his own judgment and that of those who immediately surrounded him.

Gorton watched hungrily the overall trend and the count in seats which the Liberals had to win if he were to survive as Prime Minister. In the key electorates he found hope for the survival of his government but in all electorates a reduced pro-government vote and, in a dangerously high number of electorates, defeat. From one electorate only could he derive comfort. That electorate was

St John's, Warringah. At a relatively early hour, it became clear that St John, who had not only joined Gorton's critics in describing Gorton as a "larrikin"[23] Prime Minister but who both in the Parliament and on public platforms had supplied what St John considered the chapter and verse to justify the application of that damaging description, was headed for defeat. Despite the return of his government, it was the one bright spot in what for Gorton was a black night, a night that was to release long pent-up feelings within the Liberal Party, both on the parliamentary and organisational side, and to imperil his prime ministership. When he entered the Lyneham School Hall, Gorton was reasonably sure that his government had been returned but uncertain of the extent of its majority. He paused to speak with Robert Willoughby, a short, stout cigar smoking man whose voice retained the Scottish burr of his youth, a burr that years of residence in Australia had failed to eradicate. Willoughby, a former Federal Director of the Liberal Party, had been personal assistant to Sir Robert Menzies until 1951 after which he headed the Liberal Party organisational team that had helped to bring about the unbroken procession of Liberal election wins that had marked the years from 1951 until Willoughby's retirement in early 1969. Willoughby that night was functioning, with punctilious objectivity, as an analyst of the election figures for TV stations, TCN 9 in Sydney and GTV 9 in Melbourne. Willoughby approved wholeheartedly of the Liberal Party in whose creation he had participated in 1944, but, a Menzies disciple, was reputed to disapprove of Gorton and what to Willoughby were the strange bypaths into which Gorton was leading the Liberal Party.

Waving away would-be news interrogators with a breezy "You'll get your chance in a minute", Gorton leaned across Robert Baudino, Chief of the Sydney *Daily Telegraph's* Canberra Bureau, to get Willoughby's assessment of the government's prospects. Willoughby's assessment was sober, realistic, and, as events turned out, accurate.

"At a minimum you should have an overall majority of seven which would give you a floor majority of six after you've provided a speaker," Willoughby advised. "The figures from Western Australia are very early.[24] If things go your way there, your overall majority could be fifteen. But I would not count on that. The swing against the government is so uniform elsewhere that it seems unlikely Western Australia will depart from pattern."[25]

Gorton listened intently. Outwardly he was calm and unperturbed. The only sign of strain was when he dragged deeply at a cigarette, held inverted with the lighted end in the cage of his palm and enclosing fingers. Willoughby and he discussed briefly the situation in a few individual seats. Then Gorton turned to the waiting representatives of the news media.

He was quite confident his government was returned. Its majority would be between six and fourteen. No. He did not see that the government's heavy losses were in any way attributable to the manner in which he had run the government's election campaign, or to a decline in his personal popularity with the electors. They were brought about by redistribution which had weakened many previously Liberal held seats.[26] The marked decline in the government's vote in Liberal strongholds? The natural recession from the highwater mark of 1966 when the government had been given an all time record majority in the House of Representatives.

Gorton conceded that the extent of his government's losses was unexpected. Neither he nor the Liberal Party had anticipated they would be so numerous. But the vote, he claimed, was not a personal one against his leadership. He was getting a bigger vote in his own electorate of Higgins than Holt had secured in 1966 when the government's stocks were at an alltime high. The ALP's "grab bag" of glittering but irresponsible election promises may have attracted voters. The Democratic Labor Party's continuing criticism of the government's defence and foreign policies had undoubtedly damaged the government electorally. He felt no personal responsibility for the defeat in Western Australia of his External Affairs Minister, Gordon Freeth, though it had been with his blessing that Freeth had put out without prior consultation with other government leaders a statement tacitly approving Soviet Russia's accretion of strength in the Indian Ocean area, a statement which was the straw which finally broke the back of the DLP's patience with the Gorton government.

Controlled, outwardly relaxed, impeccably groomed for his appearance before the TV cameras, with the wayward lock of hair which usually drooped untidily across his forehead smoothed back, Gorton acknowledged disappointment. But, as he rightly insisted, the fundamental in the election was that the government he led had been returned to office—a fundamental which those questioning him, excited with the ALP's revelation of its resilience and powers of electoral recuperation, were overlooking. He made no reference to his regret at the loss of so many parliamentary colleagues—an oversight that did not go unnoticed by his Party critics.

When he walked out from the hot, steamy atmosphere of the crowded tallyroom into the Canberra night, cool and fresh after a recent fall of rain, Gorton probably believed that with his government back in office, even with a drastically cut-back majority, with St John, the most vocal of his Liberal parliamentary critics, defeated, and with major rivals like Paul Hasluck, and Allen Fairhall, safely disposed of, Fairhall in retirement and Hasluck in the opulent impotency of the Governor-Generalship, his leadership problems were over for the three-year life of the new parliament whose composition the electorate was then deciding.

But, as Gorton was to discover in the days immediately ahead, that election night released forces which had long been building up in the Liberal Party and which, when released, constituted a threat to his hold upon the Liberal Party leadership and the prime ministership which he held by virtue of being Liberal leader.

These forces started to build up shortly after Gorton became Prime Minister, and they, together with the Gorton policies and style which brought them into existence, were factors in producing the pattern of the changing figures in the Canberra school that on that night of October 25, 1969, reflected Australian electoral feeling.

To have any understanding of the events that helped to produce the Liberal setback and ALP revival of that election night it is necessary to turn back the clock from October 25, 1969, to the early days of Gorton's prime ministership, when Liberal confidence was high and the ALP itself had doubts about its credibility as a possible alternative government and wondered dismally if it were on an endless downhill political slide that could end only in its extinction as a viable parliamentary grouping.

NOTES

[1] Normally, I would ignore as irrelevant the circumstances of Gorton's birth, but Alan Trengrove, in a biography of Gorton, written with Gorton's full cooperation, recorded the facts until then unknown even to Gorton intimates. Trengrove suggests that the mature Gorton can be understood fully only in the light of Gorton's childhood "insecurity" which was the product of his illegitimacy—*John Grey Gorton—an informal biography* by Alan Trengrove, Cassell, 1969, p 29.

[2] For an account of Gorton's rise to the Prime Ministership see my *The Power Struggle*, Shakespeare Head Press, 1968.

[3] When after Holt's disappearance Gorton became a candidate to succeed Holt he made it clear that if he failed in his bid for Liberal Party leadership—which would automatically give him the prime ministership —he would remain in the Senate rather than persist in entering the more demanding and competitive House of Representatives.

[4] "To get together with the boys and girls and relax a bit . . . is great . . . I like a few drinks when I'm finished work. I like a party where I can sing and dance and yarn"—Gorton, interviewed by Allan Barnes, *Age*, December 14, 1968.

5 "This is an experiment in a prime minister being himself"—Gorton, describing his approach to the prime ministership, *Age*, December 14, 1968.

6 Gorton's orchard property was at Mystic Park, Victoria.

7 My authority for this version was Gair repeating the conversation immediately after the clash and others who claimed to have witnessed the clash.

8 "Yes, I even like talking to women . . . do they want me to live in an ivory tower and meet only diplomats and politicians?"—Gorton in an interview with Allan Barnes, quoted by Alan Trengrove in *John Grey Gorton—an Informal Biography*—Cassell, 1969, p 214.

9 See Chapter 10, pp 218/240.

10 See Chapter 15, pp 382/383.

11 Mr Don Maisey, MHR for Moore in Western Australia, and other Country Party parliamentarians believed they benefited electorally from the hostility of Liberal Party voters to Gorton's political style, claiming that they did better at the 1969 elections in strong Liberal areas than in strong CP areas—Personal conversations with Maisey and other CP parliamentarians after the 1969 elections.

12 It is not without significance that long before he became Prime Minister, Gorton wrote "the centre of government resides in the Party rooms" (*Age*, August 23, 1953) and that under his prime ministership Parliament went five months, from September 26, 1969 to March 3, 1970, with only one day's sitting on November 25, 1969, and that held only to fulfil constitutional requirements.

13 For example, Menzies survived the 1961 general elections with a floor majority of one in the House of Representatives, and clearly needed to improve his standing in the general electorate. Having during the election campaign criticised proposals made by then ALP leader Arthur Calwell for a Budget deficit of £100,000,000 as "wildly inflationary" Menzies then with superb opportunism budgeted for a deficit of £118,000,000. He was returned with an enlarged majority at the 1963 election.

14 Several McMahon supporters, for example, later became ardent Gorton backers.

15 Its members adopted this title because of their belief that, as back benchers, they were, like commercially produced mushrooms, "kept in the dark and fed bullshit." It is a tribute to Gorton's intelligent use of persuasion, good fellowship, and patronage that he was able to turn a group formed originally on a frankly anti-leadership basis into a bastion of support.

16 These prospects were in some cases realised.

17 The Liberals, uneasy with what they believed had been their electoral decline while Holt was Prime Minister, wanted a successor to Holt with more electoral appeal on TV than the ALP's Whitlam.

18 Gorton was in trouble throughout the campaign in trying to explain the government's promised health scheme, which was revised after he was returned to office.

19 "The AMA agrees with us, or I believe will agree with us, that its policy, and it will be its policy, to inform patients who ask what the common fee is, and what their own fee is, so that a patient will know whether he is going to be operated on, if that's what it is, on the basis of the common fee or not."—Gorton, explaining an aspect of the proposed health scheme, Adelaide, October 14, 1969.

[20] It is to be hoped so. In the writer's view, the day when general elections are decided on TV capacity alone will be a sad day for the democratic process as practised in Australia.

[21] Gorton was almost pathetic during the election campaign on the subject of what Gorton by then clearly considered Whitlam's superior staff facilities. "Mr Whitlam's large staff—which I haven't got—helps him . . . I need some research assistance; some background speech notes. . . ." (Gorton in interview with Channel 7, Melbourne, October 16, 1969). Gorton did not seem to realise that this, coming from a man who for nearly two years commanded the full resources of the Commonwealth Public Service, resources that were not available to Whitlam, was a criticism of his own capacity for organisation.

[22] Appointed NSW Agent-General in London and knighted in 1970.

[23] The Oxford English dictionary, 1961 edition gives the definition of larrikin "A (usually juvenile) street rowdy; the Australian equivalent of the 'hoodlum' or 'hooligan'." But, personally I believe that "flash, tough, irreverent, rowdy" given as synonyms by S. Encel in an article entitled "The Larrikin Leaders" (Nation, May 25, 1968) are closer to the usual Australian understanding of what constitutes "larrikinism."

[24] Western Australian time is two hours behind Eastern Australian standard time and counting of votes in WA starts that much later.

[25] As things turned, WA went disastrously against the government. The Liberals retained only one House of Representatives seat in that State— Mr R. V. Garland's Curtin—and lost three. Willoughby's forecast of a seven overall majority for the government proved accurate.

[26] There had been a redistribution of Federal electorates in 1968. As a result of the redistribution, a number of electorates disappeared and boundaries in most were altered significantly. Malcolm Mackerras, a former Liberal Party research officer and author of "The 1968 Federal Redistribution" states "The boundaries penalised Labor to a small degree."—Australian Quarterly, Vol 41, No 4, December 1969.

CHAPTER 2

FEW men have risen to become a nation's political leader in such a macabre, yet in some ways tragi-comic manner, and with less intellectual preparation, than John Grey Gorton, Australia's 19th Prime Minister.

The macabre element rose because of a meeting one morning between the previous Prime Minister, Harold Holt, and the Speaker of the House of Representatives, William (later Sir William) Aston outside the Government Whip's office in the lobby in Parliament House, Canberra, leading to the Prime Minister's office suite. Holt was carrying his heavy briefcase. He had raced up the steps of Parliament House. When the two men met, Holt's breathing was fast, audible, and shallow. Aston anxiously asked Holt, who normally was a man who not only kept himself in good physical trim but also showed the outward signs of being in good physical condition, if he was all right. Holt assured Aston that he was suffering only from breathlessness. But there was uneasiness.[1] A prominent medico, who had Liberal affiliations but who was not Holt's usual physician, was consulted. He expressed misgivings about the state of Holt's health. The chief Government Whip, Mr Dudley Erwin, heard about the incident, though the manner in which he heard remains obscure.[2] Erwin undoubtedly believed that Holt had either had or was liable to have a heart attack;[3] Aston that his leader's health was suspect.

From this small beginning flowed events which were to help lift Gorton to the prime ministership. Both Aston and Erwin considered Holt their friend. But the two men were politicians. In politics, a dead man's shoes are not a poignant reminder of a loved one who has passed on. They are receptacles that have to be filled.[4] For the next six months, the two men, anticipating at any moment Holt's death or a breakdown in health that would force him into premature retirement, hugged what they believed to be a vital secret to their respective bosoms, and in Erwin's case set actively about the task of providing a successor. Erwin made Miss Ainsley Gotto, then 22 and his secretary, privy to his suspicions about the state of Holt's health. When Holt disappeared while bathing in dangerous and rough seas off Cheviot Beach on Victoria's

24

Mornington Peninsula on Sunday, December 17, 1967, a potential successor—Gorton—had already been flattered into a frame of mind that made him receptive to urgings that he should compete for the prime ministership, and the skeleton organisation which was to back his bid was already in existence. That skeleton organisation was set in motion and started to acquire flesh and muscle when on Monday, December 18, 1967, some twenty-four hours after Holt had disappeared, Erwin, Malcolm Fraser, young but ambitious and then Federal Army Minister, and Malcolm Scott, the Government Whip in the Senate, all of whom could see advantages for the Liberal Party or themselves in Gorton's elevation, met in the Government Whip's room and pledged themselves to work to secure the prime ministership for Gorton.

The tragi-comic element arose out of the way Gorton was cajoled and flattered into viewing himself as prime ministerial material. Both Aston and Erwin knew that there was discontent within the Liberal Party with the quality of Holt's leadership. Holt was going through one of those periods, which all politicians go through, when nothing was going right for him. He had done badly as leader at the 1967 Senate elections, been mauled badly, not so much over ministerial misuse of VIP aircraft but for telling the Parliament on the basis of incorrect information supplied to him that lists of those carried on the flights were not preserved,[5] and had allowed opposition leader Gough Whitlam to secure an ascendancy over him in parliamentary debate. Mysterious meetings of Liberal parliamentarians, meetings at which the participants discussed what they considered the defects in Holt's leadership, were being held secretly in Melbourne and Sydney. Shrewder in some ways than Erwin and with no commitment, either actual or psychological to Gorton, or at that stage to any other of the potential aspirants for the prime ministership, Aston had no desire to get involved in any antiHolt putsch or premature succession struggle. He stayed aloof. Erwin, less inhibited and already mentally committed to Gorton, made cautious soundings with Miss Gotto's assistance within the Party,[6] and found that Gorton had admirers, particularly among the younger, more impatient Liberal parliamentarians, and had been put forward, tentatively, as a leader alternative to Holt at the Sydney and Melbourne meetings. Erwin decided on a campaign designed to condition Gorton to the thought of himself as a potential prime minister.

At this stage, Gorton was a frequent visitor to the Whip's room, where Erwin, assisted by Miss Gotto, held nightly court when the Parliament was sitting. The Senate usually concluded its deliberations earlier than the House of Representatives. While Erwin and

Miss Gotto waited for the House of Representatives to get up, often in the early hours of the morning, there was ample opportunity for Erwin and Miss Gotto in concert to persuade Gorton over a convivial drink that he had the qualities and the following in the party to become Prime Minister if "anything should ever happen to Harold." For Gorton, a senator,[7] Government Senate leader by flux of time rather than outstanding quality, and administratively virtually untested except in the near sinecures of the Navy and Works portfolios and in Education where he had been under the watchful eye first of Menzies and from 1966 of Holt, it was Walter Mitty daydreaming. For Erwin and Miss Gotto, keeping to themselves knowledge of Holt's presumed heart attack, it was deadly earnest and for Erwin potentially dangerous. After a while, Erwin left the persuading almost exclusively to Miss Gotto. "I found that he'd listen to Ainsley more than he would to me or to any other man I enlisted to help in the task of persuasion," Erwin said later. "He listens to women more readily than to men."[8]

Gorton months afterwards claimed he was genuinely unaware that the talks in which he was engaging with Erwin and Miss Gotto were not the hypothetical discussions in which politicians and those on the periphery of politics, like pressmen and private secretaries engaged endlessly, but were, particularly as Erwin saw them, very meaningful. When on Friday, December 22, Federal parliamentarians assembled at the Southern Cross Hotel in Melbourne after the Holt Memorial service at St Paul's, Les Irwin, an outspoken ex-banker who served with the Australian Flying Corps in World War I and who represented the outlying Sydney electorate of Mitchell, had a few observations to make about the "treachery" of those who had organised the Sydney and Melbourne meetings to complain about Holt's leadership in secrecy instead of in the Party room. Irwin had a voice that boomed like the Cheviot Beach surf in which Holt had been lost and felt it was no occasion to whisper. Few in the noisy, crowded room were left unaware of his feelings. An account of Irwin's outburst was apparently conveyed to Gorton at a later stage and after he became Prime Minister. Gorton asked Irwin to see him. The two men met in the Prime Minister's office in Parliament House, Canberra. Gorton assured Irwin, on his word of honour, that he had not intrigued or sought to undermine Holt in any way while Holt was leader. "I'm relieved to hear that," commented the irrepressible Irwin. The two men shook hands.[9]

Still later, when, after he had quarrelled with Gorton, Erwin disclosed that Gorton was being groomed as a future prime minister for months before Holt's death,[10] Gorton took the unusual

26

step of issuing a prime ministerial statement denying that this was so. With a passion rare in a prime minister's formal statement Gorton said "I cannot understand Mr Erwin's remarks. . . . I was never approached by anyone before Mr Holt's death with any suggestion that I should work against him or stand against him. If I had been so approached, or had known of others working against Mr Holt, I should at once have told him of it. . . . I feel the implication to the contrary in the reports of Mr Erwin's statement more deeply than any allegations that have ever been made against me. They are completely contrary to the code by which I try to live."[11] The contradictory statements do not necessarily make one of the men a liar. They were probably seeing the same events from different angles. When Erwin was persuading Gorton he was prime ministerial material, Gorton was listening to what one day might be: Erwin on the other hand was thinking in terms of what he and others believed and were trying to ensure would be.

In a national sense, Gorton rose to become Prime Minister in sad circumstances. The disappearance of the likeable, good-natured Holt into the sea, which as a skindiver he had made his playground, shocked the nation. But in a narrow personal sense Gorton could not have commenced his prime ministerial career in a more auspicious manner. The drama of Holt's vanishing into the sea that he loved heightened public interest in the struggle between the surviving Liberal chieftains for the succession to his prime ministerial eminence.

Gorton had been a minor figure until then handling relatively unimportant matters in the Senate, itself relatively unimportant compared with the House of Representatives. But from Sunday, December 17, 1967, when Holt entered the water at Cheviot Beach never to reappear, until Tuesday, January 9, 1968, when the 81-strong Liberal Parliamentary Party met to elect its new leader and Australia's 19th Prime Minister, Gorton was seldom out of the public spotlight. The public reacted sympathetically.

Gorton was something new, fresh. He had an establishment background. He was educated at Geelong Grammar, Australia's closest approach to England's Eton and more expensive, and had gained his Master of Arts degree at Oxford, where he majored in history, economics and political science. He was a member of the exclusive Melbourne Club, by legend stronghold of wealth and political conservatism. Yet his accent continued to be authentically Australian—except when he said Australia which he turned, British fashion, into Orstralia—and he had no pretensions, seeming to mix more easily with the rank and file of Australians than with

27

those who aped with varying degrees of success their upper class British cousins. After Menzies, who loved royalty with an almost childish reverence and described himself as a "Queen's man" and "British to the bootheels", and Holt, unselfconsciously Australian and free from any taint of xenophobia, Gorton aggressively nationalistic—"Me—I'm Australian to the bootheels" he said obliquely mocking Menzies—had the attraction of the unusual. There was nothing synthetic about Gorton's intense nationalism. It was an Australianism that transcended state boundaries. Though he was to reveal later puzzlement in how to translate his emotional love of country into positive action, he had a vision, quite inspiring if rather confused, of an Australia, developed and wealthy, with poverty eliminated, the economic consequences of prolonged sickness removed from its people, and Australian resources preserved for utilisation by Australians rather than overseas investors. It was a vision attractive to Australians and, adding to the authenticity of his nationalism, was a war record as impressive and in some ways as romantic as that of the assassinated President John Kennedy who like Gorton survived enemy action in the war against Japan.

The war had cost Gorton his good looks. His youthful handsomeness had disintegrated in a collision with the instrument panel of his bullet damaged Hurricane, crashlanded after a dogfight with Japanese over Singapore in 1942. His rebuilt features had an ugly, homely strength, touched sometimes by melancholy. Still swathed in bandages, he spent over 24 hours in the Java Sea when the ship on which he was being evacuated from Singapore was torpedoed. Rescued by the Australian corvette *Ballarat*—with whose crew in later years he was to march in ceremonies honoring Australia's dead of World War II—he got back to Australia to undergo hospital treatment, plastic surgery on his face, service at Darwin and New Guinea, and have another crash, this time on lonely Melville Island north of Darwin where he lived like a primitive on fish and turtle eggs for five days before being returned to Darwin by lugger.

Gorton had his defects. What views flowed from his political philosophy, if he had thought one out, were uncertain. Outside the Senate his speeches had been largely ignored because of his relative unimportance. Inside the Senate since becoming a minister in 1958, he had mainly, as was his duty, read speeches supplied to him by ministers in the House of Representatives. Some believed that he was a "hawk" on the conflict in Vietnam where Australia had 8,000 troops fighting alongside South Vietnamese and United States forces; others that he was a "dove". Both schools of thought could produce quotations from his speeches to justify their beliefs. He had even before he entered politics advocated removing "from the minds of men the fear of poverty as a result of illness, accident or old age" but had not been prominent in advocating such reforms in the parliament.[12] On one subject, he was vocal. It was Commonwealth-State relationships. This issue was to create difficulties for him within his own party when he became Prime Minister.

Preservation of state rights was part of the Liberal Party mystique. When the six Australian states federated in 1901 to form the Commonwealth of Australia, only specific powers were vested in the Commonwealth. In all other matters the six states were sovereign,[13] with the High Court, set up under the Constitution, the interpreter of the Constitution and the body that decided disputes arising out of its application. Commonwealth powers were extended formally in the years between 1901 and 1969 only sparingly. Of twenty-six proposals to amend the Constitution, only five were agreed to by the voters whose will was expressed, as required by the Constitution, at referenda. But the process of time and particularly the war years, 1939/45, saw commonwealth accretion of de facto power. During the war years, the commonwealth imposed uniform taxation, reducing the states to a state of financial dependence on the commonwealth, and in the post-war period the commonwealth's right to priority of collection in the all important field of income tax survived state challenge in the High Court. In the immediate postwar period and until 1949, the Chifley ALP government continued the process of strengthening commonwealth powers at the expense of the states.

When he formed the Liberal Party in 1944 out of a number of fragmented conservative groups who shared the common features of being opposed to socialism and the Chifley ALP government of the day, Menzies listed the retention of federalism, or opposition to centralisation of power in the commonwealth, high among the party's objectives. Experience and a series of High Court judgments, particularly those which defeated attempts by the Chifley ALP government in the 1946/49 period to nationalise the Australian banking system and internal airline services, convinced Liberals that the maintenance of state rights was essential to block any further socialising acts by a future ALP government.

Gorton's views on Commonwealth-State relationships were, by Liberal standards, heretical. While Menzies had been elected in 1949 on a pledge of restoring state sovereignty, neither he nor later Holt had acted to restore the states' taxing rights, and without these rights the states continued in financial subservience to the commonwealth. But Menzies and Holt had the wisdom to pay lipservice to the principle of state rights while continuing to extend commonwealth power. Gorton, however, was more forthright. His Commonwealth-State relations sentiments commended themselves to the centralist ALP; they aroused the suspicion of Liberal supporters. Gorton disavowed the label of "centralist" but placed on record centralist sentiments. On March 26, 1953, he told the Senate "Australia cannot continue as it is at the present . . . it may be necessary for constitutional powers to be reversed so that instead of residual sovereignty residing in the states and only certain powers in the Commonwealth, certain powers might be guaranteed to the states and the residual powers might remain with the Commonwealth."[14]

While Gorton's attitudes, in some ways more appropriate to an ALP man of the depression thirties[15] than to a Liberal of the affluent sixties, resulted in some Liberals keeping a question mark after his name, Gorton by and large entered upon the prime ministership with clearly demonstrated support and sympathy from the public and from his party followers. But within a matter of weeks other question marks were to be placed after his name by men influential in the Australian power structure, and when these question marks turned into substantial doubts, they were to provide in part an explanation for the swing against the government in October, 1969, then nearly two years away.

Gorton's intellectual preparation for his assumption of his prime ministerial role had been brief. Admittedly there had been his nebulous dialogues extending over some months with Erwin and Miss Gotto on the subject of his suitability as a future prime minister. But, on the evidence of his later statements, these were not preparation, but daydreams. He did not know, as Erwin and Miss Gotto believed they knew, that Holt's days as Prime Minister were numbered. Only after Holt's disappearance and in the hectic emotion-charged twenty-two days that followed was Gorton aware that his prospects of becoming prime minister were real, and improving, and during that period he was too busy seeking the support from his 80 Liberal parliamentary colleagues that enabled him to beat his nearest rival, Paul Hasluck, by 43 votes to 38, to weigh deeply what should be his attitude, as Prime Minister, to the problems that would confront him.

When he formally took over the prime ministership on January 10, 1969, the sense of urgency died. Part of his attraction for the Liberal parliamentarians who had voted for him was their belief in his ruthlessness, energy and drive. But when he assumed the prime ministership, it was as though he had reached a goal not merely passed a milestone beyond which the effort had to be intensified. He gave the impression that he had little realisation of the amount of work involved in being Prime Minister. The cabinet ante-room where ministers assemble for a quiet drink got more use than the cabinet room. Though he was to sack two ministers—Air Minister Peter Howson and Navy Minister Don Chipp—he deferred fixing his Cabinet for six weeks on the plausible ground that before he was finally confirmed in the Prime Ministership he needed to win the by-election for Holt's old seat of Higgins, so firmly proLiberal that a chimpanzee would have been voted in provided he carried a label marked "Liberal Party" around his neck. Within a fortnight of becoming Prime Minister Gorton had made official visits to Melbourne, Brisbane, and Sydney and awarded himself a five-day vacation from the duties of his office.[16] During this period his exultant approach to the prime ministership was reminiscent of the Medici Pope, Leo X, to whom historians of the Renaissance attribute the comment "Since God has given us the Papacy, let us enjoy it."[17]

Gorton's lack of intellectual preparation for his new, exalted role soon showed in what was for the Liberals, a more serious fashion. Menzies and Holt had justified Australian participation in the Vietnam conflict by insisting that Australia had a stake more vital in a successful outcome of the Vietnam struggle than the United States. Their theme was that the United States presence and its resistance to Communist aggression in Asia was giving non-Communist Asian countries with whose future that of Australia was inextricably bound, the opportunity to establish themselves as viable political units. Australia should support the US in Vietnam. The knowledge that it had allies in the region encouraged the US to maintain an interest in Asia. Menzies and Holt rejected the ALP charge that Australian participation in the Vietnam conflict was the price Australia paid for ANZUS, the Australian-US defence alliance. Australia's participation was because "the takeover of South Vietnam would be a direct military threat to Australia and all the countries of South and South-East Asia."[18] Gorton had endorsed this Menzies-Holt assessment. On March 23, 1966, Gorton told the Senate "In South Vietnam aggression is taking place and being resisted . . . this is the basic fact on which Australia's survival ultimately depends."[19] It was from this policy base that the Liberals, under Holt, had fought the 1966 elections and won a record House of Representatives majority for the Liberal-C.P. coalition.

On February 2, 1968, Gorton destroyed this base with a few ill-chosen words at a press briefing to the Federal Parliamentary

Press Gallery. The Tet offensive by the Vietcong in Vietnam had, though militarily ineffective, captured world headlines, shaken US confidence, and intensified President Johnson's domestic difficulties with US antiVietnam critics. Gorton was asked, "In view of the latest developments (the Tet offensive), is there any suggestion Australia will increase its commitment?" Gorton replied, "Australia won't increase its commitment."[20] Asked "Have we been asked to?" Gorton said, "No." To the query "Is that a permanent statement?" Gorton replied, "As far as I am concerned it is."[21]

Menzies and Holt in the past had resisted US hints for a more sizeable enlargement of the Australian commitment in Vietnam than they were prepared to make. But they did so on the basis that Australia, geographically large but with a population of only 12,000,000, could not make heavier contributions without impairing seriously its accelerating development which, longterm, would benefit the US more than greater present assistance in Vietnam because it would enable Australia to take a larger share of responsibility for the security of its region than it was now capable of doing. But at no stage did they close the door completely and finally on the possibility of Australia as time progressed possibly extending its Vietnam commitment. In the framework of this approach, they had limited the Australian involvement without impairing their theme that the outcome of the Vietnam conflict was vital to Australia's security. Gorton's statement that Australia had reached the limit of its commitment for all time[22] made the Menzies-Holt thesis untenable and gave respectability to the ALP charge that there was no moral basis for Australia's presence in Vietnam and that the Australian presence in that wartorn country was merely an insurance cover, cynically taken out, to protect the future of the Australian-US alliance.

Gorton's statement also cast doubts on the government's credibility, already shaken by the VIP affair, as regards past statements on External Affairs-Defence issues, and caused uneasiness in the DLP, which, closer to the ALP than to the Liberal-CP coalition on domestic social policies, nevertheless had functioned as the coalition's faithful and effective electoral ally since 1955 because the DLP preferred the Coalition's foreign and defence policies to the ALP's.

At the end of six months Gorton was, if public opinion polls are to be accepted, tightening his hold upon the power point of the general electorate. A Gallup poll showed him holding fifty-three percent of the vote, three percent more than Holt received when he won his 1966 alltime record majority in the House of Representatives and ten percent better than the government's Senate vote in 1967.[23] Other political indicators pointed to the broad accuracy of the Gallup Poll. A popular central government, as Australian political history has shown, often helps state administrations of the same political hue to get elected.[24] On February 24, 1968, the day on which Gorton secured formal entry to the House of Representatives by winning the Higgins by-election, the Liberal-CP coalition, led by Liberal Mr Rob Askin, was returned in NSW with an enhanced majority. On March 23, 1968, the Liberal-CP coalition, led by Liberal David Brand, was voted back into office in Western Australia, though in this case with a majority reduced by two. On April 17, 1968, a Liberal government headed by Mr Steele Hall replaced the former ALP government in SA, thereby eliminating the last surviving ALP government on the Australian mainland and leaving the island of Tasmania with the last of the once numerous ALP administrations. But despite these successes so heartening for the Liberals, uneasiness had started to develop, Federally, within the Liberal Parliamentary Party, within the Country Parliamentary Party, and within the higher echelons of the Commonwealth Public Service.

The Liberal Parliamentary Party uneasiness arose out of the casual way in which Gorton made "off-the-cuff" statements, such as his Vietnam commitment one of February 27, 1968, the off-hand manner in which Gorton treated the Parliament and the pedestrian nature of his infrequent performances in the House of Representatives. Some Liberals were also disturbed by the development of a "cocktail cabinet"[24a] which over drinks in the Prime Minister's office or the Cabinet ante-room appeared to exercise an influence that exceeded that of the eleven senior ministers who, with the Prime Minister, comprised the formal cabinet. By June 30, 1968, Gorton had made only three speeches in the House of Representatives. One was on the subject of a Vietcong woman prisoner captured by Australian forces in Vietnam and allegedly subjected to torture by having water poured down her throat. The next was on the report of a second inquiry into a collision on February 10, 1964 between the aircraft carrier HMAS *Melbourne* and the destroyer HMAS *Voyager,* a collision in which the *Voyager* was sunk with the loss of eighty-two lives. The third was a report of his visit to the United States.

Gorton's speech on the torturing of the captured woman Vietcong was a disturbing one. Admittedly he was in a difficult position. After claiming that there was "not a scintilla of evidence" to support the charge, his new Army Minister, Phil Lynch, had conceded, after investigation, that the allegation was "substantially true".[25] As a prime minister, Gorton could be expected to deal

33

with the principle involved, and, in the interests of Australian servicemen who fell into Vietcong hands, if for no loftier reason, to insist upon observance of the requirements of the Geneva Convention that all captured enemy personnel be treated in a civilised manner. He was in a position where with complete justification he could defend the Australian Army. The Army had enabled him to do so by acting with complete propriety. On discovering the interrogation methods used by this particular serviceman and long before the matter came to public attention the Army had promptly recognised the serviceman's lack of capacity for self control and had removed him to a post that would keep him from future contact with prisoners. Gorton could have excused without justifying by pointing out that the Australian interrogator was only human and that he had recently seen in the area where the woman was captured eighteen of his comrades killed and twenty-one wounded. But instead, though admitting that the interrogator had "gone beyond the bounds of the Geneva Convention", Gorton took the line that it was only a little torture and not a particularly effective torture at that. "If the worst that happened to Australian soldiers was that somebody . . . poured a cup of water down their throats then we would not have very much to complain of", Gorton said. "The spirit of the Geneva Convention had been transgressed but it has not been transgressed . . . to the point where any real torture has been applied."[26] The speech had emotional appeal. But it was not a prime minister's speech in that it displayed inability to grasp the larger issues that were involved.

His *Voyager* speech was a competent debating effort and his report on his conversations with President Johnson in Washington in May so routine that he himself described the conclusions contained in the report as "modest".[27] Whitlam commented with some justification that they were not only modest but "exceptionally vague."[28]

But while there was Liberal uneasiness about the quality of Gorton's parliamentary prowess, there was no undue perturbation for a good reason. Whitlam, as opposition leader, had unmistakably established what might have been only a temporary but was certainly a clear parliamentary ascendancy over Holt in the weeks prior to Holt's disappearance. This ascendancy was alarming the Liberals, and benefiting Whitlam and the ALP politically. But in April, less than two months after the opening of the 1968 Parliament in which Gorton made his debut as Prime Minister, Whitlam resigned his leadership of the ALP's parliamentary wing after a frustrating and humiliating clash with the ALP Federal Executive,[29] the ALP's rather dictatorial supreme governing body between the biennial meetings of the ALP Federal Conference, the ALP's supreme policy making body. Though Whitlam re-contested the leadership and regained it by a 38/32 vote when challenged for the post by Dr J. F. Cairns, Whitlam's confidence was undoubtedly shaken. He was unable to establish the parliamentary superiority over Gorton that he had enjoyed over Holt. The "cocktail cabinet" with its potential threat to Liberal unity was more worrying to the Liberals, particularly senior Liberals, than Gorton's disappointing parliamentary performances.

The "cocktail cabinet" was more like a floating crap game than a coherent political grouping. Its composition kept changing. Gorton gave the appearance of preferring to suborn his rivals' supporters than of being preoccupied with strengthening the allegiance of his followers as a group. The favourite of today was the rejected of tomorrow. But initially the "cocktail cabinet" consisted understandably of those who had supported him most firmly in his struggle for the Prime Ministership.

When he had reconstructed his Ministry on February 26, 1968, Gorton had rewarded supporters, including individuals who had rebelled against Menzies and Holt, but otherwise had made no sweeping changes. He had eliminated two ministers, one an old enemy. When forming his Cabinet, he had also revealed a capacity for vacillation, unexpected in a man who was later and on quite numerous occasions to manifest courage, almost blind courage, and a wilful, impatient obstinacy.[30]

From the moment Gorton took over the prime ministership, it was inevitable that the then Air Minister Peter Howson would be disposed of at the first available opportunity. A scar cheeked, Cambridge educated, ex-Fleet Air Arm pilot, shot down over Malta when his Albacore and four Hurricanes attacked more than seventy German fighters, Howson, then 47, was a Holt intimate who had clashed with Gorton over the VIP issue when Holt, with greater personal loyalty than political judgment, had refused to accept Howson's proffered resignation at a time when acceptance would have got Holt out of serious political embarrassment and trouble. There had been previous trouble between Gorton, archetype of the rough, tough, and aggressively nonconforming Australian, and Howson, with his clipped English accent and punctilious regard for the proper forms. Both were Victorians, and several times Howson was credited with having thwarted Gorton moves within the Victorian State Liberal organisation. Feelings ran deep. When, just before announcing his cabinet, Gorton called Howson into the offices used by the Prime Minister in Treasury

Gardens, Melbourne, to tell Howson that he was dispensing with his services as a minister, Howson, small, neat, and precise, made no attempt to conceal his antipathy to Gorton but tried to conclude the interview on a civilised note. "Good luck to you in your new post, John," said Howson, and put out his hand. Gorton rejected the offered hand shake.[31]

Another inevitable ministerial casualty from February 1, 1968, when a later Royal Commission into the *Melbourne-Voyager* collision submitted a report which differed significantly from the report of the first inquiry into the tragic happening, was Don Chipp, then 43, an athletic, dark-visaged ex-industrial management consultant, who had been Minister for the Navy since 1966. There was no logic to this. Chipp had been a backbencher when the collision occurred in 1964. The second inquiry had been forced upon the government, rather than upon Chipp, by the tenacity of Victorian John Jess, then 41, a loose-limbed, pleasant-faced man, with a biting tongue, a sense of justice and considerable independence of mind and an attractive disregard for his prospects of political advancement or even parliamentary survival when he felt that a principle was involved. Jess was supported in his demand for a second *Voyager* inquiry by St John, a political millstone around anyone's neck in Gorton's view. As befitted a man who was later to tell President Johnson that while President Abraham Lincoln in the American Civil War had acted as he did "because the end was an end that was good", he, Gorton, was "a convinced Confederate" and would have supported the Confederacy,[32] Gorton was not one to allow logic to prevail against romanticism or prejudice. Gorton had been Minister for the Navy until December 18, 1963. With the *Melbourne-Voyager* collision taking place on the night of February 10, 1964, he had escaped being involved in the political backwash from the tragedy by not much more than a month. He was deeply antagonistic to aspects of the first royal commission. On September 23, 1964, he bitterly attacked the conduct of Mr J. Smyth, QC, who had assisted the Royal Commissioner (Sir John Spicer) at the first inquiry. "No service has been so damaged by a partial presentation of the facts, in some cases by completely unsubstantiated presentations of the facts, as was the naval service, which was improperly damaged by Mr Smyth, QC, during the course of the commission's inquiry . . . that is the only thing in this whole affair for which I accept blame," Gorton told the Senate.[33] If Gorton, not Holt, had been Prime Minister at the time Jess demanded the second inquiry, there would have been no inquiry.[34] Gorton had the emotional desire for a scapegoat, and had one available in Chipp, who suffered the added disadvantage that during the leadership struggle he had been aligned with Snedden, then a close friend of Chipp, whose vote could in certain circumstances have split the proGorton vote sufficiently to allow Hasluck to rise to the top. Chipp went out of the Ministry with Howson.[35]

Gorton was credited with desiring to rid himself also of Holt's Minister for Shipping and Transport, Gordon Freeth. A large, moustached, placid man who had been an amateur heavyweight boxer and oarsman in his youth and, like Gorton, a wartime pilot, Freeth, then 54, had campaigned during the post-Holt leadership struggle for Hasluck, a fellow West Australian whom Freeth admired, openly, enthusiastically and without envy. Gorton was not then in a position to move against Hasluck. He moved instead against Freeth, Hasluck's friend. But Gorton still had to have regard to party sensitivities. To sack Freeth so soon after he had been identified openly as a supporter of Hasluck, who had been Gorton's main opponent, would have seemed a little raw, particularly after Gorton had announced following his election "We are starting a new government . . . the book should be ruled off, and a new start made."[36] As an execution was ruled out, it was decided to lure Freeth into suicide. Gorton supporters prevailed upon Gorton to demote Freeth who had been Minister for Shipping and Transport under Holt to the comparatively lowly Air portfolio, and though there were two gaps in the cabinet ranks—one caused by Holt's disappearance and the other by the retirement on the score of age of former Supply Minister Senator Denham Henty—to promote others over Freeth's head, though Freeth as No 13 in Ministerial ranking was the next in line for advancement. The Gorton supporters believed that exasperation with such obvious and public humiliation would cause Freeth, mild but stubborn, to tell Gorton precisely what he could do with his offer of the Air portfolio. The plan might have succeeded but Freeth was forewarned. His friends pleaded successfully that he should not cut his own political throat. Freeth agreed not to. When Gorton phoned Freeth with what had been considered the demeaning and unacceptable offer of the Air portfolio he was greeted not with rejection but with a cool, "Thanks, John."[37]

Into Cabinet over Freeth's head went Senator Ken Anderson, as Supply Minister, and Malcolm Fraser, as Minister for Education and Science. Anderson, a wartime p.o.w. in Japanese hands, affable and cautious, had followed a strictly neutral line in the leadership struggle. How he had voted was anyone's guess. But the Senate needed a leader now that Gorton had moved to the House of Representatives. Anderson was the most obvious choice and as

37

Leader of the Senate needed to be in the Cabinet. Fraser, however, was a different proposition.

Six feet three inches tall, sprig of a wealthy woolgrowing family from Victoria's social and conservative Western districts, Oxford educated, Fraser's ambition was loftier than his height. With chief Government Whip, Erwin, pubkeeper, and Senate Whip, Malcolm Scott, ex-pearler turned pastoralist, Fraser had been a major and tireless organiser for Gorton in the leadership struggle. He had influenced votes in Gorton's favor, and wherever there was a string to be pulled he pulled it. Now Gorton pulled the strings. Overnight, Fraser was raised from twenty-second in a Ministry numbering twenty-six and from the Army portfolio, a junior posting, to twelfth in Ministry seniority, cabinet ranking, and the prestigious Education portfolio. With Fraser rose three other dedicated Gorton supporters who had also participated extensively in the manoeuvres which put Gorton into the prime minister's seat of authority. They were William Charles Wentworth, then 60, from NSW, Scott from Western Australia, the Senate Government Whip who with Erwin and Fraser had formed the original triumvirate which on the day after Holt's disappearance started Gorton on the road to prime ministerial power, and Senator Reg Wright, from Tasmania, who, though elected under a Liberal label had voted frequently and embarrassingly in the Senate against the Menzies and Holt government after he had been dropped as Government Senate Whip in 1951.[38]

Always restless, tirelessly energetic, a consistent rebel against both Menzies and Holt, Wentworth, descendant of an old[39] and prominent Australian family, myopic and intense, had a brilliant, erratic mind, original, questing, and determined. Starting from premises which often would not bear too close scrutiny, Wentworth could construct on them an unchallengeable superstructure of flawless logic. He had a cataclysmic view of history, a sense of horror that few shared with him, the vision of impending catastrophe, and a worldview based on a passionate hatred of communism. Yet he could be as practical as a canny housewife, and almost alone and against Menzies' formidable opposition had extracted from the reluctant coalition government a decision to build a standard-gauge railway line between Sydney and Melbourne, whose mutual transport difficulties had long been exacerbated by the uneconomic and inefficient change in the width of NSW and Victorian rail tracks at the border town of Albury.[40] Gorton, into whose leadership campaign Wentworth had flung himself with the concentrated zeal which was his hallmark, gave Wentworth the

38

promotion which Menzies and Holt had denied. Gorton appointed Wentworth Minister for Social Services and Aboriginal Affairs.

Wright, then 62, a Tasmanian lawyer, could have stepped straight from the pages of Dickens. He had a big head, long torso, and short legs, and spoke in massive, sonorous, rolling phrases. He declared himself a fervent states righter, resented the political and psychological supremacy established by the House of Representatives over the Senate for which he demanded a role larger than it had been accorded since Federation, and was prepared to fight the Menzies and Holt governments, of which he was a redoubtable critic, right up to the last ditch, which, however, he shrewdly never crossed. He was ever ready to wound but reluctant to slay. Menzies and Holt had viewed him as a rotund, troublesome but not dangerous would-be Don Quixote, who loved to tilt at windmills but who when the tilting became politically dangerous was accustomed to ride away, wisely, and disappear quietly and preferably unobserved into the sunset. He was credited with having organised the vote of the Tasmanian Liberal parliamentarians for Gorton. Gorton made him Minister for Works and Minister in charge of Tourist Activities.

Scott, brusque yet uncertain, a follower rather than a leader, personally devoted to Gorton whom he admired and held to be a "mate", was an example of the wisdom of the late Ben Chifley, Labor Prime Minister from 1945 to 1949, when he said "Never promote a loyal friend until you are confident that he can do the job because you can't later sack him without raising doubts among your followers about your own capacity for loyalty." Gorton placed himself in this situation. In 1968, he made Scott Minister for Customs. Twenty-two months later, after Scott and the Customs Department had been involved in a series of incidents, which seriously embarrassed Gorton and the government, Gorton sacked Scott from the Ministry. The sacking took place on November 11, 1969, when the Gorton post-1969 election cabinet was announced. On March 24, 1970, Scott was deprived of his pre-selection on the Liberal Senate ticket for Western Australia, after ballots conducted by the Western Australian Liberal Party State Council.[41] After a wait of nearly twenty years—Scott entered the Senate in 1949—he had with Gorton a quick rise to the top; the road down was even faster.

During the period of his cabinet making, Gorton for the first time revealed his occasional gift for vacillation. He dithered virtually until the last day over whether to appoint to the ministry Andrew Peacock, young and able, then 29, a lawyer and business man who had entered parliament by winning Kooyong after Sir

Robert Menzies retired as prime minister and from politics in 1966. One minute Peacock was "in." The next persuaders got to the Prime Minister's ear and Peacock was "out." It went on for days and it was not until just before the Ministry was announced that Peacock learned he was "out" and that a fellow Victorian, Phil Lynch, who had represented Flinders, on Melbourne's outskirts, was "in." Gorton appointed Lynch Minister for the Army.

Erwin, who though he had backed Gorton's rise to the prime ministership appears to have done so from a genuine desire to further the interests of the Liberal Party rather than to advance himself personally,[42] was left, uncomplaining, as Government Whip. But Miss Gotto, who participated in persuading Gorton that he was prime ministerial material and, later, in ascertaining for Erwin and his associates the views of the younger Liberals and which among them were potential Gorton votes, quit Erwin's office to take over, at 22 years of age, the key and responsible position of Private Secretary to the Prime Minister.

Fraser, Scott, Wentworth, Wright and Erwin became the nucleus of Gorton's "cocktail cabinet." It was inevitable that Gorton, a suspicious[43] man, should turn to them for company and comfort, particularly in his early days in the prime ministership. Of the eleven cabinet members remaining after Holt's disappearance, three—John McEwen, Douglas Anthony, and Ian Sinclair— were CP members. Excluding Gorton himself, this left only seven Liberal cabinet ministers. Of these, Gorton could be sure that only National Development Minister David Fairbairn, and Treasurer William McMahon, who was also Liberal Party deputy leader, had voted for him. Gorton was also aware that McMahon had voted for him not from affection or regard for his ability but under the duress of circumstances and after John McEwen, as Country Party Leader, had wrecked McMahon's own chance of securing the prime ministership by announcing publicly that neither he nor any of his CP colleagues would serve in a government headed by McMahon.[44] McMahon had to preserve himself in the Deputy Leadership and Treasury portfolio. It was on this basis that he had voted for Gorton. Gorton was understandably dubious about the enthusiasm of McMahon's personal support. Of the fourteen ministers outside the cabinet three—Charles ("Ceb") Barnes, Senator Colin McKellar, and Peter Nixon—were again CP members, Gorton knew that probably only two, at the maximum three, of the residue of eleven Liberal ministers had voted for him. His support had come mainly from the backbenchers, particularly the backbench senators. He had little reason to believe that he could find unqualified backing outside the back benchers, and those who had tied their fortunes to his.

But even the "cocktail cabinet" had no stability in personnel or continuity of influence. As the informal meetings took place either in Gorton's office or in the cabinet ante-room, Gorton was the host and convenor. His invitation list varied. Individual popularity among the invited and the potential invitees waxed and waned as Gorton formed new associations and reshaped his likes and dislikes in the context of changing circumstances and moods. By and large, the senior ministers, particularly the cabinet ministers, stayed aloof, uneasily conscious of the growth of an unofficial group that had access to the Prime Minister's ear in a social and unofficial atmosphere, resentful, but powerless to protest, because of the amorphous nature of the meetings, against what they considered an intrusion upon their prior right, as cabinet members, to consultation with the Prime Minister. But other ministers, appreciative that Gorton, wilful and unpredictable, held their ministerial futures in his hands under the system of ministerial selection followed in the Liberal Party,[45] gratefully joined the inner circle when summoned or permitted. Backbenchers floated around on the periphery, unimportant in their own right but influential if they could get a receptive hearing from the Prime Minister at a moment when, relaxed, he was susceptible and expansive. There was at times Jim Killen, from Queensland, an ex-jackeroo, witty, irreverent, and an amusing raconteur, a man who disguised with an air of casualness a capacity for hard slogging work,[46] who interspersed his otherwise Chesterfieldian style of oratory with colorful, earthy bush phrases and idioms, and who shared with Gorton a dislike of the somewhat puritanical, pallid, and thin featured St John. There was at times Fred Chaney,[47] from Western Australia, an ex-RAAF type like Gorton, blunt, undeviatingly loyal, and with a contempt for those who voiced their criticisms outside the party room and, sometimes, for those who complained within the party room. There was at times Bruce Graham, from Sydney, a one-legged ex-flier, who had an unshakable confidence in the merits of the F111, the United States bomber, controversial, twenty-four ordered by Australia in 1963 but still undelivered and fault prone. There were others. But they were all only part of the grouping on a tentative basis. Sometimes they were included; othertimes they were left out. It was an ad hoc affair. There were occasions when the group ceased to resemble a floating crap game and took on a resemblance to a slow moving procession passing the only fixed point of the Prime Minister.

The Country Party shared Liberal concern with the disappointing level of Gorton's parliamentary performances and with what seemed his closer affinity with his associates in the social grouping of the "cocktail cabinet" than with his formal advisers. At this stage CP parliamentarians appeared to grasp more quickly than their Liberal counterparts the implications in a statement made by Gorton on January 21, 1968, a statement which his subsequent actions suggested was not an unconsidered utterance but contained the basic Gorton doctrine on what should be the relationship of a Prime Minister to his Cabinet. Said Gorton, "There must be Cabinet responsibility on a number of matters. But I would believe that the Prime Minister, now or in the future, is not to be chairman of the committee so that a majority vote in the committee says what's going to be done. He should put to the Cabinet or the committee what he believes ought to be done, and if he believes strongly enough that it ought to be done, then it must be done."[48]

This unmistakably presidential,[49] as compared with prime ministerial, approach to cabinet government, an approach which Gorton adhered to with increasing stubbornness as the period of his occupancy of the prime minister's office lengthened and he acquired greater confidence, disturbed the Country Party. The Liberal-CP coalition had been in office for nearly twenty years. During the entire period, the CP had insisted that it was in partnership with the Liberal Party, inferior in numbers but not subservient to its larger Liberal associate, ready to negotiate or compromise when the two parties took divergent views but not prepared to accept dictation or yield unquestioning obedience. It was an alliance, unequal in some respects, but not an absorption. Even under Menzies, often autocratic but never reckless despite a personal record of unbroken electoral successes extending over close to two decades, the CP had maintained this position. There had been no problem with Holt who agreed that a prime minister though required to give leadership, was in cabinet the chairman of a committee, who accepted and implemented consensus views and decisions reached after discussion. If Gorton's presidential system of government was accepted, that was the end of the Liberal-CP partnership. Matters would not be decided in cooperation. There would be one-man rule.[50] What the Prime Minister believed ought to be done, must be done.

Though the CP was disturbed, it was not disturbed at that stage to the point that it was "prepared to rock the boat", something that politicians are seldom prepared to do unless they can see advantage for themselves or their party in so doing. Gorton was establishing himself with the general electorate. It was in the CP's interests that he should establish himself favorably. Sooner or later, there would be another general election. When there was, his standing with the mass electorate, if high, would help the CP parliamentarians to be re-elected. Besides they had immense faith in the ability of their leader, John McEwen, to see that Gorton, a relative newcomer to the coalition hierarchy, was kept under control and did not enlarge the authority of the prime minister to a degree that would reduce them from junior partners to unquestioning followers.

McEwen was unmistakably the dominating figure in the parliament which he had entered in 1934, a tall, lantern-jawed young farmer in a hurry and with the ability to get ahead. Virtually self educated—his formal education finished when he was thirteen years of age—a onetime soldier settler who without backing or bank balance had built a rabbit-ravaged eighty acre block into one of the show farms of Victoria, aloof, selfcontained, dignified, McEwen had fought innumerable complex and deadly political battles to a conclusion successful for himself and lethal for his opponents. He had presence, stature, guile and patience. But, as he had grown older, he had acquired the fixations that often bedevil ageing men. He had allowed his hates to obsess him, and he was temporarily obsessed with two hates—one for William McMahon, the Deputy Liberal leader, and the other for Maxwell Newton, a publisher of news letters and a number of small newspapers, abrasive but comparatively obscure until McEwen's pursuit of him raised him to national prominence. As well as the distraction of his hates, McEwen had another quality which weakened his capacity to handle Gorton. He was used to dealing with conventional politicians who by and large were reasonable, thought through their problems coolly and with a minimum of passion, and worked out what longterm was to the advantage of themselves and their party. Gorton was neither conventional, reasonable, patient or cool. He had superb confidence. What he wanted, he set out to get. His approach was simple. It was to get over today's hurdle, without worrying overmuch about what was on the other side. He was never quite sure what form tomorrow's hurdle would take but he was positive he could surmount it. Where another prime minister, as inexperienced as Gorton, would have leaned heavily on the shrewd, tested McEwen, Gorton leaned on nobody. He drove ahead. For all his long years in politics, McEwen had never come up against anyone quite like Gorton and as events turned out he proved incapable of restraining him.[51]

The higher echelons of the Commonwealth Public Service naturally wondered what would be their relationship with Gorton. They knew that his administrative methods as a junior minister

43

were direct. He conducted himself more like the permanent head of the department that he happened to be administering than as a minister. If he wanted something, he did not go through what the bureaucracy reverently referred to as the "proper channels." He went straight to the public servant who had what he wanted. In the wrangle between the government and the ALP over the alleged misuse by ministers and favored members of the government and opposition of planes belonging to the special VIP flight, Holt and Howson had stated that they could not make available information sought by the parliament because "Passenger manifests were not retained." Gorton, as Senate Leader, was in a difficult situation. The government was in a minority in the Senate. It could be outvoted by the ALP and DLP in combination. The DLP senators had indicated support for an ALP resolution seeking to have the Secretary of the Air Department, Mr A. B. McFarlane, called before the bar of the Senate. Howson was out of the country. Gorton took an obvious short cut which bypassed Reg Swartz, the Minister for Civil Aviation who was acting in Howson's place. Gorton phoned McFarlane. "Were there passenger manifests?" McFarlane told him that there were passenger manifests in existence. They were preserved for twelve months in accordance with an RAAF regulation. Gorton later tabled them in the Senate without explanation for their sudden production.[52] His action left Holt and Howson open to angry ALP charges that they had misled the Parliament[53] but it got the Government out of its awkward Senate plight. Gorton's boldness and forthright handling of what was a dangerous situation politically brought him a prestige that was valuable when he was seeking votes in the post-Holt leadership fight.

The public service hierarchy expected Gorton to be unconventional but not quite as unconventional as he turned out to be. He disposed of Holt's personal staff, retaining only Eggleton, not gradually and imperceptibly as was the practice but speedily and without regard for feelings. He replaced Mr Peter Bailey, a quite senior public servant, who had been Holt's private secretary with the young and inexperienced Miss Gotto. He had no respect for *amour propre*. When he overrode public service recommendations, he made public the fact that he had overridden them. He decided to replace Sir John Bunting, the permanent head of the Prime Minister's Department who had been Menzies' and Holt's senior adviser. Polite, quiet and efficient, Bunting had regard for the right of his fellow departmental heads to be kept as fully informed as possible on both government policies and their variation and was as respected a public servant as there was in the public service.

Though a permanent head has statutory protection and cannot except in abnormal circumstances be removed from his department without his consent, the Public Service tacitly agrees that a prime minister or minister is entitled to the services of the permanent head he prefers. Where a minister and permanent head cannot achieve a satisfactory working partnership—and this is seldom—there is a convention that changes are made quietly without loss of face on either side and with a minimum of disturbance. Gorton did not bother about convention. He let it be known that he did not want Bunting as permanent head of the Prime Minister's Department and was getting rid of him. As Bunting had served faithfully and efficiently the two previous Prime Ministers, public service resentment built up against Gorton not because he was replacing Bunting but because of what was considered the brutal and needlessly humiliating manner in which he was replacing him. But in the replacement of Bunting, Gorton achieved an important reform. The Prime Minister's Department among other multitudinous duties had serviced the Cabinet. The Commonwealth Public Service machine had become too big for an efficient servicing to be part of the functions of a busy and preoccupied department. Cabinet decisions took too long to reach the levels at which they were implemented, and the implementation of the decisions was imperfectly policed. Cabinet needed its own full-time servicing machine.

To get rid of Bunting, Gorton split the old Prime Minister's Department into two. One section became the Cabinet Secretariat. Bunting was appointed as its permanent head. The other section retained the title of the Prime Minister's Department. Appointed to head it was Mr C. L. ("Len") Hewitt, a long time friend of the Prime Minister.[54]

A man with an analytical, ordered mind, willing and able to work a twenty-hour day for day after day and expecting the same devoted application from his subordinates, Hewitt, then 51, was admired for his capacity, envied for his energy, and disliked, partly for his intolerance with inefficiency, partly for the ruthlessness of his drive. When Hewitt had been an assistant secretary in the Treasury dealing mostly with defence matters—it was this position that first brought him into close contact with Gorton, at that time Navy Minister—Dr Roland Wilson, then permanent head of Treasury, small in size but big of brain and possessed of an almost cruel sense of humor, recognised Hewitt's gift for merciless destruction of an imperfectly prepared argument or submission. Wilson had used Hewitt as his "tomahawk man", the man who looked at a proposition from a tough Treasury viewpoint and who when he found flaws in the supporting case said "no" bluntly and finally. This had not endeared Hewitt to a wide range of public servants who had been at the receiving end of his gift for disciplined analysis. While some public servants who worked with him swore by him, others, particularly those who had worked against him, swore at him. Hewitt had hoped to succeed Wilson in the Treasury. But after enduring the bitter experience of having his qualifications constantly denigrated he went off disappointed, to the backwater of the Universities Commission—where he was again brought into contact with Gorton, now Education Minister,— while Sir Richard Randall succeeded Wilson as Secretary to the Treasury.

Shortly after being appointed permanent head of the Prime Minister's Department, Hewitt made a series of decisions that further antagonised the higher echelons of the Public Service. He started instituting in the Prime Minister's Department a number of "think tanks", or sections, which other departments viewed as having the potential to infringe upon their jealously preserved authority. These sections were to supply policy proposals which were to cover a wide range of subjects. Hewitt also shifted his headquarters, a small thing in itself but possessed of a symbolism that heightened public service suspicion. Bunting under Menzies and Holt had worked from the Prime Minister's Department, close to but geographically separated by a few hundred yards from Parliament House where the Prime Minister had his suite. Hewitt moved into the room previously occupied by the Prime Minister's private secretary, next door to the Prime Minister's office. It was as though he was proclaiming himself as a member of the Prime Minister's personal staff and the fact that he, and he alone, was the solitary channel of communication between the Prime Minister and the Public Service.

Many of the senior public servants did not like the implication that one of their number had been absorbed into a politician's personal staff. They had taken pride in the Public Service being a body detached from politics, ready to serve any government irrespective of its political complexion and proffering advice of an essentially objective nature. Hewitt's move to them suggested a subservience that might not have existed in practice but certainly existed in their suspicions. Formally, Hewitt was the official channel of communication between the Prime Minister and the Public Service. This was inescapable. But previous permanent heads of the Prime Minister's Department had not emphasised the uniqueness of their situation. Whatever the facts of the situation, they had contrived to give the impression of being liaison minded

46

rather than "loners." Hewitt was by temperament a "loner"; the very closeness of his relationship with the Prime Minister made difficult the close and intimate liaison with fellow departmental chieftains that Bunting had maintained. Additionally, the physical proximity of Gorton, Hewitt, and Miss Gotto, and the practice of the three assembling for consultations whenever a problem developed created the illusion that the oddly assorted trio, not Cabinet, was the real government.[55] Though ministers had direct phones into the Prime Minister's office, these were used only for urgent calls. On routine matters, ministers generally sought interviews and phone contact with the Prime Minister not directly but through the Prime Minister's staff. Ministers often found that their requests for contact were not so much ignored as left unanswered. Unless they knocked personally at Gorton's door, some had difficulty in getting through to him.

These ministers blamed, probably inaccurately, Gorton's staff rather than Gorton. When they voiced privately but feelingly their discontent to their own departmental officials, they found sympathetic listeners and the legend of the Gorton-Hewitt-Gotto power grouping started to grow. This legend was to bedevil prime ministerial-public service relations in the months ahead.

NOTES

[1] I was told originally that the attack of breathlessness occurred in Erwin's office, with Aston and Miss Gotto present. I accepted this version and published it. But I now believe that the version I have set out here is the correct one.

[2] Aston probably consulted Erwin in Erwin's capacity of Liberal Party Whip upon the position that would exist if Holt's health deteriorated suddenly.

[3] Erwin's belief was based on the unofficial medical diagnosis.

[4] The former Labor Prime Minister, the late Ben Chifley used to say with grim accuracy "Rookwood is filled with indispensables." Rookwood is Sydney's best known cemetery.

[5] Gorton, then Leader of the Senate, made a public liar out of Holt by tabling the documents without explanation in the Senate on October 25, 1967.

[6] Miss Gotto had many friends among Liberal parliamentarians. She was particularly friendly with the nucleus of "The Mushroom Club."

[7] Australian prime ministers traditionally come from the House of Representatives. Gorton was the first senator to become prime minister.

[8] The significance of this Erwin remark is that it was made shortly after Gorton became Prime Minister, while Erwin was a Gorton intimate and admirer, and long before the two men quarrelled.

[9] My version of this interview is based on the account of it Irwin gave friends immediately after the interview had taken place.

[10] Sydney *Sun,* November 12, 1969.

11 Official statement, issued by PM's office, Canberra, November 12, 1969. An indication of how agonisingly Gorton viewed the implication in Erwin's statement is the fact that Gorton felt it "more deeply" than the St John allegations which were both electorally more damaging and made much earlier on March 20, 1969.

12 But Gorton was to revive these ideals and to start work on doing something particularly about the crippling cost of prolonged illness, soon after becoming Prime Minister.

13 Section 107 of the Commonwealth of Australia Constitution Act reads "Every power of the Parliament of a Colony which has become or becomes a State shall, unless it is by this Constitution exclusively vested in the Parliament of the Commonwealth or withdrawn from the Parliament of the State, continue as at the establishment of the Commonwealth, or as at the admission or establishment of the State, as the case may be."

14 Commonwealth Parliamentary Debates, Vol 222, p 1563, March 26, 1953.

15 ALP policy is for an amendment of the Commonwealth Constitution "to clothe the Commonwealth Parliament with unlimited powers . . ." ALP Platform Constitution and Rules as approved by the 28th Commonwealth Conference, Melbourne, 1969, p. 9.

16 "I am going into smoke for about four or five days. . . . I want four or five days off . . ." Official transcript of press briefing, issued by PM's office, Canberra, February 2, 1968.

17 *The Medici* by G. F. Young, Random House, New York, 1930.

18 Sir Robert Menzies, Commonwealth Representatives Debates, Vol 45, p 1061, April 29, 1965.

19 Commonwealth Senate Debates, Vol 31, p 204, March 23, 1966.

20 Gorton claimed later that this decision had been taken by the previous Holt administration and that "the Americans knew it"—official transcript of interview with Murdoch newspaper group issued by the PM's office, December 11, 1968.

21 Official transcript, issued by PM's office, February 2, 1968.

22 More than two months later, Gorton tried half-heartedly to retreat to the Menzies-Holt position, but by that time the damage was done. Answering a request from Dr J. F. Cairns, ALP, to reassert to the House of Representatives his "No more troops for Vietnam" statement, Gorton said "I am not and never could be held to be, in a position of looking years into the future but . . . yes, that was said (that the Vietnam commitment was permanently limited) and it is adhered to."—Commonwealth Representatives Debate, Vol 58, p 30, March 13, 1968.

23 The figures for the 1966 House of Representatives and 1967 Senate are given by Don Aitkin in "Political Review", Australian *Quarterly*, Vol. 40, No 1, March 1968.

24 In 1946, with the Chifley ALP government in power Federally there were ALP administrations in NSW, Victoria, Queensland, Western Australia and Tasmania.

25 Commonwealth Representatives Debates, Vol 58, p 155, March 14, 1968.

26 Commonwealth Representatives Debates, Vol 58, p 160, March 14, 1968.

27 Commonwealth Representatives Debates, Vol 59, p 1922, June 4, 1968.

28 Ibid, p 1922.

29 For a full account of this clash see Chapter five, pp 103/109.

30 This contradiction which continually reappears during the Gorton Prime Ministership makes interesting the comment, in a school report, by Dr (later Sir) James Darling, then headmaster of Geelong Grammar, on the

Prime Minister John Gorton, wearing medals earned from his wartime service with the RAAF as a fighter pilot, with his wife, Maine-born Bettina Gorton, attend a ceremonial occasion in Canberra.

Gorton and McMahon at a Premiers' Conference. The man on Gorton's right is Sir Lennox Hewitt, the public servant whose appointment by Gorton as permanent head of the Prime Minister's Department aroused Public Service resentment and suspicion.

A black night at the central tally room in Canberra. Gorton studies the results board at Lyneham High School on election night, Saturday, October 25, 1969. The Minister for the Interior, Peter Nixon, regards the camera bleakly from over Gorton's right shoulder. The bearded man is Peter Samuel, of the "Bulletin", one of the three pressmen whose stories were a link in the chain of events which cost Gorton the Prime Ministership.

schoolboy Gorton. Wrote Darling "He (Gorton) is really too wilful I think, and obstinate rather than strong minded"—p 44, *John Grey Gorton* by Alan Trengrove, Cassell, 1969.

[31] This is Howson's version of the interview given friends immediately after the interview had taken place. Asked later by the writer if Gorton had, in fact, refused to shake hands, Howson said "No comment."

[32] Gorton speaking at a White House dinner given by President Johnson— official transcript issued by the White House, May 27, 1968.

[33] Commonwealth Senate Debates, Vol 26, p 695, September 23, 1960.

[34] Page 227 *John Grey Gorton* by Alan Trengrove, Cassell, 1969.

[35] Chipp later became an ardent Gorton admirer and rejoined the Ministry as Customs Minister after the 1969 elections.

[36] Official transcript of Press Conference with Gorton, issued by Prime Minister's office, Canberra, January 17, 1968.

[37] I was in the amusing position of being informed of the plan by both Gorton supporters who wanted Freeth out and those who had warned Freeth of the reaction expected from him when Gorton made the offer of Air.

[38] "He (Wright) voted against the Liberal Party line on 133 occasions during the period from March 1952 to May 1967. Before this he was inhibited from such action as Government Whip in the Senate until dropped on March 16, 1951 and because he was an aspirant for a ministry."—"An analysis of the votes cast in the Senate against the Liberal Governments from 1952 to 1967" by W. G. Wright, Canberra 1968.

[39] D'arcy Wentworth arrived in the First Fleet in 1788. But for having aristocratic and powerful family connections, he might have arrived in chains rather than as assistant surgeon, his official position. He was reputed to have the unsocial habit, when young, of stopping carriages at pistol point on Hampstead Heath.

[40] The decision to standardise was taken in 1957 and the line opened for goods and passenger traffic in 1962.

[41] *Canberra Times,* March 25, 1970.

[42] When the elevation of Hasluck (by then Sir Paul Hasluck) to the Governor-Generalship on February 10, 1969 created a vacancy in the Ministry, Erwin recommended the appointment of Mr Fred Chaney "in the interests of the Party." Chaney, a former Navy Minister, was dropped from the Ministry by Holt in 1966. Gorton disregarded the recommendation and appointed Erwin Minister for Air and Leader of the House of Representatives.

[43] Trengrove who says Gorton read his final manuscript and who acknowledges Gorton's cooperation in gathering material says Gorton's "innate suspicion" and "nonchalant cynicism" was probably due to the childhood insecurity arising out of circumstances produced by his illegitimate birth. —P 29, *John Grey Gorton* by Alan Trengrove, Cassell, Australia, 1969.

[44] Official transcript of press conference with McEwen, issued by McEwen's Canberra office, December 20, 1967.

[45] The Liberals, unlike the ALP which elected its ministries with the ALP prime minister allocating portfolios, left the selection of a Liberal ministry and the allocation of portfolios entirely to the prime minister.

[46] Killen, as a fulltime parliamentarian, studied for and obtained a law degree. He practised law in Queensland and with typical irreverence told a jury after a judge's hostile summing up "Not all wisdom resides under a wig."

47 After his defeat in his seat of Perth at the 1969 elections, Chaney was appointed Administrator of the Northern Territory.

48 Official transcript of TV interview, reporter Robert Moore, issued by PM's office, January 21, 1968.

49 Constitutionally the position of a US president is that he "is not bound to conform to the advice of his ministers." But in the US system there are formal checks and balances upon a president's exercise of power that do not exist in the parliamentary-cabinet system of government.

50 "This (the taking by a prime minister of a major policy decision without consulting his colleagues) is a point that Australians seem reluctant to concede because it is this, more than any aspect of the cabinet system, that cuts across the accepted norm of responsibility to the party and arouses suspicions about 'leadership' which are never far from the surface in a country so self-consciously democratic"—P 263, *Cabinet Government in Australia* by S. Encel, Melbourne University Press, 1962.

51 For example, McEwen complained both to a CP parliamentary meeting and in cabinet that he had not been consulted beforehand about the Freeth Indian Ocean statement which was electorally damaging to the Coalition at the 1969 elections. If he had been consulted, it is unlikely that McEwen, acutely sensitive to electoral feelings, would have allowed the Freeth statement to have been made in the form it was made without protest.—Personal discussions with CP parliamentarians and ministers 1969/70.

52 Commonwealth Senate Debates, Vol 35, p 1634, October 25, 1967.

53 Commonwealth Representatives Debates, Vol 57, p 2819, November 8, 1967.

54 Hewitt was created Sir Lennox Hewitt in the 1971 New Year Honours List.

55 I never went along with this legend. I accept as closer to the real position a statement attributed to Gorton and allegedly made in the cabinet ante-room. Gorton was protesting against newspaper suggestions that Hewitt was Gorton's 'grey eminence' Gorton was reported as saying "I make the decisions. Hewitt does what he's told."—Personal conversations with ministers in 1969.

CHAPTER 3

DUE probably to the abruptness of his elevation, Gorton reached the prime ministership in a state of mental confusion. He wanted to enjoy the prime ministership rather than work at it. "Ideally, of course . . . the Prime Minister shouldn't have to do anything at all except go round and meet people because he ought to have ministers in charge of all various areas and leave them to do the job, and they should do it and talk to him about doing it, and he should just sit back and think about what we're going to do next, the goals we're going to reach," he rather breathlessly told a TV audience.[1] On the other hand, his desire to be an innovator and to produce reforms which he had advocated vaguely but was unsure of how to enact, and his own, suspicious nature drove him in other ways. He wanted to deepen the Australian sense of nationalism, the type of emotional nationalism that caused him to advocate adoption of "Waltzing Matilda" as Australia's national song[2] but he clearly had not thought how to achieve rather than exhort.[3] Temperamentally, he could not stand coolly aloof while ministers dealt with problems that were attracting public attention. Very early in his prime ministership when a strike of post office drivers threatened to hold up the national mails, he disregarded the advice given shrewdly by Machiavelli more than four hundred years ago that "Princes and potentates are wiser to stand at one remove from the principal negotiations and to come in at a later stage and ratify."[4] He summoned the Minister for Labour and National Service, Les Bury, the Postmaster-General, Alan Hulme, public service functionaries, and union officials to his home, and provided, readymade, a stage from which turbulent, fast talking George Slater, the main negotiator for the post office unions, could demonstrate his talent for colorful, and, in this case, industrially rewarding showmanship. The novelty of Gorton's departure from the principle of standing "one remove from the principal negotiations" enhanced his reputation for unconventionality and won him temporary applause for directness and boldness. Though it went virtually unnoticed at the time, his intervention was an indicator of his disregard for normal procedure, and of his

51

reluctance to delegate tasks to subordinate ministers, particularly tasks which brought those performing them before the public eye.

Gorton believed that his main task was to keep himself attractively before the public gaze. Though he expressed himself in a less polished manner, he had arrived at the conclusions perceptively reached by Bertrand Russell in 1938 before TV achieved the degree of penetration that was to give added weight to the Russell thesis. Wrote Russell ". . . Until very recently the (parliamentary) representative, once chosen, had considerable independent power, since men living at a distance from the capital could not know what was happening soon enough, or in sufficient detail, to be able to express their opinion effectively. Now, however, owing to broadcasting, rapid mobility, newspapers, etc., large countries have become more and more like the city states of antiquity; there is more personal contact (of a sort) between men at the centre and voters at a distance: followers can bring pressure on leaders, and leaders reciprocally can exert influence on followers to an extent which was impossible in the eighteenth and nineteenth centuries. The result has been to diminish the importance of the representative and to increase that of the leader. Parliaments are no longer effective intermediaries between voters and governments. All the dubious propagandist devices formerly confined to election times can now be employed continuously. The Greek City State, with its demagogues, tyrants, bodyguards, and exiles has revived because its methods of propaganda have again become available."[5] In other words, control of the masses gives control of the rest. It was a reversion to a simple concept of power which had an immense appeal to the direct and impatient Gorton, who saw criticism as opposition, opposition as treachery, and treachery as the thwarting of the will of the leader. This was the basis of Gorton's approach to the 1969 elections. But while it brought him back to power, it was, owing to the reduced majority his government held in the House of Representatives and to the resentment that his techniques produced within the government, a power more precariously based than that of Menzies or Holt.

But until he could demonstrate at a general election the control over the mass electorate that he believed his TV demagogery would confer, Gorton had not the control over his party that would enable him to ignore restlessness. Despite the suggestion in public opinion polls that he would have mass electorate support at a future election, this restlessness started to emerge pointedly and dangerously within a few months of his elevation to the prime ministership. It emerged openly after Gorton's visit to the United States which, though it seemed to affect Gorton's electoral popu-

52

larity only marginally, revived doubts among both government and opposition power elites, as well as in the bureaucracy, about Gorton's capacity, and produced personal hates and suspicions that influenced profoundly the trend of events then some months distant.

Gorton brought some of the trouble on his own head. He left for the United States on May 23, 1968, to see President Johnson who had announced on April 1 de-escalation of bombing in North Vietnam and his decision not to recontest the presidency. Purpose of the Gorton visit, publicly stated, was to discuss foreign affairs and defence, both delicate subjects of passionate and single-minded interest to the Democratic Labor Party, likely to be again the balance of electoral power, particularly if Gorton's confidence in the appeal of his TV personality proved unjustified.

Gorton was aware that the DLP was deeply troubled about his approach to foreign affairs and defence. In April, 1968, Gorton had had a secret conference with Bartholomew Augustine Santamaria, a little, polite-mannered man, with a lawyer's degree, a brilliant, troubled mind, and a genius for organisation. Though he was neither a member of the ALP or the DLP, Santamaria had influenced both parties profoundly. It was to break his growing influence, exerted from the background, that forces in the ALP, headed by the then Opposition Leader Dr Herbert Vere Evatt, had moved in 1954/55 against the controllers of the ALP machine in NSW, Victoria and Queensland. The moves had been successful. Santamaria's supporters and those who held views similar to those of Santamaria were ousted. But the result was the ALP split of 1955 and the creation, by the groups which supported Santamaria's implacable antiCommunism, of the DLP which from then through to 1969 constituted the electoral balance of power.[6]

A Roman Catholic but often in conflict with prominent members of his Church's hierarchy who approved neither his methods nor the departure under his influence of a sizable Roman Catholic element from the ALP which because of its high Irish-Catholic content had always had a measure of Church sympathy and sometimes the Church's active support, Santamaria was the political theorist for the National Civic Council, a largely Roman Catholic organisation, whose members were often also members of the DLP. Through them and because his lively, controversial and well written publication *News Weekly* acted as the DLP's mouthpiece, Santamaria exercised a significant influence upon the DLP despite his lack of formal membership. It was in this role that Santamaria was sent for.

The Gorton-Santamaria conference took place in the Prime

53

Minister's office in the Treasury Gardens, Melbourne.[7] The talks were apparently held at Gorton's request. Despite repeated public assertions by Santamaria and the DLP leaders, Senator Gair, from Queensland, and Senator Frank McManus, from Victoria, that the DLP was primarily interested in the problem of containing Communism in Southeast Asia and in Australian defence and that Commonwealth aid for denominational schools, necessary the Roman Catholics claimed if their school system which operated alongside the State school system was to survive, was secondary in importance, Gorton was sceptical of their protestations. He was convinced that if he promised an improvement in Commonwealth aid to the financially vulnerable Roman Catholic school system the second preference of DLP voters would continue to flow automatically to the Liberal Party, thereby ensuring for the Liberals the electoral superiority over the ALP that these votes had provided for more than a decade. He apparently gave Santamaria a pledge of improved Commonwealth aid for denominational schools.[8] The talk then shifted to defence. "His (Gorton's) attitude to Australia's defence policy was summed up in two propositions; that Australia faced only two major defence contingencies," Santamaria wrote later.[9] "The first was that in the event of a cataclysmic conflict between the USA and China, Australia would merely have to render a small token assistance in order to give the appearance of being a good ally to the US. The second contingency—covering a much longer period—concerned Indonesia."

The Santamaria article continued "It was conceivable that Indonesia might become a modern industrialised state, with the military power which would flow from this, and it might again become an enemy of Australia. In the event of hostilities, we would have to have enough military force to hold out for six months until the Americans came to our aid. 'And what if the Americans do not come to our aid?' I can still remember the shrug of the shoulders when he (Gorton) said: 'In that eventuality, there is nothing we can do'."[10]

Still complacently cherishing the belief that aid for church schools was a price the DLP would willingly accept in return for abandoning its intransigent attitude on defence and foreign affairs, Gorton made a defence assessment in the privacy of the joint government parties' room which had overtones of the Santamarian version of his conference with Gorton. Said Gorton: "The established Australian concept of 'forward defence', legitimate in its day, might have to be abandoned," Gorton said. In the place of "forward defence" might have to be substituted a concept of an

54

Australia not holding forward positions in Southeast Asia but possessed of mobile, well-armed forces that it could deploy in the area in alliance with others, or an "Israeli-type defence scheme" with personnel among Australia's civilian population trained to use arms and operate equipment kept in reserve for emergency. Defence would continue to have a high priority but it would not be given overriding priority.[11] It was at this meeting that Gorton conceded that the description "Fortress Australia" could be the description that might be applied, wrongly in his view, to the new policy. The description "Fortress Australia" was to plague him right up to polling day.[12]

His assessment undoubtedly shook a number of his followers, some of whom shared the DLP belief in the necessity to accord priority to defence requirements, particularly as Britain proposed to withdraw militarily from the Malaysian-Singapore area by the end of 1971 and as there was apprehension that the United States' determination to maintain its position in Southeast Asia was wavering, because of its prolonged involvement in Vietnam. There was, on the part of some, fear for the future of Australia, with a small population of European origin geographically located on the periphery of a disturbed and densely populated portion of the globe.

But it was Gorton's trip to the United States which hardened uneasiness into misgivings. Touchily sensitive, resentful of any suggestion that he needed advice, and openly contemptuous of the Public Service, particularly those from the External Affairs Department, Gorton listened reasonably to advice that he should take a Defence Department official to assist him in dealing with defence matters. But when it was suggested that he should also take an External Affairs official, he metaphorically bit the carpet.[13] He did not want any External Affairs types with him. They were all the same. Hopeless. He would have Hewitt with him. If he wanted any specialist advice he would get it from Sir Keith Waller, the Australian Ambassador in Washington.[14] When he was warned that Waller, of necessity, would be so deeply involved in the ceremonial side of his visit that he could function only to a limited degree as an adviser and would not have the time to study detail, Gorton brushed the warning aside. He was not taking any of those External Affairs "so-and-sos." He was adamant. In his anger that the suggestion should even be made, he now refused to entertain the thought of the Defence Department official. When he stepped on the plane, his advisers consisted of Hewitt, the press secretary Eggleton, and the 22-years-old Miss Gotto. Mr F. W. Jennings, of the Prime Minister's Department, accompanied the party, not as an adviser but to look after the travel arrangements.

Within an hour of reaching Washington, Gorton was guilty of a *faux pas*. President Johnson who spent some of his World War II years in Australia and had retained a fondness both for the country and for Australians had installed Gorton as an official guest at Blair House. As a further honor, Gorton was phoned within minutes of reaching Blair House, and invited by Johnson to be his guest on the presidential yacht on the Potomac. Gorton accepted but asked whether he and Mrs Gorton could be accompanied by Hewitt and Miss Gotto. Official eyebrows lifted. Being invited to join the President in such circumstances is rather like being asked by the Queen to Buckingham Palace. In those circumstances, as US officials pointed out to members of the Australian contingent, it is not protocol to ask to take along a public servant and private secretary. Hewitt and Miss Gotto went and the harassed Eggleton tried for the next few days to keep the gaffe from the knowledge of the Press.

But this was minor compared with what was to come. It was merely a breach of protocol. It could have been smoothed over. But on May 28, 1968, Gorton gave a press conference at Blair House. Gorton was probably tired. He had had an exhausting round of official functions and conversations. The British had announced their withdrawal from the Singapore-Malaysian area by 1971. Australia had forces in the area. Mr Lee Kuan Yew, Prime Minister of Singapore, and Tunku Abdul Rahman, speaking for Malaysia, had asked for some continuing Australian military presence after 1971 as a contribution to stability in their region.[15] In the light of Britain's 1971 withdrawal and United States' urgings that Australia should fill at least part of the vacuum left by the British withdrawal, commonsense demanded that Gorton should attempt to get some clarification from the United States' administration as to how the administration viewed its commitments under ANZUS, the rather ambiguously worded mutual defence pact between the US and Australia, which the Liberal-CP coalition claimed as the keystone in Australian defence planning.

Gorton was asked "From what Mr Bundy told us (the newspapermen) at the White House Conference, he defined the ANZUS treaty as applying to forces of all the signatories in the Pacific area. But he left ambiguous whether this would apply to Australian forces in Malaysia and Singapore under a new setup such as would emerge ultimately from the June Conference (between Britain, Australia, Malaysia, Singapore and New Zealand). Have they (the

Americans) in fact expressed any opinions on whether ANZUS does apply in that area?"

The dialogue thereafter was illuminating but not as regards ANZUS.

Gorton: I wouldn't say any definite—I don't know I can give you any definite answer to that either. ANZUS is a treaty—I think it does apply in the three defined areas.

Questioner: It does nor does not?

Gorton: I think it applies in certain defined areas. But I would want to check this with the External Affairs people before I was sure that was correct. But by and large, I think it has been, what shall I say—I cannot think of the exact words—a matter never spelled out whether it applied in the Malaysia and Singapore area or not.

Questioner: But that is exactly the point. It has never been spelled out. The point is have you made a judgment in your mind now as to whether it would apply to those two countries?

Gorton: Well, you are asking really the sort of questions which one can pursue to the point where it is the whole sort of subject of discussions. And I do not think I am free to do that.

Questioner: Can I ask you this, then. This question—was it raised with the President? Can you say that publicly?

Gorton: I do not think I am going to say anything about specific questions raised with the President.

Questioner: Possibly you would feel free to do it if I asked the question in a different context. Are you in a position now to make a judgment on the suggestions by the Tunku (and) Mr Lee, that Australian forces should remain in the Singapore-Malaysia area?

Gorton: I would answer that question (by) saying I think I am in a better position to form judgments on the whole of the area— the Far East Asian area—not just confining it to that area you asked about.[16]

At a later stage, Gorton was asked if he was under any compulsion to revise his warning to his party meetings that the forward defence policy of the Menzies era might have to be amended.

Gorton: Well, the report of what I was alleged to say at the party meeting indicated that there were a number of possibilities in front of us, but the situation was not as clearcut as it has been, and those possibilities are still possibilities. And I do feel that (as I said) at the beginning that I am in a better—I feel inside myself I am in a better position to form judgments on which of these possibilities we should eventually decide to do.

Questioner: Do you foresee a defence review in Australia, sir, after you go back.

Gorton: Not a defence review, I do not think. We will be looking at defence in the context of the budget. But, sort of, you know—I am not quite sure what you mean by defence review.

Questioner: Well, a general review of Australia's strategic position in Southeast Asia.

Gorton: Oh well—I dare say that will be a subject of cabinet discussion, yes. But that is not a strategic paper or anything, a three-year plan or anything of that kind.[17]

The Australian Press generally did not make a great deal out of this Blair House conference. Possibly those responsible for handling the reports from their correspondents back in the Australian offices were as puzzled to make out what their correspondents were talking about as their correspondents in Washington had been to make out what Gorton was talking about. If the correspondents found it unbelievable that Gorton did not know the three defined areas to which the ANZUS treaty applied at a period when he was actually talking defence matters with the United States, the major partner in the alliance, those handling the correspondents' reports almost half a world away must have found it even more unbelievable.

But the Blair House Conference brought publisher Max Newton, a former editor of the *Australian* and the *Financial Review,* into Gorton's gunsights, and produced a situation in which Newton became the target of a "Gorton hate", which months later was to culminate in a search by Commonwealth police of Newton's offices and home and to result in a Court case which Newton was to win in the immediate pre-1969 election period in circumstances politically embarrassing for Gorton and the Liberal-CP coalition government.

Irascible, irreverent, opinionated, Newton had acquired an economics degree at Cambridge in England while retaining a strident aggressive Australianism. Cambridge might have added to his education: it did not provide him with urbanity. After leaving the editorship of the *Australian* which had been started by Mr Rupert Murdoch before Murdoch invaded London and Fleet-street to challenge the British newspaper nabobs on their homeground, Newton then in his late thirties had gone into business for himself, turning out a series of news letters and minor, specialised publications. When Holt was alive, Newton had conducted an uninhibited, free wheeling political vendetta against Country Party leader, John McEwen, that matched in intensity and relentlessness any that McEwen, himself a master in the art of political infighting, had mounted in the course of his long and turbulent career. Newton disagreed with McEwen on his economic policies, particularly his tariff policies, disliked and distrusted the Trade Department which under McEwen's shrewd and forceful administration matched the Treasury in power and influence, and expressed his disagreement in forceful, trenchant language distinguished more by ferocity than by moderation.[18]

Normally very much a realist, McEwen had frequently said that he was not prepared "to fight out of his class." As McEwen regarded himself as in the top political class, this could be regarded as arrogance. But actually it was not arrogance; it was shrewdness. If McEwen engaged in a political brawl with someone his political inferior, it conferred upon the opponent a status and prestige that the opponent otherwise lacked. McEwen made a practice of dealing only with major opponents; lesser breeds he ignored.

But in Newton's case McEwen departed from the rule that he had thereto followed inflexibly. Newton was "small fry." His publications had then circulations amounting to only a few thousands. He could be ignored virtually with impunity. But Newton was attacking McEwen where he was most vulnerable. Recognising that, due to the erosion of population in rural areas whence the Country Party drew its electoral and parliamentary strength, the Country Party was slowly losing its power base, McEwen had imaginatively and boldly tried to acquire for the Country Party the backing of Australia's expanding industrial manufacturers. He could only do this by taking a tariff line, which would give benefits to Australian manufacturers. But, traditionally, the Country Party was the party of free trade. The rural sector of the economy objected to high tariff protection because it added to their costs. Until McEwen could re-educate the rural producers into acceptance of his theme that the interests of primary producers and industrial manufacturers could be combined to the mutual advantage of both groupings, he was politically vulnerable to the charge that he was "selling out" the rural producers. It was at this point of McEwen's weakness that Newton struck.

Another factor probably contributed to McEwen losing his "cool" with Newton. For a period, Newton was an admirer of baldheaded thrusting William McMahon, who, as Liberal Treasurer, had maintained the Australian economy in a healthy state since succeeding Holt in the Treasury in 1966, after Holt had taken over the prime ministership from the retiring Menzies. McEwen did not like McMahon personally. McMahon was wealthy, urban to his suede shoes, had close links with Sydney's social elite, limitless ambition, and no respect for McEwen. McEwen was also wealthy but, unlike

59

McMahon, had made his wealth not inherited it, was essentially a country man, was self sufficient, regarded the gregarious McMahon as possessed of a damaging, malice-spiced tongue, and had a distaste for the eagerness with which McMahon cultivated influential individuals whose support McEwen also sought to attract by the force of his sombre but magnetic personality. McMahon and the Treasury also had views on tariff policy similar to those held by Newton, and McMahon had opposed McEwen and his Trade Department frequently and head-on in Cabinet. McEwen seemed to vacillate between believing that Newton acted as a mouthpiece for McMahon and that McMahon was swayed in some of his economic views, particularly the views on which he was opposed to McEwen, by Newton, who had a following on economic matters both in the Commonwealth Public Service and among pressmen.

Whether prompted by a single motive or a combination of motives, McEwen at that stage had the ambition of destroying both McMahon and Newton. When Holt disappeared, McEwen announced publicly that neither he nor his Country Party parliamentary followers would serve in a government headed by McMahon as Prime Minister.[19] As McEwen had anticipated, the Liberals were much more interested in preserving the coalition and their place on the Treasury benches in the House of Representatives than in coming to McMahon's aid. Though McMahon was deputy Liberal Party leader and hence in the immediate line of succession to the prime ministership, McEwen's rejection of McMahon as the potential leader of a Liberal-CP coalition government effectively destroyed any chance McMahon may have had of rising to the top position.[20] McEwen attacked Newton as being associated with the Basic Industries Group, an organisation of woolgrowers[21] who had like Newton been criticising McEwen for his tariff policies, and for being a "foreign agent" because he did some work for Jetro—the Japanese Export Trade Organisation.

In attacking Newton in the manner in which he had attacked him, McEwen raised Newton to national prominence. Newton started to appear on TV with almost the regularity of a station announcer. Newton's publications attracted a degree of attention that they almost certainly would have lacked without McEwen's unintended boosting. When Gorton was elected Prime Minister, the Newton publications were friendly in their treatment of Gorton. Newton clearly thought that Gorton who had acquired a reputation for toughness, a reputation based more on expectation than on the Gorton record, would confront McEwen and not allow McEwen to maintain the dominance over government economic policies that Newton clearly believed he had exercised while the easier going, conciliatory Holt was Prime Minister. But there were signs by May, 1968 that Newton was growing disillusioned as neither Gorton nor McMahon, who had survived as Treasurer and who with patient dignity was trying to re-establish his position damaged by McEwen's and the CP's refusal to serve under him, were prepared to embark upon the possibly suicidal course of opposing McEwen frontally. The Blair House conference marked a change in Gorton-McMahon relationships and in Gorton's attitude towards Newton.

Newton did not have the same problem as the major press. He had plenty of space. In his publication *Incentive* of June 3, 1968, he limited his comment to a few lines. "The Prime Minister, Mr Gorton, has left the United States claiming to be in a better position to 'make an ultimate decision' on Australia's defence plans" Newton wrote. "But if the stuttering waffle Mr Gorton served up in speeches and in answers to questions during the visit are any guide, Australians should be very worried that the ultimate decision will be in Mr Gorton's hands . . . . To give readers an impression of the deeply confused state of the Prime Minister's mind, as evidenced in his American tour, we publish virtually the whole of the text of his press conference at Blair House, Washington, on May 28." *Incentive* then printed the official text of the Blair House press conference, and let it speak for itself. It was a lethal way to handle the subject. As Opposition Leader, Gough Whitlam, after quoting the section from the Blair House conference dealing with ANZUS, acidly commented in the House of Representatives: "In the passage I have quoted we have this quite extraordinary admission that the Prime Minister of Australia, on a visit to the chief partner of the ANZUS pact, had to consult with the Department of External Affairs before he could be sure what regions and responsibilities were in fact defined by the treaty. . . . Are West Malaysia and Singapore in the Pacific area covered by the ANZUS Pact . . . ? One would think that he (Mr Gorton) should have taken the opportunity to ask the United States officials and administration men whether the ANZUS treaty did cover this area. This was the prime object of the exercise; this is what he was to ascertain before going to Malaysia and Singapore this week. However, we had the extraordinary admission that the Prime Minister of Australia just cannot tell his parliament or his people what Australia's rights and obligations are under ANZUS in this part of the world."[22]

Politics is a rough game. The participants are playing for big stakes—power over their fellow men and the prestige and place in history that the exercise of power can confer. But in a democratic environment, certain conventions are observed. One convention is that justified criticism is borne philosophically and without real complaint. But Gorton gave the impression of never asking himself why he was criticised but of construing all criticism as a product of malice and a determination by some individual to wreck him politically. Gorton had previously maintained a neutral attitude towards Newton. But shortly after publication of the Blair House conference text Newton and his representatives were excluded from prime ministerial press briefings. Or, as put in the evasive phraseology of those carrying out Gorton's instructions to exclude Newton and his representatives, attendance at Gorton's press briefings was "by invitation only" and neither Newton nor his employees received invitations. Apart from Newton, a new relationship developed between Gorton and the publicity media generally, and the list of correspondents who no longer were invited to the Gorton press briefings gradually extended. Those who continued to be invited found that briefings became fewer and fewer, as Gorton found it more rewarding to flatter correspondents by inviting them individually to his office rather than to deal with them in a mass.

But, though the change in relationship between Gorton and the publicity media was important as it meant that the Gorton political style was studied more critically than it had been in the honeymoon months immediately following his elevation to the prime ministership, there were other changes much more important. Gorton realised that the prime ministership was something that had to be worked at, not just enjoyed. Doubts were emerging about the Gorton capacity for leadership.[23] What political circumstances had conferred, political circumstances could take away.

Gorton apparently did very little soul searching about the reasons for the change in the attitude of the publicity media and his own responsibility for the change. But he did a head count of his parliamentary colleagues and while the count was satisfactory he realised that he could move into peril unless he took action. He had two problems. Problem one was his public image, still unimpaired but likely to go sour unless he could produce a performance in the technical field that would match his onetime promise. Problem two was the strengthening of his position within the Liberal Parliamentary Party. He dealt with problem one by a speech to the National Press Club on June 20, 1968, a speech which was merely competent but which because it contrasted markedly with the ineptness of some of his earlier performances was hailed as a superior performance and relieved the fears of some of his followers who were beginning to believe that he was incapable even of competence.

He met problem two by attracting to his support individuals within the Liberal Parliamentary Party whom he recognised as supporters of potential challengers to his leadership if his public image turned sour and by eliminating such of the potential challengers as he could from public life. In the elimination of potential rivals he was assisted both by the personalities of the rivals themselves and by the situation then existing in the Liberal Parliamentary Party, and the Liberal Party machine.

NOTES

[1] Official transcript of TV interview by Robert Moore, issued by PM's Canberra office, January 21, 1968.

[2] Official transcript, interview with Murdoch Group editors, issued by PM's Canberra office, December 11, 1968.

[3] Gorton's nationalism made him a staunch supporter of the proposal by Country Party Leader, John McEwen, to establish an Australian overseas shipping service ("What would I rate as my greatest achievement (of 1968)? . . . One of the things . . . I am absolutely delighted about is the beginning of entering into our own overseas shipping"—Gorton, December 11, 1968). His nationalism was probably responsible for his schizophrenic approach to the problem of overseas investment in Australia.

[4] British politician R. A. Butler attributes this quotation to Machiavelli (*Bulletin,* April 4, 1970) but I confess I was both unable to identify it with or locate it in any of Machiavelli's works with which I have acquaintance. In a previous post office dispute in 1964, Menzies left the negotiations exclusively to ministers and officials and merely "ratified."

[5] Pages 201/202, *Power* by Bertrand Russell, London 1938.

[6] Professor L. F. Crisp has computed that seats won by the government on DLP preferences were: 1958 20; 1961 27; 1963 19; 1966 21; 1969 28—P 104, Australian *Quarterly,* March 1970.

[7] I learned about the conference months after it took place. I was told officially that it was a private meeting and what took place at it was also private. Mr Santamaria refused to disclose whether there had been such a meeting or discuss what took place at it. As I could not ascertain what had been discussed, and the meeting was already some months previous, I did not write anything at the time.

[8] In the 1968 budget, the government provided 27 million dollars over three years for libraries in government and non-government secondary schools, and new benefits for independent schools in the ACT and for both government and independent schools in the Northern Territory—Commonwealth Representatives Debates, Vol 60, p 41 and p 146, August 13/14, 1968.

9 Amusingly, I came across this in an article "Soviet advances and Australian policy" by B. A. Santamaria in a minor Roman Catholic publication, *Social Survey*, published in November, 1969. Mr Santamaria's only comment was that the section of the article detailing his interview with Gorton was "published by mistake."

10 "Soviet Advances and Australian Policy" by B. A. Santamaria, *Social Survey*, November 1969.

11 *Daily Telegraph*, Sydney, May 9, 1968.

12 Though he was later to attack during the 1969 election campaign, the concept of "Fortress Australia" as advanced by the ALP, Gorton never denied that he had mentioned the concept as a possibility. The maximum he would say was that he had never used the description "publicly". "I don't think I've ever used the term in any public meeting, and I don't comment on what happens inside party meetings"—Gorton, Four Corners TV interview, official text issued by PM's Canberra office, December 14, 1968.

13 The Department of External Affairs became the Department of Foreign Affairs 6.11.1970.

14 Prior to his appointment as Australian Ambassador to Washington, Sir Keith Waller was a senior External Affairs Department official. In 1970 he was appointed permanent head of the External Affairs Department.

15 Gorton disclosed Mr Lee's request in a speech officially opening the Higgins by-election.—Official transcript issued by PM's Canberra office, February 13, 1968.

16 These are extracts from the official transcript issued by PM's Canberra office, May 28, 1968. My memory is that I was the questioner in this series of extracts.

17 Official transcript, issued by PM's Canberra office, May 28, 1968.

18 "Mr McEwen stands for handouts to inefficient secondary and primary industry, a sceptical view of foreign investment, government controls . . . and the intrusion of ministerial power into economic policy in a very detailed manner"—*The Australian Parliamentary and Legislative Review*, a Newton publication, January 2, 1968.

19 "I have told Mr McMahon that neither I nor my Country Party colleagues would be prepared to serve under him as Prime Minister"—McEwen, press conference, official transcript issued by McEwen's Canberra office, December 20, 1967.

20 After the October 25, 1959, elections and nearly two years of Gorton rule, McEwen withdrew his ukase. "I made it clear that if he (McMahon) was chosen by the Liberal Party as their leader, I would not refuse to join him in a coalition. . . ."—McEwen, press statement, Melbourne, November 4, 1969.

21 McEwen described BIG as consisting of "twelve wealthy graziers and industrialists"—*Daily Telegraph*, Sydney, June 28, 1967.

22 Commonwealth Representatives Debate, Vol 59, p 1924, June 4, 1968.

23 "This anxiety about Mr Gorton's performance is reflected in the question repeated so often by Liberal members and officials 'How do you think we are going?' "—Allan Barnes, *Age*, Melbourne, April 8, 1968. If "Gorton" is substituted for "we" this was a question increasingly put also to me, particularly after Gorton's US trip.

The controversial ALP Federal Leader Gough Whitlam (left), and the former ALP Federal Leader, Arthur Calwell. There was no love lost between the two men with each distrustful of the other.

Hasluck, in the top hat and morning dress he donned for formal occasions, inspects a Naval guard of honor in his role of Governor-General. Hasluck was narrowly defeated by Gorton in a Liberal party contest which gave Gorton the Prime Ministership in 1968.

CHAPTER 4

IN periods of affluence and full employment and failing the emergence of clear-cut major issues, either internal or external, which involve deeply a significant number of voters the outcome of elections in a democracy tend to depend upon the effect upon voters of movement at the top among the active participants in politics rather than upon the reaction of the mass electorate to broad policies. Australian political history in the years between 1955, when the Democratic Labor Party split from the ALP to become the ALP's most effective critic and 1966, when with DLP assistance the late Harold Holt had secured for his Liberal-CP government a record majority in the House of Representatives, had shown the broad accuracy of this generalisation. Though the ALP had consistently produced domestic policies which super-ficially appeared to have the prospect of possessing greater appeal to the mass electorate than those supported by the Liberal-CP coalition, first Menzies and then Holt had been able to rely for electoral success upon discord within the ALP's hierarchy and the voters' suspicion, largely DLP fostered, of the ALP's defence programme and foreign affairs policies.

Gorton had inherited from Menzies and Holt affluence and full employment. The non-participants in this affluence were in a minority and geographically so dispersed as to be, broadly, politically ineffective. Mineral and oil discoveries had reduced the worry that had bedevilled generations of Australian governments on overseas funds. Development of mineral resources and the purchase, particularly by Japan, on a longterm basis of the mineral wealth with which Australia had almost overnight found itself spectacularly endowed lessened its dependence upon the fluctua-tions in overseas markets of the prices for its primary products which historically had decided the degree of Australia's prosperity. There were large issues looming. On the domestic front, it was clear that the primary industries, notably wool which for genera-tions had been Australia's largest export income earner, were running into difficulties as overseas prices not only failed to keep up with but in some cases fell below production costs. Externally, Britain's decision to withdraw militarily from the Singapore-

65

Malaysia area was a jolt to a people who though they lived on the fringe of Southeast Asia, one of the world's troubled regions, had comfortably cherished the belief that they need not worry unduly about their future in the area provided they gave support to what Menzies had described as their "great and powerful friends." Similarly, there was uncertainty as to whether the United States, the other of these "great and powerful friends", now clearly seeking to extricate itself from the impasse of the Vietnam conflict, would retreat not only from Southeast Asia but into isolation.

Though initially, due almost certainly to the maintenance of affluence and full employment, the developing issues left the mass electorate untouched and still receptively susceptible to the attractive TV projection of Gorton as a person, they started a ferment at the top which finally had its effect upon the mass electorate months later at the October 25, 1969, general elections. The personality and political style of Gorton himself and those who surrounded him in the Liberal and Country Parliamentary Parties and in the Liberal Party power structure contributed to the ferment.

When the Gorton Ministry assembled after Gorton had selected its Liberal component and announced its twenty-six members, twenty Liberal and six CP, on February 28, 1968, Country Party leader John McEwen had every reason to view himself as its dominating figure. At 68 years of age, he was the last survivor of the original Menzies' Ministry of 1949. He had just "downed" McMahon, a major power in the Liberal Party, by making impossible a McMahon bid for the prime ministership, though he had not had a final victory, as he would undoubtedly have liked to have seen McMahon ejected from the Treasury, a power point to which McMahon had managed to cling, albeit precariously. An old wolf, McEwen bore the scars of many battles, most of them successful. Shrewd, tenacious, relentless, he was backed by his powerful Department of Trade which had as its permanent head Sir Alan Westerman, energetic, able, a valuable and bold adviser, a potent force within the Commonwealth Public Service, and long an admirer and associate of McEwen. Now McEwen had aligned with him in the shape of Gorton a prime minister who distrusted and derided the conservatism of Treasury, McMahon's eroding stronghold. Additionally, McEwen had a prime minister who was relatively inexperienced and by McEwen's standards untested politically.

McEwen's personal relationships with Gorton were good. He undoubtedly would have preferred to see the External Affairs Minister, Paul Hasluck, emerge as victor from the leadership struggle which followed Holt's disappearance. But after he had

66

crippled McMahon's chance for the prime ministership by announcing that neither he nor his CP colleagues would serve under McMahon, McEwen had remained, publicly at least, studiously neutral. He had good reason to believe that Gorton would lean heavily upon him in his role of elder statesman for guidance and advice.

But McEwen made a mistake, an understandable mistake. McEwen had entered the House of Representatives in 1934, a gaunt, lantern jawed farmer, with a harsh, craggy visage that would have peered appropriately from beneath a mosstrooper's helmet, dour, aloof, unforgiving and merciless, in a hurry to get places and indifferent as to whom he trampled over in the difficult road to the top. Expelled from the Victorian branch of the CP in 1937, he had fought against or alongside nearly every major political figure in Australia for over thirty years. But always in friendship or enmity he had had to deal with men who consulted their own self-interest and who weighed the risks and possible consequences before they took action. Located as he had been for more than thirty years at the top of the Australian political pile, McEwen was aware that a politician was often quite willing to cut a colleague's political throat. But the men McEwen was accustomed to dealing with hitherto forewent the human pleasure of mayhem today if there was a risk of slipping in their rivals' political blood and breaking their political necks tomorrow. Gorton was something new to McEwen. Gorton acted not out of calculation but out of caprice. There was almost a note of pathos in McEwen's insistence nearly two years after Gorton assumed the prime ministership that the Country Party "required reassurances that significant policy decisions would always be the outcome of Cabinet discussions"[1] before agreeing to re-establish the coalition with the Liberals after the October 25, 1969 elections. It was not only a confirmation from the Ministry's longest toothed veteran of the presidential manner in which Gorton ran his cabinet; it was also a public acknowledgment that McEwen had run up against a personality that he had found himself unable to handle.

With the conventional indicators suggesting that he still had majority electoral backing, it was against Gorton's narrow electoral interests to create ferment at the top of the Liberal Party, a ferment which if it spilled down into the electorate could produce a reaction that would favor the ALP, the official Parliamentary Opposition. Policies needed to be changed: events such as the British military withdrawal from the Singapore-Malaysian area and the likelihood of a United States retreat from involvement in Vietnam, and possibly Southeast Asia, demanded such changes

67

externally and domestically. Gorton believed that it was in the national interest that the Liberals should rethink their philosophy on Commonwealth-States relationships to bring such relationships more in line with what Gorton, who wanted Australians to think in national rather than state terms, considered were modern needs. These things alone would have produced strains within the Liberal Party even if handled coolly, in a conciliatory fashion, and with judgment. Gorton added personal strains.

Either because he had unlimited confidence in his ability to hold the loyalty of electors through his TV appeal, or because he was uneasy at the stirrings within the Liberal Parliamentary Party and temporarily closed his eyes to electoral considerations, or perhaps even because he was by temperament incapable of handling the situation in a different way, Gorton took a series of actions which inevitably led to ferment in the Liberal Parliamentary Party. He set out to win friends at the bottom and to eliminate potential rivals at the top of the Liberal Parliamentary Party.

He needed friends. His Blair House conference, with its seeming revelation of his inadequacies, had been supplemented damagingly by happenings during a widely publicised Asian tour upon which he had embarked shortly after his return from the United States. It was not a happy tour. The fact that his wife, Bettina, was an Indonesian scholar, had probably intensified Gorton's interest in Indonesia, Australia's nearest and highly populous neighbour, which, as he had warned Santamaria,[2] could in certain circumstances and when industrialised threaten Australia's security. He dearly wanted to secure a non-aggression pact between Australia and Indonesia. Though warned by External Affairs officials that the time was not propitious for such a suggestion and that intensive groundwork would need to be done before his hope could turn into reality, he persisted in making the suggestion which was rejected. There were other incidents. To honor him, the Indonesian Foreign Minister Mr Adam Malik travelled to Bali where Gorton was having a two days' respite before returning to Australia. Gorton, typically but undiplomatically, took the attitude that he was in Bali for a rest and not for official purposes, and Malik was virtually ignored.[3]

While Gorton had shown no signs of positive racist tendencies[4] he was patently not at ease with Asians or people whose skin pigmentation differed from his own. He had arrogance and his humanitarianism was localised, not universal. After Senator Dorothy Tangney, ALP, Western Australia, had pleaded for Australian assistance to Tonga in the health field and argued that Australia, a fortunate country in having both wealth and stability, owed a debt to humanity in general, Gorton told the Senate ". . . I do not believe we owe anybody in that area (the Pacific) anything. What we give the people of that area is a gift . . . I do not know that I have borrowed anything from humanity in general."[5] Gorton demonstrated little sensitivity towards the feelings and difficulties of emerging and small nations, even those with close cultural, economic and administrative links with Australia.[6] This insensitivity, as much as his unconventionality, was responsible for his failure to establish the type of rapport with Australia's Asian neighbors, which the late Harold Holt had enjoyed, a rapport which was confirmed by the impressive number of Asian leaders who came to Australia for the Holt Memorial Service in December, 1967. This lack of success in Asia, coupled with reports of a series of gaffes which included confusing Australian journalist, Pat Burgess, with Communist publicist, Wilfred Burchett,[7] and engaging in a heated dispute with Burgess at a Vietnam press conference, meant that Gorton had to look more carefully than he had at his position within the Liberal Parliamentary Party.

The larger figures within the Liberal Parliamentary Party, those who possessed the potential to emerge or re-emerge as challengers were William McMahon, Deputy Liberal Leader and Treasurer, Paul Hasluck, External Affairs Minister, Allen Fairhall, Defence Minister, and David Fairbairn, National Development Minister. Other significant survivors from the Menzies-Holt period included Les Bury, Labour Minister, Alan Hulme, Postmaster-General, and the young, goodlooking Billy Snedden, Immigration Minister. But Gorton could afford to overlook the last three. Bury and Snedden had stood against Gorton in the leadership ballot, but both had been eliminated early. Bury appeared to have lost interest, and Snedden was trying to recover from the setback he had experienced from seeking to depict himself as "with it" leadership material in a manifesto that he circulated to his parliamentary colleagues and which was more appropriate as a publicity blurb for the Beatles than for a prime ministerial aspirant. Snedden was learning the hard way that it is more damaging in politics to be laughed at than abhorred. Hulme was important in Queensland but elsewhere relatively unknown.

Gorton did not have to worry unduly about Fairbairn at that stage.[8] Cambridge educated and a member of an Australian family with extensive grazing interests and a tradition of public service,[9] Fairbairn had the more attractive virtues of the Establishment. When he entered the Ministry in 1962 he had sacrificed part of his private fortune by selling off his share holdings at a low figure though he was aware that they were going to boom in price soon and refused to participate in any share dealings while he held a portfolio. He was staunch, completely honest and of high integrity. While Gorton continued to command his respect, he would serve under him with faultless and unquestioning loyalty. He had a good, though slow, mind, a tenacious memory, treated everyone from the Governor-General to the humblest messenger with the same kindly courtesy, and was painstaking in his attention to detail and in his devotion to his work. He had served in World War II, like Gorton, with the RAAF, for a period in a unit flying unarmed photographic reconnaissances over enemy held territory, and had been discharged in 1945 with the rank of Flight-Lieutenant and the Distinguished Flying Cross. He had voted for Gorton in the leadership struggle.

McMahon was a different proposition. Short, bald, nattily suited, McMahon, wealthy, a onetime playboy turned serious careerist, a physical fitness devotee who in his late fifties could beat at squash opponents years younger, had also voted for Gorton. But McMahon had not voted for Gorton from regard but for self preservation. McMahon had done so after McEwen had wrecked whatever chance he might have had of securing the prime minister-ship for himself. After McEwen had announced that neither he nor his CP colleagues would serve under McMahon's leadership, McMahon had stated in a dignified speech that, in the interests of the Liberal Party, and to avoid the risk of a breakdown in the Liberal-CP coalition, he would not contest the leadership against Gorton. After the ballot McMahon gave every sign of being prepared to serve loyally under Gorton, who had retained him in the Treasury, where he was regarded, even by his enemies within the Liberal Party, as doing a highly competent and technically accomplished job. But Gorton was suspicious of McMahon. He acknowledged that McMahon had voted for him; but he suspected that few of McMahon's followers had.[10] When publicist Newton started to criticise Gorton, Gorton accepted the McEwen thesis that Newton was acting as McMahon's literary tomahawk man, even though, amusingly, Newton was being almost as critical of McMahon at this period for what Newton considered his lack of courage in refusing to confront McEwen or to have any communication with Newton, or any of Newton's representatives.

Gorton turned on McMahon almost with relief. Politicians find scapegoats useful. Hitler and the Russian Czar had the Jews; Stalin the Kulaks. McEwen had BIG and Newton. The chieftain of a drought-hit African kraal probably uses the local rainmaker. Scapegoats are as cosmopolitan as politics and when a politician's prestige is starting to decline as valuable as oratory in providing

70

a diversion. Gorton fixed upon McMahon as a convenient scapegoat. If there was restlessness in the Liberal Party, the restlessness was unjustified: it was blamed upon McMahon's machinations. If a pressman wrote an article critical of Gorton, he did not write it because he thought the circumstances justified criticism: McMahon had inspired him to write it. If an account of what happened in cabinet "leaked", McMahon was the source of the "leak." The use of McMahon as a scapegoat for every difficulty that the Gorton government encountered reached such absurd proportions that Erwin, no friend of McMahon and at that time a rabid Gorton supporter, complained to Gorton that the antiMcMahon campaign was poisoning relationships within the Liberal Party and named a minister who was accustomed to blame McMahon for the cabinet "leaks" as the main purveyor of information to the press.[11]

Such an intense campaign extending over months would have broken the nerve of a less tough individual than McMahon. But though superficially a highly strung, tense type, McMahon had durability. He had survived a McEwen onslaught; he appeared determined to survive the Gorton blitz. Understandably, he was finely drawn at times, driven almost beyond the point of endurance, but he invariably recovered his poise and cocky aplomb. Two things stuck to him. He was a capable Treasurer, and most Liberal parliamentarians, even those who disliked him either genuinely or because it improved their prospects of promotion to appear to dislike him, recognised his professional competence. He was also as Deputy Liberal Leader in an elective position, placed there by the vote of his Liberal parliamentary colleagues and unlike other Liberal ministers[12] not dependent upon Gorton's benevolence for this post. While McMahon kept his nerve, Gorton could not get rid of him without a head-on confrontation with McMahon in the Liberal Party room, and a rocking of the Liberal boat that could be as dangerous for Gorton as for McMahon.

Hasluck was no friend of McMahon. During the leadership struggle, he had, like McEwen, told the Governor-General, Lord Casey, that he would not serve under McMahon's leadership, and applauded McEwen's action in making public the knowledge that the Country Party would not serve under McMahon. But Hasluck had stood for the leadership against Gorton and had run Gorton close, being beaten for that position by only 43 votes to 38.

A poet, addicted to reading French poetry, a historian, onetime university lecturer, and former External Affairs Department officer, Hasluck, then 64, was, like Fairbairn, a man of high integrity and complete morality, but as sensitive and vain as a young girl, confident of her good looks but despondent if they are neither

71

recognised nor extolled. Cultured rather than canny, intelligent rather than intellectual, he had all the self righteousness of the conformist and if he had a sense of humor he concealed its possession with great competence. He had no feel for the comic. When later he became Governor-General (and Sir Paul), he took to wearing a top hat. Where his predecessor, Casey, had worn his topper tilted and with a graceful, slightly gallant, *élan*. Hasluck dragged it down over his ears and dutifully presented to the world the mien of a provincial undertaker dolefully soliciting custom. He was easily upset. McMahon had beaten him for the Liberal Deputy Leadership in 1966. He disapproved of the lack of intelligence on the part of his Liberal colleagues in failing to appreciate his superior qualities;[13] he disapproved even more of the methods that had given McMahon his win. Where Hasluck had been content to let his Liberal colleagues recognise his virtues, McMahon had committed what in Hasluck's eyes was the vulgar sin of pointing out to those voting in the ballot the McMahon virtues. Gorton had done the same as McMahon in the 1968 leadership struggle. Hasluck was strong in his views; weak in endurance. He lacked McMahon's tenacity, energy, and resilience and was quickly discouraged. For Gorton he represented an easier problem to deal with than did McMahon.

Fairhall, then 59, was close to Hasluck. A fast talking, staccato ex-businessman who had lifted himself from obscurity to prominence in the radio trade before entering the Parliament in 1949, Fairhall had a wide range of admirers within the Liberal Party, including the NSW Liberal Party Secretary, John Carrick, a powerful figure in the Liberal political machine, who, possessed of a first class mind and persuasive ability, exercised a considerable influence upon Federal Liberal parliamentarians from NSW. Fairhall had excused himself from contesting the leadership against Gorton on the score of health. But he also had genuine and attractively modest doubts about his intellectual capacity for leadership. Though he had been in parliament since 1949 Fairhall described himself as "no politician." He knew the broad avenues of politics; the back alleys of politics where so much of the business of politics is transacted was for him uncharted territory. In profile he looked like Julius Caesar;[14] in action he was closer to Hamlet. Like Hasluck, he favored a "forward defence" policy for Australia. In this he was in opposition to Gorton. But where Hasluck's advocacy of such a policy was based upon political more than military factors and knowledge that both Lee Kuan Yew in Singapore and the Tunku in Malaysia considered that the physical presence of Australian forces in their area could contribute psychologically to stability in their part of South-East Asia, Fairhall's approach was cruder. Hawkishly antiCommunist, Fairhall believed that Communism had to be confronted but that the confrontation should preferably take place beyond Australia's shores.

Fairhall was volubly critical of Gorton in private conference; reticent in the cabinet room and at the conference table. Gorton had a goodhumored contempt for him. "Allen Fairhall is a man whom I can remember under three prime ministers as sort of walking round the place saying 'Oh, I am a bit fed up with politics' ", Gorton told a group of Murdoch editors. " 'There are all sorts of things we should be doing and we're not doing. There is something we shouldn't do and we have. I think I'll go back to big business.' He (Fairhall) has been doing this for years. It never means anything."[15]

But before any positive steps could be taken about Hasluck, McMahon and Fairhall, their following had to be reduced. Hasluck was the easiest to deal with. He had admirers. But due to his aloofness, he had only one really active worker in his cause. This worker was Freeth. Gorton set out to cultivate Freeth. Freeth became part of the "cocktail cabinet", accepted into the charmed inner circle, listened to flatteringly. Though later Freeth was to be accused of being a Gorton "crony" and of securing promotion to Cabinet on this basis, Freeth had a mind of his own. Freeth continued to hold Hasluck in high esteem, though an inevitable consequence of Gorton's inclusion of Freeth in the "cocktail cabinet" was an abatement of Freeth's proselytising on Hasluck's behalf. With Freeth neutralised, Hasluck was even further divorced from contact with the Liberal backbenchers with their "jowls of lard."

Fairhall's most active supporters were outside the Liberal Parliamentary Party and in the NSW Liberal Party organisation. The NSW Liberal Party Secretary, John Carrick was probably Fairhall's staunchest admirer, and possessed of greater determination and drive than the man he admired. But Carrick was a paid official and his influence was exerted obliquely rather than directly, and could be and was offset by the counter influence of Pagan, the Liberal Federal President, and Fred Osborne, the NSW Liberal President, who became impressed by Gorton's seeming willingness to listen to their views and were reluctant to accept that while he listened he seldom heeded, or, if he did, managed to hide the fact that he heeded with unalloyed success. Carrick could not be reduced to impotence: he was too capable and strategically placed in the Liberal Party machine to lose all his capacity to influence. But his effectiveness could be drastically reduced. Once it was reduced, Gorton was in a position to see that Fairhall's petulant threats of retirement, which Gorton said never in the past meant anything, could be made meaningful by further intensifying Fairhall's sense of frustration.

McMahon was a more difficult proposition. Unlike the ALP which was a harsh training ground and in which even the most junior parliamentarians were required to have a high degree of tough professionalism, the Liberal Party despite its twenty years of electoral success tended to be a grouping of political amateurs officered by a professional elite. The reason for this was that the way up was—generally—easier in the Liberal Party than in the ALP. To get parliamentary selection for the ALP, an individual had to know his way round, how to win friends and influence people, how to avoid the traps that can end a parliamentary career before it starts, and how to live, survive and advance in a rather ruthless and competitive political machine. A Liberal could get a parliamentary seat on family connections, his reputation in fields other than politics, his war service, or even his reliability for loyalty. Once in the parliament, he was expected to give undeviating and unquestioning support to the professional elite, and this was the way it mostly operated though occasionally individuals emerged who rebelled successfully to the extent that they were tolerated because Liberal loyalties were the product of attitudes rather than rules.[16] It was a system which operated satisfactorily while the professional elite was capable of self reproduction or until divisions developed within the ranks of the professional elite. Unlike Hasluck and Fairhall who belonged despite their ability to the amateur rather than the professional element in the Liberal Parliamentary Party, McMahon was unmistakably a professional. He knew politics, its back alleys as well as the broad highways, he knew power and how it operated, and he played to win and for the prize of power that winning brought, not for love of the game.

Having reduced Hasluck to comparative impotency within the Liberal Parliamentary Party by diverting Freeth from his role of proHasluck activist, Gorton and his henchmen turned their attention to Fairhall. Within the Liberal Parliamentary Party Fairhall's supporters were followers rather than thrusters; the raw material with which planners could work rather than themselves planners. Their passive admiration was likely to be transformed into aggression only under the stimulant of dynamic leadership and this Fairhall shrank from providing. Though he roared like a lion in private he performed like a lamb in public. With the active element among Fairhall's supporters outside the Liberal Parliamentary Party, mostly in the NSW Liberal organisation, anyone of influence in the NSW Liberal organisation became suspect. Carrick, particularly, was an object of suspicion. Though after Gorton's elevation to the prime ministership, Carrick had appeared to give Gorton complete loyalty he had not been an unqualified Gorton supporter during the leadership struggle. He had been mildly dubious about the practical difficulties of raising an untested senator, which Gorton had been, to the top of the government political pile. He was a man who preferred to try to control events to allowing events to control him.

Though Fairhall was likely to become a threat to Gorton's leadership under the pressure of events rather than from inclination there were signs that such events could develop. Soon after Gorton's United States' trip, advertisements appeared in the *Australian* newspaper, urging voters to write to their parliamentarians advocating Fairhall for prime minister in place of Gorton. The advertisements were the product of Gorton's inept performances in the United States and probably a reaction against the tendency he was increasingly displaying for making important policy statements "off-the-cuff" and with insufficient forethought. Gorton's followers magnified the importance of these advertisements. Though the advertisements were signed "Businessmen for Democratic Action", one of the few who publicly identified themselves as being associated with the advertisements was a flamboyant, ex-journalist Francis James. James, like Gorton, was an ex-wartime pilot with a rebuilt face. Eccentric, colorful and with a flair for bizarre publicity, James was the publisher of *The Anglican* which despite its name was James' mouthpiece rather than that of the Church of England, and though not formally in politics, he was an enthusiastic and tireless dabbler on the fringe of politics. James, who substituted an impish vitality for the political power base that he lacked, was hostile to Gorton, the Australian involvement in Vietnam, the Democratic Labor Party, and the myopic and frenetic antiCommunism which he contended the DLP was enforcing upon what he considered the more enlightened section of the Liberal Party. He was probably more mischievous than proFairhall.

Fairhall stoutly and undoubtedly accurately protested indignantly that he had nothing whatever to do with "Businessmen for Democratic Action." In putting forward his name as a possible replacement for Gorton, the group, he said, was acting without his authority or agreement. But despite Fairhall's repudiation there was in the minds of the proGorton Liberal parliamentarians the thought that Fairhall might be persuaded into taking a different attitude if the group's demand for Gorton's replacement with

Fairhall evoked a sympathetic and widening public response. Politicians expect or hope the voters will believe them; they seldom believe each other. The Gorton supporters could not bring themselves to believe wholly Fairhall's disavowal of any personal ambitions.

To contain Fairhall's admirers within the NSW Liberals and particularly Carrick, Gorton cultivated intensely Pagan, the Liberal Federal President, who though a Federal Liberal officer lived in NSW and consequently had contacts throughout the NSW Liberal machine, and Fred Osborne, the NSW Liberal President, a lawyer and former member of the House of Representatives and Air Minister, who transferred his energies to the NSW Liberal Party machine after being defeated for his Sydney seat of Evans in 1961. Both men were subjected to the "duchessing" treatment upon which a prime minister can always cynically rely for attracting even quite hard-headed politicians to his support. It is flattering to be consulted constantly and ingratiatingly by a prime minister, and to have advice listened to attentively and with seeming gratitude. It gives a sense of power, even if, as subsequent events disclose, the advice was merely listened to and not followed.

But more important within the Liberal NSW organisation than Pagan, Osborne or Carrick was the NSW Liberal Premier, Rob Askin, a former bank officer and ex-Army sergeant, rubicund, genial, with no intellectual pretensions, great competence, an intuitive sense of what people wanted and the capacity to express their aspirations for them in homely, direct language, and a belief that his NSW, the most populous and richest of the six Australian states, was being starved of the finance necessary for its legitimate and needed expansion by an avaricious and insensitive federal government, which, in control of the nation's revenues, was determined to reduce all the states to a degraded and subservient peonage.

Gorton appears to have worked out that if he could establish a rapport with Askin, he would have automatic protection against a challenge to his leadership spearheaded by either of the two New South Welshmen, Fairhall or McMahon. McMahon had followings both in Victoria, Gorton's home state, and in Queensland, which, only lightly patronised by heavy industry because of its drawbacks of distance from the larger markets and superior labor and power resources of the more populous southern states, was jealously resentful of the federal dominance Queensland believed was exercised by NSW and Victoria. But McMahon, like Fairhall, ultimately relied for his power base on NSW. Without NSW

76

backing, McMahon's strength was an irritant but not a threat. Fairhall's support was almost wholly NSW orientated.

Askin's essential practicality made Askin susceptible to Gorton's blandishments. In private, Askin described Gorton as a "centralist" who would reduce Askin's beloved NSW to vassalage. In principle and by conviction Askin was a states' righter. In practice and by nature, Askin was an able politician who if he could not get the full loaf of financial independence from the federal government and Gorton—and Askin realistically assessed that as an unlikely possibility—wanted the half loaf of expanded federal financial assistance for NSW. These two contradictory elements produced in Askin a political schizophrenia which kept manifesting itself throughout 1968. After Gorton had mauled the states heavily and threatened them with reprisals if they trespassed upon taxation fields which the Commonwealth viewed as its exclusive preserves[17] and a showdown with Gorton was narrowly averted at the Liberal Party's annual Federal Council meeting in Canberra on the issue of Commonwealth-State financial relations, Askin mounted a states' rights campaign. Askin summoned a special meeting of the State Premiers in Sydney in October to discuss and to demand a review of Commonwealth-State financial relations. This was Askin as Dr Jekyll, states' righter. But as Mr Hyde, practical politician, Askin believed that he could handle Gorton and get from him more federal money for NSW than ever he had been able to extract from McMahon while McMahon was Treasurer under Holt. Once it became apparent that the pressure Askin had contributed to building up on the Liberal Federal parliamentarians through the Liberal state organisations would produce more federal money for the states, particularly the state of NSW, Askin switched from being Dr Jekyll, states' righter, to being Mr Hyde, wheeler-dealer. While Gorton was prepared to help NSW financially, Askin was prepared to help Gorton in the NSW Liberal machine, and at vital times in public.[18]

A personal element entered into Askin's determination to support Gorton within the NSW Liberal machine. Hostility had developed between Askin and McMahon. Though proudly Australian, Askin was also a New South Welshman. He had a love-hate relationship with the Commonwealth. As an Australian, he accepted the Commonwealth as the embodiment of the spirit of Australian nationalism. As a New South Welshman, he resented what he considered its encroachment upon the sovereign rights of his native state and the inferior treatment it meted out to NSW compared with the other states, notably Victoria. He could understand though not forgive Menzies and Holt for according Victoria what he deemed to be preferred treatment. They were Victorians. But he could not understand and found unforgivable that McMahon, himself a New South Welshman and as Treasurer in a key position to get NSW more federal money, was as obstinately unresponsive to what Askin believed to be NSW's legitimate grievances as were the two Victorians.

If Gorton was prepared to give him a quid for NSW, Askin was prepared to give Gorton the quo of backing within the NSW Liberal machine, particularly if that backing was against McMahon. McMahon had leaned so far backwards, as Federal Treasurer, to be fair to the other states in his handling of the split up of federal money that he had, in Askin's eyes, been unfair to NSW, and that coming from a New South Welshman, was to Askin unpardonable. McMahon and Askin had also had a disagreement in 1968 over a twelve million dollar federal handout to NSW. There seems to have been a genuine misunderstanding. McMahon appeared under the impression that he had promised to secure NSW a loan; Askin that it was to be a grant. Askin sought Gorton's help, received his grant, and was told he was receiving it despite McMahon's opposition. From then on the Gorton-Askin relationship was held together by the cement of their mutual dislike and distrust of McMahon. Though McMahon was not removed by Gorton from his Treasury portfolio until after the October 25, 1969, elections, Askin knew well in advance that McMahon was for the chopping block of demotion. On Thursday, March 13, 1969, during a Premiers' conference, Askin had a long private session with Gorton. They discussed a proposal that would help NSW financially. Askin asked dolefully "But can you get McMahon as Treasurer to agree?" Gorton replied "Don't worry about McMahon —he's not going to be in the Treasury for long."[19]

To be completely safe, Gorton needed to reduce his four potential rivals—McMahon, Hasluck, Fairhall, and Fairbairn—to the status of political cadavers, buried, out of sight and beyond the possibility of political resurrection, even if their sepulchres were the opulence of Government House, Canberra, or a diplomatic appointment overseas. Fairbairn was superficially the least dangerous of the four. He had voted for Gorton in the leadership struggle. But he was growing disillusioned. As Minister for National Development, Fairbairn was not a member of the Cabinet's defence committee, and hence saw Gorton's attitudes on defence only when a committee recommendation came to Cabinet for ratification. But he saw sufficient of them, and heard sufficient from colleagues who were on the committee to suspect that Gorton's approach on defence issues was not markedly different to that of Dr Jim

Cairns, the ALP radical who was a major spokesman against Australian involvement in the Vietnam conflict and who advocated a "Fortress Australia" policy. Additionally, Fairbairn was not happy with the way Gorton was handling administration generally. Menzies had ordained that Cabinet submissions on large, complex issues should be circulated a week before discussion so that Cabinet Ministers would have adequate opportunity to study them in depth and to consult with their departments. Urgency sometimes demanded departure from this rule but generally it was observed. Gorton was falling increasingly into the habit of having major submissions circulated only shortly before Cabinet met. This left Gorton in a position where he and the minister sponsoring the submission were the only Cabinet members really informed about what Cabinet was discussing, which made it relatively easy for Gorton in unilateral discussions with the minister to make a decision and then enforce it upon Cabinet colleagues who had not sufficient acquaintance with the subject to offer other than tentative criticism. Fairbairn, a slow reader and a slow though solid thinker, did not like this. Nor did he like the fact that when negotiations which had the potential to cost the taxpayers millions of dollars were taking place between the government and oil companies on the government's oil pricing policy following the discovery of worthwhile Australian offshore petroleum reserves in Bass Strait Gorton instructed him not to discuss the negotiations with his department, though the National Development Department had the expertise to contribute significantly to the negotiations.[20]

Fairbairn who had broken bones in his vertebrae in a farming accident at his Holbrook property—for a time it was thought he would never walk again—had had a bout of illness. He was tired and dispirited. In November, 1968, he went to Gorton. He told Gorton "I've had it." He said that he wanted to get out. Fairbairn suggested that he might be considered as Australian High Commissioner in London where the term of Sir Alexander Downer, a former Minister for Immigration who was appointed to the London post by Menzies in 1964, was running out, or as Australian Ambassador in Paris.[21] Gorton was noncommittal. He wanted Fairbairn to stay on until after the 1969 elections. He obviously felt under no sense of urgency to dispose of Fairbairn, an attitude that he probably regretted after the 1969 elections when Fairbairn, by then completely disillusioned, refused to serve in a Gorton-headed Cabinet. Gorton told Fairbairn that there were others he wanted to get rid of, and he might have to use London and Paris as the off-loading points. Fairbairn left without getting any

79

satisfaction. His desire to quit politics and parliament receded with his return to health.

But in the interval Gorton had been discussing with selected members of his "cocktail cabinet" those he wished to see out of parliament and political running. McMahon headed the list. But there was nothing he could do about McMahon immediately. McMahon could be denigrated but not destroyed. He had a small but dedicated following within the Parliamentary Liberal Party and was respected, even by his opponents, for his capacity as a Treasurer. He had a following within the Liberal Party organisation and in business and commercial circles. He had powerful friends within the newspaper industry, including my employer, Sir Frank Packer, head of Australian Consolidated Press. The proGorton forces within the Liberal Party could not do much, but they started an underground propaganda war designed to damage McMahon's public and Liberal Party image, a war so concentrated and protracted that McMahon, months later, was to get the affirmation of silence when at a Liberal Federal Executive meeting in Canberra on November 20, 1969, he asked, "Has there ever been a campaign waged so consistently and venomously [against an individual in the Liberal Party] over the past two years as it has been conducted against me?" He was alleged to be "undermining Gorton." It was claimed that McMahon's machinations, rather than Gorton's shortcomings, were responsible for the restlessness within the Liberal Parliamentary Party. It was claimed that it was McMahon, not Gorton, who was preventing the states getting a better deal financially from the Commonwealth. It was even suggested that McMahon was about to be named as co-respondent in a divorce case. To give the story authenticity, the lady in the case was named.[22] It was a war of nerves promoted to drive McMahon despairingly from politics or into asking Gorton for a posting overseas. He kept his nerve and survived.

The others nominated for political elimination at the "cocktail cabinet" soirées were Hasluck and Fairhall, and in a more lackadaisical and less positive fashion Postmaster-General Alan Hulme, and Labour Minister Les Bury. These men were entirely different types. Hulme and Bury represented no real threat to Gorton, but they shared one thing in common. They were each identified with the Menzies-Holt regimes rather than the new Gorton era and had loyalties and associations which had their roots in the Menzies-Holt period. And Hasluck had run Gorton to a margin of only five votes in the 1968 leadership fight.

Once Freeth was neutralised by inclusion within the "cocktail cabinet", Hasluck was comparatively easy to handle. He became increasingly isolated from the Liberal Party rank and file. He was addicted to selfpity, and sulked over lost battles instead of preparing for those of the future. When crossed he was like a petulant juvenile who picks up his bat and ball in a huff and insists upon going home. In the 1968 pre-Budget discussions when an External Affairs submission seeking extra money was rejected, Hasluck gathered up his cabinet papers, announced "I will have to consider my position", and stalked out of the cabinet room. Still comparatively inexperienced, Gorton who did not want a public open clash with Hasluck worriedly asked both Fairbairn and McMahon what he should do. "Don't worry," they advised. "It's happened before. He'll be back." Within twenty-four hours Hasluck was back at his seat at the cabinet table. He made no reference to his walkout, and, tactfully, no one else did.

Though Gorton did not announce Hasluck's selection as Governor-General until February 10, 1969, Gorton had decided to get rid of him by elevating him to this post as early as late August, 1968. He had confided his intention of getting rid of Hasluck from active politics by nominating him as Governor-General to a few intimates by early September, 1968.[23] When one intimate, knowing that Hasluck's views on what should be Australia's future defence postures differed fundamentally from Gorton's, expressed doubts about whether Hasluck would accept the appointment, Gorton was reported to have commented, with typical Gorton brusqueness, "He won't have any option,"[24] the implication being that if Hasluck did not accept the Governor-Generalship he would be out of the External Affairs portfolio and possibly the cabinet.

Reports of Gorton's intention of eliminating his four senior ministers—McMahon, Hasluck, Fairbairn and Fairhall—started to spread. A "cocktail cabinet" may be a comfortable setting within which to discuss future plans but liquor also promotes loquacity. The reports disturbed the DLP, hitherto the Liberal-CP coalition's staunchest electoral allies. The DLP's Parliamentary leaders—Gair and McManus—were already uneasy over the Gorton attitudes on defence as revealed at the secret Gorton-Santamaria discussions in April, 1968, and probably disclosed to them in confidence. Hasluck and Fairhall, who shared a concept of "forward defence" and assistance to nonCommunist Asian countries, such as Singapore and Malaysia, even if it involved Australia in considerable sacrifice and some risktaking, were closer to the DLP viewpoint than Gorton. The DLP, particularly Gair, had a respect for McMahon, not only as a supporter of the Hasluck-Fairhall defence and foreign affairs line but as a tough, able politician more capable than Gorton of containing the ALP and thwarting its bid for government until it accepted the revision of its antiVietnam, isolationist defence policy which the DLP was trying to enforce. At that stage, the DLP was fairly indifferent about Fairbairn's fate. Though there was no DLP enmity for Fairbairn, he was regarded as an "old school tie", ex-officer type who, whatever his personal misgivings would march loyally to his political fate under Gorton's leadership without rebelling.

An account of proceedings within the "cocktail cabinet" also reached individuals within the ALP. All democratic politicians are talkers. It is their trade. They live by talking. Some, the less discreet, die politically because of talking.[25] Some become compulsive talkers. They cannot help talking even though on occasions it is to their disadvantage to talk, particularly when they are talking to political opponents. Capitalising on this weakness of their fellows, the shrewder parliamentarians, government and opposition, operate their own intelligence services. The more gifted in this field often know more about what is going on in the party of their opponents than they do about what is going on in their own party. They exchange items of information with members of other parties, sometimes to get an item back in return, often to damage either a colleague or to frustrate moves within their own party with which they do not agree or which they fear would, if brought to a successful conclusion, cut across their personal interests or ambitions.

Fred Daly, ALP MHR for Sydney's Grayndler, was the man who exploited the intelligence which had dribbled through to the ALP from Liberal sources. Fast talking, humorous, of Irish descent, Daly, an iconoclast and self-critic with ability and with a cynical distrust of both colleagues and opponents, a distrust justified by his own turbulent history, who scarified his Liberal opponents in public but maintained good relations with them in private, had obviously knowledge of some of the "cocktail cabinet" discussions. His information was slightly out of date and wrong, but only marginally so. Before the decision was fixed that Hasluck was to succeed Casey as Governor-General, McEwen had been mentioned in the "cocktail cabinet" as a possible Governor-General and the proposition may have been put tentatively or obliquely to him. It was not until Gorton told intimates bluntly "McEwen won't take it" that the firm decision was made to offer the Governor-Generalship to Hasluck.

On October 8, 1968 Daly asked Gorton "Is it a fact that the Deputy Prime Minister and Leader of the Australian Country Party (Mr McEwen) is to be recommended for appointment as the next Governor-General? Is it also a fact that the Treasurer

(Mr McMahon), the Minister for External Affairs (Mr Hasluck), and the Minister for Defence (Mr Fairhall) are to be appointed to major diplomatic posts abroad? . . . Are the appointments due to the violent disagreement between the Treasurer and the Deputy Prime Minister and with the Prime Minister by the Minister for Defence and the Minister for External Affairs which can be resolved only by the removal or elevation of the critics in the Gorton Ministry?"

Gorton replied "The answer to the first question . . . is no. The answer to the second question . . . is no."[26]

Gorton's answers were correct. McEwen was not to be Governor-General. Hasluck was to be. That decision had been taken in September, a month earlier. Fairhall was not to be given a diplomatic post. His sense of frustration was to be intensified to the point where his constant threats to retire, fed up with politics, a threat which Gorton had told a group of editors "never means anything", would become meaningful, and he would announce his retirement from politics and Parliament shortly before the October 25, 1969, elections. McMahon similarly was not to get a major diplomatic post abroad. He was to resist successfully the pressures built up to persuade him to apply for such a post. He was however to be demoted from his power point of the Treasury. As it happened, these events lay ahead in the future. Daly's question merely gave the broad outline of what was to come, though the detail was faulty.

NOTES

1 Official text, issued by McEwen's Canberra office, November 6, 1969.
2 See Chapter 3, page 54.
3 My authorities for this statement are pressmen who accompanied Gorton on his Asian tour and Indonesian sources.
4 Claiming that Gorton is "a man ill at ease with Asians", Maximilian Walsh, who accompanied Gorton on his Asian tour describes Gorton as having "undercurrents of mild racism"—"You ain't seen nothing yet", *Quadrant*, Nov/Dec 1968.
5 Commonwealth Senate Debates, p 1783, Vol 36, October 26, 1967.
6 Though Australia has large economic holdings, as well as long historical associations with Fiji, Gorton refused to meet Fijian leaders when returning from London in January, 1969. ". . . (He) pleaded that he was too tired. . . ."—*Fiji Times*, July 19, 1969.
7 "You ain't seen nothing yet" by Maximilian Walsh, *Quadrant*, Nov/Dec 1968.
8 Fairbairn was to give Gorton a lot of worry after the October 25, 1969, elections. See Chapter 14, p 356.

9 His uncle, James Fairbairn, Minister for Air in first Menzies government, was an architect of the World War II Empire Air Training Scheme and was killed in an air crash near Canberra aerodrome, now Fairbairn Airport, with Army Minister Geoff Street and Information Minister Sir Henry Gullett on August 13, 1940. Fairbairn's grandfather, Sir George Fairbairn, MHR for Fawkner in Victoria, was reputed to have given Arthur (now Sir Arthur) Fadden, who was later to become a Prime Minister of Australia, his first important commission as an accountant.

10 ". . . When the election was held McMahon's supporters . . . far from voting in a bloc for the Senator from Victoria (Gorton) split sharply, only three making him their choice."—p 198, *John Grey Gorton*, by Alan Trengrove, Cassell Australia, 1969. Gorton frequently in conversations after the ballot expressed the suspicion that he had received only three votes from McMahon's supporters.

11 Personal conversations with Erwin in 1969. When I asked Erwin if I could quote him as my authority for this statement he said "Yes."

12 Unlike the ALP which when in Government elects its Ministry, with the Prime Minister's only access to patronage his right to nominate which portfolios those elected by the party should hold, the Liberals, federally leave the selection of ministers and their portfolios entirely to the Prime Minister. But the Liberals elect their deputy leader in a secret ballot.

13 In a revealing line, Hasluck writes in his poem "Breaking Point" of "The politician with his jowls of lard"—*Collected Verse*, by Paul Hasluck, Hawthorn Press, Melbourne, 1969.

14 When Wentworth, Jefferson Bate (Liberal, NSW) and Fairhall sat together on the back benches before Wentworth and Fairhall were elevated to the Ministry, the three who operated as a team were known irreverently as "Mutt, Jeff and Julius Caesar."

15 Official transcript, issued by PM's Canberra Office, December 11, 1968.

16 Senator Wright and MHR William Wentworth are examples of this type of Liberal "rebel." Both frequently departed from the policy lines laid down by the Liberals' professional élite and rebelled against Menzies and Holt edicts. Though tolerated by their fellow Liberals, they were regarded askance as men who did not play the game according to the Liberal understanding of the rules. Gorton elevated both to the Ministry after he became Prime Minister.

17 "The Commonwealth will not stand by and permit its use of income tax for policy purposes to be impaired by the introduction of state income taxes"—Gorton, p 33, official report of the Premiers' Conference, Canberra, June 27/28, 1968.

18 "He (Gorton) may want to go further as regards centralisation of power than we do in the states. But he is certainly not a centralist. I know that for a fact"—Premier Askin, TV interview on Channel 9, Sydney, October 22, 1969.

19 For professional reasons, I cannot give my authority for this account of the Gorton-Askin meeting. But the information was in my possession within a short time of the meeting and was conveyed to me in circumstances that left no doubt about its authenticity.

20 Fairbairn made this charge, semi-publicly, at a Liberal Party meeting on November 24, 1969. Gorton did not deny the charge.

21 As a Cambridge student, Fairbairn spent his vacations with a French family in France. He was one of the few ministers in the Gorton government fluent in a second language.

[22] On office instructions, I asked McMahon about the persistent divorce rumours. McMahon said "At least my wife will get some amusement out of that story—I don't know anyone with the same name as the lady I'm reputed to be involved with."

[23] Knowledge of Gorton's intention to appoint Hasluck as Governor-General was conveyed to me in September but in circumstances that prevented me publishing the fact. In an argument with colleagues in October, 1968, over Governor-General possibilities, I announced that I knew who was to be the next Governor-General and deposited in the office files a sealed envelope, to be opened when the next Governor-General was announced. When opened it read "Hasluck."

[24] I have not checked whether Hasluck received this warning that he "won't have any option" with the offer of the Governor-Generalship. My request for an interview with Hasluck to get his version on this and other matters was refused.

[25] The former ALP Prime Minister the late Ben Chifley used to say "More men have talked their way out of Parliament than ever talked their way into it." The experience of Mr William Jack, former Liberal MHR for North Sydney, would seem to justify this observation. Known as "The Silent One", Mr Jack was in Parliament from 1949 to 1966. During that time he asked eight questions and made seven speeches. One of the speeches was "I move that the question be put." His majority consistently improved and he retired in 1966 undefeated.

[26] Commonwealth Representatives Debates, Vol 60 p 1637, October 8, 1968.

CHAPTER 5

THERE is an Australian political maxim that oppositions do not win elections; governments lose them. Historically, there is some support for the accuracy of this generalisation. In times of stability, full employment and reasonable prosperity, the Australian electorate has been prone to return the government of the day and to ignore the blandishments of the opposition, though often the pledges and promises of the opposition have superficially appeared more grandiose and beguiling. Formed in 1890 and hence one of the oldest Labor Parties in the world, the Australian Labor Party, turbulent and constantly rent by factions, venal yet idealistic, self destructive but possessed of enormous recuperative powers, had achieved by 1969 federal power during only sixteen of the sixty-eight years since the six Australian states had coalesced to form the Australian Commonwealth in 1901. Due to its history since World War I, a number of its leaders had formed the defeatist view that it needed crisis to secure office—the crisis of unemployment such as had secured it control of the Treasury benches in the House of Representatives during the depression years from 1929 to 1931 and the crisis of war which had seen the disintegration of the first Menzies' government in 1941 and the installation of an ALP government, which, first under Curtin, and later under Chifley, endured until 1949 when Menzies regained the power which he was to hold until his retirement in January 1966.

In December, 1967, when Holt disappeared into the surf off Cheviot Beach, the ALP Federal Parliamentary Party was led by Edward Gough Whitlam, then 51 years of age, a lawyer and wartime Flight-Lieutenant in the RAAF, elegantly tailored, straight backed and six feet three inches in height, with a facile tongue, a Man-of-Distinction air, a bourgeoisie background, hungry ambition, few friends, an arrogant petulance, and a greater gift for the deft handling of facts than of men. Flexibly inconstant in his ideological commitments, he switched sides unpredictably in the never ending ALP wars. He was constant only in his inconstancy. He had ability, but he also possessed a quality that is often more important in politics than ability—the good fortune that produced the juxtaposition of circumstances that enabled him not only to survive his

86

mistakes and personal defects but to advance. Inconspicuous for his loyalty to his former leader, Arthur Augustus Calwell, who had retired from his position of Opposition Leader after the ALP's 1966 election debacle which had given Holt the largest-ever majority enjoyed by any prime minister in the House of Representatives, Whitlam craved adulation and loyalty; he enjoyed the former but forwent the latter. In verbal encounters, he had the brittle, catty brilliance of the female characters in Noel Coward's "Private Lives." He clawed rather than punched.

On one occasion during an argument in the House of Representatives, he flung a glass of water over Hasluck, later to be Governor-General. On another occasion, he described Sir Garfield Barwick, then Minister for External Affairs and later to be Chief Justice of the High Court as "a bumptious bastard." In a clash with McMahon on the floor of the House of Representatives' chamber he called McMahon a "queen." Raised in a tougher, more fullblooded environment than that of an English drawing room stage setting, the ALP Parliamentarians found it difficult to understand, and easy to distrust, a leader who spat like a cat rather than roared like a lion.

But when Holt disappeared, Whitlam's star, and with it the ALP which was dragged behind it automatically like a comet's tail, was in the ascendancy. Whitlam had acquired an unmistakable parliamentary supremacy over Holt. This supremacy was partly due to the fact that Holt had run into a series of difficulties. Some of these difficulties were the product of external factors such as Britain's decision to devalue sterling which in turn produced strains within the coalition government, with the McEwen-led CP wanting Australia to devalue its currency also to protect the interests of rural producers, while the majority of the numerically stronger Liberal Party wanted, and insisted upon, maintaining the Australian dollar at its then level. Other difficulties were internal produced by personal and policy feuds within the Liberal-CP coalition, feuds which flourished like weeds once Menzies's restraining and dominant presence vanished from the parliament when he retired in 1966 and of which the most widely publicised was the clash between McEwen in his capacity as Trade Minister and McMahon, as Treasurer, over tariff and economic policies. Superimposed on these difficulties was Holt's temporary lapse into overcautious, fumbling verbosity which contrasted damagingly with Whitlam's crispness. In combination these factors resulted in the Holt government doing relatively badly at by-elections and in the 1967 Senate elections, setbacks which had the effect of further eroding both Holt's and his government's confidence. But much of the supremacy that Whitlam was establishing was due to Whitlam's own efforts. An indefatigable worker, cool and impressive during the lengthening periods between his fits of temper, petulance, and impulsiveness, Whitlam had concentrated upon improving the electoral appeal of ALP policy in the areas which were non-controversial within the ALP while trying to separate and reduce to a low key the policy areas which were highly controversial, and disruptive of ALP unity. Whitlam encouraged, and himself partici-pated in, the development of electorally appealing policies on economic planning, science and technology, national resources, cultural affairs, housing, health, social welfare, urban planning, transport, rural matters, aborigines' welfare, law reform, civil liberties, taxation revision, and education. At the same time, he tried, with some success, to downgrade the importance of defence and foreign affairs, issues which had affected adversely the ALP's electoral prospects in earlier elections, and though his success in his downgrading efforts was at first only marginal he was helped by the growth of antiVietnam sentiment, voiced by prominent United States' political personalities, which gave the patina of respectability not only to the staunchly antiVietnam section of the ALP led by former ALP Federal Parliamentary leader, Arthur Calwell, and Dr J. F. ("Jim") Cairns, the Victorian ALP MHR, who was Whitlam's main potential rival at that stage for the Federal Parliamentary ALP leadership, but, paradoxically, to the anti-United States section of the ALP, a section which if it did not have Communist Party sympathies at least cooperated actively with leading members of the Communist Party, strategically located within the Australian trade union movement, in the denigration of all US activities in world affairs.

But within a matter of weeks of his accession to the prime ministership, Gorton, though technically less adequately equipped for the prime ministership than Holt, heading a coalition govern-ment which in the days immediately following Holt's disappearance had publicly disclosed the bitterness of its schisms, and under distrustful scrutiny for the eccentricity of both his private and public approach to the responsibilities of his office, had clearly asserted ascendancy over Whitlam. This ascendancy was accorded him in part by Whitlam's behaviour which led to an intensification of faction fighting within the ALP, an intensification which was to assist Gorton and his government to achieve electoral success at the general elections then still more than a year distant.

The factors that led to the renewed outburst of ALP infighting were as much part of the ALP's history as Whitlam's temperament. Despite the brevity of its years in federal office, the ALP had been virtually since its formation in 1890, and probably still is, the major dynamic of Australian politics.[1] As a government, a Liberal-CP coalition theoretically had freedom of action. But it was only a theoretical freedom. Even when in opposition, the ALP determined the social atmosphere within which a Liberal-CP administration must operate unless it was to risk losing its electoral support,[2] marginally superior to the ALP's between 1949 and 1955 and thereafter superior because of the support of the Democratic Labor Party, which hived off from the ALP in the ALP split of that year. Though not always consistent in its application of its creed, the ALP's espousal of the cause of the "under dog" has influenced the outlook of the nation, not merely the outlook of ALP adherents.[3] While superficially the ALP's success in being able to fix broadly the Australian social atmosphere would seem to make the ALP more acceptable electorally to Australian voters than the Liberal-CP coalition which ruled Australia for more than twenty years after 1949, the ALP had inbuilt features which constantly caused disunity. In April, 1968, during one of these periods of disunity, Whitlam found himself on the weaker side, consistently and humiliatingly outvoted in an ALP forum. With characteristic petulance, Whitlam resigned his post as Federal Labor Leader on April 19, 1968, produced turmoil within the ALP, and presented Gorton with an advantage that persisted until Gorton involved himself in difficulties that transcended even those of Whitlam.

The high proportion of those of Irish extraction or descent in the Australian population[4] has had a large influence upon the ALP and the ALP's internal politics. From the time Britain despatched from England its unwanted convicts who were to land at Sydney Cove in 1788 and to provide the basis for the colony of New South Wales, the Irish were prominent. They were the first coherent, cohesive but originally ineffective minority around which an opposition to the parvenu aristocracy of the new colony's official and landowning classes would be formed.[5] They and their descendants provided the bulk of those Australian rebels against authority, the bushrangers who scorned "to live in slavery, bound down by iron chains",[6] and who, when the native born Currency lads replaced the old convict outlaws, added a social undertone[7] to their otherwise conventional defiance of law and conformity. They constituted the majority in the list of killed and wounded signed and supplied by Peter Lalor, himself Irishborn and the miners' "commander-in-chief", to the *Times* office in Ballarat[8] after the abortive minuscule rebellion in which goldminers, protesting against the licensing system, fought against regular soldiers and police at Eureka Stockade in 1854. They were of the dispossessed, the colonial proletariat, with a racial antagonism to their over-lords, which their fellow Australian proletarians, as yet relatively untouched by concepts of class warfare, did not share.

The Irish and the Irish-descended were the Australian Labor Party's solid electoral base, but other influences operated in the ALP's formative years. The Chartist movement of Great Britain, the utopian socialism of William Lane, the followers of Henry George, Methodist egalitarianism, the influence of English Fabian-ism (already possessed of a history of several years' agitation and teaching by the Webbs and George Bernard Shaw[9]), Australian nationalism,[10] the extending influence of the trade unions (which had attempted to move unsuccessfully in 1890 from a protective to an aggressive role) and the radicalism of the Australian middle classes (which was a hangover from the period between 1850 and 1858 when Australia became a political democracy[11]) were among the strands that combined to make the Australian Labor Party. Though originally the ALP's leaders and parliamentary members were mostly Scots and English, the ALP conscription split of 1916 resulted in the hiving off of a substantial section of this element, leaving the Irish-Australians, overwhelmingly anticonscriptionist, increasingly to fill high office in the ALP[12] and to provide the next four ALP prime ministers—James Henry Scullin, John Curtin, Francis Michael Forde and Joseph Benedict Chifley.

With their race, the Irish-Australians also brought to the ALP their religion—Roman Catholicism. They were militant but not Marxist; reformers not revolutionaries. When under the stimulus of a group which had discovered attraction in Marxist-Leninist theories the Communist Party of Australia was formed in 1920, only individuals shifted their allegiance; the overwhelming majority of the Irish-Australians stayed loyal to the ALP, despite the hardness of the times from which they, as a group, suffered most. Even during the misery of the depression era when the Communist Party benefited from the ineffectual efforts of the traditional trade union leaders to grapple with events they despairingly felt were outside their control, and secured a grip upon the Australian trade union movement that has never completely been lost, Communism could secure only a minute following politically and electorally. The Irish-Australian remained loyal to the ALP. It was only when a brilliant Roman Catholic organiser, Mr Bartholomew Augustine Santamaria, then the head of Catholic Action and later leader of the antiCommunist quasi political grouping known as the National Civic Council, decided to eliminate Communist power within the Australian trade union movement that Irish-Australian allegiance

90

to the ALP faltered. Formed primarily by the trades unions following the unions' heavy setbacks in the protracted and unsuccessful strikes of the 1890s, the ALP was basically union controlled. Whoever controlled the unions controlled the ALP. Whether or not he set out deliberately to control the ALP,[13] Santamaria by helping to organise his followers into key positions within the Australian trade union movement was securing for himself and his followers control of the ALP.

As forces within the ALP identifiable with or sympathetic to Santamaria or his dedicated antiCommunism were simultaneously trying to eject from the Federal Labor Leadership, the late Dr Herbert Vere Evatt, a brilliant, eccentric jurist who had resigned from the High Court to become Australia's wartime Minister for External Affairs and who, after succeeding Chifley as opposition leader after Chifley's death in 1951, had succeeded in defeating a referendum promoted by the then Prime Minister, Mr (later Sir Robert) Menzies, to give the Commonwealth powers to ban the Communist Party, the Evatt-Santamaria clash when it came had inevitably heavy ideological overtones. Tactically, Evatt won easily. Evatt destroyed Santamaria's power in the ALP, though, due to the tenacity with which some of the Irish-Catholic element clung to their ALP allegiance, Evatt could not destroy entirely the Santamaria influence. Evatt destroyed Santamaria's power in the ALP by branding Santamaria as the leader of groups which "adopting methods which strikingly resemble both Communist and Fascist infiltration of larger groups . . . have created an almost intolerable situation—calculated to deflect the Labor movement from established Labor objectives and ideals."[14]

Radical and leftwing forces, including the Communist Party which had an influence upon internal ALP affairs because of Communist Party dominance in some militant ALP affiliated unions, as well as some rightwing antiCommunist ALP groupings disturbed by the nibblings of Santamaria's followers at their union bastions of power and an antiSantamaria Catholic faction which had long been uneasy with what it considered the religious rather than the political basis for Santamaria's antiCommunism, rallied to Evatt's support. But Evatt's broad strategy was a failure. He had hoped to win not only the fight within the ALP but the 1955 elections on the Santamarian issue. Though he may not have consciously admitted to himself his responsibility for the change in emphasis, Evatt allowed the struggle within the ALP to turn from one against what he described as the evil influence of Santamaria upon the ALP into an antiCatholic crusade.[15] Evatt believed that for every Catholic vote within the ALP he would lose in this struggle he would gain two Protestant votes from outside the ALP. But when the antiEvatt, proSantamarian forces hived off from the ALP to form the Democratic Labor Party, they took with them, particularly in Victoria where Santamaria's organisation and influence was strongest, sufficient of the ALP's Irish-Catholic support to ensure that the ALP was debarred from winning government for years. From 1955 to 1969 the ALP consistently polled more primary votes at general elections than the Liberal-CP combination but the Australian system of preference voting enabled the DLP by giving its second preferences to a Liberal or CP candidate, to maintain the Liberal-CP coalition in office. Evatt and the ALP lost Irish-Catholic votes; they did not gain enough Protestant votes to offset these losses. AntiCatholic Protestant Churchmen applauded Evatt's antiCatholic crusade; but they and their followers continued to vote against the ALP and for the Liberal-CP coalition and its tradition of Protestant leadership.

Evatt resigned from Parliament in February, 1960, to become Chief Justice of the NSW Supreme Court, with his ambition to become Prime Minister of Australia unachieved and his longtime antagonist, Menzies, still firmly seated on the prime ministerial saddle. Calwell succeeded Evatt as Federal Labor leader; Whitlam moved up to become Calwell's deputy, beating with leftwing support[16] ALP veteran, Mr E. J. ("Ned") Ward, an implacable radical who suffered from what in the atmosphere of the times was the disadvantage of being a Catholic.

Between 1960 and 1963, Whitlam filled the role of fairly loyal lieutenant to Calwell, sharing his leader's ups and down. Calwell was Catholic, an outspoken and vigorous one who had complained loudly when in 1946 the Pope created Australian born Dr Norman Gilroy, the Roman Catholic Archbishop of Sydney, a Cardinal over Dr Daniel Mannix, the fiery, Irishborn Archbishop of Melbourne, who had fought against conscription with the ALP and Calwell in World War I. The breakaway ALP elements which later coalesced to form the DLP had undoubtedly expected Calwell, as prominent a Catholic layman as there was in Australia, firmly antiCommunist and a fervent Australian nationalist, to support them and to go with them in the ALP split of 1954/55. But influenced partly by the masterly skill with which Clyde Cameron, from South Australia, a stockily built ex-shearer and trade union secretary turned ALP Federal Parliamentarian, prematurely grey haired, with a biting, fluent tongue, a subtle, clever mind, and an intuitive grasp of psychological factors operating on his fellow ALP members, had played upon Calwell's emotionalism and passionate devotion to the Party he had joined as a boy,[17] Calwell had stayed steadfastly loyal to Evatt and the ALP at the 1955 ALP Federal Conference in Hobart where the ALP split took formal shape and by his Catholic presence contributed to the success of the leftwing, Evatt-led ALP forces over their largely Roman Catholic opponents. The DLP hated Evatt; it felt itself betrayed by Calwell, the co-religionist of many of its adherents, and in some ways DLP supporters were more malevolently hostile towards Calwell than towards Evatt. Calwell was even embarrassed in the performance of his religious duties, occasionally being the clear though unspecified subject of hostile sermons from pulpits occupied by priests who saw the DLP as the protectors of religion from the onslaughts of Godless Communism. The DLP was more implacable in its opposition to Calwell, a Catholic, than it had been to Evatt, the Protestant, whose denunciation of the largely Catholic Santamarian forces within the ALP had led to the 1954/55 split. Understandably, this left Calwell with an almost frenetic dislike of men with whom up to the split he had a lifetime of close if uneasy association.

Despite DLP hostility, Calwell had his crowded hour of near glory at the federal general elections of 1961. The Menzies' government had in the months preceding the elections allowed to develop a degree of unemployment insignificant by world standards —2.2 percent for males and 2.8 percent for females—but unacceptable to an electorate conditioned by the ALP's full employment ideals into rejection of any degree of unemployment. Additionally, the Menzies' government had introduced—belatedly and after the boom conditions that it was designed to curb had already showed signs of abating—a credit "squeeze" to reduce consumer demand and to protect the balance of payments position and then had to abandon the "squeeze" following restlessness within the Liberal Party. The Menzies' government decided at the elections to "stand on its record" and to fight on purely domestic rather than ideological issues, always electorally dangerous for a non-Labor administration in a country where the social atmosphere paradoxically is influenced more by the ALP than by its electorally more consistently successful opponents. Calwell and the ALP went within two seats of ousting the Menzies government, and it is a measure of the DLP's success in functioning as the balance of power in the Australian electorate that DLP preferences decided the outcome in the Menzies' government's favor in twenty-seven[18] of the sixty-two seats won by the government in a House of Representatives with a voting strength of one hundred and twenty-two.

Calwell was riding high. He had led the ALP closer to victory than it had been at any elections since 1949, the year in which the Chifley-led ALP administration was replaced by Menzies and his Liberal-CP coalition. But in 1963 the picture changed. The ALP again confirmed its reliable capacity for self damage.

The United States' administration arranged with the Menzies' government to construct at Exmouth Gulf in Western Australia a radio communications centre. The communications centre was to enable the United States to maintain communication with among other units, its atomic armed submarines operating in the Indian Ocean. With the facility of long practice, the ALP's policy shaping authorities split dutifully, almost straight down the centre. Half wanted to accept the installation in the belief that such acceptance strengthened Australia's defence capacity and assisted in ensuring US assistance if Australia became involved in any hostilities that might break out in its area of the globe; half, believing that the installation brought Australia into the US atomic defence system and in the event of US being involved in atomic warfare would elevate Australia into a prime target, wanted no part of the deal and a public announcement that a future ALP government would insist on the dismantling of the communications centre.

The ALP could probably have recovered from its display of disunity. With the House of Representatives entitled under the Australian Constitution to a three-year life span, elections normally would not be held until 1964. By deciding to accept the Exmouth Base, albeit conditionally and by a narrow margin,[19] the ALP removed a major point of difference between it and the Liberal-CP coalition government. It gave itself a breathing space of just under two years to turn electoral attention back to domestic matters, on which, as the 1961 election results had shown, the Menzies' government was vulnerable and the ALP's electoral prospects were better.

But while the ALP Federal conference, which then consisted of thirty-six delegates, six from each of the six state ALP branches,[20] was making its decision on Exmouth Gulf, Calwell and Whitlam committed a blunder that was to cost Calwell whatever chance he had of becoming Prime Minister of Australia and the ALP ten seats in the House of Representatives. The Federal ALP Conference met at the Hotel Kingston in Canberra. On Wednesday, March 20, 1963, when it was to decide the Exmouth Gulf issue, the conference sat late into the night. As midnight approached, Calwell and Whitlam appeared outside the hotel. Almost as though they were emphasising their exclusion from the conference, then debating a subject on which it could legitimately be argued Australia's future could depend in the event of a major war, they stood forlornly under a street lamp. Conference delegates emerged from the hotel to confer with them almost patronisingly. An extraordinary series of pictures were taken by flashlight, and appeared in the Sydney *Daily Telegraph* the following day.[21]

Menzies, an old and wily political warhorse, sniffed the breeze, and liked it. "Who is to decide vital matters involving Australia's defence and external affairs policy—the elected members of the Commonwealth Parliament or the thirty-six faceless men of the ALP Federal Conference?" he thundered. He advanced the election date. On November 30, 1963, and a year prematurely, the House of Representatives, as the senior house in the twenty-fourth parliament, went to the polls after a campaign fought mainly on the issue of the "thirty-six faceless men." Menzies' majority shot up from two to twenty-two. The ALP lost ten seats. It was from the time of this electoral reverse that Calwell dated Whitlam's disaffection and the growth of disunity in the ALP's parliamentary wing.

In a confidential report to the ALP Federal Executive,[22] Calwell, analysing the reasons for the ALP's 1966 electoral setback, wrote "Next in importance after the effects of the lying propaganda of the Liberal and Country Parties in their attempts to justify Australia's participation in the Vietnam war and the reasons for using conscripts in that cruel, dirty war, all of which frightened many estimable people into voting against us, and the vicious efforts of the jackal group (the DLP) that supports them, the factor that helped to defeat us most was the disunity in our ranks on personal and policy questions carried on during the whole lifetime of the Twenty-fifth Parliament . . . from January, 1964 until March, 1966, Mr Whitlam continued to throw the party into turmoil in the pursuit of his ambition to discredit my leadership and advance his own claims to the position." The report went on to detail what Calwell clearly regarded as acts of treachery to himself and to the ALP, subsequent to March, 1966.

A clash between Calwell and Whitlam was inevitable after Calwell had lost the 1963 elections. Whitlam was prepared to acquiesce in Calwell's leadership, waiting for time to confirm Whitlam's conviction that he was "destined to be the leader",[23] while Calwell still had prospects of being prime minister and lifting Whitlam to the deputy prime ministership. But pragmatic and flexible, Whitlam wanted power. He did not go along with what he termed the "new heresy" being voiced by Mr F. E. ("Joe") Chamberlain, the formidable and able Western Australian ALP Secretary, who, as ALP Federal President and Secretary, had since 1955 been the ALP's "strong man", federally, and a Whitlam critic. Chamberlain's attitude was "The Labor movement does not exist primarily to win elections. It exists to advance the cause of democratic socialism. We can't afford to have men running the Labor movement who will sell out on principles of the Party for a few votes."[24] Whitlam was contemptuous of this attitude. "There is nothing more disloyal to the traditions of Labor than the new heresy that power is not important or that the attainment of political power is not fundamental to our purpose," Whitlam said. "The men who formed the ALP in the 1890s knew all about power. They were not ashamed to seek it, and they were not embarrassed when they won it. . . . This party was not conceived in failure, brought forth by failure or consecrated to failure. . . . I did not seek and do not want the leadership of Australia's largest pressure group."[25]

Appreciating that for the ALP to be sure of gaining power it had to win back some of the Irish-Australian support lost after the 1955 split, Whitlam, as Calwell's deputy, had tried rather tentatively and feebly to do something about "unity tickets" in union elections, tolerated by the Victorian ALP despite a Federal ALP directive declaring them outlawed. "Unity tickets" were used when ALP and Communist Party unionists agreed to share their union's leadership, and produced "how to vote" cards on which the ALP and Communist unionists appeared jointly as candidates for the union offices which they had previously fixed upon as the entitlement of the respective parties. Such "unity tickets" because they gave the appearance of being issued under ALP auspices were often successful, particularly in Victoria, and consequently aroused suspicion of the Victorian ALP's Communist associations. They provided the DLP with seemingly firm evidence that the controllers of the leftwing Victorian ALP had a proCommunist bias. Whitlam's reformist efforts were brushed contemptuously aside. In return he was accused of seeking to intervene in the internal affairs of the trade union movement—action also proscribed under ALP rules—and his abortive attempts to promote Federal ALP intervention in Victoria[26] resulted in a Victorian-Whitlam feud that influenced profoundly both internal ALP politics and the ALP's electoral standing throughout Australia.

Even after the ALP electoral setback of 1963, Calwell and Whitlam still had one thing in common. Neither were the "pin ups" of the Victorian ALP which in 1960 after Dr Evatt's retirement had used its influence ineffectually to support Reginald Pollard, a hot tempered, peppery and lovable Victorian farmer and radical, Minister for Commerce in the former ALP government with a distinguished military record in World War I, against Calwell in

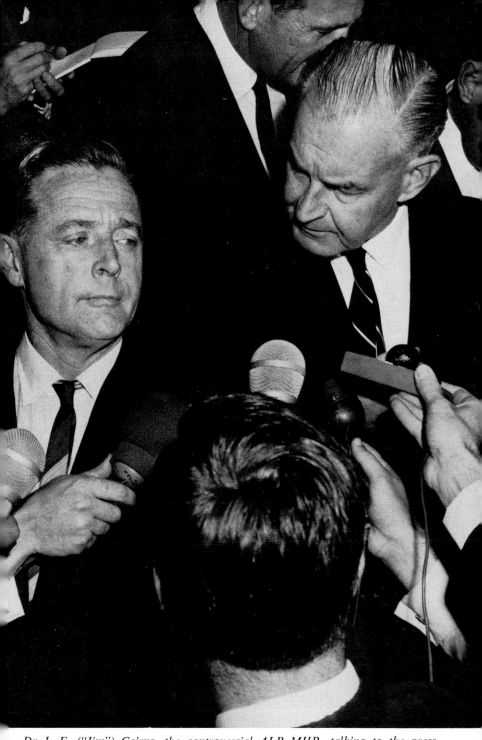

Dr J. F. ("Jim") Cairns, the controversial ALP MHR, talking to the press after he had unsuccessfully contested the ALP Federal Parliamentary leadership against Whitlam in 1968. The author, Alan Reid, is on Cairns' left.

Sir Lennox Hewitt, whose appointment as permanent head of the Prime Minister's Department and Gorton's official adviser, caused ill-feeling among sections of the Commonwealth Public Service. Gorton had earlier associations with Hewitt dating from when Gorton was Navy Minister and Minister for Education and Science.

the leadership stakes.[27] The Victorian ALP suspected Calwell for his Catholicism and his former links with the onetime ALP members who now led the DLP; the leaders of the Victorian ALP detested Whitlam for his flexible readiness to discard what the Victorians regarded as principles and Whitlam regarded as attitudes and policies which cost the ALP votes.

But on November 11, 1964, the Menzies' government, acting against the background of the Vietnam conflict where Australian servicemen were fighting against North Vietnamese and Vietcong alongside United States and South Vietnamese forces, introduced a National Service Act providing two years military service for twenty-year-olds selected by ballot. Up to this stage, Calwell had given mild support to the Australian involvement and also had expressed sympathy for the United States' position and difficulties. "The situation that 1964 has inherited (in Vietnam) obviously makes the abandonment of the military effort impossible," Calwell told the House of Representatives. "Nor do we (the ALP) advocate such an abandonment. The search for a political settlement requires negotiation and it is imperative that the anti-Communist forces should negotiate from a position of strength."[28] Even after a decision was announced on April 29, 1965, to send an Australian battalion to Vietnam to supplement a small group of Australian Army instructors who had been in South Vietnam since 1962, Calwell was relatively temperate, and again showed sympathy for the US position. While opposing the despatch of the battalion, he said "The role of Australia should have been to support the call for negotiations, and help those working towards them. Nobody underestimates the difficulties and dangers of negotiation. That is why we understood and sympathised with American efforts to secure a stronger base for negotiations."[29]

But Calwell was a dedicated anticonscriptionist. Calwell had fought on the anticonscription side during the violent, passionate political struggles over conscription in World War I—a struggle which resulted in a large section of the ALP leadership and following hiving off when the pro-conscription followers were defeated by referenda in 1916 and 1917. In 1943 with the war against Japan at a critical point Calwell, then Minister for Information, had opposed—this time unsuccessfully—proposals sponsored by his own prime minister, John Curtin, for the ALP to agree to conscription for service outside Australia and its territories but within a defined area. When the Menzies' government introduced the National Service legislation, Calwell remained firm to the attitude he had adopted through his lifetime. Whereas Whitlam, his deputy, at that time voiced objections to national

97

service only on the grounds of the lack of necessity for its introduction,[30] Calwell declared ". . . the Labor Party opposes utterly
and absolutely conscription for the youth of this country for serving
overseas in peacetime."[31] By March, 1966, the conflict in Vietnam
had become, in Calwell's eyes, "this unnecessary and unwinnable
war."[32]

Calwell's changed and changing attitudes produced a re-alignment
of loyalties within the ALP. Though Chamberlain, from West
Australia, was still federally the leftwing's largest force and main
strategist, the Victorian ALP[33] was the hard base of ALP leftwing
strength. Hitherto, Dr J. F. ("Jim") Cairns,[34] an ex-policeman
turned academic, had been the Victorian ALP's "favorite son"
and Calwell was an object of deep suspicion.

Cairns, a trim, ex-Decathlon champion, was, outwardly, tightly
controlled, impeccably courteous. He seemed to find in the
adulation of mass audiences, particularly mass audiences of young
people, a substitute for the affection he craved but could rarely
evoke from individuals with whom he had political associations.
He had secured the friendship of ALP parliamentarian, Tom Uren,
from NSW, a big ex-heavyweight boxer and former p.o.w. in
Japanese hands, who had acquired from his war experiences a
hatred of war and violence, and a steadfast belief that the quality
most needed to solve mankind's problems was goodwill. While
holding this belief, Uren, an indefatigable worker and possessed
of an intuitive feeling for how a party machine can be managed
and influenced, did not neglect organisation on behalf of those
within the ALP Uren considered to be possessed of goodwill.
Uren's attitude towards Cairns was at once admiring, exasperated
and protective. Though himself controversial because of his
identification with peace movements which came under periodic
attack because of their alleged domination by Communist Party
or Communist aligned influences, Uren was not as controversial
as Cairns. Unlike Evatt and other ALP leaders who categorised
Communism as authoritarian,[35] Cairns placed the ALP next to the
Communists in the political spectrum,[36] though he later modified
this view by declaring in a signed article[37] "I am totally against
ideological rigidity and submersion of the individual by the party
. . . ." Again modifying a previous assertion that "private property
is the foundation of all power (in Australia) and the source from
which it is derived",[38] Cairns told a Canberra audience, largely
composed of young people "You have to exercise power wherever
power is. . . . Power also exists in schools, in universities, in
factories, in government departments, in banks and everywhere
else . . . . We won our democracy by breaking laws, by changing

laws, by demonstrating in the streets . . . those who are ready to resist authority are the people who today are behind the new Reformation . . . . I sincerely hope that authority has had its day."[39] But probably what endeared Cairns most to the ALP leftwing and was his most heinous offence in the eyes of the ruling establishment was that he was one of the earliest and certainly the most able and effective opponents to Australian participation in the Vietnam conflict.

Hates and enmities decide the course of political events as well as judgment and study. When Calwell's attitude changed and he devoted his talents and leadership to opposing both Australian involvement in Vietnam and conscription, the Victorian ALP gave him the status of chief "favorite son" and relegated Cairns to second place.[40] Respectable, Catholic, with a lifetime of trenchant opposition to Communism behind him and followers within the ALP rightwing, who though they regretted his newfound affinity with the Victorian ALP declined to either criticise or oppose him because of old and valued ties of loyalty, Calwell was a more valuable ally than Cairns, despite Cairns' following among the youth and the extreme militants. Cairns was compensated for his loss of status as the Victorian ALP's "favorite son." Knowing that Whitlam was trying to replace him as Leader, Calwell set out, deliberately, to build up Cairns as his successor in the Federal ALP Parliamentary Leadership.

Though its future consequences went unnoticed at the time, this realignment of ALP forces and the pressure that both the realignment and Calwell's deliberate policy of advancing Cairns' claims to be his successor in the leadership built up on Whitlam were to be among the factors that enabled Gorton to establish the parliamentary ascendancy over Whitlam that Holt, his more experienced predecessor, was incapable of achieving.

But neither Calwell nor the Victorian ALP could prevent Whitlam winning the ALP Parliamentary Leadership after the 1966 elections when the ALP, following a disastrous clash between Calwell and Whitlam on Vietnam policy five days before polling day,[41] lost a further nine seats, reducing its strength to 41 in a House of Representatives of 123 voting members and its proportionate representation to "the lowest . . . held by the ALP since the Lyons and Lang splits in 1931."[42] When Calwell resigned after the 1966 elections, four contested the leadership ballot against Whitlam—Cairns, Frank Crean, also a Victorian, Fred Daly, the fast talking, humorous, and able radical from NSW, and Kim Beazley, a onetime schoolteacher with a strain of mysticism and a distaste for the vicious infighting at which many of his

Parliamentary colleagues excelled. In the final ballot Whitlam secured thirty-nine votes to end up with an absolute majority over Cairns, fifteen votes, and Crean, fourteen votes. Cairns was also defeated for deputy leader, with Lance Barnard, a moderate from Tasmania, who had Whitlam's backing winning the post from Cairns by thirty-five votes to thirty-three.

But with Calwell undoubtedly still fanning the flames of Victorian ALP dislike for Whitlam, and Cairns, as the months went by, breathing ever closer down his neck. Whitlam decided to attempt to capture the Federal ALP political machine, which, under Chamberlain's masterly and determined leadership, had become the dominant force in ALP internal politics, with the ALP Parliamentary wing reduced virtually to an apprehensive, wavering and impotent appendage, Whitlam had very little understanding of how a political machine worked, its intricacies, and the psychological quirks of the men who operated it and operated within it.[43] He seemed to think that speechmaking alone would decide such a struggle, without the painful, patient, and perpetual building and maintenance of a force within the machine dedicated to his interests and support.

Whitlam was helped to some extent by the reconstruction of the ALP Federal Conference and Executive which had taken place as a consequence of the public reaction against the Hotel Kingston affair when Calwell and Whitlam had waited at midnight outside the hotel while inside the "thirty-six faceless men" of the ALP Federal Conference had made the decision which theoretically could have had an effect upon Australia's future as a nation.

The then Federal Secretary of the ALP was Mr C. S. ("Cyril") Wyndham, a Whitlam ally who had faith in Whitlam's ability as a political leader; none in his steadfastness as a friend. An Englishman, Wyndham had been trained in the British Labor Party. Imported by Evatt as his press secretary when Evatt was ALP leader, Wyndham had had the disillusioning experience of being Secretary of the Victorian ALP before the ALP decided to set up a permanent Federal Secretariat and Wyndham was selected, with the blessing of Chamberlain who thought he could handle the little Englishman, to head it. Wyndham for a long time had been advocating broadening the ALP's organisational structure, particularly its Federal Conference and Executive. After the Hotel Kingston fiasco, the four Federal Parliamentary leaders—the Leader and his Deputy in the House of Representatives and the Senate Labor Leader and his Deputy—were added to the Executive which previously had consisted of two representatives from each of the six state ALP branches. A further change was that a single representative from the Northern Territory was added to bring the Executive's new strength to seventeen—the four Federal Parliamentary leaders, the twelve delegates from the states, and the Northern Territory representative. The Conference was enlarged from thirty-six to forty-seven by including the four Federal Parliamentary leaders and the Northern Territory representative and by adding the state ALP Parliamentary leader to each of the six state delegations which previously had numbered six. These moves tended to check the antiParliamentarian trend which had been a feature of ALP machine politics since the ALP split of 1954/55. Additionally meetings of the ALP Federal Conference, which hitherto had taken place in camera, were opened to the public and representatives of publicity media were admitted to Conference discussions.

Though two of the ALP Federal Parliamentary leaders—the ALP Senate Leader, Lionel Murphy, a Sydney QC, who appeared to have ambitions to emulate Gorton to the extent of stepping down from the Senate to lead the ALP in the House of Representatives, and his deputy, Sam Cohen, a Melbourne QC—had close associations with the Victorian ALP, Whitlam undoubtedly believed he could force them to support him on the ALP Federal Executive through his majority support within the ALP Federal Parliamentary Party.[44]

To get his way on the ALP Federal Executive, Whitlam had to be assured of nine votes. He had, he thought, four in the shape of the four ALP Federal Parliamentary leaders—his own vote, the vote of Barnard, his deputy in the House of Representatives, Murphy's, and Cohen's. The NSW ALP which supported him and which, under strongly antiCommunist leadership, was implacably opposed to Victoria, was another two votes. He was sure of one vote from Tasmania, where his deputy, Barnard, loyal and quietly efficient, was a powerful influence. But this gave him only seven votes that he considered certain. Victoria, Queensland, and Western Australia, with WA's Chamberlain the organising brain, were solidly against him. Among them, they had six delegates: South Australia, where the Irish-Australian content in the state population was well below the Australian average,[45] had no ideological commitment to either Victoria or Queensland, both subject to leftwing pressures, Victoria through a grouping of leftwing unions that operated under the title of the "Trade Union Defence Committee" and which decided the membership of the Victorian ALP Executive[46] and Queensland through the Queensland Trades and Labor Council on which Communist-led unions were prominent. But to attract back to the ALP some of the

101

Irish-Catholic following it had lost at the 1954/55 split Whitlam wanted the ALP to re-affirm the policy of support for state aid for denominational schools that had been ALP policy up to the split. With the Roman Catholic school system which existed alongside the state system of education visibly disintegrating, particularly in the poorer parishes, under the impact of higher costs and the post-World War II immigration programme which had added considerably to Australia's Roman Catholic population, many Catholics viewed government aid for their schools as essential if their separate school system was to survive. South Australian ALP leaders, with Clyde Cameron, Martin Nicholls, also an MHR and often a SA delegate to the ALP Federal Executive, and G. T. ("Geoff") Virgo, then SA ALP Secretary[47] to the fore, were implacably opposed to state aid for denominational schools. As state aid tended to become a symbol in the rightwing-leftwing struggle within the ALP, this gave South Australia an impetus towards the Chamberlain-Victorian group on the ALP Federal Executive, Whitlam decided to change the balance of power within the ALP Federal Executive.

He fixed on Queensland and Tasmania as the targets for his efforts. If he could get in as one of the two Queensland delegates to the ALP Federal Executive a Whitlam supporter and ensure that the second Tasmanian delegate was also of his kidney, he would have nine of the seventeen votes in all vital times and on some occasions the backing of the South Australians and Mr J. ("Jock") Nelson, the Northern Territory delegate, as these delegates' voting patterns were not irrevocably formed by the discipline of factionalism.

In Queensland, Whitlam was quite spectacularly unsuccessful. He did not understand what forces were at work within the Queensland ALP machine and what levers needed to be pulled to manipulate them. With Mr C. T. ("Charley") Oliver, NSW Secretary of the Australian Workers' Union, as NSW ALP President, Whitlam had received constant support from NSW which was his main ALP bastion. The AWU, Australia's largest and wealthiest union, had contributed heavily to the formation of the ALP back in the 1890s. It was even more important in Queensland than it was in NSW. In 1957, in temporary alliance with leftwing elements, AWU leaders had brought about the downfall of the Queensland ALP government led by Premier V. C. ("Vince") Gair[48] who had quarrelled bitterly with the AWU's leaders and resisted a direction issued by them through the Queensland ALP to legislate for three weeks annual leave for all workers, and four weeks for shift workers, in accordance with a timetable laid down

102

by the Queensland ALP.[49] After Gair's ALP government was replaced by a Liberal-CP coalition led by Frank Nicklin, CP, the Queensland AWU reverted to its rightwing stance, but its ALP power was broken. Whitlam turned to the AWU to provide him with another vote.

Whitlam's nominee to replace one of the two antiWhitlam Queensland delegates on the ALP Federal Executive was AWU Federal President and Queensland state secretary, Edgar Williams. Williams stood for the post of Queensland delegate to the ALP Federal Executive at the Labor-in-politics Convention at Surfers' Paradise in February, 1968. Williams was, in the argot of the ALP, "rolled"—badly. Out of a possible 141 votes, Williams received only 48.[50] It was a bad setback for Whitlam. It meant that for the next three years Queensland was to be represented on the ALP Federal Executive by men more in sympathy with his dedicated opponents of the Victorian ALP than with him.

In Tasmania, he was more successful. Elected with Whitlam's backing and as a publicly proclaimed Whitlam backer as Tasmanian delegate to the ALP Federal Executive was Mr R. W. B. ("Brian") Harradine, a man whose sudden elevation to the top of the ALP and whose subsequent fortunes were to influence profoundly the trend of events in the months ahead and, indirectly, the outcome of the elections in 1969.

Harradine was antiCommunist, Catholic, proState aid, pro-Whitlam, outspoken to the point of recklessness as subsequent events were to demonstrate, and able. Outwardly a mild mannered man with a clerkish air, he was bitterly, his opponents claimed fanatically, opposed to the twenty-seven, later twenty-six, leftwing unions which had broken away from the Melbourne Trades Hall and which comprised the Trade Union Defence Committee and through that committee dominated the Victorian ALP.[51] From South Australia Harradine had moved to Tasmania, where he became secretary of the Hobart Trades Hall Council.

Once Harradine became a delegate to the ALP Federal Executive, the ALP's underground presses stepped up their activities.[52] A number of documents, dealing with Harradine and his career and mostly anonymous, received wide circulation. One which appeared to be South Australian in origin claimed that Harradine had spent some years in a monastery, had held an executive position with the DLP in South Australia, and was a DLP "plant" on the ALP. Harradine was stung into a reply. In a memorandum to "Officers and Members of the State Executive, Tasmanian Section, ALP" dated April 7, 1968, a memorandum which he said was in reply to this anonymous document, Harradine wrote "Last

Monday week, Gough Whitlam in his campaign for a purged ALP which could win power in Australia for the benefit of Australian Unionists asked four members of the Victorian ALP Executive to resign.[53] They were officials of Communist-controlled trade unions. It was wrong, he (Whitlam) said, that they should be on an ALP Executive. Their membership of an ALP Executive was used by the ALP's enemies to destroy the prospects of the formation of an ALP government. Did they resign as Gough Whitlam asked? They did not. As ever, the Communist interests which they serve proved that they would rather the ALP remained in opposition for ever, as long as they had substantial influence over the ALP . . . . The real purpose of the attack (on me) is now revealed."

Harradine then added the words that were to affect both Whitlam's future and Prime Minister Gorton's election prospects in 1969. Wrote Harradine "When I go to the meeting of the Federal Executive of the ALP in Canberra[54] on April 17, the friends of the Communists intend to silence me. I have been informed that they will try to exclude me from the Executive meeting so that there will be one vote less in support of Gough Whitlam."

That part of Harradine's statement which forecast the exclusion move was prophetic. The ALP Federal Executive met on April 17, 1968. Before any other matter was dealt with, Martin Nicholls, MHR, from South Australia challenged Harradine's fitness to sit on the ALP Federal Executive after his published declaration that the Victorian ALP Executive was under Communist influence and his charge that "friends of Communists" intended to try to silence him on the ALP Federal Executive. In the subsequent divisions, Whitlam's side, which supported Harradine and his right to sit on the Executive, were outnumbered by ten votes to seven. Among those voting on the opposite side to Whitlam were his two fellow Federal Parliamentary leaders, Murphy and Cohen, and his fellow Federal Parliamentarians, Nicholls, MHR, and Senator J. B. Keeffe, who was functioning in his dual capacity as ALP Federal President, chairing the meeting, and as a Queensland delegate.

On Thursday, April 18, 1968, the two Tasmanian delegates, Harradine and Mr D. ("Doug") Lowe, then the Tasmanian ALP secretary, with the vote going constantly against them, withdrew from the Executive. Exasperated and frustrated and resenting the public humiliation that was being thrust upon him, Whitlam told the Executive "Until a Federal Conference considers the matter, I shall not appear for any candidate, other than present members, selected under present (ALP) procedures in Victoria unless I can vouch that the candidate is a fit and proper person to be an ALP member of the House of Representatives."[55] But it was clear that Whitlam was not going to get approval for the calling of a conference from an executive in which the majority was taking a savage delight in pulling out his tail feathers. Before the day was out Whitlam sent a telegram to all ALP Federal Parliamentarians. It read "Am firmly convinced that I cannot face the parliament or the public with confidence unless caucus[56] shows its confidence in me. You will have read that three times at Federal Executive yesterday Lance Barnard, Harry Webb and I were outvoted on a show of hands by Lionel Murphy, Sam Cohen, Martin Nicholls, and Jim Keeffe.[57] Such damaging division entirely nullifies McEwen-McMahon and comparable splits among opponents. Am therefore calling meeting of caucus for midday, Tuesday, April 30, when I shall resign my position (as Federal Parliamentary Leader) and recontest my position. This will permit caucus members at earliest moment and with least embarrassment to endorse their leader or substitute another. Letter will follow."[58]

Whitlam clearly thought that all he had to do was to throw down the gauntlet and he would win easily and without a fight. A Sydney newspaper, with close links with Whitlam headlined its report of the day's proceedings "Whitlam takes gamble—serious challenge to replace him as leader unlikely."[59] But there was to be a challenge, a serious one, which was to shake Whitlam's confidence badly and was to give Gorton the parliamentary ascendancy over Whitlam, an ascendancy which lasted until Gorton in turn ran into trouble with his Liberal Party and the effects of which were probably not dissipated when elections came round in 1969.

There was strong feeling against Whitlam in the caucus. But Cairns, the expoliceman who was closer than anyone in outlook to the Victorian-Chamberlain majority on the ALP Federal Executive, was viewed as an election loser. After the 1966 ALP election disaster, he had conceded "We (the ALP) have lost partly because of the thing I stand for—the (election) result is pretty much as I expected it would be."[60] After the 1966 elections when Calwell had resigned, Cairns received only fifteen votes when he opposed Whitlam for Calwell's vacated leadership. In the frantic manoeuvrings that took place in the twelve days between the announcement of Whitlam's intentions and the assembly of the caucus to vote on the leadership issue, attempts were made to persuade Barnard to stand against Whitlam. AntiWhitlam strategists estimated that if Barnard's small but crucial personal following was added to the votes Cairns, Uren, Cairns' friend and most ardent supporter, the Victorian ALP, Calwell, Chamberlain and other ALP elements hostile to Whitlam could muster Barnard could replace Whitlam as leader and Cairns could take over the Deputy leadership.

But Barnard, who had supported Whitlam consistently at the ALP Federal Executive, refused to enter the lists against his leader. He went further. He said that he would resign the Deputy Leadership if Whitlam was defeated, though, shrewdly, he covered himself against the contingency of a Whitlam defeat by reserving his right to recontest the Deputy Leadership. Cairns announced himself formally as a contender for the Leadership. From then on it was a dogfight of Herculean proportions.

Whitlam circulated a letter to all Federal ALP Parliamentarians on April 24, 1968. The letter dealt with his defeats at the ALP Federal Executive. "The Parliamentary Party bears the direct brunt of any loss of public confidence or esteem," the letter complained. "Its leader (Whitlam) was in the minority at every stage of the issue and in all attempts to find a reasonable solution. Nearly half the majority against me was provided on each occasion by four of our (parliamentary) colleagues (Murphy, Cohen, Nicholls, and Keeffe), including two of my fellow office bearers (Murphy and Cohen). All these factors created a situation which I could not ignore if I am to retain any public credit or credibility as leader of our party. Nor could the caucus ignore them if it is to retain public credit or credibility as a future government of this nation . . . . Members of the caucus who are members of the Federal Executive and Conference solely by virtue of their positions in caucus (Murphy and Cohen) have a higher responsibility. They are in effect the representatives of caucus . . . they have no right to promote the interests of a faction or a state executive at the cost of seats we hold or must win . . . those who excluded Mr Harradine did not aim simply to exclude Tasmania or even Mr Harradine. They aimed to preserve in terms of voting strength on the present (Federal ALP) executive, the position of the Victorian Central Executive. Because, as is equally wellknown to you, I have tried to secure reform of the present VCE, it was aimed at me . . . . I wish to make it clear beyond all doubt that, if you re-elect me, you will approve my efforts to secure a special (Federal ALP) Conference to deal with the foregoing matters. I would accept the position on no lower terms.[61] To do otherwise would make a mockery of all my efforts to fulfill the trust you reposed in me in February, 1967,[62] to do all I could within the framework of the party to lead us into government . . . . Even if caucus replaces me, the problems of our appalling and declining electoral performances in Victoria will still continue: the unrepresentative character of the VCE, the influence of an outside and secret body upon it, its disruptive relations with the Melbourne Trades Hall Council, its strained relations with the State Parliamentary Party, the factionalism of its official publication, the crude partisanship of its articles in the great Melbourne dailies, its inability to maintain branch membership and morale, its alienation of many scores of earnest members."[63]

Thereafter all stops were pulled out. The Victorian ALP Executive controlled the ALP preselections of Victorian Federal Parliamentarians. Only two, possibly three[64] Victorians, voted for Whitlam. One of the two was Frank Courtnay, then ALP MHR for Darebin, a Melbourne constituency. He lost his ALP preselection after he protested to the Victorian ALP Executive about Victorian ALP members visiting his home to pressure him into voting for Cairns against Whitlam. Soon after this visitation, he wanted to resign from Parliament on the grounds that politics, as played by the Victorian ALP, were "too filthy for him."[65] The second Whitlam supporter was Senator P. J. ("Pat") Kennelly, a onetime ALP Federal Secretary and ALP "Kingmaker" who had already quarrelled with the Victorian ALP, and later was to accuse it of "being sick",[66] and who was in what he proposed, and the Victorian Executive intended to make certain, was to be his last term in the Federal Parliament. The Western Australian ALP Executive, under Chamberlain's guidance, accepted "without question, the right of members of the Federal Parlaimentary Labor Party, meeting in caucus, to elect the leader of that body without direction from any state executive."[67] But having said that, the WA ALP Executive went on to blast Whitlam. "Mr Whitlam, by his repudiation of the Federal Executive and the decisions reached at its recent meeting, has broken his undertaking to the special Federal Conference on March, 1966, that he would from then on 'work within the framework of the constitution and rules of the Party',"[68] the Executive stated. "It is obvious from his letter (of April 23, 1968) to parliamentary members that he will be the judge of what is good for the ALP and that his re-election will be a mandate to follow his present course. In these circumstances, the State Executive calls to the attention of the WA members of the caucus that it is unequivocally opposed to any constitutional condition being introduced into the leadership ballot and that such a condition must be opposed."[69]

Whitlam's letter had little impact upon the four ALP Parliamentarians—Murphy, Cohen, Nicholls and Keeffe—whom it criticised. Cohen, a polite man, remained silent. Keeffe and Nicholls were unimpressed and unrepentant. Murphy told a TV audience

"Are the Parliamentarians expected to be 'yes' men or puppets and to vote in the same way as Mr Whitlam? I am certainly not a 'yes' man."[70]

Cairns also despatched a letter to all Federal ALP Parliamentarians. Dated April 24, 1968, and marked "Confidential" it branded Whitlam as "the last man" to be given greater powers. "His (Whitlam's) resignation and conduct have endangered our party because they brought completely into the public arena matters which should have been settled elsewhere within the Party's constitutional procedures," the letter read. "They have raised the question just how far can Mr Whitlam go in defying majority decisions of the Party authorities of which he is a member or with which he is in association. They raise the question: whose Party is this—ours or his? . . . In 1966 at a special conference of the Party, Mr Whitlam did two things—he apologised to the Federal Executive for his public attack on it and said 'I now undertake to work within the framework of the Party and to accept the decision of its properly constituted authorities.'[71] Mr Whitlam has failed to honor this undertaking by his present attack on party authorities and by his resignation to seek authority to override them still further should the need arise."[72]

Cairns' letter continued "I am opposed to any attempt by any man to centralise power or to dominate his party colleagues . . . there are those who believe they are being 'modern' by seeking to replace this perhaps rough and ready, but basically sound process (of conferences and executives) by one which place an elite—or even an individual—at the top, on the assumption that he knows best. This is intellectual arrogance and dangerous folly . . . . Unless harmony is established it must be obvious that the party will be in a continuing state of crisis which will place in danger the seats of many of our present members whose majorities will not stand this state of affairs . . . . I do not believe that this crisis can be solved by any one man getting more of his own way. It can be solved only by someone who can find room in the Labor Party for both those broad viewpoints, often misleadingly called 'left' or 'right'. Should I become leader, I pledge myself to achieve this aim. No one wants to see an Australian Labor government more than I do but it cannot be achieved by a continuing disregard for the socalled 'left' in the belief that it has nowhere else to go . . . . I do not think Mr Whitlam has proved himself a stable leader and an unstable leader means an unstable party. Such a leader should be the last man to be given greater power. I am sure we have a better chance of winning elections if we work together as a team rather than place our collective destiny in the hands of one man

108

. . . it would be disastrous for the party if Mr Whitlam would claim a mandate to continue what was this week called 'his war against the party.' The only effective restraint against this is the election of a new leader."[73]

The caucus met on April 30, 1968. Cairns' vote skyrocketed from the fifteen of February, 1967, to thirty-two. Whitlam obtained thirty-eight votes. It would have needed only four of the ALP Federal Parliamentarians to change their vote and the ALP would have had a new leader. Whitlam emerged from the caucus, smooth, seemingly unruffled, but a deeply shaken man.

It was these events which enabled Gorton to establish his parliamentary ascendancy over Whitlam. Normally, in a democracy like Australia, which historically has reacted in an electorally hostile fashion to a Party demonstrably divided, Gorton could have confidently expected the after effects of such a cataclysmic experience for the ALP to carry him on comfortably and success-fully to and beyond the next elections. But events in the shaping of which Harradine was more than a year later to have again a minor but significant part and Gorton's own actions were to decide otherwise. By the time the 1969 elections came round the ALP's troubles were matched if not dwarfed by those of the Liberal-CP coalition, particularly those of its leader, John Grey Gorton.

NOTES

[1] This view conflicts with that held by many Australian political scientists but I believe is historically justified.

[2] Prior to the 1961 elections, the Menzies Liberal-CP coalition departed from the ALP established concept of full employment. At those elections, the Menzies government majority in the House of Representatives declined from thirty-two to two.

[3] For example, no non-Labor government dare introduce a Budget which does not make at least a token gesture suggesting that the government is seeking to improve the lot of age pensioners. Not to do so would be to risk imperilling its electoral support even in middle-class electorates. Part of Gorton's electoral appeal was that he gave the impression of having compassion for the problems of the chronically sick, the needy and the "vulnerable."

[4] At the 1947 Census before the impact of postwar European migration and when Catholics in Australia were conceded to be generally of Irish descent, Catholics were 25 percent of those who stated their religion— Commonwealth Year Book, No 43, 1957, p 569.

[5] As early as 1796 Governor Hunter in an official dispatch to the Duke of Portland was expressing concern about "those turbulent and worthless characters called Irish Defenders who had threatened resistance to all orders"—Historical records of Australia Series 1, Vol 1, p 674.

6 "The Wild Colonial Boy"—anonymous. In *True Patriots All* compiled by Geoffrey C. Ingleton, Angus and Robertson, Sydney 1952, the "Wild Colonial Boy" is "Bold Jack Donahoe." In *Australian Bush Songs and Ballads,* edited by Will Lawson, Frank Johnson, Sydney, 1944, "John Donahue" becomes "Jack Dowling." The name changes but the Irish extraction is constant.

7 "Whitty and Burns not being satisfied with all the picked land on the Boggy Creek and King River . . . paid heavy rent to the Banks for all the open ground so as a poor man could keep no stock. . . ."—Ned Kelly's Jerilderie letter in *Australian Son—the Story of Ned Kelly* by Max Brown, Georgian House, Melbourne, 1948.

8 Peter Lalor's "Report of the killed and wounded at the Eureka Massacre on the morning of the Memorable Third of December, 1854"—*True Patriots All* compiled by Geoffrey E. Ingleton, Angus and Robertson, Sydney, 1952.

9 *A Short History of the Australian Labor Movement* by Brian Fitzpatrick, Rawson's Bookshop, Melbourne, 1946, p 102.

10 *Fifty Years of Labor in Politics* by George Weir, Industrial Publications, Sydney, 1945 quotes the *Bulletin* of July 11, 1961 as saying of the ALP "it (the ALP) wants no imported governor-generals nor borrowed generals nor hollow military pomp, no foreign titles nor foreign capitalists, and no more foreign loans, no cheap labor, nor low-priced and diseased emigrants from the slums of Europe and Asia, no more religious feuds, no National Anthem or similar doggerel, no upper house and no more party government."

11 Pointing out that the constitutions proclaimed in NSW and Victoria in 1855 were not the work of radicals, Robin Gollan writes "The explanation of the apparent anomaly lies ultimately in the quality of Australian opinion, itself the outcome less of the force of any commonly accepted radical political ideas than of a combination of unique political social and economic facts. Most Australians of the eighteen-fifties were radicals because circumstances made them so."—*Radical and Working Class Politics,* by Robin Gollan, Melbourne University Press, 1960, p 1.

12 *Australian National Government* by L. F. Crisp, Longman's, Melbourne, 1965, p 176.

13 Santamaria has consistently denied that he deliberately sought control of the ALP for his followers.

14 Official statement issued by Dr Evatt, October 5, 1954

15 To some extent Evatt was under the compulsion of events to accept this position. He was criticised by a number of Roman Catholic clerics including Dr Daniel Mannix, Archbishop of Melbourne, who complained that Dr Evatt has attacked "those men who have been most active in the fight against Communism in the trade unions and in the Labor Party"— *Catholic Action and Politics* by Tom Truman, Georgian House, Melbourne, 1959, p 11.

16 In the second last ballot for ALP deputy leadership at a caucus meeting on March 7, 1960 Ward received 32 votes, Whitlam 28, and Les Haylen, a Sydney radical whose support came from the leftwing, 12 votes. But in the next ballot with Haylen eliminated only two of Haylen's votes went to Ward. Ten went to Whitlam who defeated Ward by thirty-eight votes to thirty-four.

17 The story of the role Cameron played vis-a-vis Calwell at the Hobart Conference is too long to tell here. But it is a fascinating footnote in Australian political history.

[18] See Professor L. F. Crisp's analysis of seats won by Liberal-CP governments on DLP preferences between 1968 and 1969—Australian *Quarterly*, March 1970, p 104.

[19] The ALP decision that subject to certain conditions a "defence radio communications centre capable of communicating with submarines operated by an ally in Australia would not be inconsistent with Labor policy" was finally carried by 19 votes to 17—official Report of proceedings of the Special ALP Conference on Foreign Affairs and Defence, Canberra, March 18/20, 1963, p 15.

[20] The ALP Federal Conference, which meets biennially, is the ALP's supreme governing and policy making body. The ALP Federal Executive is the ALP's supreme governing body and interpreter of ALP policies between conferences. Contrary to British Labor Party practice, ALP parliamentarians are bound to observe the decisions and rulings of both bodies. The ALP Executive has the power to direct ALP parliamentarians on how they should vote in the Parliament, and exercised this power in 1950 when it directed ALP parliamentarians to pass the Communist Party Dissolution Bill, without the amendments that a majority of the ALP Parliamentary Party and the then ALP Parliamentary Leader, Chifley, were insisting upon and which the Parliamentary Party had the power to insert in the legislation as the ALP had a majority in the Senate. (The full text of this direction appears in *Communism and Democracy in Australia* by Leicester Webb, F. W. Cheshire, Melbourne, 1954, pp 34/35.)

[21] I arranged for these pictures to be taken, but as the man who took the pictures was an amateur, not a professional, photographer I have never revealed his identity in case he became the victim of political resentment.

[22] This document marked for distribution to members of the ALP Federal Executive was dated February 3, 1967, and up to the time of writing had not been made public.

[23] Transcript of "Seven Days" programme, ATN 7, Sydney, February 15, 1966.

[24] The *Bulletin,* March 5, 1966.

[25] Speech by Whitlam to the Victorian ALP annual conference, June 9, 1967.

[26] Under Federal ALP rule 7 (c) (VIII) the ALP Federal Executive has the power to declare that an ALP branch which acts in a manner "contrary to the federal constitution, platform and policy of the party, as interpreted by the Federal Executive" may be dissolved and a federal organisation substituted. Whitlam had to wait until September 14, 1970, before a reconstructed ALP Federal Executive was persuaded to invoke this rule to secure the dissolution of the Victorian ALP and the temporary substitution of a federal organisation. At the time of writing, the outcome of this move has not been finally resolved.

[27] Calwell, at this stage backed by the rightwing section of the ALP Federal Parliamentary party, defeated Pollard by 42 votes to 30.

[28] Commonwealth Representatives Debates, Vol 41, pp 678/679, March 19, 1964.

[29] Commonwealth Representatives Debates, Vol 46, p 1106, May 4, 1965.

[30] Commonwealth Representatives Debates, Vol 44, pp 2932/2935, November 12, 1964.

[31] Commonwealth Representatives Debates, Vol 44, p 2926, November 12, 1964.

[32] Commonwealth Representatives Debates, Vol 50, p 239, March 15, 1955.

33 Mr W. Hartley, Victorian ALP Secretary, was a Chamberlain protege appointed to his post by the Victorian ALP Executive on Chamberlain's suggestion.

34 Cairns was ALP MHR for Yarra, a Melbourne seat. When Yarra disappeared in the electoral redistribution at the 1969 elections, Cairns was elected MHR for Lalor.

35 Dr H. V. Evatt: "The objection of Labor to Communism begins with the fact that the Communist Party believes in a totalitarian form of government. . . . Communist governments resemble fascist governments" —Commonwealth Representatives Debates, Vol 18, p 1000, April 17, 1958.

36 Cairns: "We (the ALP) are situated in the political spectrum next to the Communists and they will stand for many things for which we also stand."—*Dissent*, Spring issue, 1964.

37 Signed article by Cairns, *Sun,* Sydney, July 6, 1966.

38 Curtin Memorial Lecture on "Socialist Liberty" by Cairns, University of Western Australia, June, 1960.

39 Transcript of speech by Cairns on "Australian involvement in Southeast Asia," Canberra, September 15, 1970.

40 The test came in September, 1968 when with his then seat of Yarra abolished in an electoral redistribution Cairns wanted the Victorian ALP to give him ALP preselection for Melbourne, the seat held by Calwell, then 73 years of age. But with Whitlam firmly in the Leadership saddle after defeating Cairns twice in ballots, for the leadership, one in February 1967, and the other in April 1968, Calwell was more important to the Victorians than Cairns. Cairns was given ALP preselection for Lalor, a much weaker seat from the ALP viewpoint.

41 "A labor government might keep Regular Army troops in Vietnam . . ." —Press statement by Whitlam, Adelaide airport, November 21, 1966. "At no time have we said that we will negotiate with the Americans or the South Vietnamese to prolong the stay of our regular troops in Vietnam."—Press statement by Calwell, Sydney airport, November 22, 1966.

42 Confidential report by Calwell to ALP Federal executive, February 3, 1967.

43 Not until Clyde Cameron, MHR, a machine operator par excellence, joined him in action against the Victorian ALP was Whitlam able to achieve anything substantial.

44 This belief proved unjustified. Later Whitlam was to complain "Members of caucus (the ALP Federal Parliamentary Party) who are members of the Federal Executive and Conference solely by virtue of their positions in caucus . . . have no right to promote the interests of a faction or a state executive . . ."—Circular letter from Whitlam to members of the ALP Federal Parliamentary Party, Canberra, April 23, 1968.

45 South Australia was settled by free migrants, not convicts. For a number of reasons, including a climate which was harsher than that of NSW and Victoria, it did not offer the same opportunities for advancement to the laboring classes to which the Irish-Australian usually belonged. The Catholic content in South Australia is about 20 percent; across Australia about 27 percent—Figures based on "religious denominations by sex, states and territories, census, June 30, 1960," Commonwealth Year Book, No 54, 1968, p 149.

46 After a protracted investigation the ALP Federal Executive on September 30, 1970, found "that the Trade Union Defence Committee had been

Gorton with Senator Malcolm Scott, who was one of the triumvirate who worked to raise Gorton to the Prime Ministership in 1968. Scott's rise under Gorton was meteoric. He became Minister for Customs. His fall was even more spectacular. Gorton sacked him as Customs Minister, and Scott then lost his Liberal Senate pre-selection in Western Australia.

Four apprehensive people. From left, Tony Eggleton, Gorton's Press Secretary, Mrs Gorton, Interior Minister Peter Nixon, and Gorton study the results board on election night, October 25, 1969. The Gorton-led Liberal-Country Party Coalition government had a heavy setback and survived only on a handful of votes and Democratic Labor Party preferences.

Gorton with his arm around the shoulder of US Ambassador William Crook. Crook ran into trouble when he confirmed that Gorton after a late night visit to the US Ambassador's residence had left at a relatively early hour instead of at 3 am. The US Embassy incident touched off a sustained attack by Liberal Edward St John upon Gorton's personal behaviour.

permitted to dominate the Victorian (ALP) branch and Victorian Executive."

47 Later a minister in the Dunstan ALP South Australian government which defeated the South Australian Liberal government led by Mr Steele Hall at elections on May 30, 1970.

48 Though ultimately he had accepted the decision, Gair had opposed at the 1955 ALP Conference in Hobart the rejection of the delegates from the Victorian ALP Executive dismissed by Federal ALP authority because it was allegedly under Santamarian influences. From then on powerful forces within the ALP were determined to "get" Gair, even if "getting" him resulted in the destruction of the Queensland ALP Government. Gair was expelled from the ALP when still Premier, later joined the DLP and winning a Senate seat in 1964 became the DLP's Parliamentary Leader.

49 For the details of the Gair government's fall see *Three Decades of Queensland Political History 1929/1960* compiled and edited by Clem Lack, Government Printer, Brisbane, pp 429/488.

50 *Daily Telegraph,* Sydney, February 7, 1968.

51 "He (Harradine) is the man who in April, 1968, made a public statement that there were twenty-seven 'scab unions' in Melbourne"—Undated pamphlet "Who is Mr Harradine?" issued by The Metal Trades Defence Committee.

52 The ALP has its own subterranean literature. All factions seem to share in its production. Some of the documents are original and deal with such things as an individual's political history. Some make piquant claims about the unusual sex habits of prominent ALP personalities. Some of the documents purport to be photostats of official records, such as an individual's criminal record. Some are factual; others are factual but spiced with fiction. Some are completely fictional.

53 "The representatives of these unions, which are under conspicuous Communist influence in the state, should consider whether they could not better serve their own unions and the objectives of unions and employee organisations in general by withdrawing from the (Victorian) Executive"—"Suggestions by Federal Leader (Whitlam) to Victorian Central Executive," March 25, 1968.

54 The Federal ALP Executive met in Sydney.

55 Federal ALP Executive Minutes, April 19, 1968.

56 The ALP Parliamentary Parties, both Federal and State, are called "caucuses" by ALP members and opponents alike and their meetings are usually dubbed "caucus meetings".

57 Whitlam was listing only the Federal ALP Parliamentarians who had voted with him and against him, not the full Executive vote.

58 Federal ALP Executive Minutes, April 19, 1968.

59 *Sydney Morning Herald,* April 20, 1968.

60 "Is the ALP breaking up?" by John Bennetts, *Age,* November 28, 1966.

61 Whitlam accepted back the leadership on these "lower terms." No Special ALP Federal Conference was held, and on June 7, 1968, Whitlam assured the Victorian ALP Conference that he was "not running in any way counter" to the Victorian ALP Executive"—*Daily Telegraph,* Sydney, June 18, 1968.

62 Whitlam was elected Leader in February, 1967.

63 Circular letter from Whitlam to ALP Federal Parliamentarians, April 23, 1968.

64 The third Victorian is still in the Federal Parliament. As I do not want

his political blood on my conscience if there is a resurgence of Victorian ALP power I am not naming him.

65 *Daily Telegraph,* Sydney, February 26, 1969.
66 Letter from Kennelly to Hartley, November 20, 1968.
67 Minutes of WA ALP Executive, April 29, 1968.
68 After criticising an ALP Federal Executive anti-state aid decision and describing the Executive, then numbering twelve, as "the twelve witless men" in a TV programme on February 15, 1966, Whitlam escaped disciplinary action by giving this undertaking—Report of the Special ALP Federal Conference, Canberra, March 25/26, 1966, pp 36, 64.
69 Minutes of WA ALP Executive, April 29, 1968.
70 *Daily Telegraph,* Sydney, April 24, 1968.
71 Report of the Special ALP Federal Conference, Canberra, March 25/26, 1966, p 36.
72 Cairns' letter to Federal ALP Parliamentarians, April 24, 1968.
73 Cairns' letter to Federal ALP Parliamentarians, April 24, 1968.

CHAPTER 6

FROM the day that Gorton became Prime Minister there was the likelihood of an election earlier than 1969 when the three years' life span of the 27th Parliament would normally reach its constitutional close. Three factors were operating. The first factor was vanity. Politicians are no less vain than other men. Gorton was Prime Minister, but he was Prime Minister because of the judgment of his parliamentary peers, not the voters, and in a democracy it is the voters who accord the final accolade. Until he was installed by the vote of the masses he was not prime minister in his own right. He wanted to be prime minister in his own right. Until so installed, he was inhibited. He could not rid himself with quite the same authority of Hasluck, Fairhall, and McMahon, those leftovers from the Menzies-Holt days whose experience was far more extensive than his, who represented viewpoints that he was seeking to discard, and who provided potential rallying points if opposition developed to his style of leadership and his policy changes. The second factor was advantage. After April 19, 1968 when Whitlam had petulantly stormed out from the Sydney ALP Federal Executive meeting, tossed his ALP leadership into the ring for grabs, and produced a trauma within the ALP, Gorton had an advantage. The Australian electorate had demonstrated repeatedly at elections it would not vote into office a quarrelling and divided political party. But the question was whether the advantage had to be grasped in 1968 or would continue to be available in 1969. This was a matter of judgment. The ALP was in such a state of disarray that an election during 1968 was clearly advantageous. But would the disarray continue and intensify in 1969 and be even more advantageous to the Liberal-CP coalition? As the Whitlam-Harradine-Victorian ALP issue was still unresolved this seemed not only likely, but fairly certain.

The third factor was Gorton's standing with the electorate. After only a few months of Gorton leadership, even those who supported Gorton were uneasily aware that he was unconventional, an experimenter, trying out what by Australian standards were new leadership and electoral techniques, techniques which might, long term, prove unacceptable to Australian voters. "Strike now while the iron is hot and your prestige is still high in the electorate" became the advice of these Gorton supporters, whose attitudes, while not expressly put in those words, which would have been unacceptable to their arrogantly confident leader, undoubtedly influenced marginally Gorton's thinking. Another pressure for an election earlier than normal came from those nominally Gorton's followers but who believed from the start and without giving him an opportunity to prove his quality that he had leadership defects. These critics within the Liberal Party were distrustful of his administrative capacity.

Those belonging to this antiGorton section of the Liberal Party were actuated by both self and party interest. Their analysis was that if Gorton kept on going the way he was going he would bring the ALP to power, whatever the ALP's defects. In a democracy, citizens have a choice, even if at times the choice is the dispiriting one of choosing between evils, when the wise man chooses the lesser evil as preferable to the greater. While neither Gorton nor the ALP were evil in the literal sense of the words the voters might judge that both had shortcomings. There was always the possibility that John Citizen might decide longterm that the ALP's shortcomings were preferable to those of Gorton. This position had not yet been reached. But if the old adage "oppositions don't win elections—governments lose them" was correct the position had to be watched. Gorton would undoubtedly win an election at this stage. His stocks had not deteriorated to the extent that he could lose. But in the view of Gorton's Liberal opponents they could so deteriorate. It was in the Liberal Party's interest that Gorton be brought up with a jolt, a jolt that would cause him to re-examine both his personal style and his administrative methods. This anti-Gorton Liberal section's assessment was that electoral distrust of Gorton was already sufficient to offset to some degree the image of the ALP as a party of discord. While not sufficient to overthrow the government that Gorton led, it was sufficient to cause him to lose seats. This Liberal group, cold bloodedly, was prepared to sacrifice some of its parliamentary colleagues for the government's longterm benefit. The group believed that the loss of seats might cause Gorton to revise his leadership techniques. These Gorton opponents also exercised what influence they had to secure an early election.

There were other reasons for an election earlier than normal. These reasons were not talked about. To talk about them might make the voters uneasy. Voters usually return a government when the economy is flourishing, expanding, and secure, and while there are no extensive areas of discontent. In 1968 the economy was in such a position and the areas of discontent appeared minimal. But there were some ominous clouds on the economic horizon. In the financial year 1967/68 Australia's balance of trade deficit was 222.9 million dollars a year. Australia also had a deficit in "invisibles"—shipping freights, insurance, cost of servicing overseas government loans, the outflow of dividend on foreign investments, the cost of overseas travel by Australians, and the like—of 843 million dollars. The deficit in the balance of current accounts was about 1065 million dollars. During the first three trading months of 1968 Australia had had a deficit 47 million dollars greater than in the corresponding three months of 1969.[1] But Australia's overseas currency reserves had remained unaffected because of an inflow of private foreign investment of 1159 million dollars.

The indicators, however, were that this satisfactory overseas currency position would change. Export earnings from wheat were more likely to decline than to increase. Wheat was facing a buyer's market. Wool prices were falling. While mineral exports were expected to rise in 1969 by more than 100 million dollars a year, Australia's import bill would also rise. The trade union movement was making heavier demands for a larger slice of the national cake. With employment running at a high level and no surplus labor force available to act as a restraint, the unions could and undoubtedly would turn to militancy to enforce their demands. Wage rises placing money in the hands of workers would produce a mounting demand for consumer goods as workers sought to use their higher wages to improve their living standards. This could produce an inflationary situation. If there was inflation, overseas investors might become frightened. With a slowing up in the intake of private foreign investment, 1969 could be a difficult year. Internal economic measures might have to be taken to preserve overseas funds and to check the inevitable price rises, measures against which the electors could react hostilely, particularly if a by-product of these was a falling off in employment, as had been the case in the 1959/1961 period when the Menzies' government came perilously close to electoral defeat.[2]

Gorton at this time clearly believed that he and he alone would decide when the next elections would be held. In theory, he was correct. As Prime Minister, only he had the right to approach the Governor-General and recommend the timing of the next elections. But in politics theory and practice do not always coincide. A prime minister might like to hold an election on a timetable of his fixing. But prime ministers do not control all political events within a country, only the events they are capable of controlling. Gorton seemingly was unaware of the limitation to his power imposed by events which he had allowed to develop and which had moved beyond his control. He thought he was in complete charge of the situation.[3] He allowed election speculation to develop during 1968. He went further than allowing the speculation to develop; he encouraged it by giving it the authority of his silence. He also commenced active preparations for 1968 general elections. though later he was to deny that he had done so. In early July, 1968, the Liberal Party federal organisation did a review for Gorton's guidance on both the timetable and proposed tactics for 1968 general elections.[4]

But the events which crowded in upon Gorton including reaction against some of his administrative actions, forced a revision of plans. Probably the largest single event in bringing about a revision of plans and the abandonment of the 1968 elections intention was the changing attitude of the DLP, upon whose preferences a significant number of government supporters depended for their parliamentary survival. When the chips came down, the DLP, not Gorton, controlled the situation.

But before the DLP brought things to a head with a blunt threat to divert their preferences from government candidates to a sufficient number of ALP aspirants for parliamentary seats selected for their sensitivity to Australia's defence situation[5] to keep the government in power while reducing its parliamentary majority, further strains developed within the government ranks. These strains were the outcome of specific Gorton actions. These actions, and the shape they took, were, in part, due to Gorton's dislike of the Commonwealth bureaucracy, particularly those sections of the bureaucracy that tried to insist upon adherence to time hallowed procedures and acted, or tended to act, as a brake upon any "freewheeling" tendencies on the part of independently minded ministers.

Gorton had scant respect for the bureaucracy or its sensitivities other than those sections in which he had confidence as a result of personal contact. As prior to rising to the prime ministership, his ministerial experience had been limited, these personal contacts were narrow and relatively few. Bureaucratic insistence upon what the bureaucracy reverently regarded as the orderly process of government irritated him. He was contemptuous of red tape. When he wanted something done, he wanted something done, and he grew exasperated when statutory rights, rules and regulations stood in his way. He was a "buck passer", not cynically as other politicians were who "passed the buck" because it was in their own or the government's or the party's interest to "pass the buck" but because he believed, apparently quite sincerely, that he was never responsible for the position which produced the need to "pass the buck" but that it was always someone else's fault. He blamed the bureaucracy for the trouble Holt had brought upon himself when Holt had denied—wrongly—the existence of passenger manifest for persons carried on VIP aircraft. He had no confidence in the External Affairs Department, which he had administered on occasions in an acting capacity while Hasluck was absent from Australia. He was hostile to the Treasury which he regarded as conservatively sterile. He remembered the occasions when while he was a junior minister his plans were defeated by Treasury intervention.[6] Treasury and McMahon were identified in his mind's eye. He disliked McMahon and Treasury was McMahon's power base. Hewitt, now the permanent head of the Prime Minister's Department and the bureaucrat with whom Gorton had the closest association, was a former Treasury officer. But Hewitt had quit Treasury after his qualifications to head that powerful department which had a supervisory responsibility over practically every area of policy which called for the expenditure of government funds, had been denigrated in a deliberate and brutal publicity campaign.[7] Hewitt had no reason to love Treasury.

Gorton moved in early to curb both McMahon's and the Treasury's authority. Under Menzies and Holt, the Treasurer had been left to conduct the preliminary fashioning of the Budget, with the Prime Minister dealing only with the broad principles and the essential detail before the Budget went to Cabinet. Gorton insisted that not only he, but also Hewitt, should be present throughout and take part in the construction of the Budget at every stage. In these circumstances, the Prime Minister, not the Treasurer, of necessity, had to become the dominating influence. Though McMahon had unlimited self confidence and more than the normal share of aggressiveness, a Treasurer's capacity to contradict and oppose the viewpoint of his Prime Minister in the presence of not only his own departmental officers but also the Prime Minister's senior officer was limited. McMahon got much of his own way in the 1968 Budget but only because of Gorton's inexperience. It was a very different picture thereafter.[8]

Gorton either disliked or, in the interests of promoting his image as an aggressive Australian nationalist, pretended to dislike the Treasury policy of an open door for overseas investment in Australia. "Until very recently it has seemed to me that the posture of Australia in seeking overseas capital has been the posture of a puppy lying on its back with all legs in the air and its stomach exposed saying 'Please, please, please give us capital. Oh, tickle my tummy. Oh, on any conditions' " Gorton told an Australian Club

119

luncheon at the Hotel Dorchester in London.[9] To these words, he added the rather incoherent addendum "And this (presumably the posture) is being re-examined for those who seek and wish to take the risks and the advantages that are offered by bringing in capital for new development then we are delighted and we are receptive for that capital."[10] Though almost eligible for submission as a word puzzle, these words did seem at the time to suggest that the "posture" was being re-examined, with the implication from that that there could be a tightening up on overseas capital.[11]

The Treasury's attitude at least had a basis of logic, however regretfully Australians watched overseas investors taking over Australian resources which Australians would have preferred exploited and developed by Australian capital and skills. As Uren pointed out, Australia's overseas reserves—which financed Australia's mounting export bills—had been protected during 1967/68 only by an inflow of private foreign investment of 1159 million dollars. If this inflow was cut off, either by loss of confidence on the part of foreign investors or as a result of government action, then government had to devise ways and means to make up the deficiency. Gorton wanted the popular acclaim that would come from action to protect the Australian heritage, and was prepared to talk about action in a way that he thought would secure him the acclaim. But he had no plan to meet what might be the hurtful consequences of his statements if those statements resulted in the frightening of overseas investors and the drying up of overseas investment. It was the realisation of this deficiency on his part, as much as the cavalier and flamboyant manner in which he made his decision, that brought him considerable criticism in the MLC affair, and revived uneasiness within the Liberal Party about his administrative techniques and ability to think through his problems.

On the weekend of September 21, Gorton flew in a VIP plane to Exmouth Gulf and Perth in Western Australia. Accompanying him were Hewitt and a number of pressmen. For some time, there had been rumors that an undisclosed buyer, or buyers, possibly foreign,[12] was or were acquiring a large number of shares in MLC Ltd., an Australian life insurance company which had been heavily involved in the difficulties of a major Australian trading company but which controlled 750 million dollars worth of Australian and New Zealand savings accumulated over many years and whose investment funds were increasing at the rate of 75 million dollars a year. At Alice Springs, in the heart and centre of Australia, where the plane touched down for refuelling Gorton received a phone call. Later it was to be claimed that the call came from an MLC director, who knew Gorton and was reinforcing appeals already made for the Commonwealth to come to the rescue of the company. Alice Springs, remote and as typically inland Australia as is possible to find, was the kind of place to evoke the nationalist in any Australian. Gorton had more than the average Australian share of nationalism. He also had a sense of drama and a realisation that while Australians might accept the importation of foreign capital they regretted the necessity for it, and would prefer to see Australian assets preserved in Australian hands. From Alice Springs onwards, things started to happen.

Gorton was acting Treasurer. McMahon was overseas. Later Gorton was to claim that he studied the documents on the threatened takeover before he left for Western Australia, had taken them with him, and that "it didn't just come up when we were in Western Australia at all."[13] But if "it didn't just come up" while Gorton was in Western Australia, he behaved as though it had, and produced a situation in which the charge that he was addicted to making decisions "off-the-cuff", a charge that was to plague him and damage his reputation right up to the October, 1969, elections could be levelled against him with some credibility. Over the Nullabor Plain, that harsh, featureless waterless expanse that separates Western Australians from their eastern compatriots like a petrified sea, he walked down the back of the plane and told the pressmen that there were developments regarding MLC Ltd. and that he proposed to do something about them.[14]

While Gorton was in Western Australia, there were a series of calls to the Treasury. The Treasury was against the course of action Gorton proposed. Gorton wanted to amend an Australian Capital Territory ordinance to ensure no takeover. The Treasury view was that there was no need to handle the problem in so direct a way. Such action might frighten away overseas capital, Gorton was warned. Australia had to have this capital inflow until means to fill the gap were found. Gorton might be able to take such a step when mineral exports reached the stage at which overseas capital was luxury, not a necessity. But in the interval capital inflow at current levels was needed unless Australia was to run into troubles with its overseas reserves. The Treasury had been in touch with the British Sun Alliance group. This was the group buying MLC shares. The group had stated it was not trying to take over MLC Ltd. but merely acquiring an investment as a base from which to expand its own insurance operations. The maximum needed to safeguard against a takeover was a delicate warning, not sledgehammer action.

Gorton brushed aside the Treasury's views.[15] He was going to take action. Shares acquired by overseas interest represented 36 percent of the company's total issued capital.[16] Because the real buyers of the shares[17] were cloaking their identity, and were believed to be foreign buyers, this was causing him concern. He did not believe that this accumulation of Australian capital should be allowed to fall under the control of anonymous and probably foreign interests. He was in the fortunate position that the MLC Ltd. was registered in the Australian Capital Territory.[18] He intended to have amended the Australian Capital Territory's Companies ordinance dealing with life insurance companies. On the way back to Canberra from Western Australia, Gorton and Hewitt framed a statement announcing what the government intended to do.[19]

Later Gorton was to concede that the decision he had made was against Treasury advice. "The MLC decision was made by me . . . but the decision that I reached is not necessarily one that the Treasury had advocated",[20] he said on one occasion. "Treasury tended to be not very concerned at what was happening,"[21] he said on another occasion.

The MLC decision probably improved Gorton's standing with the electorate. It confirmed his image as an aggressive Australian nationalist.[22] But it deepened the uneasiness of those within his party who had been disturbed by what was believed to be his tendency to make statements and to take action without proper reflection and prior thought as to implications and possible consequences. It also strengthened the hand of his ALP opponents. While they could claim that they were converting Gorton to the ALP outlook that Australian resources and established companies should receive protection against foreign takeovers they could also portray the manner in which he gave this protection in the MLC case as makeshift, crude, and dangerous to Australia's longterm economic interests. If Gorton secured the temporary applause of the mass electorate, the members of his own party, the bureaucracy and the ALP, who were the opinion makers, reacted uneasily to his approach.

Actually, the MLC decision came as the result of a chapter of accidents. As Gorton was later to claim, the situation did not "just come up" while he was in Western Australia. It had a much longer history. Some time before the MLC directorate had become worried about the buying which was detected through the company's share registry. Mr A. F. Deer, the MLC's general manager, opened discussions with McMahon, as Treasurer. Deer expressed to McMahon MLC's fears that the company was the target of a foreign based "raid." There seems to have been at this stage one of those breakdowns in communications that are inevitable in any big organisation, government or private. Treasury was not informed of Deer's approach to McMahon. McMahon believed that Treasury had been informed and was being dilatory in producing a report on receipt of which he could decide whether the misgivings of the MLC controller were wellbased or groundless. Verbal misunderstandings further confused the situation. It happened that Treasury was simultaneously dealing with another minor matter with which MLC Ltd. were concerned. When McMahon spoke with his senior Treasury officials and asked what progress they had made "in the MLC matter" they, knowing nothing about the approach from Deer, apparently thought he was interested in the smaller negotiations concerning MLC Ltd. The larger subject of the possible takeover of MLC Ltd. started to receive hurried attention only when Deer saw McMahon just before McMahon had to leave on an official overseas trip. On this occasion, probably disturbed over the lack of government reaction to his initial approaches, Deer produced a document setting out what MLC Ltd. knew about share movements.

McMahon sent the Deer document which contained the MLC Ltd. analysis of the company's share position and the company's fears to Treasury for urgent attention, departed for overseas, and Gorton moved in as acting Treasurer. Nigel Bowen, a Sydney QC, mild mannered and quietly spoken, with greater legal ability than political acumen, received a copy of the Deer document about the same time, probably from Deer. From then on Bowen, who was probably more preoccupied with finding some legal formula for Gorton who was determined to prevent a takeover than in performing the Treasury task of assessing the possible repercussions action of a Draconic nature might have in financial and investment circles, appears to have been Gorton's only adviser on the ministerial side, with Hewitt Gorton's main adviser on the Public Service side.

Confronted for the first time with knowledge in the shape of the Deer document that there might be an overseas takeover of MLC Ltd., knowing Gorton's misgivings about foreign investment already publicly stated and aware that Gorton impatiently regarded Treasury as conservative, obstructive, and slow moving, Treasury apparently decided to put Gorton, as its acting Ministerial head, in the picture with the utmost promptness. A Treasury copy of the Deer document was forwarded to Gorton. Gorton reacted swiftly. He was leaving for Western Australia almost immediately. Through Hewitt, he informed Treasury that he wanted a full report, including Treasury comments, available for him on arrival in Perth. His impatience may have been fed by some indication from

123

McMahon before McMahon left for overseas that the MLC matter had been or should have been receiving Treasury attention for some weeks.[23] Whatever happened at Alice Springs—the pressmen travelling with Gorton on the plane suspected that he had had a telephone call stressing the need for immediate action from someone interested in preventing a possible MLC Ltd. takeover—Gorton's determination to act decisively firmed as his plane flew across the desolation of the Nullabor plain.

It was a hectic weekend. Treasury's report was waiting for Gorton when he arrived in Perth. Bowen was contacted. He advised that, as MLC Ltd. was registered in the Australian Capital Territory, Gorton could prevent any takeover by amending the relevant ACT ordinance. Gorton was also reminded that the Commonwealth had a formidable and unchallengeable reserve power. Under Section 51 (XLV) of the Constitution, it had authority over "insurance, other than state insurance; also state insurance extending beyond the limits of the state concerned." McMahon either phoned from or was phoned at Zurich station in Switzerland while he was waiting to take a train to Basle. One version was that he was merely told by Gorton that Gorton had "fixed the MLC business".[24] But if consulted as well as informed, McMahon's objections, as revealed by his later attitude, were overruled. Treasury's recommendation that Gorton should not use a sledgehammer, which might affect the inflow of investment capital still urgently needed, to break a nut which could be easily opened in a less dramatic fashion, was overruled. So was Treasury's suggestion that all that was needed was a mild, warning statement, though Treasury could point out that Menzies had used this technique effectively when there were rumors in 1961 that a group of Hong Kong millionaires were planning to takeover Broken Hill South Pty. Ltd.[25] Treasury also suggested that Sun Alliance could hardly be classified as a foreign company in the narrow sense of the word. The group had been operating in Australia for 135 years. It had written the first life policy ever issued in Australia. Over the years it had invested many millions of dollars in Australia.[26] The Sun Alliance group was insistent that it was not seeking and never had sought to acquire a majority holding in MLC Ltd. It was proposing to extend its general insurance activities in Australia, thought this could be done in cooperation with MLC Ltd., and believed that this cooperation could be best secured by becoming a significant though not the majority sharehold in MLC Ltd. Sun Alliance's activities in Australia were wholly Australian managed and staffed. The group had been buying MLC shares at the market price for over three years. The reason it had not disclosed its identity as the buyer was that it did not wish to inflate the price of the MLC shares. The tone of the Treasury recommendation was that all that was needed to achieve guarantees from the Sun Alliance Group, probably unnecessary guarantees, that MLC Ltd. would continue under Australian control was not an atomic blast which might make foreign investors fearful but at the maximum a gentle nudge. If the technique of amending the ACT ordinance was used, the improvised nature of the decision would be underlined. This technique could be used only because MLC Ltd. was registered in the ACT. If the same circumstances involved a company registered elsewhere in Australia than in the ACT, the Commonwealth could not act similarly.

After deciding to reject Treasury's advice, Gorton did not wait until he got back to Canberra to make the announcement. As his plane flew back to Canberra on Sunday, September 22, 1968, copies of the official statement prepared by him and Hewitt up the front of the plane were distributed to the pressmen travelling at the rear. The statement announced Gorton's intention of amending the ACT ordinance dealing with life insurance companies. The amended ordinance would require nominee shareholders to reveal to the Commonwealth Insurance Commissioner the identity of the beneficial owners of the MLC shares, and would restrict persons who were not residents of Australia or companies not controlled by residents of Australia from holding more than a certain percentage of shares in MLC Ltd. Then Gorton walked down the rear of the plane where the pressmen were housed. According to the pressmen he had "a grin all over his face, like a mischievous schoolboy."

But the grin was to fade and the applause Gorton received for the decisiveness of his action was to recede. Realisation that Gorton had made his decision without any consultation with Cabinet penetrated swiftly. This realisation raised two queries. Query one was about the Gorton thesis that the Prime Minister should make the decisions on things on which he felt deeply and that Cabinet's role was merely to endorse those decisions.[27] Was this an application in practice of the presidential approach; already spelled out by Gorton in TV interviews but suspect in a community that, essentially egalitarian in character, had traditionally opposed cults of hero-leaders? Query two concerned Gorton's ability to identify policy as such. An open door for foreign investment and a refusal to take action that might make foreign investors timid or uncertain had been major policy under both Menzies and Holt. Both prime ministers had resisted with full Liberal Party backing ALP pressure as well as pressure from within the government's own ranks[28] for a modification of this policy. Yet here was Gorton during a weekend and without consultation with Cabinet making a decision which cut right across that policy.

The MLC decision was just one among thousands that Gorton was to make before he reached the October, 1969, elections. But the manner of the making of the decision, as well as the decision itself, was to linger long in the memories of both political friends and foes and to be periodically revived, as other decisions, which had an element of the "off-the-cuff" MLC decision in them, were made. Months later Gorton was still defending his propriety in making the decision he had made in the MLC affair, conceding that he had not consulted his Cabinet before he had made the decision, but pleading that this was the solitary instance[29] when he had departed from this practice of consulting Cabinet. The only excuse he produced for the failure to consult was the need for speed,[30] an excuse that seemed feeble after the Sun-Alliance group revealed that its buying of MLC Ltd. shares had extended over three years.

The decision was also to exasperate further Gorton-McMahon feelings. Gorton did not like McMahon anyway. A onetime Sydney playboy of some eminence, McMahon had shed his former habits when he entered Parliament in 1949. He had grown serious and intense. He was dedicated. He lived for politics and was engrossed in his portfolio. He fought relentlessly to maintain Treasury's influence, prestige and power. He was ambitious and would continue to be so, even though limits had temporarily been placed on his ambition by the McEwen ukase promulgated after Holt's disappearance that neither McEwen nor the CP would serve under McMahon's leadership. Gorton nursed a grievance against McMahon for not bringing him more votes when, under the pressure of events, McMahon joined the Gorton forces in the leadership struggle after Holt had vanished into the sea off Cheviot Beach. McMahon sought to avoid the humiliation of having to take the formal ministerial responsibility for amending the ACT ordinance. Apparently under McMahon's instructions, McMahon's officials tried to get Bowen, as Attorney-General and the minister who had advised Gorton throughout the MLC affair, nominated as the minister who must sign the ACT ordinance implementing the MLC decision. But Gorton was adamant. McMahon must sign. After McMahon got back to Australia, reports trickled down through the Commonwealth Public Service of a long and heated argument between Gorton and McMahon. The argument took place on Monday, November 18, 1968. It was reported to have gone on for nearly two hours. McMahon said that Gorton had

126

made the MLC decision while he was abroad. The decision was made by Gorton on Bowen's counsel and against Treasury advice. It was up to Bowen to sign the amending ordinance. Gorton said that Bowen could not sign it. The decision had already been made that the Treasurer would sign it. Finally, McMahon agreed to sign. But he asked Gorton to remember his attitude.[31]

Though a relatively minor decision compared with others that Gorton was to make later, the MLC was important for the way it made people, important people with the capacity to influence community opinion, regard Gorton in a different light. Whenever he made a doubtful decision in unconventional circumstances in the future, the circumstances were examined against the background of the MLC affair. He had made a decision against the weight of expert advice, seemingly with unnecessary speed and without consultation with cabinet. As he had done that once, he could do it again. The circumstances in which he made the decision also had an effect upon those of his parliamentary followers already shaken by his "Australia won't increase its Vietnam commitment for all time" statement after the February Tet offensive, by his dismal effort in the United States and by his disappointing performance on his Southeast Asian tour earlier in the year. They ceased being faithful, unquestioning disciples. They became doubting Thomases. Reasoning that if an election were delayed until the normal scheduled time of late 1969 Gorton might display weaknesses that would lose him—and more importantly, them— electoral support, they started pressing for 1968 elections. Other Liberals who thought that the shortcomings they considered Gorton possessed had already become evident to sufficient of the voters to make a difference but not a difference sufficient to bring about a change of government were also anxious for 1968 elections. They reasoned that if Gorton was returned with a smaller majority their own positions within the Parliamentary Party would be more secure and that the party's long term prospects would be better as Gorton would be under a compulsion to revise his attitudes and would become more receptive to advice.

But it was, basically, the DLP and not the Liberal malcontents nor Gorton who decided that there would be no 1968 election.

NOTES

[1] Mr Tom Uren, ALP MHR from NSW, set out the figures in a letter to the *Age*, dated October 9, 1968. Uren argued that they provided "compelling reasons why Mr Gorton will have an election this year."

2 In his letter to the *Age*, dated October 9, 1968, Uren forecast that if there were elections in 1968 "credit restrictions are planned after a federal election." It is interesting to note that Uren seemed to take it for granted that Gorton would win elections if they were held in 1968—the accepted view on both the Government and ALP sides.

3 This seemed to me at the time yet further confirmation of the Gorton belief that the prime ministership conferred all power, not just great power.

4 This review which the Liberals had intended to keep confidential was published in Max Newton's *Incentive*, No 164, September 9, 1968.

5 The Federal Liberal organisation showed itself more prescient than Gorton. Indirectly warning him that the DLP would prove difficult unless the government's defence policy had been decided the Liberal review which was prepared by the Liberals' Staff Planning Committee stated ". . . The committee is of opinion that such an election should be held at the latest possible date in the year, say, December 7, 1968 . . . a December election would give the government the longest amount of time in which to complete its foreign policy studies following the defence review. It would seem to be most important that the presentation of what might be a new or at least newly-aspected foreign policy should be perfectly plain and unequivocal to the electorate"—Max Newton's *Incentive*, No 164, September 9, 1968.

6 Gorton let his anti-Treasury feeling show semipublicly at a joint government parties meeting on November 6, 1968. In a debate on the Commonwealth's role in education initiated by Liberal Jefferson Bate, Gorton stated his record—fifty million dollars Commonwealth expenditure when he became Minister for Education, 170 millions when he left, and 210 millions now. Gorton said this had been achieved "despite Treasury opposition." When McMahon, then Treasurer, objected and said nobody had supported Commonwealth entry into the education field like he had, Gorton said he was not aiming at McMahon personally but "at Treasury as an institution."

7 Hewitt—understandably—resented this campaign which developed when it became known that Sir Roland Wilson was resigning as permanent head of the Treasury in 1966.

8 By 1969 the Prime Minister's dominance was established. He overrode McMahon on a number of key points and for all practical purposes he was the architect of the 1969 Budget—"I wouldn't say it wasn't quite the advice the Treasury had given me"—Gorton, discussing the framing of the 1969 Budget, ABC TV interview, August 30, 1969.

9 Official transcript issued by Gorton's office, January 12, 1969.

10 When reading a remark like this I get a certain sardonic amusement out of recalling that Gorton in an address on February 2, 1968 to the Fourth Summer School of Professional Journalism on "Communication—Key to Good Government" commented ". . . There is also a need in using the media . . . for some consideration to be paid to the use of good English."

11 There was no tightening up. Gorton set out the guidelines for overseas investment in Australia on September 16, 1969, in the House of Representatives. Gorton said "we do not believe we can or should seek to legislate in such a complex field."

12 The company allegedly engineering the takeover of MLC Ltd. was never officially identified. On a Channel 7 interview on October 11, 1970, Gorton was still describing the buyer, or buyers, as "undisclosed." In fact, the buyers were acting on behalf of The Sun Alliance Insurance

128

group, which was based in the United Kingdom and announced itself as the buyer on October 9, 1968.

[13] Gorton, Channel 7 interview, October 11, 1970.

[14] Conversations with pressmen who were in the plane.

[15] As it turned out, Treasury was unnecessarily apprehensive about the effect of direct action in the MLC case on foreign investment. The volume of foreign investment was not significantly affected by the Gorton decision.

[16] This figure apparently represented total MLC shares held overseas. The Sun Alliance group's holding at that period was about 22 percent— Gorton interview with Alan Ramsay, *Australian,* December 14, 1968.

[17] "Shares so bought are being registered in the names of nominee companies"—Gorton press statement, September 22, 1968.

[18] The ad hoc nature of the decision is shown by the fact that had MLC Ltd. been registered anywhere in Australia other than in the ACT, where the Commonwealth had complete constitutional authority, Gorton would have been forced to adopt a different procedure.

[19] Gorton press statement, September 22, 1968.

[20] Gorton interview with Murdoch group editors, December 11, 1968.

[21] Gorton interview with Alan Ramsay, *Australian,* December 14, 1968.

[22] An official summary of "The Prime Minister's Activities" during 1968 states that there was "generally popular reaction to the PM's strong move." Although there might have been an element of propaganda in this statement, it appears justified by the volume of mail received by Gorton applauding his MLC decision.

[23] This is pure speculation. I have no knowledge that McMahon raised the MLC matter with Gorton before McMahon left Australia. But it would seem a plausible explanation for the intensity of Gorton's obvious impatience with both Treasury and the Treasury's advice. Treasury's alleged "dilatoriness" on this occasion seems to have been due, as I said earlier, to one of those breakdowns in communication that inevitably happen in a large organisation.

[24] Maximilian Walsh, *Sun-Herald,* September 20, 1970.

[25] "I had some discussions with the Chairman of Broken Hill South Ltd. . . . the proposal concerning that company has been withdrawn"— Menzies, Commonwealth Representatives Debates, Vol 33, p 2083, October 17, 1961.

[26] These points were later also made by Mr R. L. Barnett, deputy chairman and chief general manager of the Sun Alliance and London Insurance group—*Daily Telegraph,* Sydney, October 10, 1968.

[27] Asked what were the Prime Minister's constitutional powers to make decisions without consulting anyone, Gorton said "Oh, they are there. You can make a decision and say that's it. Then if the rest of your Cabinet doesn't like it they can say 'Well, we won't go along with it' so that is just too bad for the Prime Minister, so he can get out, I suppose"—official transcript of interview with Murdoch editors, issued by Gorton's Canberra office, December 11, 1968.

[28] The powerful and usually effective Deputy Prime Minister and CP Leader, John McEwen, had criticised the policy of uninhibited acceptance of foreign investment as equivalent to "selling a bit of the farm each year." But the policy had been continued, unmodified.

[29] "That (the MLC decision) is the only one of all these matters that was done by me and then taken to Cabinet afterwards"—Gorton interview with Alan Ramsay, *Australian,* December 14, 1968.

30 "The MLC decision was made by me in a feeling of urgency . . . ."—
Gorton interview with Frank Davison, Perth *Sunday Times,* December
22, 1968.

31 In November, 1968, I could get no confirmation for the accuracy of this
version from either of the two principals, Gorton or McMahon. But on
things I learned subsequently I am satisfied that it is a reasonably correct
version of what took place.

CHAPTER 7

AUSTRALIAN political experience over the twenty years from 1949 suggests that a democratic government which is shrewd and flexible enough to maintain certain basics can, if politically ingenious, contrive to fight elections on issues which work to its advantage. Though the basics would probably have to vary to suit the local needs, pressures, and available resources in other democratic communities, the basics in Australia during the years between 1949 and 1966 appeared to be (a) maintenance of full employment, (b) reasonable prosperity for both primary and secondary industries, (c) steadily rising living standards for workers,[1] (d) housing programmes that would permit the majority of Australians to achieve, even on a time payment basis, the home-owning status to which they aspired seemingly as a consequence of their generally suburban style of existence, and (e) an annual recognition, however token, of the needs of the aged, sick, and the economically vulnerable, such as widows and age, invalid, and service pensioners.[2] Australia's situation was that some of these basics, including living standards and some rural prosperity, depended upon Australia's capacity to get economic prices for such of its primary products, notably wool, as competed on the world market without the benefit of subsidy and to earn overseas funds adequate enough to pay for its imports. While the three fundamentals—food, clothing and shelter—were available in Australia in potentially unlimited quantities, advances in living standards depended to a degree upon imports and these in turn depended on overseas earnings which in their turn were beyond the control of any Australian government. These earnings were determined by external factors, such as the prices received on the world's markets for Australia's unsubsidised farm products. Other Australian primary industries could be kept going satisfactorily and profitably under a messy, complicated and often economically illogical system of subsidies and government supervised marketing arrangements, provided overall external currency earnings were maintained. In the years between 1949 and 1966, Australia had periodic difficulties with its overseas earnings. But they were difficulties; not crises. This enabled first Menzies, later Holt, to maintain the basics and to seek to evolve election issues that would work to their advantage. In this exercise, they succeeded.

Broadly, Communism was the issue, sometimes the product of genuine conviction, sometimes contrived, on which Menzies led the Liberal-CP coalition to electoral victory in the elections of 1949, 1951, 1954, 1958, and 1963[3] and Holt led the coalition in 1966 to the most massive victory in Federal history. The issue appeared in many garbs but when the clothes were removed the naked figure invariably carried a hammer in one hand and a sickle in the other. In 1949, it was Communism, naked and unashamed, except for a loincloth round its middle, marked "ALP." In his policy speech at this election, Menzies after denouncing Communists as "unscrupulous opponents of religion, of civilised government, of law and order, of national security" promised that a Liberal-CP coalition if returned to power would dissolve the Communist Party and make Communists ineligible for Commonwealth employment or office in a trade union.[4] Menzies himself did not allege any association between an abortive attempt by the Chifley-led ALP government to nationalise the Australian banking system and Communism but his followers did. The CP Leader, then Mr A. W. (later Sir Arthur) Fadden, asserted that Labor and Communist objectives were essentially the same[5] and Mr W. C. ("Bill") Wentworth, who nearly twenty years later was to be a member of the Gorton Ministry, wrote in "Labor, Socialism, and Soviets" "Labor's latest proposal to nationalise the banks has shocked Australia—but it has delighted the Communists . . . all the authorities upon Soviet tactics from Lenin downwards, are agreed that the really critical step upon the road to the Soviet dictatorship is the nationalisation of the banks. Once this obstacle is surmounted, the Communist path is reasonably clear."[6]

While Menzies' proposal to outlaw the Communist Party and to "follow the party into any new form and attach illegality to that new association"[7] was probably based on his concept of the needs of the time, the year 1949 was also a particularly good one in Australia for an able and articulate politician like Menzies to exploit the national fear of Communism. During 1949, Australia had been afflicted by a series of coal and other strikes crippling in their dimensions. Troops had been called in to work open cut mines after a strike by the Communist-controlled Miners' Federation had brought heavy industry almost to a standstill, and had denied heating, lighting and all but the barest essential public transport to citizens. Chifley himself had described the strikes as "Communist inspired", had authorised a series of advertisements stating this to be so, and had taken the drastic action of putting in

132

the troops and freezing union funds. Calwell, later to be Federal ALP leader and then Minister for Information, saw the strike as "a fight between the Labor movement on one hand and the Communists on the other."[8] Though the strike was finally defeated, it together with other strikes that had also affected adversely many in the community, including workers, had given the Communist Party the appearance of massive, overwhelming industrial power.[9] Domestically, there were other factors at work, producing hostility to or suspicion of Communism in the local form. When Liberal-CP spokesmen such as Fadden and Wentworth had equated the Chifley ALP government's proposal to nationalise the Australian banking system with proCommunism, they had unexpectedly received backing from a section of the Roman Catholic hierarchy and clergy who questioned the ALP's bank nationalisation proposal "on moral grounds."[10] The Irish-Australian element, mostly Roman Catholic, was the hard core of the ALP's electoral strength. Normally, the Roman Catholic hierarchy gave tacit or open support[11] to the ALP or stayed discreetly silent. This priestly intervention undoubtedly confused those Irish-Australians who were prone to listen to the views of their Church leaders and contributed to the strains that were to produce the ALP split in 1954/55, a split which was in turn to benefit the Liberal-CP electorally in the years ahead, including 1969.

Another, probably deeper, psychological influence was operating in that period to heighten Australian fears about Communism. For years Australians had been uneasily conscious of being a relatively small community of European origin on the periphery of crowded Asia. World War II and conflict with Japan had deepened that consciousness though paradoxically public interest in external affairs developed only slowly in the postwar years. Japan's potential for aggression had been destroyed and had not revived by 1949. But rising in Asia was a new power, Communist China, from 1949 onwards under the control of Mao Tse-Tung and his Marxist myriads. British naval strength, behind which Australia had comfortably sheltered from its foundation in 1788 until World War II, had ceased to count in world affairs. It had been the United States which had protected Australia in World War II. China was Communist and believed to be aggressively expansionist. The United States was antiCommunist and a hoped for protector against future threats to Australia from Asia. These factors were to be more important in elections subsequent to 1949 but they were already shadowly present in 1949. The Communist issue in one guise or other was to pay off politically for the Liberal-CP coalition for years to come.

With his proposal to outlaw the Communist Party a major policy point, appealing strongly to an electorate resentful of the shortages produced by the continual, crippling strikes, which the ALP itself described as Communist inspired, planned and led, Menzies secured for his Liberal-CP followers an overwhelming victory in 1949, the coalition winning seventy-four seats in the House of Representatives against the ALP's forty-seven. In 1951, with the Communist issue even more prominent—Menzies again asked the electorate for a mandate to suppress the Communist Party and for a majority in the Senate where previously ALP supporters outnumbered government senators—the Liberal-CP coalition won again, dropping four of its lost five House of Representatives' seats in wool and wheat electorates where local issues proved stronger than ideological considerations but offsetting these losses with the more valuable gain of a Senate majority.

Just prior to the elections due in 1954, it looked as though the Communist issue was running out of steam. The coalition was in trouble over domestic matters. The employment situation, always key in Australian politics, was showing signs of deteriorating. The coalition had done badly at the May, 1953, Senate elections.[12] Such pointers as existed indicated that the ALP had a good chance of taking over the Treasury benches after polling day. But Menzies knew that the Communist theme still had the potential to assist him and his government. It was not dead, only dormant. Evatt, then ALP Federal Leader, had incurred the hostility of an implacably antiCommunist section of his Party because of his part in opposing successfully before the High Court[13] and at a subsequent referendum the Menzies' legislation to ban the Communist Party. It only needed a touch to bring the issue back to life. Menzies applied the touch. Virtually on election eve, Menzies announced the defection of a Soviet diplomat, Vladimar Petrov, and the setting up of a Royal Commission to investigate espionage activities in Australia. It was heady, exciting stuff. Mrs Petrov was rescued at Darwin aerodrome from the clutches of huge Soviet MVD agents by even larger Northern Territory policemen with the widebrimmed hats of frontier tradition. A sitting of the commission took place before the election. The commission's sitting produced little[14] but it evoked an atmosphere. Evatt and the ALP's leftwing were accused by innuendo rather than direct statement of association with Communism in its international aspect. It was a less convincing accusation than the earlier one that through its strength in the Australian union setup and through the unions' significant representation at and in the ALP's governing and policymaking bodies, the Communist Party exercised an unhealthy and potentially dangerous influence in ALP affairs. But the accusation had its value and the effect intended. It obscured the government's domestic shortcomings. On May 29, 1954, the Coalition limped back into office. It lost five seats, its numbers in the House of Representatives dropping from 69 to 64, while the ALP went up from 52 to 57. But the government had achieved the result it hoped for from the Petrov defection. It was back on the government benches and not on the opposition side of the House of Representatives.

In 1955 and within eighteen months of the 1954 elections Menzies saw the opportunity to restore his parliamentary fortunes to their pre-1954 level. By then the ALP split was formal,[15] with a breakaway ALP group of seven parliamentarians sitting on the cross benches in the House of Representatives. Debates were turbulent and bitter, with the ALP and the breakaway group engaged in tearing each other apart, and the government parliamentarians spectators rather than participants. Menzies decided to take his government to the country prematurely instead of waiting for 1957 by which time there was always the possibility that the ALP and the breakaway faction might have settled their difference. The Liberal-CP coalition did not play up the Communist issue and alleged ALP support for Communist policies at these elections. It did not need to do so. The breakaway ALP group, then operating as the AntiCommunist ALP and under the leadership of Mr Robert Joshua, ALP MHR for Ballarat in Victoria until the split, made coalition activity in this area largely unnecessary.[16] The Joshua-led group concentrated on the Petrov Royal Commission's report. The commission's investigations had produced little of a substantial nature. But members of Evatt's personal staff had been mentioned during the hearings, and one, Mr Fergin O'Sullivan, Evatt's press secretary, was identified as the author of one of the documents that Petrov had taken with him when he defected from Soviet Service.[17] Mr Allan Dalziel, Evatt's private secretary, was exonerated by the commission,[18] and the involvement of Mr A. T. Grundeman, another member of Evatt's staff, was so peripheral as to be farcical.[19] Evatt, however, allowed himself to get so obsessively caught up in and his own attitudes to create so much of the drama[20] at the commission's hearings that public attention was distracted from the trivial nature of many of the matters with which the commission was dealing. As a consequence, the Joshua-led group were in a position to make Evatt and the ALP's alleged association with Communists and support for Communist policies[21] significant election talking points, and succeeded in persuading their followers to follow their advice that the second preferences of the breakaway group should go to Liberal or CP candidates rather than to the ALP. The Liberals won ten seats, the CP one, and the number of ALP seats dropped to 47, giving the coalition a twenty-eight majority in the House of Representatives. But the seven ALP breakaways—Joshua, S. M. Keon, T. Andrews, W. Bryson, W. M. Bourke, J. L. Cremean, and J. M. Mullens, all Victorians and mostly representing strong ALP seats—were defeated, leaving Senator George Cole, from Tasmania, isolated in the Senate as the DLP's lone federal parliamentary representative.

Though the seven Victorian ALP parliamentarians who had sided with the breakaway, intensely antiCommunist ALP group were all defeated at the 1955 elections, the electoral support given this group in Victoria was impressive. For a while however it was thought that the group's fate would be that of earlier ALP breakaway groups—significant mass support at one election but, in the absence of representation in the House of Representatives, thereafter the inevitable withering. Only the Communists had the dedication and fanaticism to exist politically without some parliamentary representation, it was argued. Though the antiCommunist group still had Cole in the Senate this did not amount to real parliamentary representation. The breakaways were doomed to disappear as had all previous ALP breakaway groups which could not achieve adequate parliamentary representation.

This prognostication proved incorrect. Backed by Santamaria and his lively, vigorous weekly publication *News Weekly* and after 1957 strengthened by the recruitment of Vince Gair, the former Queensland Premier who lost his premiership and ALP membership while the ALP lost the Queensland State government as a result of a Queensland ALP brawl that had its origins in the 1954/55 split, the breakaway group reformed as the Democratic Labor Party. From 1958 through to October, 1969, when Gorton led the Liberal-CP forces to their narrow victory, the DLP established itself as the federal balance of power. In 1958, the Liberal-CP government owed twenty seats to DLP preferences, in 1961 twenty-seven seats, in 1963 twenty-four seats, in 1966 thirty-one seats, and in 1969 Gorton was to get twenty-eight seats on their preferences.[22] But there was a lot of water to run under the bridge and the Communist issue was to re-emerge in a much more complex form before the 1969 Gorton elections were decided.

In 1958, Menzies, a realist, was confident of being returned to office in his own right. Evatt, his opponent of a lifetime, was still indomitably struggling but now against failing health as well as political setbacks. Menzies did not hammer the Communist theme in 1958 as relentlessly as he had in previous elections. Again he

136

had no need to. His Liberal and CP followers hammered it hard. So did the DLP, much more effective in its attacks upon the ALP than Liberal or CP critics because of DLP knowledge of ALP mores and weaknesses and the intimate details of the ALP's internal history. The DLP was unforgiving. Its spokesmen had the "killer instinct" which is often the mark of ALP training and which is summed up in the savage axiom "When you've got a man down, kick him to pieces so that he never gets a chance to regain his feet." The DLP had Evatt down. It kicked him to pieces. Politically, he never regained his feet.[23]

When Evatt offered to resign ALP federal leadership after the elections if the DLP gave the ALP their second preferences, Senator Cole, on behalf of the DLP, demanded to know if this offer included an effective ban on unity tickets between ALP members and Communists in union elections, reintroduction of the ALP groups which had contested union ballots against Communist nominees prior to the 1955 split, and a withdrawal of ALP foreign policies objectionable to the DLP, policies such as advocacy of recognition of Red China, adopted at the 1955 Hobart Federal ALP Conference.[24] After Evatt had rejected Cole's terms the Liberal-CP coalition went on to improve its position still further in the House of Representatives, winning 77 seats to the ALP's 45. After the 1961 election setback when the coalition campaigned on domestic issues, virtually without mentioning Communism, and saw its Representatives' majority reduced to two, Menzies fought the next election in 1963 on the threat of Red China becoming a nuclear power while "the thirty-six faceless men" of the ALP Federal Conference were supporting the proposition that US nuclear power should be debarred from the southern hemisphere by its declaration as a nuclear free zone. In 1966, with Australia by then having forces serving in Vietnam, Holt accused the ALP of imperilling the US-Australian defence alliance by threatening to withdraw from participation in the Vietnam conflict. Turning the US-Australia defence treaty, ANZUS, into an antiCommunist symbol, Holt, with DLP support, won for the Liberal-CP coalition its greatest ever electoral victory by gaining a forty majority in the House of Representatives.

But by 1968 when Gorton succeeded Holt as Prime Minister, the Communist issue as far as its antiCommunist manifestation was concerned had undergone a change. While Australians in 1949 were conscious of living on the edge of a troubled area of the world and Evatt, as the ALP's Foreign Affairs Minister had built up an independent Australian foreign service between 1941 and 1949, the years of ALP Federal governments, Australia still suffered from a hangover from its colonial days. What went on in the world beyond Australia's shores was primarily the concern of the powers to which Australia looked for protection.[25] Australia looked to Britain for protection during the years prior to World War II. After World War II in which the United States had substituted for Britain as the protecting power, Australia looked to the United States.[26] During these years, the symbols of antiCommunism were local. They were control of the Australian trade union movement and whether it was to be Communist or ALP led, and the degree of influence that the Communist Party was to exercise upon the ALP through its ability to manipulate the delegations from ALP affiliated unions that represented the unions at ALP conferences and in ALP councils. They were whether strikes were to have a political flavor, which the Communists wanted, or to be confined to purely industrial issues, which was the ALP tradition. They were whether there should be support for the arbitration system, which the ALP supported and which had become an accepted way of settling wage and industrial disputes, or a shift to collective bargaining, a shift which the Communists favored because they were strongest in the mass unions with large memberships and a militant outlook that predated the rise of Communist power in the Australian trade union movement. A few individuals, like Evatt and Santamaria, had a world view of Communism, and their symbols, like their approaches, were different, but they were up against an inertia on the part of their followers who accepted that foreign affairs were largely the concern of others and whose attitudes were shaped by local considerations.

Even in 1954/55 when the ALP split took place, though things were gradually changing, the symbolism of antiCommunism was still largely local. In some instances the symbols had only a tenuous association with either Communism or antiCommunism, but became symbols because one of the ALP factions either opposed or supported them fiercely. State aid for denominational schools, aid which Roman Catholics insisted had to be given if the school system which the Roman Catholics operated alongside the state school system was to survive, became such a symbol.

The Roman Catholics wanted state aid. The DLP was supported by a section of the Roman Catholic hierarchy, its leaders were mostly Roman Catholic, and it depended largely upon Roman Catholic support. Automatically, the element within the ALP most virulently hostile to the DLP turned antistate aid, though state aid had been, unchallenged, a plank in the ALP's electoral platform for years.[27] This ALP element was largely left wing, secular or determinedly Protestant, and had associations with Communist

138

trade union leaders who were regarded as valuable allies in the ALP-DLP struggle. Support for state aid became a symbol of antiCommunism, and—to a lesser degree because there was the complicating factor of religious differences—opposition to state aid the symbol of proCommunism. It was all quite irrational, but irrationality is as much a feature of politics as is speechmaking. In politics, the myths are often more real than realities, and nonsense makes more sense than good sense.

Aspects of Communism outside Australia did get some attention at the 1955 ALP Federal Conference in Hobart which formalised the ALP split. The conference passed a motion advocating the recognition of Red China and questioning the use of Australian forces in Malaysia, then Malaya, to suppress Communist terrorists.[28] But the motion was passed more as a gesture of repudiation of Santamaria and endorsement for Evatt than the outcome of an upsurge on the part of a majority of the delegates of an interest in world affairs.

But by 1966 the symbols of antiCommunism were for the most part external to Australia rather than internal. There was a number of reasons for this change. Evatt had a world view on Communism. This affected his ALP followers. Santamaria also had a world view on Communism. This had an influence on the DLP, whose leaders because they were primarily concerned with Communism were predisposed towards taking a view on Communism that extended beyond Australian borders. By 1966 the ALP's leftwing had established itself firmly within the ALP machine and was not prepared to leave consideration of external affairs to the few but took its own interest. More importantly, Australia which had had a small army training group in South Vietnam since 1962 had become more deeply committed in the conflict in that wartorn country. As United States' intervention stepped up, so did Australia's. In April 1965, a battalion group totalling some 1,400 officers and men were sent to South Vietnam. In March, 1966, the Liberal-CP coalition announced the enlargement of the battalion to a three-battalion strong task force and Australia's commitment grew to 8,000 men.

Whereas earlier the DLP had tended to concentrate upon the domestic aspects of Communism, it was by 1966 primarily concerned with the Asian situation. The DLP thesis was that Asian Communism had to be contained, and Asian countries, still free of Communist domination, particularly the countries to Australia's immediate north with some of which, notably Singapore and Malaysia, Australia had long and friendly associations, had to be assisted to establish and maintain viable economies and stable, preferably democratic, governments that would produce not only steady improvement in regional living standards but the defence capacity to resist Communist promoted subversion and the southward drive of Communism. While Asian governments held the view that the physical presence of Australian troops even in the small numbers Australia could make available in their territories contributed to the region's stability, it was in Australia's longterm interests to keep the Australian troops in the region, the DLP argued.

Along with the DLP, the ALP had reacted to external events, though not without some internal turmoil. Factions within the ALP had squabbled fiercely in 1963 over the United States' proposal to establish a radio communications centre at Exmouth Gulf to communicate with US naval units, including atomic armed submarines. The argument then revolved mainly around the differing views on whether the setting up of such a station on Australian soil would bring Australia into the United States' nuclear complex, and whether, if such was the case, Australia's longterm self interests would be best served by Australian inclusion in the United States' nuclear complex. Later the quarrels took a different twist. They were over whether or not Australia should be involved in Vietnam. After the Liberal-CP coalition had introduced a system of conscription under which national servicemen selected by ballot were incorporated in the permanent military forces and sent to Vietnam, the ALP attitude against the Vietnam involvement hardened. There was a perceptible shift towards the views expounded by Cairns, who had not only consistently fought for United States and Australian withdrawal from South Vietnam but also advocated the recall of all Australian forces from Asia, including the Australian forces that had been in the Malaysia-Singapore area since the end of World War II.

In the 1960s the symbols of antiCommunism promoted by the very able propagandists of the DLP were support for Australian intervention in Vietnam, endorsement of conscription by ballot to sustain the Australian military commitment in Vietnam, backing for United States policies in Southeast Asia, maintenance of the US-Australia defence alliance, opposition to the recognition of Red China and its acceptance into the United Nations organisation until there were assurances of no military action against Taiwan, and the continuance in the Malaysian-Singapore region of an Australian military presence while the governments in that region wanted the presence maintained.

As these symbols coincided with the policies being pursued by the Liberal-CP coalition under Menzies and Holt, neither Menzies nor Holt had any real difficulties with the DLP. They could rely upon DLP second preferences going steadfastly to government candidates at general elections, and when coalition governments, at first cautiously and later more lavishly moved to give state aid to denominational schools the capacity of the DLP to direct the second preference votes of their followers in support of government candidates was strengthened.

There was, however, an element in DLP thinking that was to bring the DLP into conflict with Gorton and to prevent him holding elections in 1968. The DLP was not content in defence matters to rely as was Menzies, a product of an era when Britain's naval might provided global defence, and his government almost exclusively upon "great and powerful friends", with the United States hopefully replacing Britain, in Menzies and his government's thinking, as the greatest of these powerful friends in the post-World War II age. Though dedicatedly proUnited States and a defender of United States' antiCommunist policies in Southeast Asia, the DLP sensed earlier than other Australian political groupings the possibility of United States withdrawal from Asia and a United States reversion to a modified but unmistakable policy of isolationism.[29] DLP spokesmen argued that in the ultimate Australia's security would depend not upon its great and powerful friends whose self-interests might not at all times coincide with Australia's interests but upon Australia's own efforts and upon the stability of the region to Australia's north after the United States had withdrawn and upon the associations Australia had established and built up with the nonCommunist countries in that region. Menzies and Holt had no reason for concern about this strand of thought in the DLP: while they held prime ministerial office there had been no suggestion that the United States might withdraw from Southeast Asia.

But the world Menzies and Holt had lived in politically was not the world with which Gorton had to contend as Prime Minister. When Holt vanished into the sea off Cheviot Beach, it was as though an era had ended with his disappearance. Australia had been told, and vaguely accepted, that at some time in the future Britain would withdraw from the Singapore-Malaysia area, leaving Australia, New Zealand, and Malaysia and Singapore, with which Australians believed they had a special affinity, increasingly isolated. Gorton's first Cabinet meeting, held on January 11, 1968, the day after he was sworn in by Governor-General Lord Casey, heard British Commonwealth Secretary Thomson, specially sent from London for the purpose, announce that Britain would be out of the Singapore-Malaysia area by the end of 1971 and explain the British Government's reasons for accelerating its withdrawal programme. Of even more importance than Britain's proposed withdrawal, politically, was the emerging evidence that a growing number of people in the US, important people, people of influence and stature in politics, in academic circles, and in the administration or former members of a US administration, were doubting the wisdom of US involvement in Vietnam conflict, where Australia was also involved, a doubting that was intensified by the Tet offensive, a military failure but psychologically, because of its effect upon US opinion, a brilliant success. ALP personalities like Cairns, his friend, the ex-boxer Uren, and their parliamentary colleague, Gordon Bryant, who with a small number of private persons as well as Communist Party members and fellow travellers had long been lonely voices, unheeded as they condemned what they claimed to be the immorality of the Vietnam war, and ex-Federal ALP leader Arthur Calwell, a convert to the antiVietnam cause and possessed of all a recent convert's proselytising zeal since the introduction of conscription of young Australians for military service in the Vietnam conflict, were having an impact upon Australian thinking. More young men liable to service were objecting to the draft. University students, within whose ranks were many of the age group liable to service, objected to a system whereby by ballot a proportion of young men were plucked from the Australian community and sent to serve in Vietnam while the majority of their fellows were free to pursue careers and the community as a whole was left untouched, and without the hardships and shortages shared by a civilian population in a war in which a nation is devoting its full, not part, of its resources.

Then on April 1, 1968, President Johnson announced deescalation of bombing in North Vietnam and his decision not to recontest the presidency. DLP fears that Australia would be left longterm dependent upon its own defence efforts intensified. They had no fears about the near future. Australia was not exposed to any immediate threat. But they shared with Wentworth and other Liberals a catastrophic view of history. In fifteen, twenty years time the position might be much different than what it now was: with Communism tightening its grip in Indo-China, there was the possibility, indeed the likelihood of Communist expansion, southwards, towards Australia. They wanted a defence programme that would look ahead if not for fifteen or twenty years at least some distance. They wanted regional associations built up to provide for a future that could become uncertain.

The DLP already had misgivings about Gorton. These misgivings were fed by Santamaria, who undoubtedly gave DLP leaders, in confidence, a version of his April interview with Gorton, the interview at which, according to Santamaria, Gorton had fatalistically shrugged his shoulders and said "In that eventuality, there is nothing we can do" when questioned about what would happen in a defence emergency if the United States did not come to Australia's aid. The misgivings were encouraged by Gorton's declaration at the time of the Tet offensive that, whatever the circumstances, no extra Australian troops would ever go to Vietnam, a declaration that destroyed the argument that in the interests of Australia's future the advance of Communism had to be checked on the Asian mainland, and strengthened the suspicion that Australia was in Vietnam to assist the United States in the hope that if the day dawned when Australia needed assistance the United States would remember and reciprocate.[30] Gorton's attitudes on defence questions between April and October did nothing to relieve the DLP's misgivings.

Menzies and Holt had kept the DLP docile on defence matters by listing defence as its top priority. They consistently disappointed the DLP by appearing at times to recede from that priority. But they never abandoned it. Gorton on the other hand made it clear that his priorities were different. Asked soon after he became Prime Minister if Australia had the capacity to fill the gap which would be left by Britain's withdrawal from the Asian-Singapore area, Gorton said "We would have the capacity but we would only have the capacity if we sacrificed other needs of Australia which I, myself, think are of greater importance to Australia."[31] This determination to place other needs ahead of defence was repeated. In his 1968 Budget speech, Gorton told the House of Representatives "We do not intend to seek guns instead of growth at the cost of stunting our growth . . . the cost of defence will grow, and this will be regarded as one important need among many for the nation, though not a need which overrides all else."[32] Statements like these, coupled with the knowledge that at the joint government parties meeting on May 8, 1968, Gorton had suggested Australia might change its "Forward Defence" policy and mentioned an Israeli-type defence force, were in themselves sufficient to disturb the DLP.

But in addition to this the DLP was aware that there had been sharp differences of opinion between Gorton and Hasluck, as External Affairs Minister, and Fairhall, as Defence Minister, on defence matters and particularly over the issue of whether an Australian military presence was to be maintained in the Malaysia-Singapore area, as sought by the Malaysian and Singapore governments, after Britain had completed its military withdrawal by the end of 1971. Hasluck was later to deny that these differences existed. In August, 1968, Hasluck took the unusual step of circulating a memorandum in the Department of External Affairs which stated "Reports of differences between the Prime Minister and myself are equally misleading."[33] On November 20, 1968, Hasluck told the House of Representatives "As far as the Prime Minister is concerned, not only have I given him my utmost loyalty from the commencement (of his prime ministership) but, I am very glad to say, I have found it possible to work in the closest cooperation and in a constructive partnership with him."[34] But by November Hasluck was aware that Gorton proposed to nominate him as Governor-General, and decency demanded that he should part company with Gorton in an atmosphere of public harmony. The public record, however, apart from the reports that filtered out from the cabinet room and party meetings confirmed that there were differences between Gorton and his two ministers, differences which Fairhall who retired from politics not to a public position but to private life never sought to deny and in private conversations seldom sought to conceal.

In an international affairs debate in the House of Representatives, Hasluck reiterated that the government was prepared to discuss "the size and role of an Australian contribution to combined defence arrangements which embrace a joint Singapore-Malaysia defence effort"[35]—a clear indication that while Gorton may have revised his opinion on the desirability of maintaining an Australian military presence in the Singapore-Malaysian area Hasluck was still thinking in those terms. Malaysia's then deputy Prime Minister, Tun Abdul Razak, and Singapore's Prime Minister, Lee Kuan Yew, wanted Australian troops kept in the region after Britain's withdrawal, not that they could ensure military protection —they were and would be too small to do that—but as a symbol that would assist in promoting stability in the area. Later the Malaysian and Singapore leaders were to lose patience with what they clearly considered the evasion and vacillation of the Australian government. In Singapore the Defence Minister Lim Kim San told Parliament that Singapore could plan its defence with more precision "if it knew whether Australia and New Zealand would keep their forces in Singapore after the British pull-out",[36] the *Straits Times* asked how much longer Australia intended to wait before announcing a decision,[37] and writer Alex Josey, known to be close to Mr Lee described Australia as "dithering."[38] In Australia, Dato Donald Stephens, the Malaysian High Commissioner, stated, "If Australia does in fact decide to follow closely on the heels of the British in leaving the defence of Malaysia and

Edward St John, Sydney lawyer and MHR for Warringah, who criticised Gorton's early morning visit to the residence of the US Ambassador, William Crook, after a Federal Parliamentary Press Gallery dinner, and thereafter campaigned against Gorton's administrative methods. St John was defeated at the 1969 general election.

Cyril Wyndham, the little ex-Englishman, whose advocacy ultimately produced reforms within the ALP that re-established the status of ALP parliamentarians. Though a Whitlam supporter, he was "dumped" when a row broke out when he was intending to shift from the ALP Federal Secretaryship to the position of NSW ALP Secretary.

Liberal Federal President, Sir John ("Jock") Pagan (left) and Gorton exchange the smiles of close allies while McMahon, whose future was then uncertain, preserves a facade of indifference.

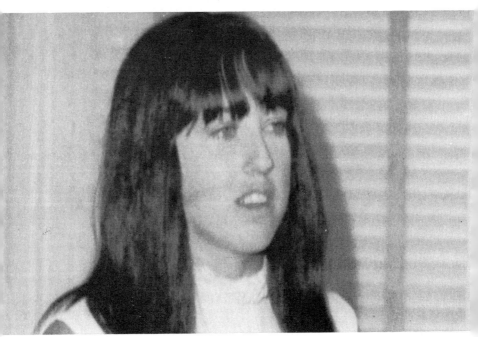

The young newspaperwoman, Miss Geraldine Willesee, who accompanied Gorton on his early morning visit to the residence of the US Ambassador, William Crook, following a Federal Parliamentary Press Gallery dinner. It was this incident that started St John upon his antiGorton crusade.

Singapore to the people of the area themselves, there will be an even greater feeling of being let down on the part of Malaysians and Singaporeans, and the confidence in Australia will be badly affected."[39] Hasluck again showed where he stood. Asked at a press conference in Malaysia whether Australia would leave with the British in 1971, Hasluck said "Before or after 1971 is not in our mind. 1971 is not a point of timetable as far as we are concerned. It is a date that is significant (only) to the British. But for the Malaysians and the Australians 1971 does not terminate anything . . . ."[40] After the Five Power Conference on regional defence between Malaysia, Singapore, Britain, Australia and New Zealand Fairhall pointed out that with Britain gone and the United States not directly involved in the region, Australia had "an important role to play in the area."[41] Fairhall also told a Government Parties meeting on August 21 that "the defence of Malaysia, Singapore, and Australia was indivisible, and that Australians were most welcome in this part of SouthEast Asia."[42]

The four DLP Senators—Gair and Con Byrne, from Queensland, and Frank McManus and John Little, from Victoria—were all ALP trained. Gair was tough and able, squat, short, in appearance a genial porker but by temperament as aggressive as a scrub bull, with a ranting, bombastic style, the faintest hint of a speech impediment, a coarse, effective sense of humor, and a pot belly that he was accustomed to pat derisively while saying "Nobody can accuse me of lacking guts", no pretensions to intellectual accomplishments but shrewdly intelligent, stubborn, fearless, principled, loyal and at times charming but with a flair for the brutal infighting of gutter politics. Byrne, a bachelor and Brisbane lawyer, a lover of good horseflesh and regular racegoer yet austere, possessed of the Celtic gaiety that is tinged with melancholy, a charitable belief, rare in politics and notably rare in the DLP, particularly as regards ALP opponents, in the good intentions of his opponents, cultivated, wellread and thoughtful, nevertheless was as tough intellectually as the others were politically. McManus, assistant secretary of the Victorian ALP before the split, was an ex-school teacher, long, lean, bespectacled, unforgiving, with a biting tongue and a memory, programmed like a computer, for hurtful aspects of ALP history and the shortcomings and misdeeds of former ALP colleagues. Little, a former Victorian ALP President and ALP member of the Victorian Legislative Council, short, square and neat, like a ship's officer in shoregoing mufti, at times vitriolic, professionally competent, an able, implacable opponent in both debate and on TV, was a good friend but a bad enemy.

145

Politically the four had lived dangerously and now accepted it as their way of life.

They were the balance of power in the Senate.[43] But their larger power was elsewhere. They knew or rather believed—for their power was precariously based, depending upon the fidelity of their followers in the electorate, a fidelity subject to renewed testing at every general election—that the forces they represented had the potential to decide whether or not the Liberal-CP coalition or the ALP would occupy the government benches. They decided "No election." Gair was deputised to make their decision effective.

Gair had had a fairly cordial working relationship with Gorton when Gorton had led the government in the Senate. But the relationship changed soon after Gorton rose to become Prime Minister. Whereas Gair had respect for Gorton, when Gorton was working under the general directions of the then Prime Minister Holt, Gair had contempt for Gorton when Gorton was freed from Holt's restraining influence. Gorton, who as Senate Leader had admired Gair's consistency and determination, also changed his feelings towards Gair. In this, Gorton could have been influenced by Senator Lionel Murphy, ALP leader in the Senate with whom Gorton had formed an association when both men faced each other as the leaders of their respective groups across the centre table in the red cushioned, red curtained Senate. Murphy, who persistently opposed his leader, Whitlam, not only in ALP Federal Parliamentary meetings but in the ALP machine, was close to the Victorian ALP, whose hatred of the DLP was frenetic and obsessive. While Gorton was toying with the thought of the premature 1968 elections, Murphy was a frequent visitor to Gorton's office. The two men would remain closeted in Gorton's inner office for quite long periods. As Whitlam was the ALP's official negotiator with Gorton, a number of government and ALP supporters formed the suspicion that during the time Murphy was with Gorton Murphy encouraged Gorton to believe that if he held a premature election he would (a) defeat Whitlam, (b) win another three years of office and (c) destroy the power of the DLP, which would suit Gorton, Murphy, possibly the government, and certainly the Victorian ALP.[44]

Much of the contempt Gair and his three Senate followers had for Gorton stemmed from Gorton's vacillation over defence issues, and the manner in which Gorton clearly believed DLP electoral allegiance could be bought. Gair and his colleagues regarded Communism and future defence needs as the major issues facing Australia. They could not point to an immediate potential aggressor. But they adhered inflexibly to the view that with main-

146

land China now Communist governed and Communism likely to expand in Asia in the years ahead, Australia had to face the possibility that by the end of a decade, possibly two, Australia could be isolated in a region of the world where Communist governments were dominant. Like Santamaria, they wanted to start preparing now against the defence contingency of ten years time. They had no faith in Britain's capacity to give Australia aid even if it wanted to, and accepted that United States' assistance would be forthcoming only if the United States considered its provision in United States' interests at the particular time it was sought. They had faith only in Australia and Australia's own efforts.

Gorton's careless certainty that they would do nothing as a party to imperil his government provided they were given the douceur of gradually extended state aid for private schools, particularly Roman Catholic schools, enraged them. They prided themselves that they had already sacrificed political careers within the ALP to establish defence and antiCommunism as the real Australian issues. While they supported and would accept gratefully from the Gorton government state aid for private schools, they would not do so at the expense of relinquishing what they considered more urgent priorities from the national viewpoint. To enforce these priorities they were prepared to risk the political careers they had rebuilt since the ALP split.

On Monday, October 7, 1968, the DLP parliamentarians met with the DLP Federal Executive in the DLP's Melbourne offices. The proposal was put up that if Gorton held an election before he had decided on a defence policy the DLP would shift its preferences in selected seats from Government to ALP candidates who were known to share the DLP's defence views. There was uneasiness. From 1954/1955 onwards, the thing that had distinguished the DLP was the tight discipline with which DLP followers had followed the advice that DLP second preference votes should go to Government, not ALP, candidates. This discipline had been most rigid in Victoria where generally when DLP candidates were eliminated and their preferences distributed, up to and over 90 percent had gone to government candidates. But it was one thing having a national policy on preferences. That was clearcut. The DLP voters knew what the leadership wanted and there was little room for confusion or misunderstanding. But to have the DLP preferences go to government candidates in some electorates and to ALP candidates in other electorates was a different matter. The DLP voters could easily make mistakes, disastrous mistakes from the DLP's viewpoint that would put the ALP in power and the

ALP, as a government, would undoubtedly seek to change the existing preferential system of voting to the simpler, "first past the post" method which would eliminate the DLP's control over House of Representatives' elections. Additionally the DLP could be unleashing forces which once released might prove ungovernable. Most of their supporters were former ALP voters with nostalgic memories of when they voted ALP. These supporters preferred ALP social policies to the Government's social policies, however much they disliked the ALP's foreign policies. A faltering in DLP consistency might provide some of them with an excuse to return to their onetime ALP allegiance. Then to determine just how many seats in which the DLP should switch preferences was a matter of delicate judgment. Here also a miscalculation as to the degree of the government's electoral unpopularity could give victory to the ALP.

"What happens if Gorton calls our bluff?" Gair was asked. "If we make the decision and, despite it, Gorton pulls on an election, we won't be bluffing," Gair told the meeting. "Once we make the decision, we'll go on with it whatever the consequences."

The DLP representatives from Victoria were particularly uneasy. They had problems. They expounded some of them. If they switched their preferences in a seat like Melbourne's Maribyrnong held for the Liberals since 1955 by Phil Stokes it might never be recovered from the ALP. It had been an ALP stronghold until the 1954/55 split. It could become one again. In how many seats should they switch their preferences? It was decided that they would leave the figure open for the further discussion that would be necessary if Gorton told them to stick their preferences up their DLP jumpers. There was a widespread view that Gorton was sufficiently reckless to do just precisely that. "We'll see," said Gair. It was decided that the DLP Executive's decision should be announced only in general terms. Delegates were asked to keep details of the decision secret. Gorton was as temperamental as an unbroken colt. If there were a public threat, he might react impulsively and pull on elections without consideration. Gair was authorised to see Gorton and to advise him, officially, of the DLP decision.[45]

On Tuesday, October 8, 1968, Gair saw Gorton in Gorton's office in Parliament House, Canberra. Gair told Gorton he was interviewing him officially as spokesman for the DLP. The DLP did not like Gorton's defence attitude. They did not like his references to "Fortress Australia" and the suggestions that Australia was contemplating abandoning such regional associations with Malaysia and Singapore as did not fit into the "Fortress Australia" concept.

148

Gorton told Gair that he had never advocated that policy. "Your statements suggest you do," Gair later reported to the DLP he told Gorton. Gorton accused Gair of making public statements that there was no difference between his defence views and those of Cairns.[46] Gair said he had not made that statement, but Santamaria had and Gorton's own words justified Santamaria making it. Gair said that if Gorton insisted on an election he and his government could not count on DLP preferences. The DLP had decided that they would recommend to their followers that they switch preferences in selected electorates. Gair named a number of electorates in which he claimed such a switch would be fatal to the prospects of government parliamentarians. Gorton reminded him that Gorton had never said there would be an election in 1968. Gair's worry was the outcome of newspaper speculation, Gorton said. The newspaper speculators had nothing to go on except their imaginations. The men parted without Gorton giving Gair any firm indication as to his plans.[47]

With no commitment either way from Gorton, the DLP went grimly ahead with its plans to attempt to switch sufficient preferences to reduce drastically the government's majority without defeating the government. Government-held seats examined were St George, Barton, and Evans in NSW, Maribyrnong and Ballarat in Victoria, Bowman, Griffith and Herbert in Queensland, Grey and Adelaide in South Australia, and Perth in Western Australia. By that stage, many government supporters were convinced that Gorton would go ahead with November 30, 1968, elections. Excitement mounted.

Gorton broke his silence on October 14, 1968. With time running out—Gorton had to make his announcement of November 30 elections to the Parliament not later than Thursday, October 17, 1968, to provide the time necessary for the issue of writs and other electoral formalities and a campaign of reasonable duration—Gorton addressed a Flinders Electorate Liberal Party luncheon at Mornington in Victoria. Gorton was as impishly coy as a young boy trying to be mysterious about his juvenile hideout. ". . . There appears to be some discussion or some speculation as to whether there is likely to be an election before the due time at which an election has to take place," Gorton told his audience. "Now the one thing that I really want to say about that is that it is quite fascinating that I have never said a word about it, one way or the other, up until this point of time. But I will let you into a secret. I made my mind up about it some time ago and I will be informing my party about it tomorrow. I think that is the proper way for this information to be conveyed—to a party meeting. It has been

149

fascinating for me to discover how people can suggest and build on things, speculate on things without really getting any indication whatsoever from people who have to decide them.[48] But we will find out about that all in good time."[49] The next day, even so well informed a newspaper as the *Sydney Morning Herald* commented "Every indication points to an election for the House of Representatives on November 30, a year ahead of schedule."[50]

On Tuesday, October 15, 1968, the day after his Mornington speech, Gorton met his cabinet at 10.30 am. "There will be no general elections this year," he told cabinet members. At 2.15 pm he walked into a meeting of the joint government parties. He repeated to the meeting that there would be no elections despite their expectations. The House of Representatives was due to assemble at 2.30. Gorton gave the reasons for his decision briefly. The major reasons were that the government had a record majority in the House of Representatives and no justification for twelve months premature elections.

At 2.30 pm Gorton entered the chamber of the House of Representatives and confirmed a weakness that had been partially concealed by his superiority over Whitlam while Whitlam was distracted by internal ALP squabbles but a weakness that was to become increasingly evident as the months passed by. Gorton was a good debater. But the points that he scored against Whitlam, Cairns and others were university type debating points, clever, facile and adroit but shallow. When talking to the Parliament he seemed to lack the understanding that Parliament, as past prime ministers knew and appreciated, was a forum from which to speak to the nation. Gorton seemed to think only of the one hundred and twenty-five members of the House of Representatives he was addressing, not the nation. He had already promoted the issue of whether or not there was to be general elections to national status by his references at the Mornington meeting. Asked by Whitlam if he were "prepared to take the Parliament and the public into his confidence on a matter on which I gather he has just reported to his party", Gorton was flippant, almost contemptuous, not just to Whitlam but also to the Parliament. "I am not quite aware of what reasons the Leader of the Opposition can advance for suggesting that this is a matter that should be discussed in Parliament", Gorton said,[51] as though Parliament and through it the nation were not the appropriate bodies to be informed of a decision on general elections, general elections left like Mahommed's coffin between Heaven and Earth by Gorton's Mornington speech. ALP MHR Martin Nicholls, pointing out that there had been reports of election discussions between Gorton and

Gair, as DLP leader, made another attempt to get an answer from Gorton to the direct question whether elections for the House of Representatives would be held in 1968.

"There were no electoral discussions between myself and the leader of the Democratic Labor Party," said Gorton. "I think what the honorable member is probably referring to is an occasion when the leader of the DLP came to tell me what his attitude was on the matter. This is quite different from discussions. A decision on this matter, I can assure the honorable gentleman, has nothing whatever to do with either the leader or members of the DLP."[52] It was the kind of needlessly evasive answer that provoked derision rather than admiration. Whitlam later described Gorton's evasions as "arch."[53]

Gorton was not prepared to talk to the Parliament but he talked freely with the news media in his prime ministerial office later in the day. The major reason against holding an election in 1968 was that the government had not had time to produce a properly prepared, studied and analysed defence policy, he said. As this had also been given by Gair as the main reason why there should be no premature election, Gorton was suspected of following the cynical but profitable maxim "when you can't beat 'em, join 'em." But then Gorton really lashed out at the DLP. He had one regret. That was that the DLP was not going to get the opportunity to do against the government what it had threatened—to give its preferences to selected ALP candidates. The DLP's threat had not influenced his thinking. "You can believe this or not as you like," Gorton said. "But the only time I wavered in favor of holding an early election was when the DLP said that. If there were anything that would have led me to have an election, it was the statements made recently by the DLP. But I realised that was an emotional reaction—not a rational one. I believe the DLP would have been completely ineffectual. I would have loved to see what happened. My sorrow is that I missed that fight. I made my judgment without taking them into consideration. They had no effect whatever on my decision."[54]

The DLP scoffed at Gorton as "belligerent." "This sort of belligerency of attitude seems politically unwise," commented the November, 1968, issue of *Focus,* the DLP's official organ. "It may seem necessary to remind the Prime Minister that Liberal and Country Party governments have no divine right to DLP preferences . . . . The extreme leftwingery of Dr Evatt and Mr Calwell and the clear danger of their irresponsible foreign policies were the determining factors in establishing a pattern of DLP preferences going to the government parties, but that pattern is not unchangeable. The DLP has always considered the response of the Liberal-Country Party coalition to the country's defence problems as being inadequate and belated."

The "non-elections" of 1968 had longterm effects, some of which continued until the 1969 elections with adverse consequences for the Liberal-CP coalition. Gorton's reputation for unpredictability[55] and political gaucherie was enhanced. The faulty psychology of allowing election fervor to build up to fever pitch and then flop soured the Liberal Party electoral machine. "The party was poised ready in late 1968 for a federal election which did not emerge," the NSW Liberal Executive reported to the NSW State Liberal Council. "The over-long period with candidates in the field made it very difficult to sustain any real campaign momentum."[56] The ALP regained from the almost childish way in which Gorton had insisted that he was in no way obliged to share his decision with the Parliament some measure of the confidence it had had in Holt's last days and Whitlam also started to challenge Gorton's hitherto unmistakable parliamentary ascendancy over himself. More importantly, relationships between Gorton and the DLP continued estranged, and DLP criticism, in some areas, particularly defence, more effective when directed against the government than the ALP's, sharpened. In the words of Mr Fred Osborne, NSW Liberal President, the DLP "had been allowed to get offside."[57] It was a costly exercise that contributed to an erosion of Liberal-CP confidence, improved the ALP's, and attracted public attention to the government's uncertainties, particularly on defence and foreign affairs.[58]

NOTES

1 Subject to the proviso that external earnings do not fall below the level needed to sustain imports at least at a static level, rising living standards for workers are an automatic feature of a full employment situation. Workers are in a position to enforce improvements so long as the independence of workers' associations is assured and continues.

2 From 1949 to 1966, Australian governments did not have to do anything substantial about these groups. To seem to be doing something was apparently sufficient to assuage the national conscience—see *The Hidden People: Poverty in Australia* by John Stubbs, Lansdowne Press, Melbourne, 1966.

3 I have deliberately left out 1961. Menzies fought that election "on my government's record". He had allowed unemployment, marginal in extent, to develop between 1958 and 1961. He won the elections but went within a two-seat margin of defeat, his House of Representatives' majority dropping from thirty-two to two.

4 Menzies' policy speech, November 10, 1949.

5 *Communism and Democracy in Australia* by Leicester Webb, F. W. Cheshire, Melbourne, 1954, p 23.

6 Extracts republished in *The Battle for the Banks* by A. L. May, Sydney University Press, 1968, pp 186/192.

7 Menzies' policy speech, November 10, 1949.

8 *Sydney Morning Herald*, July 25, 1949.

9 One of the paradoxes of Communism in Australia is that while Communists and the Communist Party have succeeded in winning considerable power in the Australian trade union movement, particularly in unions whose tradition of militancy long predates the rise of Australian Communism, and have sometimes channelled that militancy towards objectives approved by the Communist Party, the Communist Party has proved incapable of securing a worthwhile political, as distinct from industrial, following. The unionist who votes Communist in trade union ballots mostly votes ALP in parliamentary elections.

10 See pp 54/56 *The Battle for the Banks* by A. L. May, Sydney University Press, 1968, for Roman Catholic attitudes on the Bank Nationalisation issue.

11 Archbishop Mannix of Melbourne was often an open ALP supporter.

12 Though the ALP had done well at the May, 1953, Senate elections, it had not done as well as had been expected. Commenting on the vote, Professor Geoffrey Sawer wrote ". . . if a Federal general election were now held, that Party (the ALP) would still win comfortably." Sawer worked out that the ALP received 54 per cent of the total vote compared with 46 percent for the government parties—*The Australian Quarterly*, June 1953, p 104.

13 Evatt, who was a lawyer and former Justice of the High Court, appeared for the Communist-led Waterside Workers' Federation. Six of the seven members of the High Court Bench found that Menzies' Communist Party Dissolution legislation was invalid. Evatt was given the main credit for achieving this result.

14 Even after lengthy and protracted hearings which cost the Australian taxpayer 280,000 dollars, the commission produced a mouse rather than a mountain. ". . . It would appear that prosecution of none of the persons whose acts we have considered in our report would be warranted."— Report of the Royal Commission on Espionage, September 12, 1955, par 29, p 301.

15 For an authoritative, well documented account of the 1954/55 split see *The Split—Australian Labor in the Fifties* by Robert Murray, Cheshire, Melbourne, 1970.

16 However, Menzies stated "If . . . you are offered a new national leadership of the quality that emerges from the Petrov debate, it is my duty to remind you of that issue and to recall to you that policies cannot be entirely separated from the character and quality of the man who puts them forward . . . ."—Menzies' policy speech, Melbourne, November 15, 1955.

17 This document dealt with the personal habits of political journalists. I gather I was described as a "reformed drunk."

18 "There is no evidence that Dalziel improperly gave any information of a secret or confidential character to any Soviet official, either wittingly or unwittingly"—Report of the Royal Commission on Espionage, September 14, 1955, par 1002, p 273.

19 Report of the Royal Commission on Espionage, September 14, 1955, pp 40/41, 423/5.

20 The commissioners refused Evatt leave to continue representing Dalziel and Grundeman on September 7, 1954.

21 "Dr Evatt's foreign policy is clearly defeatist and based on an avowed acceptance of Communism as the way of the future"—R. Joshua's policy speech, November 10, 1955.

22 Professor L. F. Crisp's figures, given in the *Australian Quarterly,* Vol 42, No 1, March, 1970, p 104.

23 Two years later in 1960 Evatt was to retire from Federal politics, a broken man.

24 Cole, speaking in Hobart, October 22, 1958.

25 In an address in the 1950s, the Rev. E. H. Burgmann, a perceptive social observer and then Church of England Bishop of Canberra-Goulburn, commented "The Great Depression of the thirties has had a larger impact on Australian thinking than two World Wars."

26 In retrospect, it is interesting to note that the antiAmericanism which was to develop later in the ALP leftwing was absent in 1955. The 1955 ALP Federal Conference in Hobart declared "Co-operation with the United States in the Pacific is of crucial importance and must be maintained and extended"—Official report, March 1955, p 45.

27 The ALP policy of aid to "education in all its forms" was changed to aid direct to students at the Brisbane ALP Federal Conference, March 1957.

28 Hobart ALP Federal Conference, March 1955.

29 Cairns also recognised early the likelihood of United States' withdrawal. Much of his thinking seemed to be based upon the belief that the United States would be forced by internal pressures within the United States into abandoning its military commitments in Southeast Asia.

30 "It is of the utmost importance for us a small country in a dangerous world to be sure . . . that in times of stress and danger . . . we will be able to call upon the assistance of a great power, knowing that we deserve it because we have lived up to the spirit of the treaty we formed with it . . . ."—Gorton, addressing a Liberal Party rally at Parramatta, May 1969, reported in *The Australian Liberal,* July 1969.

31 Gorton interviewed on ABC TV by Robert Moore, January 21, 1968.

32 Commonwealth Representatives' Debates, Vol 60, p 573, August 27, 1968.

33 The Hasluck memorandum was issued to deny articles by myself and my colleague, Mr Peter Samuel, in the *Bulletin* of August 24, 1968. In my view, Mr Samuel's articles in the *Bulletin* over the 1968/69 period were the most authoritative on the tensions produced in Australia by the changing British and United States' policies in Southeast Asia.

34 Commonwealth Representatives Debates, Vol 61, pp 3017/3018, November 20, 1968.

35 Commonwealth Representatives Debates, Vol 58, p 452, March 26, 1968.

36 *Sydney Morning Herald,* December 20, 1968.

37 *Ibid.*

38 *Canberra Times,* December 26, 1968.

39 Transcript of speech, undated, made by Dato Stephens to the Third National Conference of Korea and Southeast Asia Forces Association of Australia.

40 Transcript quoted in article by Peter Samuel, *Bulletin,* February 17, 1968.

41 ABC TV appearance, September 1968.

42 Notes in the writer's possession.

43 The position in the Senate at this period was Government 27, ALP 28, DLP 4 and Independent 1.

44 An early election would not have suited Whitlam. Asking the question

"Who can blame Mr Gorton (if he decides on an early election)?", The *Australian* in a leader on October 14, 1968, commented "A convincing win by Mr Gorton would almost certainly jeopardise his (Whitlam's) position in the party."

45 Conversations with DLP members at the time.

46 The ALP's Dr Cairns advocated withdrawing all Australian troops from Asia, those in Malaysia and Singapore as well as those in Vietnam.

47 This version is based upon the verbal report Gair made to his parliamentary colleagues soon after his interview with Gorton. Subsequent events tended to confirm its broad accuracy.

48 In justice to my profession, I point out that questions were put ad nauseam to Gorton through his press secretary Mr Tony Eggleton. He could have killed the speculation at any stage. Instead he preferred to encourage the speculation, as he knew he was doing, by making the unvarying answer "No Comment."

49 Official text issued by PM's Canberra office, October 14, 1968.

50 The explanation for this *SMH* expectation may be contained in a later article by Ian Fitchett, as well informed a correspondent as there was in the Federal Parliamentary Press Gallery. Wrote Fitchett "When the Deputy Prime Minister and Country Party Leader Mr J. McEwen went overseas more than a month ago he was completely prepared for one (an election) taking place, having given Mr Gorton an assurance there would be no Country Party resistance."—*SMH*, October 16, 1968.

51 Commonwealth Representatives Debate, Vol 61, p 1909, October 15, 1968.

52 Commonwealth Representatives Debates, Vol 61, p 1912, October 15, 1968.

53 *Canberra Times*, October 16, 1968.

54 *Daily Telegraph*, Sydney, October 16, 1968.

55 Ian Fitchett's report was headed "Unpredictable Gorton does the unexpected"—*Sydney Morning Herald*, October 16, 1968.

56 When delegates questioned this executive reference and two candidates emphasised the desirability of being active in electorates well in advance of campaigns, it was explained "the reference was not to candidates but to actual campaigning for an election which did not take place as expected"—*Australian Liberal*, December 1969, p 16.

57 *Australian Liberal*, December 1969, p 6.

58 "When we turn to causes (for Liberal losses in 1969), I have no doubt that the first and prime cause was the confusion on our foreign policy and defence"—Osborne, *Australian Liberal*, December 1969, p 3.

CHAPTER 8

FACE in politics is like a vain woman's beauty, a matter of pride while it lasts but a source of anguish when wrinkles start to show. Gorton's decision against holding 1968 elections cost him face. The MLC decision raised doubts about his administrative methods; the "no election affair" about his political sagacity, judgment, and ability as a strategist. The mass of the electorate probably could not care less.[1] It was a "no event." But the "no election" decision affected the way in which those who were close to politics henceforward looked at Gorton—the parliamentarians, the officials who ran the various party political machines, the party activists, and, to a lesser extent, the higher echelons of the bureaucracy, who maintain a mostly detached but fascinated interest in the machinations of their political masters. It was Gorton's first real testing in the top level manoeuvres of national, domestic politics. At the best he had bungled; at the worst he had made a mess of the testing.

The groups that had a professional interest in politics did not accept that Gorton had not toyed meaningfully with the idea of 1968 elections. Such of the voting public that took any interest might or might not be persuaded into accepting Gorton's protestations that he had not allowed DLP threats to influence his judgment on the desirability or undesirability of 1968 elections. But the professionals were understandably disbelieving. They knew how things worked. They knew that the Liberal Party had been geared for 1968 elections. If Gorton had not intended to hold elections, then he had been playing "silly fellows" and they had the professional's contempt for individuals who played "silly fellows" and took risks for fun and not from calculation. They could not bring themselves to accept that Gorton had in fact been playing "funny fellows", though the flippancy or, to use Whitlam's word, the "coyness" with which Gorton refused to answer questions in the House of Representatives even after he had decided against 1968 elections gave the impression, perhaps deliberately, that he had been doing precisely that.

But whether or not Gorton had been playing "silly fellows" he had unmistakably botched things. He had allowed himself to be placed in a situation that did neither him, his image, his party, or his government any good. The Liberal political machine had been allowed to build itself up to election pitch, and once the stimulant of a proposed election campaign was removed a slump in enthusiasm and morale was inevitable.

He had permitted the DLP to emerge with enlarged status and with the public appearance of having forced the "no election" decision that the DLP, not Gorton, wanted. He had also shown faulty judgment. He had either miscalculated the intensity of DLP feeling about the government's failure to evolve defence plans and policies acceptable both to the government's own followers and to the DLP, or he had overestimated his own ability to outface a DLP bluff if, as he seemed to insinuate at the press conference he gave immediately after making his "no election" announcement to the government parties, he genuinely believed the DLP had been bluffing when it threatened to transfer its preferences from government to selected ALP candidates. Viewed from any angle, Gorton had not come impressively out of the "no election" incident.

But Gorton was courageous, dogged, and resilient. He had a quality that often marks the man who rises to the top in a harsh political environment. He was a tireless, merciless fighter, a good hater and a devoted enemy. Defeated on the 1968 elections front, he transferred his energies to other battlefields. He set out to further his plans for eliminating his potential rivals within the Liberal Parliamentary Party, to enlarge his electorally appealing image as an Australian nationalist by changing the Liberal Party philosophy on states' rights, and to support McEwen policies which had the dual attraction of being nationalistic in character and opposed to the policies which McMahon espoused and to some degree symbolised. There were elements of danger in this approach, particularly in any tampering with the Liberal Party's almost mystical belief in the necessity to maintain states' rights against the encroaching power of the already dominant Commonwealth. There was danger also in seeking to denigrate McMahon who, as well as a personal following in the Liberal Parliamentary Party, had wide Liberal Party support based upon regard for his policies and the belief that he represented a stable factor in a government which was becoming increasingly subject to the Prime Minister's unpredictability. But confident, assertive, and stubborn, Gorton was prepared to recognise danger only in an eyeball to eyeball confrontation. Only then could he be persuaded to retreat, and often the retreat was only feigned rather than real, a stratagem to secure breathing space and not an abandonment of objectives.

Gorton no longer had to worry about Hasluck. Though his

157

parliamentary colleagues were as yet unaware of it, Hasluck was a political zombie, ambulatory but in the parliamentary sense dead.[2] He was soon to be transported aloft as Governor-General and was preparing himself for his metamorphosis. But Fairhall remained, Fairhall the man who had not entered the lists against Gorton when the prime ministership was the prize but who many people held would have won if he had entered.

In his handling of Fairhall, Gorton showed himself a shrewd psychologist, with an understanding of his fellow man's weaknesses and the ability to exploit them. Fairhall was not a political animal.[3] He lacked a thick skin, had only a modest confidence in his own competence, and was sensitive. If rendered unhappy or frustrated, he would not retaliate by seeking to make his tormentors unhappy or frustrated. He would retire to the deepsea fishing which he loved, or into morose contemplation. He could soliloquise but not organise. He was a political Hamlet but neither a Cassius nor a Brutus. If pressures became sufficiently intolerable he would probably do what he was constantly threatening to do—retire from the political life for which in its cruder, more repellant backstairs aspects he was temperamentally unfitted. The pressures were put on and political life for Fairhall became increasingly intolerable.

Though he had risen high in ministerial ranking and in private life had been a successful businessman who by his own efforts had lifted himself from near poverty to comparative affluence, Fairhall had an attractive modesty. He distrusted his own capacity. He lacked the sublime certainty which usually distinguishes the political practitioner from his fellow man. He was not sure that he knew all the answers, lost when he got off the broad highway of politics and into its often squalid back lanes, and depended heavily for peace of mind upon the support of like-minded colleagues. He found his position as Defence Minister increasingly lonely after Gorton became Prime Minister; more lonely than ever when Hasluck transferred his mental attention from a minister's everyday problems to contemplation of his gubernatorial future. He became more isolated due to Gorton's virtual abandonment of a former Menzies-Holt practice.

As Prime Minister, Menzies had continued the World War II system. In wartime, defence decisions were made by a small group of senior ministers with present an elite of top advisers. Menzies preserved this practice by forming a Foreign Affairs and Defence Committee. It consisted of the Prime Minister, the deputy Prime Minister, the Treasurer, the Minister for External Affairs, the Minister for Defence, usually another senior minister, who was often the Minister for Supply, the Secretary of the External Affairs

Department, the Secretary of the Defence Department, and the chairman of the joint chiefs of staff. It was a system under which Menzies secured a body which provided continuity in defence advice. Though they waited until invited, the tradition was that the bureaucrats and service representative participated freely and uninhibitedly in the exchange of ideas.

When he became Prime Minister, Gorton allowed the committee to fall gradually into disuse. There were meetings, but they became fewer and the public service element was present only rarely.[4] Elimination of the public service element seems to have been due to Gorton's distrust of all but a few bureaucrats and to Gorton's belief that ministers should make their decisions detached as far as possible from the bureaucrats' immediate presence. A factor responsible for the committee falling into disuse was Gorton's knowledge that whatever their other differences McEwen, McMahon, Hasluck, and the departmental heads, as well as the military, shared on defence matters a viewpoint similar to Fairhall's. Like Fairhall, they believed that Australia should involve itself in regional arrangements, particularly with Malaysia and Singapore, even if those arrangements had the potential to involve Australia in some future risk. While he was reinforced with this collective, formal backing, Fairhall's confidence was maintained; without it, Fairhall could be worn down, his assurance eroded, and his sense of frustration fostered. With Hasluck, aware that he was to become Governor-General, receding imperceptibly into the political background, Fairhall was deprived, possibly without him knowing at that stage the reason, of the support of his stoutest ally, and became increasingly miserable and depressed.

As early as May, 1968, Fairhall was made acquainted with the type of problem that he was to encounter under Gorton. Fairhall was scheduled to make an important defence statement in the House of Representatives. Fairhall drafted the statement with the help of the permanent head of the Defence Department, Sir Henry Bland, a tough, able, little man, independently minded, polite but firm, who when Gorton relapsed abusively into the vernacular replied unintimidated, in kind. Fairhall and Bland were aware of the apprehensions of the Malaysian and Singapore leaders, particularly those of Singapore's Prime Minister, Mr Lee Kuan Yew, who, later, when asked his impressions of Gorton, was to comment "It's not so much the vacuum created by Britain's 1971 military withdrawal that I worry about but the vacuum in Canberra".[5] The two jointly prepared a speech which recognised the sensitivities of Malaysia and Singapore and which indicated that Australia's defence thinking was being done in a context which had regard for the interests and desires of these Asian neighbors, who, at that stage, had urged that at least a token Australian military presence should be retained in the region after 1971. The speech went to Gorton for his approval. Gorton re-wrote it, removing sections which Fairhall and Bland regarded as crucial. Fairhall sought and obtained an interview with Gorton. Fairhall took Bland with him to the interview.

Possibly fortified by the presence of Bland, a man whom nobody, not even a prime minister could browbeat into silence when he believed his duty was to speak out, Fairhall was uncharacteristically forceful. It was he who had to make the speech. It was an important defence speech. Much was at stake. Not only were government supporters uneasy about where defence policy was heading. There was also the future goodwill of Malaysia and Singapore to be considered. Fairhall said he was not going to make the speech as re-written by the prime minister. The re-written speech had some aspects that he was prepared to incorporate in his own speech. But it was without the foundations that were necessary. As re-written it was merely a shopping list, showing what Australia had acquired or proposed to acquire in the way of military equipment and strengths. It was lacking in any underlying philosophy of defence. It gave no indication to Malaysia or Singapore of Australia's future intentions and attitudes. Fairhall was sufficiently vehement to secure a compromise. When he made his defence speech, he was not able to pledge unequivocally that Australia would act in the way Malaysia and Singapore wanted it to act, which was to undertake to maintain forces in the region. But he did not close any doors. He was allowed to give a hint that that was the way Australia's thinking was inclining. "We (have) sent to Malaysia and Singapore a team from the defence complex of departments to make a thoroughgoing reconnaissance of facilities and installations, to secure data on which various alternative plans might be based", said Fairhall. With the implication that Australia would be continuing a Malaysian-Singapore commitment, this represented Fairhall-Bland thinking. But, added Fairhall, "it should not be assumed that any contribution we may make would necessarily retain the form or composition, or be maintained at the levels of the forces presently in Malaysia/Singapore."[6] This left open Australia's options and deferred to Gorton's line of thinking.[7]

Gorton and Fairhall were to have further arguments. One argument that culminated in a Fairhall threat to resign from Cabinet involved the F111. In 1963, with the RAAF's ageing Canberra bombers moving towards obsolescence, the Menzies government had ordered from the United States twenty-four F111s,

From left to right—Clyde Cameron, the South Australian MHR, who was a key figure in ALP organisational struggles, with the ALP Senate leader, Senator Lionel Murphy, centre, and Senator Don Willesee, father of Geraldine Willesee and a power in the Western Australian ALP machine.

Deciding the nation's future. ALP Federal Leader, Arthur Calwell, right, and Whitlam, back to camera and then Calwell's deputy leader, confer with ALP Federal Conference delegate, F. Waters, at midnight in the street outside the Hotel Kingston, Canberra, while inside the "thirty-six faceless men" of the ALP Federal Conference decide an issue that could be vital to Australia's security. After publication of these photographs the ALP decided to admit ALP Federal Parliamentary leaders as delegates to future ALP Federal conference discussions.

a supersonic fighter-bomber, controversial, advanced, expensive, but plagued with technical problems for years to come. Though ordered in 1963 on a promise of 1967 delivery, the F111 was still undelivered in 1968 when Gorton became Prime Minister and was still undelivered, and suspect, when the October, 1969, elections took place. With its costs constantly escalating and its future uncertain, it had been an embarrassment first to the Menzies' government, later to the Holt government, and subsequently to the Gorton government. As Menzies had announced general elections for November 30, 1963, on October 15, 1963, and the decision to acquire the twenty-four F111s on October 24, 1963, the ALP understandably alleged that the decision to buy the planes was not unconnected with the elections, and was a defensive Liberal-CP reaction to the pledge on October 22, 1963 of then ALP parliamentary leader, Mr Arthur Calwell, that if voted into office at the coming elections an ALP government would get an immediate replacement for the Canberra bomber.[8] Gorton, as Navy Minister in 1963, had fought unsuccessfully for an expansion of naval air strength, had lost out, and seen the money that might have been spent on projects he advocated earmarked for the F111s. He was apparently sour on the F111 purchase as early as 1967. In the night sessions when with Dudley Erwin, Miss Gotto, and others selected by these two to be exposed hopefully to the Gorton charm and intelligence Gorton had a drink and a gossip in the Government Whip's room after the Senate rose, Gorton unburdened himself on the F111. The project was "a bloody mess —something the government should get out of" he was reported to have said, and it was a view that when he became Prime Minister he was to repeat on occasions to his intimates of the "cocktail cabinet" over a quiet relaxing drink in the cabinet ante-room after the rigors of a hard day.[9]

In September, 1968, the government ran into parliamentary trouble over the F111. The government did not have a majority in the Senate. When the four DLP Senators—Gair, McManus, Byrne and Little—combined with the twenty-eight ALP Senators in the sixty-strong Senate, they could outvote the government's senators. The ALP and DLP combined to pass a resolution, moved by ALP Senate Leader Murphy "That there be laid on the table of the Senate all documents (or copies thereof) which constituted the original arrangements made by the Australian government for the purchase of F111 aircraft and all subsequent variations in the arrangements (with the exception of any specification or reference which would prejudice military security)."[10]

Fairhall was not a party to the 1963 decision to buy the F111s.

161

He was not then in Cabinet. The deal had been negotiated by the late Athol Townley when Townley was Minister for Defence. But Fairhall, as Defence Minister, had committed himself deeply to support of the F111 purchase. Probably like the men who made the 1963 decision he considered that the only gamble he was taking was on United States' technological skill in overcoming the defects which the F111 had developed, a reasonable gamble in view of United States' proven capacity in the past to solve technological problems.

With the ALP-DLP action in the Senate jamming the government in a nasty corner, Gorton, as befitted his temperament, preferred the bold course. He had gained kudos for his honesty and had been assisted tremendously when he was contesting the prime ministership by his action in tabling the papers on VIP flights at a time when his predecessor, Holt, and the then Minister for Air, Howson, were mistakenly insisting that passenger manifests for VIP flights did not exist. But the question was just what F111 documents should be tabled. They had become mountainous. They had to be transferred from the Defence Department to Fairhall's office in Parliament House by the truckload. Even if it were feasible to table them all in the Parliament without breaching confidences between the United States and Australian governments, it could not be done physically. Murphy's resolution had also left a loophole. The resolution left the government free to refrain from tabling any documents which might prejudice military security and it was the government that was in a position to make unfettered by considerations other than its own judgment the decisions on which documents might be deemed to infringe military security.

A quarrel broke out which was at once ferocious and low key. It was a quarrel which longterm contributed to the loss to Australia of the services of Bland and was a factor in impelling Fairhall towards his decision to retire from politics. Gorton wanted certain documents tabled. Fairhall and Bland argued that Australia had to pay regard to the fact that some of the documents were made available by the United States on the basis that they were confidential as between governments.[11] Gorton was obdurate. This was the way he wanted it to be, and this was the way it was going to be.

At this stage, the seemingly irresistible force of Gorton ran up against the immoveable object of Bland. Short, stocky, politely pugnacious, Bland, who had been a close confidante of Harold Holt and had a concept of public service which did not permit him to be associated with what he regarded as an impropriety in dealings between governments, coolly said that if the position was to be as the prime minister insisted it should be he would resign from the public service. He put this forward not as a threat but as a statement of intention. Bland apparently did not spell out the consequences that would flow from such a step. He did not need to; they were obvious. The resignation of the permanent head of the Defence Department in such circumstances would put the government in a most embarrassing position. If by any chance he stated publicly the reasons for his resignation the government could move into a dangerous position.

Fairhall was in an impossible situation. If the permanent head of his department resigned his position and the role he played in the incident that brought about his permanent head's situation would be subject to public scrutiny. He supported Bland in his viewpoint. If Bland resigned, he also would resign.

Bland had known Gorton for a long time. They had worked together on occasions. Bland had a considerable respect for Gorton's intelligence and the speed with which he grasped the essentials of a situation or subject. Bland actively liked Gorton as a person, though whether this liking was reciprocated was less certain. There was some to-and-froing. Finally a solution acceptable to Bland was adopted, and crisis averted. But the incident was to take Fairhall a further step towards retirement. Gloomily he told confidantes "If Gorton wants to work as leader of a team, he'll get all the loyalty in the world—if he goes it alone both he and us will have had it."[12]

Fairbairn was a different proposition from Fairhall. Like Fairhall, Fairbairn had not contested the prime ministership against Gorton. But unlike Fairhall, who had supported Hasluck, Fairbairn had voted for Gorton, and was not viewed, as Fairhall was, of possessing the support that might have enabled him to defeat Gorton if he had stood. Consequently while Gorton undoubtedly wanted to get rid of Fairbairn, who, like McMahon and Fairhall, was a legacy from the Menzies-Holt days there was not the same urgency to expedite his departure as there was in the case of the other two. Fairbairn was establishment and conservative, but he had the best qualities of the establishment. He was loyal, honorable, an ex-officer and a gentleman. He was eminently dependable, the type that supported the C.O. through thick and thin. But Gorton made the mistake, which many made in those days. He mistook Fairbairn's loyalty for blind loyalty and failed to recognise that if Fairbairn was confronted by a conflict between loyalty to an individual and to principle Fairbairn would adhere to principle.

Fairbairn was troubled. As Minister for National Development,

163

he had ministerial responsibility for the search for oil in Australia and also for the development of an indigenous oil producing industry once oil was found. A United States-Australian combine, Esso-BHP, had found quite spectacular quantities of oil in Bass Strait. It was expected that by September, 1970, the Bass Strait fields would be producing over 250,000 barrels of crude oil a day. The government had to decide its future policy on incentive payments to the oil industry.

An interdepartmental committee was set up. Though theoretically National Development preserved the supervisory and ministerial responsibility, represented on this committee were Treasury, Trade, and Customs and Excise. Dr P. H. Frankel, whose London-based company, Petroleum Economics Ltd., advised governments throughout the world was retained as an independent advisor. It was a conventional government procedure for handling a complex and difficult problem, which, longterm, would influence not only the search for oil in Australia but the development of domestic production and also domestic transport costs. But before long the procedure became less conventional.

The interdepartmental committee made its report. National Development prepared a submission for cabinet. Trade and Customs prepared a separate, joint submission. Though the submissions varied in some respects, they emphasised as had the interdepartmental committee report the necessity to maintain an "incentive" factor, as while the Bass Strait discoveries were substantial they were still not extensive enough to meet Australia's full domestic requirements and the need to continue encouraging exploration work still existed. Though by July he had submitted two preliminary reports, Dr Frankel's main report was still being awaited.

Then things started to take a novel twist. National Development's and the Trade-Customs submissions went to Cabinet. Gorton was to claim later that there were "quite a number of cabinet discussions"[13] which was literally true. But these discussions did not pass the "preliminary discussions" stage. No decisions were made and the submissions were not subjected to thorough Cabinet examination. Rightly or wrongly, Fairbairn formed the suspicion that Gorton had deliberately frustrated discussion so as to leave himself free of the inhibitions of a Cabinet decision for when, as he ultimately did, he took over the handling of the negotiations with Esso-BHP.[14] Fairbairn was further disturbed when Gorton instructed him not to discuss the negotiations with Esso-BHP in any way with his Department of National Development, which officially was the department supposed to possess the

164

expertise to advise the government intelligently and adequately on the subject of oil, the amount already found, the amount likely to be found, the amount needed to be found, the complexities of stimulating further discoveries and the basis on which, longterm, the best arrangements could be made with the exploring and exploiting companies. Gorton's stated reason for giving this instruction was that a highranking officer of the National Development would "leak" to the press if he had knowledge of the negotiations.[15] Fairbairn protested. He had the utmost confidence in the integrity of the officer named. It seemed wrong that a government should be denied the National Development's advice because of a suspicion that could be quite wrongly held. Gorton insisted. Fairbairn agreed reluctantly that he would carry out the direction[16] but said he felt that he had to tell the secretary of his department, Mr William Boswell[17] that the negotiations were under way. However, he would instruct Boswell that he was not to tell anyone else within the department.

Gorton conducted his negotiations with Esso-BHP with Hewitt as his only adviser.[18] When he completed his negotiations he took a wrapped up package deal into the Cabinet and, in his own words[19] asked Cabinet "Do you think this (deal) is a good one?" or "Don't you think this (deal) is a good one?", a rather intimidatory way for a prime minister to pose a query unless he expected and wanted the answer "Yes, it is a good deal." Cabinet decided it was a good deal. The government's new oil pricing policy, a wholly Gorton production, was announced to the Parliament on October 10, 1968. In November, 1968, not much more than a month later, Dr Frankel injected a piquant, new factor into the situation. Due to arrive in Australia on October 13 with his recommendations, Frankel was told that his recommendations would not be needed. By November Frankel had taken the attitude that continuance of the general consultancy agreement he had with the Department of National Development would serve no useful purpose. He commented that if Gorton had waited for his report before entering into the Esso-BHP agreement and had accepted his criticisms of the system adopted for establishing the quality price differential and his projections of overseas oil prices and freight rates then the price of petrol could have been one or two cents less than under the new Gorton agreement. But though he made these criticisms, Frankel added "The government's policy does not seem to be unsound in principle since it assures indigenous crude the opportunity of covering Australian oil demands without altogether distorting a pattern based on international prices."[20]

The oil pricing policy got a mixed reception. Some saw it as "a hit at big business in the interests of the little man."[21] Others saw it as "the great oil scandal."[22] Still others did not know what to make of it.[23]

Disturbed and dismayed at the way the government was going, unwell at that time—he still tired relatively easily as a result of the accident on his farm in which he had broken his back—Fairbairn gave Gorton the opportunity to get rid of him quietly and without fuss. Gorton did not avail himself of the opportunity. It was an opportunity which in the light of subsequent events Gorton probably reproached himself later for not seizing.

Fairbairn had discussions with Gorton about his future either in late October or early November.[24] He was disturbed but not desperate. He had misgivings about how Gorton was handling things, but he was not sure his opinion that Gorton was mishandling things badly was an unchallengable one and not colored to some extent by his feeling of depression arising from his state of health. So, understandably, he took the easier way out of his difficulties. He emphasised his personal problems rather than the fact he regarded Gorton's style as presenting him with a problem. He told Gorton he had "had it". He was exhausted. Gorton had promised him that he would split up the Department of National Development and allow it to shed the bits and pieces that had become appended over the years and were not strictly national development matters. Gorton had not kept this promise. He wanted "out." He would like an appointment as High Commissioner in London as the successor to Sir Alex Downer, whose term would shortly run out, or as Australian Ambassador in Paris.[25] Gorton was noncommittal. He expressed no regret about Fairbairn's proposed exit from the political scene. London was definitely not available. Paris was left in the air, like a slaughtered bullock hanging from a tree. Gorton told Fairbairn that he should stay on until after the next elections. Then he would see what could be done. Fairbairn received the impression that Gorton had bigger fish than Fairbairn to fry, that he was reserving the lures of both London and Paris to catch the fish he hoped to fry, and that only when that fish had been caught and fried was he interested in frying Fairbairn. Upset, disconsolate, depressed that there was no immediate escape for him from a situation about which he was increasingly worried, Fairbairn wandered around to Fairhall's office. The men confided in each other their fears about the way things were shaping. Fairhall's gloom probably did nothing to relieve Fairbairn's depression. But as far as Gorton was concerned Fairbairn was eligible for elimination whenever it suited Gorton to do the elimination. Fairbairn had offered his neck for the axe, though the price was that the block should be well cushioned. It was for Gorton to decide when the axe should fall. Gorton probably did not want too many political corpses on his hands at the one time. He was disposing of Hasluck and had prospects of disposing of Fairhall. He hoped to dispose of McMahon. Fairbairn could wait. Gorton probably judged that he was less dangerous than others. It was a miscalculation that he was to regret and to bring him trouble. But the trouble was still months ahead.

McMahon was a bird of a different feather from both Fairbairn and Fairhall. Unlike Fairbairn, he was not unwell: in fact he was in extraordinary physical condition for a man of sixty, still playing strenuous squash with talented opponents half his age and beating them. Though nervy and seemingly highstrung, he was a tough Sydneysider, as tenaciously durable, despite his background of inherited wealth and social position, as any of Sydney's gutter bred denizens. Unlike Fairhall, he could not be driven by frustration and opposition into despair and the political suicide of voluntary retirement. Nor was he the type to offer his throat willingly to the sacrificial knife. He had the strength of his own record of achievement and performance in the Treasury and the position of Liberal Parliamentary Deputy Leader, which was elective and not the gift of the Prime Minister.

McMahon and his power base of Treasury were subjected to a "squeeze" play, signalled by Gorton's insistence that he should participate from the outset not only in the policy framing of the 1968 budget but in the detail work. McEwen's dislike for McMahon was also exploited.

Gorton handled McEwen very cleverly. Gorton did not fear McEwen: it is doubtful, in fact, that Gorton knew the meaning of fear in the political sense and this was responsible for Gorton getting himself into positions which a more cautious and timid man would have avoided like the plague. But Gorton had respect for the older man, respect for his ability, for his prowess as a political infighter, for his tenacity, and above all for the following McEwen could command both within his own Country Party and among sections of the Liberal Party. He solved the problem of McEwen by allowing McEwen to secure, without prime ministerial opposition, anything that McEwen wanted and by supporting McEwen policies which McMahon and Treasury opposed. Psychologically this made it almost impossible for McEwen to confront Gorton when Gorton's techniques caused him uneasiness and concern.[26]

Both McEwen and Gorton disliked McMahon personally. This factor should not be underestimated. More decisions have gone

167

a certain way because a man has had a bad morning at stool, because his wife has been bitchy, or because he disliked the individual who was sponsoring the proposal than political scientists imagine. But between McEwen and McMahon there were also deep policy differences. The policy differences tended to revolve around tariffs in their relationship to primary industry, overseas investment, and such things as the establishment of an overseas Australian shipping line to share the lucrative Australian export-import trade, hitherto dominated by British, European, and Japanese interests. The tariff issue was particularly touchy. McEwen led the Country Party. The CP traditionally was the party of free trade, recognising that a high tariff policy excluded cheap imports, lessened competition on the Australian market and added to primary producers' costs. The McEwen-Trade attitude was that adequate tariff protection was essential, and their definition of what was adequate was generous. Primary production in Australia was not a large employer of labour, and, already intensively mechanised, would be an even smaller employer as the process of mechanisation continued. Secondary industry provided employment. Without the job opportunities provided by an expanding secondary industry, the immigration programme must slacken and development proceed at a much slower rate. When tariff barriers added to primary producers' costs, primary producers could be compensated by the payments of subsidies, either direct or indirect. The McMahon-Treasury line, which was backed by the Tariff Board, was that the McEwen-Trade thesis overestimated the importance of secondary industry as an employer. Technological advances in secondary industry were making Australian industry less dependent upon manpower which was increasingly being replaced by machines. Tertiary industries were the employers of the future. Already the United States had sixty percent of its work force engaged in tertiary industries. Australia was certain to go the same way. Primary producers were needlessly paying higher prices for a wide range of locally manufactured goods. If imports were substituted, primary producers' costs would not continue to soar as they frighteningly had been doing. The Australian tariff structure had become distorted and some industries were sheltering behind tariff walls that protected not their existence but their swollen profits. The whole Australian tariff structure should be subjected to a searching and detailed scrutiny. It was an attitude that had for McEwen the dangerous likelihood of appeal to the rural voters who maintained him and his party in the Parliament. Whenever the Tariff Board lifted its head or its voice, McEwen belted it. Such was the power of his powerful personality that while he was in the Cabinet and Parliament[27] he managed to retain the electoral support of the rural community almost undiminished.

Though he did not postulate any substitute plan, McEwen also gave the public impression that he was against the Menzies-Holt policy of an open door for overseas investment in Australia, a policy to which McMahon subscribed when he became Treasurer. As early as April 2, 1963, McEwen speaking to a Country Party conference in Victoria stated "We in this room are mostly established farmers. If we earn enough annual income we live comfortably. If we do not we could still live comfortably by selling a bit of the farm every year, and that is pretty much the Australian situation—we are not earning enough and we are selling a bit of our heritage every year." As McEwen was the second most powerful man in government until Menzies retired in 1966 and thereafter the most powerful, and the open door policy on overseas investment continued for all practical purposes unchanged through that period, it would seem that there was an element of posturing in McEwen's attitude. He collected the kudos and a measure of public approval for taking such an attitude but did nothing to change the situation that existed then and continued to exist during his term of office.[28] But his homely piece of bucolic philosophising undoubtedly had its attraction for Gorton, who himself was strongly nationalistic, and probably helped to produce Gorton's contradictory attitudes of one minute insisting upon the imperative need to secure further investment funds from overseas and the next making statements, such as those at the Australian Club luncheon in London, which, from the Treasury's viewpoint were dangerous, as they might scare away overseas investors who had a dread of uncertainty in government policies.

While he did little except moralise about the entry of capital into Australia, McEwen did evolve a scheme designed to enable Australian industry to compete on more favorable terms with overseas investors for loan funds. McEwen proposed setting up an Australian Industry Development Corporation "to marshal adequate financial resources for major expansion and development under Australian ownership" and "to borrow or to raise overseas funds in the fixed interest category on the most favorable terms possible."[29] McEwen had originally produced his scheme back in 1966. Almost contemporaneously, McMahon produced a plan for a consortium of banks to combine as the Australian Resources Development Bank with virtually the same objectives and charter. For once, McEwen experienced a setback. Cabinet preferred McMahon's scheme to McEwen's. But in 1968 McEwen had a prime minister who was prepared to give him what he wanted. On the first real sitting day[30] of the Gorton-led Parliament, March 13, 1968, McEwen revealed that he had wasted no time to get a reversal of the Holt Cabinet's "thumbs down" on the Australian Industrial Development Corporation proposal.

Questioned by Whitlam on whether he had resubmitted his Australian Industry Development Corporation scheme to the new Gorton Cabinet[31] McEwen said "The matter has not come before the new Cabinet but I have had a discussion with the Prime Minister about it."[32] The discussions were extremely fruitful, and an indication of how McEwen was to get his own way in return for the tacit understanding that he did not challenge the Gorton style. Though when the McEwen proposal went finally to Cabinet it was opposed by the former Treasurer, McMahon, by then External Affairs Minister, the then Treasurer, Les Bury, and other seemingly powerful ministers, McEwen received Gorton's backing. The 1967 Cabinet decision was reversed and McEwen's Corporation came into existence.

Entry by Australia into the overseas shipping trade was also a McEwen ambition, sought because shipping freight charges contributed to Australia's balance of payments, aggravated the cost problems of Australian exporters, and decreased their returns. Sir Alan Westerman, the energetic permanent head of McEwen's Trade Department and McEwen's principal official adviser, had long taken an interest in shipping matters. On one occasion, he had crewed, victualled, loaded, and serviced a non-existent vessel, had sailed it on paper on a voyage to the United Kingdom and back, and had emerged with the conclusion that overseas shipowners charged Australian exporters "what the traffic will bear." Westerman wanted not only modernisation of the ships in the Australian trade, a modernisation which he believed would assist in keeping shipping freights at a level lower than that achievable if ageing and outmoded ships were used on Australian services but a more dominant position for the Commonwealth in the shipping trade. A nucleus of an Australian shipping service existed in the Australian National Line, government-owned, established by the Chifley ALP government, and operating profitably on coastal routes, and occasionally doing overseas trips. McEwen, who regarded himself as the guardian of rural interests, was sensitive to freight increases. Westerman had a Messianic belief in Australia's need to modernise its shipping facilities. But Holt, who had been Treasurer before he became Prime Minister, was unenthusiastic about an Australian shipping service. Treasury had unhappy memories of the Commonwealth-owned Bay Line of ships which Australia had operated during World War I and into the

1920s. The Minister for Transport, Gordon Freeth, was reflecting both Holt's and the Treasury's viewpoint when in 1967 he told the House of Representatives: "It (the Bay Line) was not able to operate at a profit at freight rates which were being charged by its competitors who were operating at a profit . . . the most that honorable members and the country could expect if we were able to engage in the overseas trade would be for us to engage in it as a member of a conference or at least to charge conference rates."[33]

McEwen had discussions with Gorton on an Australian shipping service. Again there was a strong appeal to Gorton's nationalism as well as to his resentment against what Gorton considered Treasury's conservatism. On Tuesday, August 27, 1968, Cabinet met. A proposal was discussed to buy a forty percent interest at a cost of between thirty and forty million dollars in the British shipping company, Port Line, which would have secured Australian entry into Associated Container Transportation Ltd., [ACT], a consortium which consisted of the Port Line, the Cunard Steamship Co., the Blue Star Line, Ellerman Lines, Ben Line, and Harrison Line, and a voice in the Australia-UK European Shipping conference which fixed freight rates on the Australia-Europe shipping route. In the light of subsequent happenings, it would appear that the move was halfbaked and insufficiently considered. The ACT consortium proposed to operate fully cellular container ships. There was still dispute in Australia over whether these ships represented the most effective cargo carriers for the Australian trade, and the suspicion was to emerge later that it was precisely because they were not as suited for this particular trade as were other types of ships that the Consortium's advisers wanted to entice the Commonwealth government into a participation from which there would be no retreat. Wool was the main outward cargo from Australia.[34] If wool was not sent by cellular container vessels to the United Kingdom, the companies operating these vessels on the Australia-United Kingdom run would incur substantial losses. It was in the interests of those operating this type of operation to have the Australian government involved in the operation.[35]

In a report to the Executive Council of the Woolgrowers' Association, dated June 18, 1968 and marked "strictly confidential"[36] the Association's Shipping and Transport Committee expressed its doubts about the suitability of container ships for the carriage of wool. The committee reported "The committee has closely examined the merits and demerits of the cellular container and unit load methods, and the balance of advantages appears to

171

lie, at this stage with the unit load vessel, as long as adequate pre-stowage organisation is available and the wharf facilities are equal to those which are being provided by the Maritime Services Board of NSW and other port authorities for the cellular container operators." The Department of Trade and Industry's shipping section was reported to have recommended against the container form of shipping.[37] The Australian Meat Board which had built up a valuable trade in Australian meat exports, particularly to the United States, also questioned the benefit of the container system against unit loads.[38]

A Senate Select Committee, which under the chairmanship of Liberal Senator (later Sir) Magnus Cormack, investigated "The Container Method of Handling Cargoes" from April 1967 until June 1968 and heard 177 witnesses commented "Before any irrevocable steps are taken to place the greatest percentage of the Australia/UK Continent trade within the operational hands of two British consortia or one (if such were to be the ultimate outcome) the operators of the flexible type of shipping encompassed by Scandia vessels should be given every opportunity to prove their practical worth . . . . The absence of such opportunity and a resultant inability to reveal the maximum benefits available to Australian shippers, must only produce a field of non-competition, in relation to freight rates and services, in which cellular container operators can be the only beneficiaries[39] . . . there has been an element of haste in introducing the container system to Australia without sufficient time for adequate consultation between the many interests involved.[40]

But more importantly, the Chairman of the Australian Coastal Shipping Commission, Sir John Williams, unmistakably Australia's greatest shipping authority who had shrewdly steered the government-owned Australian National Line through fourteen years of profitable operations, preferred the unitising method to the cellular container system for the Australian trade. In an Australian National Line publicity brochure with Williams' picture on the front the ANL declared that the Scandia-type ships were superior to the British ships. Cabinet decided against buying into the Port Line but McEwen was authorised to conduct talks in London. The method of how Australia was to enter the overseas shipping trade was left open.

McEwen left for overseas and among other things discussions in London on the shipping project, on September 7, 1968. He returned on October 29, 1968. Sir Alan Westerman and the first assistant secretary of the Trade Department, Mr J. Scully, left for London in the weekend of November 17 after a conference in

172

Canberra on November 8, 1968, between Gorton, the recently returned McEwen, Westerman, and Hewitt. With Westerman and Scully in London, moves were made to induce Sir John Williams to put his impressive imprimatur upon the decisions taken by Gorton and McEwen after the Gorton-McEwen-Westerman-Hewitt meeting. The Minister for Shipping, Ian Sinclair sent for Williams. He asked him to leave, post haste, to join Westerman and Scully in London. Before he left, Williams repeated his view. He was not convinced that the cellular container operation was the best for Australia. It was essential that Australia should maintain the competitive position of the "roll-on roll-off" Scandia ships. In London, Williams was presented with two pencilled pages of figures. They represented the figures and figuring by the British shipping companies and the Department of Trade. They showed that the Australian-UK trade could be carried on with cellular container ships profitably, economically, and efficiently. Williams was asked to endorse the figures. He was told he had two days to study them. Cabinet was to meet on November 26. The Cabinet papers would be distributed to ministers only half an hour before Cabinet met. That was the plan. The ministers would have no opportunity to study them. Without Williams' imprimatur, the minister would not be in a position to argue. With his imprimatur, they would not argue. Williams refused to give his endorsement. He could not study the figures adequately in two days. He repeated his views. He was not convinced that cellular container ships were best for Australia. "Roll-on, roll-off" and Scandia ships must be allowed to show their competitive worth. The British shipping companies and the Trade Department must carry the responsibility for the figures. Without extensive examination, he would not attest either to their accuracy or worth. He also disagreed with other aspects of the proposals which still envisaged that the Australian ship would operate under the British flag but be Australian manned. Williams' view was that neither British nor Australian unions would accept such a proposal. Without union co-operation success for the venture was unlikely.

In an article in the *Sydney Morning Herald* of November 22, 1968, John Stubbs reported that Australia was to enter the shipping trade between Australia and Europe with an original investment of forty million dollars. The decision, said Stubbs, followed the Gorton-McEwen-Hewitt-Westerman conference. The government acting through the ANL intended to operate at least one container vessel within the Australia-Europe conference.

On Friday, November 22, 1968, the parliamentarians were departing from the Canberra airport for a weekend in their home cities after the week's parliamentary sitting. ALP watchers

173

amusedly watched Bury, long and lugubrious and a senior minister who theoretically should have been consulted on a policy decision of such magnitude, lobbying his fellow ministers as they waited for their planes on what they knew about the "Stubbs story." They claimed to be like him, completely ignorant of what was going on. They were not left ignorant for long. On November 24, 1968, Michael Bailey, shipping correspondent of the London *Times,* reported that the Australian National Line would take over one of three 10.7 million dollar container ships being constructed for the ACT. Bailey wrote that the announcement of Australia's stake in the British-Australia container ship service followed closed talks in London between Sir Basil Smallpiece, Chairman of the Cunard Line, and Westerman.[41]

Gorton said later that the first initiative had come from the Trade Department. But the government had not been interested in buying a minority shareholding in the Port Line. Alternative suggestions were made round the Cabinet table as to what Australia would prefer if it went into the overseas shipping trade. "From then on all negotiations were in John McEwen's hands," said Gorton. ". . . the new (shipping) proposition—which again had reached the stage with John McEwen and his department nego-tiating it, where it could be put to Cabinet for acceptance or rejection—was then put to Cabinet for acceptance or rejection and it was unanimously—virtually no discussion almost—acclaimed and adopted."[42] The "unanimous" decision was made on Novem-ber 26, 1968, two days after Bailey had announced it. There was "virtually no discussion" for a very good reason. Cabinet met at 10.30 am. The Cabinet submission recommending that Australia adopt this method of entering the overseas trade was circulated at 9 am. Ministers other than Gorton, McEwen, and the Shipping Minister, Ian Sinclair, who was a McEwen protégé had no oppor-tunity to study the submission in depth or to get the considered advice of their experts.[43]

From Gorton's and McEwen's viewpoint the operation had been a brilliant success. McMahon and Treasury, with its cautious prag-matic approach, had been frozen out from participation. Gorton, McEwen, and Sinclair held a joint press conference in Gorton's office, with McEwen doing most of the talking.

There would be two Australian 24,000 ton ships, one for the United-Kingdom-Australian and the other for the Australian-North American trade. The North American vessel was still on the drawing board. The UK-Australian one was then under construc-tion in Britain, with the British government paying one-fifth of the construction costs in subsidy. Both ships would be chartered, but at the end of five years Australia had agreed to buy the ships if the owners—Associated Container Transportation Ltd.—required Australia to do so. The ships would be British owned and fly the British flag, but would be Australian crewed and managed by the Australian National Line. The UK-Australia ship would cost about 8.56 million dollars. It was expected to bring in a gross revenue of nearly 40 million dollars in five years, much of it representing savings in foreign exchange. It would cost Australia, initially, about between 6 and 7 million dollars to enter the trade. "We are getting into this for peanuts," McEwen said, with Gorton nodding happy approval.[44]

The "peanuts" turned out to be both expensive and of dubious quality. On Thursday, April 17, 1969, half an hour after the Parliament had risen for the weekend recess, McEwen and Sinclair, in a joint statement, announced that the decision was not to charter but to buy, thereby adding another two million dollars immediately and a minimum of thirty million dollars longterm to the bill. On Tuesday, April 22, 1969, Sinclair, the most junior member of the Gorton-McEwen-Sinclair trio, was given the dubious honour of repeating the announcement in the House of Representatives.[45] Defending the government's switch from chartering to buying, McEwen told the Parliament that knowing as much about freight charges as "any other shipping operator in the world" was "the only reason why I advised the government to go into the shipping business with container vessels."[46] McEwen made no attempt to defend the view that a container service was superior to other types of shipping services, nor did he refer to the charge that the government had allowed itself to be "suckered" into association with a container service because those operating the container service wanted government pressure exerted if wool exporters turned to other than container types of ships.[47]

As time passed evidence mounted that the government had made a decision that at the most charitable could be described as injudiciously hasty and at the worst mistaken. Though Treasury's conservatism might have been distasteful to Gorton, this was an occasion on which it possibly would have had value. Sinclair himself turned critical of the shipping conference, which McEwen had said was composed of "great and reputable people." McEwen had added "Their investment is in a country which this government controls; to take us for a ride would not be a very profitable exercise."[48] Commenting on a decision by the shipping conference of which by then the government was a member, through the Australian National Line, to lift the wool freight rate by four percent, Sinclair said "I don't believe it (the freight rise) is justified because of the complete change in the nature of the ships available over the next twelve months."[49] He also told the Parliament that he doubted if container shipping would lead to the economies promised when it was first introduced.[50] The Secretary of the Shipping and Transport Department, Mr M. M. Summers, said the shipping companies had been so anxious to forestall competition that they had put themselves in a position of not having a full knowledge of the requirements of "all those on whom they depend for the successful operation of the system."[51] The Department of Trade's shipping specialist, assistant secretary, Mr R. Ramsay, who had by then resigned from the Department was described as having "always doubted the virtues of pure container shipping."[52]

In a coldly factual way, Sir John Williams, in the 1970 annual report of the Australian National Line[53] pointed up the advantages of the "roll-on roll-off" ships for the Australian trade and the constricting influence of a shipping conference operation. While Gorton and McEwen had accepted the cellular container ship on the as yet more important Australia-UK trade, Williams' advice had been accepted for the Japanese-Australia sea routes. "When Australian flag participation was first mooted, shipowners then conducting the Australian Japan trade on the 'Conference' basis were informed that the Australian National Line, in conjunction with Kawasaki Kisen Kaisha Ltd., would introduce roll-on roll-off vessels," the report stated.

Sir John Williams' report continued "In the many discussions which followed 'Conference' disputed the capacity of the Australian ships to carry the volume of cargo claimed for them . . . . Under 'conference' rules, a member who carries more freight than his allotted share in twelve monthly intervals over a four and half year agreement period must pay back any excess to those who have earned less. As forecast to conference, the *Australian Enterprise*[54] quickly demonstrated what she could do, and for the twelve months ended June 30, 1970, the commission is called upon to pay back a very substantial sum to the pool and which after taking account of establishment and other preliminary outgoings, transforms what should have been a profit into a loss for the year's work . . . . Again during the early stages, other conference members fully aware of the cargo potential of the Eastern Searoad ships and themselves favoring the 'cellular' type vessel, having previously intimated that they would restrict their proposed buildings to a '750 container' standard, built vessels to carry 1100 units instead, on the grounds that the growth of the trade so warranted, thus creating an overtonnage situation to the detriment of all. For clarification, in the Australian trade, two shipping concepts compete for cargo, i.e. the Australian development of the roll-on roll-off vessel in the Eastern Searoad Service, able to cater for any cargo save bulk; and the more restricted 'cellular' container carriers favored in this trade by the 'third flag' owners and the Japanese except 'K' Line. As it had turned out, the roll-on roll-off system backed by efficient shore facilities has by common consent been able to give better service and faster delivery to its clients and has been favored with reasonable loadings throughout . . . . The virtues of the 'Conference' system have been loudly proclaimed and certainly virtues there are. But whatever justification there may be for 'pooling shares', at a time of vast technological change such as the industry is now going through and with the need to promote and aid any new development likely to yield a more economic service, the question should be faced as to whether these members of a conference, by their voting strength alone,[55] should be able to hamstring the development of national minorities whose ships have proved their worth, by refusing a reasonable share, by overtonnaging a trade, or by any course save by providing an equal or better service."[56]

From the government's viewpoint, it was a devastating report, a report which when coupled with such extraordinary behaviour as the Cabinet being given no real time to study the relevant documents was liable to produce quite serious electoral misgiving. Fortunately for the government the report did not come out until after the October, 1969 elections had been disposed of. Nor did knowledge of other things. But the government's switch from chartering to buying its container ship for the British trade doubtlessly added to the vague public impression of confusion at the top. Nevertheless, according to the public opinion polls and to grassroot manifestations, the government's popularity continued high. In February, 1969, a Gallup poll listed 48 percent of the voters for the Liberal-CP coalition, 37 percent for the ALP, seven percent for the DLP, and two percent for independents, with six percent undecided, a very strong position for the government if the poll accurately reflected public opinion.

But as early as October, 1968, Gorton had involved himself, almost defiantly, in an issue to his handling of which can be traced with more certainty than is usually possible in politics part of the reason for the decline in his and his party's vote in the October, 1969, general elections. When the final figures were counted in October, 1969, it was found that a quite spectacular drop in the Liberal vote had taken place in what were traditionally "blue ribbon" Liberal seats, and that the Liberal vote had held up better in borderline electorates. For example, the Liberal share of first preference votes declined in Bradfield from 78.51 percent in 1966 to 63.04 percent, in Lowe from 68.88 percent to 48.21 percent, in MacKellar from 65.52 percent to 56.65 percent, and in Wentworth from 63.93 percent to 57.65 percent. In comparison with these substantial falls in Liberal support in these "blue ribbon" individual seats, the Liberal Party's overall share of first preference votes across Australia fell from 40.14 percent in 1966 to 34.79 percent in 1969.[57] The issue which contributed to these falls was undoubtedly Gorton's alleged "centralism."

Gorton seems to have "pulled on" a party fight on this issue deliberately and from long held conviction. As early as 1953 he had told the Senate that there must be a change in Commonwealth-State relations and that it might be "necessary for constitutional powers to be reversed so that instead of residual sovereignty residing in the States and only certain powers in the Commonwealth, certain powers might be guaranteed to the states and residual powers might remain with the Commonwealth."[58]

It was obvious to a political babe-in-arms that the Liberal Party could be converted to this, or a similar viewpoint, only after a long and patient process of re-education. Most Liberals, particularly the activists, were antiSocialism and supporters of private enterprise. They subscribed to the view put forward by former Prime Minister Menzies, who had virtually created the Liberal Party that "The Socialists, believing as they do and must, that a well-ordered Society should, as far as possible, be central-government controlled, are not federalists but unificationists. They stand for the abolition of State Parliaments. Indeed, they would like to abolish the Senate, which they regard as a useless excrescence."[59] Australian voters were suspicious of attempts to give the Commonwealth greater power. The voters demonstrated this suspicion at referenda. Of the twenty proposals for constitutional amendment put to the Australian electorate since Federation in 1901, all but five, and the five relatively minor, had been defeated.[60] The Liberal Party was already restive. There had been grumbles about the proCommonwealth attitudes of Menzies and Holt, when they were prime ministers, though both paid faultless and unflagging lip service to the desirability of maintaining state rights. The states' major grievance was that the Commonwealth had taken away their financial independence when it instituted uniform income tax during the war years[61] and for all practical purposes drove them out of that field of taxation. Gorton's insistence at his first Premiers' Conference that he would defend the Commonwealth's pre-eminence in the taxation field was put with a curtness that Menzies and Holt had avoided. "We believe it is wrong to impose more than one direct tax on wages, salaries and related forms of income," Gorton told the premiers. "If such a practice were to become established and to spread it would not only add to the tax burdens on wage and salary earners which already are by no means inconsiderable, but also it could give rise to all the evils of differential rates of income tax on citizens living in different states, from which the system of uniform taxation has rid this country . . . payroll taxation is an important source of national revenue and it is also an instrument which can be used to promote activities and development of benefit to our economy."[62]

Gorton had already had a warning that there would be trouble if he persisted in his attitude that the Commonwealth had to have unchallenged supremacy over the States. On October 4, 1968 the NSW Premier, Rob Askin, and the Victorian Premier, Sir Henry Bolte, had organised a special meeting in Sydney. The Commonwealth was not represented. The meeting was to organise a greatly stepped-up campaign for a thorough review of Commonwealth-State financial relations. State Liberal Parliamentarians were asked to put pressure on the Liberal Federal Parliamentarians, many of whom were sympathetic to the states anyway, to secure a revision of the Commonwealth's autocratic attitude. At this stage there was a reluctance to blame Gorton, a new Prime Minister, for the situation. Though the reverse of a centralist, McMahon, a frugal Treasurer, had tried to curb state demands for more funds by warning constantly of inflationary dangers. Gorton was prepared to give the states money so long as he retained control. The piquant situation was that Gorton, though centralist in his thinking, was generous in a paternalistic sense, prepared to hand out funds though not authority. McMahon was a states' righter but parsimonious with the taxpayers' money. McMahon started to get the blame for the Commonwealth's overall attitude. Gorton did not escape unscathed. "The Federal government's prestige has diminished since Mr Gorton became Prime Minister," Sir Henry Bolte said. "State governments have been handled in a more cavalier way by Mr Gorton and the Federal Treasury."[63] In October, 1968, Liberal Party organisational support for the premiers and state rights was clearly evident. Queensland had on the agenda for the 23rd annual meeting of the Federal Council of the Liberal Party a motion asking the council to declare "the necessity of reviewing the financial relations between the Commonwealth and the States with special reference to the share of the national taxation which the states receive."[64] NSW had a motion

179

"That this council reiterates its belief, as a party consisting of Federal and State elements dedicated to a federal system of government, that it is imperative that a special conference of the party be convened as a matter of urgency to enable study of Commonwealth-State relations to be undertaken within the confines of the party."[65]

It was an atmosphere in which a cautious man would have "ganged warily." Gorton might have had logic on his side when he considered that an allpowerful central government with specific powers delegated to the state governments would provide more efficient government than a central government with powers limited by a constitution operating over and alongside states with otherwise sovereign powers. While logic might have been on Gorton's side, history was not necessarily so.[66] Additionally, people seek things other than efficiency from government. AntiSocialists seek the means to combat socialism, and the mystique of the Liberal Party was that the federal setup in Australia provided precisely that. Other people have reservations about a powerful central government, and prefer to keep checks upon power. There is a wide variety of feeling about the existing Australian governmental system. As events were to show, the feeling among Liberals that the federal system should be preserved, even strengthened by the strengthening of the states' financial independence, was widespread. On October 14, 1968, Gorton went to a Flinders electorate Liberal Party luncheon at Mornington, in Victoria. He announced that he had made his decision on whether or not he would hold elections in 1968, and that he would announce his decision to the next day's meeting of the government parliamentary parties in Canberra. He knew that he was not going to hold elections. He must have been aware also that he would be accused of backing down because of DLP threats to transfer DLP preferences from government to selected ALP candidates. A proud and aggressive man, he would have resented the public humiliation. He also was aware of the proState rights resolutions, by implication antiGorton, to be moved at the Liberal Council meeting. He was less than tactful in his timing, and also defiant. "I speak of the need to stand and quite dispassionately survey the relationships between the various levels of government in Australia, the Australian government, the state government, the municipal government," he said. "There was a time when the party was formed when it was believed and when it was dogma and when it was unquestionable that all an Australian government ought to do was to hand out particular sums of money to Queensland, or to Western Australia, or to whoever it may be and say 'Spend these in the way in which you think best.' I do not think those conditions prevail any longer. Is it or is it not necessary that an Australian government should be charged with the responsibility of seeing that the economy of Australia as a whole is managed as a whole so that inflation is kept under control, so that deflation is met by an infusion of credit, so that overseas investment keeps coming in?"[67]

To suggest that the states should lose control of the funds over which they had the constitutional right to dictate the manner of spending was heresy among Liberals. Four days later, after he had announced in Canberra his "no election" decision, Gorton spoke at a Liberal Party dinner in the Robertson electorate in NSW. He denied that he was a centralist but admitted that what he was espousing was "heresy if it is to be compared to the 1945 constitution of the Liberal Party." He went further than he had at Mornington. "When this party was formed two and a half decades ago, there were certain dogmas accepted concerning the relations between an Australian government and the state governments which made up the divisions of this nation," he said. "They may have been right. I think they were then. They may have been wrong. But surely you cannot ossify, surely something which has been accepted two and a half decades ago, it is reasonable to say, ought to be taken out and looked at and examined again to see what a nation twenty-five years later now needs if it is properly to be a nation . . . . I don't believe that in a nation of the size we are and in a nation with the destiny we have, it is possible for any other government than an Australian federal government to have the overall control of the economy, to say whether a deficit should be large or small, to let credit run free if that is necessary or to constrict credit if that is necessary, to control taxation, to see indeed that the economic management of all our nation is run in one way."[68] With the reference to running the economy "in one way" Gorton seemed to be suggesting that it did not matter whether the voters elected in the states either Liberal or ALP governments. Direction should be from the top, from the federal administration whatever its political hue.

At the Liberal Party's Executive Council meeting on October 22, 1968, Gorton was compelled to back down. He had sought and for a while believed he had the support necessary to reject the resolution calling for a special conference to study Commonwealth-State relations. But the support was not there. The numbers were against him. Even the Liberal Party Federal President, J. E. ("Jock") Pagan who normally backed him steadfastly was against him. "As Australians we must, I believe, proceed from the basic

181

belief that a continent as large as ours can be developed adequately only with a federal system," Pagan said.[69]

The promised special Liberal Conference to examine the party's "philosophical approach to Commonwealth-State relationships" did not eventuate in the months immediately ahead. All kinds of reasons were produced to delay a report on Commonwealth-State relations. But the Liberal state premiers were to continue resentful and to spend much of their time criticising Gorton and his government for both its parsimony with funds for the states and its general "centralist" approach. Liberals generally were to continue hostile. There were to be confrontations with Gorton over his attitude both in the Federal Parliament and in the comparative secrecy of the Liberal parliamentary party room.

Though one newspaper commentator was to remark with some justice that "Mr Gorton has made it palpably unclear exactly what he wants to do—he wants to change, to reform, but he is imprecise".[70] Gorton's ambiguity, the handing out of generous sums to the states while simultaneously expressing sentiments which could be interpreted as "centralist" undoubtedly helped to lose Gorton and his Parliamentary followers votes in the October, 1969, elections, particularly in strong Liberal seats where conservatism and the Liberal mystique were strongest.

NOTES

1 Reviewing the value of the Australian Public Opinion Polls as a guide to the state of public opinion after the "no election" fiasco, Don Aitkin, senior research fellow in Political Science at the Australian National University expressed the view that since Gorton became Prime Minister "it (the Liberal-CP Coalition) has looked almost invulnerable . . . ." *Australian Quarterly,* March 1969, Vol 41, No 1, p 76.

2 "Paul has been an absolute tower of strength over the last month"— Gorton, speaking to Murdoch group editors, significantly on December 11, 1968, after Hasluck had been made aware by individuals then close to Gorton, if not officially by Gorton himself, that he was to be the next Governor-General.

3 The late Sol Rosevear, Speaker of the House of Representatives from 1943 to 1949, once described a fellow ALP parliamentarian as "the perfect politician—all hide and no conscience."

4 "Until recent times, most major defence issues were dealt with by a cabinet committee. Often . . . senior civilian and military advisers would be in attendance. Many observers would wish the practice resumed"—Sir Henry Bland, former Secretary of the Defence Department, Roy Milne Memorial Lecture, Perth, September 29, 1970.

5 Mr Lee, a man with a fine cutting edge to his tongue, made this comment in slightly varying words to several Commonwealth Ministers. He is

reported to have made a comment upon the same lines to Hasluck, by then Governor-General, when he visited Hasluck and had a long tête-à-tête with him during the Canberra Five-power Conference, June 1969. I was unable to secure an interview with Sir Paul Hasluck to check the accuracy of this report.

6 Commonwealth Representatives Debates, Vol 58, p 1075, May 2, 1968.

7 For professional reasons, I cannot give my authority for this version of the Gorton-Fairhall-Bland discussions.

8 Commonwealth Representatives Debates, Vol 40, p 2070, October 22, 1963.

9 Conversations with Gorton intimates in 1967 and 1968.

10 Commonwealth Senate Debates, September 17, 1968, Vol 38, p 695.

11 Overtones of the Gorton-Fairhall-Bland discussions came through Fairhall's speech to the House of Representatives after the documents were tabled. Said Fairhall ". . . the Australian-American alliance . . . is characterised by the most extraordinary mutual confidence and trust. If we were to accede to the demand for publication of information confidential between our governments merely to assist the opposition's cheap political attack, one must expect an end to other than formal and hard business type arrangements as between Australia and the United States for the future." The reference to assisting "the opposition's cheap political attack" was clearly a mollifying sop, thrown in to appease Gorton.

12 Incidentally Bland's retirement was announced soon after Fairhall announced his retirement as Defence Minister.

13 Official transcript of Gorton interview with Murdoch Group editors, issued by Gorton's Canberra office, December 11, 1968.

14 Fairbairn stated these suspicions to a Liberal Parliamentary Party meeting, November 25, 1969.

15 If the named National Development Department officer ever gave any pressmen more than a polite greeting, I was not fortunate enough to be one of them. Personally, I would doubt if this particular officer would tell a pressman the time of day without first checking that he was empowered by regulations to do so.

16 "On this you gave me instructions not to discuss the matter with my department"—Fairbairn, addressing Gorton, Liberal Parliamentary Party meeting, November 25, 1969.

17 Boswell left the secretaryship of the National Development Department to become Australian Deputy High Commissioner in London in 1969.

18 After the Esso-BHP negotiations were completed, ministers grumbled—in private—that Gorton had talked with Cabinet on a quite different level from the real level on which he was conducting his negotiations.

19 Official transcript of Gorton interview with Murdoch Group editors, issued by Gorton's Canberra office, December 11, 1968.

20 Article by Ken Davidson, Australian, November 29, 1968.

21 Official summary of Prime Minister's activities, issued by Gorton's Canberra office for 1968.

22 Article by Alan Ramsey, Australian, November 25, 1968.

23 With no pretensions to any economic expertise, I belonged to this group. The Canberra Times, November 29, 1968, summed up the uncertainties of this group in a leader which stated "If the world price (of oil) does rise, then the Prime Minister will have made a bargain indeed and we will all cheer, but the consensus is that just the opposite will occur."

24 I can pinpoint the discussions to the extent that they took place before

November 13, 1968. I first heard about them on that date, though not in the detail set out above. Both Gorton and Fairbairn confirmed later that discussions had taken place.

25 Fairbairn who had lived during university vacation with families in France spoke French fluently.

26 The fact that McEwen had long had concern about the Gorton style was revealed publicly after the October, 1969, elections when McEwen demanded as a term for the re-establishment of the Liberal-CP coalition government that "significant policy discussions would always be the outcome of Cabinet discussions."—Official statement issued by McEwen's Canberra office, November 6, 1969.

27 McEwen in late 1970 announced that he would retire from the Parliament and politics in January, 1971 and adhered to that timetable.

28 "Out in the countryside in the past seven years, he (McEwen) has been down on foreign investment . . . but when we come into this house . . . (he) follows government policy"—ALP MHR Tom Uren, Commonwealth Weekly Representatives Debates, No 8, p 2208, May 14, 1970.

29 Commonwealth Weekly Representatives Debates, No 7, p 1589, May 5, 1970.

30 The opening day of the Parliament, March 12, 1968, had been occupied wholly with tributes to the vanished Harold Holt.

31 The fact that Whitlam asked his question at such an early stage in the new Parliament's life suggests that Whitlam had prior knowledge that there had been discussions on the corporation between Gorton and McEwen.

32 Commonwealth Representatives' Debates, Vol 58, p 29, March 13, 1968.

33 Commonwealth Representatives' Debates, Vol 56, p 1378, September 27, 1967.

34 "Wool constitutes approximately one-third of Australia's export trade to the UK and the Continent, by volume, and approximately one half by value"—Report of the Senate Select Committee on container cargoes, June 1968, p 19.

35 "At the same time (1968) tensions within the (shipping) conferences had raised the probability of a breakaway by some European operators. Such developments could not have done other than bring about a sharp reduction in freight charges"—Whitlam, Commonwealth Representatives' Weekly Debates, No 18, p 2597, October 21, 1970.

36 Despite this marking, copies of the report were sent to relevant Commonwealth Ministers and Departments.

37 The Bulletin, May 3, 1969.

38 Extracts from a letter setting out the Australian Meat Board's preference for the unit load system and sent to the Meat Importers' Council in Washington were published in an article by James V. Ramsden in The Australian Financial Review, February 27, 1970.

39 Report of the Senate Select Committee on Container Cargoes, June 1968, pp 12/13.

40 Ibid., p 5.

41 Canberra Times, November 25, 1968.

42 Gorton interview with Alan Ramsey, Australian, December 14, 1968.

43 Conversations with ministers at the time.

44 Notes of Gorton-McEwen-Sinclair press conference, November 26, 1968.

45 Commonwealth Representatives' Debates, Vol 62, pp 1287/1289, April 22, 1969.

46 Ibid., p 1366, April 23, 1969, Describing the government's explanation

for operating its own instead of chartered ships as "confused and inept" Peter Long in an article in the *Canberra Times* commented that thirty million dollars expenditure was "an expensive way to obtain information."

47 "The Scandinavians . . . once they bring their vehicle deck or 'roll on—roll off' ships into business . . . will compete the pants off the container ships being run by the British and the continental lines and the Australian National Line . . . the question being asked is whether the Australian government will use pressure on the Scandinavians to stick to the conference for fear of them taking cargo away from the ANL's container ship. That would be the ultimate 'irony' "—*Bulletin*, November 7, 1970.

48 *Sydney Morning Herald*, November 7, 1968.

49 *Daily Telegraph*, Sydney, July 30, 1970.

50 *Australian*, October 20, 1970.

51 *Australian*, October 20, 1970.

52 *Bulletin*, November 7, 1970.

53 Tabled in Parliament, October 20, 1970.

54 "The Australian Enterprise," a roll-on roll-off vessel of 14,082 tons d.w. inaugurated the Eastern Searoad Service between Australia and Japan in August, 1969.

55 The Australian National Line was also outvoted on the Australia-UK Europe Conference.

56 Annual Report of the Australian National Line, Australian Coastal Shipping Commission, 1970.

57 This analysis was produced by John Bennetts in an article in the *Canberra Times*, 1970.

58 Commonwealth Parliamentary Debates, March 26, 1953, Vol 221, p 1563.

59 "The Foundations of Australian Liberalism," a lecture delivered by Sir Robert Menzies, Perth, May 12, 1970.

60 Commonwealth Representatives Handbook, 1968, Sixteenth edition, p 654.

61 Uniform income tax was introduced by the wartime Curtin ALP government.

62 Conference of Commonwealth and State Ministers, Canberra, June 27/28, 1968, pp 33, 34.

63 *Canberra Times*, December 13, 1968.

64 Article by Ian Fitchett, *Sydney Morning Herald*, October 14, 1968.

65 *Ibid*.

66 Though certainly all powerful it can hardly be claimed that the governments of Nazi Germany, Fascist Italy, or Communist Russia were more "efficient" in the wide sense than governments which have operated under the restraints of a federal system, a judiciary independent of the administration, or the democratic electoral system.

67 Official transcript issued by Gorton's Canberra office, October 14, 1968.

68 Official Transcript issued by Gorton's Canberra office, October 18, 1968.

69 *Sydney Morning Herald*, October 22, 1968.

70 Alan Ramsey, *Australian*, October 25, 1968.

CHAPTER **9**

IT is hard to get to the top in politics. But once at the top in a parliamentary democracy it is hard for any force other than that of the voters to dislodge a leader from his position of pre-eminence. The leader as Prime Minister has not only the power conferred upon him by his high office; he is the dispenser of patronage, of advancement, and of jobs. He is buttressed in his position by the hopes, ambitions, venalities, and self-interest of his followers. If he does not succeed, they do not succeed, and they risk the descent into the anonymity from which they have struggled. Only rarely does a palace or parliamentary revolt succeed against the leader of a democratic government. There were only two examples in Australia's federal history. One was when Stanley Melbourne Bruce replaced William Morris Hughes in 1923 as Prime Minister, the result of a brilliant coup engineered by Sir Earle ("Doc") Page, the giggling surgeon-grazier, with the clear mind and confusing tongue who led the Federal Country Party from 1921 to 1939. The other was the deposition of Mr (later Sir) Robert Menzies from the prime ministership in 1941, this time with Page working in informal partnership with Hughes, the man he had earlier deprived of the prime ministership, to secure Menzies' prime ministerial scalp.

Page's first experiment in the political assassination of a prime minister succeeded spectacularly. Bruce, the Page-created Prime Minister, lasted until voted out in the general elections of 1929, and during Bruce's six-year reign, Page was a dominant figure in the government, which was referred to, even in official publications, as the Bruce-Page administration. Page's second excursion into the highly specialised field of prime ministerial liquidation was a failure. Firstly Menzies was succeeded, not by Page or by the would be Lazarus of the resurrected Bruce by then ten years absent from the Parliament,[1] as was the plan,[2] but by Mr (later Sir) Arthur Fadden. Fadden, a genial, Queensland accountant and extrovert, whose flair for politics came more from the seat of his pants than from intellectual study, and who, decent, straightforward, and "a mate", had resigned from the Country Party after a brawl with Page over the way Page was undermining Menzies.[3]

Fadden's government lasted in the words of Chifley "forty days and forty nights", from August 29, 1941 to October 7, 1941, and was followed by eight years of ALP rule. Memories of how short-lived had been the Fadden regime after Menzies downfall was a factor in assisting Gorton to keep control of his followers. Even those who developed misgivings about Gorton subsequent to the 1968 leadership ballot had no desire to "down" Gorton if the price was to be loss of office as in 1941 and the installation of an ALP government in power for an indefinite period.

As a consequence, Gorton continued to shock with impunity the more conservative of his followers, accustomed after seventeen years of Menzies and two years of Holt to conventionality in the conduct of the prime ministership. On September 30, 1968, Gorton breezily, almost challengingly, told a Western Australian audience "You ain't seen nothing yet",[4] and then proceeded to demonstrate that he was not indulging in an idle boast. To another audience, more than 2,000 miles distant, in Maitland, NSW, where he had flown after his Perth appearance, he revealed a weakness that he was to manifest through to the 1969 elections. Though words are part of the professional equipment of a democratic politician, Gorton was too busy, or too indifferent, or too self-assured to prepare a speech carefully and with precision.[5] He got to his feet and just let the words flow. He told his audience that he did not know the population of Australia in 1949.[6] He told the same audience, almost certainly NSW to a man and well aware that Governor Phillip and his motley band of officials, marines and convicts had formed the first British settlement in Australia at Sydney Cove in 1788 that the "first settlement was made at Port Phillip"[7] where, nearly 600 miles south of Sydney, Melbourne had its starting point in 1835.

Then on October 17, at a delicate stage in the Paris negotiations over the bombing by the United States of North Vietnam, Gorton attended the John McCallum-Googie Withers' play at a Canberra theatre. After the performance Gorton went backstage to meet the performers. The Parliament had been sitting. It adjourned at 11.19 pm. Some time after midnight, Gorton reappeared at Parliament House. Most of the parliamentarians and pressmen had gone home.[8] Gorton wanted to call a press conference. There was reason to believe that he had been smarting for some time because of suggestions that Australia, despite supporting the US with Australian troops in Vietnam, was not consulted in any meaningful way on, or even informed of, any significant adjustment of US policy in Vietnam. Gorton wanted to make public the fact that on the cessation of bombing, a major policy change, he was consulted.

187

Only two pressmen could be found, Allan Barnes, of the *Age,* and Ken Braddick, of Australian United Press. They provided Gorton with his audience at what later became derisively known as "the midnight press conference."

There had been rumours that a Vietnam bombing halt was about to take place. But with the aim of securing a successful outcome to the Paris negotiations secrecy was being maintained. No participant in the negotiations had made an official statement. Gorton was the first person who was in a position to know what was going on who confirmed that a bombing halt was likely. He told Barnes and Braddick that there was only one obstacle in the way of the bombing halt. Later Gorton was to say ". . . Braddick's (story) was a little bit the more interpretative, I think, than Allan Barnes' and this led to this allegation of official confirmation of something."[9] But Gorton's "midnight press conference" was undoubtedly resented by those who were handling the negotiations and who considered the negotiations to be at a stage as yet too delicate for public comment. Whitlam, aware of this reaction, later commented with some legitimacy ". . . his (Gorton's) personal vanity took a higher priority than the world's hope for peace in Vietnam . . . his actions and indiscretions might well have sabotaged those negotiations and dealings."[10]

While there was uneasiness among Liberal and CP parliamentarians about such things as this, it was only uneasiness, and uneasiness in politics is meaningless unless it crystallises. The thing which could have produced the crystallisation was defence, and the formal abandonment by Gorton of the "forward defence" policy enunciated by Menzies and Holt and supported by both Liberal and CP parliamentarians who believed that despite Britain's announced decision to withdraw from Malaysia/Singapore by 1971 Australia should continue to keep forces in that area of the world while Malaysia and Singapore insisted that such a presence would be a contribution to the stability of the region. This uneasiness never crystallised. Gorton did a complete volte face. Many reasons have since been advanced for this volte face, including the firmness of Hasluck, Fairhall, and McMahon. But Gorton's belief was that "the centre of government resides in the party rooms",[11] and he was probably more sensitive to the views of the mass of his parliamentary followers than to those of individual ministers. Two meetings of the Government Parties' Defence Committee took place towards the end of the November, 1968, parliamentary session, meetings which persuaded Gorton that if he did not accept the view that Singapore and Malaysia had to be assisted, even in such action involved the abandonment of his

"Fortress Australia" concept, he might lack the support and capacity to maintain the supremacy of his position in the government parties' room.

John Jess, the Liberal chairman of the Government Parties' Defence Committee, did not like nor approve of Gorton. Jess was forthright, independently minded, prone to moments of despair, but a fighter. He had contempt for some of the Byzantine manoeuvrings that had put Gorton into the prime ministership. He said what he thought, forcefully and without regard to its effect upon his political future. Jess' room was near to Senator (later Sir)[12] Magnus Cormack's room in the Commonwealth Parliamentary Offices in Melbourne. Though he had managed to stay fairly well in the background, Cormack, a former president of the Victorian Liberal Party, had used his influence as a Liberal Party patriarch to get Gorton elevated to the prime ministership. Unrealistic in some ways, Jess objected to those who set out to get what they wanted by organisation rather than open advocacy. He watched with distaste those who filed in and out of Cormack's room, some from other states, as votes for Gorton were lined up during the leadership struggle. Rather typically, when he was told that Dudley Erwin, in 1968 a vote chaser for Gorton, had warned Howson, then Minister for Air "If you don't vote for Gorton you'll have no chance of being in Gorton's cabinet",[13] Jess had phoned Hasluck, with whom his sole association across eight years had been to nod "Good day" and told Hasluck "You have my vote." Jess had strong views on defence and the necessity for joining in regional arrangements such as Malaysia and Singapore were anxious to enter into with Australia.[14]

There were over thirty government parliamentarians, or about a third of the coalition's parliamentary strength, at each of the two meetings of the Defence Committee with the Prime Minister. One of those present was Jefferson Bate, the Liberal member for Macarthur, a big, powerful man, with mutton chop whiskers, a clumsy gait, and a peasant's earthy shrewdness in political though not financial matters. Though theoretically he should have belonged to the landed aristocracy—the original Bate arrived free in the Colony in 1806 and the family acquired some of the choicest land on NSW's South Coast—Bate kept his feet firmly in the Australian soil, which he worshipped, closely in touch with the bread and butter problems of not only his own but others' electorates, and had a political intuition that was often sounder than the intellectual figurings of his parliamentary colleagues. He had a slow but thorough mind, was absurdly generous, a painstaking speaker more impressive in committee discussions than in the Parliament, and a respecter of no one.

There seems at first to have been a tendency on the part of some of the participants in the committee proceedings to curry favor with Gorton and his known inclination to avoid commitments in Asia, an inclination which may have been strengthened by his own experiences in World War II when he was evacuated, wounded, from Singapore a few days before thousands of his fellow Australians fell as p.o.ws. into Japanese hands. Initially the view was taken that the principles of war laid down that troops should not be maintained at the end of long lines of communication. These communications could be threatened and cut. Once they were cut the troops were vulnerable. Maintenance of Australian forces in Asia would be the maintenance of forces at the end of vulnerable lines of communication. It was better that Australia should not have a presence in Asia. Australia should concentrate upon defence of the Australian mainland. This would produce economy of effort, strong internal lines of communication, easier logistics and advantages to Australia.

At some stage, Bate seems to have exploded. He said "For Christ's sake, this is not a military organisation but a political committee. We are dealing with politics, not the principles of war. Most of us here have seen military service. But don't think we are military experts. We are not. We have to discuss this in terms of politics. For God's sake. On the way we are talking here now we might as well accept the ALP's policy and get out of Asia. How about the Singaporeans and the Malaysians? They want us there to help them achieve stability in the area. Stability is crucial. But it won't come because of a decision based exclusively on military factors. The decision has to be made on a political basis before the military factors are considered."

When Gorton said "I will not for a political decision risk one Australian life" Jess tried to pull Bate up. Jess told Bate, "Don't go on with that, Jeff—this is a military appreciation." But Bate refused to be silenced. He insisted "I'm a parliamentarian, not a military expert. We've got policies which we believe that it is in Australia's interests to maintain and I'm trying to get them across to the Prime Minister. As for the PM saying that he would not risk one Australian life for a political decision, that's the kind of thing that was said when Hitler marched into Czechoslovakia. And because a political decision was not made then Hitler killed twenty-six million." When Jess again tried to get Bate back on to the military rather than the political problem, Gorton intervened. "No, let him go on—this is interesting," Gorton said.

190

After Bate's outburst, the situation changed. One by one, Jess went around the table seeking the views of each of the government parliamentarians present. To a man, they opposed "Fortress Australia" concept and urged that Australia should participate with Malaysia and Singapore in pursuing stability in the area. And if pursuit of that objective demanded that Australia should respond to the wishes of Malaysia and Singapore and maintain forces in the Malaysia/Singapore region then those forces should be maintained even if it involved risk for Australia. It was a case of weighing risks and also responsibilities to neighbors who had the same ambition as Australia which was the preservation of peace and stability in the area, and on balance it was preferable to take a minor risk to avoid creating the far more major risk of upsetting the stability of the area.

By December 12, 1968, after months of indecision, Gorton rejected the "Fortress Australia" proposition. This concept of everyone getting back inside Australia and never getting out again was ridiculous, he said. It was the approach of the ALP's Dr Cairns.[15] He proposed to see President Nixon subject to the President's convenience between March and April.[16] Talks with President Nixon would be valuable. But the defence forces would not have to wait for these talks. Australia had consulted with the Malaysian and Singapore governments on its plans after 1971.[17] But Gorton still refused to say precisely what Australia intended to do, and despite Gorton's claim that Malaysia and Singapore had been informed of Australia's plans after 1971, both the Malaysian Prime Minister, Tunku Abdul Rahman, and the Malaysian Deputy Prime Minister, Tun Abdul Razak, insisted that they had no knowledge of Australia's future defence plans. "Australia has given Malaysia no clue to its defence intentions after Britain's withdrawal in 1971," said the Tunku.[18] "Malaysia would like to know Australia's and New Zealand's real position on their commitment (to Malaysia and Singapore) in case of trouble," said Tun Abdul Razak.[19]

But after his two meetings with the Government Parties' Defence Committee, ministers noted a change in Gorton's attitude in their discussions with him. There was not a great deal of discussion in Cabinet. When defence subjects were brought to Cabinet, they were presented rather to secure Cabinet's official endorsement than for examination. There was very little objection to this procedure. Those cabinet ministers who were not members of the Cabinet's Foreign Affairs and Defence committee tended to take it for granted that the decisions which they were being called upon to ratify had been probed in depth and thrashed out thoroughly by the very senior ministers who comprised the committee's members. Those who were on the committee had been consulted either unilaterally or in groups and because of these consultations failed at this stage to appreciate how the committee, as an instrument of defence policy, had almost imperceptibly receded into the background with meetings getting increasingly infrequent. Even those who had noticed how things were shaping were reluctant to complain.

Though superficially an untested political parvenu compared with the veteran and wily Menzies, Gorton was feared far more than Menzies had ever been. Menzies' ministers knew that Menzies would consult his own self-interest, and the government's and the Liberal Party's longterm political well-being before he indulged his personal prejudices and moved against any of them, and would not stir up needless strife. Provided they operated within this known context, their positions were secure and the only thing they had to fear was Menzies' personal displeasure. But Gorton consulted only his whims and even the most powerful among ministers were not safe, as Hasluck found when he had the Governor-Generalship offered to him with the suggestion that it was that or "out", and as McMahon was to find after the 1969 elections when, though McMahon wanted to retain the Treasury, was Deputy-Leader of the Liberal Party with probably the majority of the Liberal Party wanting him to retain the Treasury in the administration of which he had proved outstandingly successful, and with Gorton's political fortunes at a sufficiently low ebb to make a person of a different temperament cautious and tentative, Gorton forced McMahon to accept the External Affairs portfolio and a reduction in political power. If any of the ministers complained about Gorton taking into his hands almost complete control of defence issues, it was only occasionally as when Fairhall protested against Gorton's re-writing of his 1968 defence speech and later joined Bland in threatening resignation if Gorton insisted upon getting his way over the tabling of the F111 documents.

On February 25, 1969, Gorton reached a new peak of popularity within the Liberal Parliamentary Party. On that day Gorton announced "We are prepared to maintain . . . forces of all arms in that area (Malaysia and Singapore) after the British withdrawal —without setting any terminal date. The forces planned to be retained will consist of two squadrons of Mirages, totalling in all 42 aircraft, and stationed at Butterworth in Malaya, except for one section of eight aircraft which will be stationed at Tengah in Singapore. In addition, both ourselves and the New Zealanders will each maintain a naval ship in the area at all times for the

On opposite sides of the ALP political fence, F. E. ("Joe") Chamberlain,
ALP Federal "strong man", who detested ALP Federal Leader, Gough
Whitlam, and NSW ALP President, C. T. ("Charley") Oliver, who supported
Whitlam, chat seemingly amiably at an ALP Federal Executive meeting.

R. W. B. ("Brian") Harradine and the then ALP Tasmanian Secretary, D. Lowe, at the ALP Federal Executive meeting at which Harradine was not permitted to take his seat as a delegate. Harradine's ejection caused Whitlam to resign as ALP Federal Parliamentary Leader and was responsible for the 1968 ALP leadership struggle.

Peter Howson, a wartime pilot like Gorton, and a close friend of the former Prime Minister, Harold Holt, was stripped of his portfolio as Minister for Air when Gorton took over the Prime Ministership in 1968. Howson and Gorton disliked each other.

purposes of protection and not merely for the purposes of training. Further, we are planning to maintain, in conjunction with New Zealand, a two battalion organisation of ground troops of which the Australia component excluding personnel required for head-quarters, communications and the Jungle warfare training school in Malaya to which we shall contribute will be approximately 1200 men."[20] Commenting on the decision, Sir Alan Watt, Director of the Australian Institute of International Affairs and a former permanent head of the External Affairs Department, virtually re-echoed Bate in emphasising the political rather than the military aspect of the decision. Watt pointed out that Gorton in an earlier statement had said "it is much easier for a country which is to be assisted to believe that it will be assisted if forces from the country which may provide such help are there and visible." Watt used the illustration of how the "insistence by European countries that American forces should be stationed in Europe (even token forces in Berlin)" to underline how political rather than military decision had operated successfully to give Europe confidence. ". . . The Prime Minister's courage in publicly endorsing a policy which during the preceding year he had appeared to question if not to reject deserves recognition," Watt wrote approvingly.[21]

With almost pathetic gratitude, the Liberal parliamentarians turned from their worries about Gorton's clash both with the States and with the Liberal Party organisation over Commonwealth-State financial relations, and about Gorton's inadequate per-formances as a speaker and his unconventional methods of administration. When they have interests at stake, politicians grasp humanly at any straw. This was the "new" Gorton, fulfilling the promise they believed he had shown when they elected him Prime Minister. From here on things would be different. The Liberal-CP coalition had again asserted its essential difference from the ALP on defence and foreign affairs issues, issues which had been so valuable electorally to the coalition in the 1966 elections. Gorton's parliamentary followers breathed a sigh of relief. They could see a less troubled future opening out before them.

As they saw it, Gorton had rejected the ALP concept of defence embodied in a Victorian Fabian Society pamphlet written by Lance Barnard, the ALP's Deputy Leader and parliamentary spokesman on defence matters. The pamphlet published in January 1969 stated "The basic contention of the Labor Party is that Australia's strategic frontiers are its natural boundaries. It is strategically invalid to spread Australia's military strength thinly through South East Asia." Endorsing the attitude taken by some government parliamentarians in the early Government Parties'

Defence Committee discussions with Gorton, Barnard had added "Furthermore the great island mass of Indonesia effectively interposes between Australia and South East Asia; this fact of geography should be accepted and the decision taken not to pre-position substantial land forces in Malaysia and Singapore." Now the government parties were back to where they had been under Menzies and Holt; possessed of a defence and foreign affairs policy which differed from the ALP's in other respects than simply Vietnam and which gave promise of a maintenance of links with Singapore and Malaysia, links that could assist in promoting stability in the region. Gorton's popularity rating improved within the government ranks; so did his public standing, according to the Gallup polls. In October, 1968, the Gallup Poll's reading of the public pulse was 47 percent for the Liberal-CP coalition, 41 percent for the ALP, 7 percent for the DLP, 2 percent for independents, and 3 percent undecided. By April, 1969, the Gallup Poll reading was 49 percent for the Liberal-CP coalition, 38 percent for the ALP, 7 percent for the DLP, 2 percent for independents, and 4 percent undecided.[22]

With his position re-established in the government parties' room —"the centre of government", as Gorton had called it—Gorton was able to concentrate upon the task of eliminating forces which he resented or feared. His only inhibition was that he did not want too many political corpses cluttering up the landscape at the one time and too obviously. He had already made arrangements for Hasluck to be buried politically in the sumptuous obscurity of Yarralumla, the Governor-General's official residence set in exten-sive, guarded grounds on the southern outskirts of Canberra. Fairhall was being driven into a nervewracked state of nailbiting frustration. Fairbairn had already offered his neck, dutifully, for the executioner's axe, and could be disposed of at any time. Of his principal rivals, only McMahon, durable, nervy but patient, sensitive but not suicidal, was as yet untouchable.

Asked a long time later why his cabinet changes were not made as a "clean sweep" but done over a period, Gorton confirmed that the reason he had not acted was because he did not want a plethora of political cadavers having to be buried in a mass grave with a single ceremony. "I won't mention names . . . but they were senior ministers of considerable standing in the party and the country . . . more conservative than I was on many matters . . . and changing them all round straight away I think could have had more detrimental effects than good ones," he said.[23] But Gorton seized the opportunity presented by Hasluck's political interment to do a bit of minor surgery, this time on a lesser rival, Billy

Mackie Snedden, then 43, Minister for Immigration and Leader of the House of Representatives. Snedden looked like a matinee idol, aging but distinguished, with greying temples, convivial habits, an unfailing gift for unconvincing hyperbole, fashionable side levers, an addiction to "mod" talk, and an insatiable ambition. Snedden had stood for the leadership against Gorton, Hasluck and Bury, but had been "done" as crisply as a well fried chicken. He drew some status from being Leader of the House. Gorton decided to relieve him of the position and the status. Gorton could justify the move. Barnard, ALP deputy leader, with whom Snedden had to negotiate to secure reasonable cooperation from the Opposition so that the House of Representatives could function with passable smoothness, constantly complained that Snedden was not so much interested in a deal as in an advantage. Those government parliamentarians who believed that their political futures were bound up with Gorton's well-being viewed Snedden as having ideas above both his political station and his native ability.

But before Gorton deposed Snedden, Gorton, who had been absent from Australia attending the Conference of Commonwealth Prime Ministers in London from January 5, 1969 to January 28, 1969, had discussions with Gordon Freeth, then Air Minister, and with Dudley Erwin, the government whip. Hasluck's elevation to the Governor-Generalship was to be announced on February 10. Gorton told Freeth that he was to be promoted to the Cabinet replacing Hasluck as Minister for External Affairs; Erwin that he was to succeed Freeth as Minister for Air.

Freeth was later to be accused of having secured his promotion because he was a "Gorton crony." But he probably was given his promotion because far from being a "Gorton crony" he was his own man, with a mind of his own, considerable stubbornness, and an activist, not so much in his own cause as in the cause of those he admired. During the leadership struggle, he had campaigned openly, tirelessly and unstintingly for Hasluck, his fellow West Australian for whose integrity and ability he had a profound respect. A big placid man Freeth was not easily overawed or intimidated. In his day he had fought with Country Party Leader, John McEwen, a most formidable antagonist for any challenger. Freeth was not friendly with McMahon. When McEwen had turned "thumbs down" on McMahon during the leadership struggle by announcing that the Country Party would not serve under McMahon as Prime Minister, Freeth had been among those who applauded McEwen's propriety in making public this antiMcMahon decision. Said Freeth "In my view, Mr McEwen acted with complete correctness . . . it would have been intolerable that such a decision . . . should be concealed from the Liberals when they were about to elect a new leader."[24] But as well as being Air Minister, Freeth since Gorton's entry upon the prime ministership had acted as Minister assisting the Treasurer, who was McMahon. It was not beyond the bounds of possibility that Freeth, even if he did not like McMahon as a person, might as a result of this enforced association with McMahon end up respecting McMahon's professional ability, and, once Hasluck had departed from the political scene, transfer to McMahon the active loyalty he had previously reserved for Hasluck.[25] Freeth was being flattered by being included periodically in the informal consultations of the "cocktail cabinet." But he was not a man notable for his vulnerability to flattery. He had a sense of humour and a mild cynicism that protected him against this form of subversion. Despite his seeming placidity, he had energy and fearlessness. Wisdom dictated that he should be removed from the zone of exposure to McMahon's daily influence.

The appointment was quite extraordinary in more ways than one. External Affairs was recognised as a particularly sensitive portfolio, particularly at that time with the position changing rapidly in Vietnam, under the influence of the new US President, Mr Nixon, and Malaysia and Singapore planning anxiously for discussions in which Australia was to participate on the situation created by the British military withdrawal from Southeast Asia by the end of 1971.

No politician can be an expert on everything. The range of subjects is too vast. Even the most brilliantly endowed with brains and application cannot be a specialist in every field, a lesson which Gorton had not yet learned but which was to be brought home to him painfully before he faced the electors in 1969. ALP Prime Minister John Curtin had intervened in economic matters only broadly and had left the detail to the specialist, Treasurer Chifley. When Chifley succeeded Curtin as ALP Prime Minister, he had dealt with External Affairs only broadly, and had left the details also to the specialist, External Affairs Minister Dr Herbert Vere Evatt. Menzies, as Prime Minister, looked for informed advice from the specialists before making up his mind, and reserved as his exclusive preserve only the political decisions, and even there consulted before acting. Menzies' successor, Holt, similarly recognised there were areas in which the most he could acquire was a broad knowledge, and sought and welcomed advice in the fields in which he felt unsure. Whatever his qualities in other directions— and Freeth had been a reasonably good Minister for Transport and for Air and assistant to the Treasurer—he did not pretend to

196

be an expert in international affairs. As opposition leader Gough Whitlam was to point out after the official announcement of Freeth's appointment to the External Affairs post Freeth had never been identified with an interest in international affairs. "I have been looking up when Mr Freeth last spoke on External Affairs," Whitlam said. "I had to go back quite some time." Claiming that the only external affairs debate in which Freeth had taken part was eighteen months previous and on a minor subject that was more political than international, Whitlam added "Looking back, I can't think there was ever a minister with so little interest in the subject or (so little) seniority in the ministry to have this portfolio."[26]

But extraordinary as was the appointment to such a sensitive portfolio of a man who though in parliament since 1949 had shown only a marginal interest in international affairs the conversation between Gorton and Freeth when Gorton told Freeth he was appointing him External Affairs Minister was even more extraordinary.[27] Freeth, rather diffidently, pointed out that international affairs was hardly his forte. He knew the government's broad policy, supported it wholeheartedly, and was capable of defending it from political platforms. But he had not studied the detail of international affairs. He had concentrated upon economic service and domestic matters, and was quite confident of his ability to handle himself adequately in these fields. But international affairs were for him a new area of activity.

Gorton was unperturbed. He was sure Freeth could make a good fist of the External Affairs job. Anyway, he was giving him the portfolio only until the general elections later in the year. After that he would appoint somebody else. He thought he would put in either Malcolm Fraser[28] or Ian Sinclair.[29] Both appealed to him as potential External Affairs Ministers. But he did not want to put either one of them in at this stage. He had his reasons for not wanting to put them in as yet.[30]

The novelty of this approach seems to have diverted Freeth, temporarily. Freeth said that to go into a portfolio for only a few months and with the knowledge in the back of his mind that he was to be shifted within a very short time was disconcerting. It took away the incentive to get down to deep and intense study of the portfolio. Then Freeth came back to his original theme. He thought his value to the government was on the economic or service side. These were the things he had studied and knew most about.

Gorton assured him that he would get him back on the economic side at the first opportunity. He recognised that Freeth's talents were better suited to the economic side. Opportunity to come back to the economic side would present itself after the general elections. There would be movement. Unspoken but unmistakable was the suggestion that McMahon would not be in the Treasury after the elections[31] and that Freeth would be considered for that key post. It was an attractive bait to be dangled under the nose of any redblooded, ambitious politician and Freeth was those things. Freeth accepted the position of Minister for External Affairs.

Then came the turn of Dudley Erwin, the government Whip. Though Erwin had been with Malcolm Scott and Malcolm Fraser a foundation member of the "Gorton for Prime Minister" Club which was formed immediately after Holt's disappearance into the sea off Cheviot Beach, a club joined at an early stage by Magnus Cormack, Senator Reg Wright and William Wentworth, Erwin and Cormack had received no reward for their services. Scott had been made Minister for Customs, Fraser promoted to the Education Portfolio and, more importantly, raised overnight from tailend ranking in the ministry to cabinet eminence. Wentworth had been lifted from the back benches to become Minister for Social Services and Aboriginal Affairs. Wright had been made Minister for Works. Erwin had not and did not expect any award. Even now when it was clear that Hasluck's lift to the governor-generalship would mean promotions that would leave a position vacant at the bottom of the ministry list, Erwin suggested to Gorton that it be filled by Western Australian Liberal MHR, Fred Chaney, a Gorton supporter who had been Navy Minister from 1964 to 1966, but who had lost his position in a cabinet reshuffle after the 1966 general elections.[32]

Gorton told Erwin that he did not intend to appoint Chaney to the vacant ministerial post. Erwin was going to get the job. He was going to be Minister for Air. Furthermore, Gorton said, Erwin would be appointed Leader of the House of Representatives. Gorton was not satisfied with the job that Snedden was doing as House Leader. Snedden spent too much time on other activities. The government was not getting its legislative programme carried out smoothly and on time. No, Snedden had not asked to be relieved of the job. He, Gorton, was relieving Snedden of it. He wanted somebody he could trust. He also wanted Erwin to continue to be his eyes and ears.[33] He would not be giving Kevin Cairns, who was assistant government whip, the whip's job. Cairns was a McMahon supporter. Victorian Liberal MHR Max Fox was to become chief government whip. He did not know how Cairns would take this, but he did not particularly care. Cairns could stay on as assistant whip, if he wanted to. That was up to Cairns.

When on February 10, 1969, Gorton announced Hasluck's

appointment as Governor-General and his elevation, as Sir Paul Hasluck, to knighthood and the other consequential moves, the rumbles started. Gorton got off lightly over the elimination of Hasluck from the political scene. When such a high office as the governor-generalship is involved, the conventional hesitate to suggest that not only a knighthood but the Royal Order of the Boot Upstairs has been bestowed. Some did not allow the grandeur of the office to inhibit them. Santamaria, the able, controversial publicist who figured prominently in the 1954/55 ALP split and modernly had close associations with the DLP commented gloomily "Under Sir Robert Menzies and Mr Holt, the foreign policy Mr Hasluck was called on to conduct (as External Affairs Minister) was clear and purposeful, even if the purpose was limited . . . . Since the advent of Mr Gorton, clarity and purpose have vanished . . . . He (Hasluck) was temperamentally incapable of challenging Mr Gorton. So he decided to go. For him, the governor-generalship was an honorable way out of the impasse."[34] The *Sydney Morning Herald,* editorially probably Australia's most influential newspaper, said austerely "It is difficult to escape the feeling that the calibre of the government as it now stands is the weakest it has been for many years. With Sir Paul Hasluck's departure it lost the services of perhaps its ablest and most experienced member . . . . However skilfully the Prime Minister may have strengthened his own position, he has manifestly not strengthened his team . . . . Of course, if the Prime Minister's authority was all that mattered, one would have to admit that his changes have been master strokes of pragmatic political realism. There is now, to put it bluntly, no credible alternative to his leadership: no doubt Mr McMahon still has his ambitions, but with Mr Fairhall in the background and with Mr McEwen on the way out[35] all other conceivable rivals are either too young or inexperienced."[36]

Though, basically, it was the elimination of Hasluck from the political scene that was most resented, not too much could be made of that because, formally, Hasluck's political demise could be presented as a promotion upstairs. The complaints had to be made about Freeth and Erwin. Knowing that Freeth had been admitted on occasions to gatherings of the "cocktail cabinet", aware that he had never had pretensions to any expertness in the field of international affairs, and regarding his promotion to the External Affairs portfolio as a piece of pure cynicism, Liberal parliamentarians were disturbed. But out of loyalty to their party, they did their grumbling in private. Snedden's supporters and admirers did not like his replacement by Erwin as house leader. They considered

199

that Snedden was being demoted because he had the temerity to contest the leadership against Gorton. Les Irwin, pokerfaced, put on the agenda for a meeting of the government parties an item reading "Leadership of the House of Representatives." Irwin, a tubby ex-bank manager and like Gorton an ex-flier but from World War I when aeroplanes were delicate things of canvas and plywood thought, unlike Gorton, that Snedden had done a good job, and that some appreciative recognition of his services should be placed on record. Irwin was talked out of going on with his party room agenda item. He was seen by several ministers. He was told that the situation was "a bit explosive." If he went on with his agenda item he might "put a match to the fuse."[37] Irwin, who though direct and outspoken, was not a troublemaker, agreed to withdraw his agenda item.

An illustration of just how explosive was the situation was a conversation between Jess and the new government whip, Max Fox. Part of Gorton's troubles was quite a number of Liberals believed that he made his appointments to the ministry upon the basis of loyalty rather than ability. Scott, the former senate whip who with Wright and Cormack had played a major role in mustering to Gorton's side the Senate vote that, basically, was responsible for lifting Gorton to the prime ministership, had been rewarded for his services with the Customs portfolio. Scott was seldom out of trouble in that administration. Scott also represented several House of Representatives' ministers in the Senate. Fairbairn, an easy going man, still at that stage Minister for National Development, was driven to complain several times about clumsy, inaccurate, or misleading answers given by Scott on National Development matters.

What became known as "The Hoffmann Affair" brought Scott, and Gorton, into the firing line. The affair had highly comic elements, but matters of principle were also at stake, including the role of the Australian Security Intelligence Organisation, a security body operating in secrecy, set up originally by the Chifley ALP government, and revealed during debate on "The Hoffmann Affair" as extending its operations, with Gorton's blessings, from security to commercial spying.

Central figure was Gerard Charles Hoffmann who had been a senior Customs official. Some eight years earlier, Hoffmann had been approached by a foreign embassy. In the words of a letter from Hoffmann to Scott, a letter handed to Mr Bruce Alexander, Scott's secretary, on November 11, 1968, " . . . Mr Carmody (permanent head of the Customs Department) knows that I was approached by a foreign embassy to provide them with confidential customs information and that my immediate reporting of this incident led to my wife being used as an ASIO agent within that embassy and my employment as courier and contact with the ASIO."[38] The wife, Mrs Mary Hoffmann, who was working at the Japanese Embassy, then started her ASIO operations. Her brief was "to copy anything that seemed important". She proceeded, according to her own story,[39] to copy any material she could lay her hands on. She had no idea of the value of the material which she purloined. Most of it related to trade matters. When she had completed her three years work at the Japanese Embassy, she was invited by ASIO to continue her activities at the Indonesian Embassy and the United Arab Republic Embassy.[40] Mrs Hoffmann herself gave a richly comic touch to her female James Bond activities. During part of her employment at the Japanese Embassy she was pregnant. Asked how she got the pilfered documents out of the Embassy, she said "Well, I usually had them concealed on my person. Sometimes I had them in my handbag. Ah, mostly on my . . . on my self . . . er . . . as I . . . I was about six months pregnant and I had maternity frocks on and it was quite easy to conceal it under. This all sounds peculiar[41] but really . . . uh . . . it didn't seem so at the time; it seemed just natural."[42]

Mrs Hoffmann's unusual pre-natal duties were revealed almost by accident. Publisher Max Newton, McEwen's bête noir and increasingly Gorton's, was known throughout the Commonwealth Public Service as dedicatedly hostile to McEwen. Anyone in the Commonwealth Public Service hostile to either McEwen or McEwen's Trade Department—and Trade, which was a thrusting, bustling department with scant regard for hurt feelings, made many enemies in its own right—was aware that Newton would receive happily any material, official or unofficial, authorised or unauthorised, that could be used advantageously in Newton's crusade against McEwen. Newton was getting some very good "leaks" of unauthorised material both from Trade and about Trade's activities. *Incentive,* a Newton publication, had published on November 11, 1968 the first reference to Mrs Hoffmann's ASIO activities. Newton had also published some confidential material on tariffs. The Commonwealth Police understandably was trying to find out where the "leaks" were coming from. First, Treasury, whose views on tariffs were opposed to those of McEwen and Trade, was investigated, without result. The investigators moved on to Trade, and various officers there were interviewed. In the course of this investigation, the officers came across an irregularity which had no association with Newton, an irregularity that led them to Hoffmann in the Customs Department.

From there the sequence of events was detailed to the Senate by Scott on April 16, 1969. Said Scott "On September 27, 1968, my department recommended to the Public Service Board that Mr Hoffmann be dismissed as he had been found guilty of charges of improper conduct[43] under Section 55 of the Public Service Act. On September 30, Mr Hoffmann appealed against his punishment. The Appeal was heard on October 23 and 24, and the decision to dismiss Mr Hoffmann was confirmed. On October 30, an authority of dismissal, to be effective from the expiration of November 15, was issued by the Public Service Board. On October 30, Mr Hoffmann was notified of the decision by my Department. On November 11 Mr Hoffmann wrote to me, having first tried to obtain an interview through Mr Whitlam's office.[44] He had been advised to put in writing what he wished to say. I passed Mr Hoffmann's letter, without comment, to my department on November 12. On November 14, Mr Hoffmann saw the chief officer of my department and submitted his resignation. The resignation letter was sent that day to the Public Service Board. On November 15, informal advice was received from the Public Service Board that Mr Hoffmann's resignation had been accepted . . . . On November 20 formal advice of acceptance of the resignation was received from the Public Service Board . . . . On November 26, I gave a brief interview to Mr Hoffmann. That was the first time I had seen or spoken with him."[45]

Though Gorton insisted that allowing Hoffmann to resign in such circumstances and after the decision to dismiss him had been taken conformed with Public Service regulations and with Public Service Board practice,[46] the ALP, with Whitlam as its spokesman, claimed that there was "a certain plausibility" to the allegation that Sir Charles Spry, head of ASIO, intervened to get Hoffmann permission to resign after his dismissal had been formally gazetted. Whitlam also alleged that security had exceeded its charter[47] which Barnard, Whitlam's deputy, later stated as "to obtain, correlate, and evaluate intelligence relevant to security" and that commercial operations, such as those in which Mrs Hoffmann had publicly stated she had engaged, were "completely outside the Act [whence ASIO drew its authority] and the ASIO charter as it has always been defined in this house."[48] Gorton retorted "It is the essence of counter espionage to discover whether information is being supplied and the sources from which it comes, and no apology whatever need be made for taking action of that kind."[49] Gorton had already made publicly statements of this kind earlier. These statements had drawn from the *Australian* an acid editorial which asked "Just what is ASIO's role?" "Mr Gorton is way off course when he says that 'surely no Australian could object' to Mrs Hoffmann's 'counter-espionage in Australia's interests' and that the Labor Party is doing Australia a disservice by its objections," the editorial commented. "Industrial espionage is not its (ASIO's) role, and it is Mr Gorton who is doing Australia a disservice when it implies that it is so."[50] Scott added another contradiction to the affair. On February 26, 1969, Scott talked about the "gravity" of the offence for which Hoffmann was first dismissed and later allowed to resign.[51] But on March 5, 1969, Scott revealed that his November 26 interview at which Hoffmann presented him with a Bible was to enable Hoffmann to thank Scott and the officers of Scott's Customs Department for having "obtained for him a job in Sydney." Interjected ALP Senator Cavanagh "At nine thousand dollars a year."[52]

Scott had not been responsible for the pregnant, emotional Mrs Hoffmann being employed by ASIO as Australia's commercial lady spy within the Japanese Embassy.[53] Her recruitment had taken place long before he had been elevated to the ministry. But he botched badly the handling of Senate questions about the dismissal of her husband, Mr Hoffmann, and contributed to the impression that the government was staging a burlesque of a rather comical James Bond thriller. Scott was a friend of Gorton, a man who was given his promotion to the ministry because he had assisted Gorton win the prime ministership. Dudley Erwin was a friend of both Gorton and Scott, and had also assisted Gorton to win the prime ministership. Erwin shared in the back-wash of feeling against Scott. He had another problem. A number of Liberals who had voted for Gorton in the leadership struggle believed they had been given a promise that they would receive the next vacancy in the Ministry. They had not got the vacancy. Erwin had. These disappointed aspirants to ministerial office could not openly show their resentment of Gorton. To do so would cost them any hope of appointment to the next ministerial vacancy. They could, with impunity, show their resentment of Erwin. They proceeded to do so.

It was against this background that Jess had his conversation with the new whip, Max Fox. Jess was neither a disappointed ministerial aspirant, nor a supporter of Snedden whose friends believed that he had been deprived of his post as Leader of the House of Representatives in an arbitrary and humiliating manner Jess was simply a man who spoke his mind. Jess told Fox that he wanted to congratulate him, genuinely, upon his appointment as government whip. However, as Fox's duties included liaison with the Cabinet he could take Gorton a message. The message was that after Erwin's appointment Gorton could not rely upon him for uncritical support. He was sick of the "cronyism and double standards." Erwin might turn out all right, despite being a friend of Gorton. But Scott had not. He had gone to Scott about the case of a twenty-years-old Melbourne girl prosecuted in Brisbane for bringing in a transistor. There were only twenty dollars in duty involved. The girl's father admitted she was in the wrong and offered to pay the duty. Scott had "turned sanctimonious" and said the law must be observed.

Jess contrasted this treatment with that accorded Hoffmann, who had in Scott's words committed an offence of some gravity against Public Service regulations but had been found a job. Jess aired his contempt witheringly in the House of Representatives. "I direct a question to the minister representing the Minister for Customs and Excise," Jess said. "Having just returned from the Minister for Customs and Excise and having been advised by the minister that as the law must be observed and must take its course concerning a young female teacher who made one mistake and brought in one transistor radio, the duty on which would be twenty dollars, and then having read in a newspaper that the department had recommended one gentleman who also has made only one mistake for a job in private enterprise at a higher salary, I ask: Can the minister tell me what justification there is for what appears to be a double standard?" As the Interior Minister Peter Nixon, who represented Scott in the House of Representatives, went to answer Gorton whispered something to him, urgently. "Have you got your riding order?" asked ALP MHR Tom Uren, interestedly, across the chamber of the House of Representatives. Nixon said that he would refer the question to Scott. "From what the Prime Minister has just said, I am not at all sure that there is a deal of accuracy in part of (Jess') question," Nixon added.[54] As there was little doubt that Jess had seen Scott, that Scott had told him that the law must take its course, that Scott on his own admission had helped to get Hoffmann a job in private enterprise, and that a young lady was in trouble over bringing into Australia a transistor radio on which the duty would be twenty or so dollars, it is difficult to see how Jess' question could be described as inaccurate.

Jess' attitude was something for which he had already prepared his party electorate council at an unpublicised Melbourne meeting with that body. Jess had told the committee that he was gravely concerned about the decline in public morality and morale within the Liberal Parliamentary Party. He did not like where it was going on defence, its equivocation and evasion. He did not like the double standards that were being observed. But the ALP did not represent an alternative government in his view. He was

204

convinced ALP policies, particularly on foreign affairs and defence, were bad for Australia. It was this knowledge that the ALP did not represent an alternative government that would be good for Australia that was inhibiting him. Nevertheless, he proposed to continue speaking his mind. He might even get to the point where there would be an independent Liberal—himself—in the House of Representatives. But he would await events. He could get out. But he did not think this provided a solution. Jess's Liberal council endorsed his attitude.

From mid-1968 through to March 18, 1969, the movement at the top of the government parties was constant, dramatic, turbulent, and of a type that could be expected to have had some impact upon the mass electorate, even though economic conditions in Australia continued to be buoyant, employment was full, wages rising, the external currency situation satisfactory, and difficulties restricted to pockets, relatively small in the general context but growing as with world markets growing more competitive for some primary products and returning less for others, notably wool, the rural section of the economy showed a downward turn. Offsetting the difficulties within the government parties was the weakness of the ALP, still unsure and licking its wounds after the Whitlam-Cairns contest for the leadership in April, 1968, and wracked by fresh feuds and hatreds.

Whitlam, anxious to get ALP support for state aid for denominational schools and aware that without support for such a policy the ALP would have only a remote chance of winning back any substantial section of the Irish-Australian element that had turned against the ALP in 1954/55, was feuding bitterly with the Victorian ALP, which was dogmatically and doggedly antiState aid and antiWhitlam. Calwell, the former leader, had clashed head-on with Cairns over who was to take the safe ALP seat of Melbourne after Cairns' own seat of Yarra had disappeared in an electoral distribution, and had defeated Cairns, who though given ALP preselection for the less secure seat of Lalor, appeared to have temporarily lost interest in the ALP's quest for federal power and was concentrating upon the promotion of demonstrations against Australian involvement in the Vietnam conflict, demonstrations which despite the feeling in Australia against the Vietnam war, particularly among the younger, university students who were liable to be conscripted to serve in Vietnam, revived suspicion among the more conformist of Australian voters about ALP radicalism and its possibly Marxist origins. South Australian MHR, Clyde Cameron, a significant figure in the ALP's Parliamentary Party and political machine, was pursuing publicly a vendetta against the rightwing controllers of the Australian Workers' Union in which he had held office as SA State Secretary before he entered the Parliament in 1949 and which was Australia's largest and wealthiest union and a midwife at the birth of the ALP in the 1890s. Senator Pat Kennelly, an oldtime ALP "Kingmaker" was describing the Victorian ALP as "sick." Harradine, the Tasmanian antiCommunist, was being pursued relentlessly and denied the seat on the ALP Federal Executive to which he had been elected by the Tasmanian ALP Conference. If the government was in a mess, ALP affairs were messier.

With the attention of the voters still seemingly largely concentrated on the more obviously turbulent, lethal, and well publicised[55] struggles within the ALP, there was no indication that the Liberal-CP coalition, or Gorton, was losing significant public support. The findings of the April 1969 Gallup Poll were that the Liberal-CP coalition with 49 percent support held a comfortable 11 percent advantage over the ALP whose support was 38 percent.[56] Without attributing infallibility to the poll which in Australia at least has a record of reasonable accuracy, this assessment conformed with other indicators, including the judgment of party analysts. The same Gallup Poll also showed the DLP holding 7 percent of the vote, a credible figure as the DLP had consistently rolled up a vote of this proportion, or higher, at general elections since the 1954/55 ALP split. If these figures were anywhere near right, the government could win its way comfortably back to government at the next general elections. Only danger was if the DLP switched its preferences from the Liberal-CP coalition to the ALP, and this was unlikely. Despite the DLP's misgivings about Gorton and his government, the DLP, like Jess, preferred the government's defence and foreign affairs policies, imperfect as the DLP and Jess viewed them to be, to the ALP's.

But on March 19, 1969, Bert James, MHR for Hunter in NSW, an ex-NSW detective-sergeant, 260 lbs in bulk, with a voice that boomed like a cell door drummed on with outsize handcuffs, and a belligerent supporter of peace movements, rose at 10.45 pm in his place in the extreme back bench on the opposition side of the House of Representatives and made a seven-minute speech. The speech was about an article purporting to give details about Gorton's personal conduct published in a Sydney newsletter called "Things I hear" and written by Mr Frank Browne. Though the then Clerk of the House of Representatives Mr Frank Green advised that no breach of Parliamentary privilege was involved, Browne with a Bankstown building contractor, Raymond Fitzpatrick had been committed by the House of Representatives to jail for three months in 1955 following a Privileges Committee Inquiry into articles assailing the then MHR for Reid Mr Charles Morgan written by Browne for the Fitzpatrick-owned *Bankstown Observer*.[57] Rather unctuously, James finished his speech by saying "It disturbs me somewhat to think that such things could be written about a person who holds the highest position in this nation. I have no doubt that the Prime Minister could clear the air in regard to this shadow that has been cast on his integrity by this magazine. I have no doubt that the matter will soon be clarified to the satisfaction of members of the house and those who had the unpleasant experience of reading this damaging article."[58] James' speech was not nearly as important as the things it started. Speaking immediately after James, Liberal Jim Killen[59] pointed out that James had "put forward as his chief witness, the darling of the Crown case, Frank Browne."[60]

As the House of Representatives had jailed Browne in 1955, it was unlikely to accept him as a reliable witness in 1969. But the James speech brought other dramatis personae upon the scene, and had effects which continued for a long time. From March 19 onwards, the Gallup Poll figures for the ALP were constantly improving and support for the government steadily eroding.[61] The broad accuracy of the figures was to be confirmed on October 25, 1969, when the nation went to the polls.

NOTES

[1] Bruce became the first Australian Prime Minister defeated at general elections when in 1929 he lost his seat of Flinders in Victoria to Mr Edward Holloway, who was to become a minister in wartime ALP administrations.

[2] For an account of these extraordinary machinations see *Truant Surgeon* by Sir Earle Page, Angus and Robertson, Sydney, 1963, pp 270/278.

[3] *Ibid.*, pp 280/281.

[4] Address to the 68th annual general meeting of the Western Australian Chamber of Manufactures, official transcript, issued by Gorton's Canberra office, September 30, 1968.

[5] ". . . what struck me most in the first month or two (as Prime Minister) was the enormous importance everybody seemed to place on every word one spoke"—Gorton TV interview with Peter Martin, Channel Seven Network, October 11, 1970.

[6] The population in 1949 was 7,796,479. It took me precisely half a minute to look it up in the Commonwealth Year Book, No. 43, 1957.

[7] Address to the Paterson Federal Electorate Conference, Maitland, September 30, 1968.

[8] I unfortunately was one of the early home goers so this account is second hand.

9 Gorton, TV interview with Peter Martin, Channel Seven Network, October 11, 1970.

10 Commonwealth Representatives' Debates, Vol 61, p 2428, November 5, 1968.

11 *Age,* Melbourne, August 23, 1953.

12 Cormack was knighted in the 1970 New Year's Honours List. The citation was "for long political and public service."

13 Howson who voted for Hasluck was dropped from the new Gorton Ministry, announced on February 28, 1968.

14 ". . . The Australian presence in Malaysia and Singapore . . . is not to threaten anyone . . . (it) is useful as a general stabilising force . . . . It would be good for Australia and good for us too."—Dr Goh Keng Swee, Singapore Minister for Finance, press conference, Canberra, January 3, 1969.

15 Cairns had advocated a "Fortress Australia" defence policy. The DLP had earlier accused Gorton of adopting "the Cairns line."

16 The US was urging Australia to fill at least part of the vacuum that would exist in the Malaysia/Singapore region after Britain's 1971 military withdrawal.

17 *Daily Telegraph,* Sydney, December 12, 1968.

18 *Sydney Morning Herald,* February 7, 1969.

19 *Canberra Times,* February 16, 1969.

20 Commonwealth Representatives Debates, February 25, 1969, Vol 62, p 35.

21 "Australian Defence Policy in South East Asia after 1971" by Alan Watt, Pacific Community No 1, June 1969.

22 *Herald,* Melbourne, May 22, 1969.

23 Gorton, TV interview with Peter Martin, Channel Seven Network, October 11, 1970.

24 *Sydney Morning Herald,* December 28, 1967.

25 Subsequent events suggest that McMahon and Freeth did establish some rapport. After Freeth was defeated for his WA seat of Forrest at the 1969 general elections and as a consequence ceased to matter politically, McMahon was instrumental in securing for him appointment as Australian Ambassador to Japan.

26 Whitlam, Press Conference, Canberra, February 13, 1969. Freeth himself made no claim to specialised knowledge of foreign affairs. On August 17, 1967, Freeth said, "Tonight, for the first time in seventeen years in this Parliament, I am taking part in a debate on a paper on foreign affairs." Commonwealth Representatives Debates, Vol 56, p 257.

27 When I asked Freeth, by then out of the House of Representatives and Australian Ambassador-designate to Japan, to confirm the broad accuracy of what follows he said "No comment." But significantly he refused to say it was inaccurate.

28 Fraser, a Liberal, was then Minister for Education and Science.

29 Sinclair, a CP MHR, was then Minister for Shipping and Transport.

30 Even then, Gorton may have had in mind that he might not be able to dispose finally of McMahon and was keeping External Affairs as a portfolio to which he might be able to exile McMahon at some future date without unendurable fuss.

31 Despite his protests, McMahon was ejected from the Treasury and became

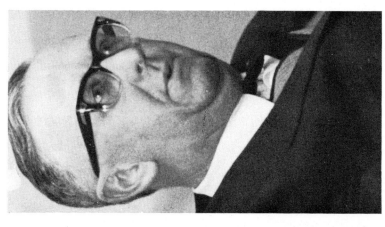

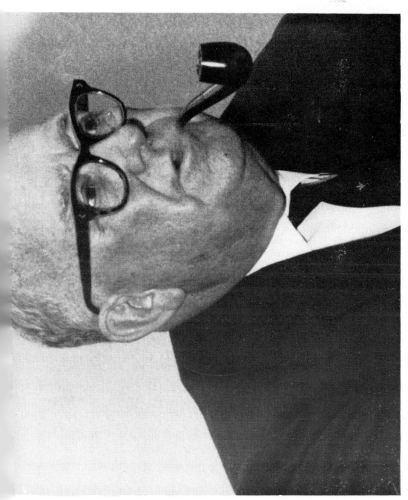

The Democratic Labor Party's Parliamentary leader, Senator Vince Gair (left), ex-Premier of Queensland. Right, Frank McManus one-time schoolteacher and ALP official in Victoria, now deputy leader of the DLP.

ALP Federal Parliamentary Leader Gough Whitlam at a press conference. Watching worriedly from the background is Whitlam's deputy Lance Barnard.

the Minister for External Affairs (later Foreign Affairs) in the Cabinet reconstruction that followed the 1969 General Elections.

32 Chaney who lost his seat in the House of Representatives at the 1969 general elections was shortly afterwards appointed Northern Territory Administrator.

33 As whip, Erwin had responsibility for keeping the Prime Minister informed of moves within and any discontent that arose within the Government parties.

34 B. A. Santamaria, TV commentary "Point of View," February 16, 1969.

35 At this stage, McEwen had announced that he intended to retire, and would not lead the CP to the 1972 elections.

36 *Sydney Morning Herald,* February 14, 1969.

37 Personal conversations with ministers and Irwin at the period.

38 Quoted by ALP Senator Cavanagh—Commonwealth Senate Debates, Vol 40, p 842, April 16, 1969.

39 Mrs Hoffmann's account of her activities was published in the *Daily Telegraph,* Sydney, during March 1969.

40 This is Whitlam's précis of Mrs Hoffmann's *Daily Telegraph* articles, given to the House of Representatives on March 18, 1969.—Commonwealth Representatives Debates, Vol 62, p 571.

41 "If I were associated with an embassy I would never again employ a woman wearing a maternity frock—ALP MHR Fred Daly, Commonwealth Representatives Debates, Vol 62, p 579, March 18, 1969.

42 Mrs Hoffmann, TV interview with John Moses, Channel Nine Network, March 10, 1969.

43 In Hoffmann's letter to Scott, Hoffmann stated ". . . during evidence (at the appeal hearing) he (the Crown Prosecutor) also stated that the Crown knew there was no gain for me of any kind in my action and no criminal proceedings were ever contemplated against me . . . (it was) one error in seventeen years"—quoted by ALP Senator Cavanagh, Commonwealth Senate Debates, Vol 40, p 842, April 16, 1969.

44 This seems to have been the ALP's first formal contact with the Hoffmanns. Mrs Hoffmann was seen by Mr Peter Cullen, then Whitlam's secretary. Cullen was shown by Mrs Hoffmann a letter intended for the Prime Minister. The letter referred to Mrs Hoffmann's association with ASIO. Cullen later stated publicly he took no copy of the letter and government spokesmen accepted this denial—Commonwealth Senate Debates, Vol 40, p 845, April 16, 1969.

45 Commonwealth Senate Debates, Vol 40, pp 835/836, April 16, 1969.

46 Commonwealth Representatives' Debates, Vol 62, p 573, March 18, 1969.

47 *Ibid.,* p 571.

48 *Ibid.,* p 576.

49 *Ibid.,* p 574.

50 *Australian,* March 10, 1969.

51 Commonwealth Senate Debates, Vol 40, p 114, February 26, 1969.

52 *Ibid.,* p 284.

53 The Japanese, a people who prize efficiency, understandably and good-humoredly treated the whole thing as a very big joke.

54 Commonwealth Representatives' Debates, Vol 62, pp 457/458, March 6, 1969.

55 Despite their attacks upon "the capitalist press," ALP members are more prone than the Liberals to use the press mercilessly, intelligently, and

incessantly as a weapon in their endless, often picturesque and always energetic internecine disputes.

56 *Herald,* Melbourne, May 22, 1969.
57 See *Servant of the House* by Frank Green, Heinemann, 1969, pp 155/162. and *Parliamentary Privilege in Australia* by Enid Campbell, Melbourne University Press, pp 155/161.
58 Commonwealth Representatives' Debates, Vol 62, p 695, March 19, 1969.
59 Then a backbencher, Killen was Minister for the Navy after 1969, and again a backbencher in 1971.
60 Commonwealth Representatives' Debates, Vol 62, p 695, March 19, 1969.
61 *Herald,* Melbourne, October 11, 1969.

CHAPTER 10

PRESIDENT JOHNSON announced the Vietnam bombing halt on November 1, 1968. The Federal Parliamentary Press Gallery held its annual dinner on the same night. The Gallery's guest of honour was the Prime Minister, John Gorton. Twice while the dinner was under way, the United States Ambassador to Australia, Mr William Crook, phoned the hotel at which the dinner was being held. There had been tension during the day. Crook felt he had perhaps been a little late in giving Gorton the information Gorton had wanted about the bombing halt. Through Mr Tony Eggleton, Gorton's press secretary, Crook had invited Gorton to call in after the Gallery dinner and whatever the hour at the US Embassy for a drink, a drink that would show Gorton was not upset about what had happened.[1]

There were about forty pressmen at the dinner. Miss Geraldine Willesee, 19, employed by Australian United Press and a daughter of prominent ALP Senator, Don Willesee, from Western Australia, was the lone girl at the dinner. She was the only female journalist employed at the time in the Press Gallery. At some time late in the evening and after the dinner was over, Gorton said he was ready to give Miss Willesee a lift home.[2]

At a time that was to become a subject of controversy, Gorton left with Miss Willesee. Gorton's car driver was Mr Ray Coppin. Gorton was alongside Coppin in the front seat. Eggleton and Miss Willesee were in the back seat. They reached the US Embassy at probably a quarter to twelve or midnight, and left half an hour after that, according to Gorton's original figuring which he was to change later.[3]

They reached the Embassy about 1 am and left about 3 am according to Miss Willesee, in a statutory declaration issued at her home-town, Perth, on March 21, 1969. After leaving the Embassy Miss Willesee was driven to her flat and dropped. Gorton was driven to the Lodge, official residence of the Prime Minister in Canberra.

It was from these events—and times—and from the arguments that were to develop from the events and about the times that emerged the controversy which was to rage around Gorton

211

from then until election day, October 25, 1969. James' speech was to recede into the background, but he had acted as a catalyst. Other forces were released, and in an indirect way I may have been responsible for the whole thing.

Because I was an older member of the Gallery and probably because I had known her father, Senator Willesee, for many years, Miss Willesee used on occasions to consult me on professional matters. Some days before the Press Gallery dinner was held, Miss Willesee came to my office in the Press Gallery to see me. She was wondering whether she should go to the dinner. Her brother, Michael Willesee, also a member of the Gallery and a prominent ABC TV personality, would not be there. She might be embarrassed as the only female present. What was my advice? Should she go to the dinner?

In the light of what subsequently happened and the fact that Miss Willesee lost her job as an outcome, my advice was extremely poor and my sense of anticipation non-existent. I told her that she and every young journalist should go. At these functions the guest speaker usually turned anecdotal. There was no news in what they said. But they gave most revealing glimpses of how politics really operated and how great questions were resolved, often not for the weighty and solemn reasons that journalists and historians gave, but because some powerful individual had had a grievance against another powerful individual, a grievance sometimes obscure or trivial in its origins, and was determined that, come hell or high water, his opponent was not going to get what he wanted, irrespective of the merits of his case. The speakers usually gave fascinating revelatory glimpses of the life that went on in the backstairs of politics. I recalled speeches made at such functions by former prime ministers like Lyons, Curtin, Chifley, Menzies, and that most colorful of figures, William Morris Hughes, diminutive in stature but intimidatory, with a diabolical tongue, a flamboyant vocabulary, and an irrepressible cynicism. The fact that Miss Willesee was female did not matter. We had had lone females present at such functions in the past. Their presence had not created any problem. She had the same rights as any member of the Press Gallery, and should exercise them. Whatever inequalities existed elsewhere, equality of the sexes existed in our profession. As for her being embarrassed, I would be there, and would keep an eye on her. If there were an incident that threatened her with embarrassment, I undertook to stamp heavily on the toes of whoever was responsible. I would not be making a night of it. I would be leaving early, probably immediately after the guest of

212

honour had departed. She could leave with me. I would drive her home.

My assurances and undertakings turned out to be worthless. On the day of the dinner, I was ill. I considered absenting myself from the dinner, but I had not seen Gorton at one of these functions before. There was hostility, politely veiled, but unmistakable, between him and some members of the Press Gallery who, like a number of Gorton's parliamentary colleagues, disapproved of Gorton's methods and techniques. I was interested to see how Gorton would handle himself. I went to the dinner.

Gorton's speech was rather pedestrian which was understandable. He had had a hard day. It was certainly anecdotal, but in the personal rather than the political sense. After the dinner, Gorton and the Gallery members moved into an adjacent area for drinks. I had not eaten at the dinner, but I felt worse. I stayed chatting for a while, but Gorton showed no signs of leaving.

The President of the Gallery at that time was Mr Jonathan Gaul, a man much younger than I was. A very talented journalist, Gaul worked at that time for the *Canberra Times*.[4] As might be expected in an organisation which consisted of highly individualistic people who had strong views on everything and who, particularly when warmed with good wine and food, conducted their arguments with fervor, there had been incidents, some rather colorful, at previous Press Gallery dinners. Believing that an older man, like myself, could more easily persuade disputing younger members of the Gallery into conformity than one nearer their age groups, Gaul had asked me to stay on until the Prime Minister had departed. I explained to Gaul that I was feeling rather unwell. I then offered myself as a candidate for consideration as a contributor to "Famous last words". After studying the assembly, I told Gaul, "Nothing is going to happen tonight—it is as respectable as a curate's picnic." Gaul agreed that there was no necessity for me to linger. I made my adieux to Gorton, and moved across to Miss Willesee. Again following the "famous last words" tradition, I explained that I was not well and was leaving early. "But you're enjoying yourself, Geraldine," I told her. "There's no need for you to leave. Everything is going very nicely. Why don't you stay on for a while? I'm sure someone'll give you a lift home when you want to go." A number in the group immediately around us gave assurances that they would see that she got a lift home. I left with my colleague, Robert Baudino.

The next day, an account of Miss Willesee's and Gorton's midnight visit to the United States Embassy was all over Canberra. In its original form, the account was given some nasty and malevolent twists. Gorton was depicted as arriving at the Embassy with the uninvited Miss Willesee, hammering on the door, demanding drinks and behaving in such a fashion that Mrs Crook who had gone to bed, refused to come downstairs to greet her belated guest, unwelcome at that hour, and more unwelcome when accompanied by a young and uninvited female. A version of this story came to the ears of persons in the management echelon of Australian United Press, Miss Willesee's employers.

AUP's management decided that Miss Willesee's presence on their staff was an embarrassment, and, if the US Embassy incident was publicised, could be a serious embarrassment.[5] Mr Ken Braddick was the chief of the AUP's bureau in the Press Gallery at Parliament House. He was instructed to tell Miss Willesee that the AUP was dispensing with her services. The formal justification to be given her was that there was to be "a reconstruction of the Bureau." A very unhappy Braddick descended from the Press Gallery and went to the office of Eggleton, Gorton's Press Secretary. Braddick told Eggleton of the distasteful task that had been assigned to him. Eggleton's office was just along the lobby from Gorton's office in Parliament House. Eggleton went to Gorton and told him of what was happening to Miss Willesee.

Gorton's reaction was immediate. He told Eggleton to get Mr A. T. Shakespeare on the phone at once. Shakespeare, a veteran newspaper proprietor and the former owner of the *Canberra Times,* was an AUP chieftain. He was also a Canberra legend, shrewd, at times testy, but universally respected. He was also bluntly outspoken and not likely to be intimidated by prime ministers with whom he had rubbed shoulders and, as the champion of Canberra, crossed swords frequently during his long newspaper career. Gorton said he would ask Shakespeare to have the instruction to Braddick withdrawn. Eggleton advised Gorton against intervention. Shakespeare might view such intervention as unsought interference in AUP affairs. Shakespeare could be choleric. He was just as likely to give the Prime Minister a blast as a hearing. If it got out that the Prime Minister had intervened—and Shakespeare was as likely as not to complain angrily if Gorton intervened in something that, basically, was AUP and not prime ministerial business—it would give the incident an importance and significance that at present was lacking. Gorton accepted Eggleton's advice. He did not phone Shakespeare. Miss Willesee left her AUP employment. Despite her reputation as a competent journalist, Miss Willesee had some difficulty in getting another job. Probably to Gorton's chagrin, Max Newton, whom Gorton by now disliked intensely, offered Miss Willesee a job. Newton may have had an eye to the future. But he had also shown in the past and was to show in the future that he had feeling for an "under dog"[6] and anyone caught up helplessly in a difficult situation. Miss Willesee accepted the job. After a period, the incident, which received little publicity, appeared to have been forgotten. An interesting facet of this period when the time at which Gorton and his party left the US Embassy had no particular significance was that Eggleton, quite openly and casually, told pressmen that Gorton, Miss Willesee and he had left the Embassy at 3 am.[7]

In retrospect, I realise that I should have grasped earlier than I did that the US Embassy incident was far from forgotten. It was not dead; merely dormant. On Thursday, March 6, 1969, I was approached by Edward St John in the newspaper reading section of the Parliamentary Library.

St John, then 53, was a Sydney QC. He was Napoleonic in stature, thinfaced and lipped, precise of speech and manner, religious, abstemious in his habits, bespectacled, proud of what he considered to be his morality and high principles, and possessed of a Savonarola-like zeal to secure their adoption by others, a zeal which earned him a high reputation and a wide berth. Stripped of his horn-rimmed glasses, his sharp features would have been appropriately framed within a monk's cowl or jutted out fittingly from under a high sugarloaf Puritan's hat. He took pride in his descent from Oliver St John, a kinsman and close friend of Cromwell, who had made his reputation as counsel for John Hampden in the Ship-money case and who, as Chief Justice under the Commonwealth, had refused to participate in the trial of Charles I because he could not recognise the acts of a House of Commons, forcibly purged by Cromwell's army.

Austere and righteous, humble of mien, but arrogant of mind,[8] as convivial as a shrouded side of beef hanging in a chilling chamber, a man who appeared to crave the approbation of the serious minded[9] and addicted to John Donne and Biblical quotations, St John was hardly the type to appeal to Gorton, a man who liked the relaxation of parties, a few drinks, the company of handsome, sociable women, and the bawled songs of a wartime airforce mess. St John was a "do-gooder" not in the broad political sense, as Gorton said he wanted to be, but in specific directions. St John was prominent in the Australian section of the South Africa Defence and Aid Fund, a body which provided legal aid to those who suffered under South Africa's apartheid laws and financial aid for the sufferers' dependants, and was critical of those who supported Rhodesia in the Parliament, among whom was Jimmy Killen, Irish descended, a man who enjoyed life, had exuberance as well as diligence, loved laughter, the clash of wits, a convivial drink and a hearty, uninhibited brawl, and was close to Gorton. Killen and his friends who by this time mostly supported Gorton, viewed St John, who when seeking election for the "blue-ribbon" Liberal seat of Warringah had been ferociously opposed by extremist rightwing Liberal forces, as naive, sanctimonious and superior.

Additionally, St John had antagonised Gorton when St John made his maiden speech on May 16, 1967, while Holt was still Prime Minister. Gorton had been Navy Minister until December 18, 1963. On February 10, 1964, less than two months after Menzies shifted Gorton from the Navy to the Education portfolio, a collision took place off the NSW coast between the Royal Australian Navy aircraft carrier, *Melbourne,* and the RAN destroyer, *Voyager.* The *Voyager* was cut in half and sank with the loss of eighty-two lives. A Royal Commission, established to inquire into the collision, found the *Voyager* the cause of the collision but was critical of Captain R. J. Robertson, commander of the Melbourne. Appointed to a shore job, Captain Robertson resigned from the Navy, as "a matter of principle."[10] The government had refused to pay Robertson a pension, though Robertson had given thirty-five years of gallant and unblemished service. John Jess was convinced, as were many RAN personnel, that Robertson was treated unjustly, and had been fighting valiantly but vainly to persuade the government to hold a second inquiry into the *Melbourne-Voyager* collision. Gorton was implacably opposed to an inquiry and was to claim later that if he had been Prime Minister in 1967, there would have been no second inquiry.[11]

In his maiden speech, St John supported Jess' demand for a second inquiry. The speech was a parliamentary tour de force. It received wide acclamation.[12] After a debate in the government parties' room the next day, May 17, 1967, the government felt it had to yield to the pressure produced by St John's speech. On May 18, 1967, Holt announced that there would be a second *Voyager* inquiry.[13] The report of this second inquiry was presented to the House of Representatives on March 13, 1968, after Holt's disappearance, and Gorton's appointment as Prime Minister. The report completely exonerated Robertson. It said he was "free of any criticism."[14] One of Gorton's first tasks as Prime Minister was to announce the "act of grace" payment of 60,000 dollars, free from income tax, as compensation for the pension rights that Robertson had sacrificed when he resigned "on principle" after being, in his view, wrongly criticised by the first *Voyager* Royal Commission Report.[15] As there would have been no inquiry and

216

no 60,000 dollars compensation for Robertson if Gorton had been Prime Minister when St John made his speech, this could hardly have endeared St John to Gorton. St John had subsequently been critical of the government over other things, and though I did not know it at the time, had already on February 20, 1969, had discussions with Gorton about the US Embassy incident.[16]

After St John approached me in the newspaper reading room of the Parliamentary Library, we discussed a number of things. I was interested in a speech St John had delivered on February 24, 1969, to the Federated Taxpayers' Association of Australia. The speech was entitled "Commonwealth/State Financial Relationships —possible solutions to the problem." In that speech, he had made a cryptic reference to McMahon's future. He had said, "I know that this audience will not think that I am expressing any merely fulsome praise if I say in passing that he (McMahon) is probably the best Treasurer the Commonwealth has ever had. Let us hope that he survives for a long time to come." In common with everyone else in Parliament House, I was aware that McMahon's prospects for survival as Treasurer were not bright. As soon as Gorton could conveniently fit a noose around the McMahon neck he would hang him. But I had not talked with St John since he had made the speech. I was curious to find out whether St John had specific information about McMahon's future, information that I lacked. St John said that he had no specific information. But he was sure beyond doubt that Gorton would get rid of McMahon as Treasurer at the first opportunity. Gorton did not want a strong Treasurer. He wanted to be his own Treasurer. St John thought Gorton would be hopeless as the de facto Treasurer. He was too "slapdash" in his methods and would not listen to advice. St John said that he had put the reference to McMahon into his speech in the hope that it would make Gorton aware that McMahon was admired both in the Parliamentary Liberal Party and in the community generally for his work as a Treasurer. Not that he really thought that Gorton would be deterred from getting rid of McMahon as Treasurer. Gorton was not the type to be deterred. Once he set his mind on something he was like an irresponsible child. He wanted it and was determined to have it, even though it would do him more harm than good to have it.

Then St John really opened out. He said that a number of backbenchers were seriously disturbed about Frank Browne's article in "Things I Hear" which had appeared during the parliamentary recess. He did not like the Prime Minister placing himself in positions which contributed to notoriety being associated with his name. He was opposed to Gorton's presidential style of

217

government. His fear was that in its disorganised state and because of its disorganised state the ALP could lose further seats at the forthcoming elections and Gorton would misinterpret this as an endorsement for his style of government. The newspapers were protecting Gorton—covering up his mistakes and failing to report things that the public were entitled to know. Take the Willesee incident. Every pressman in Canberra knew that Gorton had taken a young lady, uninvited, to the United States Embassy and had stayed there talking and drinking until the small hours of the morning. Yet not a line had been written about it.

I argued that a prime minister, like any other politician, or citizen for that matter, was entitled to a private life. I was not interested in Gorton's private life. What he did in his spare time was his business, not mine. I was interested in anything and everything he did in the public domain or in his official capacity. This was a legitimate interest, to which I was entitled as both a citizen and a newspaperman, and I would always insist upon my right to take this interest. As for Gorton's visit to the US Embassy, I had been assured that it was a private pre-arranged party. When Gorton, Eggleton and Miss Willesee had arrived there, Ainsley Gotto and Jeff Darman, one of the Embassy's attachés, were already present listening to records with Crook. Crook was about as respectable a churchgoing, conforming character as it was possible to find. The only thing that puzzled me was that there was no reference to Mrs Crook being present at the party. Even if she had gone to bed, an ambassador's wife could be expected to get up for a prime minister. There could of course be a simple explanation. But if Gorton wanted to take a young lady to a private party, that was his affair. It might be indiscreet for a man in his position to do so, because some gossip about it was inevitable, but I could not get worked up about it. It hardly seemed big enough to kick up a fuss large enough to bring down a government. The ALP obviously did not think so. ALP parliamentarians had undoubtedly heard accounts of the incident just as St John had, and the measure of the importance that they had attached to it was that they had done nothing about it.

St John said that my thinking was too black and white. A prime minister's private life could not be separated from his public office. There were grey areas where they overlapped. He believed the incident after the Press Gallery dinner when Gorton took Miss Willesee, uninvited, to the US Embassy was in the grey area, part of Gorton's public life. How could it be otherwise? Gorton was Prime Minister. Crook was US Ambassador. The visit had taken place on the day President Johnson had announced the bombing halt. There had been strain that day between the two men, strain between the head of the Australian government and the official representative in Australia of the US, Australia's most important ally. Crook had phoned Gorton at the Press dinner asking for a meeting, admittedly in social surroundings, but a meeting to relieve strain between two men each significant in their government's structure. Was that not official? Did the meeting not have the potential to relieve the strain or, if things did not go well, increase the strain between these two significant men? That there had been strain was an unchallengeable fact. He, St John, had told Gorton "face to face" that he had behaved badly in the Willesee incident.[17]

St John expressed the view that there were two reasons why the ALP had done nothing about Gorton and his unconventional behaviour such as taking Miss Willesee to the US Embassy in the circumstances in which he had taken her. One reason was that there were individuals on the ALP side whose personal conduct was open to criticism. From self-interest, they did not want to promote a "mud-slinging" contest. The other reason was that the ALP was a very weak opposition. St John was obviously troubled. He said that the ALP's weakness as an opposition imposed a heavy responsibility on Liberal backbenchers. They had to function as critics of the government even if they did not want to. They had to do it in the national interest. A strong opposition made for good government. When the formal ALP opposition was weak, the Liberal backbenchers had to compensate for that weakness. Otherwise government would deteriorate. But the position as regards Gorton could not go on indefinitely. Labor or "somebody else" sooner or later would "turn a bucket."[18]

In retrospect, I can see that I missed the peg on which I could have hung a newspaper story—St. John's "face to face" confrontation with Gorton. I had taken a mental note of the "or somebody else". But I regarded St John as a bit amateurish in his politics. In my view, anyone who was really going after the Prime Minister would not base his case on the iniquity of a prime minister taking an uninvited guest to an embassy party, however indiscreet the circumstances, and however late the hour. It was interesting, as a gossip item, but lacked durable substance. He would pick on things much more substantial in the policy and administrative fields —and Gorton in his fifteen months of office had provided quite a selection—and use the embassy incident, if it was considered as having any value at all, merely as an illustration of Gorton's personal unconventionality. I thought that St John was having a good, oldfashioned bellyache, nothing more, and as soon as one of his shrewder friends pointed out the weakness in his case, and the rather strained emphasis he was putting on the embassy incident, would write the incident off as having dubious value in any antiGorton crusade. I misjudged St John. Where the earlier St John had sensibly stayed aloof from the Charles I Execution and thereby had given himself a partial safeguard against the possibility of a Stuart Restoration, the modern St John was prepared to proffer himself as Gorton's would-be political executioner, without qualification.

James' March 19, 1969, speech, which drew on Browne's "Things I Hear" raised, in a blurred way, four matters. The first one was that the United Kingdom magazine *Private Eye* had intended running during Gorton's January visit to London for the Conference of Commonwealth Prime Ministers an article dealing with Gorton's private life, that the CIA had bought the rights to this article from *Private Eye,* and that the CIA had sold the rights to this article to publication in Africa, Europe and the United States.[19] There had been rumors before Gorton departed for London that *Private Eye* was preparing such an article.[20] But little attention was paid to this matter which received its coup de grace when *Private Eye* spokesmen announced publicly that *Private Eye* had not only not sold any article to the CIA but had never had such an article to sell to anyone.

The second matter raised was an alleged incident at Chequers night club in Sydney. Gorton visited Miss Liza Minnelli, the American singing star, in her dressing room. But the editor-in-chief of Australian Consolidated Press, Mr David McNicoll, as well as Mrs Gorton and Mrs McNicoll had been with Gorton at Chequers that night. McNicoll published an account of what had happened.[21] McNicoll had been the host. The McNicolls had been to a dinner party at Government House and had invited Mr and Mrs Gorton after the dinner to hear Miss Minnelli sing. Miss Minnelli had presented "her usual magnificent performance" according to McNicoll. Mrs and Mr Gorton had expressed the wish to meet Miss Minnelli, had been introduced, and subsequently Gorton had talked with Miss Minnelli in her dressing room, with others, including Mrs Woolnough, Miss Minnelli's mother-in-law, present. As McNicoll described it, it was a pleasant, normal evening, with the Prime Minister meeting the star of the show and being politely and probably sincerely applaudatory of Miss Minnelli's performance. By the time James made his speech, Miss Minnelli was back in the United States. She indignantly said that she knew nothing whatever about untoward incidents at Chequers and that anyone who said there had been anything untoward was indulging in "a pack of lies."[22] After Miss Minnelli's statement and McNicoll's account of what had happened at Chequers the so-called Chequers incident was not raised again.

The third incident was one that occurred in Bali during Gorton's 1968 Asian tour. It was all terribly vague. Gorton either deliberately or from indifference — he disliked the constant presence of a "shadower"—"lost" his security guard, Mr Ray Whitrod. Mrs Gorton was disturbed, and had emissaries scurrying in all directions. Gorton was finally located strolling in the hotel gardens with Miss Gotto. There was an argument between Gorton and Whitrod. Whitrod, a precise, soberminded man, with a strong sense of duty and responsibility, made no attempt to disguise his feeling about the Prime Minister's disdain for his personal safety and casual attitudes. When Whitrod subsequently resigned his position as Chief of the Commonwealth Police, and accepted a post, first as Northern Territory Police Commissioner and later as Queensland Police Commissioner, Whitrod's departure from the Federal scene was attributed to this argument. This incident overshadowed the far more serious charge that Gorton, who was determined to have a holiday break before he returned to Australia, had treated casually local Indonesian authorities in Bali, and has been needlessly offhand with Indonesian Foreign Minister, Adam Malik, sent specially by the Indonesian government to Bali to assist Gorton make his stay there more pleasant. But the Bali incident was also allowed to drop from sight. It was the fourth matter raised in James speech, the US Embassy incident, that was to be used as a test of Gorton's credibility and which was to provide him with the most trouble.

What happened immediately after James had made his speech was, in itself, important. It was that starting point in the deterioration of relations between Gorton and Erwin, hitherto Gorton's most loyal supporter within the Liberal Party, and was to contribute further to rancor between Gorton and McMahon. With James having done a tongue-in-cheek, mock Uriah Heep "bucket" job on Gorton, Liberals Jim Killen and Tom Hughes, a Sydney QC, who then held the "swing" seat of Parkes,[23] attacked both James and the worthlessness of Browne as an authority. Killen said, "It will be a sorry day for the Parliament of Australia and it will be a pathetic day for the people of Australia if on no more reliable authority than that of Frank Browne, whose pen will go to the highest bidder this Parliament is to be asked to say, 'Well, we are prepared to inquire into the nature of this alleged blackmail'."[24]

But it was Hughes who provoked a situation that he did not

221

intend to bring about. Hughes said, "The accuracy of this man Browne may best be judged from another passage in his libel sheet of January 31, 1969, where, referring to a book written and recently published by Mr Alan Reid,[25] he states that a good deal of what was in the book about the Prime Minister was excised on legal advice. I want to tell the House—I hope that it will give me credit for being reasonably honest—that I read the book in its original transcript form. I have read the book in its printed form and I say without equivocation that in its printed form it contained not one syllable which reflected in any way upon the Prime Minister. We all know that in its now printed form it contains not one sentence and not one syllable that reflects personally upon the Prime Minister . . . I was the first person to read it after it had been typed."[26] Then Hughes added the words, "Let somebody on the other side rise to disown the Honorable Member for Hunter (James). If nobody does so, we all will know that the Labor Party is muck raking at the bottom of the political bucket in the knowledge that it cannot do any better."

Fred Daly, from Sydney's Grayndler, was the only member of the ALP's Federal Parliamentary Executive in the chamber of the House of Representatives. A mischief-maker of great eminence, Daly, who shot words out as rapidly as a perfectly functioning machine gun did bullets, sensed opportunity. Later he was to add to the uneasiness among Liberals on how their parliamentary leaders had handled the situation by insisting, straightfaced and innocent, that all he had proposed to do was to make a "humorous" speech. But Daly's humour could be as devastating as a hand grenade exploded in a confined space. When Daly, who had already spoken in the adjournment debate, said "The Honorable member (Hughes) has asked for someone on the Opposition side to speak. I ask for leave to make a speech in reply . . ."[27] the Speaker, Sir William Aston, asked, "Is leave granted?" Erwin, in his capacity as Leader of the House, said, "No." The former Opposition Leader, Arthur Calwell, an aged but highly experienced parliamentary warhorse, smelt blood, battle, and advantage. "I move that so much of the standing orders be suspended as would prevent the honorable member for Grayndler (Daly) making a second speech on the motion for the adjournment of the House," Calwell said.[28]

It was 11.11 pm. Gorton was in his office where he had heard the James' speech and the replies by Killen and Hughes over his amplifier system. With him were Malcolm Fraser and Miss Gotto. Max Fox, the government whip, kept running between the chamber of the House of Representatives and Gorton's office, looking for instructions. Gorton wanted to go into the chamber and speak. Fraser and Miss Gotto were persuading him not to. This left McMahon the senior minister in the chamber. McMahon was encouraging Erwin to stick to his decision not to allow Daly to speak. Later Erwin was to claim that so were a number of other substantial figures on the Liberal side, including Fred Chaney. Calwell insisted upon a division.

The state of the parties in the House of Representatives was then Liberals, 61; CP, 21; and ALP, 42; a majority for the Liberal-CP coalition of 40. But when the division was counted, the vote was 42/all. Fifteen members had crossed the floor of the chamber of the House of Representatives to vote with the Opposition. They were NSW Liberals, W. T. Arthur, C. W. Bridges Maxwell, Dr M. G. Mackay, and E. H. St John, SA Liberals, Miss Kay Brownbill and D. S. Jessop, Queensland Liberals, Kevin Cairns, E. N. Drury, Donald Cameron, W. T. Gibbs, and D. J. Killen, Victorian Liberal, M. W. Lee, and CP MHR's, S. E. Calder, Northern Territory, Don Maisey, Western Australia, and I. L. Robinson, NSW. In the absence of the absolute majority of the 124-strong House of Representatives necessary to suspend standing orders, Speaker Aston ruled that Daly could not be heard.

The debate dragged on until 12.03 am, with McMahon and Malcolm Fraser who by this time had entered the chamber defending Gorton's integrity and assailing James. As soon as the Speaker put the formal motion "that the House do now adjourn" and left the chair, Fraser flew at Erwin. He called Erwin all the stupid fools he could put his tongue to, for seeking to gag Daly. He blamed Erwin for the fifteen government members crossing the floor. McMahon joined in the argument. "Don't talk to Dudley that way, you long streak," said McMahon. Then glancing up at the press galleries where the pressmen were watching, fascinated, he lowered his voice, which, however, was still audible to those watching and listening above. "If you want to quarrel with Dudley, get outside and do it more discreetly," McMahon said. Fraser, flushed with anger, walked out of the chamber.

For Erwin, it was the start of the road out. Though it took Erwin a long time to recognize what was taking place, Gorton's attitude towards him changed from there on. Gorton blamed him for handling the situation in such a way as to prompt St John to launch against the Prime Minister a series of attacks which continued until polling day, October 25, 1969. Instead of being resentful against those who had joined with St John in supporting the move designed to get Daly an opportunity to make a second speech, Gorton not only supported their action but cultivated

223

those among them whom he believed would back him in any trouble that might emerge within the Liberal Party because of his unconventional behaviour. Hughes was the only one morally committed to vote in Daly's support. He had challenged an ALP spokesman to disown James at the moment when Daly was the only senior ALP MHR in the chamber, and consequently Hughes could hardly vote to prevent Daly from speaking. But the others were in a different category. They voted for a variety of reasons, and normally would have incurred the Prime Minister's anger. As it was, selected ones were marked out for advancement and patronage.[29]

From then on, Gorton got involved in a series of happenings that did nothing to stimulate confidence in his credibility. Leaving out altogether the propriety of taking a young lady, indeed anyone, uninvited to the US Embassy, at the hour he had taken Miss Willesee, he demonstrated the same slipshod approach on the times at which he had arrived at and left the US Embassy as he had in other aspects of his administration. With his customary boldness in moments of tension and stress, Gorton had grasped firmly the nettle of party unease. At 12.45 pm on Thursday, March 21, 1969, he hastily convened a Liberal Party meeting. Earlier in the Parliament, Gorton had defended himself on the Liza Minnelli incident, but had not referred to any other incident. After McEwen in turn had vigorously defended Gorton, describing him as "this distinguished man",[30] the government had gagged the debate, with St John the only Liberal voting with the Opposition for its continuance. At the Party meeting, Gorton said, "I shall be here for only thirty seconds. You heard my denial of the allegations and the fact that Miss Minnelli has also denied them. I ask for a vote of confidence." From the back of the room, St John said, "Sir, I don't agree." Gorton said, "I'm not here to discuss it with you . . . you can do what you like." The meeting, which lasted twenty-seven seconds, carried the vote of confidence with standing applause. St John remained seated. It was a fighter-pilot's technique; a fast approach, a quick fusillade of shots, and then up and away. But St John was not yet finished.

On the same night, March 20, 1969, St John rose on the adjournment. He was determined to make a mountain of the US Embassy molehill. Later he was to admit that his tactics were wrong. "Rightly or wrongly I felt that this was not the time to embark on a full dissertation on the matters that had been causing us (some Liberals) concern," St John wrote later. "I still hoped that the party would take effective action and it would be unnecessary to wash all the dirty linen in public. I restricted myself

therefore to the events of the night of the Press Gallery dinner . . .
Perhaps I was unwise or unfair to myself in thus restricting
myself."[31] Boiled down, what St John alleged was that Gorton
and his party had arrived at the US Embassy at 2.30 am and left
at 5.30 am. He believed "that such conduct could only be calculated gravely to prejudice our relationship with the United
States."[32] If St John's times subsequently were demonstrated to
be significantly wrong, Gorton's times proved even more wrong.
For some reason which has never been explained, Gorton did not
consult with Eggleton who was present throughout and who as
early as November when the time was unimportant, had fixed
their departure time from the US Embassy at 3 am, with Coppin,
who drove the party, or with the Lodge security man who recorded
Gorton's arrival time at the Lodge after he had left the US Embassy. Instead Gorton said vaguely, "I would imagine—I would
think—that we probably arrived at the American Embassy at a
quarter to twelve or twelve o'clock, or sometime . . . and that we
left about half an hour after that . . . It is an interesting exercise
in how something which I believe is a perfectly reasonable and
proper thing can be twisted, turned and slimed over . . ."[33]

The US Ambassador, Mr William Crook, got caught up in
the controversy. In an official statement, issued on March 20,
1969, Crook said he had invited the Prime Minister to "come by
the Embassy for a drink later that evening with myself and Mrs
Crook. The Prime Minister dropped in about midnight for a
social visit and departed about a half-hour later."

After Miss Willesee had issued on March 21, 1969, her statutory
declaration which put their arrival time at the US Embassy at
1 am and their departure time at 3 am, and Gorton had confirmed
this by stating that an official record at the Lodge showed he
returned home at 3 am,[34] Crook on March 26, 1969, put out
another official statement. It said, ". . . A stop watch is not used
on visitors at the American Embassy residence . . . I take this
means to again refute all charges of impropriety on behalf of my
government and all suggestions that anything but a most decorous
social visit occurred in my home. No further comment will be made
on this subject."

Gorton was lucky that St John's approach to politics was
amateurish. As early as February 25, 1969, St John had shown
in his address to the Federated Taxpayers' Association of Australia that he had misgivings about Gorton. A shrewder man would
have attacked Gorton in the areas where he was most vulnerable—
on examples of his slipshod methods both in speechmaking and
administration, his disdain of Cabinet, his fostering of trouble

within the Liberal Party by his ambiguous attitude on State rights, and so on—and used the US Embassy incident merely as an illustration of Gorton's unconventionality rather than as the basis of a charge. By Friday, March 21, 1969, St John had realised his mistake. He tried to widen the basis of his criticisms. He criticised Gorton's handling of the Commonwealth Public Service which he described as being "apprehensive of the building up of the power complex within the Prime Minister's Department—the Gorton/ Hewitt complex . . . they (public servants) are reaching the point where they have to wonder whether they should give their honest impartial advice or whether perhaps they shouldn't say something they know will be acceptable." He expressed his concern "about the policy or lack of policy in relation to overseas investment, the lack of definition in policy, the lack of any clear guidelines to business." He dealt with the Prime Minister's presidential approach. "We see a pattern of conduct which points to the conclusion that the Prime Minister wishes to assert his authority in every direction you care to name, against the States, against the Public Service, within the Party, within the Cabinet; in every direction where he can possibly assert his authority."[35] But having nailed his flag to the mast of the sinking US Embassy affair, St John was manoeuvred into a position in which he found it impossible to switch his pennant to another more seaworthy craft. Those elements within the Liberal Party dedicated to Gorton were determined that St John would go down with the US Embassy ship, whose fighting capacity he had gravely overrated.[36]

St John was not only amateurish. He was a willing, indeed an anxious, martyr. By March 24, 1969, Mrs Gorton had produced what she described in the heading as "Comment on current events." It was a bowdlerised version of a William Watson verse. One of Australia's top public relations men was staying at the Lodge. She had overridden both his and her husband's advice. They both wanted her to stay aloof from the argument between her husband and St John. But Mrs Gorton had insisted. Through Eggleton's office she put out the verse which read —

"He is not old, he is not young,
The Member with the Serpent's tongue,
The haggard cheek, the hungering eye,
The poisoned words that wildly fly,
The famished face, the fevered hand —
Who slights the worthiest in the land,
Sneers at the just, condemns the brave,
And blackens goodness in its grave."

Mrs Gorton was not the only one to move against St. John. All over Australia the Liberal establishment was mustering to Gorton's defence. The April, 1969, issue of the *Australian Liberal,* mouthpiece of the NSW branch reported, "Immediately (the Liberal) State council met on March 21 for its monthly meeting, a motion from the floor proposed that the council should pass a vote of confidence in the leadership of the Prime Minister. The NSW Liberal Party President, Mr F. M. Osborne, asked if there was any opposition, and when there was no response, declared the motion carried unanimously. Similar motions were carried in the following week by other State divisions and the terms of the motion were then telegraphed to the Prime Minister." On March 24, 1969, the Liberal Party Federal President, Mr J. E. Pagan, in an official statement, said, "As Federal President, I completely support my colleagues on Federal Executive, who, as presidents in their own particular States, have already affirmed in the most positive terms, their confidence in, and loyalty to, the Prime Minister. Indeed the opinion of the Liberal Party organisation throughout Australia utterly repudiates Mr St John's tactics and attitudes. I have never before witnessed such an immediate and unequivocable reaction from the State divisions of our party."

St John was scheduled to meet Warringah Liberal Federal Electoral Conference on Friday, March 28, 1968. With the might of the Liberal Party mobilising against him, it was obvious that he was for the "chopper" unless he could demonstrate that he had support sufficient to give the Liberal Party mandarins second thoughts about the wisdom of martyring him. But St John not only seemed to welcome martyrdom. He gave signs that he wanted to be the sole starring attraction at his own auto-de-fe.

A meeting of the Liberal Federal Parliamentary Party was held at Parliament House, Canberra, at 9.30 am on Thursday, March 26, 1969. The Liberal leaders were determined that St John should be destroyed for all time. There had been continuous consultations between Gorton, Pagan, Fraser, Fairhall and others, with Miss Gotto fluttering in the background like an attractive butterfly hovering over a bed of stinging nettles. McMahon had been frozen out. Fraser had voiced the suspicion that in some Machiavellian way McMahon had engineered the whole incident to discredit Gorton. Gorton originally proposed vacating the chair at the Parliamentary Party meeting. But this would have put McMahon into the chair, something that Gorton did not want. While Gorton's vacating of the chair might on one hand give the impression that St John was being dealt with impartially by his parliamentary colleagues, Gorton decided on reflection that it was more likely to be interpreted as weakness on his part. But,

227

though McMahon was the Liberals' Deputy leader, Gorton decided to make Fairhall his main defender. Gorton rationalised this by pointing out that Fairhall was the minister with whom, according to St John, he was at daggers drawn. Fairhall was therefore the appropriate minister to speak. Gorton had approached Fairhall to speak. Fairhall had agreed. Robert Cotton was called in.

A former Liberal Federal and NSW President, Cotton was a strong organisation man. Cotton held the belief that where an individual threatened the existence of a Liberal government or the Liberal Party the individual had to be ruthlessly destroyed. Cotton agreed to move a motion. The motion read "(a) that this meeting of members of the Parliamentary Liberal Party strongly deplores and dissociates itself from the disloyal public attacks made by Mr St John on the Prime Minister and the policies of the government, (b) that this meeting express full confidence in the leadership of the Prime Minister, and (c) that in the circumstances the meeting calls upon Mr St John to consider his position and expresses its wish and its belief that he should withdraw from the Parliamentary Party, should not attend Party meetings, and should openly operate as an independent."

It was in the political sense a clever motion. It combined almost inextricably a call for a declaration of confidence in Gorton, a declaration for which Gorton undoubtedly had majority support, with an implied demand for St John either to quit the Liberal Party or accept the discipline that his refusal to quit would inevitably bring in its train. But the meeting did not go precisely to the plan evolved by the Liberal masterminds, and it could have gone really badly but for St John's masochistic urge towards self immolation.

Gorton opened the meeting. He said it was a special meeting called to deal with the position of himself and St John. The position had to be resolved. The matter was now open for discussion. Cotton referred to the wide respect and admiration for the Prime Minister throughout Australia, an admiration confirmed by the Gallup poll.[37] Cotton then moved his resolution. NSW Liberal Jeff Bate interjected that the motion was "stupid, dangerous, and bungling." It should be in two parts. The motion as it stood had the potential to make a martyr out of St John.

Len Bosman, a Sydney restauranteur, who had won the marginal seat of St George for the Liberals, appealed to Gorton not to accept Cotton's resolution. Bosman was friendly with St John. He was also a stubborn, determined man, who had reservations about Gorton's leadership. Bosman said that if the Prime Minister accepted the Cotton resolution, Gorton would compound blunders already made. Nevertheless, whoever convened the meeting should be complimented. The meeting gave the party the chance to get together to straighten out its difficulties. He appealed to Gorton and the Liberal parliamentary leaders to let the heat diminish, and to go back to a position before St John was projected into the situation. While the Prime Minister was entitled to go out of the room with the knowledge that he had the full confidence of the party, the party, however, had its problems. He appealed to Gorton and the party to solve these problems and adjust the differences. In the long-term, this, rather than any heresy hunt, would be in the best interests of Gorton himself and the Liberal Party.

After Bosman spoke, Gorton said that he could not allow the position to remain as it was. The party had to express itself for the Prime Minister or for St John. He said that he accepted Cotton's resolution. If the party wanted him to carry on, he must have the party's complete loyalty.

WA Liberal Fred Chaney, who was to be defeated at the coming 1969 elections[38] said that St John's attitude sickened everyone. The Party had not brought about the present situation. It was St John. St John was the one fellow out of step among 59.[39] It behoved all members to remember the great responsibilities and the colossal task the Prime Minister had. The Prime Minister had all kinds of problems on his plate, including the inhibitions of some members of Cabinet about State rights. Members had to back him. Anyone with a glass chin ought to be out of politics. St John was a sad case. He, Chaney, for one, did not appreciate being called a sycophant by St John.[40] Chaney also complained about Miss Willesee's name being brought in. He said the Willesees were a wonderful family. Gorton had been a fighter pilot. When he went out on missions, he wanted to know that he could depend on the men who were flying on his wings. He was entitled to the same kind of loyalty and support from others.

St John said he was sorry Chaney applied the word "sycophant" to himself. There had been sycophants among those who had interjected when he spoke on Thursday, March 20. But he did not include Chaney in that group. He had not mentioned Miss Willesee's name. The person to blame for Miss Willesee's notoriety was the Prime Minister. The Prime Minister should have thought about the notoriety that might accrue to Miss Willesee and taken appropriate action on the night of the Press Gallery dinner to see that he did not create the circumstances that caused the gossip. He recognised the danger of the Liberals losing electoral support. On the other hand, the conduct of the Prime Minister and his policies, or lack of them, could cause a great erosion of Liberal support anyhow. In the long run it was for the benefit of the party to face up to the situation now and before it got worse. Faced with "this intolerable rising tide of scandal and gossip", a group of ministers should have got together and told Gorton to stop the conduct that was giving rise to the gossip and scandal. If the rumours were false, they should have insisted on action being taken to stop the scandal sheets and scandalmongers.

Gorton invited St John to air his complaints about his appointments. St John said there was every justification for a man appointing his own friends to ministerial rank if they were well qualified people. It was an entirely different thing if inadequately equipped people were appointed to the highest posts in the land. He referred to the replacement of Snedden by Erwin as the Leader of the House of Representatives. He criticised the "unceremonious" way in which Sir John Bunting had been removed from the Prime Minister's Department and Hewitt installed in his place. There was the appointment of Mr A. B. McFarlane, as a Public Service Board Commissioner, even though McFarlane had not been one of the three recommended by the Chairman of the Public Service Board, Sir Frederick Wheeler, for appointment. Not only had Gorton made the McFarlane appointment, but he had publicised the fact that McFarlane was his personal choice, and not a Public Service Board recommendation—a complete departure from precedent and a deliberate underlining of his determination to maintain "one-man" rule. The Prime Minister consistently disregarded public service advice. Gorton did not want advice; he wanted submission. The Prime Minister had made the oil decision without waiting for Frankel's report.

St John said he had discussed with the NSW Liberal Secretary, John Carrick,[41] what he should do about Gorton's "one-man" rule. Carrick had advised him to talk with Gorton. This he had done. His talks with Gorton had not lessened his fears; they had intensified them.

A Victorian Liberal, Mervyn Lee, who had a close association with St John—they were members of an all-Party grouping of Christians—moved that the resolution should be in two parts. Bate repeated that the resolution should be in two parts—one dealing with the Prime Minister and the other with St John. It was essential that Gorton be given unanimous support. He had succeeded as a prime minister. He had been elected to contain Whitlam. He had done that successfully. He had established himself as Whitlam's superior right from the time he participated in the *Voyager* debate. His performance in the censure debate in which Whitlam had failed so dismally, had set the seal on his performance. As for the appointments about which St John complained—Erwin's promotion to the Air Ministry and as Leader of the House and Snedden's demotion—Bate advised St John to read Jenning's *Cabinet Government*. It was part of a prime minister's strength that he could appoint whom he liked to cabinet. He, Bate, might have some reservations about some of Gorton's appointments. But he could not but support the Prime Minister's right to make such appointments as he, the Prime Minister, judged to be in the best interests of the country and the government.

Bate said that he thought the move against St John was, as he said earlier, "stupid, bungling and dangerous." The Liberal Party was a democratic party, not authoritarian like the ALP. Liberal parliamentarians had the right to act independently. Any action against St John should be taken within the context of Liberal principles. It was not for the Liberal Parliamentary Party to deal with St John. It was not even for the NSW Liberal Party Executive to deal with him. St John represented Warringah in the Federal Parliament. This was a matter between St John and the Warringah electoral council.

McMahon said that all must leave the room with dignity and unity. The personal life of the Prime Minister was a matter for himself. Members always had the right to express criticism. But the criticism had to be expressed within the context of the interests of the party. If, after expressing their criticisms, members were not satisfied, they had the right to withdraw. That was traditional in the Liberal Party. St John could not remain in the party and carry on as he was carrying on. It was up to St John to make up his mind. St John had said that he would not attend further party meetings until he had made up his mind. This was not good enough. St John had to make up his mind. He, McMahon, saw nothing in the gossip about the Prime Minister that should affect in any way his support for the Prime Minister.

Fairhall criticised St John strongly but there was a strange ambiguity in his closing remarks. Fairhall said that nobody opposed members of the party criticising the party or its leaders when they thought the criticism was justified. But that did not confer licence on them. St John went too far in these things. St John had expressed doubts about the F111, the plane Australia had ordered from the United States for the RAAF. He, Fairhall, had gone to great pains to get St John full information. So had his officials. They had answered every point he raised. Yet, despite that, St John had gone into the house, and criticised the government's insistence upon persisting with the F111 programme. The Prime

Minister was the leader. To wreck him was to wreck the government. It was not for one man to wreck the government. Australia was in highly formative years. Its leaders had to live up to a high ethical code. A member should never denigrate the Prime Minister. To do so was to denigrate Australia. St John had put the party in the position that it had to express its loyalty to the Prime Minister. That should never be. It should be taken for granted that the Prime Minister had the party's full loyalty.

Fairhall then took a strange line. He called upon St John to examine his position and his loyalty. He said that St John was "too independent." St John said, "Alan, you may be right. It may be that I can't give up a lifetime of independent thought, action and judgment." Fairhall then gave St John an accolade that under normal circumstances would have been prized in the Liberal Party, theoretically and in its own eyes the custodian among the Australian political parties of independence of thought and public morality. "You are too independent and too pure of heart," Fairhall told St John.[42]

But while St John may have been "too independent and too pure of heart" he was certainly too politically naive, or anxious for martyrdom in splendid isolation, for his own good when the crunch came. In any political party of any size, there is always a group prepared to vote against the leader for one reason or another, provided their vote is secret and cannot be proved against them. The Liberal Party was no different from any other party. There were about a dozen who could be relied upon to cast a vote against Gorton whatever the issue, provided the vote was in secret, and they did not have to put their hands up publicly and be identified. As it was, there was support for the motion being put in two parts, support which was not pressed but which suggested that there were elements in the room which while not prepared to vote frontally against Gorton were nevertheless prepared to try to thwart any action being taken against St John. Queensland Liberal, Kevin Cairns, the government's assistant whip, asked for a secret ballot. Gorton agreed that there should be one. Members were entitled to vote as they pleased, he said. Gorton's supporters were startled. They knew nobody would vote with St John in public. But in a secret vote, St John might collect sufficient support to show that there was substantial backing for his antiGorton attitude.

St John then cut his own political throat. In a public vote he could get one vote—his own. In a secret vote, he could not do worse, and almost certainly would do better. He had nothing to lose except his uniqueness. With great nobility and no acumen, he rejected the secret ballot. "I stand alone," said St John. "I am the only dissenter. I am quite content that you don't take a vote and you don't take a secret ballot. You can now say that everyone but St John joined in expressing complete confidence in your leadership."

St John left the room and started on the Via Dolorosa which led first to his confrontation with his electoral conference in Warringah, and then to his defeat at the 1969 elections. His reception by the Warringah electoral conference must have shaken the Liberal Party chieftains. As he entered the conference hall where the Warringah delegates were gathered, he was greeted with "sustained applause."[43] But he was not there to fight but to announce, with fatalistic resignation, his withdrawal from the party brawl. He said he would represent Warringah as an independent for the rest of his time in the Parliament. He would not attend meetings of the Parliamentary Liberal Party. He would not run as an endorsed Liberal candidate as long as Gorton remained Prime Minister. He said reasons for surrendering his Liberal endorsement had nothing to do with the possibility of conference delegates voting against him. He had made his decision, despite widespread assurances of support. He felt it would be quite wrong to attend meetings of the Liberal Parliamentary Party, or stand for election as an endorsed Liberal candidate while ever the party retained as its leader a man whose policies and conduct he had repudiated.

St John listed four reasons why he would not serve under Gorton as Liberal leader. The first was the strong tendency towards one-man rule evidenced by Mr Gorton's ministerial appointments, his attitude to the Public Service, and his tendency to make decisions and foreshadow policy without adequate consultations with Cabinet ministers, public servants, or outside experts. The second reason was Gorton's conduct on the night of November 1, 1968, exemplifying many of Mr Gorton's characteristics as parliamentarians had come to know them. The third was that Gorton had sought to mislead the Parliament and through it the public about the events on the night of November 1, the night of the Press Gallery dinner. The fourth was the departure, often without proper deliberation or consultation, from traditional Liberal policies particularly on defence, Commonwealth-State relationships, and overseas investment. Ironically the conference thanked St John for his devotion to the electorate of Warringah, and expressed its "warmest thanks."[44]

From there on, St John started to recede into the background. He continued to address meetings, particularly meetings of univer-

233

sity students. He also encouraged the students' newspapers, which were seemingly uniformly hostile to Gorton, to continue their criticisms of the Prime Minister. He had undoubtedly had his effect upon Gorton's public image. A Gallup poll taken in October, 1969, claimed that the proportion of electors who approved of Gorton as Prime Minister had fallen from 64 per cent to 44 per cent since April, 1969. The poll reading was that only 64 per cent of Liberal-CP voters approved of Gorton in October, 1969, compared with 77 per cent in April, 1969.[45] St John's blast against Gorton and the consequences that flowed from it and the incidents with which he dealt also unleashed other forces, which in turn produced reactions within the Gorton government that had their effect upon the 1969 elections outcome.

In her statutory declaration of March 21, 1969, young Miss Willesee, with national prominence forced upon her, told what appeared to be a straightforward story of her visit to the US Embassy on November 1, 1968. Her account differed from Gorton's in only two significant respects. Gorton had said that Miss Willesee had asked him for a lift. Miss Willesee said she did not ask the Prime Minister or anyone else for a lift home. Gorton had asked her if she wanted a lift home. Both of them were probably telling the truth as they recalled it five months after the event, and it was a minor point anyway. Miss Willesee's account of the times also differed from Gorton's. Gorton said they arrived at the US Embassy about midnight and left a half hour later. Miss Willesee said they arrived at about 1 am and left at 3 am. Miss Willesee's times turned out to be the closer to accuracy. Otherwise the statutory declaration revealed what was already known. Gorton enjoyed female company. Instead of driving Miss Willesee home and then going on to the US Embassy, he had preferred to take her with him to the Embassy where, according to Miss Willesee, "Mr Gorton and I were together at one end of the room talking, and Mr Crook, Mr Darman, Mr Eggleton, and Miss Gotto were talking and dancing to music from a record player at the other end of the room." Miss Willesee's statutory declaration added "My conversation with the Prime Minister centred around the Vietnam bombing halt which had been announced that day, and also Australia's participation in the Vietnam war, conscription, and general politics. We also discussed newspapers and the Press Gallery and had some private conversations . . . When we left the embassy, the ambassador remarked on how pleased he was that we had come and said, 'We must do this more often'."[46]

But when Miss Willesee went to work for Max Newton after her dismissal from AUP, things changed. McEwen hated Newton, who regarded McEwen's economic policies, particularly his tariff policy, as liable to lead to economic disaster. Newton hit at McEwen where it hurt the hardest. He kept repeating that McEwen's high level tariff policy was sending primary producers broke, an accusation that if sustained could have cost McEwen and his CP dear in country seats where declining prices for rural products were reducing many formerly affluent farmers and graziers to parlous dependence upon the banks and wool companies for the maintenance of any kind of a living standard. Newton's staff, like Newton, a cheerfully irreverent and abrasive group, dredged up anything they could use against McEwen and used it with the same devotion as McEwen used anything he could find against Newton.

McEwen's hatred had infected the Cabinet. Despite the fact that Newton's publications had only a relatively small circulation, ministers became quite irrational when Newton's name was mentioned. By this stage, Gorton, whom Newton contemptuously "rubbished" as a "lightweight" had for Newton as deep a hatred as McEwen. Newton continued on his way, with brash assurance. Whenever he could get his hands upon a confidential government or Liberal document—and known as a free-wheeling critic of the government, Gorton, and McEwen he got his hands on quite a few, fed to him by elements within the administration who had a grievance against the government, Gorton, or McEwen—he published them in full, flauntingly, and in a manner which further enraged his enemies within the government.

Trailing his coat insolently, Newton had published in the May 13, 1969, issue of Management Newsletter under the heading "Report of Confidential Government Cable" an account of talks between the Australian Ambassador to France, Mr Alan Renouf, and the French Foreign Minister, Monsieur Debre. He also about the same time published something quite innocuous about the Primary Industry Department, administered by Doug Anthony, the CP Deputy leader, usually one of the cooler headed of the Cabinet ministers. Anthony complained in Cabinet about Newton getting access to confidential documents, and wondered why something could not be done about Newton. It was like dropping a lighted match into dry grass. There was a flare of hatred. Cabinet decided to instruct the Commonwealth Police to search Newton's premises.

It was a mistake. The Federal Parliamentary Press Gallery had stayed aloof from the Government-Newton arguments. So had the Australian Journalists' Association. More importantly, so had newspaper managements, several of whom had a grievance against Newton, a one-time editor of the *Financial Review,* which was published by the *Sydney Morning Herald* Group, and the first editor of the *Australian,* published by the Murdoch group. But if Newton could be "got at" and successfully intimidated in this manner, so could the employees of any newspaper group. Under instructions from the Attorney-General, Nigel Bowen, QC, Commonwealth Police searched not only Newton's business premises but his home. The police ransacked cupboards containing Mrs Newton's clothes and the Newton children's toys. In the past other organisations had had their offices searched. But this was different. It was a man's home. Some major justification was needed for the government to invade in such an arbitrary fashion the privacy of a man's home, and the government had no such justification.

Where Newton formerly had numerous enemies in the Federal Parliamentary Press Gallery, who disapproved of his news-getting methods, the desire of journalists to maintain the principle that Gorton had enunciated in a speech to the fourth summer school of Professional Journalism on February 2, 1968, brought Newton support. In his speech to the summer school, Gorton said, "I believe the governments ought never to seek to suppress news or information, whether those governments feel it is for the moment to their advantage to do it or not to their advantage to do it." Both the President of the Canberra District of the AJA, Mr Gordon Burgoyne, and the President of the Federal Parliamentary Press Gallery, Mr Jonathan Gaul, drew attention to this enunciation of principle by Gorton in letters to Gorton, authorised by their respective organisations. Burgoyne's letter, dated May 26, 1969, three days after police had searched Newton's home and premises, stated, "The District expresses its deep disquiet that on a matter of demonstrably minor significance the government was prepared to breach the principle that a citizen's home is invaded only in extreme circumstances and when the interests of the state and the community are vitally involved. The (Canberra AJA) committee has been shown a copy of one of a number of documents seized by the Commonwealth police, which does not deal with Commonwealth administration, but is purely political. Seizure of such a document, in its view, constitutes an attack on every citizen's right to comment freely and with impunity from the law on political events."

Gorton's reply to Burgoyne's AJA letter was singularly unconvincing. Dated June 5, 1969, it made no reference to the AJA's claim that among the documents seized was at least one that was purely political. It merely expressed thanks for "your letter of May 26 expressing your Association's alarm at the action taken by the government to attempt to discover which public servant had broken the law by providing Mr Newton with a classified cable from one of our ambassadors," and drew the AJA's attention to a prime ministerial statement made in the House of Representatives on Tuesday, May 27, 1969. In this statement, Gorton said, ". . . There has been some suggestion that other pressmen need fear this kind of action and that in some way this action was taken to stifle criticism . . . this organisation (Newton's) has been involved in criticism of one kind or another over a long period of years . . . no action has ever been taken. I would not expect that it would be taken against that or any other press organisation. But when that information could only get to them with some breach of the Crimes Act, it is a matter that requires investigation. No pressman who follows only legitimate methods of obtaining information need fear any action."[47]

In a press conference at Bendigo on June 3, 1969, Gorton defended the government's action by saying that the issue of search warrants under the Crimes' Act was not new. "For example," he said, "this was done by Dr Evatt (Attorney-General in wartime and immediate postwar ALP governments) when he sent people into the home of a man called Rupert Henderson to discover documents and discovered them and sentenced the person concerned to gaol." Either Gorton had a lapse of memory or had a mental aberration. From London, Mr Rupert Henderson, who had been general manager of the *Sydney Morning Herald* while Evatt was a Minister, denied that his home had ever been searched. It was possible that at some time papers in his care had been asked for. But he was unaware of the facts stated by Mr Gorton and believed there had been some confusion.[48]

The *Australian,* normally not sympathetic to Newton, stated in an editorial on May 29, 1969, "The operation of the Crimes Act, according to explanations given to Parliament this week, means that no aspect of Federal government activity may be communicated to the public unless the government approves . . . The Attorney-General, Mr Bowen, appears to sum up the government's attitude in two sentences, 'In the public service, which runs the nation's affairs, to pass out information is a breach of the Crimes Act. This is so whether the information is classified or unclassified —it does not depend on classification' . . . If these all-embracing implications are not to be read into the government statements this week, several possibilities emerge. The government may have been previously unaware of the dragnet effect of the Crimes Act (though it cannot claim now to be still unaware of it). It may have established somewhere its own set of rules to define 'acceptable' as against 'actionable' public revelation. Or else it has a useful law to allow it to wield extraordinary powers whenever it has a mind to do so (as in the case, it would seem, of Mr Maxwell Newton)."

But even worse was to follow. Under search warrant, Newton's bank accounts were examined. The government was allegedly looking for information that would enable them to trace and stop "leaks" of information to Newton and his organisation from public servants. How a payment by Newton to journalists working openly as journalists could have anything to do with public service "leaks" is beyond my comprehension. But records of payments by Newton to journalists were taken. It is a well-known practice in the newspaper industry for journalists to do "foreign orders." They do work in their own time and outside their normal working hours for publications which do not compete with the publications which employ them, and are paid for such work. Some organisations accept the right of the journalists they employ to do such work, provided it does not compete in any way with the journals produced by the organisation that employs the journalist. Other organisations do not like their employees engaging in "outside" work, even if it is a noncompetitive area as far as their publications are concerned. Details revealed during the search of Newton's bank accounts of cheques paid by Newton to Canberra journalists were given, quite improperly, to some people in very high places. Attempts were then made to "lean on" the journalists who had done these "foreign orders" for the Newton organisation. Those journalists whose organisations were indifferent as to whether or not they did "foreign orders", provided they did the work for which they were formally paid efficiently and well, just laughed. Those whose jobs might have been in peril if their employers were informed of their "outside" activities were frightened. It was a crude, ungentle form of blackmail that journalists, even those who did not do "foreign orders" resented, particularly as the information had been secured in a manner which left any citizen who came into conflict with the power of government virtually defenceless.

Newton, for once, appeared worried, as well he might be. Sections under the Crimes Act which had application to his case carried penalties of up to seven years imprisonment. But Newton fought back. He took the Commonwealth to court, challenging the validity of the warrants under which the documents had been seized. Mr Justice R. W. Fox in the ACT Supreme Court quashed the warrants under which the searches were made on the grounds that they were invalid, and, later on September 8, 1969, ordered the return to Newton of exhibits, documents, and other things seized in Commonwealth police searches on May 23, 1969, and June 5, 1969.[49]

In an exchange with Mr R. J. Ellicott, QC, the Solicitor-General, who appeared on behalf of the police, the nominal defendants, Mr Justice Fox, a judge of impeccable politeness and infinite patience, made two interesting observations on June 24, 1969. Ellicott had said, "Public policy is a very important matter in these days of increasing crime." Said the learned judge: "Of course there are very great questions when you come to public policy. The attitude of the courts in the past undoubtedly has been that if there is to be an intrusion of this nature it should be clearly authorised by the legislature and the procedure indicated by the legislature should be followed. The courts exist of course to protect the citizen— I suppose this is their prime function—against excesses and wrongful acts by the Executive . . . If Executive discretion is to be substituted for law, Parliament must say so in clear terms."[50]

Playing in a tough game against tough opponents, Newton also played the game toughly. His enemies had the power; he had his native wit. Miss Willesee by that stage had been working for him for some time. She made a second statutory declaration, duly witnessed by a Commissioner for Affidavits, on June 2, 1969. Unlike her previous affidavit which had a detached quality, the second statutory declaration had an emotive element, which may in part have been due to Miss Willesee's gratitude to Newton in giving her a job when she had lost her job with AUP and was not securing a response from other prospective employers, nervous of her period of national prominence. The first two paragraphs in the second statutory declaration read, "I, Geraldine Margaret Willesee, of 197 Adelaide Terrace, do solemnly and sincerely declare:

"In view of what I consider unwarranted, damaging, unfair and unjust attacks on my employer, Mr Maxwell Newton, by the Prime Minister, Mr John Gorton, through the undemocratic Crimes Act, I feel it has become necessary to enlighten the public and the press on certain aspects of our Prime Minister's character."

Newton played it shrewdly. The reference to the necessity to "enlighten the public and the press" suggested that, with Miss Willesee's approval, he intended to use the statutory declaration. But apparently he planned to use it only as a last resort and if the government jammed him inescapably in a corner. After his earlier experiences with the Commonwealth police, he probably did not keep the statutory declaration on his premises or in his house. He put it somewhere safe, and then allowed the story to "leak" that he held it and if pushed to the point of desperation would use it.

His ploy paid off. The fact that he held the document scared the hell out of a lot of people in the government. I know of at least one prominent Liberal MHR who intervened on Newton's behalf and warned the government that the government's very existence would be at stake if the government persisted in persecuting Newton, forced him into a corner, and brought about publication of the statutory declaration. From then on the pressure on Newton started to ease perceptibly. Ministers did not love him any more than they had. The setback of the Fox judgment made them reluctant to get involved in another, similar imbroglio. But knowledge of the existence of the statutory declaration also had its effect. Ministers did not know what it contained; they were fearful of what it might contain.

A copy of the declaration came into my possession.[51] Part of it was merely an extension of things that Miss Willesee had spoken of in her earlier statutory declaration. For example, a section of the declaration read, "On the night of November 1, 1968, I was taken home, after being taken for social drinks between 1 am and 3 am at the American Embassy in Canberra by the Prime Minister. Although what I have stated in my previous statutory declaration —that the Prime Minister offered me a lift home—is true, what his suggestion actually was, was that we leave the press gallery dinner to attend the Red and White Ball[52] which was on the same night. In conversation with Mr Gorton he said, 'I have been invited to the Red and White Ball. Would you come with me? There'll probably be gossip, but who gives a damn what they think. It'll probably be a good ball. Do you want to come?' It is now common knowledge that Mr Tony Eggleton talked him out of going to the ball and common knowledge that Mr Gorton then invited me for drinks with him at the American Embassy." The remainder of the statutory declaration is more controversial. It purports to detail part of what Miss Willesee described in her March 21 statutory declaration as "private conversations." Newton did not produce the statutory declaration prior to the 1969 general elections which was the threat he held over the government's head. He had no reason to. The government was leaving him alone.

In itself, the US Embassy incident was comparatively unimportant, though Gorton's handling of it and his carelessness over the times did nothing to improve his reputation for precision. The searching of Newton's premises and home was more important because it revealed the government's sensitivity to criticism and the fact that it was prepared to use a Draconic law, like the Crimes' Act, in pursuit of a vendetta and over a comparatively minor "leakage" of information. But, more importantly, from the elec-

Commonwealth police search the premises of publisher Maxwell Newton, after confidential government documents had appeared in Newton publications. Newton, in pullover, watches what the police are doing. The man behind Newton is Mr Peter Kelly, then working for Newton but formerly McMahon's press secretary.

From left to right — Sir James Plimsoll, then permanent head of the External Affairs Department, Hasluck, then Minister for External Affairs, Fairhall, then Minister for Defence, and Sir Henry Bland, then permanent head of the Defence Department, at

toral viewpoint, both incidents directed public attention to the movement that was taking place at the top of the government pile on leadership, defence, foreign investment, and a variety of other matters, including Commonwealth-State relationships. Once that movement became a subject of public interest, the other factors that would help normally to keep a government in power—full employment, affluence, generally good economic conditions apart from the declining rural industries, and a relatively ineffective opposition—ceased to operate to the extent that they would otherwise have done.

To add to the troubles of which the Gorton government was still sublimely unaware, its ALP opposition started to take on for the first time for years the semblance of an alternative government.

NOTES

1 This is Gorton's own version—Commonwealth Representatives' Debates, Vol 62, p 792, March 20, 1969.

2 Gorton said Miss Willesee asked him for a lift. Miss Willesee said Gorton offered her the lift.

3 My own experience suggests the difficulty in recalling times accurately months later. I drove the head of the *Daily Telegraph* Canberra Press Bureau, Mr Bob Baudino, home from the dinner. I had not had a drink and Baudino was cold sober. I thought I got home about 11 pm; Baudino said that he got home about midnight. My wife confirmed that Baudino's time was correct; Mrs Baudino thought my time was correct.

4 Gaul later went to work for Max Newton.

5 I would have preferred to have seen AUP take the view taken later by Miss Willesee's father, Senator Willesee. Willesee commented that he would expect any young reporter worth his or her salt to be glad to have access to the Prime Minister, repository of innumerable stories.

6 When Mr Cyril Wyndham, former ALP Federal Secretary, ran into trouble with the ALP and seemed "on the outer" with everyone, Newton gave Wyndham a job in his organisation.

7 I have a note dated "Thursday, November 28, 1968" which gives the departure time at 3 am. I have always been puzzled why, if Gorton was unsure of his times, as he stated later he was, he did not consult with Eggleton, his driver, Coppin, his security guard, or the guard at the Lodge gates *BEFORE* he committed himself in the Parliament to times which later proved incorrect.

8 Freeth, then Minister for Air, and like St John, a Liberal, said of St John on October 10, 1968, "From this honorable gentleman (St John) emanates an odor of sanctity in this House which is quite nauseating"—Commonwealth Representatives' Debates, Vol 60, p 1828.

9 While admittedly written at a time of great stress, St John's book, *A Time to Speak*, Sun Books, Melbourne, 1969, is a pointer to how urgent was his need for approbation.

10 Official letter dated August 27, 1964, from Robertson to Admiral W. H. Harrington, Chief of the Naval Staff—quoted in *One Minute of Time* by Vice-Admiral Harold Hickling, Sun Books Pty. Limited, Melbourne, p 199.

11 *John Grey Gorton* by Alan Trengrove, Cassell, Australia, 1969, p 227.

12 Though I appreciated the Parliamentary effect achieved by St John's maiden speech, the speech did not impress me as a piece of logic or analysis. I thought that for a lawyer, St John too readily accepted allegations as established facts. But my view was that of a very small minority.

13 Commonwealth Representatives' Debates, Vol 55, p 2309, May 18, 1967.

14 Commonwealth Representatives' Debates, Vol 58, p 32, March 13, 1968.

15 *Ibid.*, p 33.

16 *A Time to Speak* by Edward St John, Sun Books, 1969, p 174.

17 It must have been one of my off-days. I missed the implication in St John's "face to face" remark. Only much later did I realise that St John indirectly and probably unintentionally was telling me of his confrontation with Gorton, later revealed as having taken place on February 20, 1969.

18 In Australian political argot to "turn a bucket" means to attack someone on personal grounds, usually of a slightly scandalous nature.

19 The rather involved suggestion in this was that under Gorton, Australia was a less valuable ally to the US than under Menzies and Holt. The US Administration, working through CIA, wanted to destroy Gorton, but not the Liberal-Country Party Administration. I remember thinking at the time that if there were anything in this it would make the CIA one of the clumsiest, bumblefooted organizations ever established by any government.

20 In her statutory declaration of March 21, 1969, Miss Willesee revealed that Gorton phoned her father, Senator Willesee, and said he (Gorton) had information that a story about himself was to be published in *Private Eye*.

21 *Daily Telegraph*, Sydney, March 21, 1969.

22 *Ibid.*

23 After Parkes disappeared in the 1968 electoral redistribution, Hughes won pre-selection for the strong Liberal Sydney seat of Berowra.

24 Commonwealth Representatives' Debates, Vol 62, p 697, March 19, 1969.

25 *The Power Struggle.*

26 Hughes had been a friend of mine long before he entered politics. He had appeared professionally on my behalf in several cases. He had advised me on some documents which I had proposed to use in *The Power Struggle*; documents which did not involve Gorton in any way. He also advised me on some legal aspects of *The Power Struggle*. To the best of my recollection, he was the only individual outside myself and a typist who read *The Power Struggle* before it was sent to the publishers. As he said, "neither the transcript nor the printed book contained anything that reflected personally on Gorton."

27 Commonwealth Representatives' Debates, Vol 62, p 696, March 19, 1969.

28 *Ibid.*

29 After the 1969 elections, Hughes became Attorney-General and Killen, Minister for the Navy. Arthur, who lost his seat, was appointed to Gorton's staff, as a research officer.

30 Commonwealth Representatives' Debates, Vol 62, p 742, March 20, 1969.

31 *A Time to Speak* by Edward St John, Sun Books, 1969.

32 Commonwealth Representatives' Debates, Vol 62, p 792, March 20, 1969.

[33] *Ibid.*

[34] *Ibid.,* p 826, March 25, 1969.

[35] Transcript of St John's press conference, March 21, 1969.

[36] St John seems at this stage to have formed the belief that I was trying to sabotage his press conferences by pointing up the weaknesses in his position. One question colleagues said he objected to was "Taking 1 am as a yardstick, why in your view is everyone who says the PM left the Press Gallery dinner earlier than that a sycophant or a liar and why is everyone who fixes the PM's departure time later than 1 am a man of integrity and truth?" I was not trying to sabotage. I was merely trying to work out how his thinking operated.

[37] A Gallup Poll in February, 1969, showed 74 percent of Liberal-CP voters approving of Gorton as a Prime Minister—*Herald,* Melbourne, May 20, 1969.

[38] The Gorton government then appointed Chaney Administrator of the Northern Territory.

[39] Chaney was understating the Liberals' numbers in the House of Representatives, then 61.

[40] Derided by government supporters when criticising Gorton's US Embassy visit, St John had said, "Honorable members may laugh as much as they please; they are mere sycophants"—Commonwealth Representatives' Debates, Vol 62, p 793, March 20, 1969.

[41] Carrick was elected to the Parliament in November, 1970, as a NSW Senator.

[42] No outsiders are admitted to the meetings of any of the major Australian parliamentary parties. Pressmen fit pieces together, like assembling a jigsaw puzzle to get a picture of what goes on in the secrecy of the party rooms. For the above account I have drawn heavily upon notes I made at the time.

[43] *Daily Telegraph,* Sydney, March 29, 1969.

[44] Article by Jonathan Gaul, *Canberra Times,* March 29, 1969.

[45] *Herald,* Melbourne, October 14, 1969.

[46] Apparently it was a night for highly quotable "Famous Last Words"—see this chapter, p 213.

[47] Commonwealth Representatives' Debates, May 27, 1969, Vol 63, p 2237.

[48] *Sydney Morning Herald,* June 4, 1969.

[49] *Sydney Morning Herald,* September 9, 1969.

[50] From notes taken during the hearing, Mr C. D. Pearce, Senior Lecturer in Law, Australian National University, described the Fox judgment in Newton's favour as "a welcome stand against excess of police power and interference with the liberty of the individual. It is to be hoped the decision will act as a constant reminder to other judges of the role they must play if we are to sustain our claim of being a free society."—*Australian Law Journal,* October 30, 1970, Vol 44, p 482.

[51] Because of professional considerations, I am debarred from saying how the copy came into my possession.

[52] A social authority assured me that a prominent charity held a Ball on November 1 at a hotel near the one where the Press Gallery had its dinner.

CHAPTER 11

BY-ELECTIONS are not good election barometers in Australia. Since the six states federated in 1901 to form the Commonwealth of Australia, and up to 1970, only once and then in quite extraordinary circumstances had a Federal government, whatever its political complexion, won a seat from its opposition in a by-election poll. This was in 1920 when quite unjustly ALP MHR, Hugh Mahon, was expelled from the House of Representatives for attacking British rule in Ireland. Assailed as a traitor, not to his own country, Australia, but to Britain, Mahon was defeated at a by-election contested on December 18, 1920. With this solitary exception, historical precedents suggest that governments can usually expect their votes in by-elections to be down. But when their votes are down, governments still panic.

With St John making his well-publicised attacks upon Gorton and his conduct of national affairs throughout March, 1969, a by-election was held on April 19, 1969, to fill the seat of Curtin in Western Australia vacated by Hasluck when he became Governor-General. The St John criticisms probably added to the anti-government bias always perceptible in Australian by-election polls. Curtin was mainly middle class, staid, conformist, and a Liberal stronghold. In 1955, the ALP had not bothered to oppose Hasluck. In 1958, Hasluck's absolute majority over his ALP and DLP opponents was 10,589. In 1961, when the Liberals were at their post-1949 nadir and Calwell came within two seats of toppling Menzies, Hasluck had a 10,355 advantage over the combined ALP-DLP vote. In 1963, Hasluck's absolute majority was 19,782, and in 1966 7,984. Mr Ramsey Victor Garland, an accountant, was the Liberals' replacement for Hasluck. If he had held Hasluck's vote, it would have been a miracle. Hasluck was a veteran, known, respected, and admired. Garland was young and a newcomer. When the vote was counted, Garland had a 350 vote margin over his ALP and DLP rivals. Two things about the vote were interesting. Though voting was compulsory and those failing to do their electoral duty were liable to a fine, the voters stayed away from the polling booths in droves. Only 80.80 percent of those enrolled cast votes. The ALP did not improve its vote, which was down by more than a thousand compared with 1966. The DLP, which tended to be identified with puritanism,[1] nearly doubled its votes. It had apparently picked up most of the defecting Liberals. The explanation for the vote going to the DLP rather than the ALP may have been that a percentage of Curtin's Liberals wanted to register disapproval of Gorton and his government without voting for the ALP. The DLP may have been more attractive to estranged Liberal voters than the ALP because DLP defence and foreign policies, broadly, coincided with those of the antiGorton section of the Liberal Parliamentary Party. The dispute within the ALP, then being conducted with an even more than usual degree of picturesque intensity, may have also contributed to the vote going to the DLP rather than the ALP.

But on June 7, 1969, Liberal Party strategists decided with relief that the St John criticisms were losing their effectiveness and electoral hostility to the Gorton government declining. On that day another by-election poll was conducted, this time in Bendigo, Victoria, to fill a vacancy caused by the retirement from the House of Representatives, officially for health reasons, of Mr Noel Beaton, an ALP MHR. A tall, slender ex-athlete, with an exquisite wit—Beaton was the first to describe the F111 as "a flying opera house"[2]—Beaton was the ALP's spokesman on rural matters. He had had his difficulties with the leftwing Victorian ALP Executive. While the Victorian ALP Executive could mostly, though not always,[3] count upon safe ALP constituencies returning their nominees, the position was different in rural seats, such as Bendigo. In such seats, the ALP candidates to win had at least to appear to be moderate rather than leftwing. Beaton was a moderate. He was also suspected by the Victorian ALP Executive of being a supporter of Whitlam, whom the Victorian Executive hated and with whom it had been conducting a running battle for years. Beaton was both conscientious and a worrier. Brushes with the Victorian ALP Executive, occasioned by his support in caucus votes for Whitlam, undoubtedly contributed to the deterioration in his health, which improved and continued to improve from the time he quit his parliamentary post. Beaton had won at the 1966 elections with a 1,489 majority over his Liberal and DLP opponents. Andrew David Kennedy was selected by the ALP as its banner bearer when Beaton retired. On this occasion, 93.58 percent of those enrolled voted. The ALP's vote was down by over 3,000; the Liberals by less than 1,000. The DLP vote was virtually static, and Kennedy won by only 670 after preferences had been distributed. On the same day, June 7, 1969, a by-election was held in Gwydir, NSW, to replace CP MHR, Ian Allan, an

245

elongated six feet five inches tall, onetime broadcaster, who had resigned to take a post with the War Graves' Commission. The CP's replacement was Ralph Hunt, then a 41-years-old cherubic faced grazier-farmer, chairman of the NSW Country Party since 1964, and one of the CP's most promising younger men. Allan had won by 9,289 votes in 1966. Hunt held the seat for the CP by 2,820 votes. But Gwydir was a seat in which votes were influenced by what was happening about wheat, already a problem as extensive harvests elsewhere in the world resulted in contracting markets for Australia, and wool, for which prices were eroding threateningly. Additionally Hunt had been opposed by Roger Nott, a formidable local candidate who had been a successful and respected Minister for Agriculture in a NSW State ALP government. The government attributed the reduced government vote in Gwydir to local factors, and Nott's candidature. After Bendigo, the Liberals, understandably, formed the conclusion that the political tide was again flowing in their favor. The ALP despondently thought the same.

Apparently believing that they had little to lose and no chance of winning government in 1969, ALP chieftains intensified their feuds. While personalities were important, underlying their incestuous violence were ideological considerations. There was disagreement on practically everything, except social services, which, with the traditional adherence to the name "ALP" which had an almost mystic quality in ALP eyes, provided the hard cement holding together the shaky ALP structure. There was disagreement over Australia's involvement in the Vietnam conflict. The former ALP leader, Arthur Calwell, Cairns, the ex-policeman turned academic and politician, Clyde Cameron, onetime shearer and union secretary and a mischief maker of great talent, Tom Uren, a former boxer and peace movement advocate and Gordon Bryant, radical in the ALP tradition, but possessed, unlike so many of his contemporaries who observed double standards, of a single set of values, wanted all Australian forces withdrawn from that war torn country. So also did the Victorian ALP machine under its antiAmerican leftwing leadership, the Queensland ALP machine, dominated by the Queensland Trades Hall where various Communist groups, by then dividing into proMoscow, proPeking and Italian line groupings, had influence, and Western Australia, under the guidance of onetime ALP Federal "strong man", F. E. ("Joe") Chamberlain, the WA ALP secretary. Supported by the majority of the ALP Federal Parliamentary Party who after twenty years of opposition wanted to quit the frustration of opposition and achieve government, by the NSW ALP machine, whose rightwing leaders

246

had not only the same ambition but a sympathy with the United States caught up almost inextricably in the Vietnam conflict because of the US desire, shared by these rightwing ALP elements, to halt the southward advance of Communism in Asia, and by Harradine and Harradine's followers in the Tasmanian ALP who held that the Victorian ALP was unhealthily under Communist influence, Whitlam would not commit himself to an unqualified declaration that a future ALP government would withdraw Australian troops from Vietnam and Southeast Asia. Liberal-CP governments had won previous elections on issues associated with the Vietnam involvement and foreign policy; he did not want to give the Gorton government the opportunity to repeat these successes. In the benevolently approving eyes of his ALP supporters a pragmatist who was realistically seeking federal power in the interests of the ALP and its thousands of loyal electoral supporters, in the eyes of his ALP opponents an unprincipled opportunist who would sacrifice the most time hallowed of ALP beliefs or anyone, friend or foe, to his craving not so much for power as for the prestigious status of the prime ministership, Whitlam equivocated, twisted, stalled, or evaded. But sometimes he was forced into a position where he had to give answers, and, when he did, his ALP opponents did not like the tone of these answers, and their hostility deepened.[4]

"The only way (Australian) troops can come back now is if there is a settlement, if there is an armistice" Whitlam told a TV interviewer. To the specific question "Mr Whitlam, would you withdraw Australian troops from Vietnam now?" Whitlam in the same interview had said "No",[5] making this one of the rare occasions when he was direct.

Whitlam was equivocal also on Malaysia and Singapore. Calwell and Cairns were firm on removing all Australian armed forces from Southeast Asia. But Whitlam said that while a future ALP government would remove ground forces from the Malaysia-Singapore region it would be prepared to keep RAAF squadrons in the area. "I think air forces, naval forces, army advisers and so on are in a different category to Australian soldiers who were never integrated with the Malaysian forces and who have only been there as part of British forces," Whitlam told a press conference on January 29, 1969, on his return from an overseas tour. Said Whitlam "They (the Malaysians and Singaporeans) are used to having Australian troops there. I think there is a feeling in Malaysia: 'It is bad enough the British leaving in breach of arrangements; we don't want to lose the Australian ones as well'."[6] Though later, Whitlam was to accept the Calwell-Cairns-Chamberlain-Victorian ALP view, which was backed in some

247

respects even by so loyal a Whitlam supporter as Whitlam's deputy leader, Lance Barnard, and to come out firmly against both the Vietnam involvement and the stationing of any Australian forces in Malaysia and Singapore, the fact that the ALP was talking with two voices at the one time did not enhance the ALP's electoral standing.

The disagreements on Vietnam and foreign policy, at the hard core of which were diverging viewpoints on how the ALP should view Communism in a world context, spilled over in the domestic arena. Calwell, Cairns, Uren and Bryant supported mass demonstrations of protest against the Vietnam involvement, as did the Victorian and WA ALP, unreservedly, and the Queensland ALP, more cautiously. Whitlam, backed by the NSW ALP, wanted all demonstrations to be under ALP control and argued that in a parliamentary democracy like Australia, foreign policy must and should be decided in the parliament and by the duly elected government of the day, and not in the streets, however impressively the streets were packed with resentful dissentients who could only prove themselves to be a majority if they voted at the polls and by due constitutional process for the ALP to take over the government of Australia. As early as 1967, when demonstrations were planned against the visit to Australia of Air Vice-Marshal Ky, of South Vietnam, Whitlam had fled, unheralded and unsung, to the sanctuary of the Barrier Reef, remote and beautiful and insulated by distance from the political turmoil of Sydney, Melbourne, and Canberra. Whitlam had left Calwell and Cairns, both good demagogues, Calwell in the rousing fashion of a by-gone age and Cairns, quieter, in the modern style demanded by the broadcasting microphone and amplifier systems, to function as the ALP's spokesmen. On numerous occasions thereafter, Whitlam displayed his ability to fade discreetly into the background while demonstrations not purely ALP controlled were either contemplated or under way. This habit did not endear him or his policies to the ALP's leftwing.

The provision of state aid for private schools, though seemingly divorced from the main ideological struggles, had become an integral part of them, and a disruptive, controversial issue that constantly produced passionate dissension within the ALP. The DLP and the Irish-Catholic element, which still adhered loyally to the ALP, supported state aid for private schools, from which the main beneficiaries would be the Roman Catholic church which alone among the denominations sought to operate a fullscale school system alongside the more massive state school system. In some states, the Roman Catholic school system educated up to and sometimes over twenty percent of the state's children. Those within the ALP opposing state aid for private schools included individuals who held that religious segregation of children and adolescents in schools was not in the community's best interests and Protestants who could see the Roman Catholic Church, with its more numerous schools, getting from state aid an advantage superior to that of other denominations.[7] The major opponents of state aid within the ALP were Chamberlain, the dominating ALP figure in Western Australia, the Victorian ALP, whose secretary, Mr W. Hartley was chairman of the ALP's Federal Education Committee, and the South Australian ALP, headed by MHRs, Clyde Cameron and Martin Nicholls.

Whitlam and the NSW ALP supported state aid for denominational schools. The ALP's leftwing contended that as far as Whitlam was concerned this support was the product of opportunism, not conviction. Though predominantly Protestant in its leadership and originally implacably anti-state aid, the Menzies government had been converted to the principle and had given aid to private schools from taxpayers' funds in ever enlarging amounts as its dependence upon DLP electoral support intensified in the 1960s. This had two effects. It enabled the DLP to direct the second preference votes of its followers with even greater authority to Liberal-CP parliamentary candidates. It also persuaded the Irish-Australian element, socially more mobile in a community of increasing affluence and ceasing to be so markedly a lesser privileged proletariat, to regard the Liberal-CP coalition more favorably. The ALP leftwing argued that Whitlam was not so much interested in bettering the position of the poorer Roman Catholic schools, as in winning back some of the votes lost to the Liberals and to the DLP on the state aid issue.

Few, if any, holds are barred in an ALP brawl. "After much consideration, I think it best that I should not write a special article for *The Western Sun*[8] on that awful splurge which appeared in the *The West Australian* in December depicting Whitlam as the leader of the 'goodies' and you and I as the leaders of the 'baddies'," Calwell wrote to the WA ALP Secretary, "Joe" Chamberlain, in a letter which gives an indication of the vigor with which ALP feuds are conducted. "It is not possible to write an objective article without clashing with Whitlam's views and Whitlam's opinions, and, although I have no respect for him nor his opinions, it might not be a good thing from a party point of view to start an argument with him in a party journal at this stage. I think it best to wait until the Federal Executive has decided its attitude to the splendid resolution, unanimously adopted, by your executive on the question of demonstrations[9] because, after that, we should have the backing of the executive and he (Whitlam) will then have to fall into line . . . . Very few people in Canberra seem to think of anything other than holding their seats and securing the return of a Labor government at any price—and that means at the sacrifice of any, or even every principle. Democracy in Australia is in a very sick condition . . . . The West Australian and the Victorian executives are the two best executives in Australia . . . ."[10]

Even before Whitlam had succeeded Calwell in the ALP Federal Parliamentary leadership, in 1967, the Trade Union Defence Committee (TUDC) in Victoria had revealed its feelings very nakedly. The TUDC was a grouping originally of twenty-eight, later twenty-six Victorian unions, some of them Communist officered and controlled which dominated the Victorian ALP. For years spokesmen for the TUDC including one of its major leaders, Mr Percy Johnson, had denied that the TUDC, which had no official ALP status, was the major power within the Victorian ALP. But in September, 1970, after an exhaustive inquiry the ALP Federal Executive by ten votes to seven found that the TUDC had decided who would sit on the Victorian ALP Executive, the ALP's principal governing body in Victoria. The Federal ALP Executive declared "non-existent" the Victorian ALP branch on the grounds that "the TUDC has been permitted to dominate the Victorian branch and the Victorian executive . . . ."[11] But from the time Whitlam was contending for the leadership and up to and after the 1969 general elections, the TUDC was still in a position to make Whitlam's ALP life a misery and did so. "Will witless Whitlam win?" the TUDC asked in a typical headline in its publication *Scope*,[12] when discussing Calwell's possible successor as ALP Federal Leader. "Next month should decide whether Mr G. Whitlam, who publicly called the top Executive of his own party 'the witless twelve' will become leader of the Federal Parliamentary Party," stated the *Scope* article. "If the candidate who the anti-Labor dailies so obviously want as Federal leader of the Labor Party is elected, can he expect to continue receiving previous helpful boosts . . . so far as at least one candidate for leadership is concerned, on this occasion the depth of party division is unprecedented."[12]

In another rather typical ALP document, this time anonymous, Whitlam was accused of having attended a "secret meeting" in Victoria. "On the night of April 25, 1968, Mr Gough Whitlam made a special visit to Melbourne," the document read. "It was to attend a secret meeting of a sinister group whose real aim is to capture, by any means, control of the Victorian Central Executive. This group has been discredited by the rank and file representatives at successive annual conferences. Our informants tell us that the meeting was held at the home of one of the group—Mr John Button, a solicitor of 1 Oak street, Hawthorn; that there were about eight there, including Mr Dick McGarvie, Queen's Counsel, and a Mr Barney Williams of the Bank Officers Association. Gough Whitlam was there . . . . Of interest to those with long memories is the fact that (Senator) Pat Kennelly was there. Of course many loyal Labor Party members would not be aware that this secret organisation has a long term aim—a *rapprochement* with the DLP after they get control of the local executive. Remember Kennelly's statement not so long ago favoring a deal with the DLP, a front for Santamaria's Civic Council? Is this why Harradine, of Tasmania, is defended?"[13]

But ideological considerations were also crisscrossed by a bizarre series of hates during 1969 which complicated even further the ALP's already desperately complicated situation. Calwell hated Whitlam and lost no opportunity to humiliate and belittle him. Originally, Calwell had supported Cairns as a desirable replacement for Whitlam in the leadership. But after Cairns had first announced that he would retire from the Parliament if he did not receive the ALP preselection for the Melbourne electorate which he was contesting against Calwell because his own seat of Yarra had disappeared in an electoral distribution and then, after defeat, had tamely accepted ALP preselection for the less acceptable seat of Lalor, Calwell acquired from this incident a mild contempt for Cairns, who gave the impression that he had retired, hurt, into his parliamentary shell as a result of his defeat. Calwell's view was that Cairns lacked "toughness". An ALP oldtimer whose opponents had frequently had him down on the floor with his face kicked in, Calwell had respect for the ALP tradition that next day the loser should be back on his feet, fighting. Calwell also had a dislike for Cameron, whom he regarded as a troublemaker and who had attempted to secure ALP federal intervention in Victoria to take the ALP Melbourne preselection from Calwell, and hand it to Cairns.

Outwardly highly controlled, a man who deliberately tried to maintain an appearance of impassiveness, Cairns, who had allies but few intimates, maintained a cool detached courtesy in his dealings with Whitlam, who middleclass and conformist, envied Cairns' appeal to the ALP's leftwing and tried to insist that on some issues he was "to the left of Cairns". Though Whitlam on occasions seemed to repudiate Cairns and his views, particularly on Vietnam and on demonstrations, Cairns went on his way,

251

uncomplaining and seemingly unruffled. But at rare moments when he let down his guard, Cairns revealed that he had not revised his opinion expressed during the ALP leadership struggle which followed Harradine's exclusion from the ALP Federal Executive that Whitlam was "unstable . . . the last man to be given greater power". Clyde Cameron, sometimes pro-Cairns but always pro-Cameron, never allowed his tolerant and mildly amused personal regard for Whitlam to interfere with his ALP operations. Ruthless, dogged, highly intelligent, a man who enjoyed manipulating men and events, one of the few among the Federal ALP Parliamentarians with an understanding of the workings of the ALP machine with which he had been associated most of his adult life, Cameron had been conducting over twenty years an effective, demoralising vendetta against the rightwing controllers of the Australian Workers' Union, Australia's largest and wealthiest trade union, in which Cameron had been a prominent official until elected to the Parliament in 1949.

Normally, as he was frenetically anti state-aid Cameron could have been expected to maintain indefinitely an alliance with the antiWhitlam Victorian ALP with whose leftwing views he was in sympathy and which was the spearhead of the anti-state aid campaign in the ALP. But in 1969 at a Sydney ALP Federal Executive meeting, the Victorian delegates, with William Hartley, the Victorian ALP Secretary as the main spokesman, refused to support Cameron against AWU leaders who had complained to the ALP Federal Executive about Cameron's attacks in the Parliament on AWU leaders, leaders who included the AWU NSW Secretary, C. T. ["Charley"] Oliver, then NSW ALP President and a NSW representative on the Federal Executive. Thereafter, it was war to the death, and Hartley and Cameron drifted apart, until in 1970, with the 1969 elections disposed of, Cameron became the floor leader of moves within the ALP Federal Executive which led to the dissolution of the Victorian ALP branch, a Federal takeover of Victorian ALP affairs, and a consequent ejection of Hartley from his positions of power within the Victorian ALP.[14]

Other enmities within the Federal Parliamentary Party and the ALP political machine followed the same confusing and bizarre pattern. Though a New South Welshman, Senator Lionel Murphy, QC, the ALP leader in the Senate, was allied with the Victorian ALP and, consistently opposing Whitlam on the Federal Parliamentary Executive and in the ALP Federal caucus, was suspected of nursing the ambition to emulate Gorton by stepping down from the Senate to take over from Whitlam ALP leadership, and the possibility of one day being prime minister. Murphy had a close

252

association with Gorton, formed when Gorton led the government in the Senate and Murphy was Gorton's opposite number leading the ALP in that august chamber. Divisions within the ALP parliamentary leadership kept emerging constantly. While not supporting the personal aspects of St John's attack upon Gorton, Whitlam had nevertheless been studiously neutral and not defended Gorton's behaviour while being critical of such Gorton actions as came within the context of Gorton's prime ministerial office. Murphy sprang to Gorton's defence. In the Senate on March 20, 1969, the morning after his ALP colleague, James, had raised the question of the Frank Browne allegations in the House of Representatives, Murphy purported to ask a question of the Government Senate Leader, Senator Ken Anderson. It was not a question but a statement.

Said Murphy "Will the leader of the government inform the Prime Minister that as leader of the Opposition in the Senate I wish to make it known that I believe that these allegations are completely and utterly untrue and I accept without reservation the Prime Minister's statement that his conduct has been entirely proper? If I may have the indulgence of the Senate, I would like to say that it is a fact of political life that everyone who holds a high political office, such as the prime ministership, is surrounded by rumours and gossip, sometimes of the most extraordinary nature, which tend to excite public imagination . . . . Will the leader of the government accept that while the Opposition may differ with the Prime Minister on public affairs it does not seek to displace him or to injure him on the basis of matters which, even if they are true, have no relationship to his public office?"[15] Gorton appreciated Murphy's support. But it was a direct slap at Whitlam, and Whitlam's attitude. But for the intervention of Calwell, there would have been an open rift at a caucus meeting on April 16, 1969, when the feeling over what was viewed as Murphy's constant undermining of Whitlam's authority manifested itself heatedly. Kennelly, a Whitlam supporter, criticised Murphy for going into the Senate and upholding Gorton against the attacks by St John while Whitlam was simultaneously upbraiding Gorton in the House of Representatives. "Let us speak with one voice at least in election year," Kennelly said.[16] Calwell, unusually benevolent, intervened to smooth things down.

Others besides Murphy did not trouble to disguise their antagonism to Whitlam and what they considered his "namby pamby" attitudes. The ALP was deeply divided over the planned establishment of a joint Australian-United States satellite base at Woomera in remote Central Australia. The base had been established in an atmosphere of secrecy. At a press conference on April 23, 1969, Fairhall, in his capacity of Defence Minister, had said "The functioning of the station will make a contribution to free world defence, but I wish you would not ask me how."[17] The ALP suspected that it was part of a prewarning system for rockets from Asia fired against the United States across the South Pole area, and was one in a series of US-Australian arrangements that was fitting Australia into the US atomic defence system, thereby making key installations in Australia targets in the event of an atomic war.[18] Whitlam was prepared to criticise the government's secrecy, but not its decision to agree to the establishment of the base within Australian territory. Sydney MHR, Fred Daly, who never bothered to conceal his dislike for Whitlam protested in a meeting of the Federal ALP Parliamentary caucus that the base was contrary to ALP policy which laid down that the southern hemisphere should be a nuclear free zone. Daly wanted the government attacked not only for its secrecy over the base but for agreeing to the establishment of the base and an announcement made that a future Federal ALP government would renounce any agreement entered into by the Gorton government for the setting up of atomic bases in Australia. A compromise was agreed to. If the government's attitude on secrecy was unsatisfactory, the ALP would decide whether to adopt a stance of complete hostility to the establishment of the base.[19] But then Whitlam decided to play "clever fellows". When the debate took place on April 29, 1969, he made an agreement with Erwin, government leader in the House of Representatives, for an unusual arrangement. After each side, Government and Opposition, had put up four speakers, there would thereafter be two government speakers to each opposition speaker and the debate would finish at 9.30 pm. This was to cut Daly and Calwell out of the debate, so that they would not have the opportunity to point up publicly the deep divisions within the ALP.

Realising that the government was being advantaged by the debate, which was revealing ALP divisions, Erwin moved for the debate to be continued after 9.30 pm, the hour at which Erwin had earlier agreed with Whitlam to end the debate. Despite angry protests from his own followers, Whitlam objected. He wanted such a damaging debate ended quickly. When the vote was taken on whether or not the debate should be extended, Daly refused to line up with the ALP which had sullenly accepted Whitlam's insistence that ALP MHRs must vote for the ending of the debate. Daly walked out of the chamber of the House of Representatives, and refused to vote. Quickly grasping that the government was in danger of not securing the absolute majority of the House of Representatives—62—needed for a vote to suspend standing orders so that the debate could be continued, Whitlam himself also walked out of the chamber. To suit their mutual convenience, the Prime Minister and Whitlam, as Opposition Leader, had a permanent arrangement. When one was not present to vote, the other refrained from voting. Amid shouts of "You're breaking an agreement", Gorton walked into the chamber and voted despite Whitlam's disappearance. "All pairs off" said Gorton curtly.

Henceforward, relations between Gorton and Whitlam, not particularly cordial at any time, were never again the same. Whitlam later complained that in voting in the manner he had, Gorton had broken "a long-established practice." Whitlam served notice that he would vote in all future divisions whether or not Gorton was voting. Gorton re-entered the chamber as Whitlam was making his threat. "My lord has come," quipped ALP MHR, Edward Peters. Whitlam could not restrain his catty, Noel Coward type of wit. "It is better than lurching in as he last did on such an occasion," said Whitlam.[20]

But of greater consequence to Whitlam at this stage than any estrangement from Gorton was the continued hostility being shown to him from within his own party. One of his most acidulous critics was Senator John Wheeldon, from Western Australia, who had a close association with WA ALP Secretary "Joe" Chamberlain. Wheeldon shared with Chamberlain a contempt for Whitlam. Possessed of a biting, lacerating tongue, Wheeldon, short and slender, a solicitor, fearless, impatient, and exasperating, had dressed down Whitlam, six feet three inches and built proportionately, like a schoolboy at the 1966 Special Federal ALP conference in Canberra at which Whitlam was compelled to apologise for taking an anti-ALP Federal Executive stance on the issue of state aid for private schools and compelled to give an undertaking that he would now "work within the framework of the party and accept the decisions of its properly constituted authorities."[21] Wheeldon continued to treat Whitlam with the insulting superiority of a headmaster dealing with a delinquent schoolchild. "We have a truly impressive gift for taking attitudes that antagonise everyone," Wheeldon told Whitlam patronisingly during one of the numerous caucus arguments on state aid that took place during 1969.[22]

Fortunately for Whitlam, his opponents within the ALP Parliamentary Party while unitedly antiWhitlam differed among themselves on other issues. Calwell, Daly and their followers were against any relaxation in Australia's immigration policy which restricted the entry for permanent residence of people from Asian countries and those whose skin pigmentation differed from people of European extraction. They argued that the problem of racial tensions had not been solved elsewhere in the world and until it was solved elsewhere Australia should not import the problem of which it was free by the accident of history which resulted in Australia having been colonised principally from the British Isles and later from Europe. Cairns, Wheeldon, and their sympathisers believed that the Calwell-Daly attitude was based on racialism rather than pragmatism and wanted a relaxation of the barriers reared against nonEuropean immigration—one of the few things on which they saw eye-to-eye with a section of the DLP, their most obdurate enemies.

There were other differences that tended to divide the anti-Whitlam group, including differences on tariff policy, what should be the ALP attitude towards mass demonstrations,[23] and whether the Victorian ALP was of longterm value to, or an incubus on, the advancement of the ALP's leftwing. But it was outside the parliament and in the ALP political machine that Whitlam had his real troubles. There were incidents involving the ALP Federal Secretary, Cyril Wyndham, who, rather pathetically unaware that in Australian politics there were no friendships, only alliances, believed that Whitlam was a friend, Harradine, the Tasmanian antiCommunist who, having put his political neck on the chopping block in Whitlam's cause, was prepared to fight on in the mistaken belief that Whitlam would support him, and Hartley, the Victorian ALP Secretary who was also Chairman of the Federal ALP's education committee and was uninhibited about opposing Whitlam determinedly on state aid for private schools whatever the disastrous electoral consequences accruing to the ALP from a confrontation on that touchy issue in an election year.

An Englishman, short, slight, London bred, principled, Wyndham had been imported to Australia by Dr Evatt in 1957 as Evatt's press secretary. He was then 27-years-old. A former secretary to a onetime general secretary of the British Labor Party, Mr Morgan Phillips, Wyndham acquired an admiration for Chamberlain, who during the significant years of the ALP split which started in 1954/55, was Evatt's able and ruthless "hatchet man" in the internecine war against the ALP grouping that later coalesced into the DLP. Though only a modest performer on a public platform and thwarted in his parliamentary aspirations, Chamberlain, shrewd, patient, implacable, was one of the best committee and conference tacticians in the ALP. As a result of

Prime Minister Gorton gives McMahon a quizzical, tolerant smile and a handshake after Gorton has triumphed over McMahon and Fairbairn in the post-1969 elections leadership struggle.

Minister for Defence, Sir Allan Fairhall (left), who held different views from Gorton on defence and who did not re-contest the 1969 elections, and the Minister for External Affairs, Gordon Freeth, who lost his seat at these elections.

Gorton (left) watches as his former rival for the Prime Ministership Sir Paul Hasluck is sworn in as Governor-General. Mrs

Chamberlain's patronage, Wyndham was selected from a field of thirteen aspirants to become Victorian ALP Secretary in 1961. Raised in the British Labor Party tradition, Wyndham, unlike the normal ALP state secretary who was a power point in his own right, believed that he could function as a party bureaucrat, impersonally serving the executive which appointed him. In 1963 Wyndham became the ALP's first full-time federal secretary, filling a job that had been done previously only on a part-time basis.

Wyndham applied himself zealously to the task of reforming the ALP in a way that had the potential to appeal to Australian voters and to end what was then the ALP's fourteen years term in the frustrating wilderness of opposition. In the federal arena, the ALP fervently advocated "one vote, one value." But in its internal management, the ALP was still a state orientated party. At meetings of its Federal Conference, the ALP's supreme policy making and governing body, the six delegates from Tasmania, with a population of 371,000 and five Federal electorates within its boundaries, and the six delegates from Western Australia, with a population of 836,000 and nine Federal electorates within its boundaries, had the same voting rights as NSW with a population of 4,200,000 and 47 Federal electorates within its boundaries, and Victoria with a population of 3,200,000 and 32 Federal electorates within its boundaries. The same position, with the smaller states having equal power with the larger states, operated on the then twelve-man strong ALP Federal Executive, the ALP's supreme governing body between ALP Federal Conferences. To secure a wider based conference, Wyndham advocated the inclusion in the conference, with full voting rights, of the federal parliamentary leaders, and representatives from each of the one hundred and twenty odd federal electorates, and from federal unions. Wyndham also advocated changes in the ALP Federal Executive structure. His proposals would have reduced the power of the ALP bureaucrats from the smaller states, enhanced the importance of NSW and Victoria, and lessened the ability of machine operators like Chamberlain to manipulate numbers. Gifted, talented and resourceful individuals like Chamberlain may have retained their power, but they would have been forced to rely on persuasion rather than the compulsion of an artificially contrived majority constructed on the base of innumerable deals. Chamberlain opposed the Wyndham proposals. But Wyndham, though he could admire a man for his ability and drive, was temperamentally unsuited to be anyone's creature. He was very much his own man. Chamberlain's path and Wyndham's started to diverge.

These paths diverged further when Chamberlain, at a crucial

257

time from a state electoral viewpoint, organised, and headed, a much publicised Federal ALP incursion into NSW to oppose a proposal by the NSW ALP government, which had then held office in NSW for twenty-five years, to give extended state aid to private schools. Wyndham could see no justification for putting at risk the existence of a state ALP government in the furtherance of an internal ALP brawl. In 1965 the seemingly securely entrenched ALP NSW government was defeated by a Liberal-CP coalition led by Rob Askin who was then installed as NSW Premier. Rightly or wrongly, Chamberlain's state aid intervention was blamed for assisting to bring about this result, and relations between Chamberlain and Wyndham worsened.

By 1969 Wyndham had achieved only one reform in ALP structure, and that, ironically, under official Chamberlain auspices. Bowing to the inevitable and with mass ALP sentiment clearly favoring such a move, Chamberlain had made a virtue of necessity. At a special ALP Federal Conference, convened in Adelaide on Tuesday, August 1, 1967, Chamberlain had moved an amendment to a report of the Federal Executive on party reorganisation. Chamberlain's amendment provided that the Leader and deputy Leader of the Federal Parliamentary Labor Party, and the ALP Leader and Deputy Leader in the Senate, should be added to the Federal ALP Conference as full delegates. It also provided that each of the six state ALP branches should henceforward be entitled to send seven delegates to an ALP Federal Conference, one of whom would be either the state parliamentary leader, or his nominee as approved by the state ALP Executive. Chamberlain's amendment further provided for the Leader and Deputy Leader of the Federal Parliamentary Labor Party, and the ALP Leader and deputy Leader in the Senate to be added to the ALP Federal Executive.

It was a revolutionary move which restored the balance, heavily weighted for years in the ALP machine operators' favor, back in favor of the parliamentarians. Hitherto an ALP Federal Conference had consisted of thirty-six delegates, six from each of the six states. No parliamentarian had sat on a Federal Conference by right. Such parliamentarians as had become conference delegates had become so because of their ability to ingratiate themselves with, or because of their personal influence within, the ALP machines in their home states. Now the four Federal ALP parliamentary leaders and the ALP parliamentary leaders in each of the six states sat by right in the conference—a total of ten in a conference which, with a representative from the Northern Territory now also included, numbered forty-seven. The parliamentarians had a different attitude from the ALP machine bureaucrats. The parliamentarians were more sensitive to the hopes and aspirations of the general electorate. They wanted to win government. The ALP machine bureaucrats were less concerned with winning government than with maintaining their positions and power within the ALP machine. Despite their numerical inferiority, the parliamentarians, generally prominent in public life and accustomed to handling public affairs, were now placed in a position to persuade the conference into having regard for mass electoral feeling and against making decisions in a crude, tactless way that would antagonise the general electorate. Their presence at the Federal ALP Conference held in Melbourne from July 28, 1969, to August 1, 1969, helped considerably to improve the ALP's public image, something that was considerably to the ALP's advantage when the electors went to the polls to vote in the general elections on October 25, 1969, only three months later.

But there was still a lot of water to go under the bridge before the Melbourne ALP Federal Conference was held. It was at the 1967 Adelaide special conference that the parliamentarians' position on the ALP Federal Executive had been strengthened. Until then the ALP Federal Executive, the ALP's paramount governing body between the biennial federal conferences, had consisted of twelve delegates, two from each of the six states. With the four federal parliamentary ALP leaders and a representative from the Northern Territory added, it now numbered seventeen. But it was a body in which tension continued at a high level. Murphy and his Senate deputy, the late Sam Cohen, though parliamentarians, and technically junior to Whitlam and Whitlam's House of Representatives' deputy, Lance Barnard, usually sided with the Victorian ALP and the Victorian ALP secretary, Hartley, who hated Whitlam, against Whitlam and his NSW supporters. Murphy, a New South Welshman, was *persona non grata* with the NSW ALP machine controllers, who, if they had had the power, would have had him deprived of his Senate ALP preselection, a deprivation which would have almost certainly have resulted in his disappearance from the Federal Parliament. Murphy, one of the leaders of the NSW "outs", understandably regarded the Victorian ALP, with whose leaders he had a close association, as his real power base within the ALP structure. Cohen, a Victorian, was dependent upon the Victorian ALP Executive for his Senate ALP preselection. What the Victorian ALP Executive gave, the Victorian ALP Executive could take away. To a degree that the right-wing controllers of the NSW ALP had never matched, the leftwing Victorian ALP Executive had exhibited complete ruthlessness in

259

"rubbing out" opponents to its viewpoint and those who defied its directives or wishes. Chamberlain had an association with Murphy and the Victorian ALP, and, through the Victorian ALP, with Cohen, and usually masterminded the tactics of this group. The then ALP Federal President, Senator J. B. ("Jim") Keeffe,[24] a Queenslander, who as often as not also functioned as a Queensland delegate when he exercised voting rights, loathed Whitlam and the rightwing grouping which supported him and was far from reluctant to contribute to Whitlam's embarrassment. The South Australian delegates, with Clyde Cameron's presence even on occasions when he was not formally a delegate to the ALP Federal Executive always shadowily in the background, were steadfastly opposed to Whitlam and his backers on state aid for denominational schools. The ALP at this period was like a bag of snakes, full of holes, with the unhappy Wyndham trying to prevent the snakes escaping and poisoning the ALP's electoral prospects.

By 1969, Wyndham was a tired, exhausted man. He had spent years seeking to revive the ALP's electoral fortunes, and indications were that there was little prospect for their revival for years to come. Despite its imposing title, the ALP Federal secretaryship was a minor ALP power point. Held in conjunction with another post, such as the secretaryship of a state ALP branch, it was useful, as Chamberlain had found when he was both ALP Federal Secretary and WA ALP Secretary. But in isolation it gave power to a manipulator, like Kennelly, who had been ALP Federal Secretary while Chifley was ALP Prime Minister, rather than to an organiser, and Wyndham was essentially an organiser.

On March 12, 1969, just a week before James "dropped the bucket" provided by newsletter publisher, Frank Browne, on Gorton in the House of Representatives. Mr W. R. ("Bill") Colbourne announced his retirement as NSW ALP Secretary. Colbourne, an ALP veteran and Whitlam supporter, had fought alongside Curtin and Chifley, who later became ALP prime ministers, in earlier ALP splits. But Colbourne's final years had been bitter ones. Despite having given faultless loyalty to the ALP, he was suspected by the ALP's leftwing of having DLP sympathies and while being constantly assailed by the DLP was consistently attacked by the ALP's leftwing for these alleged DLP leanings. Though under sustained pressure from the ALP's leftwing and with its influence correspondingly reduced, the NSW ALP branch was still, from an ALP viewpoint, the most significant branch in the ALP structure, wealthier and with more members, than any other. Wyndham decided to move from the ALP Federal secretaryship where he did not have a real power base to the NSW ALP, where, as secretary, he would have a real power base.

Despite his twelve years in Australia, his eight years in the ALP machine, and his realism in other directions, Wyndham was in some ways still naive. He thought that there were friendships in politics, not just alliances, and that associates give loyalty and backing, even when such loyalty and backing could affect adversely their political futures. He was to learn otherwise, unmistakably, and the hard way.

I liked the little Englishman, who had worked like a drover's sheep dog to rehabilitate the ALP. I knew that there were powerful figures on the ALP Federal Executive with whom his popularity would be at zero now that he was formally allying himself with the NSW ALP rightwing. I was also aware of the mores of the ALP. In faction fights, no efforts are spared to discredit an opponent. When a defeated faction vacates an office it takes with it as many records as it can carry. On occasions it has even taken the office fittings and light bulbs. Whatever records are left behind are combed thoroughly for material to use pitilessly against the dispossessed. Wyndham was operating the federal office on a shoestring budget. He was overworked. His office was understaffed. He was bound to have committed sins of omission rather than commission, such as operating accounts without the number of signatories required by some ALP rule which was observed in the breach rather than punctiliously but which could be quoted against him. "Get your books audited before you vacate your office," I advised him.

At first Wyndham did not believe that his opponents would seize on such things to discredit him. I pointed out that I was probably better acquainted with ALP habits in faction fights than he was. He agreed that he should follow my advice. But he was depressed and lassitudinous. I got the impression that the death wish was upon him, and that he would not do anything about protecting his well-being. As it turned out, he did nothing. As it also turned out, he had committed sins of omission.

Chamberlain wanted the federal secretaryship. Though not key in the ALP power structure, it was a valuable outpost of power. It was useful for the gathering of information. Information was important in a faction fight, as Chamberlain well knew. But there were individuals within the ALP who though they admired Chamberlain's ability were fearful of his ruthlessness and the damage he could do to the ALP electorally by insisting upon the observance to the letter of ALP law and lore. Cameron and Senator J. P. ("Jim") Toohey, from South Australia, went to work on Mr M. ("Mick") Young, thirty-three years old, a powerfully built ex-shearer and AWU member, with a golliwog's shock of black hair, and a face that was a map of Ireland. Young had become SA ALP Secretary. He was radical but tolerant, goodhumored but firm, with a courteous easygoing manner, a sense of humor and extensive patience. Wyndham was moving into the NSW ALP secretaryship shortly. Cameron and Toohey persuaded Young to stand against Chamberlain for Wyndham's vacated post. Young did. With three Federal ALP delegates—Barnard, Beazley, WA, and D. Lowe, Tas—absent, Young and Chamberlain deadlocked seven-all in two ballots. Chamberlain conceded the post to his younger opponent, as yet unidentified firmly with any of the feuding ALP factions.

Young had none of the earmarks of a vindictive man. But he was a new vigorous broom sweeping clean. As was inevitable with a secretary as overworked and drawing upon the resources of as understaffed an office force as Wyndham, there were errors of omission. Both Young and the Federal ALP Executive sought explanations from Wyndham. But Wyndham, tired and dejected and also, to some degree disgusted, refused to make explanations. If the people for whom and alongside whom he had fought on the ALP Federal Executive were not ready to defend him, then he was not going to defend himself. He was "fed up", disgusted, and disillusioned.[25] Whitlam made a halfhearted attempt to come to his aid. On May 22, 1969, Whitlam sent a wire to Young, in Young's capacity as ALP Acting Federal Secretary, stating "Business of House prevents me attending Federal Executive (meeting) this afternoon. Am gravely concerned by wording and recommendations of Finance Committee . . . Am strongly of opinion that these words are an injustice to person named and a legal hazard for any person using these words . . . Gough Whitlam".[26]

The ALP Federal Executive understandably ignored Whitlam's intervention, confined as it was to a telegram more pious than forcible. At pages 165 and 166 of the official record of the ALP Federal Conference held in Melbourne between July 28, 1969, and August 1, 1969, appeared an item reporting that on May 22, 1969, the ALP Federal Executive had scathingly criticised Mr Wyndham's administration of the ALP Federal Secretariat finances. Bowing to the inevitable, the NSW ALP Executive dismissed Wyndham from his post as NSW ALP Secretary on May 27, 1969. Reporting the dismissal to the NSW ALP Executive on May 30, 1969, the former NSW ALP Secretary, Colbourne, said that Wyndham had not been seen at his office since May 21, 1969. Wyndham had given no reason for his nonattendance. Colbourne said that Wyndham had been advised of his dismissal by registered mail.[27] Despite the fact that on May 23, 1969, the ALP Federal Executive

262

in a formal report had said that there was no suggestion of misappropriation of funds,[28] Wyndham's enemies within the ALP continued to "feed out" to anyone who would listen highly damaging material against Wyndham, which contained a grain of truth extensively embroidered.

Max Newton, not the most diplomatic of defenders, sprang to Wyndham's defence. Said Newton "I have been a longstanding friend of Mr Wyndham and he and I have discussed over recent months the possibility of him joining the Newton organisation in some capacity.[29] I know he has been very unhappy in recent weeks and illtreated, maligned, and smeared by members of the ALP Federal Executive. In my view this is a shabby reward for the years of service he has given to the Labor movement."[30] To some extent Wyndham had intensified his difficulties by his own fatalistic and embittered attitude. Young was one who felt he had a clear conscience on the matter. "As acting general secretary of the ALP, I am deeply alarmed at Mr Max Newton's public attack upon the Federal Executive of the ALP in its relations with the former general secretary, Mr Cyril Wyndham," Young said. ". . . All decisions appertaining to the general inquiry held by the Federal Executive were unanimous, and the composition of the Federal Executive, containing no fewer than seven federal members of parliament, including two QCs (who are well aware of the laws of natural justice),[31] one state member of parliament, and five branch secretaries, does not read like a tribunal which would be interested, as Mr Newton suggests, in illtreating, maligning, or smearing any member of the ALP. Mr Wyndham well knows that he was given every opportunity to attend the Federal Executive meeting to take part in the discussions—it was his decision not to do so . . . I would think it very wise if Mr Newton did not continue with his provocations for if he does we will have to re-assess our position on what should be made public."[32] The loss of such an important official in such circumstances rocked the already disorganised ALP. But there was something else with the potential to be even more electorally damaging for the ALP.

Harradine, the Tasmanian antiCommunist, whose expulsion from the ALP Federal Executive had led to Whitlam's resignation from the Federal ALP leadership and the subsequent leadership contest between Whitlam and Cairns that Whitlam had won only by a 38/32 majority, had been advised by Whitlam to apologise to the ALP Federal Executive and to repudiate the suggestion that he had insinuated that there were "friends of the Communists" on the ALP Federal Executive who would try to secure his ejection from that august body. Whitlam urgently needed Harradine's vote on the Executive. A QC, Whitlam worked out a letter to conform with the requirements of the resolution passed by the ALP Federal Executive on April 17, 1968, that "until such time as he (Harradine) completely and unreservedly withdraws the statement . . . and unreservedly apologises to the Federal Executive for his conduct, he is not a fit and proper person to be seated on the Federal Executive of the ALP."[33]

The letter drafted by Whitlam for Harradine was sent to Wyndham, as ALP Federal Secretary in May, 1968. The relevant portion read ". . . It is now clear that the Federal Executive was referring to the following sentence in my document: 'When I (Harradine) go to the meeting of the Federal Executive of the ALP in Canberra[34] on April 17, the friends of the Communists intend to try to silence me. I have been informed that they will try to exclude me from the Executive meeting.' "

Harradine's letter continued "A person reading this statement could conclude that, in my view, there were friends of the Communists on the Federal Executive itself. I completely and unreservedly withdraw that statement. As I said on Thursday afternoon, April 18, page 23 of the (Federal ALP Executive) minutes: 'I regret any imputation which members may feel reflected upon them personally.' I would draw attention to the following passages from the minutes for Wednesday morning, April 17: 'I have not said nor do I mean that there are friends of the Communists on the (Federal ALP) executive' (page 12) . . . I explained that I used the term 'friends of the Communists' in the sense in which I used it in the third section of the document, viz. 'The authors of the document are Communists and friends of Communists (foot of page 12), and the reference to friends of Communists was to those who had prepared the anonymous document[35] . . . I would also draw attention to these passages in the Federal ALP Executive minutes: 'He was prepared to say or do anything in his power to clarify the issue. He did not mean or intend any reflection on the Executive' (page 14), and 'He was prepared to state to the Executive so far as the Federal Executive was concerned there was no Communist influence' (page 21). I unreservedly apologise to the Federal Executive for my conduct in releasing the document to the press.[36] Yours sincerely, R. W. B. Harradine."

Whitlam had the legal qualifications: the antiHarradine, antiWhitlam forces the numbers. At meetings of the ALP Federal Executive held from August 5 to August 7, 1968, the executive by majority vote and with Whitlam voting with the minority decided "That this meeting of the Federal Executive resolves that the letter from Mr R. W. B. Harradine to the Federal Secretary under date May 3, 1968, does not meet the requirements of the Federal Executive decision made on April 18, 1968: 'That until such time as he completely and unreservedly withdraws the statement made in the document and unreservedly apologises to the Federal Executive for his conduct, he is not a fit and proper person to be seated on the Federal Executive of the ALP,' and that he be informed accordingly."[37]

Left and Communist officered unions made it clear that if Whitlam persisted in his support for Harradine, who had got into his original troubles by paraphrasing comments already made publicly by Whitlam against the Victorian ALP and supporting Whitlam's call for reform of the Victorian ALP, the Harradine trouble would be extended to the Australian Council of Trade Unions (ACTU) and to the trade union movement generally. Whitlam was threatened with a withdrawal of leftwing union financial support in an election year. Whitlam dropped Harradine like a hot potato. The Tasmanian ALP Conference, which elected yearly the two Tasmanian delegates to the ALP Federal Executive and the six Tasmanian delegates to the ALP Federal Conference, to be held in Melbourne in July/August, 1969, was to meet in February, 1969. Harradine reluctantly allowed himself to be persuaded that so as not to damage the ALP's electoral prospects in the general elections due later in 1969 he should not re-nominate for the position of a Tasmanian delegate to the ALP Federal Executive. Whitlam and his deputy, Barnard, who was a Tasmanian, breathed sighs of relief.[38] But at the last moment, Harradine bailed up. Accused of all kinds of things but never charged with an offence against the ALP though ALP rules provided ample opportunity for the levelling of formal charges, Harradine refused to reconcile himself to acceptance of the position of "a second class ALP member."[39] Just before nominations closed, he nominated for a position as one of the six Tasmanian ALP delegates to the ALP Federal Conference. He topped the poll, and cheering and hand clapping greeted the announcement of the count. No figures were revealed but it was believed that Harradine had a big lead over his opponents.[40]

The leftwing and Communist officered unions immediately implemented their threat. A successful union official and industrial advocate, Harradine was secretary of the Hobart Trades and Labor Council and a member of the ACTU interstate executive, on which the leftwing then had a 9/7 majority. A highly organised, intensive, and largely anonymous and subterranean propaganda blitz was organised against Harradine. It was stated that he had spent some

265

years in a monastery,[41] had held an executive position in the DLP in South Australia,[42] and had criticised Mr R. J. ("Bob") Hawke, then industrial advocate but soon to become President of the ACTU, for writing an article in *The Federal Law Review* which had been used by employers against union wage claims in a case in which Harradine was appearing for the unions.[43]

By nine votes to seven, the ACTU Interstate Executive censured Harradine on May 13, 1969. Though he was supported by his local Tasmanian organisations, he had become a liability for Whitlam. A petition was circulated in Queensland, Western Australia, and South Australia as a preliminary to debarring him from the July/August Conference. The petition accused Harradine of making unfounded attacks on Hawke, and described Harradine as being "this recent acquisition from the Democratic Labor Party."[44] Harradine refused to back down further. He said that he had not been asked to withdraw his reference to the Victorian ALP being under Communist influence and had no intention of doing so.[45] The July/August Federal ALP Conference was easily the ALP's most important pre-election gathering at which, normally, the ALP would display its political wares and seek to convince the mass of voters that it represented a government alternative to the reigning Liberal-CP coalition, Harradine could wreck the show. Constitutionally, Harradine had every right to attend the conference. He had been elected, democratically, by the Tasmanian ALP Conference. There was no ALP rule that would enable the federal ALP authorities to force Tasmania to provide an alternative or proxy delegate in his place. Harradine's physical presence at the conference would require his ejection if his opponents persisted in their determination to exclude him, and such action, in election year, could seriously impair the ALP's electoral prospects.

As it was, the Harradine affair, even without Harradine's formal ejection from an ALP Federal Conference, had already probably affected the ALP electorally adversely, and could be viewed as of assistance to the Liberal-CP coalition in helping the coalition to regain the electoral dominance that, with DLP support, it had enjoyed for years. On May 10, 1969, while the ACTU was convulsed by the antiHarradine moves, Tasmanian voters went to the polls to vote in a State election. The ALP had been in power in Tasmania for thirty-five years. The Tasmanian Premier, Eric Reece, a onetime ALP Federal President, was a respected and able administrator, middle of the road, eminently balanced, and a man who, despite his State's relative unimportance as Australia's smallest state, was a major and impressive figure at Premiers' Conferences in Canberra, where, with the Prime Minister presiding, the Commonwealth and States conducted their formal negotiations on taxation reimbursement, Commonwealth grants to the States, the split up of loan moneys, and discussed and made decisions on problems of mutual interest that needed either Australia-wide co-operation between Commonwealth and States, or fell into the legislative no-man's-land where Commonwealth and State powers either ran jointly or merged inseparably. When the Tasmanian vote was counted, the ALP had won 17 seats and the Liberals 17 seats in the 35-strong Tasmanian House of Assembly. An independent, Mr K. O. Lyons, member of a Tasmanian family which had long been prominent in Tasmanian politics and which had supplied a pre-war prime minister to the Commonwealth in the shape of the late J. A. Lyons, who headed a nonALP administration from 1932 until his death in 1939, was the balance of power. On May 22, 1969, Lyons decided to throw in his lot with the Liberals. On May 26, 1969, the new Liberal government, headed by Mr W. A. Bethune as Premier, was sworn in, and for the first time since pre-World War I Australia was without an ALP government, federal or state. In Queensland where local issues were paramount but the Harradine affair may have also had a marginal influence, the Country Party-Liberal coalition which had held office for twelve years was returned as the state government with its majority reduced by only one at elections held on May 17. From the Liberal-CP viewpoint, the electoral omens were again propitious.

With the ALP Federal Conference its major showcase during election year, 1969, the ALP had another problem, as touchy as that of Harradine, and possessed of the same potential for electoral damage. The years of incessant squabbling over state aid for private schools had undoubtedly affected ALP morale, soured a significant section of its supporters, and contributed to the erosion of its mass vote. A fresh feud had broken out. Hartley, spokesman for the Victorian ALP, was at Whitlam's throat over a pledge given by Whitlam at a Sydney meeting attended mainly by Roman Catholic parents that an ALP government would make an emergency grant of fifty million dollars for schools in the 1970/1971 Budget, with half the amount to go to non-government schools.

There had been angry disputes at meetings of the ALP's National Advisory Committee on Education. The meetings were held at the Collingwood Town Hall, Melbourne, on Saturday, June 21 and Sunday, June 22, 1969. The Chairman of the Committee was Hartley; Whitlam was a rank and file member. The meetings were nominally in camera, but, as was usual in the ALP, leaked like a sieve.[46] Hartley was inflexibly antiState aid. Whitlam wanted State aid: without it, he argued, the ALP would never again be presented

267

with the chance to form a government in a country in which nearly twenty-five per cent of the population were Roman Catholics who believed that Roman Catholic schools could not continue to exist for long unless they received state aid.

The committee was split into three groups. One group, headed by Hartley, was against state aid for private schools and wanted all available resources devoted to improving state schools. Another group led by Whitlam, wanted state aid for private schools on a basis of equality between the state and the private school systems. A third group was not unwilling to give state aid to private schools but only if the needs of the state school systems had priority. Delegates argued that some non-state schools were wealthy and did not need aid. In fact they needed aid less than many state schools which were operating at only thirty percent efficiency. There were even different degrees of "need" between needy state schools and needy non-state schools. Were non-state schools to be given priority over state schools? Whitlam was asked.

Whitlam launched into a defence of the principle of state aid to non-state schools. He said that he had given a pledge that a future ALP government would provide an emergency grant of fifty million dollars, half to go to state schools and half to go to non-state schools. Rejection of state aid would put him, as ALP Federal Leader, in an impossible position. If the ALP Federal Conference, due to start its meeting in a month's time, decided against state aid he would not be the leader of the ALP at the forthcoming elections. "Do you mean that you are going to resign again?" asked Wheeldon, the WA Senator, who as well as being against state aid delighted in sarcastically needling Whitlam. Wheeldon was then described as "laughing derisively". A compromise was reached. By ten votes to three, the committee decided to recommend that ALP policy continue to provide for state aid, but with the rider that a national inquiry be set up to examine the education needs of both state and nonstate schools.[47] But it was still open for conference to reject state aid for private schools, or to add conditions that would make its provision meaningless.

To add to Whitlam's discomfiture, Hartley had reported Whitlam to the ALP Federal Executive for having disclosed publicly decisions of the ALP's Education Committee, and Murphy, the Senate Opposition Leader, had mauled him savagely at a caucus meeting on March 26, 1969. Both incidents had their starting point in Whitlam's pledge of fifty million for schools, half to go to private schools. Murphy accused Whitlam of failing to report to the caucus an ALP Federal Parliamentary Executive decision restricting Whitlam's capacity to offer state aid. Of the two complaints,

Hartley's was the more serious. At meetings held between March 11 and March 14, 1969, the ALP Federal Executive had resolved "That all members of Federal (ALP) Policy Committees be advised that all deliberations and recommendations of the committee are strictly confidential and are not to be made the subject of outside discussion or press releases until committee reports are formally presented to Federal Conference."[48]

If Hartley, spokesman for the Victorian ALP Executive with which Whitlam had been in unforgiving dispute for years— Whitlam had among other things suggested that individuals who were from Communist-officered unions should resign from the Victorian ALP Executive—could establish a case against Whitlam, Whitlam would be put in the position of appearing to defy the ALP Federal Executive, always a touchy situation for an ALP Parliamentary Leader and a particularly touchy one when the seeming defiance touched on the emotive subject of State aid for denominational schools.

But for once luck, a commodity with which the ALP had not been superlatively endowed for many years, was on the ALP's side. The ALP Federal Conference met at the Hotel Chevron in Melbourne on Monday, July 28, 1969. It met in an atmosphere of considerable tension. Present were only forty-six of the forty-seven delegates entitled to be present. They were the four Federal Parliamentary Leaders, Whitlam, Barnard, Murphy and Cohen, Mr J. ("Jock") Nelson from the Northern Territory, seven delegates from each of five states, and six delegates from Tasmania, with the local State ALP Parliamentary Leader included in each of the six state delegations. Harradine had been delayed by a wage case in Hobart, where he was functioning in his capacity as Secretary of the Hobart Trades and Labor Council. But the news media were announcing that Harradine would seek entry to the conference on the Tuesday when his business in Hobart was expected to have been concluded.

After the Hotel Kingston imbroglio of 1963 when Calwell, then leader, and Whitlam, his deputy, had been kept waiting under a streetlamp at midnight while inside the conference resolved what should be the ALP's attitude to the establishment of a United States radio communication station at Exmouth Gulf, an issue which could effect materially both Australia's future defence and its relationships with the United States, the ALP decided to open its conference to the news media. After some minor initial difficulties at the 1963 Perth Conference,[49] the ALP opened its conferences to the news media and to the public and thereafter was able to claim that, unlike the Liberals whose policy making bodies

269

met behind locked doors, the ALP did its policy making and policy shaping openly and exposed to the public gaze, a claim that undoubtedly was assisting to improve the ALP's public image. However, the Hotel Chevron conference, understandably, opened in camera. The ALP wanted to dispose of the Harradine affair in private.

The first matter always dealt with at an ALP conference is credentials. It is usually a formality. Delegates at an ALP conference get to know each other well over the years. They usually can trace each other's political lineage back until it disappears into the mists of childhood or adolescence. They know who has authority to speak firmly on behalf of the state branch he represents and who is present merely as an obedient vote. On this occasion, the matter of the credentials was far from a formality. Young, in his capacity as acting ALP Federal Secretary—as he also functioned as one of the seven South Australian delegates he wore two hats, taking one off to fit on the other as the occasion arose—told conference he wished to move a motion which embodied a recommendation from the ALP Federal Executive. He produced a list which showed the forty-seven accredited delegates. He then moved "That the credentials of all delegates listed on the sheet with the exception of that of Mr R. W. B. Harradine be accepted. That Federal Conference accepts the decision of the Tasmanian State Executive that it has no power to disturb the decision of the State Conference which appointed Mr Harradine as a delegate to this Conference. However, we are of the opinion that Mr Harradine is not a fit and proper person to be seated as a delegate at this Conference and his credential be rejected." Mr G. T. Virgo, a former secretary of the South Australian ALP branch,[50] seconded.

Mr Eric Reece, who until two months earlier had been ALP Premier of Tasmania moved an amendment. The amendment read "That Conference accepts the credentials of the seven delegates from each state branch and the delegate from the Northern Territory Executive in accordance with the entitlement conferred by Rule 6(a) of Federal Conference rules". Mr M. Everett, another Tasmanian, seconded. Martin Nicholls, MHR, a SA delegate, raised a point of order that the amendment was a direct negative of the motion. The Chairman, Senator Keeffe, Qld, rejected the point of order. Mr F. Taylor, another Tasmanian, supported the motion. Mr Tom Burns, the Queensland ALP secretary, moved that the question be put. Mr W. Brown ,[51] from Victoria, seconded. The amendment was put and declared lost on the voices. The motion was put and carried on the voices. The delegates had been watching Whitlam with unabashed curiosity. He may not have voted for the motion. But he certainly did not vote, or speak, against it. It was clear that Whitlam would do nothing to prevent the executioner's axe falling on the neck of the man who had put his head on the chopping block in Whitlam's cause. The Conference breathed a sigh of relief. Delegates had known that Whitlam had intended to sit by, passively, as a spectator, while his erstwhile supporter was politically decapitated. This deal had been worked out between Whitlam and the Conference managers, but it was feared that at the last moment Whitlam might display symptoms of squeamishness and evoke public sympathy for Harradine, deserted by those who in the past had incited him to take the stand for which he was now paying the price. The news media were then admitted to the Conference room. As the representatives of the news media trooped in, they noted an empty chair where the Tasmanian contingent was seated. The chair remained unoccupied for the remainder of the Conference.

Harradine's behaviour from there on, oddly, assisted the ALP. Harradine arrived from Hobart on the Tuesday, threatening that if he were barred from taking the seat at the Conference to which he was constitutionally entitled under ALP rules he would make public details of a "plot" against him. There was no plot as such, though plenty of antiHarradine propaganda. The ALP powers that be, Whitlam included, had agreed that Harradine was expendable and he was being expended. Harradine visited the hotel where the Conference was sitting, gave letters setting out the ALP constitution position as he saw it, to the assistant-Victorian ALP Secretary, Glyde Butler, for distribution to delegates, but made no attempt otherwise to claim his seat. On Thursday, July 31, 1969, friendless except for supporters on the impotent Tasmanian delegation, he abandoned the unequal struggle. "I am not prepared to fight over a square foot of hotel space," Harradine said[52] as he walked finally from the hotel foyer.

The delegates, particularly the parliamentarians, recognised the advantage accruing to the conference from this anti-climax. The anti-climax had a psychological effect even on those most bitterly opposed to Whitlam. Having avoided one crisis, the delegates tried seriously to avoid a further one. The parliamentarians took over the conference. Beazley, a thinfaced, serious man, an ex-school teacher, religious and as impressive a speaker as the ALP had in the Federal Parliament, was prominent in the debates on social issues and aboriginal affairs, and sounded a high moral note. Don Dunstan, a former Premier of South Australia and a man who was destined to be Premier of that state again, added to the tone as did Whitlam, Murphy, Clyde Holding, leader of the Victorian

ALP Parliamentary Party, and other parliamentarians. Wyndham was absent, but his initial spadework in getting the parliamentarians with their electorally appealing approach to issues and problems was paying off for the ALP.

The Conference dealt thoroughly and soberly with such things as advancement of aborigines, legal and constitutional reform, and civil rights, national development, improved social welfare, abolition of the means test for age pensions and the introduction of a national superannuation scheme, rural matters, industrial reform, problems created by automation in industry, improvement in communications and the arts. With the government's health scheme showing serious defects, the ALP produced its own plans for a health scheme to provide free hospitalisation, medical, pharmaccutical and dental services for all, to be implemented when an ALP government came to power. There were minor clashes. The ALP advocated the abolition of the Senate. Murphy, who had used the Senate as an ALP power point and tried to claim equal power for it with the House of Representatives, sought revision of this longheld ALP policy. Whitlam was quite firm. He wanted to see the end of the Senate. The issue was stalled. A further conference would look at it.

Only issues likely to produce major clashes were education and foreign affairs. The conference managers handled foreign affairs cleverly. They relegated debate on the ALP External Affairs and Defence Committee report to the end of the agenda so that when it came up it would be handled under the pressure of time and with brevity. But there could be only one belated major item. To have two emotive items placed at the end of the agenda would have been too raw, and would have done more damage than good. The Conference faced up to the education issue. It was the one on which Whitlam had threatened to quit the ALP federal leadership if state aid for denominational schools was rejected.

The education debate grew heated. Though the debate was on recommendations that did not deal directly with state aid for private schools in so many words, every delegate present was aware that the fundamental in the debate was in fact state aid for nongovernment schools. Clyde Cameron, MHR, from SA, made a speech which Chamberlain, himself an ardent anti state-aider, was to describe later as being "a speech in which you could hear the faggots crackle."[53] Cameron, who had arranged for TV cameras to carry his speech to the nation, said that it was "morally indefensible and constitutionally very doubtful" whether a Commonwealth government, ALP or of any other political complexion, could use public funds "for the propagation of any faith." Said

Cameron "There's no doubt that what we are doing now is propagating the Catholic faith. There would not be one Catholic school left open if you said they (Catholics) could not teach religion . . . I sympathise with any parent, whether he is a Lutheran or a Catholic, or whether he has some other odd kind of religious faith who wants his children to be brought up in that particular faith. But let them do it at their own expense . . . There are too many short cuts today by people of all denominations who want to get religion instilled into the minds of their children the cheap way, the easy way . . . there is a great groundswell of opposition coming from parents with children attending state schools. They can see the government schools being starved already. They see a great national party now coming forward and saying 'If you vote for us, then we are going to give more of the available public funds for education to the nongovernment schools, which must mean less for government schools.' I believe there is a backlash now among the public and that when we go to the next election on this kind of policy we will be defeated because there are more voters sending children to understaffed government schools than there are sending children to understaffed Catholic schools. This thing is going to hit you bang in the face at the next election. I believe there are many people—nobody at this conference of course[54]—but people inside various political parties who are supporting state aid not because they believe in state aid because I know there are some agnostics and atheists among politicians who do not believe in any religion but supporting it for one reason and one reason only. They think there are votes in it. There are no votes in it. You are going to lose votes."[55]

Things started to happen when Chamberlain moved a seemingly innocuous amendment to a motion for adoption of that section of the Education Committee's report setting out what the committee considered to be the Commonwealth's constitutional powers in the field of education. Chamberlain, an old dog and a shrewd tactician, moved that this section of the Committee's report should be accepted by the conference only as "an opinion of the committee." Design was to leave a loophole for the antistate aiders by reducing the ALP authority of a subclause recommended by the Education Committee. The subclause read: "The Commonwealth can make grants to the states for the provision of buildings, equipment, and services and the training and payment of staff in all forms and at all levels of education, government and nongovernment." Wheeldon, the WA Senator, antiState aider, Chamberlain admirer and consistent "needler" of Whitlam, seconded the Chamberlain amendment. Wheeldon was a lawyer. So also was Murphy. Whitlam supported the original committee recommendation. But feeling was mounting. Whitlam was refused an extension of his speaking time by conference — an almost unprecedented rejection for a federal ALP leader. Murphy opposed the original recommendation.

A onetime Attorney-General in a NSW ALP government and intimate of former ALP prime minister, the late Ben Chifley, Reg Downing, also a lawyer, proceeded to "monster" Murphy and Wheeldon. Downing accused Murphy and others of "not being completely honest" in their opposition. Wheeldon and Murphy demanded withdrawals. Downing's withdrawal was more insulting than his original statement. "I unreservedly withdraw," said Downing. "I am only astounded at the lack of legal competence of the lawyers who expressed the view that the Commonwealth was constitutionally debarred from giving by grant financial assistance to all forms of education, nongovernmental as well as governmental." Murphy commented audibly "Now, it's on." Wheeldon complained that Downing was indulging in personalities. Both asked for withdrawals. Downing again withdrew but in terms that Wheeldon refused to consider an apology.[56] A measure of the way feelings were getting out of hand is an entry in the official report. The report reads ". . . the Chairman (Senator Keeffe) appealed to delegates to refrain from indulging in personalities and advised Conference that any such repetition would necessitate this (education) committee report being dealt with in committee."[57]

Chamberlain's amendment was defeated, with eighteen votes in favor and twenty-seven against. William Hayden, from Queensland, moved an amendment "That the Commonwealth should seek to use its powers to make grants to the states for the purpose of providing building, equipment and services and the training and payment of staff in all forms and at all levels of education, government and nongovernment." Keeffe ruled him out of order. The Committee's recommended motion, which basically only did what Chamberlain wanted said that it did which was to express the committee's opinion[58] that the Commonwealth was capable of making grants to assist education whether government or nongovernment, was then put. It was a tied vote, 22 all. Under ALP Federal Conference rules, a tied vote was decided in the negative. The anti-state aiders had won the first round. But they lost the subsequent decisive rounds.

The next key recommendation was for "The Commonwealth to establish an Australian Schools Commission to examine and determine the needs of students in government and nongovernment primary, secondary, and technical schools and to recommend

274

grants that the Commonwealth should make to the states to assist in meeting the requirements of all school-age children on the basis of needs and priorities." Mr I. Cathie and Mr George Crawford, both Victorians, moved and seconded that the words "government and nongovernment" should be deleted. Mr Frank Waters, from Queensland, moved, and Hayden, from Queensland, seconded an amendment reading "Provided political indoctrination of children be not allowed to take place in both government and nongovernment schools where finance to maintain such schools is provided by the Federal government." The Cathie-Crawford amendment was lost, nine voting for it and thirty-four against it. The Waters-Hayden amendment was also lost, with fifteen in favor and twenty-three against. The recommendation was endorsed by thirty-two votes to ten.

But Whitlam was not completely out of the woods on his fifty million dollar emergency grant for education, half to go to non-government schools. Under the heading of "Urgent programming" the education committee had recommended the pledge that "A federal ALP government will make emergency grants to provide adequate standards of operation within the shortest possible time, including the numbers and qualifications of teachers, the size of classes, standards of school buildings and facilities, and the level of financial assistance to students through scholarships."

When this recommendation was being debated, Young slipped in a quiet amendment. He moved "Notwithstanding any other provision of the (ALP) policy or (ALP) platform, any emergency grant made by the Commonwealth for education shall be such as to give government schools a sum which is not less per student than any other grant made to nongovernment schools." Whitlam did not like it. It had the potential to prevent him implementing his fifty million dollar emergency pledge' on education, with half to go to nongovernment schools. On the basis of Young's amendment, government schools had to get three times as much as private schools because government schools educated three times as many children as did private schools. But Whitlam had been forewarned of what Young intended to do. He was aware that without the backing of Young, part at least of the South Australian delegation, and those who would follow Young's lead, he had no chance of carrying the day. He followed the old political adage "When you can't beat 'em, join 'em." He seconded Young's amendment, which was then carried unanimously.

Whitlam emerged from the Conference to go on TV and to save face by improvising brilliantly. The Conference move had been made to force him to abandon his pledge that half of the fifty million dollar emergency grant would go to private schools. When Chamberlain had asked: "Does that dispose of the fifty million dollar emergency grant, half to go to non-state schools" Whitlam replied "I have nothing to add to what I've already said on this subject." But at a combined TV-press conference, held soon after Young's amendment became ALP law, Whitlam said that he interpreted the Young amendment not as a decision to reduce the amount—twenty-seven million dollars—that a future ALP government would provide for private schools but as one which required him to increase the amount the future ALP government would make available to government schools. Instead of a fifty million dollars emergency grant for education, a future ALP government would make available a one hundred million dollar grant, twenty-seven million dollars to go to nongovernment schools, and the balance of seventy three million dollars to go to government schools. Mainly through his own facile improvisation, Whitlam had got himself "off the hook" on the state aid issue, and had produced a situation in which a future ALP government was empowered to give state aid to private schools. He met the difficulty that a future ALP government was obliged to reserve the lion's share of any emergency education grants for the larger, more heavily patronised state school system by increasing the size of the carcass available for consumption. He hailed the Conference decision as a personal triumph: his triumph was in the way he adjusted the decision to what he believed were his and the ALP's electoral needs.

With the emotive state aid debate out of the way with a minimum of damage to the ALP and some kudos for himself, Whitlam took some knocks when the report of the ALP Foreign Affairs and Defence Committee was presented. But the conference was drawing to a close, the debate was relatively brief, and Whitlam's setbacks went almost unnoticed. There was a minimum of debate, and the debate was constantly interrupted by departing delegates, moving around and making their adieux. The time factor was helpful to the ALP. In the past delegates had fought tirelessly on foreign affairs issues and revealed the party's quite fundamental divisions on Vietnam and aspects of Southeast Asia policy. But Chamberlain still indomitably insisted that it should be his view, not Whitlam's, that should prevail on Vietnam.

Whitlam moved for the discharge of a series of items, dealing with Australia's involvement in the Vietnam conflict, including one from Victoria which declared "All Australian military forces should be withdrawn forthwith." Whitlam moved for the replacement of these items by a resolution which asserted merely "the party's resolve to work to end the war (in Vietnam) and to end Australian participation in it," and that "the Vietnamese should undertake without undue delay responsibility for affairs in Phuoc Tuy province (where an Australian task force was operating), and in adjacent areas and Australian armed forces should be withdrawn from Vietnam." Chamberlain moved, and Virgo, from South Australia seconded an amendment "that on the party becoming a government it will take immediate action to notify the United States Government that all Australian forces will be withdrawn from Vietnam." Whitlam argued in vain for retention of his original motion which would give a future ALP government greater flexibility. But when the vote was taken, he did not even bother to seek a show of hands, and the Chamberlain-Virgo motion was carried. Whitlam's defeat by Chamberlain was virtually ignored as delegates made their hurried departures to catch planes and trains. It might not be the way great national affairs should be considered but it is the way in which they are often considered when they interfere with personal convenience and travel arrangements.

From the ALP's viewpoint, it had been a highly successful conference. After the Harradine fiasco and after the dangerous hurdle of the Education Committee report had been crossed, there had been a minimum of dissension. Whitlam had projected himself impressively.[59] The ALP had emerged from the conference with the appearance of a possible alternative government. It was an appearance that was to help it improve its parliamentary representation and to reduce that of the Gorton Liberal-CP coalition when Australia went to the polls in a general election three months later on October 25, 1969.

NOTES

[1] On occasions, the DLP has been described humorously as drawing much of its support from "the Methodist wing of the Catholic Church."

[2] The reference was to the Sydney Opera House, still then uncompleted and costing astronomically more than the amount originally estimated.

[3] Victorian ALP Executive "favorite son" candidates were sometimes beaten by independent candidates with an ALP background in what normally would have been extremely safe ALP State seats.

[4] "I don't start with the proposition that we withdraw. That was put by my predecessor (Calwell) when countering an equally foolish policy by Mr Gorton's predecessor (Holt) . . . each was a futile policy"—Whitlam TV interview, Channel 9 Network, February 18, 1968.

[5] Official transcript issued by Whitlam's Canberra Office of TV interview on the ABC programme, Four Corners, February 26, 1967.

[6] Official transcript issued by Whitlam's Canberra office of press conference, January 29, 1969.

[7] Figures issued by the Commonwealth statistician on January 13, 1969, showed that Roman Catholic schools educated 82.5 percent of all pupils

277

at nongovernment schools in Australia—*Daily Telegraph*, Sydney, January 14, 1969.

8 *The Western Sun* was the ALP's official organ in Western Australia.

9 The WA ALP Executive had passed a unanimous resolution calling on Whitlam "to organise regular, mass anti-Vietnam demonstrations throughout Australia."

10 Calwell's letter which appears to have been written on February 20, 1970 is typical of the subterranean, clandestine documents that go the rounds in the ALP. Someone gets hold of a letter like this and circulates it. People like myself who have shown an interest in ALP affairs get these documents mostly from anonymous senders. These clandestine ALP documents include photostats of police records, scandalous matter about individuals' private lives, as well as political material. Occasionally some of the documents are forged, but most, when checked, turn out to be genuine.

11 Motion moved by Clyde Cameron, MHR, SA, seconded by Senator Ken Wreidt, Tasmania, Federal ALP Executive meeting, Melbourne, September 14, 1970.

12 *Scope,* January 26, 1967.

13 The anonymous ALP scribe seems to have been accurately informed on the fact that such a meeting took place and that those named were present. Button, McGarvie, and Williams were prominent Victorian ALP personalities opposed to the then Victorian ALP Executive.

14 Hartley regained part of his ALP power when in May, 1971 he won back his positions of Victorian delegate to the ALP Federal Conference and ALP Federal Executive.

15 Commonwealth Senate Parliamentary Debates, Vol 40, p 507, March 20, 1969.

16 *Daily Telegraph,* Sydney, April 17, 1969.

17 Quoted by Whitlam—Commonwealth Representatives' Debates, Vol 63, p 1414, April 29, 1969.

18 In a written reply to questions from Whitlam Gorton disclosed Australia had agreed to the installation in Australia of seventeen defence and scientific projects. Two projects were operated solely by other countries— the United States and United Kingdom—and in four US installations Australia had entitlement only to "participation"—Commonwealth Representatives' Debates, Vol 65, pp 1011/1012, September 9, 1969.

19 *Daily Telegraph,* Sydney, April 30, 1969.

20 Commonwealth Representatives' Debates, Vol 63, p 1470, April 29, 1969.

21 Report of the Special Federal ALP Conference, Canberra, March 25/26, 1966, Canberra, p 36.

22 *Daily Telegraph,* Sydney, September 24, 1969.

23 "Members of the party should not give the false and damaging impression that under a Labor government foreign policy would be determined at mass meetings or by public petitions"—Whitlam, in letter to Chamberlain, December 18, 1969.

24 In 1970 Keeffe was replaced as ALP Federal President by Mr Tom Burns, Queensland ALP Secretary.

25 Personal conversations with Wyndham over this period.

26 From a copy in the writer's possession.

27 *Australian,* May 31, 1969.

28 *Canberra Times,* May 24, 1969.

29 Wyndham later joined the Newton organisation as a political and industrial writer.

278

[30] Press statement by Newton, May 26, 1969.

[31] Young overlooked the fact that one of the QCs on the ALP Federal Executive—Whitlam—described the Finance Committee's antiWyndham report as "an injustice to the person named" in a telegram to Young, in his official capacity as Acting Federal ALP Secretary, on May 22, 1969.

[32] Press statement by Young, countersigned by Keeffe as ALP Federal President, issued on May 27, 1969.

[33] Official report, ALP Federal Conference, Melbourne, July 28 to August 1, 1969, p 162.

[34] This particular ALP Federal Executive meeting was held in Sydney not Canberra.

[35] This is a reference to an anonymous document, probably of South Australian origin, which was circulated against Harradine in Tasmania and provoked his reply which referred to the "friends of Communists."

[36] The "unforgiveable sin" in the ALP is not so much to "leak to the capitalist press" as to be found out to be "leaking to the capitalist press." In apologising for "releasing the document to the press" Harradine was doing himself less than justice. He may have released the document to the press after it had already been published. My impression is that the *Daily Telegraph* was the first to publish the Harradine document. It appeared under my byline on April 9, 1968. My original copy of the Harradine document came from a source other than Harradine.

[37] From a copy in the writer's possession.

[38] Personal conversations at the time with those involved in the Harradine negotiations.

[39] *Age,* Melbourne, February 21, 1969.

[40] *Canberra Times,* February 21, 1969.

[41] "As is well known . . . I did spend several years after matriculation studying Philosophy, Sociology, and History at St Paul's Catholic Student House in Glen Osmond (SA). Of this fact I am proud, although it does cause some embarrassment to have to admit being unable to succeed in studies of this nature"—Harradine memorandum to officers and members of the Tasmanian ALP State Executive, April 7, 1968.

[42] ". . . I am prepared to admit to whatever association I had with that party (the DLP) ten years ago. Since when did the ALP act on the principle that a member's political allegiance ten years earlier should be a disqualification from membership of the ALP today?"—Harradine memorandum to officers and members of the Tasmanian ALP State Executive, April 7, 1968.

[43] "All I did was to write a note (to the ACTU) complaining of the article" —Harradine, *Sydney Morning Herald,* March 18, 1969.

[44] *Canberra Times,* March 12, 1969.

[45] *Daily Telegraph,* Sydney, August 7, 1968.

[46] I have a copy of the minutes of these meetings in my possession.

[47] From notes made at the time, and, in part, from the minutes.

[48] Official Report of ALP Federal Conference, Melbourne, July 28/August 1, 1969, p 164.

[49] I was not admitted because I would not give an undertaking that I would remain in the conference room when the conference went into secret session. I considered it the ALP's responsibility to safeguard its secrets, and I did not propose to help safeguard them by being made privy to them. After experience of the system in operation, the rest of the news media also walked out. Thereafter the ALP imposed no restraints and ALP-news media relations were amicable.

[50] Mr Virgo later became a minister in the Dunstan South Australian ALP government.
[51] Brown shortly afterwards became a Victorian ALP Senator replacing the Senate Deputy Opposition Leader, Sam Cohen, who died soon after attending the Conference.
[52] From notes made at the time.
[53] Chamberlain described Cameron's speech in this way at the ALP Federal Executive meeting in Broken Hill in August, 1970.
[54] Cameron had a nice gift for sarcasm.
[55] From notes taken at the time.
[56] From notes taken at the time.
[57] Official Report, ALP Federal Conference, Melbourne, July 28 to August 1, 1969, p 146.
[58] The ALP's Education Committee was only in a position to offer an "opinion." If there were ever a legal challenge to the Commonwealth's authority to spend public moneys in this fashion, the decision would be made by the High Court of Australia, which under the Constitution was given responsibility for deciding such matters.
[59] Whitlam indulged in the luxury of his catty, drawing-room type of wit only once during the course of the conference. This was when he described Senator Cohen as "always torn in a conflict of disloyalties." Otherwise Whitlam kept himself under tight control.

CHAPTER 12

ONE school of thought in Australia holds that the outcome of general elections is settled months before polling day. This school contends unless there is a Zinoviev letter[1] type of situation, which can evoke a near hysterical response from the mass electorate, election campaigns are merely tribal rituals whose main value is to maintain the fervor of the faithful. The theory behind this is that the voters have formed well before the general elections an impression of the performance, meritorious or otherwise, of the government of the day and only something momentous, like violent movement among the parliamentary elite, or, as in 1954, the defection of Vladimir Petrov from the Soviet Embassy and the insinuations that followed that the ALP had close links with Soviet diplomats, can change that impression. The late Ben Chifley, a former ALP prime minister, belonged to this school and tended to confirm the validity of the school's thesis when some months before the general elections of 1949 at which he and his ALP government were defeated he allowed to develop an impression of doctrinaire rigidity due to the inflexibility with which he adhered to his determination to nationalise the Australian banking system and to maintain petrol rationing, introduced originally as a wartime measure and continued long after the war ended, despite claims by such as the then CP Leader, Arthur Fadden, that petrol rationing could be abandoned without wrecking Australia financially.[2]

The veteran Federal Director of the Liberal Party, J. R. ("Bob") Willoughby, who was the major "backroom" organiser of Liberal election planning in the successful Liberal years between 1951 and 1966—Willoughby retired from the post of Liberal Federal Director in early 1969 after finding it difficult to work with Gorton—was, like Chifley, a disciple of this school of thought. Interviewed when he was retiring, Willoughby expressed his scepticism about the influence of election campaigns on the final election result. He expressed the belief that the outcome of a federal election "is settled three months before polling day."[3] Judged on his election tactics which were put into operation months before polling day, Menzies, electorally the most successful of all Australian prime ministers up to his time, held a similar

281

view, though he did nothing to discourage the Liberal tradition that his government's return was due to his superb election campaign performances and fine oratory of which he was justifiably proud.

In 1969 all the traditional Australian criteria—full employment, rising living standards, a satisfactory overseas funds position, and an ALP opposition still suspect as divided, financially irresponsible, and antiAmerican at a period while the bulk of the Australian electorate regarded the United States as a substitute for Britain as the potential military guardian of an Australia situated on the fringe of a troubled Southeast Asia—pointed to the relatively easy return of the Liberal-CP government at the coming elections. The St John antiGorton crusade seemed by mid-year to have lost its momentum, and, provided Gorton could avoid future personal embarrassments which would revive the disquiet caused by the St John condemnation of Gorton's techniques and methods, was only a marginal threat. There were other, seemingly larger trouble spots.

With large wheat harvests in the significant wheatgrowing countries, the government was making wheat payments only on a quota of production, and Australia's markets overseas were contracting and less rewarding. Wool prices were on a downward slide. But the full impact of the wheat crisis had not been felt by wheatgrowers. There was uneasiness but, as yet, no panic. Provided the general elections were held before wheat was harvested and presented for storage, reaction against the government in wheat and other rural seats was likely to be minimal. The government could expect to live off the fat of wheatgrowers goodwill, still lingering on from the years of plenty. Woolgrowers, though clearly concerned with the situation in their declining industry, had not manifested any mass inclination to switch from support of the Liberal-CP coalition to the ALP; ingrained suspicion of the ALP's allegedly "socialistic" approach to rural problems was too deeply embedded in the political mores of woolgrowers, by tradition conservative, for that to happen quickly. Due partially to Gorton's own attitudes and his political minuet of first retreating from the Menzies-Holt foreign policies and then advancing towards them when political pressures developed, the Liberal-CP coalition's defence and foreign policies no longer gave the coalition the clear electoral advantage over the ALP the coalition had enjoyed for years in these policy areas, and, due both to overseas happenings, particularly in the United States, where hostility to the Vietnam involvement was manifesting itself increasingly, and Gorton's almost formalised advances and retreats, growing numbers of

Australian voters were clearly beginning to question Australian involvement in the Vietnam conflict, and whether it had a moral basis, as well as being in Australia's longterm interests as both Menzies and Holt had successfully maintained. But while defence and foreign policies were less of a plus for the Liberal-CP coalition than they had been in the past they were still on such indicators as public opinion polls and Commonwealth and State election and by-election results far from being a minus.

After the succession of "frights" Gorton had been given—the DLP threat of a selective preference switch if general elections were held in 1968, the need to revise his defence approach in the light of the Government Parties Defence Committee-DLP attitude, and the reaction within the Liberal Party to the promotion of Hasluck to the Governor-Generalship and the consequent promotion of Freeth to External Affairs Minister and Erwin to Air Minister and Leader of the House of Representatives—Gorton might have been expected to abandon temporarily his plans to get rid of McMahon, Fairhall, Fairbairn and others, and to have refrained from promoting any violent movement at the top of the Liberal-CP coalition until after his government was safely re-established in office with an unthreatened three years term in front of it. But at this stage Gorton still had a limitless faith in the efficacy of his own TV virtuosity. He appeared to believe by sheer force of personality and by impressing upon the electorate that here was a prime minister who was determined, come hell or high water, both to be "boss" and his own uninhibited self, he could secure his own return as Prime Minister and the return of his coalition government. He did not seem to understand that there is an interplay of events, and that one event can produce a chain reaction.

Fairhall had been put under strain before on the F111 issue and now he was to be put under even more severe strain. The late Athol Townley was Defence Minister and Fairhall was not even in the cabinet, which made the 1963 decision to buy from the United States twenty-four of the ill-starred F111s, then to cost one hundred million dollars and to be delivered by 1967.[4] But during his period as Defence Minister Fairhall had identified himself, dedicatedly, with support of the F111 programme. Nothing could shake him. In August, 1967, Fairhall quoted approvingly an article which praised the F111 in most flamboyant terms and described the plane as "the Cadillac of the air."[5] The F111 was a subject on which he became hypersensitive. He reacted to criticism of the F111 as though it were an attack upon his personal honour and integrity. He was despondently aware that

283

Gorton lacked his zeal for the F111 programme, and regarded it as a political embarrassment, as delivery dates continued to be postponed and the cost estimates rose to two hundred and seventy-three million dollars before 1968 ended.

I became involved in the F111 affair quite innocently. Gorton was due to leave Australia for talks with President Nixon in Washington, on Thursday, May 1, 1969. On previous occasions, my newspaper, the *Daily Telegraph,* had sent me to the United States to cover visits to that country by Menzies and Holt. I had also gone to the United States to cover Gorton's May, 1968, visit to Washington and was present at the Blair House press conference of unhappy memory.[6]

Earlier, in the last week in April, I had been talking with a parliamentarian who was one of Gorton's intimates. He asked me if I was going to Washington with Gorton. I said my office had decided against sending me. He said that it was a pity. There would be at least one good political story in Washington. Gorton was going to discuss the future of the F111 programme with the Nixon administration. Though I pressed him, he professed to know nothing more than that. But he was quite certain that there were going to be discussions on the F111. He had had that on "the highest authority." Without mentioning names he conveyed that his "highest authority" was Gorton.

Parliamentarians often like to convey that they are "in the know." This is why journalists on occasions get to know more than they are supposed to know. I was not very interested. It seemed to be inevitable that while visiting Washington, Gorton would make inquiries about the progress of the F111 programme. That would be routine. But I was sufficiently interested to inquire further. I walked around to Fairhall's office several times, but missed out on seeing him. On each occasion, he was either out or had officials with him. I was on my way back again to his office when I met a man whom I had known for many years. He was in a position of great authority, and was certain to know what was happening about the F111 situation.[7] We discussed Gorton's plans in the US and what he intended to do about the F111. Later I was shown a document.[8] It was a voluminous document. There was technical stuff which I neither understood nor attempted to understand, but the recommendations were quite clear. They were that Australia should reject delivery of the F111 unless the United States Administration met what boiled down to two Australian conditions. The conditions were that the United States guarantee to carry on the F111 programme across the life period of the plane with the RAAF, a life period which the Australian government believed it was entitled, in view of earlier US assurances, to fix at fifteen years, and that in the event of the United States being unable to hold to this guarantee, Australia should get compensatory treatment on the price of replacements, spares and such things. I was told that this approach had been "approved". Such was the authority of the document and the individual to whom I had spoken that I did not bother further about seeing Fairhall. I felt there was no need. I wrote a story which said that the Australian government would reject delivery of the F111 unless the Nixon Administration agreed to meet Australian demands, which set out the two basic Australian demands, and which concluded "Unless the guarantees from the US were unequivocal and in a form that they could not later be repudiated, Australia should reject acceptance of the aircraft, the authorities advised".[9]

I saw Fairhall the next day. Fairhall said "Someone has sold you a pup with the F111 story your paper published this morning". Fairhall added that Gorton would not be discussing the F111 in the United States. It was possible that the plane might get a mention. But it would be only a mention. Gorton could not have meaningful discussions. He did not have the data on which meaningful discussions could be held. There was no document. With most ministers, I would have just sat back and listened, secure in the knowledge that there was a document, that there would be discussions and that I would be justified by events. But I liked Fairhall. I said, "You're the Minister. You should know what is going on. But there is such a document. There are going to be discussions. I'd advise you to check your lines of communications. Somebody is being sold a pup, and I don't think it is me." Fairhall reiterated that there was no document,[10] and there would be no F111 discussions.

But there were discussions, and the discussions focused on the points emphasised as fundamental in the document—the lifespan of the F111 in the RAAF and the US Air Force and the guarantees sought by Australia on the availability of spares for the Australian aircraft during their fifteen years life expectancy. Gorton had his F111 discussions in Washington with US Secretary of Defence Malvin Laird. After these discussions, Gorton said his purpose had been only to establish whether there were problems in relation to Australia's F111s becoming "orphans".[11] He said it was still "odds on" that Australia would get the aircraft.[12] Gorton told a Washington press conference that a re-examination of the F111 project was being conducted also on the provision of spare parts for the Australian aircraft.[13]

285

Immediately on his return, Gorton reported to the Parliament that the Chief of Staff of the United States Air Force, General McConnell, "was emphatic that . . . (the F111) would be in service until 1980 and probably much longer".[14] Gorton added that the United States Air Force expected that the F111 wing carry through box, which in its earlier version had developed faults, would be tested to 8,000 hours, or two aircraft lifetimes, by July when it was intended to remove current restrictions on the aircraft. "However, the original contractual arrangements called for testing for 16,000 hours, and I made it clear that we would not wish to take delivery of our aircraft ourselves until that period of testing had been satisfactorily completed," Gorton said.[15] Less than three weeks later, Gorton said that the RAAF was looking at American aircraft which could act as alternatives to the F111. The RAAF's assessments, involving a "variety of aircraft" had been carried out for "quite some time", Gorton said. The assessment was a matter of "ordinary prudence and natural routine". Australia would only accept the F111 "if they meet our specifications and last as long as we expected them to last when we bought them".[16] On September 23, 1969, Fairhall said ". . . The United States has guaranteed Australia that all necessary replacements and modifications will be made to the wing box to give it (the F111) a life span of fifteen years".[17]

Happenings involving the F111 were to embitter Fairhall further. Much later, and after he had quarrelled with Gorton and consequently could not be accepted as a completely unbiased witness, Erwin was to say of this period when, as Air Minister, he was familiar with some of the defence decisions in which Gorton was involved, "Fairhall was being frozen out of many of the things that had to do with defence". But there is also some independent evidence that if he was not being "frozen out", Fairhall was certainly not being informed to the extent that he was entitled and could be expected to be informed. On July 2, 1969, Gorton gave a background briefing to a group of pressmen.[18] The next day a number of newspapers came out with stories that read most authoritatively. The reports were unanimous that Australia wanted an assured operational life of fifteen years for the F111s it had proposed to acquire from the United States. The reports dealt with the different interpretations placed upon 8,000 hours of testing and 16,000 hours of testing by the US and Australian advisers. The reports also dealt with other technical aspects of the F111 problem. Two press colleagues, one, Barry Wain, from an organisation other than the one for which I worked and the other from an associated publication, informed me that they had phoned Fairhall in Newcastle to get further clarification on the differences between the Australian and the Pentagon claims. Both reported Fairhall as saying "I know nothing about those figures—they're a lot of rubbish". When one of those who phoned told Fairhall that he was positive that the figures had emerged from Gorton's July 2, 1969, briefing, Fairhall said he found it hard to believe. Fairhall claimed that he had not been aware that such a briefing had taken place.

On May 12, 1970, with Fairhall then retired from politics, Malcolm Fraser, Fairhall's successor as Defence Minister, contributed yet another instalment to the F111 saga. Said Fraser "The aircraft is at the moment quite unacceptable to Australia and to the Royal Australian Air Force . . . It is possible that proof and structural testing and US flying later in 1970 and 1971 could produce evidence that we would never get an F-111C acceptable to us . . . it is not until December, 1971, at the earliest that we would be able to make a decision concerning the likely ability of our aircraft to reach 100 percent of our required performance . . . at the best it would look like getting F-111C aircraft fully operational some time in 1974".[19] But by that stage, Fairhall had "tossed it in" and it was Fraser who was walking the F111 Via Dolorosa.

Fairhall's F111 tribulations, in isolation, were insufficient to persuade Fairhall to seek the solace of retirement and escape from the rebuffs and disappointments inflicted upon him, not by the electorate nor even a majority of his Liberal parliamentary colleagues, but by events, events in which Gorton played the leading role. In mid-1969, and virtually until the day he announced his retirement, Fairhall kept insisting upon his determination to contest in the Liberal interests his seat of Paterson at the coming general election. But his disillusionment was growing more intense; his frustration more obvious. In June, 1969, he was an unhappy, bewildered man.[20]

Originally, Fairhall's adherence to the Menzies-Holt policy of "forward defence" in Southeast Asia, which resulted in Australian troops being stationed in that area of the world continuously since the end of World War II, had an element of crudity. A business man rather than a politician, Fairhall tended to see things in black and white. Fiercely antiCommunist, he saw Communism advancing southward down the Asian continent and approaching Australia. China to him was "a new China—Communist, militant, aggressive".[21] Sooner or later, Communism would have to be confronted and its southward march contained. If that had to happen, it was in Australia's interests that the confrontation should take place as distant from Australia's shores as could be managed. This type of thinking was at the basis of his firm, unwavering support for Australian involvement, with the United States, in the Vietnam conflict. "The vital importance of stopping Communist aggression must surely be all the more obvious when it is realised that Communist subversion and open terrorism is already going on in an organised way in Laos and Northern Thailand," Fairhall told a NSW Liberal Party rally at Gosford on April 18, 1966. "If South Vietnam falls to Communist aggression, the rest of Southeast Asia inevitably will follow."[22] Later, when justifying Australian involvement in Vietnam, he was to repeat the same theme in a more refined form. "It is fortunate for the free world that the United States has assumed, even if with reluctance, the burden of counterbalancing Communist expansion . . . today the United States holds the line in Southeast Asia from Okinawa to Thailand," Fairhall said in an address to the fourth annual dinner of the Imperial Service Club in Sydney on April 1, 1969.[23]

But stimulated probably by Hasluck's greater sophistication—Hasluck, as External Affairs Minister, and Fairhall, as Defence Minister, worked together closely — Fairhall's approach had widened. He had become interested not only in the containment of Communism, but in the promotion of stability in Southeast Asia, and particularly in the Malaysia/Singapore region. He developed an immense sympathy for those trying to find answers to the problems confronting Malaysia, and conceived an admiration for the Tunku, as Malaysian Prime Minister, and his tough, able little deputy, Tun Abdul Razak, battling pragmatically to cope with the difficulties of a country that in 1969 had to deal not only with Britain's 1971 withdrawal, but with racial conflict as Malaysians and Malaysians of Chinese extraction clashed and rioted. Like Hasluck, Fairhall had a profound respect for the dynamic Lee, Prime Minister of Singapore. Fairhall accepted that morally as well as from self interest Australia had to "give our Asian friends the practical evidence of our concern for their welfare . . . sympathetic noises from us are of limited value". Fairhall told his Imperial Service Club audience in Sydney on April 1, 1969, "There are risks (for Australia) in maintaining a presence in the Malaysian/Singapore area. They have been assessed. We must take them."[24]

Fairhall appears to have been genuinely convinced of the correctness of the views expressed by the governments of Malaysia and Singapore that the retention of Australian forces in the Malaysia/Singapore area after the British military withdrawal in 1971 would assist the stability of the area. "It has been argued that this (Australian contribution) does not represent a significant

David Fairbairn, the "quiet rebel", facing a barrage of cameras and micro-phones after announcing following the 1969 general elections that he was no longer available to serve in a Ministry headed by Gorton. Fairbairn had previously served under Gorton as Minister for National Development.

William McMahon (left) studies his then Prime Minister, John Gorton, appraisingly. Gorton had just defeated McMahon and David Fairbairn in the leadership ballot after the 1969 elections and McMahon was shortly to be stripped of his Treasury portfolio and relegated to the Foreign Affairs portfolio.

military force, and, in the face of a major overt attack, that would be true," Fairhall told the July 7, 1969, Sydney meeting of Liberal Party Parliamentary candidates." But this criticism overlooks completely the by-products of the appearance in Malaysia and Singapore of Australian and New Zealand military forces. Certainly the governments of the two countries (Malaysia and Singapore) do not underrate their value. First of all the economic and social problems of the region can be solved only by the encouragement of industrial development. Industrial developers are nervous and any contribution to the military security of the area will go a long way towards solving the economic and social problems particularly of Singapore . . . It is therefore for the best economic, military, and political reasons that we propose to base our troops in Singapore."[25] Holding this view, Fairhall, initially with Hasluck, and later with Freeth, had put in a lot of preliminary work to try to make a success of the Five-power Conference held in Canberra on June 19, 20, and 21, 1961. The Conference met in seeming harmony; it broke up in anger. Gorton had been largely responsible for the anger.

In some ways, Gorton was quite insensitive. He did not seem to be conscious of, or concerned about offending, the susceptibilities of those with whom his office obliged him to deal. He was blunt, sometimes almost offensively so. For example, when a group of pensioners sought to halt him on his way into Parliament House he said "All you want is more dough",[26] which was probably true, but needlessly hurtful to and denigrating of people who believed, rightly or wrongly, that they had justice on their side. When St John talked with him on February 20, 1969, about the Willesee-US Embassy incident, Gorton, apparently quite genuinely, believed that St John left him reassured and blamed the mishandling of a parliamentary situation by Erwin, not himself, for the fact that St John subsequently gave the incident a public airing. Later, after the elections, when Fairbairn in a private interview with Gorton expressed disquiet about the election's and the dissension Gorton's approach to Commonwealth-State relations was producing in the Liberal Party, Gorton failed to realise that Fairbairn was deeply concerned about the way the government was going, and, as a consequence, did nothing to allay Fairbairn's misgivings, but, in fact, intensified them.

The Five-Power Conference gathered in an atmosphere of reasonableness. The Deputy Malaysian Prime Minister, Tun Abdul Razak, led the Malaysian delegation, the Singapore Prime Minister, Mr Lee Kuan Yew the Singapore delegation, the UK Defence Minister, Mr D. W. Healy, the British delegation, the NZ Prime

Minister, Mr Keith Holyoake, the New Zealand delegation, and the Minister for External Affairs, Gordon Freeth, and the Defence Minister Allen Fairhall, led the Australian delegation. Both Singapore and Malaysia were disappointed over decisions Australia had already made. Commenting on the Australian decision to move its ground troops from Malaysia to Singapore, Lee said the Australian troops would be welcome in Singapore but they would have been more effectively deployed in West Malaysia.[27] Tun Razak said Malaysia was disappointed with Australia's decision to base its troops in Singapore, rather than Malaysia, but would not press the matter further.[28] Malaysia had another reason for disappointment. The Philippines was claiming Sabah as Philippine territory. Though Australia recognised the boundaries of Sabah and that the people of Sabah had exercised an act of free choice when they decided to join Malaysia rather than the Philippines, Hasluck and Fairhall, and later Freeth, has explained to Malaysia that, despite this, Australia was not committed automatically to the involvement of Australian troops in the event of armed conflict breaking out with the Philippines though "by the same token it didn't necessarily exclude the use of those forces in the event of aggression being committed against Malaysia".[29] Malaysia had accepted the Australian attitude, in the language in which it was put to them by Hasluck, Fairhall, and Freeth, with disappointment, but without violent resentment. Gorton put something quite different to the Malaysians in quite different language—strong language.

With the difficulties they had with the Philippines at that time over Sabah, the Malaysians were understandably sensitive to anything that could worsen their position in that dispute. Gorton had a real horror of Australian troops getting involved in racial disturbances in Asia. This was one reason why when announcing the retention of Australian servicemen in the Malaysia/Singapore area after Britain's 1971 withdrawal, he and his government had insisted (a) that the forces would remain there only while "their presence continues to be actively desired by the governments of the countries in which they are stationed", (b) that any decision to employ the forces would be a matter to be determined by the Australian government "at the time and in the circumstances of the time",[30] and (c) that the troops would be available, not for the maintenance of law and order which was the responsibility of the government concerned but "to oppose any insurgency which is externally promoted, which is a threat to the security of the region and which is beyond the capacity of the forces of Malaysia and Singapore to handle".[31] With the position on Sabah already spelled out, Gorton could have let the matter rest there. Instead he elected to tell the Malaysians, in effect, that Australia was not contemplating getting involved in any circumstances in the Malaysian-Philippines dispute over Sabah.

There was a certain symbolism attached to the words "the defence of Malaysia and Singapore is indivisible". Australia had asked Malaysia and Singapore to reach agreement on that point before Australia made its decision to retain troops in their areas after 1971, and the Malaysians and Singaporeans had reached agreement. Twice in his opening speech to the Five-Power Conference Gorton used the word "Malaya" instead of Malaysia. "These (Australian) forces are there under the concept that defence against external attack is, as far as Singapore and Malaya are concerned in our view, indivisible," Gorton said.[32] As Sabah was not part of the peninsula of Malaya, the implication in this was that Australia was "bailing out" for all time from the Philippines-Malaysian dispute, not as first Hasluck and Fairhall, and later Freeth, had told the Malaysians merely preserving its options. Even Gorton's closest advisers thought that he had made a verbal slip. But when questioned Gorton said that his reference to "Malaya" in place of Malaysia was "quite deliberate". Gorton added "I meant what I said and I said what I meant."[33]

As Australia's Pontius Pilate-like washing of its hands as far as the Sabah dispute was concerned had the potential to stiffen the Philippine's attitude, the Malaysians were understandably upset, and, like Fairhall, more than slightly bewildered. The Deputy Malaysian Prime Minister, Tun Abdul Razak, sought Gorton out at an official reception to say "Prime Minister, I believe there were some mistakes in your speech today." After Gorton replied "No, I don't think so", Razak said "Mr Prime Minister, you are out of date".[34] Coming from a country which was projected into national history as the penal colony of New South Wales and only later when it was beginning to acquire selfrespect as a nation was identified as Australia, Gorton could have been expected to appreciate the resentment that could be evoked by applying the title Malaya, used when the peninsula was a British possession, to the independent country which Malaysia had since become. After this the Conference fell to pieces as a symbol of five-power unity, though work, viewed as worthwhile by the participants, was done on the practical side of organising the defence potential of the area. Tun Abdul Razak was outspoken about his resentment. Lee, a realist, disappeared from the conference on the plea of a stomach upset, but spent two hours talking at Government House with Hasluck, an old friend, and, according to Lee's entourage, making comments on Gorton and Gorton's inconsistencies, which, if correctly reported, must have made Hasluck wonder whether he had done the right thing in deserting politics for the impotence of his gubernatorial splendour.

Freeth and Fairhall clearly thought that their Prime Minister had misinterpreted the Australian Cabinet decision on Sabah, though they, loyally, did not say so in so many words. Said Fairhall "What we have done is in fact to make a reservation about our possible involvement in what we regard as a domestic issue as between Malaysia and the Philippines to be sorted out by diplomatic initiatives on Malaysia's part. But if there should be an act of aggression . . . we would probably take a different view".[35] The dialogue between Freeth and questioners at a press conference held immediately after the conference's official communique was issued showed how far apart Freeth and Gorton were in their interpretation of the Cabinet decision.

This is the revelatory dialogue—

Freeth: We haven't excluded the possibility that they (Australian forces) may be used (in support of Malaysia) if there is an act of aggression against Sabah. I don't think that leaves the situation in any doubt.

Questioner: Then why talk about Malaya, sir? What was the point of making the distinction?

Freeth: Don't ask me to explain the words the Prime Minister used. He was using words which were used in his speech in February, and they were used then to make it very clear, as I understand it, that we were committed to a rather greater extent to defend the territorial integrity of (the peninsula of) Malaya, but that we were not committed in regard to Sabah, and I think that was why he made that distinction. But don't ask me to read his mind precisely in the form of words he used.[36]

Gorton made no attempt to modify his attitude, or to restate it in the context that Freeth and Fairhall were insisting was the correct context. In words which seemed rather emotive, as neither Malaysia nor Singapore had questioned the Australian government's right to decide when Australian troops in their area would be available for use, and which appeared to re-echo his statement to the Government Parties' Defence Committee "I will not for a political decision risk one Australian life", Gorton said that Australia was giving no "blank cheque" for the defence of the Malaysia-Singapore area after Britain's withdrawal in 1971. With what on the surface was needless vehemence, Gorton added "We are not giving blank cheques for the use of Australian youth and the killing of Australian youth unless we are sure this is done to prevent aggression, to prevent attack, and not merely to become involved in racial fights in a particular area itself . . . We are not giving blank cheques for the use of Australian youth unless they are under our control . . . It is well and necessary that everyone should understand this because there could then be no danger that, in the future, Australia could be accused of a breach of faith".[37]

Gorton's motive was undoubtedly of the purest—to make it clear that Australia was not going to get involved in Asian strife which had a racial basis. But as the Sabah dispute had a territorial content, it is hard to see why he felt under compulsion to express this thought so trenchantly in regard to the Philippines-Malaysia dispute and in a fashion which the Malaysians were certain to regard as offensive. The Principal Secretary of the Malaysian Ministry of Foreign Affairs, Mr Zain Azraai, said that the Malaysian delegation was going home "to think about the discussions". Both Malaysian and Singapore delegates were "absolutely in accord" on questioning the credibility of the Australian commitment that had arisen from the Five-Nation Conference, Mr Azraai said. The use of the word "Malaya" had surprised the Malaysian delegation.[38] By June 24, 1969, Singapore and Malaysian newspapers were telling their readers that they must no longer depend on Australia. Some emphasised the need for selfhelp; others said that Malaysia must look for new friends.[39]

As far as domestic politics were concerned, Gorton again confirmed the impression that the government was unsure about its defence policy and that there was dissension among the government's parliamentary *élite*. The DLP was merciless. In *Focus,* the DLP's NSW mouthpiece, the question was asked "Can Mr Gorton be trusted in foreign policy". The *Focus* article continued, "What diplomatic blunder can we expect from Mr Gorton next? Will he start talking of the 'East Indies' in a conference with Mr Malik (of Indonesia)? But Mr Gorton was not only guilty of an unnecessary and insulting offence against diplomatic protocol, he was also laying down Australian policy in an unnecessary manner and generating quite avoidable annoyance. The DLP agrees with the Australian government that we should avoid a provocative sounding commitment to defend the disputed Sabah territory against the Philippines. This would not contribute to stability and harmonious relations within our region. On the other hand there seems to be no reason whatever for Mr Gorton to harp on the point that it seeks to avoid an automatic commitment to the defence of Sabah against the Philippines. Mr Gorton has said many times that our forces in Malaysia can only be

293

deployed at the command of the Australian government . . . Surely this in itself is an effective enough precaution against any automatic commitment . . . Mr Gorton has firmly ruled out support for West Malaysia against possible aggression from the Philippines whereas his ministers have said something quite different, namely that Australia will make no guarantees but does not rule out the possibility of helping. Past experience suggests that Mr Freeth and Mr Fairhall are expressing the line agreed on in Cabinet, and that Mr Gorton is out on his own again in this matter".[40]

The *Focus* article added "The trouble is that Mr Gorton has renounced the principle of decision making by Cabinet, asserting for himself the right of the Prime Minister to dictate when he thinks the issue important enough. So no one knows where Australia stands . . . Indeed there must be suspicion that Mr Gorton has been deliberately aiming to generate dissension between Australia and its Asian allies. He is a 'Fortress Australia' man by instinct and would still like to opt out of Asia like the left-wingers in the ALP. After all, only after months of efforts by Liberal colleagues, DLP men and journalists was Mr Gorton dragged by the scruff of his neck into making the February 25 statement affirming the continuance of 'Forward Defence' in the form of maintaining forces in Malaysia and Singapore. Now he is acting as though he wants to sabotage 'Forward Defence' by making it impossible for our allies to tolerate the presence of Australian forces. He insults them deliberately and repeatedly. He lays down conditions for the use of Australian forces which make it very difficult for the local governments to justify their presence to their electorates".[41]

Gorton's confidence did not waver. With the favorable Bendigo by-election results under his belt, the government's setbacks in the Gwydir and Curtin by-elections rationalised out of existence, the CP-Liberal government voted back into power in Queensland, the ALP government voted out in Tasmania, and Gallup polls still showing his government holding a commanding lead over the ALP,[42] Gorton sought to promote further movement at the top of the government pile. He sent for Fairbairn. Fairbairn was not long back from overseas. As guest of the French government, Fairbairn had toured French nuclear centres, and arranged an agreement, announced on June 16, 1969, for technical cooperation between France and Australia, which had bought French equipment for its Atomic Energy Research Establishment at Lucas Heights, near Sydney, in the peaceful use of nuclear energy and for fuller exchange of information, and research workers. After leaving France, Fairbairn went to London, where he stayed with the Australian High Commissioner in London, Sir Alex Downer, an old friend and a former parliamentary colleague.

Gorton had changed his mind. Earlier when Fairbairn, unwell and depressed, had asked Gorton for an appointment either as Australian High Commissioner to the United Kingdom or Australian Ambassador to France, Gorton had been noncommittal and had told Fairbairn that he wanted him to stay on until after the general election.[43] Now he wanted Fairbairn to go to London as High Commissioner, replacing Downer in October.[44] He gave no reason for his change of mind. It may have been that by this time Gorton realised that Fairbairn was beginning to be critical of the way government was being conducted, though this was unlikely as Gorton generally was too preoccupied with his own plans to be perceptibly sensitive to the feelings and reactions of others. More probably Gorton had worked out that he could win the coming elections comfortably whatever the movement at the top and wanted Fairbairn's portfolio of National Development as a prize he could confer in a post-election cabinet reconstruction on a supporter whom he preferred to Fairbairn.

But Fairbairn had recovered his health. He had also grown distrustful of Gorton's administrative methods and was not particularly anxious to receive patronage from Gorton's hands. Though the high commissionership in London, where he had many associations, was a wonderful plum to be dangled under his nose, Fairbairn had publicly given his electors an undertaking that he would be standing at the next general election for his seat of Farrer in southern NSW. Fairbairn had an old-fashioned belief that when a pledge was given it had to be honored. Fairbairn told Gorton he could not accept the post. He had given his word that he would stand for Farrer. He must keep his word. He could not and would not go back on his word.

Gorton argued. Fairbairn added another factor. When he, Fairbairn, was recently in London, Downer had told him that Gorton, when in London for the Commonwealth Prime Ministers' Conference, had given Downer an assurance that he would continue Downer as High Commissioner until June, 1970.[45] Downer was a personal friend. Fairbairn said that he would not do anything to damage Downer or upset his plans. Gorton said he had no memory of giving Downer this assurance. Gorton consulted with Hewitt, the head of the Prime Minister's Department. Hewitt confirmed that Gorton had given Downer that assurance. Hewitt produced a letter from Downer asking Gorton to confirm this assurance in writing. Fairbairn was stubbornly determined not to accept the post. Gorton yielded. He could not afford a by-election before the general election. Fairbairn left, having refused what Australian politicians usually regard as one of the richest prizes obtainable.

In July the heat switched to McMahon. A tireless worker with antennae sensitive to movement within the business community as well as the employment and trade union situation, McMahon had been a successful Treasurer, both economically and politically. Except for the weak points in the rural economy caused by overseas fluctuations rather than domestic management, the economy was strong, stable and the national growth rate encouraging. Despite Uren's pessimistic forecasts,[46] overseas currency holdings were satisfactory. As Prime Ministers, Menzies and Holt had discussed with their Treasurers and then with Cabinet the philosophy of the Budget but once that had been settled, left to the Treasurer the settlement of details other than those in which the Prime Minister had, because of their nature, to take a supervisory interest. Gorton had changed that. He did not like the Treasury; he liked McMahon less. He had insisted upon participating in the detail of Budget making in 1968. At that stage, he was circumscribed by his inexperience. The 1968 Budget was still essentially a McMahon and Treasury document. By 1969 Gorton's confidence had been established. The 1969 Budget was largely his product.

Gorton and Cabinet accepted the Treasury Budget philosophy. McMahon stated the philosophy in his Budget speech. "From an economic point of view, the prospects are basically favorable," McMahon said. "The new resources being opened up must add increasingly to output both for domestic use and for export. Our productivity will continue to rise. Migrants are pouring in and the work force is building up rapidly. We are attracting a good flow of capital from overseas. Our reserves are reasonably strong and, despite monetary and trade disturbances abroad, our exports are growing, diversifying and reaching out into still wider markets. This provides a margin of safety. It gives us some scope and time for any adjustments needed to keep the economy on a sure and steady course ahead." But having said that McMahon got down to basic Treasury thinking. "The broad promise of future growth does not however reduce, or change essentially, the continuing problem of economic management, that is, of keeping the national effort close to the limit of available resources but not allowing it to exceed this limit. The problem is with us this year in characteristic form. Rapidly though our supplies of labor, equipment, and materials are increasing, demand is right up with them and is growing fast."[47]

It was a philosophy of expansion but careful expansion.

296

McMahon had earlier in his Budget speech spelled out the economic position, as he and the Treasury saw it, in some detail. "At the end of December, 1968, the seasonally adjusted figure for persons registered for employment was 67,439 and for unfilled vacancies 36,866—a difference of 30,573. By the end of June, the corresponding figures were 55,308 and 44,411 respectively so that the gap between the number registered for employment and unfilled vacancies was reduced to 10,897. This tightening occurred despite the big migrant inflow and the continuing addition of large numbers of married women to the employed workforce. There is no sign yet that pressure in the labor market is being reduced," McMahon said. "On the contrary, the information available to us indicates a continued tightening. An unwelcome feature of the rising pressure on resources has been the over rapid increase in costs . . . the consumer price index increased by 2.9 percent during 1968/69. The nonfood groups in the index increased by about 3.75 percent—a much faster rate than in 1967/68 . . . the money supply in the form of trading and savings bank deposits and notes and coins in the hands of the public increased by 1,169 million dollars, or 9.1 percent. The increase in the previous year was 8.3 percent . . . the labor market is now much tighter than it was a year ago. Practically all the additions to the workforce will have to come from the ranks of school leavers, married women entering the work force, and newly arrived migrant workers . . . The rate at which incomes are rising leaves no doubt that consumption expenditure will continue to gain strength. Consumption normally accounts for about 60 percent of gross national expenditure so that even a small acceleration in its rate of growth can add substantially to the demands on domestic output and imported supplies . . . Present conditions in capital markets abroad suggest that it would be prudent to allow for a reduction in capital inflow this year . . . any tendency for demand to outrun supply in the home market will have adverse effects on the balance of payments . . . These reserves are fortunately strong enough to enable us to cope with a temporary oversea payments deficit."[48] Without being pessimistic in any way, it was a philosophy of carefulness.

Gorton and Cabinet accepted the philosophy, but Gorton did not accept the detail. McMahon budgeted finally for a deficit of only 30 million dollars compared with a deficit of 386 million dollars in 1967/68. Pensioners received an extra dollar a week at an estimated cost of 58.4 million dollars in a full year, the fertiliser subsidy went up to 50 million dollars or 19 million dollars more than in the previous year, and government undertook to double its contributions to wool research and promotion, with the government's contribution not to exceed 27 million dollars a year average for the three years subsequent to July 1, 1970.

Free health benefits designed to assist the more vulnerable section of the community—they were given to family groups of at least two units, excepting those of pensionable age,[49] where the family cash income did not exceed 39 dollars a week—were budgeted for at a cost in a full year of 8.1 million dollars, and per capita grants to independent schools, 35 dollars per pupil for primary schools, and 50 dollars per pupil for secondary schools, were to cost 24.5 million dollars in a full year. A tapered means test, whereby single pensioners would have a eligibility for some pension until their means reached 40 dollars a week, and married couples, both being pensioners, had some eligibility until their joint means reached 70 dollars a week, was introduced at a cost 49.1 million dollars in a full year. But defence expenditure was reduced by five percent, from 1,165 million dollars in 1968/69 to 1,104 million dollars—and this, politically, as Gorton was to find later was important because of the effect it had both upon some of his own followers and upon the DLP.

While the Budget was being framed, Gorton and McMahon had frequent disagreements. McMahon, wisely, kept his own counsel. But those among Gorton's supporters who shared Gorton's dislike of McMahon did not attempt to disguise their jubilation at the consistency with which Gorton was overruling McMahon and getting his own way, and they made known the fact that Gorton was overruling McMahon. Even Dr Malcolm Mackay, an ordained clergyman who had forsaken a fulltime career as a churchman to become politician and businessman and who had an admiration for McMahon's ability and judgment, was innocently enlisted into the antiMcMahon camp. Mackay had strong views on the rights of pensioners. Himself the product of a family with limited financial resources, he believed that the state owed a duty to those who had been unable to provide adequately for their old age from a lifetime of work which had returned them only a modest income. Mackay was a prominent member of the Government Parties' Social Services Committee, which had made a detailed study of the tapered means test proposal. During the pre-Budget discussions, Gorton summoned Mackay to discuss the tapered means test. Mackay explained how he saw the scheme. He was in favor of it. Gorton later told intimates that he had commented to Mackay "A number of senior ministers have doubts about this tapered means test. They call me a dictator. Well, they could be right as far as this issue is concerned. I'm going to get

298

my way". When this version of their conversations got some currency, Mackay confirmed to his intimates that Gorton had—in substance—said this during their interview.

McMahon bowed to the inevitable. Constantly under suspicion — unjustified in McMahon's view — resented, and belittled, McMahon was anxious in the interests of the government and the Liberal Party to avoid confirming in any slight way the impression of conflict in the government's top echelon of ministers. It was election year. McMahon recognised there was much more at stake than hurt vanity. There were the seats of colleagues and, as McMahon like most parliamentarians at that time could not visualise the ALP having any chance of replacing the Liberal-CP coalition as the Government, the size of the government's majority. McMahon was a professional; he played to win not to indulge his idiosyncrasies. Though the philosophy of the Budget was his and Treasury's, some of the most important details were not. Closing his Budget speech, McMahon made Gorton a peace offering. Gorton was being credited with being the main architect of the Budget. Said McMahon "I think it is one of the best Budgets I have known to be introduced in the twenty years I have been in the House".[50] If Gorton recognised this as a peace offering, he gave no sign, either then or later.

The ALP seized upon the political weakness of the Budget. In former years, the Liberal-CP coalition had attacked the ALP's election promises as "financially irresponsible". This superior attitude had undoubtedly materially assisted the Liberal-CP Coalition electorally. Yet here was the Government proclaiming that the utmost care had to be taken as Australia was poised on the edge of an inflationary situation, but simultaneously proposing measures which from a Liberal-CP viewpoint could only be interpreted as stimulants to inflation. Referring to the obvious electoral appeal that the government clearly expected some of the proposals to have, Opposition Leader Whitlam said, "The Treasurer, Mr McMahon, could have saved everybody's time by making his Budget the election manifesto for his party".[51] The Deputy Opposition Leader, Lance Barnard, said "In an inflationary economic context, the government has found resources for a wide range of fiscal measures. In the light of this Budget, the government should never dare to question how Labor would pay for its election pledges".[52] Such statements had their psychological effect. When two months later, the government went to the people, government spokesmen made only halfhearted, soon abandoned attempts to use the tactics of previous years and to question the worth of the ALP's election promises on the basis of "Where is

299

the money coming from?", a query that had rendered the Liberal-CP coalition valuable electoral service in the past.

The Budget possessed for the government the minus pointed up particularly by Barnard. It weakened the claim that the government was more cautious with its budgeting than the ALP was with election promises. But on August 14, 1969, just two days after the presentation of the Budget, Gordon Freeth, as External Affairs Minister, made a speech that was to be for the government a pure, unalloyed minus, not so much because of what it said but the way in which it was said and the effect it was to have. The speech was on international affairs. Two months later the speech was to contribute to the loss of the Western Australian seat of Forrest which Freeth had held almost effortlessly in the House of Representatives since 1949 and to the decline of Gorton's and the Liberal-CP coalition's majority in that chamber from forty to seven. Freeth was not wholly to blame for the adverse effects the speech produced; nor was the External Affairs department which either compiled the original draft for him, or assisted in its compilation.[53] As Freeth had explained to Gorton when Gorton appointed him Minister, External Affairs were not his forte.[54] Because it was not his forte, he was not as acutely aware as he might have been otherwise of nuances to which the DLP was almost morbidly sensitive. The Budget, with its five percent reduction in the defence vote, for which the DLP leaders blamed Gorton, not McMahon,[55] confirmed, in their suspicious minds, that Gorton on defence matters was "a man of drift"[56] who had agreed to a policy of assistance to Malaysia and Singapore with their defence needs only because such a policy had been forced upon him by combined Liberal-DLP forces, and who fatalistically accepted that, unless the United States came to its aid, Australia in a crisis could not defend itself.[57] This assessment of Gorton had overtones of Santamaria's assessment of Gorton, following Santamaria's private interview with Gorton as long ago as April, 1968,[58] though the DLP parliamentarians' antiGorton attitude was also influenced by events subsequent to the Santamaria interview. Freeth's speech, or at least that section of it that roused DLP ire, might have gone comparatively unnoticed but for the Budget announcement that defence spending was to be cut back. Following so quickly upon that announcement, it was waving a red rag enticingly under the nose of already angry bulls. The DLP bulls charged, headlong and, as it proved, damagingly from an electoral viewpoint.

The section of Freeth's speech which functioned as a matador's cape to the DLP whose fervently antiCommunist members, collectively and individually, abhorred the color red read "I turn

300

now to the subject of the Soviet Union in Asia". It was a provocative subject; it continued to be a provocative subject in the context of Australian domestic politics. "During the past year or so there has been increasing interest and activity by the Soviet Union in the Asian region," Freeth reported. "Examples are the movements of ships of the USSR Navy in the Indian Ocean; the development of diplomatic and trade contacts with Malaysia and Singapore; and Mr Brezhnev's speech in Moscow on June 7 when he told the World Conference of Communist Parties that the Soviet Union was 'of the opinion that events are putting on the agenda the task of creating a system of collective security in Asia'. The Australian and USSR governments have also been in contact, both in Canberra and in Moscow, on matters of bilateral interest and also in discussing wider issues. Mr Gromyko, the Foreign Minister of the Soviet Union, said in a speech in Moscow to the Supreme Soviet on July 10 that 'the prerequisite and potential for an improvement in our relations with Australia exist'. The Australian government has naturally kept those and related developments under observation. Australia has to be watchful, but need not panic whenever a Russian appears. It has to avoid both facile gullibility and automatic rejection of opportunities for cooperation". Asked the ALP's Dr Cairns, across the chamber: "Why don't you tell Erwin that?"[59]

"It depends how often, how many, and what sort, doesn't it?" Freeth retorted. "The Australian government at all times welcomes the opportunity of practical and constructive dealings with the Soviet Union, as with any other country, and this has been the basis of our approach to each issue. In principle, it is natural that a world power such as the Soviet Union should seek to promote a presence and a national influence in important regions of the world such as the Indian Ocean. The limited degree of naval penetration of this area up to date was described by me in answer to a question earlier this week.[60] Reason for concern arises when the scale or methods or objective of the promotion are calculated to jeopardise our direct national interests, or to endanger the general security and stability of the area. In judging this, we cannot cast out of our minds the Russian intervention in Czechoslovakia and the pernicious doctrine of 'limited sovereignty' which the USSR attaches to other Communist states."[61]

Freeth started to move into deeper waters. "If cooperation can be maintained or strengthened among countries of the region— including of course Australia—we will have made important advances towards ensuring that Southeast Asia will not be a source

301

of weakness in the total pattern of world security. If the Russian proposals prove to be in line with these general objectives and would assist to facilitate their achievement we would naturally consider them with close interest . . . A substantial withdrawal at present of American strength would leave in the region a weakness which might very well tempt Peking to press southward or let it feel free to make moves against its northern neighbour. Such a situation would not be in the interests of anyone in the region, nor, indeed of the Soviet Union, nor of the world."[62]

There were two special features to this speech. Firstly, Freeth cleared it with Gorton, who made some minor alterations but did not change it substantively. He did not seem to realise what its explosive potential would be when it hit the solid wall of DLP opposition to any collaboration with Communist governments. Secondly, though there was no hard and firm practice under Menzies and Holt, the principles of an important external affairs statement had been generally either discussed by Cabinet, without the actual statement being discussed, or the statement had been referred to senior ministers for their scrutiny and endorsement.[63] On this occasion, the statement was not referred to anyone, not to Fairhall, who as Defence Minister, had already expressed views on the subject, and not even to the CP Leader, John McEwen. McEwen was angry. McEwen had as shrewd a political brain as there was in the Parliament, and more experience under his belt than any parliamentarian on the government side. An old and guileful campaigner, he would for a certainty have realised the reaction that the speech would evoke not only from some of the government's own supporters, but from the DLP, and he did not want this kind of dangerous reaction in an election year. Though the speech might have emerged unchanged in substance, it would have been much more differently worded if McEwen had been consulted. Questioned by parliamentary followers at a Country Party meeting held on August 20, 1969, McEwen said grimly that he had not been consulted on the Freeth statement. If he had been consulted the statement would not have gone out in that form. He agreed with those who thought it "ill advised". He was not intimidated by the DLP, he said. On the other hand, he saw no reason to offend needlessly and in election year a political grouping which was a useful ally at election time. He repeated the same views forcibly in the Cabinet, and told Cabinet but really Gorton that he wanted no repetition of the incident.[64]

As well as the CP, for whom McEwen acted in this issue as the complaining safety valve, a section of Liberal Party and the entire DLP went "up the wall". The height to which they climbed was encouraged by two things. Fairhall had already expressed views on the Soviet presence in the Indian Ocean, which contained none of Freeth's cosy overtones, but which projected a strong note of warning. Addressing a meeting of the Liberal Party's parliamentary candidates in Sydney on July 7, 1969, Fairhall had said "There appears no immediate military threat to Australia's interests, although it would be imprudent not to recognise latent possibilities for a quick change in that situation. In the immediate future, global war must be assessed as unlikely, except by mis-adventure, But other matters occupy our thinking and I put them in no particular order of priority in referring, firstly, to Russia, her growing interest in the Middle East and the increasing appearance of Russian naval strength in the Indian Ocean. The Soviet is clearly promoting closer relations with India in particular, but also with other nations in Southeast Asia. We must keep in mind Russian support of the North Vietnamese, without which the war in that country would have long since finished, and Russian technical and military support for Indonesia in the days of Sukarno".[65] The second thing was the prompt reaction of the Soviet Embassy in Canberra. Without apparently waiting to check back with Moscow, thereby creating the impression that the embassy had foreknowledge of the contents of the Freeth speech[66] the Embassy issued a statement. The Embassy statement said that Russia shared Australia's concern as expressed by Mr Freeth about the adventurist policies of the leaders of China. Russia strongly disagreed with Australian foreign policy on Vietnam, and the Australian government's assessment of the Warsaw treaty countries' actions in Czechoslovakia. "The most interesting moment in the speech for us is of course the expression of the Australian government's desire to develop Australian-Soviet relations and also cooperation of the two countries in the international arena in search of solutions for international problems including the problems of Asia. We have noted with satisfaction the part of the statement which says that 'the Australian government at all times welcomes the opportunity of practical and constructive dealings with the Soviet Union'. We also noted the positive attitude of the Australian government towards the Soviet proposal for collective security in Asia and its sober reassessment of the Chinese provocations against the Soviet Union. We share the concern expressed by the minister about the adventurist policies of the Peking leaders".[67]

The Soviet Embassy statement continued "Territorial claims of the Peking leaders to the neighbour countries, their chauvinistic treatment of the Chinese people in the spirit of hatred to other

303

nations graphically show their fargoing designs. We think that the realistic approach of the Australian government towards the Soviet Union will open up good opportunities for further development of our bilateral relations and cooperation of our two countries in preserving international peace and security".[68]

On August 19, 1969, just five calendar days after the Freeth statement and with only the weekend and two working days intervening, Fairhall announced his retirement from politics. He would not contest his seat of Paterson at the coming general election. Fairhall had always lacked the "killer" instinct. He was a conformist. For all his misgivings, voiced privately, continuously, and moodily, he had never embarrassed either Gorton or the Government in public. He wanted to get out, but he wanted to get out according to his own standards and "decently". He said he was getting out because he doubted if his health would stand the wear and tear of another term. He said that he had told Gorton six months ago that he was "seriously thinking of retiring". As he had been thinking "seriously" of retiring and voicing the thought in conversations with more than Gorton for years this was undoubtedly accurate. Fairhall added that three months ago he had told Gorton he had "definitely" decided to retire.[69] When it was pointed out to Fairhall that this statement conflicted with public pledges he had given in recent weeks that he would stand in Paterson in the Liberal interest, Fairhall produced probably the most truthful confession ever made by any politician. "Now and then you have to make a liar of yourself to save a situation," Fairhall said.[70] Fairhall left ambiguous whether he was doing his lying to protect the government from a hostile reaction because of his resignation, or when he said that he had told Gorton of his intention three months earlier, or when he had made his pledge that he would stand for Paterson at the coming elections. There was a heated clash between Fairhall and a representative of the news media at a Fairhall press conference called immediately after the formal announcement of Fairhall's proposed retirement. Fairhall was asked if his retirement so close to a general election could be interpreted as an act of disloyalty to the government. "I have reasons of my own, and I do not have to tell them to you—not everything is in the public domain," Fairhall said.[71]

Fairhall denied that there was any inference to be drawn from the fact that he was announcing his retirement only five days after Freeth's speech. There was no difference between his approach and Freeth's. He (Fairhall) had made a speech only a few weeks ago to Liberal candidates about a continuing threat

Two of the "old guard" who had been Ministers under Menzies and Holt. Postmaster-General Sir Alan Hulme, left, and the elongated Leslie Bury, who became Treasurer when Gorton ejected McMahon from that post.

Dudley Erwin, flown from Melbourne to Canberra because of an ALP censure vote against the government, hobbled to the chamber of the House of Representatives on a foot with a bone broken. Erwin helped Gorton become Prime Minister but later accused Gorton of being too much under the influence of Miss Gotto's political advice.

from China and Russia.[72] Such a threat might not emerge. But it was wise to keep an eye on it. This did not mean the Russians were coming down to take charge of Australia. There was no need to man panic stations. Nor was the recent five-power conference the reason for his retirement. Gorton's use of the word "Malaya" had not caused any diplomatic friction. The Five-Power Conference had been "wellhandled". There was no particular issue on which he was leaving Parliament. He just "chose" to go. The timing of his announcement was related to the election.[73]

The combination of the three things—the Budget cut in the defence vote, Fairhall's resignation, and Freeth's statement—was too much for the DLP. It went berserk. Gair, as DLP parliamentary leader commented: "The real reason for Fairhall's retirement is that as a man of great political integrity he cannot stand by to see Australia's defences denuded or accept the government's change of policy in relation to the Soviet Union. He (Fairhall) sees Australian defence and foreign policy lying virtually in ruins and is not prepared to sit among them[74] . . . The Prime Minister . . . is living in a world of fantasy. The DLP believes that Australia has nothing to gain and a lot to lose by the Soviet Union's presence in Southeast Asia. He (Gorton) should know by now that it is an easy matter to correct an error in domestic policy but it is almost impossible to correct a mistake in international policy . . ."[75] Addressing the DLP NSW branch annual meeting, DLP Senator John Little said that the DLP was prepared to "crucify" the Liberal Party. Independent candidates with a "reasonable defence policy" would receive DLP second preferences. "If it is necessary to fight the Liberal Party in the interests of Australia and destroy it as we destroyed the ALP fifteen years ago[76] we will tell them we have picked up the challenge. We crucified a lot of good men politically (in 1954/1955) and did it without regret. I would like to think we would not have to do this sort of thing again. But in the last fortnight a lot of events have occurred which have indicated that the choice is no longer ours." Little added that "Australia with its resources and the spirit of its people could create a defence situation which would not pay outsiders to attack". Asked how the DLP would allocate its preferences if a sitting Liberal, who was a Catholic, was opposed by an Independent who was a nonCatholic, Little said "Throughout this country we have politically slaughtered more Catholics than members of other denominations. If there are any more lined up with the enemies of Australia, we will have great pleasure in destroying their political careers also".[77]

Santamaria set out the DLP position in a colder and more

logically reasoned form. In an address,[78] interestingly to the National Civic Council, of which he was national president, and not to the DLP of which he claimed not to be a member, Santamaria drew attention to several aspects of Freeth's speech, as supplemented by a question and answer interview with Peter Samuel in the *Bulletin* on August 30, 1969, and by Gorton in a TV interview with Mike Willesee on the ABC's "Four Corners" TV programme on August 30, 1969. Santamaria pointed out that Freeth's August 14 statement had said "the Australian and USSR governments have also been in contact both in Canberra and Moscow on matters of bilateral interest and also in discussing wider issues". Santamaria claimed that these "wider" issues went really wide. "In August last year, at approximately the same time as the Soviet invasion of Czechoslovakia, . . . some professionals in the Australian Foreign Affairs Department began to show an interest in some kind of collective security," Santamaria wrote. "External Affair's new proposals—to look at the Russian entry into the region with a more benign eye—would have sprung from the realisation that the American presence in Asia was now likely to be withdrawn or at least seriously changed in form . . . External Affairs drew the conclusion that we might look for new friends; and while it probably had few illusions about the Soviet, the proposal to explore its Asian plans can only mean that it considered that here might be a substitute for the failed British and Americans. On June 7, Brezhnev, one of the two Soviet leaders responsible for the rape of Czechoslovakia, addressed the Conference of World Communist Parties and he formally . . . said 'We are of the opinion that the course of events is also bringing to the fore the need to create a collective security system in Asia' . . . Mr Freeth's statement drew attention to (this) Soviet proposal for a system of collective security in Asia . . . the statement also justified the appearance of the Soviet Union in our vicinity (by saying) 'In principle it is natural that a world power such as the Soviet Union should seek to promote a presence and a national influence in important regions of the world such as the Indian Ocean area . . . it appears that at this stage the Soviet Union itself is exploring the reactions of other countries before trying to convert the idea into any firm or detailed proposal."

Said Santamaria "What Mr Freeth did not mention, and might have mentioned, was that Soviet feelers had, to this point, met with almost universal coldness. The Indonesian newspaper *Nusantara* on June 17, 1969, condemned 'the expansion of Soviet influence in this part of the world'. India had stated that it wanted the Indian Ocean neutralised and all great powers excluded from it. Mrs Gandhi was to repeat this on September 12. Japan had coldly refused to consider any arrangement which might involve it in the Soviet's conflict with China. In fact, the Australian suggestion that the Soviet proposals should be explored was the first sign of welcome to come from any country in the region. Unwittingly, Australia constituted itself as the entering wedge of Soviet influence".

Santamaria then drew attention to two statements in the Freeth interview with Samuel. Freeth had said "There hasn't been a clear distinction drawn between the Russian desire to have a Communist Southeast Asia and the Chinese desire to have a Communist Southeast Asia . . . There had been competition between Russia and China as to who would have the predominating influence. But there now seems to be some change in emphasis on the Russia part to a desire to prevent Chinese Communism expanding into Southeast Asia. We read into that, as following on that, a Russian desire to prevent Southeast Asia going Communist because if it goes Communist it will be dominated by Chinese Communism. So to that extent we have some common ground with the Russians".[79]

Santamaria claimed that Freeth had advanced several novel propositions. One was that there was a qualitative difference between Russian and Chinese Communism which was to say that Chinese Communism was worse than Russian Communism. Another was that Russia was a member of the international community whereas China was not—"whatever that may mean". The third was that Russia wanted to stop not only the expansion in Southeast Asia of Chinese influence but it wished "to prevent Southeast Asia going Communist because if it goes Communist it will be dominated by Chinese Communism so to that extent we have some common ground". Commented Santamaria "Mr Freeth thus seriously believes that the Soviet has become an anti-Communist force in Asia . . . The Soviet plan for Asia aims at a physical reality—Soviet military power—of which the security pact or alliance is only the legal and diplomatic form".

Santamaria added "Having established herself in the Mediterranean, pre-eminent in the Middle East, increasingly dominating the Red Sea states and the Persian Gulf, increasingly influential in India, the Soviet is now moving systematically to become the dominant—indeed the only—naval power in the Indian Ocean. If the Soviet achieves this monopoly of naval power, she will ultimately be in a position to supply arms, land troops, to provide air cover and naval support for any local Communist or other minority coup in Indonesia or any Southeast Asian state . . . .

307

Those who say that the Soviet would never behave this way in Asia —once her physical power was well established—have forgotten several inconvenient facts. She did invade Czechoslovakia on August 21 last year. She threatens to behave in the same way towards her former ally, China. She has made the same threats towards Indonesia. She still insists on a Communist victory in Vietnam. To all this, the Gorton Government's answer, when it was originally formulated, sounded eminently reasonable. We can't do anything to stop the entry of Soviet power into the Indian Ocean and Southeast Asia. Agreed. We do not, at this stage, know whether that power, once it exists there, will in fact be hostile to us. (Mr Gorton has since revised this, but one suspects only for the election.) When it shows itself to be hostile to us, then we will do something about it. It sounds eminently reasonable; yet on examination it is transparent nonsense . . . What you say you can't do today while there is time you expect to do tomorrow when there is none . . . . What was surprising was that the Australian government turned out to be the only government in the Asian region to think the Soviet proposals deserving of discussion. What was equally surprising was that the Australian government should not have realised that such a proposition should have a substantial impact not only upon Australia's international relations, but on her internal politics as well."

Santamaria then spelled out a threat, a threat that in itself was a course of action which the DLP was later to follow. ". . . someone has an obligation to act effectively to bring the government to a sense of reality. No risk whatsoever must be taken that an ALP government will be returned to office. Within the framework of that over-riding objective, unless the government meets the second —and the basic defence problem—practically in the policy speech, a small but effective demonstration of disapproval should be made by withholding preferences in less than half a dozen carefully selected seats."

Survival is the first law of politics. The law applies with equal rigidity to a backbencher as to a prime minister. Gorton believed that he could survive and enable the government he led to survive by appealing through TV and over the heads of the disturbed sections of his party and the DLP to the mass electorate. Some of his followers believed that they could survive only on the votes of the DLP. Liberals, whose views on this matter of Soviet naval intrusion into the Indian Ocean were closer to the DLP's views than to their own government's views, were quite open about their outraged feelings. Even before the DLP threat of withdrawal of preferences was voiced, outspoken Les Irwin, from Mitchell, in

Sydney, had said his piece. Said Irwin: "I am disturbed by the present overtures to the Soviet. In fact I am bewildered and astounded. The Russians are not coming into the Indian Ocean for health reasons, or for the benefit of Australia. We should not give our neighbors in the area the impression that we are welcoming the Russian presence. The Russians would only use our acquiescence to their presence to persuade our neighbors that they also should acquiesce. I don't like it. This attitude is not in Australia's best interests."

The assistant Government Whip, Kevin Cairns, sought an interview with Gorton. He was granted one on September 10, 1969. Cairns told Gorton he, Gorton, lacked "a strategic concept." Cairns, a Queensland dentist, was a Roman Catholic of working class origins. His father had been a trade union official. Short, bespectacled, studious, Cairns who had a specialised interest in economics was critical of what he considered to be Gorton's ad hoc approach to financial problems. Cairns' seat of Lilley was lower middleclass and had a high DLP content. Cairns had an affinity with some of the DLP parliamentarians, particularly with Gair, a fellow Queenslander, who had been highly regarded as an administrator and admired for his stubborn adherence to principle when he was an ALP Premier in Queensland. Gorton wanted to discuss with Cairns DLP attitudes to his policies. Gorton probably worked out that Cairns could influence the DLP parliamentarians into taking a more sympathetic attitude towards him and his government. Cairns said he was not interested in DLP policies. But he was very interested in government policies. It was the government that he expected to support with his vote in the House of Representatives. He could not support Gorton's present defence and foreign policies, implicit in which was the "Fortress Australia" concept. Cairns came out of the interview feeling that he had "got nowhere." Later he told intimates that once it became clear he was not going to use his influence with the DLP parliamentarians to "softpedal" on the Gorton-Freeth policy Gorton had "merely waffled on."

In his interview with Gorton, Cairns was apparently only restating views which he had already put forward elsewhere. In August, 1969, a précis of Cairns' speech to the Lilley area Liberal Executive[80] which re-endorsed Cairns as Liberal Party candidate was circulated in Queensland, where the State Liberal branch was showing signs of being mountingly critical of Gorton. The Lilley Liberal Executive meeting seems to have taken place some time in July, 1969. In the précis, which conformed with Cairns' known views, Cairns stated that he was not going to campaign on social

309

service issues at the coming general election, whatever line Gorton took. Important as he regarded social services as being, "regionalism" was even more important to Australia. It would decide Australia's future and in fact whether Australia would have a future. The précis reported Cairns as saying "The old Australian Workers' Union principle of 'one out, all out' is clearly adapted to our foreign policy. If one sinks in Southeast Asia, we all sink. That was Menzies' and Holt's interpretation of our position. It does not appear to be that of the present Prime Minister, Mr Gorton. . . . Most tragically there has been an erosion of will in Australia as well as in America, as an outcome of the January Tet offensive in Vietnam this year. The Tet offensive had as its greatest casualty in Australia the Opposition Leader Mr Whitlam. But I fear it also had its effects on the will and judgment of our present Prime Minister. Many have forgotten that strategically, militarily, and politically, the offensive was a failure for the Vietcong and the Communists in South Vietnam. But it was not a failure elsewhere. Whether the Tet offensive was an excuse or the reason for a basic alteration in Australian attitudes I do not know. But that our strategic assessment has changed subsequent to it is undeniable . . . . I hope you appreciate the significance of the differences in attitudes which are developing concerning foreign policy and its appendage, defence policy. These differences could be grave, very grave . . . the results may be very distressing to some of us in the (Liberal) Party. I do not intend to change. In other words, if there is a fight on, I do not support what appears to be the present attitudes. I will take the fight to its logical conclusion."

On September 11, 1969, the day after his interview with Gorton Cairns voiced his attitude publicly. Said Cairns ". . . to say 'Well, we ought to give the diplomatic green light or we ought to afford a tacit acceptance for another Communist power (Russia) to replace Communist China in her area of interest in Southeast Asia' . . . is a doctrine with which I just cannot go along."[81]

Irwin and Cairns were only the tip of the Liberal iceberg. Quite a number of Liberals were upset by the tone of the Gorton-Freeth declaration, some because ideologically they were in agreement with the DLP about the stupidity in taking an attitude that would encourage Soviet aspirations in the Indian Ocean area and discourage Southeast Asian countries trying to produce a situation that would militate against those aspirations, and others because of the electoral consequences that could follow what they considered to be the needless exasperation of DLP feelings. Among the number upset were McMahon, still Treasurer, Fairbairn, still

310

Minister for National Development, Peter Howson, a former Minister, John Jess, chairman of the government's defence committee, Sir John Cramer, a onetime Army Minister and as one who had participated back in the 1940s in the founding of the Liberal Party quietly influential, Dr Malcolm Mackay, who said straightout that his election manifesto would vary in defence matters from the line followed in the Gorton-Freeth statement, and others.

Acting on his concept that "the centre of government resides in the party rooms"[82] Gorton took action to see that more of the iceberg did not rise above sea-level. He started on a retreat from Moscow, which at times seemed more disorganised than that of Bonaparte's but which in the immediate outcome was more successful. Where Bonaparte survived but lost his throne, Gorton survived and kept his. Soon after Freeth had made his August 14 speech, Freeth had left for the United States to lead the Australian delegation at the opening on September 16 of the 24th Session of the General Assembly of the United States. On September 18, 1969, he was to speak at an American-Australian Association luncheon in New York. Copies of his speech were circulated in advance to the publicity media in Australia. Gorton saw the speech. In it, Freeth defended himself—mildly—against DLP and Liberal Party criticisms about his Soviet statements. He repeated the substance of those statements, though in verbiage less provocative to the DLP. Gorton phoned him in the United States and told him to cut out all references to the Soviet. The instruction was relayed back to the External Affairs Department. The External Affairs' officers patiently contacted the news media late at night. But by that time most of the first editions of the morning papers had gone to press. It was too late to withdraw the Soviet references. Freeth was advised. He decided to retain the references. The affair attracted even more attention to the incident.

But the retreat was already in full swing. Said Gorton ". . . Our ultimate security in Australia would be threatened by the establishment of any Russian naval or military bases anywhere in our own regions. We feel that any military alliance between Russia and a country in our own region would pose a threat to ourselves. We cannot forget Czechoslovakia and Hungary and the Berlin airlift and all the sorry chapters of the past. We have no intention, nor have we ever considered the remotest possibility of any military understanding between ourselves and the Soviet Union or any active military involvement by Soviet Russia in any collective security arrangement among the countries to our north. For we think that would be dangerous for us. This should be made

311

clear. I hope it has now been made clear."[83] But the marauding Cossack squadrons of the DLP kept pressing menacingly on Gorton's exposed flanks. They were determined to keep the retreating government troops on the retreat. The Deputy DLP Parliamentary Leader, Frank McManus, announced that a decision on how the DLP would allot its preferences in the forthcoming general election would be taken on the content of the election speeches given by the Government's Gorton and the ALP's Whitlam. "We have decided we will have our own opening after we have heard the policy speeches of Mr Gorton and Mr Whitlam," McManus said. "Then we will be deciding what we shall do with our preferences." McManus added that the DLP would make Australia's defence, security, and foreign affairs policies vital issues at the forthcoming election.[84] What the DLP wanted to extract from Gorton and his government was (a) an increase in the defence vote, (b) an undertaking against participation in Soviet inspired pacts in Asia, (c) confirmation of the maintenance of the "forward presence" in Malaysia/Singapore, (d) the building of a naval base at Cockburn Sound in Western Australia, and (e) the maintenance of a "naval presence" in the Indian Ocean.[85] With the assistance of Country Party Leader, John McEwen, who maintained a cautious liaison with the DLP through the DLP's Parliamentary Leader, Vince Gair, and who wanted DLP preference for CP seats, particularly in Victoria and Western Australia, and whose broad views on defence were not markedly dissimilar from the DLP's, the DLP was to get what they wanted, with the exception of an increased defence vote.

Other things were happening on the domestic as well as the foreign affairs-defence front. The wheat situation was deteriorating. In the last week of August, both Australia and the United States cut their wheat prices, intensifying fears that the world was on the brink of a wheat price war. Wool prices were declining steadily. Australia's 60,000 wheatgrowers were to begin harvesting the 1969 wheat crop in September. The crop was expected to reach 500 million bushels, and the government was prepared to pay only on a quota figure of 357 million bushels. The International Grain Agreement, which McEwen, as Country Party Leader, had insisted was Australian wheatgrowers' impregnable bastion, was showing signs of crumbling.

Don Maisey, a tough and tough looking wheatgrower, who represented the Western Australian seat of Moore in the CP interests, was highly critical of the government's wheat policy, for which he blamed his leader, McEwen. Maisey, as a member of Australian Wheat Board, had negotiated the contracts with mainland China which had turned China into a major customer for Australian wheat. He was highly respected, and recognised as an authority on the wheat industry by both government and ALP parliamentarians. He was opposed to McEwen's wheat policies, which he claimed, by raising prices for local consumption, merely added to general farming costs, while penalising the impecunious and vulnerable section of the Australian community, which relied heavily for nutrition upon wheat products. It was recognised that while reasonably temperate in his criticisms in 1969 in recognition of the fact that it was election year, Maisey could break out damagingly at any time. Others in the CP, including Robert King, from Wimmera, in Victoria, were uneasy about wheat policies, and could provide Maisey with a readymade and destructive following.

After a CP meeting on August 20, 1969, Maisey was summoned to McEwen's room in Parliament House, Canberra. There had been rumors that Maisey would repudiate his CP allegiance, and contest Moore as an independent. Maisey said that he would be running as a CP candidate unless CP endorsement was taken from him. There had also been a rumor that the CP would take away his endorsement because of his opposition to the McEwen-inspired government wheat policies, and Maisey was getting in first. Maisey was assured that his CP endorsement would not be interfered with. Asked if he wanted CP ministers visiting his electorate to assist him during the election campaign Maisey said bluntly "No." Maisey pointed out that McEwen had not participated in the 1966 Senate election campaign when the WA Country Party had done "all right" and secured third place for a CP Senator.

In the middle of these happenings, Gorton announced Saturday, October 25, 1969, as the date of the general elections. Before he announced it in the Parliament on August 20, 1969, Gorton announced it in the Government Parties' room. Though in his Budget speech the next day, August 21, 1969, Gorton did not mention defence, he did not hesitate when asked at the Government Parties' meeting what he considered the basic issue or issues in the forthcoming elections. "Defence," Gorton said. Gorton said that the government and the ALP were in flat disagreement on three vital areas of defence. Where the government was determined to maintain ANZUS and the Australian-US alliance to the point of accepting joint bases in Australia, the ALP was prepared to repudiate the spirit of ANZUS and to dismantle those bases. This was point of disagreement one. Where the government was committed to maintaining both an interest and armed forces in the Singapore-Malaysia[86] area at the request of the Singapore and

313

Malaysian governments, the ALP was pledged to withdraw them. This was point of disagreement two. Where the government would not sign the nuclear non-proliferation treaty in its present form, the ALP was pledged to sign it, even though such signing could adversely affect Australia's longterm defence interests. Gorton said that having brought forward a Budget, he could see no reason for waiting another four weeks[87] to go to the country at a later date. "Having presented our Budget, we are placing it before the people for them to pass judgment," Gorton said. His election campaign would be mainly on television. He would find it difficult to attend individual electorates. But if his presence was needed and it was possible he would try to attend campaign meetings.[88] In the Parliament later, Gorton said the House of Representatives would be dissolved at noon on September 29, election writs would be issued on that date, and nominations would close on October 7, 1969.

Until Parliament adjourned on September 26, 1969, Gorton enjoyed himself. The Australian Medical Association Gazette had criticised the value of Whitlam's and the ALP's outlined medical scheme, which proposed a complete cover for medical, pharmaceutical, hospital, and dental services, and which, Whitlam claimed, in total would cost no more than the existing health scheme and would cost individuals slightly less. The Liberals, under Gorton's guidance, had a pleasant week in Parliament "rubbishing" the ALP scheme.

Gorton also announced details of a new Queensland sugar agreement,[89] told Parliament the Commonwealth was prepared to lend Queensland eighty million dollars over a six-year period for the construction of a Central Queensland power station,[90] and when the High Court made a judgment that made it illegal for the States to collect some of the receipts tax they had been levying in some cases for years and which in total brought them in revenue of about seventy million dollars in 1969/70,[91] gave assurances that the Commonwealth would cooperate in overcoming this problem. Gorton also appeared on a major TV show on August 31, 1969[92] in which, reverting to his former laconic style of speech and answering questions, relaxed, directly and with seeming ease, he made a good impression and emerged again confident of his TV virtuosity, a virtuosity that would enable him to appeal successfully over the heads of both political opponents and nominal supporters to the mass of the Australian public.

Supremely confident—as at that period was nearly everyone else connected with politics—that he and his government would be returned on polling day, October 25, 1969 with at worst a slight paring down in their majority, Gorton adhered to the last to his determination to be a prime minister who would behave as he wanted to behave. On September 1, 1969, he took off for a week's fishing at Exmouth Gulf with Western Australian prawning magnate, Michael Kailis, whose "fishing trips, his excellent seafood cuisine, and rough cut brand of informality have already charmed several state and federal politicians."[93]

But the calm warm azure waters of Exmouth Gulf and its environs were far different from the cold troubled waters within which Gorton was to be fishing for the next two hectic months in which Gorton was to survive both the general election and a challenge to his leadership by only narrow margins and as a result of his own dexterity, doggedness and courage.

NOTES

1 The Zinoviev letter, allegedly sent by the President of the Communist Third International to the British Communist Party instructed the party to support the Anglo-Soviet trade treaties, and ordered preparation for military insurrection. It was published in Britain four days before polling day for the 1924 general British elections and at a stage when it was believed that the British Labor Party had prospects of retaining government. The British Labor Party lost forty-one seats and the Tories won government.

2 Fadden justified his claim. As Treasurer in the Menzies' post-1949 government, he lifted petrol rationing, and the Australian economy continued prosperous.

3 *Canberra Times,* February 1, 1969.

4 I have always had a certain sympathy with those who made the 1963 agreement. Though the agreement made with the United States was almost incredibly loose on the financial side (see the careful résumé of the F111 transaction given to the House of Representatives by Malcolm Fraser, then Minister for Defence, on May 12, 1970) the only fundamental gamble being taken was on US technical "know-how", superficially a very slight gamble in view of the proven US ability to solve technical problems, quickly and satisfactorily.

5 Requoted derisively by Whitlam against Fairhall—Commonwealth Representatives' Debates, Vol 63, p 2338, May 28, 1969.

6 See Chapter 3, pp 56/58.

7 The emphasis changed so quickly that it was difficult for an "outsider" to keep reasonably well informed.

8 Fairhall later told me that he "knew" where this document had come from. He said it had its origins in the US Embassy in Canberra. I was never able to work out why he believed this. The document I saw contained nothing to suggest it was a US Embassy document.

9 The story appeared in the *Daily Telegraph,* Sydney, May 2, 1969.

10 There were some mysterious happenings involving documents dealing with the F111 over this period. I have so far been unable to establish what precisely happened to one document which was marked to be delivered by safe hand and only to a person with the highest security

315

clearance. I have reason to believe that a copy of this document went with Gorton to Washington.

11 In other words, Gorton wanted a guarantee that the US would continue with its production of the F111 during the lifetime of the Australian twenty-four.

12 Official summary of the Prime Minister's 1969 activities, issued by Gorton's Canberra office.

13 *Canberra Times,* May 10, 1969.

14 This was the guarantee Gorton sought that the US would continue producing the F111 for at least ten years, and preferably the fifteen years, sought by the Australian government—Commonwealth Representatives' Debates, Vol 63, p 192, May 15, 1969.

15 Ibid.

16 *Daily Telegraph,* Sydney, June 7, 1969.

17 *Australian,* September 29, 1969.

18 I was not present at this briefing, and my knowledge is confined to what I read in the newspapers the following day.

19 Commonwealth Weekly Representatives' Debates, No 8, pp 1987/1993, May 12, 1970.

20 This is from personal observations and conversations with Fairhall during 1969.

21 Official text, Fairhall addressing Liberal Party Parliamentary candidates Conference, July 7, 1969.

22 Official text issued by Fairhall's Canberra office.

23 Official text issued by Fairhall's Canberra office.

24 Official text issued by Fairhall's Canberra office.

25 Official text issued by Fairhall's Canberra office.

26 This happened on August 13, 1969, the day after the Budget, in which pensioners got a dollar a week rise, was introduced in the House of Representatives.

27 *Daily Telegraph,* Sydney, June 19.

28 Ibid.

29 Freeth, interviewed by Robert Baudino, Channel GTV-9, Melbourne, June 23, 1969.

30 On February 25, 1969, Gorton in a section of his speech dealing with Sabah said that a decision on the use of Australian troops would be made "in the light of our judgment of all the circumstances at any given time" —Commonwealth Representatives' Debates, Vol 62, p 37.

31 Commonwealth Representatives' Debates, Vol 62, p 36, February 25, 1969.

32 *Daily Telegraph,* Sydney, June 20, 1969.

33 Gorton repeated that the Malaya reference was "deliberate" in a TV interview, Channel HSV-7, Melbourne, July 6, 1967.

34 *Bulletin,* Sydney, June 28, 1969.

35 Transcript of Freeth-Fairhall press conference, June 20, 1969.

36 Transcript of Freeth-Fairhall press conference, June 20, 1969.

37 *Sydney Morning Herald,* July 1, 1969.

38 *Daily Telegraph,* Sydney, June 21, 1969.

39 *Sun-Pictorial,* Melbourne, June 24, 1969.

40 *Focus,* Sydney, July 1969.

41 *Focus,* Sydney, July 1969.

42 The June, 1969, Gallup Poll figures were Liberal-CP 50 percent, ALP 40 percent, DLP 7 percent, others 3 percent—*Herald,* Melbourne, October 24, 1969.

43 See Chapter 8, p 166.

44 Fairbairn apparently was one of the earliest to be given a hint that Gorton was planning to hold an October election.

45 Downer had his term extended for another twelve months after 1970.

46 See Chapter 6, p 128, Notes 1 and 2.

47 Commonwealth Representatives' Debates, Vol 64, p 43, August 12, 1969.

48 Commonwealth Representatives' Debates, Vol 64, pp 31/33, August 12, 1969.

49 Aged pensioners were eligible for a special Pensioner medical service.

50 Commonwealth Representatives' Debates, Vol 64, p 43, August 12, 1969.

51 Ibid., Vol 64, p 384, August 19, 1969.

52 Ibid., Vol 64, p 194, August 13, 1969.

53 Santamaria was to claim later that the first draft was prepared by the then permanent head of External Affairs, Sir James Plimsoll—undated address to National Civic Council.

54 See Chapter 9, pp 196/198.

55 McMahon had admirers in the DLP. This did nothing to endear McMahon to Gorton.

56 Gair described Gorton in these words—*Sydney Morning Herald,* January 20, 1969.

57 There is a certain irony in Gorton having served in the RAAF in World War II while the four DLP Parliamentarians—Gair, McManus, Byrne and Little—though critical of him on defence matters, were nonmilitary men.

58 See Chapter 3, pp 53/54.

59 Air Minister Dudley Erwin, earlier on the same day, had said that Uren, Cairns' best friend in the Parliament, had had "very close associations" with members of the Soviet Embassy. Uren, as a soldier in the Australian army had served in Malaya in World War II, and spent several years as a p.o.w. in Japanese hands. Since 1962, Uren had fought doggedly a series of protracted court cases—in which a column I wrote in the *Bulletin* was an issue—to defend his reputation against charges which had their nonlegal starting point in a speech made by Erwin in the Parliament on November 29, 1962. On August 14, 1969, after Uren had spoken and said justifiably he had "cleared" his name, Erwin withdrew and accepted unreservedly "what the honorable member (Uren) has said tonight"—Commonwealth Representatives' Debates, Vol 64, pp 307/310, August 14, 1969.

60 After setting out the relatively small scale of Russian naval activity in the Indian Ocean area, Freeth had told the Parliament "Up to the present, although there has been an increasing Russian interest, it poses no threat to any Australian interest"—Commonwealth Representatives' Debates, Vol 64, p 8, August 12, 1969.

61 Commonwealth Representatives' Debates, Vol 64, pp 311/312, August 14, 1969.

62 Commonwealth Representatives' Debates, Vol 64, pp 312/313, August 14, 1969.

63 Gorton denied this, stating, "I don't know of any occasions . . . where statements on foreign policy ever went through Cabinet or to Ministers other than the Prime Minister"—TV interview, official text, August 30, 1969.

64 From conversations with CP parliamentarians at the time.

65 From official text issued by Fairhall's Canberra office.

317

66 DLP Senator Byrne hinted at this suspicion publicly in the Senate—Commonwealth Senate Debates, Vol 41, p 661, September 10, 1969.

67 *Sydney Morning Herald,* August 16, 1969.

68 *Sydney Morning Herald,* August 16, 1969.

69 It may not be without significance that "three months ago" was around the period of the five-power conference, held from June 19 to June 21, when Gorton made his "Malaya" references.

70 From notes made at Fairhall press conference, Canberra, August 19, 1969.

71 Ibid.

72 Fairhall was either again operating on the basis "Now and then you have to make a liar of yourself to save a situation", or had taken the unusual step of refraining from reading Freeth's speech. Far from regarding the growth of Russian influence in the Indian Ocean as "a threat", Freeth had described it as "natural that a world power, such as the Soviet Union should seek to promote a presence and a national influence in important regions of the world such as the Indian Ocean area."

73 From notes taken at the Fairhall press conference, August 19, 1969.

74 Official text issued by Gair's Canberra office, August 19, 1969.

75 *Canberra Times,* September 10, 1969.

76 Little was referring to the ALP split of 1954/55 as a result of which the DLP hived off from the ALP. It was a DLP article of faith that this hiving off was because of the successful operation of proCommunist influences on ALP foreign, defence and industrial policies.

77 *Daily Telegraph,* Sydney, August 25.

78 I have a copy of this address with the date, and where the address was given, carefully blacked out. Internal evidence suggests the address was given early in October, 1969.

79 *Bulletin,* Sydney, August 30, 1969.

80 I have a copy of this précis. Cairns refused to confirm that it was an accurate précis of what he said. But, significantly, he refused to deny that it was an accurate précis.

81 Commonwealth Representatives' Debates, Vol 65, p 1206, September 11, 1969.

82 See Chapter 1, p 22, Note 12.

83 Official text, address to Gorton's Kingston electorate Liberal Party rally, Glengowrie, South Australia, September 12, 1969.

84 *Australian,* September 5, 1969.

85 "Struggle on Two Fronts: The DLP and the 1969 Election" by B. A. Santamaria, *Australian Quarterly,* December, 1969, No 4, Vol 41, p 41.

86 I checked carefully and repeatedly to ensure that Gorton had reverted to "Malaysia" instead of the "Malaya" he had used during the five-power discussions in June.

87 Normally elections would have been held in November. But by that time the wheat harvest would be piling up.

88 *Daily Telegraph,* Sydney, August 21, 1969.

89 Commonwealth Representatives' Debates, Vol 65, pp 2004/2005, September 25, 1969.

90 Commonwealth Representatives' Debates, Vol 65, pp 2075/2076, September 26, 1969.

91 Senate Weekly Debates, No 11, p 2432, June 12, 1970.

92 Interview by Mike Willesee on the ABC's "Four Corners".

93 *Australian,* September 4, 1969.

CHAPTER 13

ARISTOTLE said a long time ago "Man is by nature a political animal." Because they themselves are political animals, politicians tend to accept this as a statement of fact. But it is demonstrably not fact. Some men are political animals. Others are not. If politics have to do with government, who should conduct it, how it should be organised, and the purposes for which it should be carried on—and that seems to be what it is all about—only a relatively few in the community are consistently and continually involved. The majority, like Dr Pangloss and his world weary associates in their later years, concentrate upon cultivating their personal gardens. As a rule, these home gardeners are interested in the effects which government has upon their lives, or such decisions as governments make which affect their lives, only when government or its decisions intrude upon them unmistakably. Failing a near catastrophic happening which impinges or threatens to impinge, momentously, upon their individual lives, a catastrophe such as mounting unemployment with the potential to add them to the jobless, depressed economic conditions or inflation that could affect adversely their living standards or produce hunger, a war whose consequences are felt by a significant section of the community, or a changing or threatening social atmosphere which erodes their feeling of security and safety, their interest, when they have any, is vague or sporadic.[1] But, under a democratic parliamentary system, the voters, unlike Pangloss and his companions on their eighteenth century Turkish farm, have some enticement not to let the political world pass by completely, because they are proffered on occasions, triennial in Australia, the opportunity to pass judgment upon their national government and to choose whether it, or some alternative political grouping, shall continue to operate as the government after polling day. To meet this situation, they rely upon impression. Without a dramatic happening, such as the Zinoviev letter in the United Kingdom in 1924 or the Petrov defection in Australia in 1954, impressions are formed over a period. They do not emerge overnight.[2]

There was no catastrophic situation existing in Australia in late August when Gorton announced that October 25, 1969, would be election day. "The economy was bursting with health, exhibiting a remarkable rate growth of six percent at constant prices, with inflation low at three percent. The registered unemployed were less than one percent of the work force in every state" was the description of the then situation by Alan Hughes, lecturer in political science at the University of Melbourne.[3] "Confidence in the economy was high, and rose higher as mineral discoveries followed one another at regular intervals," was the judgment of Don Aitkin, Senior Research Fellow in Political Science at the Australian National University. "The war in Vietnam was cooling off, and if that was, on balance, likely to favor the ALP, polls still showed substantial support for the government's stance. The most delicate problems were all in the rural sector, the lifting of the embargo on the export of merino rams and the imposition of quotas on wheat production being the most notable . . . ."[4] These assessments by two academics were re-echoed by other qualified judges. Politicians, who worked off the seats of their pants, intuition, study of statistics which showed trends, and personal observation, shared this view of Australia as an affluent, expanding society. Even opponents of the government did not challenge this picture of affluence; what they challenged was the inequality with which the affluence was being distributed over the community. There were areas of need, real need, and in some cases poverty, but the sufferers were impotently distributed across the Commonwealth, and located generally in constituencies held by Opposition parliamentarians. The casting of their votes against the government would merely contribute to the size of an ALP win not to a government loss. The general expectation at that time was that the government would be returned comfortably, with at worst its parliamentary strength only slightly diminished.

But over the months before Gorton's announcement that the general election would be held on October 25, the mass of voters had been given opportunity to form an impression. The impression undoubtedly was of a Liberal Party which itself had doubts about Gorton's leadership qualities, and of a government which was unsure of where it was going, or where it wanted to go, on defence, foreign investment, relationships with the states—which provided the citizen with the basic services, such as transport, housing, education, hospitals, sanitary services, and the like—and uncertain as to how it should handle such difficult and complex problems as the decline in the rural industries. And to strengthen this impression of questionable leadership, indecision, and irresolution, the major criticisms were coming not from the ALP, the formal

320

opposition, but from within the government ranks and from within the Liberal Party.

Liberal and government associated individuals and organisations had for months been assailing Gorton and his government persistently and consistently. Those attacks deepened and intensified after St John had made his abortive and amateurish attack upon the Prime Minister's personal conduct and administrative methods. Gorton's supporters had succeeded in burying St John in the unconsecrated ground of isolation, and were to bury him still deeper by securing his defeat at the October 25 election in his seat of Warringah, but his ghost went marching on. Unlike St John, those who followed in St John's ghostly wake, did not concentrate upon Gorton's personal idiosyncrasies, but, more dangerously from Gorton's viewpoint, complained about his method of conducting government.

The Country Party "can no longer tolerate centralism either by force under Whitlam or centralism by stealth and suffocation under Gorton",[5] Mr G. F. Freudenstein, the Country Party Minister assisting the NSW Premier and Treasurer, Askin, told a Country Party rally at Lockhart, the centre of a wool and wheat rural area in southern NSW. Whether the CP worked in a coalition or exercised its complete individuality it must be ever watchful for the signs of centralisation of power, Freudenstein said. "Power in many hands is power in safe hands," he said.[6] NSW Premier Askin supported his CP assistant. Attacking centralism in Canberra, Askin told the Liberal Party's NSW Convention in Sydney that centralism was a "disaster". "It smacks more of Socialism than Liberalism," Askin said. Askin blamed this "centralism" for many of NSW's difficulties. "A man has been landed on the moon, but sewerage hasn't reached my own electorate of Collaroy yet," Askin said.[7] NSW feeling towards Gorton was not improved when it was revealed that Gorton had refused an invitation to address the NSW Liberal Conference, whose political activities covered the forty-five Federal seats within the boundaries of NSW but instead had elected to attend a dinner in the Kingston electorate of Liberal MHR, Miss Kay Brownbill, in South Australia where even if he had a statewide effect with his Kingston appearance only twelve seats were exposed to his political blandishments.

In Victoria, the Liberal Premier, Sir Henry Bolte, who had led the Victorian Government since 1955, was openly and often publicly hostile to Gorton and his government. The Queensland Liberal machine was estranged. The Western Australian Liberal machine was critical. The expressions of dissatisfaction were paraded before the public in various ways. On the few occasions when Gorton sought publicly to combat these expressions of disapproval he succeeded only in attracting to them further public attention. A typical occasion was when members of the Liberal North Sydney branch at a meeting on September 3, 1969, not much over a month before the general election was scheduled to take place, agreed to send to federal and state Liberal parliamentary members and to Liberal Party officials a letter on Federal-State relations which cast doubts on whether Gorton adhered to Liberal philosophy in his approach to this emotive and divisive issue. The letter drew attention to the Federal platform of the Liberal Party which provided for "the maintenance unimpaired of the federal system of government with appropriate division of powers between the Commonwealth and the States as most conducive to the progress and well-being of Australia, the development of her territories and resources, and the democratic protection of the freedom of the individual". The letter concluded, "If the Prime Minister wants the loyalty and confidence of the members of the Liberal Party, he should be prepared to give his loyalty and confidence to the party platform."[8]

Gorton discussed the North Sydney attack in a telephone conversation with Askin, who had to leave a meeting of NSW Liberal parliamentarians to take the call. Gorton said later the branch which agreed to issue the letter was only one among twenty-five Liberal branches in North Sydney, and only fourteen people had been present at the branch meeting which agreed to the dispatch of the letter.[9] Still later the NSW Liberal Party claimed officially that the North Sydney Liberal Federal Electorate Council had dissociated itself from the letter.[10] But Mr George d'Avagour, president of the Liberal North Sydney branch, claimed that he had had a "great number" of letters after the branch's letter had been circulated. "Out of these, only three Federal members implied or indicated their support for the policies of the leader of the Federal Parliamentary Party (Gorton)" d'Avagour said. "A number of letters criticised the timing of the North Sydney branch letter which, it was feared, tended to jeopardise the party's electoral prospects. Other letters, dozens of them, unanimously supported the stand taken by the North Sydney branch . . . . Mention has been made . . . that the North Sydney Federal Electoral Council subsequently dissociated itself from the Branch's letter. . . . The fact is that the council was represented in that context by four office bearers only". . . . At the subsequent general meeting of the conference on November 21, 1969, three of the officebearers resigned, and a member of the North Sydney branch was elected Vice-President of the Conference.[11]

With such mutinous stirrings in the ranks of the Liberal Party, and with the DLP, the firmly loyal electoral auxiliaries of the Liberal-CP legions while Menzies and Holt generalled the Liberal-CP campaigns discontented and no longer completely reliable, the coalition did not look like the political army that had conquered almost effortlessly for twenty years and had held for that period, with only occasionally a meaningful challenge, the dominating citadel of federal government. The subject population which had access once every three years to the arms of a vote undoubtedly started to look at their rulers with more critical eyes and in a different light. As a consequence of the ambiguous and frequently contradictory attitudes taken by Gorton, as the government's political commander-in-chief, on Vietnam, defence, foreign investment, Southeast Asian involvement, Commonwealth-State relationships and a number of other issues, with the questioning of Gorton's leadership style and mode of administrative operation, and with the disappearance from the political battlefield, overnight, without preliminary warning, and in circumstances which left the Liberal rank and file uneasily disturbed, of such respected figures as Hasluck and Fairhall, the credibility of the government had declined. Australian voters may not have had a knowledge in detail of what had happened and was happening. But they had been furnished with ample material to form a revised impression, however vague, of the Liberal-CP coalition in action, and broad impressions rather than detailed study are, almost certainly, the factors that decide how many individuals vote in a democratic election when conditions on the economic and employment front are reasonably good and stable. Furthermore the ALP forces had improved if not their electoral position at least their public image. After their successful July/August Federal Conference and once the ALP Victorian branch, which Whitlam himself had constantly depicted as controlled by an unrepresentative leftwing grouping which was not entitled to be considered as fit to take over government, either federal or state, had been deducted, the ALP had emerged if not as an alternative government at least in an electorally less repellant light than had been the case since the ALP split of 1954/55.

But, despite these factors, parliamentary and machine politicians, government and opposition alike, were slow to realise that at the coming general election the traditional criteria—full employment, community affluence, impressive national growth, no issue, either domestic or external, of a magnitude seemingly sufficient to sway votes away from the government on a significant scale—would not apply to ensure the easy return of the government, with at

323

most its parliamentary majority only slightly depleted. It was to the rural seats, particularly the rural seats which relied for their prosperity upon wool and wheat, that the opposition strategists pinned their hopes, and even there their hopes were not notably high, as it was recognised that the full impact of adverse wool and wheat conditions would not be felt fully for some time, and that rural seats, traditionally conservative, reacted only when crisis was upon them, not when crisis was merely anticipated.[12]

Clyde Cameron, the ALP MHR from South Australia, with a talent for manipulation and a tongue barbed with fish hooks, was one of the few parliamentarians I encountered who sensed well before August, when Gorton announced the election date, how the electorate was moving. I have notes of a conversation I had with Cameron in June, 1969. Cameron said that he did not profess to know what was the situation in the other states. The only state of which he was prepared to speak with any authority was South Australia, his home state. But he was as certain as ever he had been of anything in politics that the ALP was going to win back from the Liberals the SA seats of Adelaide, Kingston, and Grey. It would also win Hawker, the new SA seat created in the recent electoral redistribution. Given any slight local advantage, it would also win Sturt, despite Ian Wilson having won the seat for the Liberals in 1966 with a vote of 31,479 to 15,941 over the ALP and his father, Keith Wilson,[13] having held the seat for the Liberals in 1963 with a 26,469 votes to 18,264 over the ALP. The position in South Australia would change from eight seats to three in the Liberals' favor to a minimum of seven seats to five in the ALP's favor, and possibly eight seats to four in the ALP's favor.[14] If the position in the other states were anything like that in South Australia, the ALP would either win, or go very close to winning the general election.

I argued that Cameron was indulging in wishful thinking. All the classical criteria for the return, relatively unscathed, of a government, was operating against his forecast. There was no unemployment, living standards were rising, and the effects of the rural slump had not been fully felt even in the areas which would be the first affected by such a slump and certainly the slump had not yet been felt outside these areas. The ALP had no chance of winning. It started behind scratch in Victoria where the Victorian ALP branch was suspect, and the DLP had its strongest hold. With the ALP holding only nine Victorian seats, and unlikely to pick up more than one or two extra, the Liberal-CP coalition started with an advantage of thirteen to fifteen seats, a big margin in a chamber numbering only 125, and one which the ALP was not likely to overcome with the gains it might make in the other states.

Cameron agreed with everything I said. But he argued that I was overlooking one factor. The uneasiness that existed among those whom he described as "in the know" about Gorton's administrative methods had reached grassroots level in South Australia at least. He was quite convinced of this. The uneasiness might not have penetrated to grassroots level elsewhere but it had in his state. It was the factor for which I was not allowing, he said. This uneasiness was widespread. It cut across class barriers, and even political allegiances. He reiterated that he could not speak with assurance of the position in other states. But South Australia would return a minimum of seven ALP MHRs, possibly eight, to the coalition's five, more probably four.

But when the 26th Federal Parliament ended its existence on September 26, 1969, amid the customary flurry of backslapping panegyrics, Gorton and his followers were still in a mood of supreme confidence. Whitlam was to deliver his policy speech in the Sydney Town Hall on October 1, 1969. With the nonchalance of certainty, Gorton was contemptuously to delay and to deliver his on October 8, 1969, in Melbourne before not a mass audience but a handpicked group of parliamentary and party followers. The first chastening note was produced by the Gallup Poll.[15] The poll, the first taken since August, 1969, was finished after Whitlam's October 1 policy speech, but before Gorton delivered his. The poll figures showed a swing away from the Liberal-CP coalition. In August the figures had been Liberal-CP 46 percent, ALP 41 percent, DLP 5 percent, and other 3 percent. The October figures were Liberal-CP 42 percent, ALP 45 percent, DLP 5 percent, and others 3 percent.[16]

Whitlam's speech on October 1 was very competently stage-managed. The organisation had been good. The section that was televised showed a young, attractive, and enthusiastic audience. Blessed with good looks and a fine presence, Whitlam was impressive, restrained, lucid, and—sparingly—scathing as when he asked why should Australia trust a party whose leader had responded to the most momentous event of recent times in Australia's region with the observation "We are not the sheriff but are part of the posse"—a reference to a Gorton statement made to describe Australia's role in the Southeast Asian region after the announcement of Britain's 1971 military withdrawal.[17]

Whitlam's speech, later to be referred to by Gorton as "a grab bag of promises", was designed to be electorally appealing on the domestic side. Whitlam undertook that if returned to power an

ALP government would abolish the means test on pensions over a six-year period, provide a national superannuation scheme, embracing the retired, widowed and invalid, and immediately increase all pensions by one dollar. The interest burden on home-owners, particularly young couples, would be reduced, a uniform building code would be introduced, rationing of war service homes would be ended, and the Commonwealth would make a fresh housing agreement with the States to make special provision for urban renewal and housing for the aged. University fees would be abolished, and the Commonwealth would accept responsibility for advancing education in both state and private schools. Subsidised preschool centres would be set up. The Liberals' multiplicity of voluntary health funds would be replaced with a single Common-wealth Health Insurance Fund. Taxpayers would contribute one and a quarter percent of their taxable income to the fund, with a ceiling of 100 dollars for a family. Everyone would receive from the fund complete payment for hospital care, including medical care, in whatever type of hospital ward their doctors advised. They would receive back 85 percent of their doctor's fees if they paid themselves, or, alternatively, they would not have to pay anything to their doctors if the doctors chose to send their accounts direct to the fund. An ALP government would review tax schedules to make the progressive system of tax apply in practice as well as in principle. It would create a fund to finance development, establish a Ministry of Northern Development, and suspend all mining and drilling on the Great Barrier Reef. It would "renegotiate the hurried and hushed agreement with Esso-BHP, negotiated personally by Mr Gorton, on the eve of what turned out to be the non-election (in 1968)" to ensure that Australian petrol users were not penalised by the use of Australian petrol. Whitlam also promised that a future ALP government would take steps to relieve the position of the hard-pressed wheat and wool industries.[18]

Turning to Vietnam, Whitlam pledged that with an ALP govern-ment in power there would be no Australian troops in Vietnam after June 1970. As Prime Minister he would go to Washington to give every assistance to the United States in its effort to extricate itself "honorably and quickly from a disastrous and deluded war" while his deputy, Lance Barnard, would go to Saigon to begin arrangements for a takeover of the Australian area of responsibility in the Phuoc Tuy province by the South Vietnamese army. An ALP government would sign the Nuclear Nonproliferation Treaty, and look forward to resumption of "open, honest and constructive relations with Malaysia and Singapore after the avoidable misunderstandings of the past year." Service conditions would be improved.[19]

Gorton had already made arrangements with Mackay to hold a Liberal Party dinner at a sporting club in the Sydney suburb of Ashfield the night after Whitlam had spoken, so that he might have an opportunity to answer Whitlam. Still the Prime Minister who "did what he liked when he liked", Gorton was photographed having a drink with club habitués, and trying his hand at darts while upstairs the Liberal assembly waited. In his speech, Gorton acted as though the issue he had nominated as the major one for the Australian voters to resolve—defence—would be the one upon which he would be concentrating during the campaign. "Mr Whitlam's speech is irresponsible because of the attitude it takes to the Australian position in the world and to the future of Australia," Gorton said. "I believe we were right as a people to go in to help South Vietnam when we did. At that time, unquestionably, there was aggression against a small nation. Any small nation crushed by aggression presents a danger to other small nations—and we are a small nation. We should try to see that aggression, whether Communist or Fascist, does not succeed. . . . We are right to be in Vietnam now. The United States could not have done more than it has done to try to bring peace to Vietnam. It has suggested elections in which candidates of any kind could stand. It has been rebuffed even on the withdrawing of its troops. I do not believe that the United States will leave that nation in the lurch. Now as the President of the United States is calling for continuing resolve, calling on Americans not to buckle but to stand firm so that their enemies will have no choice but to negotiate for peace, the leader of the alternative government in this country (Whitlam) says that if he is elected he will go to the United States at Christmas and arrange for the immediate withdrawal of all Australians assisting the United States and Vietnam to attain their objective. In history there cannot be a more abominable example of abandoning a proper objective and imperilling our future security."[20]

Gorton said Australia was interested in helping people to Australia's north build up their living standards and defence potential. "If other countries there (to Australia's north) were overrun or endangered this would be an ultimate danger to Australia itself," Gorton said. "We could not take over the defence of the region to the extent that Britain had done previously but we would contribute and maintain in that area, as a visible expression of our interest and willingness to help against external aggression, some forces, naval, ground and air, while also main-

327

taining in Australia forces with mobility capable of backing up those in the area. This decision was hailed as wise and helpful by the United Kingdom, the United States and countries in the area itself. But the alternative leader of the government (Whitlam) has stated that if he were elected he would withdraw at once all those ground, naval and air forces. . . . There will scarcely be any action more designed to tarnish our national image or to make sure that now and in the future those in the region to the north look on us with some contempt and much misgiving."

Though defence issues were the keynote of Gorton's Ashfield speech, Gorton dealt also with Whitlam's domestic proposals. He described the ALP health scheme as a "meretricious, badly presented, uncosted, change daily health scheme." "I call it change daily because every time we point out a fault a new scheme is presented," Gorton said. Gorton also attacked the ALP's proposals for a national superannuation scheme, and for abolition of the means test. The ALP's promises would run into hundreds of millions of dollars if fully implemented. "If these proposals were adopted, if 370 million dollars are used to abolish the means test (on pensions) instead of abolishing poverty, as we would seek to do, then the offers on one hand would be taken away by inflation tomorrow," Gorton said. "They (the ALP's proposals) would lead to galloping inflation, making it impossible to bring in the migrants we need for national development, making those overseas look askance at a country which elected someone with such a peculiar economic approach and regard us as a nation in which there should not be investment for development."[21]

Gorton recorded his policy speech at GTV Channel 9, Melbourne, on October 5, 1969. He still had overwhelming confidence in his own TV ability. He brushed aside the advice of well-meaning professionals. He knew how to perform on TV. He wanted to be himself. When the policy speech was screened on October 8, 1969, he failed to communicate. He was wooden, unconvincing, stilted. The audience on to which the camera occasionally moved included John McEwen, William McMahon, and other senior Liberals, as well as their womenfolk and Mrs Gorton. The men were a particularly lugubrious lot. They looked as though they were present not as claquers but as professional mourners, lamenting the passing of a dear one with practised but artificial tearfulness. If the Chifley-Willoughby thesis was correct and the majority of voters had made up their minds on how they would vote on impressions received some months earlier, those among the TV watchers who had decided to vote against the government were given no visual reason to change their intention.[22]

Despite the emphasis given in his Ashfield speech to defence, Gorton assumed a defensive role and the concentration in his policy speech was upon domestic matters. "Our task is to protect Australians against inflation and the increased burdens of income tax," Gorton said. "Our task is to continue immigration, to continue the inflow of developmental capital, to continue full employment, to ensure that we do not try to do more than we have the men and resources to accomplish. This must and will be overriding. Others may make glittering and irresponsible promises for which you will, in one way or another, pay. We will not." It was all very laudable but hardly inspiring. Gorton then proceeded to make a few promises of his own. "Our aim will be so to reduce personal income tax, over the three years period beginning with the next Budget, that at the end of that time we will be providing relief to lower and middle income earners, of the order of two hundred million dollars as compared with the amounts which would be payable to them under the present income tax structure."[23] Gorton said. "Because lack of water is one of the greatest limitations on Australia's growth, we shall set aside one hundred million dollars over the next five years to be spent in cooperation with the States . . . . We shall, during the next Parliament, take Australia into the atomic age by beginning the construction of an atomic plant at Jervis Bay to generate electricity."[24]

Gorton moved on to things that gave promise of assisting his parliamentary followers electorally. He undertook to develop the Port of Darwin at a cost of sixteen million dollars,[25] to build the Port Augusta/Whyalla railway at a cost of eight million dollars and the Port Pirie/Adelaide Railway at an estimated cost of thirty to fifty million dollars over two years,[26] and to establish an Institute of Marine Science at Townsville, with an early priority research on the Great Barrier Reef, at a cost of about three million dollars.[27]

On the social services side, Gorton's principal pledge was in the health field. Said Gorton, "We are well advanced in negotiations with the medical profession and the health insurance funds so that all patients will be assured of medical benefits more closely related to doctors' charges. Commonwealth medical benefits will be increased so that the difference between the benefit entitlements and the common fee charged by doctors will not at any time exceed five dollars even for the most complicated and costly surgical procedures. For simpler procedures which are less expensive the difference between the benefits and doctors' common fees will be very much less. This is estimated to cost the Commonwealth some sixteen million dollars. The successful introduction of these proposals will mean that no section of the community which is prepared to insure itself need fear hardship from the cost of medical services." An amount of one million dollars would be provided as initial capital for an Australian Film and Television Development Corporation which would make loans to film and television producers for the making of films and programmes in Australia with a significant Australian content. On tariffs, Gorton came down on McEwen's side of the fence in the squabbles about the degree of protection that ought to be accorded Australian industries, squabbles which had divided both the government and opposition parties. The Tariff Board, the autonomous body set up to advise the government on tariffs, had indicated that there were upper limits beyond which tariff protection should not and could not go without damage to the general Australian economic fabric. This had aroused McEwen's ire and condemnation. Said Gorton "The government does not accept any predetermined upper limit to the level of protection which might be accorded. The decision in each case must be determined by the government and by the government alone in the light of circumstances of any particular case."[28]

Defence occupied only three of the nineteen pages covered by the Prime Minister's policy speech. The DLP had asked for an increased defence vote. Said Gorton, "Adequate defence is the rock on which national security stands. Without it, debate on internal matters could be academic. Over the years ahead, we shall maintain and increase our defence capacity." The DLP had asked for an undertaking against participation in Soviet-inspired pacts in Asia. Said Gorton, "We will continue to support the concept of a regional security pact in that region (to Australia's north) in which we will participate. But we will exert all the influence at our command to prevent participation by Russia in such an arrangement. We believe that our security would be threatened by the establishment of any Russian naval or military bases in that area. We believe that any military arrangement between Russia and a country in our region would pose a threat to ourselves. For we cannot forget Czechoslovakia and Hungary and other occupied nations, and we believe that Russian Communism still has as its objective the spreading of its system throughout the world." The DLP had asked for confirmation of the maintenance of the "forward presence" in Malaysia/Singapore. Said Gorton, "Australia cannot fail to be affected by what happens in the nations in the region to our north. What affects their security can ultimately affect our security. We will therefore adhere to our decision to maintain in the region of Malaysia/ Singapore forces of all arms—and will maintain in Australia a capacity for swift additional assistance." The DLP had asked for the building of a naval base at Cockburn Sound in Western Australia. Said Gorton, "We have decided that we should begin the planned development of a naval base at Cockburn Sound in Western Australia. We . . . will begin construction next financial year. Thereafter the naval facilities will be progressively installed over a period." The DLP had asked for the maintenance of a naval presence in the Indian Ocean. Said Gorton, "We shall strengthen the Navy with the types of ships the Navy advise us they most require—including the new light destroyers and fast combat support ships asked for by that service . . . . Learmonth Airfield in Western Australia is to be upgraded to an operational base on the Indian Ocean. We believe that broad considerations of Australia's geo-political position and national development point to the conclusion that naval support facilities in Western Australia will also be required in the future. Our fleet numbers will increase and we will have to take an increasing interest in the Indian Ocean as the British withdraw."[29]

Gorton threw the DLP a bonus. "We shall not sign the Nuclear Nonproliferation Treaty until we are sure that it is an effective treaty, that it provides real protection to its signatories, and that Australia's security in the future is not endangered," Gorton said.[30] This was also something that commended itself to the DLP which had consistently opposed signing the pact and when mainland China had unveiled itself as an atomic power had advocated Australia developing its potential to turn itself into a nuclear power if the need ever arose.

Though he did not know it at the time, Gorton won the election with those three pages of his nineteen pages long policy speech. On Professor Crisp's analysis, the government won twenty seats after DLP preferences were distributed. With the Gorton government's majority when voting finished only seven, the government won five vital seats—Evans and Phillip, in NSW, and Griffith, Herbert and Lilley, in Queensland—on the fidelity with which DLP preferences went to the Liberal candidates. In Evans, Liberal Dr Malcolm Mackay with 24,294 primaries was still behind the ALP's James Monaghan, with 25,371 primaries, when DLP Kevin Davis' 3,274 votes were split up. Of the 3,274 DLP votes, 2,806 went to Mackay against 468 to Monaghan to give Mackay his 27,100 to 25,839 win over Monaghan. The pattern was similar in the other four seats. As David Fairbairn said after the elections, "But for the support of the DLP, the government would have been annihilated."[31]

Having got its pay-off, the DLP paid off. Santamaria reported the pay-off in these words, "The DLP kept a careful eye on the time-schedules associated with the election. Mr Gorton's policy speech was scheduled for October 8. Accordingly the DLP scheduled its own policy speech for five days later—October 13, and its announcement of the preferences for one day later again— October 14, a full eleven days before the election. Thus the DLP had time to satisfy itself as to whether the Prime Minister would make the necessary concessions and time to make and to publicise any favorable preference decision in sufficient time before the election. Once the Prime Minister's undertakings were given in the policy speech, the DLP at once clarified its preference position. In fact, it took notice of the slide in government support and announced its preference decision on October 10, four days before it had originally planned."[32]

Though Gair had announced on October 10, 1969, that the DLP would not give any of its second preferences to the ALP, its backing for the government was unenthusiastic. Wherever it could, it directed its preferences to other than official government candidates. It gave its second preferences in Warringah to Independent Liberal, St John, now Gorton's most implacable critic, and in Denison in Tasmania to Michael Townley, another Liberal Independent who was a nephew of the former Minister for Defence, the late Athol Townley.[33] In Victoria, the key state, it directed its preferences to sitting government candidates, but in seats so strongly held for the ALP that it did not matter DLP preferences were directed to a breakaway ALP group, the Independent Labor Alliance, which campaigned in opposition to the Victorian ALP Executive, which controlled the Victorian ALP branch.[34] DLP preferences went to the Country Party in six of the eight three-cornered contests involving Liberal, CP, and ALP candidates.[35]

With the policy speeches disposed of and the DLP having told its supporters where they should allocate their preferences, the leaders of the major parties—Gorton and Whitlam—embarked upon the rigorous ceremonial of an Australian election campaign. They visited every state. Gorton's Boswells estimated that he travelled more than ten thousand miles, mostly by VIP plane, and Whitlam, who also had a VIP plane at his disposal, travelled probably further, as he had started a week earlier. Gorton spoke at ten public meetings, took part in some twenty-five television programmes, and gave about a dozen radio talks.[36] Later the *Australian Liberal,* official organ of the NSW Liberal branch, in its November, 1969, issue commented, "In Sydney, it was regretted that the only public meeting which Mr Gorton addressed in NSW was the successful one at Hurstville on October 22." This Liberal "regret" was understandable. On TV, Gorton was heavy, lifeless, and leaden. He was turgid and wordy, and often incomprehensible. His press conferences were not much better. In Adelaide, he tried to explain the government's health scheme. Though his Minister for Health, Dr Jim Forbes, was in Adelaide and standing by awaiting a call, Gorton, typically, preferred to do the explaining himself. By the time he had finished explaining, his listeners, many of whom had thought they were acquiring an understanding of the intricacies of the government's health proposals, were more confused than when Gorton had started on his explanations. Gorton's best moments were at public meetings when his audiences were either hostile, or had hostile elements. At such moments, Gorton the fighter emerged and he showed to his best advantage.

Having got off on the wrong leg, Gorton found it almost impossible to get back on to balance. In Adelaide, he allowed Andrew Jones to portray himself as the South Australian Federal Parliamentarian whose company Gorton sought and who was one of Gorton's major advisers. Jones was a brash, young man who had been elected to the national parliament at twenty-two years of age when he unexpectedly beat ALP veteran, Joseph ("Joe") Sexton, for the seat of Adelaide at the 1966 general election. In the heady atmosphere of privilege conferred upon him by his parliamentary status, Jones developed a liking for a convivial glass and succumbed to the attraction of parliamentary amenities. Attributing to others in a more magnified form a fondness for the pleasures that he himself enjoyed, he told a meeting of young Liberals that the Parliament was an assembly of "idlers and boozers"—an indiscretion for which he had to apologise publicly.[37] But he discovered in himself a quite remarkable talent as a TV performer, and in TV sessions could make men of greater intellectual pretensions look fools and himself appear gifted, forthright and well-informed.[38]

Jones triumphantly paraded Gorton on an Adelaide TV session on Tuesday, October 14, 1969 as an intimate and an admirer. On Thursday, October 16, 1969, Jones was charged in the Adelaide Magistrates Court with driving while being so affected by liquor or a drug as to have ineffective control of a car and driving while his blood contained point 08 percent or more of alcohol.[39] In normal circumstances this may not have affected either Jones' or the government's South Australian electoral position. In fact it could conceivably have assisted Jones and enhanced his reputation. Australian voters in the past had shown themselves sympathetic towards legislators who shared their own human weaknesses, though more often in less inhibited New South Wales and Queensland than in reputedly straitlaced South Australia. But Jones's legal adviser, Mr P. J. Rice, secured from a South Australian Supreme Court Judge, Mr Justice Travers, an order directing the magistrate to prohibit publication of Jones' name until after commencement of the trial on November 4, 1969, the post-election date to which Jones' legal advisers had secured an adjournment.[40] This produced an immediate hostile reaction. The view was taken that there was one law for the ordinary citizen, and another for the politically privileged.[41]

The suppression proved ineffective. In states other than South Australia, Jones' name was coupled with the incident. For example in NSW, Mr J. P. Flaherty, an ALP State Parliamentarian, referred in the Legislative Assembly to the "Federal Member of Parliament who was picked up drunk in South Australia." "I speak of Mr Andrew Jones, who has been charged with driving under the influence of alcohol,"[42] Flaherty said. As Flaherty was speaking under parliamentary privilege and publication was therefore lawful, Flaherty's statement was widely publicised, and the South Australian electorate was informed not only of the incident, but, more importantly, of the suppression of Jones' name. This could have been the local advantage which Cameron had believed was all that was necessary to enable the ALP to win Sturt from the Liberals,[43] which the ALP proceeded to do.

Gorton made a series of errors almost as fundamental as getting himself identified in the South Australian mind with such an uncertain quantity as Andrew Jones. While the mass of voters may have decided before the election campaign how they were going to vote, an election campaign has value for the manner in which it sustains the fervor of the faithful, needed to man the booths and hand out a party's "how-to-vote" cards on polling day. With the campaign well under way, Gorton complained of Whitlam's superior access to research material. Gorton appointed Eric White, a well known, very able, and respected public relations authority to assist him in researching his speeches. "Mr Whitlam's large staff—which I haven't got—helps him," Gorton said. "You see, I have never delivered a speech that I haven't written myself. I doubt very much if Mr Whitlam has ever delivered a speech he wrote himself. I need some research assistance, some background speech notes and this is what this man (White) is doing and that is all he is doing."[44] Asked how he reacted to Gorton's claim that

334

he wrote all his speeches himself, Whitlam, who had spent the campaign lampooning Gorton for Gorton's frequent lapses into near incoherency, quipped "That is one of the few Prime Ministerial statements of this election that I find credible."

Gorton did not seem to realise what a damaging admission that he was making with his reference to Whitlam's superior facilities for research. By implication he was saying that Whitlam's speeches were better researched than his. He was also saying that Whitlam could attract and organise a personal staff that was superior in both quality and organisation to his own. Without appearing to realise what he was doing, he was reflecting upon his own administrative capacity. Gorton was also confirming his contempt for the Commonwealth Public Service. Though fully available to him were the resources of the Commonwealth Public Service, with within its ranks some of the most brilliant minds in Australia, virtually all there to be seconded, if required, to his personal staff, he preferred to operate without their assistance or advice and to underline the charge made by St John that he was disdainful of guidance except from individuals whom he valued for qualities other than those of sagacity, balance, and shrewdness. His attitude may not have swung a vote one way or another but it certainly affected the eagerness of Liberal Party supporters, whose services he and his government required for the donkey work of manning booths and distributing Liberal "How-to-vote" cards on election day.

A number of Liberal and CP parliamentarians decided to secure their own survival rather than rely upon Gorton to procure their survival. Gorton was fortunate that they did. They secured not only their own survival but as it turned out the survival of Gorton and the Gorton-led Liberal-CP coalition. In Evans in NSW, Mackay, as he announced he would do, even before the policy speeches were delivered, followed his own foreign affairs and defence policies, and secured the loyalty of DLP voters in his electorate to the extent that when their preferences were distributed they went overwhelmingly in his favor.[45] Others followed suit. In Queensland, Liberal Senator, Ian Wood, put out an advertisement for Kevin Cairns. Wood was an aging bachelor, toughminded, a North Queenslander, and undeviating "states righter" who had clashed with Menzies on important issues, had an independent outlook, had voted frequently against the government in the Senate, respected consistency in either friend or foe, and was an implacable opponent of Gorton. The establishment within the Federal Parliamentary Liberal Party would have dearly liked to have disposed of Wood and to have taken away from him his Liberal preselection as a Queensland senator. But he was too strongly entrenched in his native state for them to take that risk; he would almost certainly have held his Senate position as an independent and without Liberal endorsement. So they left him alone.

The Wood-Cairns advertisement amounted to a repudiation of Gorton. The Queensland Liberal branch had shown itself antagonistic to Gorton. It considered that he wanted in his Cabinet and Ministry and around him only "yes-men". The Wood-Cairns advertisement read "Kevin Cairns is not a yes man. Senator Ian Wood, the rebel senator, said last night, 'He (Cairns) is a fighter for the people of Lilley and for Queensland. Keep him as the member for Lilley to keep on fighting for you.' " The Wood-Cairns advertisement did not mention the word "Liberal" nor was Gorton's name invoked, though Gorton was in Brisbane to address one of the rare public meetings he addressed during the campaign when the advertisement actually appeared.[46]

Other government candidates tailored their campaigns not to that of the Prime Minister but what they considered the feelings and aspirations of their electorates. For example, CP MHR Ian Pettitt, whose seat of Hume in South NSW was a "swinger", ALP from 1943 to 1949, CP from 1949 to 1951, ALP from 1951 to 1955, CP from 1955 to 1961, and ALP until 1963, conducted his own personal campaign. Pettitt concentrated upon explaining, supporting, and defending the government's formal policies, both internal and external. After the elections, Pettitt was to attribute the government's reduced vote to public reaction against Gorton and his administrative methods. In Gwydir, another CP-held seat, Ralph Hunt distributed campaign material which showed that, like Pettitt, he was fearful of being engulfed by an antiGorton flood. Hunt gave prominence throughout his campaign to defence, foreign policy, and other issues on which the government differed radically from ALP policy to a degree only matched by Gorton in the final stages of the campaign. Hunt retained his seat, as might be expected, but with an absolute majority of thirty-two in an electorate where, since 1949, government candidates had counted their excess votes in thousands. Pettitt also held his seat, by 855 votes, a surprising outcome in view of the general swing against the government in NSW of 7.9 percent. In Herbert, in Queensland, where redistribution had weakened the seat and the sitting Liberal, R. N. ("Duke") Bonnett needed a progovernment swing of at least one percent to hang on, Bonnett fought a highly localised campaign, emphasising defence, a sensitive issue in Queensland uneasily aware of a troubled Asia to its near north,

A pensive McMahon, attending a ceremonial occasion in the Senate, sits in the splendid isolation that marked his existence during the three-year Gorton regime. In front, from left, Sir John McEwen, Gorton, the Government leader in the Senate, Sir Kenneth Anderson, centre, McMahon, at back, from left, the Minister for Air, Senator Drake-Brockman, the Minister for Civil Aviation, Senator Robert Cotton, the Minister for Works, Senator R. Wright, and the Minister for Housing, Senator Dame Annabelle Rankin.

Gorton with NSW Premier, Rob Askin, a one-time Gorton ally, who turned sour and hostile when Gorton threw him, in Askin's words, "to the electoral wolves" in the 1971 NSW State elections.

Gorton and McMahon leave their hotel when in Singapore in 1971 to attend the Commonwealth Prime Ministers' Conference. The attractive young lady on the left is Miss Ainsley Gotto, Gorton's private secretary, who, while Gorton was PM, became important in the Commonwealth's power structure.

and won. Though Bonnett's primary vote of 19,738 was behind the ALP's 21,318, the DLP which had received 5,181 primary votes was steadfastly loyal to him with their preferences, and he won by 23,897 votes to the ALP's 22,340.

Even government MHRs in safe government seats became aware of the chilliness of the electoral breeze as the campaign advanced towards the D-day of October 25. I was in Adelaide on Tuesday, October 14, 1969, to report the South Australian section of Gorton's campaign. In the street near the hotel where I was staying, I met Geoffrey Giles, MHR for Angas. Giles, a wartime RAAF flight lieutenant, had been a member of the South Australian Legislative Council from 1959 until in 1964 he resigned to contest the Federal seat of Angas at a by-election. Giles was a calm, placid man, a cattle breeder who rolled his own cigarettes, and was not prone to panic. His majority in the 1966 general election was almost 18,000. Giles said there was clearly rural discontent. Fortunately, his ALP opponent was "a non-rural type" which mattered in Angas, essentially a rural constituency. Giles, who after the election was to be promoted by Gorton to the position of assistant government whip, said he was "following his own line" on foreign affairs and defence. Giles held Angas. But his majority dropped to under 7,000.

An interesting feature not so much of the campaign as of what emerged from the campaign was the sense of grievance that developed within the proGorton section of the Liberals over what they considered to be the hostile attitude of the press and pressmen to Gorton as an individual. Personally, I do not think there was a great deal of hostility. There were those among the pressmen who did not love Gorton with any undying affection, but love is not important to a prime minister. It is respect that matters. The press certainly reported Gorton's mistakes and there was undoubtedly some irritation when he made statements, particularly on the government's complex health proposals, which were virtually incomprehensible. But the press was merely reporting his errors, not producing them spontaneously, and the attitude of the proGorton faction within the Liberal Party after the election suggested that they were more anxious to find scapegoats than explanations for the government's declining popularity. Menzies had never been particularly popular with either press or pressmen. But he did not complain because they did not manufacture for him a favorable public image: he produced his own. He also saw that he did not make the blunders upon which his critics could seize. Though in the 1969 election I was mostly involved in reporting speeches and press conferences, did not do nearly as much commenting as I did in earlier elections, and did most of my commenting subsequent to the elections, my attitude during the election campaign was strongly criticised at later Liberal Party postmortems, and I became in some mystic way responsible for contributing to the government's declining fortunes.[47]

The Australian Liberal, mouthpiece of the NSW Liberal branch, which at the managerial level at least was proGorton, set out with some realism what it considered to have been the factors which produced an election result far more adverse from the Liberal viewpoint than was either expected or that historical criteria suggested should have been the final result. "Immediately after the election of the House of Representatives last month, many observers suggested that Mr Gorton's style of leadership was largely to blame for the result," the publication stated. "This view was taken by many wellknown political commentators. Mr Gorton himself admitted that in some respects he could be to blame. Many Liberals felt that various aspects of his leadership since he was selected to succeed the late Mr Harold Holt were disturbing. There was some public criticism of the strategy of the campaign and of Mr Gorton's television appearances. One overseas observer, Dr David Butler, said in the *Bulletin* that 'a man who misjudges election strategy[48] is going to misjudge political situations that confront him in office', a comment that was interpreted more as a warning to the Liberal Party than a prediction. In addition to the leadership and personality aspects, other possible causes of the swing against the government which were being suggested were—

"• The inevitable reaction from the massive and record majority of 1966.

"• The effects in some seats of the redistribution.[49]

"• Failure in the past year to emphasise sufficiently and continuously the reasons for Australia's fully vindicated participation in the war in Vietnam and for the retention of national service.

"• Undue concentration at the outset of the campaign on domestic policies, which, however important in themselves, were of lesser concern to a majority of Australians than the crucial issues of security, defence, and foreign policy, and the consequent alarm of the Democratic Labour Party whose preferences were known to be decisive in several seats.

"• The ALP's 'grab bag of policies'—Mr Gorton's apt description.

"In all states, also, it was felt to be unfortunate that the demands of the states for a greater share of available funds had not received greater consideration," *The Australian Liberal* continued. "Late in the campaign the Prime Minister acknowledged the issue of Federal-State relations as important."[50]

While Gorton was in the eyes of the more devoted and emotional of his Liberal followers being buffeted mercilessly by an unfeeling and unsympathetic press, or, in the view of opponents within the Liberal Party, making the Liberal Party carry electoral responsibility for his own self-inflicted wounds, Whitlam was having a comparatively easy passage. The usually effective question applied by a Liberal-CP government to ALP election promises, "Where's the money coming from?" was asked, but got nowhere. Reason for this appeared to be a breakdown in liaison between Gorton and his Treasurer, McMahon. McMahon estimated that such of the ALP's promises as could be costed provided for an outlay of 540 million to 640 million dollars a year.[51] Gorton's estimate was that the ALP's "irresponsible and halfbaked" promises would cost 850 million dollars a year.[52] Gorton, in Adelaide, said the discrepancy was because McMahon had costed the ALP's pledge to abolish the means test at 281 million dollars which was its cost in its first year when an ALP government would take its initial step towards abolition whereas he, Gorton, had costed it at 570 million dollars which would be the cost when the ALP scheme was fully operative.[53] As Gorton flatly refused at any stage during the campaign to say that he would reappoint McMahon as Treasurer, this and other disagreements between Gorton and McMahon, such as on the cost of building a standard gauge railway between Adelaide and Port Pirie, undoubtedly heightened Liberal uneasiness, and helped Whitlam marginally. "Mr Gorton not only refuses to say who, if the Liberals are reprieved, would be the Treasurer, but he also refuses to name his Minister for Defence, or his Minister for External Affairs," gibed Whitlam. "The public is being asked to support a one-man band when the bandwaggon has staggered and stuttered to a stop."[54]

By this stage, ALP parliamentarians had the scent of office strongly in their nostrils. ALP MHR Dr Jim Cairns, who had opposed Whitlam for the ALP leadership in 1968, made it more difficult for the Liberals to get any response to their traditional query of "Where's the money coming from?" by contributing a sober, responsible, and balanced statement when sharing a platform with Whitlam at the Dandenong Town Hall in Victoria. Said Cairns, "We have told you what we are going to spend our money on. We believe all these things are essential, needed, and owed. But the basis on which the money will be spent will be determined by Gough Whitlam, as Prime Minister, and by the

339

ALP as the government. If we find that we can't afford to implement our programme in the first year then we will cut it back. If we find we can't fully implement it in the second year we will cut it back rather than cause inflation, which would injure the Australian people. Never in the history of Australia has an ALP (government) been responsible for inflation. Where inflation has emerged, it has been an anti-ALP government that has been in office."[55]

Whitlam's bad moments during the campaign came on the ALP's foreign policies, particularly as they applied to Malaysia and Singapore, from the atmosphere of suspicion he had assisted in building up around the leftwing Victorian ALP Executive, and from his former leader, Arthur Calwell. On the stationing of Australian forces in the Malaysian/Singapore area, Whitlam sailed perilously close to defying ALP policy. The ALP platform stated that "no plans for the stationing of armed forces in other countries are now feasible or acceptable."[56] Whitlam sought with some adroitness to have the best of worlds—not to antagonise the leftwing elements within his party and simultaneously to benefit from the Australian sentiment that if the stationing of Australian troops in the Malaysian/Singapore area was thought by governments there to be to their advantage then they should be so stationed, a belief that, rightly or wrongly, was felt to be held by the great majority of Australians. Whitlam said that an ALP government would keep RAAF and Australian naval units in the Malaysia/Singapore area. Questioned about the ALP Federal Conference decision which laid down that no Australian forces of any service should be stationed overseas, Whitlam said "Stationed, yes. But conference confirmed the attitude . . . which I put all along. That is that our Air Force should be used to train the Malaysian Air Force, not to replace it or to be a substitute for it. Yes, I would station our Air Force at Butterworth (in Malaysia) to train the Malaysian Air Force."[57] As it was on the eve of the general election and the ALP's leftwing also now hoped to participate in an ALP government, Whitlam was not challenged, as he had been so frequently in the past by leftwing ALP elements, on his rather elastic interpretation of ALP policy.

On the question of the Victorian ALP Executive, even Whitlam's most acrobatic skating around and over thin ice was not wholly successful. His own lethal words were there facilely ready for use against him and the Victorian ALP. Asked by a questioner whether it was not a fact that he had said of the Victorian ALP Executive that it included "an influential number of men who have flouted ALP policy on unity tickets in trade

340

union elections, who have organised and led political strikes in defiance of the ACTU, who have disregarded and repudiated ALP and ACTU policy on the manning of ships to Vietnam . . . and that it is disgraceful that these men should be on an ALP Executive which can influence or appear to influence (ALP) Federal policy and selections", Whitlam answered, weakly, "I was addressing the 1967 Conference of the ALP in Victoria—it was not the present Victorian (ALP) Executive."[58]

But the Victorian ALP was the soft, vulnerable underbelly of the ALP as Whitlam had himself pointed out in the past and was to rediscover on October 25 when the ALP's hopes of forming a government, despite Victoria's weakness, were thwarted. Whitlam tried vainly to provide some shield for the ALP's soft underbelly. "There have been two meetings of the Federal (ALP) since then (1967)," Whitlam said. "The Party's structure has been reformed since then. I did have, in the past, cause to complain about some attitudes expressed by, and policies promoted by, the Victorian branch of the ALP. They appeared to me at times quite unduly anti-American and anti-Catholic. The attitudes which they pursued have been rejected by the top forums of my party, and the Victorian branch accepts the Party's (Federal) policies. At the last two Federal Conferences, it has been quite clear what the party's policies are on all these things. The Victorian Executive has accepted those policies, and it is effectively pursuing the party's federal policies, and has chosen some excellent candidates, whom I am confident will be elected to the House of Representatives."[59]

Whitlam had another headache. In circumstances and with a timing that was reminiscent of his own performance when in 1966 he cut across the declaration of his then leader, Arthur Calwell, that an ALP government would withdraw Australian forces from Vietnam immediately, Calwell, now a backbencher, pointed out Whitlam's evasions on defence and foreign affairs. Whitlam, said Calwell, must follow ALP Federal Conference decisions on Vietnam, defence, and national service. Foreign affairs and defence would be the issues which would decide the election. Calwell listed the things that an ALP government would have to do if elected to office. It would have to release immediately from service all military conscripts, free all people jailed for offences under the National Service Act, and bring back Australian troops from Vietnam by Christmas. "This ALP programme allows no time-table or deferment," said Calwell. "Mr Whitlam is contorting ALP defence and foreign affairs policy in an attempt to maintain an air of electoral respectability. Let us be quite honest about this. When the CP leader, Mr McEwen, said an ALP government would

341

wreck the National Service Act, he never said a truer thing. We will wreck it. There will be nothing left."[60]

"The ALP has opposed Australia's participation in the filthy (Vietnam) war from the beginning, and opposed the Gorton government's continued commitment to that war," Calwell added. "We have always regarded United States intervention in Vietnam as criminal as anyone else's intervention in another country. Many Australian Pharisees get all worked up about Russia's intervention in Czechoslovakia. Where is the difference?" Calwell repudiated a plea by Whitlam for demonstrators and young people not to display their feelings at meetings held by the Prime Minister. "I urge all young people and demonstrators to go along in force to all government, DLP, and, if necessary, ALP meetings if they want to make their views felt and heard," Calwell said. "I want the demonstrations to be orderly, but this coming week may be the last chance of the young people to have their say. Whatever leaders say, I do not counsel them not to show their feelings at Mr Gorton's meetings. Such action is entirely undemocratic—undemocratic nonsense. The lives of young Australians are more important than the abolition of the means test, or any other domestic issue. This issue must be fought on Vietnam, defence, and foreign affairs on which ALP policy is quite clearcut. An ALP government won't be waiting until June, 1970, to bring back Australian troops from Vietnam. We'll have them back for Christmas."[61]

Normally, Calwell's statement would have been the signal for the ALP leftwing to jump savagely on Whitlam. But for the first time since 1954/55 leftwing ALP leaders had a vision of power, of imposing offices, of wide ministerial desks, of staffs that would work to their bidding, of status and of their usually harshly kicked haunches plumping luxuriously into the soft leather back seats of chauffeur-driven limousines. Whitlam, uncharacteristically, restrained himself from flinging a metaphorical glass of water in Calwell's offending face. The ALP's leftwing studiously looked the other way; conscience and consistency have ever been early casualties in a power ploy when power comes within reaching distance. But though the Calwell outburst went almost unnoticed it may have had the marginal effect that kept Whitlam from the prime ministership. If defence and foreign affairs were issues operating in Gorton's and the government's favour, Calwell's brutal candour probably assisted to resolve the uncertainties of the doubters.

Gorton either sensed or was persuaded into again placing the emphasis upon defence. When Whitlam, on a Brisbane TV session, said that an ALP government would not replace the Third Battalion, whose period of service in Vietnam was drawing to a close, with the Fourth Battalion, then training in Queensland for Vietnam service,[62] Gorton hit back. Gorton said he had discussed withdrawal with the United States. But it was on the basis that Australia would be phased into any possible United States withdrawal. "We don't want to be left there until the last if ever—and it is an if—the United States decides to withdraw," Gorton said. Asked what would happen if the Third Battalion was not replaced, Gorton said ". . . they (the ALP) are endangering the two battalions that remain. It will certainly make them far less militarily effective. They would not have sufficient rest. They would be subject to attack when tired."[63]

In his final press conference, on election eve, October 24, at the Hotel Sheraton, in Melbourne, Gorton reviewed his election campaign. In a future campaign and with the experience of the 1969 campaign under his belt, he would still not be enthusiastic about public meetings. He did not think he would have more public meetings. "I might have one more if I replanned the campaign," Gorton said. "I don't want to go around the suburbs and have a couple of hundred listless listeners like Whitlam has." He thought it had been a "scurrilous" campaign. "I think there has been a fairly organised smear campaign on for a long time," Gorton said. "The campaign has been aimed mainly at me. I don't know about other candidates. I don't know who is behind this campaign. I would hope it has not been effective. I don't think there is room for this sort of thing in Australia. I don't think there is any way to stop such campaigns. I believe the Australian people are not affected by them. I think it is rather revolting that that sort of thing should happen. It reminds you of little white frog-bellied things scurrying around in the sewer. I would not say it unduly distresses me personally. Literature has been put out, photographs circulated, and that sort of thing.[64] I think it is all part of the same thing as the St John allegations." Gorton said he was not particularly unhappy with the reporting of the campaign. "But I query some of the comments of some of the reporters," he said. "But I am not disturbed by this."[65]

Gorton could not see any campaign lessons for him emerging from the events of the previous few weeks. "I don't think I should have given the policy speech in any different way," Gorton said. "A policy speech as such ought to be one that can be put before the people in a composed, coherent way without being broken up. There are meetings I like better than doing that sort of thing. But I still think it is probably the best way to do it as the policy speech is designed to put programmes before the people for the next three years. We can't have the stooge faithful at public meetings the way our principal opponent (Whitlam) can. So I think we will continue to do it that way." Gorton did not make any forecast on how many seats the government would win by, but he had no doubt that his government would win.[66]

On the following day, October 25, 1969, polling day, the formula devised by Gorton of a prime minister being his uninhibited self and the other ingredients—the blunt "no more Australian troops for Vietnam" reaction to the Tet offensive that changed the whole concept of Australian involvement in Vietnam, the hesitation over what should be Australia's attitude to the contribution of troops to the Malaysia/Singapore area, Gorton's novel and authoritative approach to cabinet government, and the domestic matters of shipping, oil, foreign investment, and other things, including the disappearance of Hasluck and Fairhall from the political scene and McMahon's dubious ministerial future, which Gorton's cabinet approach had brought in its train and which had distinguished the Gorton régime from those of its predecessors —were fed into the power crucible of a general election. Fed in with them were the counterbalancing elements of an ALP suspect in Victoria, an ALP leader who gave greater loyalty to his ambitions than to such followers as Harradine, the ALP's policies on defence and foreign affairs, and an Australian economy still affluent, expanding, yet stable. The Gorton formula was to prove successful. Gorton and his government were returned to power, but at a heavy price and only just successful.

In the four seats which finally decided the election outcome and gave the Gorton government its majority of seven in the new House of Representatives—Phillip and Evans in NSW and Lilley and Griffith in Queensland—the proLiberal margin over the ALP was only 5,076 votes out of an Australian total of 6,273,611 recorded votes, and even then most of the 5,076 decisive votes were not primary votes for the Liberals, but second preferences from the DLP.

Sir William Aston, Speaker of the House of Representatives, won Phillip for the Liberals by 440 votes, Malcolm Mackay won Evans by 1,261 votes, Kevin Cairns won Lilley by a 1,771 margin, and young Donald Cameron won Griffith by a 1,604 margin. When the final results were posted, the government had lost fifteen seats, and the ALP had won seventeen—the fifteen won from the government, the new seat of Hawker in South Australia, and Batman in Victoria following the retirement of Captain Sam Benson, an independent, master mariner, and onetime ALP MHR who had broken with the ALP after insisting upon defying an ALP instruction to the contrary and maintaining his membership of an allegedly nonparty organisation, supported by both prominent Liberals and DLP members, and known as the Defend Australia Committee. The Liberal-CP coalition also had the mortification of experiencing a 6.8 percent adverse swing, the largest ever recorded against any government since the bleak depression days of 1931.

But if success is measured by the winning of a majority of seats in that chamber of a parliament in which a majority determines the political complexion of the government of the day—and that is what a parliamentary electoral contest is all about—the Gorton experiment had proved successful, though costly. It was the high cost that was to produce a troubled aftermath for Gorton, an aftermath which from the viewpoint of the Liberals had the potential to make the price of the Gorton experiment, despite its success, prohibitively high.

NOTES

[1] This, of course, is a purely personal view. But newspaper surveys, casual street TV interviews, and even some academic studies tend to confirm the accuracy of this view.

[2] "All of us know one thing. What we do in the months and years before a campaign wins or loses the election. What we do in the last few weeks does not have much value"—John Carrick, NSW Liberal Secretary, *The Australian Liberal*, p 13, April 1970.

[3] "Political Review: The Federal Elections" by Alan Hughes—*The Australian Quarterly*, December, 1969, Vol 41, No 4, p 16.

[4] "The 1969 Federal Election" by Don Aitkin, *Politics*, May 1970, Vol 5, No 1, p 45.

[5] *Sydney Morning Herald,* July 18, 1969.

[6] *Sun-Herald,* Sydney, September 14, 1969.

[7] Gorton seemed always to understate the emotional appeal of state chauvinism. Though myself a centralist who has sympathy with the early Gorton thesis that the Commonwealth should have supreme legislative powers and the States delegated powers. I find my chauvinism emerges if I think that NSW, my home state, is not getting "a fair go" at Premiers' Conferences. This is the irrational factor in politics that many politicians and most political scientists seem to underrate.

[8] *The Australian Liberal,* November, 1969, p 4.

[9] *Commonwealth Representatives' Debates,* Vol 65, p 1145, September 11, 1969.

[10] *The Australian Liberal,* November, 1969, p 4.

[11] *The Australian Liberal,* December, 1969, p 13.

[12] At the October 25, 1969, election, the rural seats stayed solidly pro-government. Only in Murrumbidgee, where the ALP's Al Grassby had a personal triumph and a voting swing of 20 percent in his favour was there any change.

13 Keith Wilson retired from the Federal Parliament in 1963, and his son, Ian, won the Liberal preselection for the 1966 elections.

14 Cameron's forecast turned out to be accurate. The ALP won eight South Australian seats to the government's four.

15 I am not a "poll" man. I distrust them and prefer to work "off the seat of my pants," But the Australian Gallup Poll has a fine record of accurate forecasting.

16 *Herald,* Melbourne, October 11, 1969.

17 Whitlam also described Gorton as "a Prime Minister who represents nobody except himself, speaks for nobody in his party except himself, and, as far as one can gather, speaks to nobody except himself"— Whitlam's policy speech, October 1, 1969.

18 Whitlam's policy speech, Sydney, October 1, 1969.

19 Whitlam's policy speech, Sydney, October 1, 1969.

20 *The Australian Liberal,* October, 1969.

21 *The Australian Liberal,* October, 1969.

22 The Liberals later conceded this to be so. See "Campaign Survey", *The Australian Liberal,* December, 1969, p 1.

23 Gorton implemented this promise within twelve months, remitting the two hundred million dollars in taxation in the 1969/70 Budget.

24 Gorton's policy speech, Melbourne, October 8, 1969.

25 CP MHR, Sam Calder, whose Northern Territory seat was regarded as "dicky", was returned with unexpected ease at the October election to become·one of Gorton's seven majority in the House of Representatives.

26 These pledges had no apparent influence upon the South Australian seats.

27 Liberal MHR Robert Noel ("Duke") Bonnet, whose Queensland seat of Herbert, which took in Townsville, was also regarded as "shaky", survived the October election.

28 Gorton's policy speech, Melbourne, October 8, 1969.

29 Gorton's policy speech, Melbourne, October 8, 1969.

30 On February 18, 1970, Gorton announced that Australia had decided to sign the treaty, but did not propose to ratify the treaty until matters of concern to Australia had been clarified to Australia's satisfaction—Facts and Figures, No 105, p 65.

31 Fairbairn press conference, November 3, 1969.

32 "Struggle on Two Fronts: the DLP and the 1969 election" by B. A. Santamaria, *The Australian Quarterly,* December, 1969, Vol 42, No 4, p 41.

33 St John and Townley were both defeated.

34 The Independent Labor Alliance had no significant electoral impact.

35 Article by David Solomon, *Australian,* October 15, 1969.

36 Official account of Prime Minister's 1969 activities issued by Gorton's Canberra office.

37 *Commonwealth Representatives' Debates,* Vol 55, p 1575, May 2, 1967.

38 I only remember seeing Jones once on TV. This was the judgment of Cameron and other South Australian ALP supporters, who disliked Jones but who had suffered the mortification of watching him "demolish" on TV some quite imposing ALP personalities.

39 *Daily Telegraph,* Sydney, October 17, 1969.

40 Ibid.

41 "It is a pretty pass where parliamentary candidates can be protected from the results of their own misdemeanours"—Whitlam, Perth, October 17, 1969.

346

[42] Jones pleaded guilty and was fined 140 dollars and had his driver's license suspended for nine months—*Sydney Morning Herald,* November 5, 1969.

[43] See this chapter, pp 324/325.

[44] TV interview with John Boland and John Fitzgerald, Channel 7, Melbourne, October 19, 1969.

[45] See this chapter, p 331.

[46] *Courier Mail,* Brisbane, October 20, 1969.

[47] See Chapter 15, p 334.

[48] My view was that the Prime Minister did not have an election strategy, but a personal strategy only.

[49] These were Gorton's reasons for the adverse result but later he said "One has to expect a swing when the government has a record majority, but . . . not one of the magnitude that happened in the states outside Victoria"—Gorton, at Higgins' poll declaration, November 5, 1969.

[50] *The Australian Liberal,* December, 1969.

[51] *Daily Telegraph,* Sydney, October 13, 1969.

[52] From notes taken during Gorton's Tasmanian visit, October 15, 1969.

[53] From notes taken during Gorton's South Australian visit, October 13-14, 1969.

[54] Whitlam press conference, Adelaide, Ocotber 20, 1969.

[55] *Daily Telegraph,* Sydney, October 10, 1969.

[56] Official report, ALP Federal Conference, Melbourne, July 28/August 1, 1969, pp 157, 217.

[57] Whitlam, TV programme "Meet the Press", Brisbane, October 12, 1969.

[58] Whitlam, National Press Club Luncheon, Canberra, October 22, 1969.

[59] Whitlam, National Press Club Luncheon, Canberra, October 22, 1969.

[60] *Daily Telegraph,* Sydney, October 18, 1969.

[61] *Daily Telegraph,* Sydney, October 18, 1969. Whitlam had fixed June, 1970, as the time when an ALP government would bring back Australian forces in Vietnam.

[62] "Meet the Press", Brisbane, October 12, 1969.

[63] *Daily Telegraph,* Sydney, October 20, 1969.

[64] The student press put out a number of antiGorton photographs and issues. In the main the student and university press seemed to support St John fervently.

[65] Gorton press conference, Melbourne, October 24, 1969.

[66] Gorton press conference, Melbourne, October 24, 1969.

CHAPTER 14

THE Gorton experiment might not have succeeded completely but it was certainly not a failure. Gorton was back in office which was the main purpose of the exercise. By the middle of the week following polling day, October 25, it was clear that the Liberal-CP coalition had not only been authorised by the majority of Australian voters to continue administering the Federal Government for the ensuing three years, but had been given in the House of Representatives an overall majority of seven, which was a floor majority of six when provision had been made for the appointment of a Speaker to preside over the House of Representatives' deliberations. It was a more than adequate margin under normal circumstances to allow the Liberal-CP combination to function without fear of parliamentary challenge from the Opposition. But circumstances were not normal. The government's electoral losses and relatively poor performance at a time when economic, employment, affluence and other conditions suggested that a better performance might be expected was the catalyst which released antiGorton forces which for some time had been building up slowly but inexorably both within the Liberal Parliamentary Party and within the Liberal Party political machine.

The Liberal Party losses had been heavy. In the previous House of Representatives, numbering 124, the strengths of the various political groups, when St John was counted with the Liberals, were Liberals 60, CP 21, ALP 42, with the independent Captain Sam Benson, from Batman in Victoria, supporting the Government on its defence and foreign policies though originally elected, in 1962, as an ALP MHR. This had given the government a majority of 40 on many issues, and theoretically[1] a clearcut 38 party majority on all issues. In the new House of Representatives, increased to 125 MHRs after an electoral redistribution in 1968, the Liberals numbered only 46, their CP partners in government 20, and the ALP 59. There were no independents or representatives of the minor political groupings. St John had been defeated in Warringah. Benson had retired from Batman. Though the CP had lost Murrumbidgee with a spectacular fifteen percent swing of the vote to the ALP's flamboyant but capable Al Grassby, pocket-sized, moustached, slender, Italianate in appearance and Italian speaking in an electorate peopled by many voters of Italian descent, but English born and Australian raised, as sharp in speech and mind as in his colourful "with it" dress and an astute and tireless organiser, the CP had emerged from the election almost as powerful as it went into it. In a threecornered contest between a Liberal, a CP and an ALP candidate, the CP's banner bearer, Frank O'Keefe, had won Paterson, the seat formerly held for the Liberals by Defence Minister, Allen Fairhall, now in the obscurity of retirement. The decline in CP strength from 21 to 20 was because of the disappearance of the CP seat of Lawson in NSW in the 1968 electoral redistribution.

In NSW, the ALP won from the Liberals a total of five seats, Barton, Eden-Monaro, Riverina, Robertson and St George, in Victoria, the ALP's weak spot for fifteen years, only Maribyrnong, in Queensland Bowman, in South Australia Adelaide, Grey, Kingston, and Sturt, in Western Australia Forrest, Perth and Swan, and in Tasmania Franklin. Additionally, the ALP won the new seat of Hawker in South Australia, and regained Batman in Victoria following the retirement of the independent Benson,[2] to give the ALP an overall gain of seventeen seats. In NSW, the government had barely held its own with only a 23/22 seat advantage over the ALP. In Queensland, where a 5.3 percent[3] swing against the government had been unevenly distributed and Liberal MHRs like Bonnett, Kevin Cairns, and Don Cameron had survived by individual effort and because of their good relations with the DLP, the government's seat advantage was 11/7 over the ALP. Only in Victoria, which Liberal Premier Bolte, no particular admirer of Gorton, rubbing salt unctuously into the Gorton electoral wounds, described as "The brightest jewel in the Liberal crown" did the Liberals have an overwhelming supremacy, with twenty-three seats to the ALP's eleven.

An analysis of the percentage figures was also depressing for the Liberals. Compared with the 1966 vote, the figures across Australia showed a decline of 6.5 percent for the Liberals, a decline of 1.3 percent for the DLP, and an improvement for the ALP of 7.2 percent. In NSW, the Liberal-CP vote was down by 7.9 percent, in Victoria by 3.7 percent, in Queensland by 5.3 percent, in South Australia by 12.0 percent, in Western Australia by 6.8 percent, and in Tasmania by .6 percent. The Liberal-CP coalition had obtained only 43.5 percent of the total Australian vote compared with the ALP's 47.2 percent, while the DLP had secured 6 percent and the smaller political groups and independents 3 percent.

349

The defeat of the Minister for External Affairs, Gordon Freeth, in Forrest in Western Australia, from 1949 onwards regarded as an unassailable Liberal stronghold, was another bad shock for the Liberals. Freeth was the author of the August 14, 1969 statement, which had dealt in a conciliatory and moderate fashion with mounting Soviet interest in the Indian Ocean area, which had aroused DLP ire, and for which Gorton had to accept the status of co-author as he had "vetted" the statement, made some alterations, approved the text and authorised its publication without consultation with Cabinet or even consultation with such senior members of it as McEwen and McMahon, both politically perceptive and astute, or Fairhall, who had an interest as Defence Minister.[4] Gorton sought to minimise the national significance of Freeth's defeat, and to attribute it not to the August 14 statement for which he had co-responsibility, but to local factors. Asked if he accepted any responsibility for Freeth's defeat as he had been the only member of Cabinet or the Ministry involved in the preparation of the Soviet-Indian Ocean statement, Gorton said "No. I don't." Gorton added, "I think they have local problems there (in Western Australia) that they were arguing about rather than national problems, and (these local problems) had quite an effect on the vote there."[5] Gorton made no attempt to explain why, when the government vote in Western Australia had fallen by 6.8 percent, Freeth had been singled out and his vote had fallen by 10 percent, making him the only minister to receive such exceptional and punitive treatment at the voters' hands.[6]

After a normal Australian general election, there is generally a brief cessation of activity within the ranks of the victorious political group or groupings rather like the pause, dealt with in the De Quincy essay, between Duncan's murder by Macbeth and the resumption of normal life with the knocking on the gate. During this period of quietude, the parliamentary members of the victorious party or parties are less interested in election post-mortems than in trying to get for themselves, or, if they have no chance themselves, for their intimates, a share of the political booty in the shape of ministerial appointments and parliamentary positions which confer high pay, status, extra secretarial assistance and the privilege of unlimited access to government cars. Having won, or won back, the political Papacy, their human and understandable ambition is to get as much authority over as large a portion of its temporal domains as their ingenuity, talent for toadyism, and manipulation of their fellows can secure.

While this is going on in the winners' ranks, the defeated party tends to engage in a sullen and resentful examination of the reasons for its defeat, usually using its leadership as the scapegoat, unless, even though defeated, it has made advances which turn its parliamentary followers' eyes from the disappointing present to the glittering promises of a rosy future.

But it had not been a normal election and post-election happenings did not follow a normal course. Despite the large gains, not anticipated when the 26th Commonwealth Parliament ended its sittings on September 26, just a month before polling day, achieved under Whitlam's leadership, the ALP facade of unity imposed by electoral necessity, speedily collapsed. Gorton also got no breathing space. His experiment had produced unanticipated by-products. Events crowded in on him with kaleidoscopic rapidity.

Having led the Liberal-CP coalition back on to the government benches, Gorton, never notably sensitive to atmosphere, appeared to believe genuinely that there would be no real challenge to him in his position as Prime Minister. During the election campaign, he had said that he would have to accept personal responsibility for the result of the election. But he had said this within a context of the government possibly losing the election. Quite realistically, he pointed out that winning an election, even with a reduced majority, was not the same thing as losing an election. He did not know of any serious opposition to himself within the Liberal Party. He did not accept any responsibility for Freeth's defeat. If what he regarded as a misinterpretation of Freeth's August 14 speech had contributed to Freeth's defeat that was "completely unfortunate". He did not regard the vote as a vote against his leadership. He had had a look at the vote in Higgins, the electorate he represented in the House of Representatives. "They seem to me to be rather better figures than the 1966 vote," said Gorton. "That was the seat where I was standing." Gorton was asked "What about the overall vote?" Gorton shrugged his shoulders. "Well, I think you can only judge (whether there was a personal vote against the Gorton leadership) on the sort of vote you get in your own seat," said Gorton. "The vote (in Higgins) appears to be as good or better than in 1966 (when the former Prime Minister, the late Harold Holt, contested the seat). It was an extremely good vote in that area."[7] Gorton said he could not judge whether TV had been a great success or not. "You can't tell what might have happened without it," he said. In a future campaign, he might start a day earlier and have a meeting in his own electorate. "Apart from that I don't think I would do a great deal differently," he said.[8]

But if Gorton did not know of any serious opposition to himself within the Liberal Party, there were others who sensed that opposition was coming. Gorton had three major sources of strength within the Liberal Parliamentary room. One source of strength was the twenty-six strong Ministry. For all his boldness and disregard for longterm consequences, Gorton was not able to do precisely what he liked with those who had the status of Liberal Party chieftains. He was reckless, but not completely reckless. He had a sense of self-preservation which emerged whenever his supremacy as Prime Minister was threatened, and, as he had shown in his dealings with the DLP and with his own followers when they took an implacable stand on such things as cooperation with Malaysia and Singapore in defence, would retreat from a hopeless position abruptly and at a speed which made overtaking impossible. His weakness was that his temperament and his tendency to confuse stubbornness with strength encouraged him to trap himself so often in hopeless positions from which he had to make disorganised retreats. But with Hasluck and Fairhall retired from the political scene, and Freeth defeated, Liberal Party chieftains who were also Federal Parliamentarians, were getting thin on the ground. Only McMahon and Fairbairn, from NSW, and, to some extent, the Postmaster-General, Alan Hulme, from Queensland, qualified among the ministers for such a rating. The other ministers had neither party room nor extra-parliamentary power bases. They were Party nonentities, and, with the possible exception of Malcolm Fraser, the Defence Minister, who appeared to have an unusual personal relationship with Gorton, a relationship which produced no sign of consciousness of inferiority from Fraser, they either knew they were Party nonentities or were prepared to behave as Party nonentities.

The Prime Minister was in effect their power base. They depended on his goodwill for the retention of their highly-prized ministerial posts and for the privileged position and the power conferred upon them by such posts. Their dependence upon his goodwill was at once part of Gorton's strength in the Liberal Party room and a contributing factor to Liberal weakness. They feared him and his unpredictability, and fearful men make poor advisers. Individual ministers were prone at times to complain, privately and discreetly, about Gorton's "centralism" in his approach to Commonwealth-State relations; they failed to recognise how he had, despite the formal continuance of the cabinet system, centralised power in the Prime Minister's office. Because they had no independent existence, even those ministers most critical of Gorton in private would continue to support and back Gorton in the open forum of the Liberal Party room until they were absolutely certain that the numbers were present in the

352

Mr Jefferson Bate, Liberal MHR, Mrs Gorton, Gorton, and Dame Zara Bate toast each other. Dame Zara was the widow of the former Prime Minister, Harold Holt. Bate was among the group who threatened to vote against the Liberal-CP coalition unless Gorton vacated the Prime Ministership.

Politicians and service chiefs in less turbulent times. Right to left, General Sir Thomas Daly, then Chief of the General Staff, Malcolm Fraser, then Minister for Defence, General Sir John Wilton, Admiral Sir Allen Fairhall, then Minister for the Army,

party room to "down" him—a thing of which no man could be completely certain until the vote was actually taken and counted. Provided Gorton could keep intact his other two sources of strength, the Ministry would continue to be a source of Gorton's strength.

Gorton's second source of party room strength was the support he could command because of his control, as Prime Minister, of patronage. Just as every one of Napoleon's soldiers metaphorically carried in his knapsack a marshal's baton, every parliamentarian carries in his brief bag a pair of striped pants, the seat of which is tailored for intimate and enduring contact with the deep cushioned chair behind an imposing ministerial desk. There is nothing reprehensible about this. Politicians become politicians in the main because they are convinced they know what is good for the nation and sometimes what is good for the world, as well as what is good for themselves. Politicians become Parliamentarians in a parliamentary democracy generally because they want to be ministers and part of a government. They are aware that it is from behind a ministerial desk that they can best impose the policies and plans which they know with superb certainty are in the people's interests. There are few exceptions to the general rule that every man who enters Parliament sees himself if not as a future prime minister as a future minister. This produces its own psychology. When in 1799 Thomas Jefferson wrote "Whenever a man casts a longing eye on offices, a rottenness begins in his conduct", the American statesman may have overstated the point he was making with his use of the word "rottenness". But he was describing accurately a prime minister's capacity to elicit support when a ministry is selected arbitrarily by the Prime Minister and not elective in any way. Liberal ministers were selected by the Prime Minister. He answered to no one for his selections. With Fairhall gone and Freeth defeated, there were two ministerial vacancies dangling enticingly under the noses of those avid for office. There might be other vacancies, as yet unrevealed, depending on the Prime Minister's whim or judgment of those dispensables already in the Ministry. Human nature being what it is, those who demonstrated their loyalty to the Prime Minister by consistent, unwavering support in the party room believed they were more likely to receive a ministerial job than those who turned critical. Those prepared to show their loyalty in the hope of future preferment were a sizable section of the Liberal Parliamentary Party.

Gorton's third source of party room strength was unique to him. It derived from his twenty years sojourn in the Senate. As

353

it was a strength that had an emotional basis, it should theoretically have been less enduring and less reliable than the strength Gorton drew from the self-interest of the Ministry and the ambitious. But the irrational element, the element that has repeatedly defeated the theoretician since man emerged from the primeval jungle to experiment with and develop methods of government, operated. The strength Gorton drew from the backing of the government senators was probably his most reliable and main party room strength. Australian senators have a highly developed inferior complex vis-à-vis their parliamentary colleagues in the House of Representatives. Like MHRs, Australian senators are not chosen, but elected by the vote of the people. The senators like to have ignored the fact that, unlike the MHRs, they are elected, for the most part, because of the party labels they carry, not as individuals,[9] and they resent the superior powers, authority and prestige of the House of Representatives, and the reservation of the larger, juicier plums of office, because of tradition and practice rather than constitutional necessity, for House of Representatives' members. Gorton had become the Senators' symbol, a man who had risen to the prime ministership not in the conventional way through the House of Representatives but from the Senate.[10] With Gorton as Prime Minister, the Liberal senators for the first time in Australian history functioned within the Liberal Parliamentary party room not as individual Liberal parliamentarians but as a formidable power block. With Liberal numbers in the Liberal parliamentary room depleted and the depletions having taken place exclusively within the ranks of Liberal members of the House of Representatives, Liberal senators comprised a third of the party's parliamentary strength. Exercise of their strength collectively gave them a heady sense of power. They no longer felt inferior to the Liberal MHRs. Provided they could be kept as a cohesive and coherent grouping, Gorton was safe against any challenge to his authority within the Liberal party room.

A Gorton supporter intent on keeping the Liberal senators as a cohesive and coherent grouping was Senator Magnus Cormack, then 63, a Victorian grazier and clubman, unobtrusively well groomed and with the faintly casual manner of a man of distinction. A manipulator of some eminence, Cormack who had been president of the Victorian Liberal Party operated in a quiet, gentlemanly fashion. But he was as ruthless as any of his coarser mannered colleagues. Cormack's association with Gorton predated Gorton's 1949 entry into federal politics. Cormack had been a major figure in establishing the Liberal Party and breaking CP political power in northern Victoria and had used the young

Gorton as one of his instruments.[11] Maintaining discreet but strong links with sections of the Victorian Liberal machine, possessed of influence with a number of Liberal senators, a manoeuvrer who preferred to work in the shadows than in strong sunlight, Cormack had played a significant, largely unpublicised part in getting Gorton elevated to the prime ministership after Holt's disappearance into the sea off Cheviot Beach in December 1967. His proGorton efforts had received no recognition prior to the 1969 election.[12] His reward had been the personal satisfaction that politicians like Cormack desire from being contributors to the shaping of large events.

When, during the election campaign, indications emerged that it was possible that things were not going for Gorton and the government as well as had been hoped and might be expected, a meeting of Liberal senators was called for Wednesday, October 29, four days after polling day. The meeting had unusual aspects. It was called not by Senator Ken Anderson, the Liberal from NSW who had succeeded Gorton as Government Senate leader, but by Cormack. Anderson was absent from the meeting. The meeting was called for Melbourne and the locale was not the usual parliamentary or Liberal party office, but Cormack's club—the Australian Club. Though the purpose of the meeting was stated to be the innocent one of giving Liberal senators the opportunity of discussing prospects for the 1970 Senate election in the light of the results achieved by the Liberal-CP coalition at the 1969 general election, the invitation list was selective. Wood, the independent minded Queensland Senator, who was openly contemptuous of Gorton's competence as a prime minister, was not invited. Nor was Senator Alexander Lillico, a Tasmanian, a quiet, dignified man, also possessed of an independent mind and not amenable to intimidation from any source. There were other notable absentees. However, fourteen of the twenty Liberals in the Senate mustered on the Australian Club's exclusive premises on October 29.

But before the senators assembled for their meeting, things had started to happen in Canberra, the nation's capital, to which Gorton had returned on polling day after casting his vote in his electorate of Higgins. Fairbairn had an interview with Gorton on Tuesday, October 28. Fairbairn was a troubled man. He was also a principled man. Though reputedly an extremely wealthy man, he was only moderately so. When elevated to the Ministry at the age of 45 by Menzies in 1962, he had disposed entirely of his share holdings at a period when the share market was at a low ebb, and thereafter had steadfastly refused to participate in any

355

financial dealings which could be viewed as impinging, however indirectly, on his ministerial office. Though his grazing property, Dunraven, near Albury in South NSW was a show place and he was regarded as a highly efficient farmer, Fairbairn's income had contracted drastically with the decline in wool prices. Now 53 years of age, he was probably dependent to a degree he had never depended before upon a ministerial salary, at that time, for senior ministers such as Fairbairn, 8,500 dollars a year, with a tax free allowance of 3,600 dollars a year, a travelling allowance of thirty dollars a day, and such money-saving perquisites as unlimited access to government cars, free telephones, free air travel, and the like. But as his subsequent actions revealed, Fairbairn was not troubling about financial matters. He was concerned about other things. Fairbairn was a fervent states righter. He had also developed a distrust of Gorton's administrative methods since Gorton had prohibited him from informing his department, theoretically the department with the expertise to proffer informed advice, of the negotiations that Gorton, aided only by Hewitt, had conducted with Esso-BHP on oil pricing in the Bass Strait fields.

There were two versions of the Gorton-Fairbairn Tuesday interview. One was put out by Gorton at a press conference held soon after Gorton had received from Fairbairn on the afternoon of October 30, 1969, a telegram which read, "After deep thought and consideration have reluctantly decided that I will not be available to serve in any future cabinet headed by you." At this October 30 press conference, Gorton said Fairbairn had not given at their Tuesday meeting any indication of what he had in mind. When he had received Fairbairn's telegram, he thought at first it was a hoax. He had thought that if Fairbairn had such an attitude Fairbairn would have written or talked to him. Gorton said he had a complete recall of the conversation. Fairbairn had asked what were his Cabinet intentions concerning him. Gorton said he replied that he had told nobody what they were getting and he would not tell Fairbairn. According to Gorton's version, the question of Fairbairn accepting an appointment as Australian High Commissioner in London was discussed then. Gorton gave no indication that it had been discussed also prior to the elections.[13] On this occasion Gorton said that Fairbairn had said that he did not feel that he wanted the job any more.[14]

Fairbairn did not at any stage put out an official version of his conversation with Gorton. A man very conscious of the proprieties, Fairbairn apparently revealed details of the conversation only to those with whom he felt that the conversation had to be discussed in the national interest. After his talk with Gorton, he went off,

356

a very unhappy man, and had conversations with McEwen and other senior colleagues whose attitudes could have a bearing upon the future. A version of what he had told them was the substance of the discussions between Gorton and himself then started to circulate. According to this version,[15] Fairbairn expressed to Gorton the belief that the deterioration in Commonwealth-State relations had assisted to bring about the election result, so adverse from the government's viewpoint. Gorton had replied that he did not subscribe to this view. He did not consider that the issue of Commonwealth-State relations had had any significant effect upon the election result. He did not intend to be influenced by the election result as far as Commonwealth-State relations were concerned. He did not intend to change his attitude. Fairbairn in his recital of the conversation produced an alleged Gorton phrase which had clearly shaken him. "Whitlam went to the electorate on a centralist policy, did all right, so why should I reshape mine?" Fairbairn reported Gorton as saying. Gorton also refused to consider changing his personal style of government. It had not been his personal style which was responsible for the government's setbacks, he said. It had been electoral redistribution, Whitlam's promises, and the war in Vietnam.[16] In fact, if the government had behaved in the pre-election period as he, Gorton, thought it should have behaved and if he had not been led into misjudgments by "poor advice" the result would have been much better for the government. From here on, he, Gorton, would not be listening to any more of this "poor advice" but would be running the government "as I want it run". As Fairbairn believed that some of the policies, particularly the defence and foreign affairs policies, on which Gorton had gone to the electors had been virtually forced on Gorton by either the DLP or the stubbornness of a relatively small group of government backbench parliamentarians, Fairbairn had another cause for worry. Fairbairn's fear was that if the Gorton style of government went unchallenged and Gorton ran the government "as I want it run", Gorton would insist upon defence policies particularly being revised to make them conform more closely with his personal viewpoint.

From McEwen, Fairbairn got a sympathetic hearing, but no reason to believe that McEwen at that stage was prepared to force a change in the Gorton style of government. Though easily the most experienced and shrewdest parliamentarian in the CP, McEwen was not above listening to, and taking advice from men years his junior if he was convinced that their advice was worthwhile. There was a ground swell gathering strength in the CP. Ian Pettitt, the CP MHR for Hume, stated publicly that Gorton's bad public image was responsible for the government's setbacks.[17] Later Don Maisey, the CP MHR from Moore, in Western Australia, who was critical of McEwen's wheat policy, was to come out and express the hope that McMahon would replace Gorton as Prime Minister.[18] Other CP personalities phoned McEwen on Monday, October 27, 1969, and attributed the government's bad showing to hostility within the electorate, not to the government or the Liberal Party, but to Gorton. McEwen sent for the three young men he was nurturing for responsible, trained participation in CP leadership when he retired. They were McEwen's deputy, Doug Anthony, then 39 and Minister for Primary Industry, Ian Sinclair, then 40 and Minister for Transport and Shipping, and Peter Nixon, then 41 and Minister for the Interior.

McEwen and his younger colleagues discussed the situation soberly and thoroughly. McEwen reported to his CP colleagues that he had talked with Gorton. He had formed the impression that Gorton had "seen the light" and in future would listen to advice before making decisions and taking action. McEwen and his young men decided it was in the best interests of the Liberal-CP coalition that they "should not rock the boat". Public recriminations would only serve to further weaken the government and the Liberal-CP coalition's standing in the electorate. They would be supporting Gorton against any move from within the Liberal Party to the extent that they would be proffering this "don't rock the boat" advice to those who approached them. When Fairbairn was given this advice, he said he was not nearly so concerned about the future of the coalition as about the country. He gave McEwen his version of his conversation with Gorton. In view of this conversation he could not accept advice that nobody should "rock the boat," he said. He might consider that advice if it were only the future of the government, the coalition, and the Liberal Party at stake. But he thought Australia's longterm interests were at stake.[19]

The CP political machine generally followed the lead given by McEwen and his three young lieutenants. The NSW branch of the CP took the attitude that CP members should stay aloof from any Liberal Party leadership dispute, so as not to embarrass the Liberal Party after its severe electoral reverse, and in order to close the ranks and to generate a feeling of loyalty on the part of the CP to its Liberal partner in the federal coalition administration. But this approach did not prevent expressions of private, antiGorton opinions on the part of CP members.[20]

In his only public references to the Tuesday, October 28, conversations, Fairbairn gave no hint of what was said but merely described his reactions. "When I saw the Prime Minister (on Tuesday, October 28) I was hoping to find some feeling of concern on his part as a result of the election debacle, and some readiness to adjust or review policies, some action to call together immediately his senior Liberal colleagues," Fairbairn said. "I came away with the unfortunate feeling that nothing had changed, and in the future nothing would change. In particular the Prime Minister seemed to believe that no problem existed in the field of Commonwealth-State relations . . . . Considerably depressed in my mind, I flew home alone the next morning and spent the day pondering what to do."[21]

While Fairbairn, a conformist but a conformist with a conscience, was on his grazing property, near Woomargama, wrestling with the problem of where lay his duty and whether loyalty to his leader and to his party should override what he considered important to the national interest, the Liberal senators assembled at Cormack's club in an atmosphere of some tension. By that stage it was known that Fairbairn had seen Gorton and had left his presence disturbed. There was no certainty about what Fairbairn would do, but there was a possibility that he would do something, and from his actions might come a challenge to Gorton and his leadership. The senators' meeting, which originally had been to study what lessons for the 1970 Senate elections were contained in the previous Saturday's general election result, turned into a drive to ensure that the Liberal senators' overwhelming support for Gorton and his leadership was maintained.

Present at the meeting were several influential Liberal senators, Cormack himself, Robert Cotton, then the Government Senate Whip[22] and others. The meeting turned into a postmortem on the general election and into an examination of Gorton's post-election position. It was argued that Gorton had led the government to the election. What the voters had passed judgment on was a government led by Gorton. Any move to replace Gorton now after the vote had taken place would, if successful, be an indefensible breach of faith with the electorate. It would be equivalent to the Liberal Party foisting on the electors a prime minister who had not been voted for as a prime minister but as a junior member of a team led by Gorton who would have to be retained as Prime Minister if political decency was to be preserved. To replace Gorton as Prime Minister in such circumstances would split the Liberal Party hopelessly. It would be only a matter of time before the ALP took over the reins of government.

But the proGorton senators could not keep the ranks of the Liberal senators completely solid for Gorton. Present at the

359

meeting was Senator Dame Ivy Wedgwood, who had shared the Victorian Liberal Senate ticket with Gorton from 1949 until Gorton quit the Senate to contest Higgins in 1968 after he had succeeded both to Holt's prime ministership and to his vacant Victorian seat in the House of Representatives. Dame Ivy had been a stalwart of the Victorian Liberal Party since its foundation. An early liking for the young airman, with his battered face and gallantry with women, had been replaced by distrust and disillusionment. Dame Ivy[23] viewed her former Senate colleague as too impetuous and too arrogant, disdainful of advice and capable of the petulance of a small child when confronted with obstacles that a more patient and painstaking man would study with care before tackling. She had respect for the quickness and sureness with which he could absorb the difficult details of an individual problem but little regard for his ability to fit the problem into the broad context of community needs. She and two others expressed themselves in a way that led shrewd judges[24] to report to Gorton "Eleven of the fourteen are your votes, but three of those present, and Dame Ivy is one of those three, will if given the chance vote against you."[25]

From then on criticism started to build up against Gorton in the Liberal Party political machine. Some of the harshest criticism came amusingly from individuals who were seeking to defend Gorton but who, like Gorton himself, did not study the implications in what they were saying. Fred Osborne,[26] then NSW Liberal President and a staunch Gorton defender, told the annual meeting of the Liberal NSW Council on November 28, 1969, "I have no doubt that the first and prime cause (of the swing against Liberal candidates) was the confusion in the electorate on our foreign policy and defence."[27] As Gorton had undoubtedly been the major contributor to confusion in these areas, this was more like an attack on, than the defence of, Gorton that other sections of Osborne's speech showed clearly it was intended to be. Osborne went further.

Osborne listed Federal-State relationships as the issue next in importance to foreign policy and defence during the campaign. Wrangling between the Commonwealth and the States had affected profoundly the election result, he said. As Gorton was again the major contributor to controversy in this field with statements which the Premiers, rightly or wrongly, interpreted as an endorsement of "centralism", this could also be taken as rather dubious support for Gorton. Osborne also drew attention to the fact that the DLP had "been allowed to get offside", but made the point that this was "not entirely our (Liberal) fault". He thought "the leadership of the DLP was foolish."[28] Osborne said a final factor in bringing about the antigovernment swing had been the personal attacks "on the Prime Minister and Mr Gorton's standing in the community during the campaign". The effects of St John's attacks during six months on Gorton had helped to undermine public confidence in the Prime Minister, Osborne said. The electorate, however, had rejected St John who had received about 10,500 votes compared with 25,756 for a young and relatively unknown Liberal candidate.[29] There had been effort, money and intensive action behind St John's campaign, but the electorate had rejected him "contemptuously". In Higgins, Gorton had been given a tremendously high vote by his own constituents. "The Prime Minister deserves our profound sympathy," Osborne said. "He has been the subject of an unbalanced and unreasonable series of consistent attacks. He and Mrs Gorton have worked incessantly to make themselves known to the people of Australia."

Osborne did an analysis of the election result, an analysis the validity of which was challenged by two articles in the same issue of *The Australian Liberal* of December, 1969 as reported his speech to the NSW Liberal Council. Said Osborne, "The severest swing against us was among the elderly people and the well-to-do. The swing was most restricted in areas where young people congregate and means are moderate . . . the Liberal loss was practically nil amongst what is termed the 'artisan' group and there was a considerable gain to the Liberals in what are described as the 'lower income groups'. . . . The younger voters resisted the swing most."[30]

As it happened, Osborne and the NSW Liberal establishment could keep the "oldies", who in some cases were very definitely in the "well-to-do" bracket, on the Liberal NSW Council in line and not publicly antiGorton. But the Liberal establishment could not control the young Liberals. At a Liberal Youth Council meeting[31] in October, held immediately after the general election, an urgency motion, sponsored by Messrs McCarthy (Strathfield) and Kops (Eastwood), called for a vote of no confidence in the capacities of Gorton as party leader and Prime Minister. The state chairman of the Liberal Youth movement, Mr Peter Fitzgibbon, ruled that a debate on such a motion was beyond the power of the Liberal Youth Council. The Council, however, by suspending its standing orders, carried a motion of dissent from the chairman's ruling, and debate proceeded. Messrs Quilty (Killara) and Olsen (Hornsby) moved a motion of confidence in Gorton. Principal arguments in favor of a non-confidence vote were that the Prime Minister's personal style of government and poor relations image

361

had contributed to the reverses of the party, *The Australian Liberal* reported. "Speakers against the motion denied this, stating that they opposed any attempt to dictate to federal parliamentarians the choice of a leader, which was entirely their (the parliamentarians') own prerogative." The McCarthy-Kops non-confidence motion was carried by 31 votes to 27, and the Quilty-Olsen confidence motion was lost by 21 votes to 34. An immediate rescission motion had the effect of holding the decision on the table until the November meeting.

By the time the November, 1969, Liberal Youth Council meeting came round Gorton had been re-elected Prime Minister, and the Liberal powers-that-be wanted the no confidence motion expunged from the records. Liberal Youth Council State President, Peter Fitzgibbon, vacated the chair to ask for the withdrawal of the no confidence motion. "We hit the opposition for six on the issue of behind-the-scenes control of its parliamentary members," Fitzgibbon said. Yet here was the Liberal Youth Council presuming to do exactly the same thing. *The Australian Liberal* reported Mr Kops (Eastwood) as saying that he felt no reasons had yet been given to make the party or the council change its earlier vote. Mr Ruddock (The Hills) spoke against the concept of party unity where it meant sacrifice of principle. A secret ballot was agreed to. "(The ballot) resulted in a convincing reversal of the earlier no confidence vote," *The Australian Liberal* reported austerely. But *The Australian Liberal* did not give the figures that emerged from the ballot. Nor did it report any of the participants in the debate as speaking in defence of Gorton. It merely had the speakers insisting upon adherence to the principle that the selection of a Liberal parliamentary leader was entirely a matter for the Liberal Parliamentary Party.

But there were other more serious stirrings than in the NSW Youth Council. In Queensland, Gorton had always been suspect. Believing that Queensland already suffered from federal neglect, Queensland Liberals considered that further centralisation of power in Canberra would intensify that neglect. On Friday, October 31, the Queensland Liberal Party assembled for its first post-election meeting. About thirty members of the executive, including the Postmaster-General Alan Hulme, were present.

The Queensland Liberal Party President, Eric Robinson, said that he was not seeking to stifle any delegate's freedom. But he asked that there should be no emotionalism. Delegates should approach the discussion coolly and in an analytical manner. As a consequence of this appeal, there was no personal, as distinct from political, criticism of Gorton. The closest approach to personal criticism came from a woman delegate who said that a Liberal leader should not only act in a "responsible" manner but should display a measure of dignity and show publicly a realisation of the importance of the Prime Minister's office. Other delegates re-echoed this viewpoint.

Among the Gorton critics were Gordon Chalk, who was the Liberals' Parliamentary Leader in Queensland and also Deputy Premier and Queensland Treasurer since 1965, Dr A. W. Hartwig, a former Queensland Liberal President,[32] and three Queensland Liberal Party vice-presidents. There was no outright support for Gorton and only a mild defence of Gorton from Hulme and from the area representative for Moreton, the seat held in the House of Representatives by Jim Killen, who was a Gorton supporter. Speakers said that Gorton had electorally reached the point from which he could not make an electoral comeback.[33] Unless Gorton was replaced as Liberal Party leader, the Liberal-CP coalition government faced destruction and the Liberal Party annihilation. While the electorate generally had no criticism of basic Liberal policies and approaches, many voters were suspicious of Gorton and his methods. Liberals were even more suspicious than ALP voters. Gorton had shown himself incapable of understanding or unwilling to understand the issues of defence, foreign affairs, Commonwealth-State relations, and other matters.[34]

Speakers said that Gorton had disregarded advice on campaign strategy given to him by the Liberal organisation. He had persisted in following guidelines that were exclusively his own. Robinson reported that the Queensland Liberal Party had protested to Gorton while Gorton was in Adelaide during the election campaign that he, Gorton, was neglecting the issues of defence and foreign affairs. It was only after this protest that Gorton had given any emphasis to defence and external matters. Speakers said that Gorton might have given some emphasis to defence and foreign affairs after Queensland's intervention but even then he had shown inadequacy in presenting the government's viewpoint on these matters. To a claim from Hulme that Gorton had been "a victim of the press",[35] delegates retorted that Gorton and his ministers should have been able to phrase their statements so that they could not have been misinterpreted. The press could not be blamed for Gorton's incoherencies.[36]

The Queensland Liberal Party Executive directed Robinson to express at the forthcoming Federal Liberal Party Executive meeting, scheduled for November 20, 1969, in Canberra "dissatisfaction, disapproval and distrust" of Gorton's leadership. The decision was virtually unanimous. Robinson was also asked to

363

convey this view to the Liberal Party Federal President, J. ("Jock") Pagan as soon as possible so that the Liberal Federal organisation would have "no illusions as to where Queensland stood in the present Liberal Party leadership crisis."[37] On the same day as the Queensland Liberal Party Executive met, Kevin Cairns, then assistant Government Whip announced publicly "I am not prepared to serve even in the humble position of Deputy Government Whip under Mr Gorton. I believe the fate of the Liberal Party is involved in the coming ballot."[38] Senator Ian Wood indicated that he would be voting against Gorton along with Cairns. Nigel Drury, the quietly spoken but influential MHR for Ryan, a Brisbane seat, said he would not commit his vote until his conscience dictated his attitude in the party room at the Liberal Party meeting, which Gorton had summoned for Friday, November 7, 1969. Though originally Hulme immediately after the election had said he would support Gorton, Hulme retired into his shell and refused to commit himself further on the issue. But Gorton was not completely without support in Queensland. Killen came out as a devoted Gorton supporter, as less exuberantly did "Duke" Bonnett, MHR for Herbert, and young Don Cameron, MHR for Griffith.

"The Liberal Party did absolutely nothing (in the election campaign) to exploit the superb policies of Mr Gorton," said Killen.[39] "And now, because of their own inadequacy they are seeking to impale John Gorton."[40] Bonnett was terser but made where he stood very apparent. "As far as I am concerned, Gorton gets a go," said Bonnett.[41] "Without qualification, Mr Gorton is the nation's real leader in Parliament," said Cameron.[42] Outside Queensland, those who expressed an opinion were mainly pro-Gorton. After rumors had spread that Malcolm Fraser, then Education Minister, who had been lifted over the heads of many of his colleagues to cabinet rank after he had helped Gorton to rise to the prime ministership, was contemplating challenging the Prime Minister, Fraser hastily put out a public statement. "I will not stand against the Prime Minister," said Fraser.[43] "We won this election with John Gorton as Prime Minister. After the party meeting has been held, I am completely confident that he will be forming a new government in which I hope to have the opportunity of serving Australia under his leadership."[44] Billy Snedden, then 43 years of age and Immigration Minister, with the looks of an ageing matinee idol and limitless ambition, had hopes of getting the Treasury from which an increasing number of Liberals believed Gorton would eject McMahon at the first opportunity, probably on November 11.[45] Snedden said that he hoped no one would nominate for leadership in opposition to Gorton. "I would like to see John Gorton elected unanimously," said Snedden.[46] Peter Howson, the former Air Minister, who had been dropped by Gorton when he formed his Ministry in 1968, was among the few who publicly applauded Fairbairn's action in refusing to serve in a ministry under Gorton's leadership. Said Howson, "I admire a man who has the guts to stand up and be counted for deeply held convictions on his part."[47]

NOTES

[1] I say theoretically because Liberal discipline within the House of Representatives is not as tight as that of the ALP's and on occasions the government had defectors.

[2] Indicative of Gorton's pre-polling day confidence was his disinterest in Benson's future. Recognising that only Benson was capable of keeping Maribyrnong out of ALP hands, a prominent Liberal, wisely "running scared", worked on the assumption that the government might need Benson, who supported the government on defence and foreign affairs issues, after polling day. The Liberal persuaded Benson to reconsider his retirement decision, which Benson agreed to do provided Gorton gave him assurances of a minor nature. After waiting outside Gorton's office for an interview for three days, Benson "gave Gorton away", and insisted on retiring—Personal conversations with Benson and the Liberal negotiator over the period.

[3] I have relied upon the percentages worked out by Malcolm Mackerras in his article "Another Second Preference Government" in the *Australian Quarterly,* December, 1969, Vol 42, No 4.

[4] "Well, it (Freeth's statement) was not really a defence statement. It's hard to draw the line, I suppose, between defence and foreign affairs"—Gorton, TV interview on the ABC's "Four Corners" programme, August 30, 1969.

[5] Gorton press conference, August 26, 1969.

[6] Don Aitkin estimated the anti-government swing in seats held by Liberal Ministers at 6.4 percent, compared with 7.4 percent in Liberal backbenchers' seats—*Politics,* May, 1970, Vol 5, No 1, p 51.

[7] The 1969 Higgins figures were Gorton 30,191; ALP 14,868; DLP 4,208; Australia Party 1,598; others 77. The 1966 Higgins figures were Holt 23,918; ALP 9,510; DLP 4,370. Higgins had lost 9,500 voters to Henty and acquired 25,000 new voters from Fawkner in the 1968 electoral redistribution.

[8] Gorton press conference, October 26, 1969.

[9] The ALP's leftwing has recognised this fact of Australian political life. Because of their strongly leftwing leanings, some leftwing ALP leaders might not be able to win a seat in the House of Representatives, where the individual factor is much more important than it is in the Senate. So these leftwing ALP personalities get an ALP preselection for the Senate, and then get into Parliament, not as individuals, but because they carry the ALP label and are virtually anonymous.

[10] Gorton was the first Australian senator to become Prime Minister.

11 Gorton was a member of the Country Party until 1947—*John Grey Gorton* by Alan Trengrove, Cassell, 1969, p 98.
12 Cormack received a knighthood in the 1970 New Year's honors list for "long political and public service."
13 See Chapter 12, pp 294/295.
14 *Daily Telegraph,* Sydney, October 31, 1969.
15 What follows is, of necessity, third hand. Fairbairn refused flatly to discuss his conversation with Gorton, or even to say whether the version which follows was accurate or inaccurate.
16 Despite his election criticisms of the ALP for advocating the withdrawal of one of Australia's three battalions, and his declaration that this would endanger the two remaining battalions, Gorton on December 16, 1969, announced Australia would reduce its Vietnam commitment when the US made its next withdrawal. To protests that this justified the ALP attitude he had condemned as near treason during the election campaign, Gorton retorted, "The people have turned against us on Vietnam."
17 *Australian,* October 28, 1969.
18 *Daily Telegraph,* Sydney, November 3, 1969.
19 I wrote virtually this in the *Daily Telegraph,* Sydney, October 31, 1969. I cannot reveal my sources without breaking confidences.
20 I reported in the *Daily Telegraph,* Sydney, October 29, 1969, that the CP organisation considered Gorton's personality was major in producing the electoral reverse. In a carefully worded public statement, the NSW CP Chairman, Mr L. A. Solomons, MLC, after discussing the election figures said "They (the figures) reject Mr Alan Reid's contention in the *Telegraph* today . . . . In situations such as we are now facing in the federal sphere, we support our leaders, not denigrate them."
21 Official statement, issued by Fairbairn at a press conference, Melbourne, November 3, 1969.
22 Cotton was appointed Minister for Civil Aviation in the Gorton ministry announced on November 11, 1969.
23 In a letter dated January 30, 1970, announcing her intention of not recontesting the 1970 Senate election, to Mr R. Southey, Liberal Federal President, Dame Ivy said she had informed Gorton of her intention to retire at the end of her present Senate term "some considerable time ago."
24 There is reason to believe that both Cormack and Cotton reported to Gorton their assessments of what support there was for him at this meeting.
25 From conversations at the time with participants in the meeting and with Gorton intimates.
26 Osborne was MHR for Evans until defeated at the 1961 general election.
27 *The Australian Liberal,* December 1969, p 3.
28 As the DLP lost nothing except 1.3 percent of the vote at the election and established very clearly the Gorton government's dependence on DLP preferences for its very existence, a hardheaded political judgment might be that the DLP was not nearly as "foolish" as the Liberal elements which needlessly estranged the DLP.
29 The "young and comparatively unknown" successful Liberal candidate was Michael McKellar, 30, an agricultural scientist. The final figures in Warringah gave McKellar 25,799, the ALP's Thomas Reynolds 11,884, and St John 10,589.
30 *The Australian Liberal,* December 1969, pp 1, 3, and 6.

31 The attendance was "the smallest . . . for more than twelve months"—
   The Australian Liberal, December, 1969.
32 Hartwig later made a public statement that the Liberal Party needed
   renewed enthusiasm for the ideals of the Party and "this must come
   either from a marked change of heart from the leader, or by a new
   leader"—*Daily Telegraph,* Sydney, November 3, 1969.
33 This of course was an overstatement. Politics, like horseracing, has a
   glorious uncertainty.
34 From conversations at the time with participants in the Queensland
   Liberal Party executive meeting. I reported the substance of these
   conversations in the *Sunday Telegraph,* November 2, 1969.
35 This was a view held by many Liberals. See Chapter 15, p 384.
36 *Daily Telegraph,* Sydney, November 3, 1969.
37 From conversations at the time with participants in the Queensland
   Liberal Party Executive meeting.
38 *Daily Telegraph,* Sydney, November 1, 1959.
39 Killen was appointed Minister for the Navy in the Ministry announced
   by Gorton on November 11, 1969.
40 *Daily Telegraph,* Sydney, November 3, 1969.
41 Ibid.
42 Ibid.
43 Fraser was promoted to Minister for Defence on November 11, 1969.
44 Official statement put out by Fraser's Canberra office, October 28, 1969.
45 Snedden missed out on the treasuryship but was promoted to Minister
   for Labor on November 11, 1969.
46 *Daily Telegraph,* Sydney, November 1, 1969.
47 Ibid.

CHAPTER 15

THE drama shifted to Melbourne, the Mecca of Australian race fans on the first Tuesday in November when the Melbourne Cup is run. Almost as much political lobbying as horse watching was done by the politicians assembled at Flemington race course as the day progressed and the Cup went to the hardfinishing Rain Lover, starting at nine to one.

It was during this period that McEwen, able, subtle, and well versed in the art of fishing rewardingly in troubled waters, started to move. Originally, after consultations with his three young CP lieutenants—Anthony, Sinclair, and Nixon—McEwen had decided that it was against the coalition's interest to "rock the boat". But the "boat" was rocking violently, not because of any CP movement but because of the Liberal restlessness. McEwen decided that as the boat was already rocking he might as well add to the violence of its swings.

McEwen was in the fix that the more farsighted and shrewder head of a Scottish border family must have been in when law and order was first being enforced in the historically turbulent border-land between Scotland and England. McEwen believed in consistency in government. Consistency could only come if there were constant consultations and the management of affairs was not left to the whim of one man. But that one man, in this case, Gorton, in return for being left to go his own way had given McEwen virtually everything he wanted. It was a case of law and order, or the opportunity to pick up across the border the exciting plunder of fat Sassenach cattle. Both prospects had an appeal to McEwen, a mosstrooper by temperament and a methodical man by training. On this occasion, he subdued his mosstrooper tendencies. He plumped for law and order. He did this by lifting his veto on McMahon, imposed in late 1967 when immediately after Holt's disappearance into the sea, he announced that neither he nor his CP colleagues would serve under McMahon as Prime Minister. It was a warning to Gorton that the history books are as full of the allegedly politically indispensable as cemeteries are of those once viewed as irreplaceable. McEwen probably worked out that his action would either secure the displacement of Gorton as Prime Minister or have the effect of curbing Gorton's propensity for unilateral decision making if Gorton survived.

McEwen used a technique that he had used before. A proud man, he would not go to McMahon to tell him that he had lifted the veto. If he did that it would be equivalent to acknowledging that he had made a mistake in 1967 when he imposed the veto. He wanted McMahon to come to him to ask that the veto be lifted. So an old standby of McEwen's was produced. This standby was an anonymous and unidentified journalist. Out of the blue, this journalist asked McEwen if McEwen would take the same attitude now as he had in 1967 if McMahon became a candidate for Liberal leadership. McEwen answered. As his reply was too important to be left the property of one journalist, it was released generally.

McEwen withdrew his veto on McMahon after Fairbairn on Monday, November 3, 1969, had committed himself irrevocably to contesting the leadership against Gorton. Fairbairn made his declaration at a press conference in Melbourne. "The die is cast," Fairbairn jested. "For me it's Sydney or the bush, or in other words, Kirribilli House (the Prime Minister's Sydney residence), or Woomargama (the little town near Fairbairn's Riverina farming property)." Fairbairn said his loss of faith and confidence in the Prime Minister had been "building up for some months". If Gorton were re-endorsed this would be a good thing. The Liberal Party would know where it stood. But he felt that the party should have a choice. He would be happy if other candidates came into the field because this would give the party a wider selection. But it seemed to him that there had been under way an operation to try to prevent anyone else standing against Gorton.

Fairbairn said he thought Gorton should be replaced as Prime Minister because he believed there were aspects of Gorton's policies reacting against the Liberal Party and the nation. He was strongly opposed to Gorton's views on Commonwealth-State relations. He believed in the federal system. "There was recently a get together of Commonwealth and State ministers in Sydney arranged by the Liberal Party to try and see if we couldn't bury the hatchet between the Commonwealth and the States," Fairbairn said. "We buried the hatchet all right—right in each other's backs." He was not a stalking horse for Mr McMahon in any way. He had made up his own mind to contest the leadership. He would be running if he got only one vote—his own. "It has been a tremendous decision to make," Fairbairn said. "I'm sure anyone would realise the horror of coming to a decision like this. But

369

eventually you say, 'Well, what can I do that is best for the nation.' "

Fairbairn said he had not discussed his challenge with McMahon prior to making his decision. He had made his announcement about his attitude to the Prime Minister and of his intention to contest the Liberal leadership. Only after he had made that announcement did he ring McMahon and tell him of it. He believed that if there was any change to be made in Liberal leadership it must be made now. He had a very high regard for the quality of McMahon's work as Treasurer, and the ability McMahon had shown. "I think it is very largely due to McMahon that the economy of the nation is in the position it is in today," said Fairbairn. "If by any chance I win the prime ministership I would want to retain him in office as Treasurer because I just don't believe there is anyone else who could do as well as he does."[1]

Fairbairn said he was perfectly prepared to serve under McMahon as Prime Minister. He believed that cabinet should be more of a team than it had tended to be. "Most importantly, the government must . . . not be excessively influenced by a handful of individuals," Fairbairn said.[2] He would not discuss a report that he thought a number of policies had been forced on Gorton against his will by Cabinet and that there was a danger that Gorton would go back on these policies, particularly the decision taken to keep Australian troops in Malaysia and Singapore, a decision taken after long delays. "To answer that would be violating cabinet secrecy," said Fairbairn. "The question impinges on cabinet secrecy and cabinet responsibility. But occasions when a prime minister does not get his way in Cabinet are inevitable. I've served under three prime ministers. I've seen Sir Robert (Menzies) get up with great aplomb and defend very strongly something with which he personally did not agree. But cabinet as a team had produced the decision. One man must work as part of a cabinet, and I feel that we just haven't tended to do this quite as much as we should. It is no good having one brilliant person. I believe team work is better than individual brilliance. I hoped that others would have brought their names forward. This decision has caused me considerable worry and concern. Perhaps it should have been made by someone else. Nevertheless I feel that I do have some qualities with which I would hope to be able to lead the nation. Basically it is a prime minister's policy which sets the pattern. Certainly this is the case where you have a prime minister who believes that he should keep a very strong control rather than have more of a team effort."

Fairbairn said some people had been saying that the Liberal parliamentarians might be able to change the views of the Prime Minister, others that Liberals must hope and pray, and others that Liberals must not "rock the boat". Fairbairn said his view was that if the boat had a hole in it, the hole must be plugged or the boat would sink, irrespective of whether or not it was rocked. He had nothing whatsoever personally against the Prime Minister. Asked if he would rather see the Liberal Party in opposition than Gorton as Prime Minister Fairbairn replied "Good heavens, no."[3]

McEwen's reliable, unidentifiable, and anonymous journalist then got into the act. Asked if Fairbairn would be acceptable to him as prime minister, McEwen said, "I would certainly be quite happy to form a coalition government with him." McEwen then responded to a question about McMahon and whether his attitude was the same as he had taken in January of 1968 when Gorton was elected Liberal Party leader. McEwen replied austerely, "As Mr McMahon has not announced himself as a candidate, there is no need for me to comment on situations which do not at present exist." McEwen then moved on to the real meat. Asked if this meant that McMahon would need to declare his candidature first and only then learn McEwen's attitude, McEwen said "This is not the position. Mr McMahon and I have been for years on an amicable daily relationship, working together as Cabinet Ministers on christian name terms. I am not playing any cat and mouse situation on an issue of such great importance to the stable government of this country. I am sure that if Mr McMahon is concerned to know my attitude he would come and see me. Last year I told him in a personal conversation why I was taking the attitude which I then did. My desire and intention is to act correctly in the public interest." As an insurance to cover all contingencies, McEwen added "I have already stated publicly that if Mr Gorton is to carry on as Prime Minister on the decision of the Liberal Party, I would work with him to establish good and stable government for the country."[4] McEwen's references to McMahon were virtually an invitation to McMahon to first see McEwen and then throw his hat into the leadership ring.

As McEwen had anticipated, it did not take McMahon long to respond to McEwen's invitation. Within minutes of reading McEwen's statement, McMahon left his Melbourne hotel for McEwen's Melbourne home. For McMahon, apart from anything else, McEwen's new attitude was a belated vindication. McEwen's implied withdrawal of his 1967 veto was an official confirmation that the veto had originally been imposed, not because of any impropriety in McMahon's conduct of his office as Treasurer, but for other, more personal reasons. McEwen and McMahon had a friendly discussion at McEwen's home. After these discussions, McEwen said ". . . I made it clear that if he (McMahon) was chosen by the Liberal Party as the Liberals' leader, I would not refuse to join him in a coalition, subject to having a satisfactory understanding with him on a variety of matters."[5] Immediately after he had his discussions with McEwen, McMahon announced that he was entering the leadership contest. Said McMahon, "After reading Mr McEwen's statement this afternoon, I had a discussion with him. It was friendly and in general terms. I am sure that if I were successful in the ballot for the leadership of the Liberal Party, there would be no objection from him . . . . I have informed Mr Gorton that I intend to submit my name to the ballot."[6]

With McMahon and Fairbairn both in the arena, headcounting started in earnest. Headcounting is always difficult, even in the ALP where it has the status of a fine art. It is even harder in the Liberal Party, where there is an element of amateurism, particularly in the lower echelons, and a prim schoolgirlish belief that there is something vulgar about votes and it is not nice to know the result of a vote. Also politicians do not like to commit themselves publicly even though they have committed themselves mentally, because it is not only pleasant after the event to say they supported the winner, but dangerous to their future prospects to be identified with the loser. At the stage McEwen moved in, my estimate was that Gorton had a minimum advantage of possibly eight, certainly seven, over the combined McMahon-Fairbairn vote. MHRs were split almost evenly and Gorton's majority depended on senators.

Gorton, who had taken an almost offhand attitude since the election, suddenly seemed to realise that with the McMahon-Fairbairn combination ranged against him, and McEwen moving from a position of support into neutrality at best and possibly hostility, he needed to adopt a more positive and conciliatory attitude. Otherwise the waverers might turn against him. Gorton held out the olive branch to the Liberal Parliamentary Party at the declaration of the Higgins poll on Wednesday, November 5, 1969. He took a line that had a strong appeal to the Liberals, the majority of whom liked to view themselves as loyalists and the prototypes of officers and gentlemen, despite their years in politics. Gorton nominally addressed a gathering of his electors in the street outside the office of the Commonwealth Returning Officer for Higgins. Actually, he was talking to the MHRs and senators who made up the Liberal Parliamentary Party. "The swing was much greater than we expected," said Gorton. "One has to expect a swing when the government has a record majority. But not one when you lose thirteen or fourteen seats. And not one of the magnitude that happened in the States outside Victoria. This is an indication that, while the government has been returned, the electorate is not completely satisfied. There is some dissatisfaction shown by the vote. It is necessary for that to be identified and rectified. This will be the task of my government, assuming it is my government, and I am confident it will be my government. My government will examine our policies so that in the next (general) election we can win overall as well as you have allowed me to win here (in Higgins). This we pledge ourselves to do. We shall examine all our policies searchingly for that purpose."[7] It was a public declaration that if re-elected Liberal Party leader, the post-election Gorton would be a reformed character.

Gorton's words were virtually a direct reply to Fairbairn, who had said on November 3, 1969, that he had come away from his interview with Gorton on Tuesday, October 28, 1969, three days after polling day "with the unfortunate feeling that nothing had changed and that in the future nothing would change." Political correspondent Ian Fitchett reported "Members of the antiGorton camp said tonight that, although the Prime Minister had spoken in the briefest of terms today, there were several waverers in the party who would be impressed by what he had said and who would probably now support him. They said that it was noteworthy that Mr Gorton had not placed any of the blame for the election reverse on his own shoulders, but that this probably would not matter to the wavering element, which was probably larger than generally accepted. This element was truly perturbed at the prospect of removing a prime minister in office, and would not need much argument to refuse to do so."[8]

Time was starting to contract. The vital Liberal Party meeting which was to decide the leadership was to assemble on Friday, November 7, 1969, two days after Gorton had made his declaration of poll speech. Even McEwen with his genius for timing could not beat the march of time. Nevertheless McEwen made one further move. It was a move that could not in any circumstances be helpful to Gorton. Endorsing criticism by Fairbairn that Gorton was "excessively influenced by a handful of individuals" and that "one man must work as part of a cabinet", McEwen on the eve of the Liberal Party meeting stated publicly that his party "required reassurances that significant policy decisions would always be the outcome of cabinet discussions."[9]

McEwen had long privately bemoaned Gorton's predilection for taking major policy decisions without consultations with his senior colleagues, and at the maximum in consultation with low-rated members of his "cocktail cabinet". Though, as he had been able to get his way on a number of things which the CP had wanted, McEwen had turned a blind eye to a number of actions taken by Gorton on an individual basis, McEwen still could not bring himself to approve of these individual forays. McEwen had been hostile about the "Russia in the Indian Ocean" statement put out by Freeth on the eve of the elections, with Gorton's approval but without consultations either with McEwen or Cabinet. To McEwen, experienced, knowledgeable, and possessed of an understanding of how the Australian electorate was likely to react, issue of the Freeth statement was just "plain stupid".

To McEwen, the Gorton-Freeth statement was another example of how Gorton departed from Cabinet government in favor of personal government. McEwen told a group of CP parliamentarians on Wednesday, August 20, 1969, that he had complained trenchantly in Cabinet about such a major change in policy being made without consultation with Cabinet or with him as CP leader and a partner in the coalition. He had also complained about the "almost unbelievable stupidity" of releasing such a statement on the eve of an election without wider consultations than those which had occurred between Gorton and Freeth. In making public his statement that the CP had "required reassurances that significant policy decisions would always be the outcome of cabinet discussions" McEwen again used the technique of responding to questions asked by some unidentified questioner. He thereby avoided the appearance of seeming to produce the statement spontaneously. He made it clear that he was replying to a questioner, but did not identify the questioner in any way. McEwen's statement, in part, read "Mr McEwen was asked today if he anticipated any difficulty in reaching agreement with Mr Gorton or either of the other candidates on the terms of reforming and continuing the coalition. Mr McEwen said he saw no reason why there should be any difficulty in this regard. . . . Mr McEwen said that what the Country Party required was an understanding on general policy objectives in the traditional character and an accepted recognition of the fact that rural export industries were at present in a phase of very considerable difficulty due to constantly growing internal costs which reflect the general Australian prosperity, while at the same time the prices of many products in export markets were low and with a downward tendency." McEwen then let fly his body punch. "Mr McEwen said that his party required reassurances that significant policy decisions would always be the outcome of Cabinet discussions,"

374

the statement said blandly. The statement went on to outline conventional demands—an extra minister for the CP now that the Liberals had failed to maintain their comparative numbers, and four CP ministers in Cabinet, as against the present three. McEwen said that he intended to retire in about twelve months, and another CP Minister in Cabinet would mean than an extra CP minister would be gaining the experience of cabinet membership. "This was a simple, practical contribution to good experienced government, with no prestige aspect intended, and he could see no reasonable person objecting to it," the statement concluded.[10]

McEwen's statement had at most only a marginal impact upon the sixty-five Liberal MHRs and senators who assembled on Friday, November 7, 1969, to vote on leadership. It had come twenty-four hours too late to have an effect. Many of the Liberals had not read it. They were too worried about what they should do and how they should vote in the leadership ballot to be concerned about anything else. It was only after they had re-elected Gorton as leader and emerged from the party room that the implications of the McEwen comment about requiring reassurances that all future significant policy decisions would be the result of cabinet discussions penetrated.

Even before the meeting started the McMahon-Fairbairn camps were aware that Gorton held a majority of three, probably four, over their combined vote. In view of this deficiency in votes, word was passed around among the McMahon-Fairbairn supporters "Turn on a blue—it's our only chance." The advice to "turn on a blue" allegedly came from McEwen, an interested spectator from his office further down the government lobby from the Liberal Party meeting room of the day's happening. But there was a breakdown in liaison. Liberal Jefferson Bate, from NSW, whose views on Commonwealth-State relations had brought him into conflict previously with Gorton in the party room, kept trying to get the call. When he thought something important was at stake, Bate was ever willing "to turn on a blue". But Liberal veteran, Sir John Cramer, a former minister who had participated in the formation of the Liberal Party back in 1944, though not a Gorton supporter, urged that the leadership issue should be decided without discussion. Discussion, he thought, might turn acrimonious and damage Liberal Party relationships for years to come. Cramer's suggestion was accepted eagerly by the proGorton forces. They believed they had the numbers to "down" McMahon and Fairbairn. They did not want to risk having defectors as a result of a party room wrangle. Three scrutineers were suggested— Senator John Marriott, from Tasmania, and MHRs Bruce Graham, from NSW, and Nigel Drury, from Queensland. The three candidates, Gorton, McMahon, and Fairbairn, said that these scrutineers were acceptable to them. Gorton was chairing the meeting as was normal in his role as Prime Minister. Gorton said that as he was a candidate he thought it proper that he should not act as chairman. The party unanimously decided that the meeting should be chaired by the Speaker of the House of Representatives, Sir William Aston.

Aston briefly announced the purpose of the meeting. It was to elect a leader. Ballot papers were distributed. The scrutineers pledged that they would reveal to no one, not even the Prime Minister, the result of the vote. They undertook to destroy the ballot papers as soon as they were counted.[11]

The scrutineers left the party room. They crossed the government lobby and disappeared into the office of the Government Whip, Max Fox. As the minutes then inexorably started to tick away, the proGorton forces became increasingly uneasy. At the previous ballot when Gorton was elected leader in 1968 following the drowning of former Prime Minister, Harold Holt, the count had taken only a few minutes. At the end of a quarter of an hour, there were whispers of "He (Gorton) is in trouble." But the solid backing of the Liberal senators in the maintenance of which Government Senate Whip, Robert Cotton, had been a major influence saved Gorton. The scrutineers returned to the room. It had taken them sixteen minutes to count the vote. A sheet of paper was handed to Aston. Aston read out that Gorton had been elected leader by an absolute majority. There was handclapping and cheers.

Gorton said he was pleased and proud that the Liberal Party had re-elected him leader. He thanked party members for the trust they had reposed in him. McMahon said that Gorton had been elected leader, and consequently became Prime Minister of Australia. McMahon asked party members to give their unqualified allegiance to Gorton and to ensure that there were no divisions within the party. If there were feelings before, they now should be forgotten. The Liberal Party should look at its problems with generosity of mind. It should not matter who voted for or against anyone. Having made its decision, the party should now work together as a team. If it did this it would win back the kind of support it had in 1966. Cramer made a similar appeal for unity, and loyalty.

A ballot then proceeded for the deputy leadership. The contestants were McMahon, Hulme, and Snedden. With the position between the proGorton forces and the McMahon-Fairbairn camp

376

tightening, the proGorton forces had felt they needed Snedden's votes for Gorton, even if they were only a handful. The proGorton forces encouraged Snedden to run for the deputy leadership on the basis that the vote for him in the deputy leadership would duplicate the vote given Gorton in the leadership ballot. "Mr Gorton accepts my candidature (for deputy leadership), and would not be displeased if I won," Snedden told a press conference on Thursday, November 6, 1969, a conference at which Snedden had said also that it was traditional that the Liberal deputy leader should be Treasurer, the portfolio then held by McMahon.[12]

But the moment Snedden had delivered his vote, which contributed to Gorton's survival in the leadership battle, the inevitable happened. In the subsequent ballot for deputy leadership, Snedden's ministerial rivals, though proGorton, were not prepared to see Snedden promoted over their heads by edict of a party vote. These rivals cynically switched their votes, and McMahon was elected on the first ballot. It took only three minutes to count this ballot against the sixteen minutes to count the ballot for the leadership.

Immediately the balloting was over, the proGorton forces spread the report that Gorton had won by fifteen votes, or 40/25. The three scrutineers—Marriott, Drury, and Graham—honored their undertaking. They refused to tell anyone the precise vote. One scrutineer is reported to have made the unguarded remark that the vote for Gorton was "overwhelming" but this may have been a calculated indiscretion. With Gorton back in the saddle, it was to the Liberal Party's advantage to give the impression that he was more firmly back in the saddle than a close vote would have suggested. I believe that I have since identified a minimum of thirty, possibly thirty-one, who voted for either McMahon or Fairbairn, which would have made the final vote 35/30, or 34/31. But while the Liberals preserve their Boy Scout attitude on votes and with the ballot papers destroyed, the vote now cannot be known with complete certainty. But the sixteen minutes it took to count the leadership vote compared with the three minutes for the deputy leadership vote tends to confirm that the vote was closer to my 34/31 than to the 40/25 originally put out by the pro-Gorton supporters.

After a luncheon adjournment, the Liberal Party met again to consider a proposal put forward by Victorian Liberal MHR, Alex Buchanan, for a ministry elected by the party instead of one arbitrarily selected by the Prime Minister. Gorton said he had already made his position clear. He would accept an elective ministry if the party decided that it should have one. But while there were pros and cons he himself did not think an elective

377

ministry was a good system. Senator George Branson, from Western Australia, said an elective system would put ministers under intolerable pressure. Anyway, the present was not an appropriate time to deal with such an issue. Gorton commented, grimly "It is an appropriate time." Having had a win earlier in the day, he wanted another win while he still had the numbers supporting him.

John Jess, from Victoria, an MHR who was critical of Gorton's ministerial appointments, said that the elective system had worked successfully for the Victorian Liberal Government. He could not see that it would put ministers under more pressure in Canberra than in Melbourne. "It would be the end of the Mushroom Club," commented the outspoken Les Irwin, referring to the group of government backbenchers who dined together as the "Mushroom Club" and had been turned by Gorton into a cave within the party, a cave whose members always supported Gorton and were as reasonably assured of promotion as anyone could be in the uncertain world of politics in which loyalties can change faster than fashion. Tom Hughes, from NSW, who was a member of the "Mushroom Club", suggested that a party committee should be set up to study an elected ministry. Hughes[13] said that the present system of appointment to the Ministry being the Prime Minister's prerogative should continue for the lifetime of the present Parliament, and a change, if a change was recommended, should operate in the lifetime of the next Parliament. "That's a real Kathleen Mavourneen" commented the irrepressible Irwin. "If we go on the way we're going, we mightn't be selecting ministers but the members of an opposition executive." Killen commented that the move was contrary to the constitution of the Federal Liberal Party. Gorton said that the organisational difficulty could be overcome. During a discussion on a possible special status for senate ministers, Jess, an antiGorton man who clearly resented the role that the Liberal senators had played in preserving Gorton in the prime ministership, grew caustic. "It is a pity that the senators do not have to face the people directly instead of living off No 1 and No 2 places on the party's senate tickets," said Jess. "I hope there is not going to be more block votes by people who do not have to face the people." John McLeay, a South Australian MHR, said he was against elective ministries. "They encourage malcontents," said McLeay. "Define malcontents," snapped Jess, a man with a quick temper and an impatient disposition. "You're one," retorted McLeay. The proposition finally voted on was that the party elect nine House of Representatives ministers and two Senate ministers, with the Prime

378

Minister appointing the rest of the Ministry and deciding who should be in Cabinet.

With those in the Ministry hoping for a continuance of prime ministerial patronage and a number of those not already in the Ministry hoping to be in the Ministry to be announced within a few days and in one of the ministerial vacancies caused by the retirement of Fairhall and the announcement by Fairbairn that he was not available to serve again in a ministry headed by Gorton, the way the vote would go was inevitable. It went that inevitable way. The elective proposition was thrown out.[14]

At his press conference after he was re-elected leader, Gorton was on top of the world. He was again completely cock-a-hoop. He had the wonderful temperament which gave him confidence that, if he could overcome the problems of today, tomorrow's problems would be equally soluble. Yes, he had lost four senior ministers in the last year—Hasluck to the governor-generalship, Fairhall to retirement, Freeth by defeat, and Fairbairn by withdrawal. But there was plenty of talent in the party. It would be a good thing to bring some of that talent up to the top.

McEwen's requirement that future major policy decisions would always be made after cabinet discussions?[15] He had seen the two sentences in McEwen's statement which made reference to that. The sentences did not represent precisely what he had discussed with McEwen. He thought they were "a kind of shorthand". But his attitude was that he knew of no occasion when policy decisions had been taken without cabinet discussions except one—when he took action to protect the MLC.

Why did McEwen think it necessary to make the request for such a reassurance? Gorton shrugged. "I can't read McEwen's mind," said Gorton. Was not Freeth's Indian Ocean statement a matter for Cabinet? Gorton shrugged again. "That's right," he said, rather mysteriously. "I think it was not a policy change. It was interpreted as policy change when in fact it wasn't."

When would he begin an examination of government policies? The party would wish to express its views on the subject, but he would expect to be examining things with ministers before another Liberal Party meeting. It would take some time. It was not for him to make a move about Fairbairn deciding not to serve in a ministry under his prime ministership. It was not up to him, also, if Cairns said he would not be deputy government whip.

What lessons had he learned from the election? There was clearly some dissatisfaction in the electorate. That dissatisfaction needed to be identified and then rectified. The government's first task was to identify it. "I can only say I am not of or in the

379

establishment," said Gorton. "I think my policies might change. I think they would need to. But I think it's unlikely they would change in a conservative direction." Could there be unity after the bitterness of the last few weeks, and would McMahon remain Treasurer? "Have you noticed any bitterness or recrimination coming from me or anyone else—coming from McMahon?" Gorton asked. "I have not seen it. I think everybody has the right to stand for leadership of the party. That right has been exercised and the party has made its judgment." As for McMahon and the Treasury, he would prefer to wait until things had been finally decided.[16]

McMahon, uninvited, intruded into the Gorton press conference. With professional competence, he virtually took over the conference. Gorton, with arms folded, glared down at McMahon who was sitting in the chair Gorton had vacated. If looks could have killed, McMahon would have been the first talking cadaver to star on TV. Said McMahon, "I can assure you of our complete loyalty to John Gorton and the will to unity that we should work back to having exactly the same kind of majority that we earned in 1966 . . . . We will be working together as a team to make certain that not only in the parliament, but before the bar of public opinion we win the kind of support we have enjoyed in the past and which I am sure we will win in the months to come."

Asked if he wished to remain Treasurer, McMahon replied that he would not express a view about that, and then proceeded to express one. "Of course, it is always my wish to remain Treasurer," said McMahon. "But I don't want to be trying to commit the Prime Minister. It is his jurisdiction as to what he does there."[17]

McMahon's boldness in stating that he wanted the Treasury did not pay off. It might have succeeded with a more careful man than Gorton. Many Liberals admired McMahon's competence as a Treasurer, and to remove him might cause trouble. A more cautious man than Gorton would probably have worked out that he should occupy himself with the mending of fences rather than in the creation of a situation that could, conceivably, lead to further convulsions within the already convulsed Liberal Party. But Gorton was determined to get rid of McMahon from the strong point of the Treasury, possession of which had enabled McMahon to confront Gorton with the authority of knowledge and the backing of a team of highly qualified public service advisers and administrators.

When on November 11, 1969, Gorton announced his ministry McMahon had been shifted from Treasury to External Affairs.[18] Bury, much more amenable to Gorton's authority, had been moved from Labour and National Service to the Treasury. Fraser had been promoted to Defence Minister. Two who had been effective in rallying support to Gorton had been raised to the ministry, Cotton as Minister for Civil Aviation and Killen as Minister for the Navy. Hughes had been made Attorney-General. Victorian Liberal MHR Don Chipp, the Navy Minister dropped from the Ministry by Gorton in 1968, was brought back as Customs Minister. Liberal MHR, Andrew Peacock, from Victoria, then 30, was brought in as Minister for the Army and Minister assisting the Prime Minister. Queenslander Reg Swartz, formerly Minister for Civil Aviation, was promoted to Fairbairn's vacated job as Minister for National Development. Snedden received a pay-off for his support. He became Labour Minister and replaced Erwin as Leader of the House of Representatives.

McEwen got what he wanted. Victorian CP MHR R. N. ("Mac") Holten became the CP's seventh minister. Holten went into the Repatriation portfolio. Senator Tom Drake-Brockman, from Western Australia, filled the CP vacancy caused by the retirement from the Ministry of NSW veteran CP senator, Colin McKellar. Drake-Brockman became Minister for Air.

Gorton dropped three ministers, MHRs C. R. ("Bert") Kelly, from South Australia, who had been Navy Minister, and Dudley Erwin, from Victoria, and Senator Malcolm Scott, from Western Australia. Erwin and Scott had been members of the Fraser-Erwin-Scott triumvirate which had done the organising work that had brought Gorton to the prime ministership in 1968. Scott, a pathetic figure in some ways,[19] who had been in more trouble than Speed Gordon while Customs Minister, went quietly. Erwin, who had been Air Minister, raised a storm which in some ways assisted Gorton. Erwin's complaints distracted attention from McMahon's ejection from the Treasury. Erwin blamed Miss Ainsley Gotto, his former secretary, who had moved up to become private secretary to Gorton when Gorton took over the prime ministership, of "poisoning" the Prime Minister's mind against him. Erwin had been told that one of Gorton's relatives had said that women always found it easier than men to "get through" to Gorton and because of his experiences Erwin believed this implicitly. He claimed that the Prime Minister had acted on Miss Gotto's advice "because he had no other advice". Erwin also claimed that because of Miss Gotto he could not get in to see Gorton, and neither could other ministers. Erwin suggested Miss Gotto deliberately kept ministers away from Gorton to strengthen her influence with the Prime Minister. Gorton needed a trained staff to help him, said Erwin. Gorton had excellent people in the head of the Prime

Minister's Department, Mr Len Hewitt[20] and his press secretary, Mr Tony Eggleton. "But he needs so many more—research workers, and so on to feed him material, to keep him out of the trouble he has been getting into," said Erwin. "In the last election, we travelled the countryside in a one-man band with a little girl trying to feed the Prime Minister the material he should have had from experts," said Erwin. "It's just not good enough for the nation."[21] In their 1969 Christmas letter, signed by Erwin and his wife, Joan, but clearly written by Mrs Erwin, reference was made to Erwin being "unceremoniously dumped from the Ministry". The letter continued "The publicity that followed, and the necessary limited revelations came as a shock to the public, but we have lived with this for a long time and did not attempt to expose the situation without a great deal of thought. In his own way, God has salvaged us from that den of iniquity. After a year of accusations and a great deal of smoke, it seems incredible to me that the Australian public still doesn't suspect fire."

Erwin was soon presented with another grievance, this time much more clearcut in its nature. It was "leaked" that Erwin had asked Gorton for an appointment as Australian Ambassador to the United States.[22] His application had been rejected. Erwin was understandably furious. "Only two people knew of the conversation —myself and the Prime Minister," Erwin said. "I was staggered to see the report in today's papers. It was strictly private. I would not have expected it from a man in the position of Prime Minister." Told the report had not been sourced, Erwin said he believed Gorton was responsible for the release. Erwin said the "leak" must have come from Gorton. "This has been purposely given out," Erwin said. "The Washington posting was mentioned, but the Prime Minister failed to add . . . that he could not allow Ballarat[23] to be turned into another Corio."[24]

Before things could settle down, Gorton still had two further hurdles to overcome. He had a meeting with the Liberal Party Federal Executive on November 20, 1969, and an election postmortem meeting with the Liberal Parliamentary Party on November 24, 1969. Despite the delicate matters with which the executive dealt, the executive meeting was kept at a low-key level. Later the Liberal Federal President, Pagan, claimed that Gorton was not "personally" criticised at the meeting. But some fairly straight talking was done.

Oddly, some of the most critical views were expressed by Osborne, the NSW Liberal President. A strong proGorton man, Osborne was clearly trying to be helpful. Osborne dealt with such matters as the need for a better presentation of the differences between the Liberals and the ALP on defence and foreign affairs, and for improvement in the relationships between the Federal Government and the Liberal State Governments, the deterioration in which had been a factor in producing the adverse Liberal vote. Osborne said he had been instructed to say something to the Prime Minister that was more on the psychological and personal than the purely political side. It concerned the style, character and actions of the Prime Minister. A prime minister who had a drink with "the boys in the bar" would get approval. But he would not attract votes. The swing voter wanted dignity, a leader he believed he could rely upon and who was stable under the most difficult conditions. They wanted a leader who was a little aloof and who set a standard.[25]

On the question of the press, the executive was a little hysterical. Speakers said that the press had "ganged up" on Gorton. The suggestion was made that Alan Reid in some manner was connected with a group which might have international overtones and which campaigned against Gorton.[26] Because of this group, the Liberals and particularly the Prime Minister had been confronted by an unfavorable press. A member of the federal parliament was named as the man who had given Reid an "account" of what had happened at two Queensland Liberal meetings at which criticism of Gorton had been voiced. Eric Robinson, the Queensland Liberal President, said "Well, I don't know who gave the information to Reid. But I have got to say this. The parliamentarian who has been named was not at either meeting." Gorton said "He was at one of the meetings." Robinson replied "No, he was not at either of the meetings." Gorton said "Well, he must have got it from somebody else, and passed it on to Reid." Robinson said "Well, I don't know about that, but he wasn't at either of the meetings." Gorton asked Robinson why he did not deny that the statement that the Queensland Liberal Party Executive had instructed Robinson to express "dissatisfaction, disapproval, and distrust" of Gorton's leadership.[27] Robinson replied "Well, I couldn't deny them." Gorton said "But you just said that a resolution was not passed." Robinson said "Well, that is perfectly true. There was no resolution before us (the Queensland Liberal Party Executive). But there was a unanimous decision."

After the Executive meeting, Pagan said the Liberal Party Executive recognised that the voting public had taken the opportunity to rebuke the government. As far as the Liberal Party was concerned "that message had been received loud and clear." The executive had identified several factors as contributing to the Liberal reverses. The Liberal campaign should have been longer.

There should have been more public meetings. The medium chosen for the policy speech—TV—should be changed. Gorton's policy speech had been badly produced and did not meet with universal approval. Though the presentation of the speech had been criticised, there was not one word of criticism of what was said or how it was said. The Liberal Party needed to improve Commonwealth-State relations. While there was no doubt that the great issues facing Australia were defence and external security and it was the government's intention to maintain in those areas a forward looking posture, Liberal policies could be improved in other directions.[28]

Pagan added that the Liberals had missed out on the importance to young married people of health, education, housing, and such things. These matters had had more electoral importance than the Liberals had placed on them. The Liberals would be giving them "great attention in the near future". The Australian people were looking forward to some excitement in Liberal policies—a little risk taking. The Liberals, and particularly the Prime Minister, had confronted an unfavorable press. When it was pointed out that the allegedly "unfavorable" attitude that the executive believed it had detected in the press might have stemmed rather from faulty Liberal policies or inadequate performances by its spokesman than from press attitudes, Pagan said "I won't be drawn on that." Pagan said the Prime Minister agreed with all the points raised and identified improvements that could or should be made in the future. "We are a party that learns from adversity," Pagan said.[29]

The aftermath of the Gorton experiment in electoral management spilled over into the Liberal Party meeting on Monday, November 24, the day before the Parliament met for the one-day sitting required by the Constitution before it adjourned until March 3, 1970, giving Gorton and his disorganised followers an opportunity to regroup in the sanctuary of a parliamentary recess. At this Party meeting, Fairbairn explained why he had made his decision not to serve again in a ministry headed by Gorton and Gorton defended and explained past actions to which Fairbairn objected.

Fairbairn charged Gorton with having frozen the Department of National Development out of the negotiations with Esso-BHP about the price to be paid for the oil extracted from the Bass Strait field discovered and developed by the Esso-BHP combination. Fairbairn said that, as Minister for National Development, he had been instructed by Gorton to keep the negotiations secret from his department. Gorton and the permanent head of Gorton's department—Len Hewitt—had taken charge of the negotiations.

Robert Baudino, chief of the "Telegraph" Canberra Bureau (left) and Peter Samuel, Canberra representative of the "Bulletin". With Alan Ramsey, of the "Australian", they wrote the stories which produced the government reactions and led to Gorton's replacement by McMahon as Prime Minister.

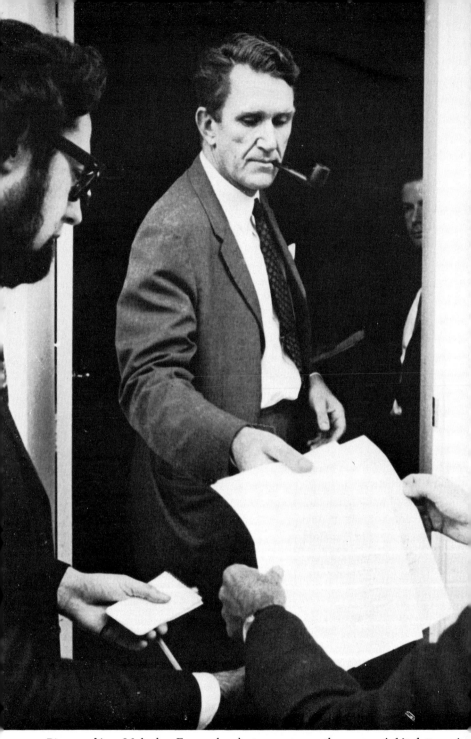

Pipe-smoking Malcolm Fraser hands to pressmen the copy of his letter of resignation as Minister for Defence. Two days later Gorton resigned as Prime Minister.

As a result the "expertise" of the Department had been wasted and the negotiations handled entirely by two men. "You and Mr Hewitt handled everything," said Fairbairn. "There had only been inconclusive Cabinet discussions on this matter." When Fairbairn said that Gorton had acted unilaterally and without consultation with Cabinet in a number of instances, Gorton challenged Fairbairn to say what instances he was referring to. Fairbairn said "If you are freeing me from my cabinet oath of secrecy, I will."[30]

Fairbairn said an example of Gorton's penchant for unilateral actions was Freeth's statement on the Russian presence in the Indian Ocean, issued by Freeth after it had been approved only by Gorton. Another example was Gorton's unilateral action to protect the MLC insurance company. Yet a further example was Gorton's statement immediately after taking office of no further troops for Vietnam in any circumstances. "That was a decision of the Holt government," interjected Gorton. "The decision was no further troops at that time—you were answering something you were not asked," Fairbairn said. Another example was Gorton's pledge that he would prevent drilling for oil on the Barrier Reef. It was not known whether legally Gorton could keep that promise, said Fairbairn. An interdepartment committee was actually examining the Commonwealth's legal situation. Fairbairn said that this kind of approach was demoralising the public service. It was undermining the service's integrity and morality. The public service's fears were shown by the vote in the Australian Capital Territory at the recent election. Canberra's voters had supported the ALP MHR, Mr Jim Fraser, as though Canberra were a coalmining and not an administrative city. Public servants were leaving the service, frustrated and resentful. "Name them," challenged Gorton. "Sir Harry Bland, secretary of the Defence Department,[31] for one," said Fairbairn. "He is the only one," commented Gorton. "There was my own permanent head, Mr Boswell,[32] who was so frustrated and resentful, he left to take up a post in London," Fairbairn said. Fairbairn said he was also troubled by the deterioration in Commonwealth-State relations and the fact that diplomats representing their countries in Australia were "brushed off". They could not see the Prime Minister. One diplomat had waited twelve months to see Gorton. "I am disturbed by the growing lack of morality and integrity in the parliament which feeds on things like this," Fairbairn said. Fairbairn said that the Commonwealth was seeking to interfere in the detailed workings of the States, duplicating administration, instead of approving things and leaving the states to work out the details.

Gorton said he was accused of interfering in details. This was not so. He had interfered with the universities. If left to their own devices, professors and deans of faculties would have luxury suites better than in any hotel in Australia. He did not apologise for interference there.[33]

Gorton said that in regard to Commonwealth-State relations, the Liberal state presidents had now agreed to have the six state Liberal branches make recommendations to the Liberal Party Federal Executive. He was confident that after these and other recommendations which the Commonwealth would produce had been received, a formula could be worked out giving justice to the Commonwealth and the States. Fairbairn had mentioned that the Liberals had suffered at the last election because he, Gorton, had quarrelled with the DLP. He did not remember quarrelling with them. They had quarrelled with him and with the government because defence spending had fallen off. The reason defence spending had fallen off was because of the failure by the defence services to order materials and supplies. The Freeth statement had not been submitted to Cabinet. But it was merely a restatement of a point of view that had been frequently restated. He had not submitted the MLC matter to Cabinet. He had had to act quickly to protect an Australian company with immense assets being taken over by overseas interests. On the Esso-BHP agreement there had been voluminous files, and it was necessary to act quickly. As for the complaints about the treatment of diplomats it was not the custom overseas for them to be received by the prime minister.

Peter Howson, the former Minister for Air, who had supported Fairbairn in his challenge to Gorton's leadership, was also critical. Liberal support from young voters had fallen off by between 40 and 60 percent at the recent general election, Howson said. Similarly, the Liberals' urban following had fallen away. There had been inconsistencies in Defence and Foreign Affairs policies, particularly as regards Malaysia and Singapore. There had been no logical, consistent, and coherent government statement on health or state aid for private schools. There should have been a dialogue with the state governments, not a monologue by the Prime Minister.

Gorton said that his statement on the stationing of troops in the Malaysia-Singapore area was a firm commitment. But the government did not want Australian troops used internally and involved in the dispute in east Malaysia with the Philippines. The government's health scheme had not been completely finalised. He agreed that a solution must be worked out as speedily as possible. Cabinet was working on this. The meeting petered out inconclusively.

With 1969 drawing to a close, Gorton got his first lucky break for months. With the ALP Parliamentary Opposition inflated with its electoral successes, Whitlam had shown arrogant confidence, marred by slight flashes of petulance, during the one-day sitting on November 25, 1969, of the House of Representatives. But even Whitlam's electoral successes could not keep subdued his opponents in the Victorian ALP. The ALP started to show signs of disintegration, a disintegration which in 1970 was to intensify and which was to climax in a takeover of the leftwing Victorian ALP branch by ALP Federal authorities urged on by Whitlam and organised by Clyde Cameron, a takeover which was intended to break the power of the former Victorian ALP controllers among whom Mr George Crawford, Victorian ALP President, was prominent.

On Monday, December 15, 1969, a meeting in Melbourne of fifty-two union shop stewards and delegates, representing 150,000 trade unionists and chaired by Crawford, passed a resolution calling on Australian national servicemen in Vietnam to "lay down their arms in mutiny against the heinous barbarism perpetrated in Australia's name". On Tuesday, December 16, Gorton was in the happy position that he could once again draw attention to the ALP's internal troubles. If the ALP did not "want a Communist victory in South Vietnam" Whitlam should "at once condemn and dissociate himself from the resolution passed in Melbourne," Gorton said. On Sunday, December 21, 1969, Whitlam disowned the resolution in a letter to Chamberlain, secretary of the Western Australian ALP. Said Whitlam, "(This Melbourne) Vietnam resolution . . . is not and never could be ACTU or ALP policy."[34] From there on, the government's internal troubles tended to lessen while the ALP's internal troubles tended again to intensify.

The Gorton experiment, the experiment of a prime minister being himself, of behaving as he felt like behaving, of running a government as "I want it run", of making the major decisions on which he felt deeply and then expecting his Cabinet and his party followers either to endorse his decisions or to get rid of him, of trusting nobody who disagreed with him and of being eternally suspicious, and of appealing over the heads of colleagues and opponents to the masses through the medium of TV, had, temporarily, run its course. It had been for Gorton a successful experiment in that it had given him a further term as Prime Minister. But it had been a costly experiment. It had cost him the prestige of a substantial parliamentary majority, and the friendship of men like Erwin who had started him on his upward climb to the prime ministership. It had surrounded him with timid, frightened sycophants scared of holding their positions, and had exposed him to charges of inconsistency, eccentricity and dogmatism. It had estranged large sections of his party and left him heavily dependent for his continuance in the office of Prime Minister upon things which he could not control—the weakness of his official Opposition, the ALP, and the support, already grudging, of the DLP. But it had succeeded in its prime object— restoring Gorton to the prime ministership.

But the experiment only appeared to be over. On the personal side, it was over. Gorton retired into discretion and conventionality. But politically it was far from over. To experiment was part of Gorton's temperament. And he was following in a large tradition. Men, or at least those men who are political animals as well as men, have been experimenting with forms of government since men emerged from the jungle to live in organised communities. While their mechanically minded fellows have advanced within relatively few generations to the point where the world is crowded with their ingenious gadgets and men now walk on the moon, the political experimenters have not moved far from the metaphorical jungle which is nearly as close now as it was physically in the long ago.

From October 1969 onwards Gorton tried valiantly to fit himself into the mould of a conventional politician, functioning within the restraints imposed by a parliamentary democracy with a Constitution interpreted by a High Court possessed of a tradition of independence and a Federal system under which the central government had specified powers and the six States were otherwise sovereign. But Gorton found his new role difficult. He had weaknesses of perception[35] as well as temperament. Despite the warnings given by the election results and the post election happenings within the Liberal Party room, he still failed to recognise the strength of the power points that existed outside of and apart from the mass electorate and the Liberal Parliamentary Party room, external power points whose influence affected in turn the tightness of his control over his personal power points of the mass electorate and the Party room. He continued to act as though he could afford to ignore the residual power of the Parliament, confront the States with impunity, antagonise sizeable sections of the extra-Parliamentary Liberal Party organisation, and escape the consequences. He persisted in regarding confrontation rather than re-education and patience as not only the most satisfactory but virtually the only means of resolving political problems. He was a man of direct action operating in an environment where history, experience and tradition had placed checks on the exercise of power by men of action in the belief that men of action may be activated as much by a desire for dominance as by good intentions.

These weaknesses were to cost Gorton the prime ministership.

NOTES

1 From notes taken at Fairbairn press conference, Melbourne, November 3, 1969.
2 Fairbairn refused to elaborate this cryptic statement.
3 From notes taken at Fairbairn press conference, Melbourne, November 3, 1969.
4 Official statement issued by McEwen's Melbourne office, November 3, 1969.
5 *Daily Telegraph,* Sydney, November 4, 1969.
6 Official statement issued by McMahon, Melbourne, November 3, 1969.
7 From notes taken at Gorton's declaration of poll speech, November 5, 1969.
8 *Sydney Morning Herald,* November 6, 1969.
9 *Daily Telegraph,* Sydney, November 7, 1969.
10 *Daily Telegraph,* Sydney, November 7, 1969.
11 From conversations at the time with participants in the Liberal Party meeting.
12 Snedden press conference, Canberra, November 6, 1969.
13 A distinguished QC and leader of the NSW bar, Hughes was to be made Attorney-general by Gorton five days later.
14 This account of the November 7, 1969, Liberal Party meeting is from notes made at the time of conversations with participants in the meeting.
15 An ironic touch was while McEwen was making this request, Les Bury, as Labour Minister was publicising proposed changes in the Commonwealth Conciliation and Arbitration Act of a major nature not cleared by Cabinet—Article by Maximilian Walsh, *Sun-Herald,* November 9, 1969.
16 Gorton press conference, Canberra, November 7, 1969.
17 McMahon at Gorton's press conference, Canberra, November 7, 1969.
18 "All epitaphs are supposed to be pithy and there should be no difficulty in writing this one: 'He (McMahon) was too good at the (Treasury) job'."—The Financial Editor, *Sydney Morning Herald,* November 11, 1969.
19 Scott shortly afterwards lost his Western Australian Liberal Senate preselection in part for his support of Gorton policies considered "centralist" in WA.
20 Mr Hewitt became Sir Lennox Hewitt in the 1971 New Year's Honors list.
21 "The Medieval Court of John Gorton" by John Hamilton, *Age,* Melbourne, November 14, 1969.
22 *Daily Telegraph,* Sydney, November 18, 1969.
23 Ballarat was Erwin's Victorian seat.
24 Corio was a Victorian seat lost by the Liberals to the ALP's Gordon Scholes when Hubert Opperman, the former Immigration Minister, resigned in 1967 to become Australian High Commissioner in Malta.
25 From notes taken at the time of conversations with participants in the meetings.

26 This reference left me completely mystified. I had probably done less commenting in the 1969 election than in any previous election. As I think the bulk of my colleagues would confirm, I "lone wolf" and do not get involved in groups. My only international association is that I am a Rugby union fan.

27 "Mr Robinson refused to confirm or deny earlier reports that the Executive had instructed him to express 'dissatisfaction, disapproval and distrust' over Mr Gorton's leadership"—*Sydney Morning Herald*, November 6, 1969.

28 Pagan press conference, Canberra, November 20, 1969.

29 *Daily Telegraph*, Sydney, November 21, 1969.

30 From notes made at the time of conversations with participants in the meeting.

31 Sir Henry Bland's retirement to become effective in March, 1970, was announced soon after Fairhall announced his retirement as Defence Minister in September, 1969.

32 Mr R. W. Boswell, permanent head of National Development, moved to become Australian Deputy High Commissioner in London in 1969.

33 From notes made at the time of conversations with participants in the meeting.

34 *Canberra Times*, December 22, 1969.

35 "I probably wasn't a good politician . . . ."—Gorton, interviewed by Alan Trengrove after Gorton's resignation as Prime Minister, *Sun-Pictorial*, Melbourne, March 13, 1971.

A Note from the Editor

The material up to this point had been received, and was being set, when the dramatic events of March 10th, 1971, took place. I prevailed upon Mr Reid to leave this material unaltered, so it has not been pruned, nor has it been embellished, by 'hindsight'.

We were pleased when we saw how few of the major issues would have been altered and how many of the minor events were no more than indicator straws showing the currents.

V.S.B.

POSTSCRIPT *1*

THROUGHOUT history, politics has been a precarious career. Men who one day exercised great, sometimes supreme, political power have become either corpses or political nobodies the next. John Grey Gorton's ejection from the prime ministership of Australia was in this tradition. On Tuesday, March 2, 1971, Gorton was Prime Minister, unchallenged and seemingly unchallengeable, a man who has outfaced and put down a series of rebellions within the ranks of his own followers so successfully that on Tuesday February 2, 1971, just a month earlier, Senator Ian Wood, of Queensland, had failed to attract a single supporter when he tried to re-hoist the flag of rebellion. Supreme, again confident, with the barons of his Ministry cowed and submissive and would-be rebels effectively crushed, Gorton appeared assured of retention of the prime ministership at least until he had to face the electors at general elections in 1972. On Wednesday, March 10, 1971, eight days later, Gorton was no longer Prime Minister.

To the last day of his term as Prime Minister, Gorton lived up to his reputation which was that he was not only unconventional but unpredictable. Other men contributed to the pageant of his passing from the prime ministership. But he was his own executioner, not only figuratively but literally. Not only was he and he alone responsible for the circumstances that brought about his removal from the prime ministership at a time when his hold upon that prestigious and powerful office seemed firmer than at any time since the 1969 general elections. But he himself dropped the axe which cut off his prime ministerial head. With the Liberal Parliamentary Party divided 33/all on a vote of confidence in his leadership, he cast his vote, as chairman, in favor of "No confidence". Then with the boldness and bravado that had been the hallmark of his three years as Prime Minister he stood for the deputy leadership of the party which had just ejected him from the prime ministership, and convincingly wrested that consolation prize from a party too wracked by emotion at that moment of time to weigh intelligently the implications of its contradictory performances.

In politics, the elimination of powerful personages other than

392

when the elimination takes place because of natural causes, or, in a democracy, because of the verdict of the electorate, is usually planned either by the personality himself or by his enemies. Menzies planned carefully the timing and circumstances of his retirement from the prime ministership in 1966. Opponents of the late Dr Herbert Vere Evatt planned to procure his departure from leadership of the ALP to the political aloofness of the NSW Supreme Court in 1960. The list could be extended almost indefinitely. But sometimes the element of deliberation, or planning, is absent. Things happen without plan and because of a series of incidents that are unplanned. Gorton's downfall was not planned by his opponents. It happened because of things he either did or did not do. He was the architect of his own misfortune.

A quarrel with Malcolm Fraser, then 40 and Minister for Defence, the solitary survivor as a minister of the Fraser-Scott-Erwin triumvirate which had done so much to secure Gorton's elevation to the prime ministership in 1968, was a part, an important part, of the lead up to the events which culminated in Gorton's enforced relinquishment of the prime ministership. This quarrel was a vital quarrel in the series of quarrels which were to break Gorton's grip upon the prime ministership to which he had clung firmly despite demoralising electoral setbacks, both Federal and State, setbacks which boded ominously for the prospects of the coalition government if led by Gorton at the 1972 general elections.

Gorton and Fraser did not go their separate ways until after the 1969 elections and until after Fraser had supported Gorton when Gorton was under challenge from McMahon and Fairbairn for Liberal leadership and the prime ministership. Following the 1969 elections which saw the coalition's thirty-eight majority reduced to seven in the House of Representatives and Gorton's triumphant emergence from his struggle against McMahon and Fairbairn, Gorton realised that to maintain his position within the Liberal Parliamentary Party he had to do something about Commonwealth-State financial arrangements. Even the proGorton Liberal parliamentarians were worried by the electoral damage done in the airing of their grievances against the Commonwealth by the six State Premiers, all either Liberal or CP, until the ALP under Premier Don Dunstan regained a place in the Australian political sun as the government of South Australia after the South Australian State elections of May 30, 1970.

Gorton did something about Commonwealth-State finances. He had to. With McMahon out of the Treasury after the 1969 elections and replaced by Les Bury, who was clearly dominated by Gorton, Gorton could no longer use McMahon as the scapegoat and blame McMahon for Commonwealth parsimony with funds for the States. At the June, 1970, Premiers Conference, Gorton turned generous. Though South Australia, which had a month before voted into office an ALP government, got nothing and, two million dollars worse off than in the previous year, was described by Dunstan as the victim of a vengeful and politically motivated operation, the other Liberal and CP governed states were treated handsomely by the standard of previous years. After the June 1970 Premiers' conference the states, as usual, protested against their niggardly treatment by the Commonwealth but with the exception of Dunstan's their protests lacked the fervor of even near sincerity. Commented economist Kenneth Davidson ". . . the Premiers should be laughing all the way back to their respective treasuries. Instead they have spent yesterday evening in crying poor mouth. The only state that has any real cause for complaint is South Australia."[1] Gorton's action temporarily took the heat out of the internal Liberal squabbles on Commonwealth-State financial relations and appeared to improve the Liberal-CP coalition's electoral standing.

But Gorton failed to recognise that Commonwealth-State financial relations were only one aspect of Commonwealth-State relations generally. His nationalistic outlook and his seeming compulsion to get his way by confrontation rather than by persuasion had already put him in conflict with the states on another issue, an issue which raised questions of government morality, which led to the first breach with Fraser, and which ultimately was to contribute to Gorton's downfall as Prime Minister. This issue arose from an arbitrary Commonwealth decision, made after the 1969 election and without consultation with the States, to exercise sovereign control over the resources of the sea bed off the Australian coast to the outer limits of the continental shelf. Until then the State Governments had believed that they held the sovereign rights from low water mark to the outer limits of the shelf. Involved were mineral rights, though not rights over offshore petroleum discoveries as these rights had already been fixed by agreements between the Commonwealth and States.

Fairbairn protested. As Minister for National Development and prior to his resignation from the Gorton Ministry, he had been authorised by Cabinet to enter into negotiations with the States. As the Commonwealth's negotiator, he had agreed that there would be further consultations between the Commonwealth and the States before the Commonwealth acted. But after his resignation as Minister for National Development the Commonwealth had decided to go ahead with its plans without honoring its commitment to consult with the States. "I have heard it argued that the undertaking I entered into was not legally binding on the Commonwealth," Fairbairn said. "I flatly refuse to accept that argument. Has public morality in this country declined to such a degree that an agreement entered into by the Commonwealth is not binding unless it is legally enforceable? If that is the position we have come to a pretty despicable state of affairs. Is it believed in Australia today that the word of the Commonwealth government means nothing unless those to whom this word is given have some legal means of enforcing it? How could anyone ever trust us again if that is the position? What is the worth of an electoral promise? The voters are not given a pledge in a legally enforceable form. They have to rely upon our honor, and if we have no honor we have nothing."[2]

The States added their complaints. NSW, Victoria, South Australia, Western Australia, and Tasmania were critical, resentful, and pugnacious. Queensland, with its pride in the Great Barrier Reef, one of the great natural wonders of the world, which the Commonwealth legislation threatened to remove from Queensland and place under Commonwealth control was particularly outraged. The Queensland Acting Minister for Mines and Attorney-General, Dr Peter Delamothe, deputy leader of the Liberal Party in the Queensland government, commented curtly, "There has been an arrant and, I believe, considered breach of faith on the part of the Commonwealth."[3]

Despite the complex nature of the proposed legislation, seemingly of interest only to fervent state righters and mining companies with offshore interests or ambitions, a Parliamentary crisis built up on the issue of government morality. On May 15, 1970, Dr Rex Patterson, a Queenslander, who acted as ALP spokesman on primary industries and mining matters, moved a motion of censure in the House of Representatives. The motion read "That the Prime Minister and his Cabinet lack of the confidence of the House because they failed to honor a commitment made to the States by the previous Minister for National Development, acting for and on behalf of the Commonwealth government, that there would be further consultations with the States before the Commonwealth government introduced legislation on the territorial sea and continental shelf."[4]

Fairbairn said that he would support the ALP amendment. The Chief Government Whip, Max Fox, was advised that Bate, from NSW, Howson, from Victoria, Cairns, from Queensland, and others were considering following Fairbairn across the floor of the

House. It would need only four to cross for the government to go down. Defeated in a censure motion, the coalition government might be forced to a general election at a time when its electoral standing was ominously low. Gorton refused stubbornly to vary his stance. He wanted the legislation and he was going to go on with it whatever the consequences. His attitude suggested that he believed Fairbairn, Howson, and the others would wilt at the last moment.

Aware of rumblings within his own Country Party, particularly from Queensland CP members, McEwen was not as confident. Negotiations were opened with the "rebels". Howson acted as their spokesman. Fairbairn could not be shifted. He had made his stand: he would not retreat from it. The others were not so implacable. They were prepared to accept a compromise, though not one that would leave Fairbairn isolated and publicly discredited. McEwen and Howson worked out several compromise resolutions. They were taken to Gorton in his Prime Minister's office just a few yards from the House of Representatives' chamber where the public drama was taking place. Gorton tossed them contemptuously on the floor. But it was evident that those who supported Fairbairn in his viewpoint were weakening.

Gorton's stubbornness was justified. When it came to the crunch, with the possibility of the government falling as a consequence of their actions, Fairbairn's supporters folded. They threw Fairbairn to the wolves. They accepted a resolution which read "This House does not believe that there has been any failure on the part of the government to honor any commitments." In other words, Fairbairn had been wrong when he claimed that the government had in fact failed to honor a commitment. The maximum Fairbairn's supporters could extract from Gorton was a face-saving excuse for Fairbairn being wrong. "The House acknowledges that when the government decided to change its policy on offshore authority by legislating to take control from the low water mark to the continental shelf, the government did not, at that time, inform the states of this change of policy which had been the subject of consultations between the Minister for National Development and the State ministers." The resolution continued: "It is of the opinion that it is this fact which has led the honorable member for Farrer (Fairbairn) feeling justified in believing that an undertaking that there would be further consultations which he gave to the states has been dishonored."[5] Howson moved this as an amendment to Patterson's motion of censure, which it then replaced. Bate seconded it. Government supporters, with the exception of Fairbairn, supported the Howson-Bate amendment.

The amendment was carried by 63 votes to 57. The Parliamentary crisis was over, and Gorton's position within his Party strengthened immeasurably. He had shown his capacity to outlast his opponents whom he had shown up as weak-kneed, vacillating, uncertain, and the makers of empty threats.

Firmly in the Liberal Parliamentary Party saddle, Gorton started to apply the spurs. He was stubbornly determined to push on with the offshore legislation over the opposition of Fairbairn, Bate, Howson, Cairns and the others and without further consultation with the states. It was at this stage that Gorton and Fraser started to quarrel. Fraser expressed the view that Gorton was needlessly antagonising the States and splitting the Liberal Party. Fraser had no criticism to offer on policy. He supported the Cabinet decision that the Commonwealth should have control over offshore mining and the resources of the seabed between low water mark and the continental shelf. But Fraser argued that Gorton could get what he wanted by negotiation rather than confrontation. Gorton was being divisive, picking needless fights with the States and his Parliamentary followers, fights which could be highly damaging to the Liberal Party and the coalition government, electorally. Gorton turned on Fraser savagely.

Again McEwen intervened, again effectively. Ten minutes before a key government parties meeting at which Gorton had proposed to announce baldly that he was going on with the offshore legislation whatever the consequences, McEwen informed Gorton that he could not guarantee that there would not be CP defections if Gorton went on with the legislation. Sullenly, Gorton accepted a situation that he could not change. He could browbeat members of his own party into submission. But the browbeating of CP members who had McEwen's powerful protection was a different matter. The legislation was quietly shelved. But Gorton blamed Fraser for his setback and also for securing McEwen's intervention. Relations between Gorton and Fraser, his onetime supporter and admirer, were never again quite the same.

When Gorton survived the McMahon-Fairbairn challenge to his leadership after the 1969 elections, some of those who supported him then agreed that they would reconsider their attitudes after the 1970 Senate elections. They conceded that Gorton had been largely responsible for the Liberals' electoral reverses in 1969. But they had trust in his intelligence and flexibility. He had probably learned from his mistakes, they argued. He was courageous, stubborn, a fighter. He had high intelligence, doggedness, resilience, an attractive concept of Australian nationalism, and the ability to handle Whitlam in the Parliament if not on the hustings, and should benefit from the 1969 election campaign and acquire the ability to deal convincingly with Whitlam from public platforms as well as in the chamber of the House of Representatives. If he did not improve and the 1970 Senate elections again demonstrated that he was a deadweight that the Liberal Party and coalition government could not carry without courting electoral annihilation in 1972 when the next general elections for the House of Representatives were due, then the position could be re-assessed and Gorton if necessary replaced in the prime ministership with another leader.

But after the happenings in the offshore crisis, this attitude was no longer tenable. Fairbairn had stood his ground stolidly and determinedly. But those who supported Fairbairn or the viewpoint he represented had revealed their weakness. They had done something which is fatal in politics. They had made a threat, the threat of voting against the government on the floor of the House of Representatives, but, when confronted, they had crumbled. They need no longer be regarded as a credible and coherent opposition to Gorton within the Liberal Party. They could be treated as discontented, disaffected, irritating, but impotent individuals, who would bark but not bite. As those who supported Fairbairn and the Fairbairn viewpoint included also potential McMahon supporters, McMahon and Fairbairn could not with any reality be considered as having sufficient strength within the Liberal Parliamentary Party to replace Gorton in the prime ministership, however badly Gorton did at the Senate elections. Only a catastrophic blunder on Gorton's part, a personal blunder for which he and he alone could be blamed, could alter that situation, and such a blunder was unlikely. After his experiences in the St John incident, Gorton was behaving with greater circumspection. With Gorton very much in control of the Liberal Parliamentary Party, and with McMahon and Fairbairn discarded from leadership calculations, Gorton was confirmed in his belief that head-on confrontation was the most effective way of solving difficulties. With the Gorton-Fraser quarrel on the offshore legislation either unknown or dismissed as only a temporary rift in their political alliance, Fraser started to be talked about in Liberal Parliamentary circles as future leadership material, but, significantly, as a possible successor to Gorton not as Gorton's replacement, which had been the context in which McMahon and Fairbairn had been hitherto discussed.

Recognising the weakness of their position and, understandably, not anticipating that Gorton was still capable in the light of the lessons which they believed he must have imbibed from his traumatic experiences of perpetrating mistakes of a magnitude sufficient to affect his party room dominance, the antiGorton forces in the Liberal Parliamentary Party in effect dispersed to concentrate upon protecting their positions as individuals. The more vulnerable of them were under heavy threat. The proGorton element within both the Parliamentary Party and the Liberal Party machine ordained their elimination. They turned their attention to survival.

In Victoria, moves started to strip Jess and Howson, two of Gorton's most consistent critics, of their Liberal preselections for their seats of Latrobe and Casey. Bate's Liberal preselection in his NSW seat of Macarthur also came under threat. Bate, married to Dame Zara, the widow of the former Prime Minister, Harold Holt, was a fervent state righter. Additionally, Gorton's supporters believed with some justification that Bate had knowledge of and resented the internal Liberal Party manoeuvres to replace Holt with Gorton even before Holt disappeared when he went swimming in the troubled surf at Cheviot Beach in December, 1967. Bate found that high ranking Liberals who were Gorton followers were inspiring moves against him and urging his replacement in his seat of Macarthur. In Queensland, Kevin Cairns was protected to some extent by the open hostility of the Liberal Party machine in that state to Gorton's administrative methods and alleged "centralism" and by the fact that his Brisbane seat of Lilley was a "swinger" which probably only Cairns could retain because of the assistance given by DLP preferences, a party with which Cairns had links through his friendship with its leader, Senator Vince Gair, the former Queensland Premier, and because of his sympathy for its strongly antiCommunist policies. Even Fairbairn was put under pressure. But in his case it was more psychological than anything else. He was told constantly that as he disagreed with Gorton and Gorton policies he should, as an honorable man, quit politics completely rather than hold, while a Parliamentarian, to attitudes that could damage the Liberal leader and hence the Liberal Party generally. It was an appeal to Fairbairn's essential decency, an appeal which produced in Fairbairn a conflict of loyalties, with loyalty to his beliefs on one side and loyalty to the government and his party on the other. But the proGorton forces could not move frontally against Fairbairn. Like Senator Wood, in Queensland, Fairbairn's grip upon the loyalty of his electorate of Farrer was too strong.

Almost to a man—Jess, who was never prepared to abandon what he considered to be a principle to pursue self-interest, Wood, and Howson were possible exceptions—the antiGorton Liberal parliamentarians decided that they had no alternative but to march fatalistically to the 1972 elections under Gorton's leadership. They judged that their opportunity to change the leadership had passed.

For nine months, their judgment appeared to be vindicated. The voters went to the polls for Senate elections on Saturday, November 21, 1970. It had been a dull campaign, understandably, as the outcome would not affect the position in the House of Representatives and hence would leave the position of the government unchanged. The leaders of the opposed political groupings, Gorton and Whitlam, could hardly make promises. An ALP Senate win would not put Whitlam and the ALP in a position to implement such promises because the ALP would still not control the House of Representatives, whose majority group or groupings determined the political complexion of the government of the day. For Gorton to make promises contingent upon the Liberal-CP gaining majority support in the Senate vote was unreal. Possessed of a majority in the House of Representatives, he was already in a position to implement promises. The leaders concentrated upon extolling the merits of their respective parties, and pointing to the weaknesses they believed they detected in their opponents.

Gorton turned in a workmanlike performance, which compared more than favorably with his lacklustre showing in the 1969 elections. However, when the Senate results became known, it was clear that neither of the major political groupings had done well. The ALP vote had been 46.95 percent of the total at the 1969 general elections. Its Senate vote was down by over four percent to 42.22 percent of the total vote. That was bad enough. But the Liberal-CP showing was even more inglorious. The Liberal-CP's vote in 1969 had been dismal. Then it had received only 43.33 percent of the total and had to rely upon DLP preferences to retain its majority in the House of Representatives and the government. But if the Liberal-CP vote was dismal at the 1969 general elections, it was abysmally low at the Senate elections. The Liberal-CP vote fell to 38.18 percent, the lowest point in the Liberal Party's twenty-odd years of existence. It was as though a large number of voters preferred to vote for anyone rather than government or ALP candidates. Though their policies were poles apart, the DLP, which supported Australian military intervention in Vietnam, and the Australian Party, a minor political grouping which opposed Australia's participation in the Vietnam conflict, amassed large votes. The DLP, with 11.11 percent of the national vote, secured the re-election of Senator Gair in Queensland and

400

The tables turn.
As Governor-General, Sir Paul Hasluck, and a gratified McMahon walk out from Government House after McMahon was sworn in as Prime Minister on March 10, 1971. Gorton, from the rear, fixes his eyes on his former deputy leader who has now taken over Gorton's former office.

The Premiers' Conference "Under New Management".
Mr W. McMahon (Prime Minister), Sir John Bunting (Secretary, Prime Minister's Department), Mr R. Snedden (Treasurer)

Senator McManus in Victoria, and succeeded in getting elected Senator John Kane in NSW, where previously the DLP had obtained votes, which, while decisive in deciding the outcome in the government's favor in key House of Representatives' electorates, had not previously given the DLP much hope of securing Senate representation in its own right.

An independent, Michael Townley, who, however, had previous Liberal associations and was a son of a former Tasmanian Liberal Opposition Leader, Reg Townley, and the nephew of the former Commonwealth Minister for Defence, Athol Townley, was elected in Tasmania. Western Australia returned a Senator, Sydney Ambrose Negus, whose sole policy plank appeared to be abolition of probate, though later Negus was to add to this a spirited advocacy of government licensing of brothels.[6] Neither of the two major political groupings, the coalition or the ALP, had done well. But while the ALP had taken a beating, the Gorton-led Liberal-CP coalition had taken a thrashing. Morale was at a low ebb when the Liberal Parliamentary Party gathered in Canberra on Tuesday, February 2, 1971, to conduct a post-Senate election postmortem.

With the antiGorton elements within the Liberal Parliamentary Party still dispirited after the debacle of their stand on the offshore minerals issue, Gorton's leadership was not under real threat, despite the Liberals' fears that they were sliding inexorably towards annihilation in 1972. Gorton was riding temporarily a small wave of success and the Liberals, Micawbers like all politicians and ever hopeful that some fluctuation in political fortunes would save them from electoral extinction, were pathetically grateful. In January, at a meeting of Commonwealth heads of government in Singapore, where Britain's decision to sell maritime arms to South Africa was an issue and for a while it looked as though Australia's immigration policy, which gave open door treatment to persons of European origin but only restrictive and restricted entry to Asian and other migrants, would come under criticism, Gorton had performed competently. Even there, however, there had been blemishes.

Gorton had decided to take McMahon, his deputy leader and Foreign Affairs Minister, with him to Singapore. But McMahon was treated in a humiliating fashion. He was not invited to join Gorton in the VIP RAAF plane in which Gorton and his personal entourage flew to Singapore. Instead McMahon was left to find his own way to Singapore on a commercial service. At the Singapore hotel where Gorton and McMahon stayed, McMahon originally was to be housed on the same floor as Gorton. When this was discovered, a readjustment was made, McMahon was

401

banished to another floor, and word about his relegation to "servant's quarters" was derisively and hurtfully leaked to a section of the press.

McMahon, though a sensitive man in many ways, was also a professional. The past three years had hardened him, and he had grown accustomed to minor humiliations. His sense of humor had developed, and, though he might have resented the slights, he endured them without complaint. Thoroughly professional, he took pride in his technical competence. He was determined to do a good job both for his own satisfaction and because he believed that he owed that much to Australia, to the government, and to the Liberal Party. Despite the slights, which may have been engineered as much by Gorton's entourage as by Gorton—though the entourage must either have known that such slights would not cause Gorton displeasure or that Gorton would support these actions if McMahon sought a showdown—McMahon showed no signs of anger or hurt and for the duration of the conference Gorton and McMahon worked in unusually close professional harmony.

There was another incident in Singapore which heightened suspicion about the degree of influence exercised over Gorton by his youthful private secretary, Miss Gotto. Gorton had respect for what he believed to be Miss Gotto's political acumen. It was accepted as a fact of life among Gorton's personal staff that if there were disagreement between Gorton and Miss Gotto on an issue there was absolutely no chance of getting a decision from Gorton until there had been a reconciliation of viewpoint. When the formal business of the day was over, Gorton and Miss Gotto used to settle down in the Prime Minister's inner sanctum to discussion of serious matters, both political and administrative. Eggleton, Gorton's press secretary and one of the few persons Gorton had inherited from the Menzies-Holt régimes whom he had retained in his personal service, was among the very few who were welcome to join such sessions. But Eggleton seems to have eschewed these intimate seances as much as possible. A very proper man, Eggleton probably disliked the ferocity with which personalities were dissected and their futures preordained by such a narrow and, with the exception of Gorton, unimportant gathering, and the manner in which complex and highly technical subjects were examined on a personalised basis of near primitive simplicity. Gorton confided professionally in Miss Gotto to a degree to which he did not seem to confide in anyone else, and she was privy to nearly everything, and her advice sought, on most things that happened in the Prime Minister's inner office, which under the administrative procedures Gorton favored was the main locale of government action during Gorton's three years' prime ministership.

The rare visitors, additional to Eggleton, who occasionally participated in these after official hours soirées confirmed that they were planning rather than pleasant sessions, for assessment rather than sociability, and for decision making rather than relaxation. They were part of a pattern. While Gorton seemed to prefer to talk with women rather than men, he paid them the compliment of discussing with them the serious questions of the day. With the exceptions of Eggleton, and briefly, Malcolm Mackerras, who left the post of research officer in the Liberal Party machine when Gorton was Minister for Education and Science to join Gorton's ministerial staff, but who was swiftly frozen out, males had not figured prominently on Gorton's personal staff. Throughout his ministerial career, Gorton had had female secretaries. During the 1969 election campaign, Eggleton had been his only male companion. Gorton appeared to listen more diligently to the views of his political friends' womenfolk than to his male political friends. In the book *Inside Canberra* by Don Whitington and Rob Chalmers, the co-authors, under the heading "Killen, Denis James" state ". . . according to Killen, the Prime Minister would rather discuss politics with Killen's teen-age daughter than with him (Killen)."[7]

In Singapore, Gorton told the news media that he intended to make an important speech at the Commonwealth heads of government conference. The speech needed some preparation. But there was a disagreement between Gorton and Miss Gotto. Miss Gotto withdrew from participation. The system immediately clogged up. Other members of Gorton's personal staff and the advisers who hover round the periphery for consultation found that what happened in Canberra when there was disagreement between Gorton and Miss Gotto was being repeated. They could get no guidance or instructions on what was expected of them. Finally, McMahon made the speech. The news media was baffled as to why McMahon had been allowed to appear as a personality on such a prestigious political stage, from which, normally, he would have been jealously excluded. But due to this bafflement, the significance of the incident passed without public comment.

But while, with the exception of Wood, nobody was prepared to question formally the quality of Gorton's leadership, there was deep uneasiness at the February 2, 1971, Liberal Parliamentary Party meeting, an uneasiness that was not confined to the anti-Gorton elements within the party. Not only was there the unease arising from the Senate poll with its revelation that Liberal support was at its lowest level ever. Gorton had discovered inflation, and was setting about halting its developing strength. But there was the same inconsistency and fuzziness about his handling of the issue as had marked his handling of previous issues.

Fears had developed about the inflationary situation when figures revealed that there had been a 1.9 percent increase in the cost of living index in the December quarter of 1970, and this had been followed by a six percent national wage rise awarded by the Commonwealth Conciliation and Arbitration Commission. Prices were rising sharply and obviously. Speculation started about the extent of possible increases in government service charges and in taxes as a counter inflationary measure. As far as taxes were concerned, Gorton was in a difficulty. In the 1970 Budget, he and his government had reduced income tax on individuals at the rate of 289 million dollars in a full year, but at a flat rate of some ten percent up to incomes of 10,000 dollars a year, tapering off thereafter and cutting out altogether at incomes of 32,000 dollars a year, with the consequence that it was the middle and higher income earners, not the lower income earners, who were the main beneficiaries.

On his return from Singapore, Gorton held a Cabinet meeting, from which emerged a series of decisions, announced by Gorton in a TV address to the nation on Friday, January 29, 1971, virtually the eve of the Tuesday, February 2, 1971, Liberal Party senate elections postmortem meeting. In his TV report, Gorton said that inflation, while "a very real problem for discussion" had been "a little overdramatised, perhaps".

Nevertheless Gorton said that the government intended to take action so that the inflationary situation would not get out of hand. The government would take this action in several ways. It would reduce government spending. It would encourage the postponement of private investment in plant and equipment. It would stimulate competition by strengthening the Trade Practices Act. It would discourage over-award payments by employers buying peace with militant unions. This discouragement would be procured by use of the Trades Practices Act, and, possibly, by lowering tariffs and bringing such employers competition in the shape of cheaper imported manufactures. In the case of the Trades Practices Act, its successful use as an anti-inflationary, competition stimulating weapon depended upon a favorable High Court judgment and, in the absence of such a favorable judgment, upon the uncertain outcome of a referendum designed to secure from the voters the necessary Commonwealth powers. Gorton blamed inflationary pressures in the building industry upon demand due to the inflow of overseas capital for the specific purpose of building

404

office blocks, and indicated that such investors would be required to discuss their plans and proposed starting dates for building with the Treasury.

From the outset, the credibility of the government's analysis of the causes of the mounting inflation was open to challenge. No study had been made of the degree to which overseas investment in the non-dwelling field of building construction was straining that industry. Treasury had not been consulted on this aspect. Three weeks later the credibility gap widened further. The government announced that it did not intend to do anything in this area. Developers were not to be restrained. It was a virtual admission that the government's original decision had been taken with insufficient examination and was based on faulty information and premises. Nor was confidence enlarged by the manner in which the cuts in government spending had been decided. Ministers and public servants found that the cuts had been made on an almost offhand rule of thumb basis. It was almost impossible for Ministers and public servants to discover who was responsible for the decisions and to whom they should appeal to secure revision of enforced economics which were so shortsighted and in the long-term damaging to the national economy as to verge on the ludicrous. It was against this background that the Liberal Parliamentary Party assembled for the senate postmortem.

Liberal Harry Turner, from NSW, had formally set down on the Liberal Party meeting agenda the item "Loss of support in Senate election and means of regaining it". Though a prickly and in some ways difficult man, who had supported Jess when Jess was striving in what he believed to be the interests of natural justice to get a second inquiry into the *Voyager* naval disaster and who resented the continual erosion of parliamentary authority over the Executive, Turner could hardly be described as "a rebel". A member of the NSW Legislative Assembly from 1937 until 1952, Turner was probably bitter that despite his considerable experience he was passed over for promotion to ministerial rank in favor of lesser experienced colleagues by in turn Menzies, Holt and Gorton. But he represented Bradfield, a Liberal stronghold on Sydney's North Shore, and was more a traditionalist than an innovator. Turner was clearly genuinely trying to help rather than hinder. He wanted the Liberals to have prospects of being returned as the government in 1972, and was constructively suggesting ways in which that this might be achieved rather than seeking to identify Gorton as the architect of the Liberal decline. He started by complimenting Gorton upon his performance in Singapore.

Turner spoke for nearly three quarters of an hour. He had

405

clearly been impressed by the criticisms advanced by a Liberal branch in his electorate that among the reasons for the government's electoral decline were "lack of objectivity—aimlessness—no goals". He told Gorton that the government's secretive and offhand method of formulating and presenting policies was fundamentally defective. The Westminster House of Commons' practice was greatly superior. When dealing with complex subjects, the House of Commons practice was to appoint an expert committee, to publish its report, to state in a White Paper the government's policy, adopting or rejecting particular recommendations, to allow time for public discussion, and to conclude the matter with informed debate in Parliament, followed by legislative or executive action.

Turner continued that government policies would be better devised and more readily accepted by the voters if formed and definitively stated against the background of independent factual information and reasoned analysis in depth, officially published in advance and convincingly related to the decisions taken. Turner listed defence, Commonwealth-State relations, the volume of immigration intake, economics, financial management of the nation's affairs, and other areas in which the government did not possess clear, reasoned-through policies. Turner also criticised the government's methods of administration, and claimed that the functions of departments should be constantly overhauled.[8]

Gorton, who later was to boast semi-publicly to pressmen "Every time a head was raised (in the party room), I kicked it", lashed out. Turner did not understand the position. The government had policies on everything Turner had raised. The government had a policy on defence. It had announced what it was going to do on defence in conjunction with Singapore, Malaysia, New Zealand, and Britain. It had policies on Commonwealth-State relations. He had stated them repeatedly. It had policies on economics, financial management, and, in fact, on everything Turner had mentioned. If these policies were not getting through to the voters, then public relations had broken down. Liberal backbenchers had to take their share of blame for this. As far as Commonwealth-State relations were concerned, they were going to be a problem until time immemorial. They had always been a problem. They always would be a problem. Gorton called upon McMahon, then Foreign Affairs Minister, and Lynch, Immigration Minister, to answer specific points in Turner's speech.

McMahon, understandably, did not deal at any length with the policy issues. He had increasingly been squeezed out of participation in such matters. He concentrated upon answering Turner's charge that the functions of departments were too seldom overhauled by describing what he personally had done. As Air Minister,[9] he had reorganised that department, McMahon said. The reorganisation had been a success. As Labour Minister,[10] he had reorganised that department. That reorganisation had been a success. As Treasurer,[11] he had reorganised that department. That reorganisation had been a success. As Treasurer, he had sought to keep Liberal parliamentarians informed of the financial assistance that the Commonwealth was giving to the States. Copies of the document which contained this information still existed. He was sure that the current Treasurer, Les Bury, would make them available to anyone requiring them.

McMahon said he was now in the process of reorganising the Department of Foreign Affairs. He was positive that this reorganisation would be a success. The reorganisation would help to remove some of the Turner complaints about the lack of precision in the foreign affairs and defence area. Lynch said a study in depth was being done on the impact of the current volume of immigration upon the Australian economy and community. Turner wanted studies in depth. Such studies could not be completed overnight. There would be no undue delay in the completion of this immigration study.

Fairbairn said that a major factor in the government's electoral decline was its obvious inconsistency. The government was now talking about inflation. The 1970 Budget had allegedly been designed to prevent such an inflationary situation emerging. But it had been the government itself which had wrecked the strategy of the Budget with expenditure of hundreds of millions of dollars after the Budget had gone through the Parliament and with subsequent ad hoc decisions which also added to expenditure.

Adhering to his policy of kicking every head the minute one was raised in the Party room, Gorton immediately challenged Fairbairn to identify the expenditure to which he referred and also the alleged inconsistency and ad hoc decisions. He also challenged Fairbairn's statement that "hundreds of millions" of dollars were involved.

Fairbairn said that the decision to pay receipt duties tax to the states, expenditure on propping up the wool market, and rural reconstruction outlays would account for millions of dollars outside the Budget. The discussions degenerated in an argument between Gorton and Fairbairn as to whether Fairbairn had originally stated that the extra expenditure had been provided for by the Budget or subsequent to the Budget. Gorton said that it was not hundreds of millions of dollars as Fairbairn had claimed. Fairbairn's complaint that expenditure had gone up in the Budget was incorrect.

Jess said that the Prime Minister was "nitpicking" and playing with words. Jess said he could provide examples of inconsistencies. He reminded Gorton that Gorton had virtually accused Whitlam, as Opposition Leader, of being disloyal to the Australian troops in Vietnam by suggesting the withdrawal of one of the three Australian battalions serving there. Gorton had said that this would gravely imperil the safety of the two remaining battalions. Yet only a few weeks later Gorton had announced the withdrawal of the third battalion. Gorton said that circumstances in Vietnam had changed between the time Whitlam advocated the withdrawal of the third battalion and his announcement of the withdrawal. Fairbairn said that only a couple of months had intervened. An argument broke out as to when Gorton had revised his stance and virtually accepted the Whitlam case for withdrawal of one battalion.

Jess said there were other examples of inconsistency. The government would reject a backbench viewpoint in the Liberal Party room. It would take the line that it had made a decision and would stick to it. But when the decision got to the Senate and the ALP combined with the DLP[12] the government always found it expedient to change its mind and adopt the course originally suggested by Liberal backbenchers. The government changed its mind when it was forced to, but would not listen to the warnings of Liberal members. If the government went on the way it was going it would more than likely be defeated at the general elections in 1972. The leadership left much to be desired.

Having kicked Turner and Fairbairn verbally in the head, Gorton went on to kick Jess in the head. "If the government is defeated in 1972, it will be because of speeches like the one you have just made," Gorton said. He expressed the belief that such speeches as Jess's were made in the hope that they would get out from the privacy of the party room and to be made public so that they would damage him politically. The implied accusation must have infuriated Jess, who, forthright, impatient, and fearless, punctilious in preserving the secrecy of the Party room, was inhibited in putting his views in the open forum of the Parliament only by his loyalty to the Party.

"Are you telling me to leave the party?" Jess asked. "You can do what you like," Gorton said. Jess subsided. Later, he told friends that he was tempted to walk out of the party room. But he had decided that he should not do so. He was loyal to the government and to the Liberal policy and believed it was for Australia's good that a Liberal-CP coalition should govern Australia, rather than the ALP whose policies and general

408

attitudes, particularly on foreign affairs, he viewed as contrary to Australia's longterm interests. His criticisms were not of the Government and the Liberal Party but of Gorton and the manner in which he thought Gorton was managing the country and distorting government and Liberal Party policies.

Peter Howson, from Victoria, said that he supported both Fairbairn and Jess in their belief that inconsistency, or the appearance of inconsistency, was responsible for much of the government's electoral trouble. Rightly or wrongly, the voters had an impression of government inconsistency. The government in its 1970 Budget had planned for a domestic surplus as an anti-inflationary measure. Heavy expenditure had been promised subsequent to the Budget. The fact that the proposed expenditure was outside a Budget context was, politically, irrelevant. So much had been promised that the impression was abroad that the government was indifferent as to whether there would be a budget surplus or deficit. The government could no longer rely complacently upon DLP preferences bridging, and more than bridging, the gap between the ALP's vote and the Liberals' vote. This technique could be successfully worked only if the Liberals could maintain their primary vote at a reasonable mass level. But their primary vote was slipping to a point at which DLP preference votes, however large and however solidly directed towards Liberal candidates, would have no effect. In fact, the position might be reached in some electorates where the DLP primary vote would one day, perhaps soon, exceed the Liberal primary vote. The senate vote had shown that there were a million Australian voters now without attachment to either of the major political groupings. The government should strive for consistency to get at least some of these to return to their Liberal attachment.

Wood was neither impressed nor intimidated by Gorton's head-kicking tactics. An earthy, unpretentious man, a bachelor and travel agent, who had made a minor fortune from the Australian mining boom and rode a bicycle for years around his native Mackay, in Northern Queensland, Wood prided himself on keeping in close touch with grassroots feelings in his electorate. This gave him two advantages. He had confidence in his judgment about electorate reactions, and the Liberal hierarchy, which resented his independence of mind, could not strike at him through his Queensland voters, who supported him loyally and would probably support him as loyally as an independent as a Liberal candidate. Wood had decided even before he entered the Party room that in the Party room he would ask Gorton to resign the prime ministership, and, if, as he expected, Gorton rejected his "request", to move a motion seeking party support for his request. Wood opened his speech mildly.

Wood said that the meeting had not been called to give anyone the opportunity to be nasty to someone else. It had been called to discuss why the Liberal Party had done so badly at the senate elections. All kinds of reasons had been given as to why Liberal Party support had fallen away. But nobody had mentioned the major reason. The major reason why the Liberal Party vote had gone down was that the voters simply would not vote for John Gorton. If there were to be any realism in the Liberals' analysis of the adverse senate election result, that fact had to be faced. The senate election had been a contest between Gorton and Whitlam. Gorton had symbolised the Liberal Party. Whitlam had symbolised the ALP. The voters did not like Gorton. Every testing he, Wood, had made confirmed that viewpoint. Fortunately for the Liberals, the voters liked Whitlam about as much as they liked Gorton. This was why such a substantial vote had gone to the minor political groupings, particularly the DLP, which, whatever its other faults, had consistency. But in the different circumstances of a House of Representatives' election and even with the advantage of Whitlam leading the ALP, the Liberals would need a miracle to survive the 1972 elections. Miracles did happen in politics. But without a miracle, the Liberals would be out of power in 1972. The Liberal Party should not have to rely upon a miracle. It should recognise it had elected the wrong man to the leadership in 1968 when it put Gorton into the prime ministership as successor to the late Harold Holt. The members of the Liberal Parliamentary Party should acknowledge their mistake.

Wood said that the party needed a new look and a new leader. Gorton had had three years' testing in the leadership. He had been tested and found wanting. He was calling upon Gorton to resign.

Gorton interrupted Wood. "Would you like to move that as a motion?" he asked Wood. "Yes, I will," said Wood. Gorton said he would accept it as a motion. He looked around the room. "Is there a seconder?" he asked. There was a second's tense silence. Nobody moved. Gorton called the next speaker.

From there on, the heat went out of the debate. Young Don Cameron, MHR for Griffith, in Queensland, who had an admiration for Gorton, said when Gorton was elected Liberal Leader and moved into the prime ministership he was very much a new boy and had made mistakes. But he was learning. The general tone of the discussions changed. Members said that the party must get behind the Prime Minister and support him. Otherwise the fears about the outcome of the 1972 elections would prove justified. Gorton had faced and was facing political problems greater than those which had confronted either Sir Robert Menzies, or the late Harold Holt during their terms in the prime ministership. Unless he was supported, the government would be defeated in 1972. Gorton said that he recognised inflation as a major danger to Australia. He pledged that he would cure inflation in 1971, whatever unpopularity some of the required action might bring him or the government. He thanked members for the expression of their views, and the meeting ended. "The meeting proved . . . an exercise in futility," wrote Turner in his letter to the *Sydney Morning Herald* of February 4, 1971.

But, with Wood unable to secure a seconder for his motion calling upon Gorton to resign as Prime Minister, Gorton left the Party room undisputed master of the Liberal Parliamentary Party. Though his grip upon the loyalty of the electorate might be weakening, as the senate results tended to suggest, Gorton's hold upon the party was tighter. McMahon was being thrust successfully into the Party background. Fairbairn had again failed to get any significant support in an open confrontation with Gorton in the party room, a confrontation from which Gorton had emerged as the clearcut victor. The so-called "rebel" element which included Howson, Jess, Wood and a few others had been shown up as impotent and, when the crunch of Wood's motion came, vacillating, divided and weak. From here on it could be assumed that the "rebels" would be passive. It was in their interests not to make further trouble. Everything pointed to Gorton leading the government at the 1972 elections. If his image was further damaged such damage would imperil not only the government but the "rebels'" own parliamentary survival as individuals.

Gorton used his reasserted strength promptly and with a boldness that bordered on recklessness. The Askin-led Liberal-CP government in NSW and the Brand-led Liberal-CP government in Western Australia were within three weeks of state elections. Askin had state elections coming up on February 13, 1971, and Sir David Brand elections on February 20, 1971. Gorton had a meeting arranged with the Premiers on Thursday, February 4, 1971, only two days after he had triumphantly outfaced and outfought his critics within the Federal Liberal Parliamentary Party. The States had been worse hit than the Commonwealth by the six percent national wage rise, and by rising costs. Unlike the Commonwealth, they did not receive the benefit of the extra income tax returns flowing from the community's inflating incomes. They were facing heavy deficits. Of the six Premiers, four—Askin, in NSW, Bolte, in Victoria, Sir David Brand, in Western Australia,

411

and Walter Bethune, in Tasmania—were Liberals. One, Johannes Bjelke-Petersen, in Queensland, was Country Party. Don Dunstan, in South Australia, was the solitary ALP Premier. All, Liberal, CP, and ALP alike, were looking to the Commonwealth for assistance.

With the Commonwealth already pledged by Gorton's January 29, 1971, TV address to the nation to a slower rate of expansion of Commonwealth spending, Federal Cabinet agreed that the rate of expansion of States' spending should also be contracted. But, sensibly, Cabinet decided that the States' rate of spending could not be altered overnight without severe dislocation. Cabinet agreed to some thirty million dollars being made available to assist the states with their deficits. But Gorton and Treasurer, Les Bury, were, as usual, left with a wide area of discretion, essential for negotiations with the State Premiers, who, opportunist and shrewd, were clever, wily and experienced negotiators.

But Gorton was getting obsessively preoccupied with the inflation problem. There appeared to be two factors which contributed to this preoccupation. He had received wide applause from both the publicity media and taxpayers, always cynical about the wastefulness and extravagance of government departments, for his decision to restrain Commonwealth spending. But he also believed firmly that the "little people", particularly pensioners, were the main sufferers from inflation, and held that the checking of inflation was more vital to these people than pension rises.

On the morning of his conference with the Premiers, Gorton summoned Bury and Treasury officers into consultation. He told them that he proposed to give the states nothing. He went into the Premiers' Conference. The State Premiers, with the exception of Dunstan, who either suspected the shape of things to come or had been tipped off privately about the shape of things to come, agreed that the premiers should meet in camera. Askin and Brand probably did not want matters raised in public which could be used against them by their opponents in their state elections. The press was excluded.

Gorton told the premiers that the Commonwealth would give them nothing to assist them with their deficits and warned them not to expect anything from the Commonwealth in 1971. The states would have to cut back on their planned rates of expansion and carry their own deficits. Gorton assailed the states for failing to provide in their budgets for foreseeable increases in expenditure. Some states had done so. But the others had just come along to the conference as they had been accustomed to do for years expecting the Commonwealth to "pick up the tab". The Common-

wealth was not going to do so, Gorton said. In the present inflationary situation the states would have to carry their own deficits.
Gorton rejected claims that the Commonwealth's attitude would
mean that the states would have to cut down their recruitment of
teachers, nurses, policemen and other essential State Public
servants. There would be no reduction except in their planned
rate of expansion, he claimed. He quoted examples of the rates at
which the states had expanded. He said that he was not particularly worried about the states' warning that the Commonwealth's
action would create a pool of unemployment. The employment
situation was tight. There was plenty of employment in the private
sector. If there were a cutback in government spending in the
building industry, the effect would be to release labor for the
private sector. There would not be unemployment, but there would
be less pressure on private employers to provide overaward
payments.

Askin and Brand pleaded for better treatment. They had state
elections coming up within a matter of days. If Gorton adhered
to his stand, he would in effect be cutting their political throats.
Gorton was adamant. In a luncheon discussion, Gorton made
only one concession. He would agree to another meeting of the
premiers in April. The fact that they would have another
opportunity to resubmit the states' case for greater access to
Commonwealth funds would give them a talking point during their
coming state elections. But, Gorton added, ominously, "I give no
commitments."[13]

Askin left Canberra for Sydney, declaring, semi-publicly that
Gorton had thrown him to the wolves, electorally. He announced
that he was returning to denounce Gorton. The *Sydney Morning
Herald* re-echoed Askin in its editorial columns. " 'Autocratic' was
Mr Askin's word for the Prime Minister's behaviour, and it was
absolutely justified," declared the *Sydney Morning Herald* leader.
"It is monstrous that the States should have to bear the brunt of
the Commonwealth's anti-inflationary measures, which themselves
were made necessary by Commonwealth policies (or lack of
them). Mr Askin is entitled to feel that he has been badly, almost
unforgivably, let down by the Federal Parliamentary Leader of
his own party, and even by the party itself . . . . The suddenly
applied weight of Gortonian centralism must, of course, bear
heavily on state election issues and policies. If anyone ever really
doubted the Commonwealth's overwhelming influence on price
levels and the cost of living he must by now be satisfied. When
the Commonwealth puppet master makes a gesture, the states
twitch, willy-nilly, at the end of the string. The South Australian

413

Premier, Mr Dunstan, that expert in price control, has already said flatly that his state will have to pay for services (such as recruitment programs for nurses and teachers) which Mr Gorton wants to cut back. Taxes and service charges will have to be increased—motor registration fees, drivers' license fees, some death duties, land-tax, transport fares, electricity charges and harbour dues are possibilities."[14]

Despite his threat, Askin, as earthy as a pig's wallow, did not waste time and energy upon recriminations. He recognised that he was fighting for his and his government's survival. Applying his considerable talents, he ran a shrewd, colorful, and intensive campaign. When brought an advertising programme, he said, curtly "Double that programme." Though his recent health had been indifferent, his exertions were prodigious. Due largely to his efforts and the reputation he had established since his elevation to the NSW Premiership in 1965, he and his government survived on polling day, Saturday, February 13, 1971, but only marginally, with the NSW Opposition Leader, Pat Hills, justifiably refusing to concede defeat for days, so close was the result in decisive electorates. In Western Australia, a week later, the Brand-led Liberal-CP administration was ejected from the government benches it had occupied since 1959, and replaced with an ALP government led by 69-years-old John Trezise Tonkin.

Askin's estrangement altered the balance of power within the Liberal Party machine. In his previous leadership troubles, Gorton could count on Askin's support. Askin could influence votes, and did, on Gorton's behalf, inside the Federal Liberal Parliamentary Party. Askin had the ear of several Federal Liberal Parliamentarians from NSW electorates. He had persuaded these Liberals to support Gorton in previous party crises. He had been punctiliously and valuably loyal to Gorton. He had expected loyalty and assistance from Gorton in return, particularly on the eve of elections in NSW. Gorton's indifference to his electoral well-being and to his government's prospects of political survival infuriated him. There are few lasting enmities in politics, and fewer lasting friendships or alliances. Askin might again give Gorton assistance and support. But henceforward it would be grudging support, based upon political necessity, not a personal attachment. But after the February 2 Liberal Party meeting from which he had emerged stronger than ever Gorton undoubtedly judged that he would not need Askin's assistance again, at least not until after the 1972 general Federal elections when the leadership issue might re-emerge but when circumstances were likely to be much different. Safely ensconced in his citadel of the Liberal Parliamentary Party, Gorton was unassailed and seemingly unassailable. He obviously felt that he no longer wanted or needed Askin's assistance. He gave Askin no assistance but on the contrary an electoral burden that was only just within Askin's capacity to survive. He was on the top of the political pile and he judged he no longer needed Askin to help him stay there.

NOTES

[1] Article by Kenneth Davidson, *Australian,* June 26, 1970.

[2] Commonwealth Representatives, Weekly Hansard, No 7, pp 1897/1898, May 8, 1970.

[3] Ibid., p 1901.

[4] Commonwealth Representatives, Weekly Hansard, No 8, p 2246, May 15, 1970.

[5] Commonwealth Representatives, Weekly Hansard, No 8, p 2305, May 15, 1970.

[6] *Age,* Melbourne, December 14, 1970.

[7] Killen said the same thing to me. A Gorton admirer, Killen was apparently unaware of how revelatory a glimpse he was giving of the Gorton personality, and how it tended to confirm the Erwin comment "He listens to women more readily than to men" (see Chapter two, p 26).

[8] It has to be remembered that meetings of parliamentary parties are held in private. Accounts such as the one I am giving here are built up from fragments, like a mosaic. In Turner's particular case, my knowledge is supplemented by a letter he wrote to the *Sydney Morning Herald* and which appeared on February 4, 1971.

[9] McMahon was Minister for Air from 1951 to 1954.

[10] McMahon was Minister for Labour and National Service from 1958 to 1966.

[11] McMahon was Treasurer from 1966 to 1969.

[12] The government was in a minority in the Senate and relied upon the DLP for the passage of its legislation. In association, the ALP and DLP could outvote the government senators.

[13] From the author's notes, made on February 4 and February 5, 1971.

[14] *Sydney Morning Herald,* February 8, 1971.

But Gorton underestimated his own capacity for self-destruction. On Thursday, February 25, 1971, started the chain of unexpected and unplanned political events, which were to culminate thirteen short days later in Gorton's resignation from the prime ministership and his replacement by William McMahon, the durable, little man who for once played no role in happenings but was merely an onlooker until Gorton's own actions, and the Liberal Party's reaction to them, raised him to the political purple of the prime ministership and the eminence which he had craved but which he had thought he had no longer any hope of achieving.

I select Thursday, February 25, 1971, as the starting point because on that date I gave advice which almost certainly resulted later in the interview on the following Monday, March 1, 1971, between Gorton and the Chief of the General Staff, General Sir Thomas Daly, a 58-years-old professional soldier, with a distinguished service record and a fierce pride in the Australian Army, an interview that was to lead on to the resignation of the Defence Minister, Malcolm Fraser, the Liberal Party crisis, the resignation of Gorton, and the elevation of McMahon.

On Thursday, February 25, 1971, I was in the position that I had to leave Canberra for Sydney at the weekend to participate in a "Meet the Press" TV programme on Channel Nine on Sunday, and then cover on assignment a series of meetings of the ALP Federal Executive in Sydney, meetings which were expected to last until the Thursday or Friday of the following week. Robert Baudino, Chief of the Daily Telegraph Canberra Bureau, asked me what I knew about alleged strain between Fraser, in his role as Minister for Defence, and the Army. I said that I did not know much. I did not want to overstate what I knew. There was always a bit of strain between a Defence Minister and the services, particularly when a Defence Minister was doing his job properly. I knew that there had been an argument going on for some time between Fraser and the Army over the location of army bases. Fraser wanted one in Western Australia, but the Army wanted it in Victoria, somewhere close to Melbourne.[1] The Army was stalling. Fraser was turning cartwheels because he could not get costings

416

from the Army. Then there had been the recent row over what was alleged to be the Army decision to wipe out its civil aid programme in Vietnam within twelve months, contrary to government policy. Fraser was angry about that. I recalled that Fraser had made statements recently in the Parliament about this. I knew a few other things, but they were only minor. My knowledge in this area was not very great, I told Baudino.

Baudino said he had a story that strain between Fraser and the Army had intensified recently. Fraser was getting really angry. The row over civil aid in Vietnam was quite fierce. Fraser had let it be known that he believed the Army had deceived him by attempting to end civil aid without Government knowledge or authority. The Army had not mentioned its civil aid proposals at regular meetings with the Australian Ambassador in Vietnam. Fraser did not trust completely the reports he was getting back from the Army in Vietnam. Baudino said he had not got the full story. But he proposed working on it.

I asked if the story would keep until I got back to Canberra from Sydney. Baudino said he did not think so. Fraser had been briefing pressmen about what was happening and his state of mind. He was sure that Peter Samuel, of the *Bulletin,* David Solomon, of the *Australian,* and Alan Ramsey, of the *Australian* had been briefed. He thought that Wallace Brown, of the *Brisbane Courier-Mail,* and Hugh Armfield, of the *Age,* might also have been briefed.

At this stage, I made a mistake. I did not ask Baudino if Fraser had briefed him. Pressmen preserve jealously the confidences with which they are entrusted. They do not like being asked to reveal their sources, even by close working colleagues. I took an interest in defence matters only when they became important politically. Baudino usually dealt with defence matters that had a technical content. Baudino had a professional relationship with Fraser. Whenever Fraser had previously done briefings, which every minister is entitled to do so long as he confines the briefings to the area of his ministerial responsibility, Baudino had been one of those who had been briefed. I took it for granted that if Samuel, Solomon, and Ramsey, and probably Brown and Armfield, had been briefed by Fraser, Baudino had also been briefed by Fraser. I was wrong; Baudino had not been briefed by Fraser on this occasion. But there were aspects of the story I did not like. "If the story won't keep until I get back (from Sydney), I suggest that you try and have a word with Gorton before you file it," I advised. "He could have an angle that puts a different emphasis on the story."[2] I left for Sydney.

417

Baudino's story appeared in the *Daily Telegraph* on Tuesday, March 2, 1971. It said that the Joint Intelligence Organisation was reporting on Australian Army activities in Vietnam. Fraser had told colleagues he did not trust Army reports reaching Canberra. He had let it be known he believed the Army had been deceptive over an attempt to end civil aid in Vietnam. Army authorities at regular meetings with the Australian Ambassador in Vietnam had not mentioned civil aid. The Army had been trying to present him with an accomplished fact as far as the ending of civil aid in Vietnam was concerned. The Army hid the operation so well that the Joint Intelligence Organisation had not referred to it in its reports. Baudino reported Fraser as having said in discussions with colleagues that the Army had always been hostile to a programme of civil aid in Vietnam. When Fraser was Minister for Army, he had had on a visit to Vietnam to insist determinedly before he was permitted to see the man in charge of the civil aid programme at that time. The Army had always resisted attempts to transfer National Service specialists to civil aid work. The Army had protested initially but Joint Intelligence was now reporting on the operations of the Australian Army in Vietnam. Units of Joint Intelligence were based in Vietnam. The Joint Intelligence Organisation, under the directorship of a civilian, Mr R. Furlonger, was officially described in the Commonwealth directory as having been established "to advise the defence committee and/or Chiefs of Staff committee on intelligence matters". Fraser received reports direct from a member of the Joint Intelligence Organisation each week.

But even before the story appeared in the *Daily Telegraph,* things had started to happen in Canberra, things far more important than the newspaper stories which touched them off.[3] On Monday, March 1, 1971, Baudino who had been working on the story since my departure to Sydney believed that he had amassed sufficient information to justify a story. Following my advice, he asked to see the Prime Minister. He went to the Prime Minister's office at about 3 pm. Baudino gave his version of what happened on a "Meet the Press" TV programme on Channel Nine, Sydney, on Sunday, March 7, 1971. In Baudino's words "I sat down opposite the Prime Minister. At that stage I had an unwritten story. I only had shorthand notes, and went through points in the story with the Prime Minister. In particular, I dealt with claims that the Australian Army in Vietnam had moved out of its area of tactical responsibility."

Baudino continued "I told Mr Gorton that I would be writing a story along these lines. I also mentioned that the Chief of the

General Staff, Sir Thomas Daly, allegedly had taken a decision early in December that civic aid would be phased out in Vietnam within twelve months. Mr Gorton at that stage did not refute the story in any way. In fairness to him, I must say he made no comment whatever on it except to say that if there were an attack on the Army or on Sir Thomas Daly he would come to their defence . . . . At six o'clock that night I had an inquiry as to whether the story had been written and whether I had sent it to Sydney, and I said that I had. I had a request from a member of Mr Gorton's staff (Mr Eggleton) could he please see copies of the story. . . . I supplied Mr Eggleton with these copies, and they were returned to me an hour later. I would say they had been seen by the Prime Minister and photostated."[4]

But even before Eggleton asked if he might look at a copy of Baudino's story, Gorton was starting to move into deep and dangerous waters. Miss Gotto maintained a rapport with certain members of the Federal Parliamentary Press Gallery. After Baudino had seen Gorton, contact was made with these pressmen. They were quizzed. The object clearly was to find out if they had been briefed by Fraser and what Fraser had said in his briefings. Normally, Eggleton would have done the contacting of pressmen. But after his return from Singapore and with Gorton seemingly firmly and unchallengeably seated in the Liberal Party leadership saddle, Eggleton had accepted a better paid post in the Commonwealth Secretariat, with headquarters in London and a prospect of escape from the twenty-four hours-a-day job that he had filled since his original appointment by Menzies seven years earlier. Gorton had accepted philosophically that Eggleton was entitled to better his position and had released him without argument and with his best wishes for success in his new career. But from the day he announced his resignation, Eggleton, though still functioning as the Prime Minister's press secretary, found that he was not being given access to information as freely as before. The contacts with the pressmen were made by Miss Gotto, without Eggleton's knowledge. Nor was Eggleton told about the vital meeting which took place between Gorton and Daly on the same Monday after Baudino had seen Gorton. Eggleton learned about it the next day from pressmen.

The same atmosphere of almost furtive, self-satisfied secrecy was maintained on Tuesday, the day on which Baudino's story was published in the *Daily Telegraph*. It was as though Fraser was being encouraged to dig his own political grave and deliberately left with the impression that he was doing only a drainage job. Fraser saw Gorton on the Tuesday morning. Fraser had already conferred with the permanent head of the Defence Department, Sir Arthur Tange, and prepared a statement dealing with the Baudino story. Gorton made no mention to Fraser of the fact that he had seen Daly on the previous evening and had committed himself to an unquali- fied defence of the Army, before hearing Fraser and possibly hearing that Fraser had justified grievances and evidence of the Army ignoring or departing from government policy on the civil aid programme in Vietnam. Fraser did not learn about the Gorton- Daly discussions until Wednesday, when he was told about them by Daly, who, understandably, as he was aware that Fraser had seen Gorton subsequent to his discussions with the Prime Minister, appeared to take it for granted that Fraser had been informed about the discussions and acquainted with their general tenor.

After his talk with Gorton, Fraser issued a denial of the Baudino story, a denial which laid considerable stress upon the fact that the Joint Intelligence organisation was not reporting to him upon the Army's activities in Vietnam. But the denial was in such equivocal terms as to prompt the editor of the *Daily Telegraph* to add a footnote to the report of the denial which appeared in the *Daily Telegraph*. The footnote read "Mr Fraser appears to be splitting hairs. From his own (denial) statement, it is obvious that his department has been receiving Joint Intelligence material covering the Australian forces in Vietnam." As yet, the incident was only a minor one, with Fraser losing some political skin and having some damage inflicted upon his public image but nothing more.

But on the same day, Tuesday, a party of pressmen, with Baudino one of the pressmen, travelled by plane to and from Shepparton in Victoria with Gorton. Gorton went to Shepparton to participate in the Murray by-election, made necessary after Gorton returned from Singapore by the retirement of the ageing veteran, Sir John McEwen, from Cabinet, Parliament, and the Country Party leadership. Douglas Anthony had replaced McEwen as Country Party Leader, deputy Prime Minister, and Minister for Trade, and Ian Sinclair, who had been challenged unsuccessfully by Peter Nixon, now Minister for Shipping and Transport, had taken over Anthony's vacated portfolio of Primary Industry and the CP's Deputy leadership. Throughout the Shepparton trip, Gorton showed signs of being pleased with himself and life in general. Even before they had stepped on the plane, the pressmen were aware of the Gorton-Daly meeting on the previous evening, though they had no details of what was discussed.[5] But by the time the plane returned to Canberra, the pressmen believed that they had justification for believing that Fraser had been "done

420

over" by Gorton at the Gorton-Fraser meeting earlier in the day. They were also given cause to believe that Fraser had originally wanted to issue the statement on the Baudino story under his Department's authority, but not in his own name, that Gorton had insisted that as Fraser's name had been mentioned in the Baudino story that the statement should go out in Fraser's name, and that the Fraser statement was not the statement as originally prepared by Fraser and Tange but a statement virtually dictated by Gorton. In other words, Fraser had been put very firmly "in his place". The pressmen had the impression that Gorton was weeping no tears about Fraser's discomfiture but was rather enjoying it.

On Wednesday, Peter Samuel produced a story in *The Bulletin* which had overtones of the Baudino story, but set out in greater detail the alleged circumstances which had produced tension between Fraser and the Army, particularly as far as the Army's operations in the civil aid area in Vietnam were concerned. As members of Fraser's personal staff had been saying quite openly that Fraser had given Samuel a briefing on this subject, the fact that Fraser had briefed Samuel was widely known in the Federal Parliamentary Press Gallery. Fraser issued another rebutting statement, and departed for Tasmania. The incident was still, relatively speaking, minor, an operation designed to cut Fraser "down to size", and still lacking the ingredients of a major crisis.

But the ingredients of a major crisis were soon added. I was still in Sydney covering the ALP Federal Conference but keeping in touch with what was going on in Canberra and handling the Gorton-Fraser stories for the *Daily Telegraph,* the newspaper for which I worked. I was curious about what had transpired at the Gorton-Daly discussions. The primary sources were Gorton and Daly, the two men who had participated in the discussions. But both men were bound to have discussed at least the broad outline of what had been said in the privacy of the Prime Minister's office with colleagues and staff. On my experience, it was always best to have some inkling of what was said in such circumstances before approaching one of the primary sources. There were two lines of approach. One led down from Gorton. The other led down from Daly. Working over the telephone from Sydney, I got only a scanty and third-hand version of what allegedly took place between Gorton and Daly. Daly was supposed to have assured Gorton that at no stage had the Army sought to sabotage the civil aid programme in Vietnam. Daly was also reported as having told Gorton that what was happening was neither good for the Army nor for Army morale. What I had was too innocuous and flimsily-based to justify a story. Daly's remark about the Army and Army morale was the kind of natural thing that an Army leader would say under such circumstances. I did not write anything on the Gorton-Daly discussions.

But, in Canberra, Alan Ramsey, of the *Australian*, was also working on the story. I do not know which line of inquiry Ramsey followed, the line leading down from Gorton or the line leading down from Daly. But I do know that Ramsey, subsequently, gave the impression that he was genuinely convinced that the information he had been given came from a source that was in no way inferior in authority to the two primary sources, Gorton and Daly. That information was political dynamite. It was that in the course of his conversation with Gorton, Daly had accused Fraser of "extreme disloyalty to the Army and its junior Minister, Andrew Peacock".[6]

Ramsey handled the problem presented to him by the version he had been given of the Gorton-Daly conversations with professional competence and propriety. Ramsey clearly recognised that the version, as he had it, must involve Fraser and Fraser's administration of the Defence portfolio. If Daly had in fact made the statement about Fraser and his relations with the Army and Peacock, and the Prime Minister had agreed with the Daly statement, then clearly Fraser could not be continued as Minister for Defence. Ramsey prepared a typewritten memorandum. It read "From Alan Ramsey. I am told that the PM called General Daly to his office on Monday to ask him about press and other reports of growing differences of opinion between Army, specifically the military, and Defence. Daly replied by claiming that these differences were being deliberately leaked to the press by Fraser and his Department. He accused Fraser of extreme disloyalty to Peacock and claimed that it was all part of a campaign to discredit Peacock for purely political motives (or words to that effect). He was very bitter about Fraser and gave details of what he saw as instances where the Army (and, by responsibility, Peacock) had been wrongly blamed for 'mistakes' embarrassing to Fraser as head of Defence. Among these: The military guard for Delacombe,[7] certain aspects of the civic action controversy. The other side of the coin is that Defence (or, at least, certain officials) claim that the military strongly resents Fraser, because of what has been described as his brusque, no-nonsense attitude. These people also see Fraser as certainly the most active, the most involved, and the best minister the Department has ever had. I want to ask the PM: (a) Did he call Daly to his office? (b) Did he question him about Army v Defence? (c) Did Daly reply as I have set the matter out? (d) Did he call Fraser in yesterday to tell him to 'sort the matter out'? (e) Has he discussed the matter with Peacock?"[8]

Ramsey gave his memorandum to Eggleton at about 1.25 pm on Wednesday, March 3, 1971. Eggleton told Ramsey that he would give the memorandum to Gorton and let Ramsey know later whether Gorton would see him. Eggleton went along the lobby from his office to Gorton's Prime Ministerial office. Gorton and Miss Gotto appear to have been the only two people in Gorton's office at the time. Eggleton read out the significant point in Ramsey's memorandum—that Daly was alleged to have said that Fraser had been guilty of extreme disloyalty to Peacock, and by implication to the Army. I have reason to believe that Eggleton told Gorton that he was not suggesting that Gorton should tell a lie. But if Ramsey's story was wrong, it should be denied firmly and promptly and publication prevented by this means. To allow publication of a wrong account could bring serious repercussions. Gorton was noncommittal.

At that stage, Gorton was in a position to refuse to see Ramsey. If he refused to see him, Ramsey would have to re-assess his position. Ramsey would have to decide whether his source was so authoritative that he could publish the version he had of the Gorton-Daly conversation without having discussed it with Gorton, the major of the two primary sources. Or Gorton could see Ramsey. If he saw Ramsey he could (a) deny the accuracy of the Ramsey version of the Gorton-Daly conversations, which almost certainly would stop publication as few journalists would publish a version of a conversation which was denied in advance by the major of two participants in the conversation, or (b) confirm directly the accuracy of the Ramsey version, or (c) confirm indirectly the accuracy of the Ramsey version by refusing to comment on its accuracy when it was clear that it was in both Fraser's and Daly's interests to deny the accuracy of the version if it was wrong.

Gorton chose to see Ramsey. Gorton saw Ramsey at 1.55 pm on Wednesday, March 3, 1971, in Gorton's office. Gorton and Ramsey talked together for about fifteen minutes. On the desk in front of Gorton was Ramsey's memorandum. The two men went through Ramsey's questions one by one. According to Ramsey's subsequent statements, confirmed later by Gorton himself, Gorton would not comment upon anything said by Daly in the Gorton-Daly Monday interview. "He (Gorton) made no other remark about the allegations I had attributed to General Daly," Ramsey wrote in the *Australian* of Friday, March 5, 1971. "Nor did he attempt to discourage me in any way from publishing the story based on the statement (memorandum) I had given him." Ramsey went away, confidently and justifiably believing that Gorton had confirmed his story in the indirect way that so many stories are confirmed in politics. Ramsey wrote his story. It appeared in the *Australian* of Thursday, March 4, 1971.

Ramsey's story set out (a) that Daly had accused Fraser of extreme disloyalty to the Army and its junior Minister, Peacock, (b) that Daly had told Gorton that he, Daly, believed that the Army was being discredited as part of a political campaign against Peacock, and (c) that Gorton had told Daly that he knew the reports to be wrong and that he would not allow them to go unchallenged.

After Ramsey's story was published on the Thursday morning, Gorton did what he had refused to do on the previous day when face to face with Ramsey. He said that the allegations in the *Australian* article that Daly had criticised Fraser were "untrue". "At no time did Sir Thomas Daly 'denounce' the Minister for Defence, or accuse him of disloyalty to the Army or the Army Minister," declared an official Gorton statement issued on Thursday, March 4, 1971.

On the next day, Friday, March 5, 1971, came the article that was key in the whole affair. Ramsey reproduced in the *Australian* the five-question memorandum he had put in to Eggleton, and reported part of his conversation with Gorton in the interview that followed his submission of the memorandum. "The Prime Minister, Mr Gorton, had the opportunity to repudiate before it was published a report I wrote in the *Australian* yesterday," Ramsey's article stated. The fat was in the fire and from there on the fat fizzled fiercely.

On the same day, March 5, 1971, as Ramsey published his account of how he had sought confirmation from Gorton of his version of the Gorton-Daly conversation, Gorton confirmed that he had seen Ramsey before Ramsey had published the story[9] that Daly had accused Fraser "of extreme disloyalty to the Army and its junior Minister, Peacock."

But, said Gorton, he had not misled or deceived Ramsey in any way. "A refusal to make any comment on a journalist's speculation cannot be held to be misleading or deceiving," Gorton said.[10] Gorton made no attempt to explain why, before publication and when a denial would almost certainly have prevented publication, he did not consider a journalist's "speculation" merited a denial, whereas, after publication, he had judged the same journalist's speculation as meriting a long and detailed reply in which he had described the Ramsey version of the Gorton-Daly conversation as "untrue" and said that "at no time did Sir Thomas Daly 'denounce' the Minister for Defence or accuse him of disloyalty to the Army or to the Army Minister."[11]

Fraser, as Defence Minister, was in an impossible position. Behind his back and before he had been consulted on a matter for which he carried ministerial responsibility, Daly, representing the Army, had virtually been told by the Prime Minister that in any conflict with Fraser the Army would receive the Prime Minister's backing against Fraser.[12] Fraser returned from Tasmania on Friday, March 5, 1971, and had an unhappy 90-minute meeting in the Prime Minister's office. Neither Gorton nor Fraser would discuss what had transpired at this meeting. But for the first time Gorton, who until then had appeared to be enjoying both himself and Fraser's discomfiture, seemed to realise that he was heading into dangerous waters. The ALP was threatening a censure motion against the government in the House of Representatives. To some extent, Gorton's personal position was protected by the ALP's belief that Gorton was a vote loser for the Liberals.[13] The ALP did not want to do anything that would bring about Gorton's deposition from and replacement in the prime ministership. But that ALP attitude could alter under the pressure of events. Said Gorton "It appears that the whole question (of the Gorton-Fraser-Army row) will be the subject of discussion in the Parliament next week. I do not propose to make any (further) comment on any aspect until that time."[14]

Although Gorton realised by Friday, March 5, 1971, that he was heading for dangerous waters, he later claimed that he did not perceive just how dangerous those waters were. "I didn't know there was any crisis until Fraser stuck in his resignation on Monday," Gorton said in a special interview with Alan Trengrove after he had lost the prime ministership. "That's when I started hearing warning bells. He (Fraser) took the telephone off the hook and I left a message for him to ring me and he didn't."[15] If Gorton did not hear warning bells until the Monday, he must have been tone deaf. As early as the Saturday, I learned that Fraser was taking advice from various people, that that advice was that the clear breakdown in trust between Gorton and Fraser was threatening not only the Liberal-CP government and the Liberal Party itself but the Government's 1972 election prospects, and that Fraser was being counselled that his only way out with dignity and the restoration of his credibility was by resignation from his Defence portfolio. I did a lot of legwork. I found that Fraser was not only listening to that advice but showing an inclination to take it. I wrote this and the fact that pressure was on Fraser to resign in the *Sunday Telegraph* of March 7, 1971. If Gorton

425

heard nothing about Fraser's intentions, and had no worry about them, until the following Monday his intelligence service within the Liberal Parliamentary Party must have either been non-existent, inferior to mine, or broken down badly at a crucial period.

There was to be a further happening on that Sunday night to which proGorton Liberal parliamentarians were to attach what I believe to be an exaggerated importance and which was to cause the proGorton Liberal parliamentarians to advance the theory that Gorton's replacement as Prime Minister was not the result of his own actions but the successful outcome of a "Packer"[16] plot, with "Alan Reid as the hatchet man".[17] With Baudino and Samuel, I appeared on that Sunday night on the TV programme "Meet the Press" on the Packer-controlled Sydney TV Station, Channel Nine.

By this stage, there was considerable public interest in what was going on in Canberra. Mr King Watson, producer of "Meet the Press", tried to arrange that Ramsey, Baudino, and Samuel, each of whom had written a newspaper story which had become part of the Gorton-Fraser issue, should be in Sydney to appear on the programme to explain how they became involved. I was not on the programme nor scheduled to be. I was to return to Canberra on the Sunday to report the events of the next week. But on either the Friday or the Saturday, Watson asked me to stand by. He was not certain that he could get Ramsey for the programme. Ramsey was unsure about whether or not he could appear. Watson would need somebody to explain the significance of the Ramsey story. I would have to fill in for Ramsey if Ramsey was unavailable. Ramsey was unavailable. I filled in.

In the course of the TV interview I was asked whether Liberal parliamentarians were going to do anything about Mr Gorton's position. I replied that this depended on what Fraser did. If Fraser resigned and stated the reasons for his resignation—and I believed there was a strong possibility that Fraser would do this—there could be a successful revolt against Gorton's leadership. I also said "The test here will come with Mr Fraser. If Mr Fraser accepts this (the happenings of the past week), he becomes henceforward a (Gorton) puppet in the same way as—I don't say this offensively—the Treasurer, Mr Bury, has been reduced to a (Gorton) puppet."[18] A number of proGorton supporters believed that Fraser made up his mind to resign after watching the "Meet the Press" programme, and hearing that remark.[19] This interview became part of the mythology of the "Packer" plot.

On Monday morning, March 8, 1971, a Cabinet meeting was held in Parliament House, Canberra. Word spread that Fraser was absent from the meeting, an absence that in itself was significant. The unflappable Eggleton parried questions with his habitual urbanity. At 1.45 a cryptic statement was issued in the Press Gallery: "Mr Malcolm Fraser, Minister for Defence, said today that he would seek leave to make a statement in the House (of Representatives) tomorrow, Tuesday, March 9, 1971, immediately after question time." As Fraser was still describing himself as "Minister for Defence" it was obvious that he had not yet resigned. But as he was in a position to issue a statement in Canberra it was equally obvious that he was in a position to attend the Cabinet meeting if he so desired. He was clearly preparing for his resignation. Unknown to the press as yet, ten minutes after Fraser had issued his statement, Fraser's private secretary, Mr Dale Budd, and his press secretary, Mr Barrie Gillman, delivered a letter to Miss Gotto for transmission to Gorton. A copy of the letter also went to Anthony in his capacity as Country Party Leader. The letter, dated March 8, 1971, read "My Dear Prime Minister—This letter is to advise you that I have considered the events of recent days carefully and deliberately. I regard your conduct as Prime Minister as one which indicates significant disloyalty to a senior Minister. Such a situation is not tolerable. I therefore resign, and will be delivering a letter to his Excellency, the Governor-General, tomorrow morning. I intend to seek leave to make a statement after questions tomorrow. Yours sincerely, Malcolm Fraser."

Within less than an hour, the contents of the letter were known to some pressmen. Fraser blamed the Prime Minister's office for the premature release of the contents of the letter.[20] Fraser heard a report of his resignation at 4 pm while listening to radio newscasts at his Canberra home. In the meantime, Cabinet was meeting. The more vocal members of Cabinet were vehement in their support of Gorton, though some of the shrewder ones were significantly silent. Gorton extracted a pledge from McMahon that he would not contest the leadership against him if a revolt flared. Hulme volunteered to drive to Fraser's home to see if a reconciliation was possible. In the interval, Gorton tried to phone Fraser.

Gorton could not get Fraser on the phone. Fraser's phone gave the engaged signal continuously. Later Gorton was to express the suspicion that Fraser had taken the phone off its cradle. Fraser, meanwhile, had phoned the Governor-General and arranged an appointment. Fraser drove off to Government House at 4.20 pm. At 4.25, only minutes later, Hulme arrived. But he was too late. The opportunity for reconciliation had passed. When Fraser returned at 5.30 after seeing the Governor-General and submitting his resignation, Fraser released his letter of resignation. For Gorton the warning bells were not only ringing loudly but the rocks were perilously close.

Originally, the Liberal Party meeting on Tuesday, March 9, 1971, had been set down for 11.30 pm. But between 10.30 am and 11.30 am there had been a meeting between Gorton and Fraser in Gorton's office. Then Gorton spent some time with the leader of the Country Party, Anthony, and the government Chief Whip, Max Fox, from Victoria. The consultations between Gorton and Anthony produced the scuttlebutt that Gorton had resigned as Prime Minister in favor of McMahon. The patient, imperturbable Eggleton went to see the Prime Minister and came back with the quote in Gorton's name "I deny that." At 11.30 the Liberal Party meeting was delayed for an hour. Gorton's supporters were obviously checking their numbers. It was clear that only a miracle would prevent yet another leadership showdown.

The Liberal Party meeting started at 12.30 pm. With the Parliament due to meet at 2.30 pm, the party meeting could be of only brief duration. This suited the Gorton supporters. The briefer the meeting the less chance there was of it becoming uncontrollable. The Liberal parliamentarians would have to be in the House of Representatives. The ALP had indicated its intention of moving a vote of no-confidence. As yet it was not known whether it would be a vote of no-confidence in the government or in Gorton. The Gorton supporters had hoped it would be in the government. They knew that the government could survive such a vote. They were less confident of surviving a vote of no-confidence in Gorton.

In the Party room, Gorton explained his position and claimed that he had acted properly throughout recent events, even though he had refrained from denying Ramsey's story when presented with the opportunity to do so before publication. Fraser gave his viewpoint on recent events, a viewpoint far from flattering to Gorton. Fraser mentioned a grievance which until then was not known to such of his Liberal parliamentary colleagues as were not members of Cabinet. Fraser claimed that Gorton, without consultation with Cabinet and possibly illegally, had been responsible for the creation of a situation which could have involved Australian troops in firing on Papua-New Guinea natives. Fraser cited this as yet another example of the way in which Gorton was destroying the Cabinet system of government. Fraser was to repeat and elaborate on this grievance later that day in the Parliament. Both men kept themselves under tight control. Though they were dealing with explosive material, explosive enough to blow the government sky high, they spoke in such quietly conversational tones that those in the party room had to ask them several times to "Speak up." Senator John Marriott, from Tasmania, made a valiant but hopeless attempt to persuade the party to affirm confidence in Gorton before the meeting closed. But Howson, Jess, and Turner said that, until they heard the full facts, the Prime Minister could not count on them voting to support him in the House of Representatives. With others still wanting to state their positions, the meeting adjourned, with nothing settled but with an assurance from Gorton that there would be a further meeting before a vote was taken in the Parliament.

The drama shifted from the semi-private pond of the Liberal Party room to the goldfish bowl of the House of Representatives. Whitlam was enjoying the spectacle of the Liberal Party tearing itself to pieces, a practice at which the ALP was adept. The ALP had not announced its parliamentary intentions. Whitlam had been given discretion to decide ALP tactics according to his judgment of how events were developing. The House met at 2.30 pm. At 2.33, after Prayers, Whitlam moved the suspension of standing orders.

Said Whitlam "I should think that everybody would agree that these matters about which the honorable member for Wannon (Fraser) has made statements outside the House are of more immediate importance to the public—more immediately in the minds of honorable members—than the other matters which would normally intervene."[21] Gorton said he had no objection to the suspension of standing orders. But he took it that the suspension would be such that there would not be just the one statement, Fraser's, but at least two. It was the serving of notice that he also intended to speak. "Yes," said Whitlam. He also took it that there would be at least two statements. The motion for the suspension of standing orders was passed.

Fraser rose to his feet. For the first time for years he was speaking from the back benches. Superbly groomed for the occasion, exquisitely tailored, just the right amount of pocket handkerchief emerging from his breast pocket, the thick mop of hair topping his six feet three inches of height carefully slicked down, Fraser's tone was almost conversational. But his content was lethal. With cool quietness, Fraser went through the earlier events in which he, Gorton, Baudino and Samuel were involved. Then he came to the Ramsey story. "One sentence (from the Prime Minister) would have killed the report," Fraser reminded the Parliament quietly. "The Prime Minister, by his inaction, made sure that it would cover the front page. As I have indicated in my letter of resignation, I found that disloyalty intolerable and not to be endured . . . I wish to say something about loyalty. My responsibility through the Government is to this Parliament and through it to the people of Australia. My ultimate loyalty must be to Australia. What is meant by 'loyalty to the Army'? Does anyone mean that that requires a Minister to defend every act of commission or omission of the Army or does it mean that it ought to be defended when it is unjustly accused? If there is anyone in this House who believes that loyalty to a service requires uncritical and universal support of its activities, that is not a concept that I can embrace for it would be a denial of parliamentary authority."

With that statement, Fraser had gone to the nub of the issue. Gorton's interview with Daly, and his acceptance, without previous consultation with Fraser, "that the allegations against the Army were false, that I had the utmost confidence in the Army and its commanders, and that I wanted Sir Thomas Daly and the Army to know this" was not only, in Fraser's words, an act of "significant disloyalty to a senior minister." More importantly, it was the repudiation of the principle, vital in a parliamentary democracy, that military forces were subject to civilian control through the authority of a Minister of State responsible to the parliament and, ultimately, through the parliament to the nation. It was also yet another example of Gorton's inability to appreciate and to work within the confines of a cabinet and parliamentary system of government.

Fraser was frank about difficulties between himself and the Armed Services. "I do not deny that there have been differences of opinion—the press has labelled it 'abrasion'—with some service relationships in Canberra," he said. "But I assert that any Minister for Defence who seeks to do his duty will have to seek to move people from old views and from views which may not embrace the total defence concept." Fraser went on to specify areas in which there had been differences of opinion between himself and the Services, particularly the Army. ". . . there has been some implication that the Army is an independent organisation," said Fraser. "Of course it is not . . . the ultimate decision and responsibility belongs to the Minister for Defence and his immediate advisers. . . . No Minister for Defence can carry this heavy task unless he has the active support of the Prime Minister. Unless he has that support he cannot maintain an adequate authority over the Services. If they feel there is an appeal direct to the Prime Minister, the co-ordination of policy and the chain of command disintegrate." As Fraser proceeded he grew more lethal

430

though his voice did not rise at any stage above conversational level. "It should not be thought that act (by Gorton in not killing the Ramsey report with one sentence of denial) alone has brought me to this point," Fraser said. "Since his election to office, the Prime Minister has seriously damaged the Liberal Party and cast aside the stability and sense of direction of earlier times. He has a dangerous reluctance to consult Cabinet, and an obstinate determination to get his own way. He ridicules the advice of a great Public Service unless it supports his view."[22]

"Let me give one example," Fraser said. "Little notice was taken of a press statement issued by the Prime Minister on July 20, 1970, concerning the call out of troops in New Guinea. Nobody knew of the unpublicised drama of the previous week. During the Gazelle Peninsula crisis in Papua and New Guinea[23] there was a possibility that the police would not be able to contain the situation. A course of action had been set in train that had as its central point the possibility of a serious confrontation with the Mantaungan Association. This plan was not discussed by Cabinet. The first I heard of the matter was when I was asked to arrange for a call out of the Pacific Islands Regiment on July 14. I immediately took advice from my Department and the Defence Committee. Part of the advice was to the effect that the legal consideration for a call out had not been fulfilled. I made it plain that I would not sign such an order until the legal considerations had been fulfilled and until Cabinet had been consulted. After some days the Attorney-General (Hughes) flew to Port Moresby, and, on his return, I received his advice. Cabinet met on Sunday, July 19, at the Lodge.[24] With Cabinet authority I then signed that call out order. The Prime Minister had resisted Cabinet discussion from the outset. The attitude was 'This is the course I want and that is all there is to it'."

Fraser added further details. "It is also not known that a letter from the Minister for External Territories (Barnes), saying that both he and the Administrator (of Papua-New Guinea) considered it appropriate for the call out order to be revoked by a further recommendation to the Governor-General, was sent to the Prime Minister. I received a copy on September 16, and I supported it in my own letter to the Prime Minister on September 17, 1970. Despite this, the Prime Minister has refused to allow adequate Cabinet discussions to decide whether or not the original order should be revoked. It still stands, and, possibly, illegally. This was an important matter. It involved not only the possibility of the Pacific Islands Regiment being used but also its subsequent reinforcement from Australia. It could have involved Australian

431

troops having to fire on people from Papua and New Guinea. The Prime Minister did not believe that Cabinet discussion was warranted."[25]

Fraser wound up with a denunciation of the man whom he had helped to lift to the prime ministership. "The Prime Minister, because of his unreasoned drive to get his own way, his obstinacy, impetuous and emotional reactions, has imposed strains upon the Liberal Party, the Government, and the Public Service," Fraser concluded. "I do not believe he is fit to hold the great office of Prime Minister, and I cannot serve in his government."[26]

In his reply, Gorton did not deal at length with Fraser's charge that the capacity of the Defence Minister to "maintain an adequate authority over the Services" had been lessened by recent events. He agreed with Fraser's concept of how the defence services of Australia should be run. But, said Gorton, very much was expected of the Armed Services. "They are expected to be at all times subject to the direction of the civil power—completely subject," he went on. "They are an arm wielded by their commanders but only for the purposes decided by the government of the day. They are expected to refrain from any political activity and to make no public comments or statements themselves even in their own defence if they see themselves denigrated in the newspapers. This is their duty in a democracy. This is essential and an essential duty for them to perform. But in return there is an equal duty on governments. The Armed Services must not be allowed to be denigrated or criticised without proper basis. If that happens the government has a duty to come to their defence and to refute that criticism. If, of course, there is a proper basis for criticism then that should be laid open and corrected. I think this is the only decent and proper way in which a government can act in relation to its own armed forces. This is not, as some newspapers have suggested, taking the side of the generals. It is protecting the whole of the Army against criticism when that criticism is undeserved, and I believe there is a duty to do that." Gorton said that he did not think that Fraser could claim that at any time he was interfered with or in any way obstructed or not supported in carrying out the general concept of the functions of the Ministry of Defence vis-à-vis the Services.[27]

Gorton then concentrated on aspects of the three newspaper stories, which had become part of the issue. He confirmed that he had seen Baudino on the Monday afternoon. Just why Baudino had wanted to see him he did not know. "It is a most unusual thing to have happened," Gorton said. Gorton said he did not want Daly to wake up the next morning to read against him by

432

name an accusation of what would have been a dereliction of duty and to find that the *Telegraph* was accusing Daly of this action. He had phoned Daly and asked Daly to see him so that he could forewarn Daly of what he might see in the press the next morning and to let Daly know his own views as head of the government. These views were that there was "nothing to go on alleging that these accusations (against the Army) had come from the Department of Defence, or Mr Fraser since they were based purely on rumours in the Press Gallery," that he, Gorton, "knew" that these allegations against the Army were false, and that he wanted Daly and the Army to know this, and to know that the allegations would be denied "at the highest level". "I attempted incidentally, to ring Mr Fraser, not for him to take action on this matter, but again to warn him that he might see something of this kind in the paper the next day but he (Fraser) was not available at the time."[28] Gorton said that when he saw Fraser the following morning "there was no dissension, no discussion, no disagreement."

Gorton conceded that in hindsight he now had no doubt that not denying, before publication and when he had the opportunity to do so, the Ramsey story that in the Gorton-Daly discussions Daly had accused Fraser of "extreme disloyalty to the Army and its junior Minister, Peacock", was an "error". He should have denied the story. "The matter on which I would not comment at all was Mr Ramsey's suggestions as to what General Daly might or might not have said," Gorton told the Parliament. "I believe it wrong to do this, to make comments or affirmations, or denials in cases like this. I think this is so whether the person who is a third party is a general, an admiral, a politician, a civil servant or a businessman."[29]

"I am told now that if I had taken some such action (as denial) the story would never have been printed," Gorton said. "That might or might not be true. Who knows? Who can tell? It is quite possible that it might well have been printed under the heading 'This is the story the Prime Minister tried to kill.' But that is by the way. I would still have been more pleased if I had taken that action. . . . I thought it wrong to discuss or comment with Mr Ramsey on what a third party had said and Mr Ramsey replied 'Fair enough'."[30]

While Gorton was speaking, Ramsey was standing behind where I was sitting in the Federal Parliamentary Press Gallery. Ramsey leaned across me. In a loud voice, thickened with tension, he said "You liar." Ramsey's words were clearly heard in the chamber below the Press Gallery. They were picked up by the sensitive microphones on the floor of the chamber. They were

433

broadcast throughout Australia.[31] Startled members looked up from the floor of the chamber to the Press Gallery. There was a second's stillness and then the rustle of excited voices. Whitlam talked hurriedly with members of his front bench as Ramsey left the Press Gallery. But Gorton continued unperturbed. He said that he did not have as clearly in his mind as he would have liked the circumstances surrounding the request that the Pacific Islands Regiment, not Australian troops, be placed on readiness to go at a moment's notice to the Gazelle Peninsula to prevent civil disorder generally. He then read from notes, which had been passed to him. The notes contained dates and material which tended to confirm Fraser's version that he, Fraser, had insisted that there should be Cabinet discussion of the order providing for the call out of the Pacific Islands Regiment. "I would not deny that when the former Minister for Defence was talking to me on this matter, I was doubtful whether the group of ministers concerned was sufficient to do this, or whether there needed to be a full Cabinet meeting," Gorton said. "The Minister for Defence pressed his view that there should be a full Cabinet meeting. He certainly argued with me for a while—I think quite cogently— and there was a full Cabinet meeting."[32]

When Gorton resumed his seat, Whitlam again moved for the suspension of standing orders, this time so that the House could next day bring Ramsey before the House to be dealt with for his interjection. The ALP was clearly with justifiable opportunism trying to get put on the official record why Ramsey had felt impelled to interject "You liar" when Gorton was giving his account of his conversation with Ramsey. The debate on this particular incident was deepening into acrimony when Gorton stood up. Gorton said his press secretary, Eggleton, had received from Ramsey a communication which Ramsey had given him, Gorton, authority to use. Gorton said that Ramsey had just telephoned Eggleton in "a great state of emotional upset." Gorton added "I am quoting what Mr Eggleton says . . . Mr Eggleton says 'He (Ramsey) says that he lost control of himself in a quite inexcusable way. He apologises most humbly and he realises that his action was very wrong. The reason for his outburst was that he thought you had generalised rather on your own comments to him that day, while you certainly did quote him correctly. What he meant when he made his outburst is that you had been unfair. There was no question of you being a liar. He agrees that he did in fact say 'Fair enough'."[33]

Gorton said that as far as he was concerned that was apology enough for him. He suggested that the motion for the suspension

434

of standing orders so that a further motion for Ramsey to be summoned before the House to be dealt with for his interjection be withdrawn. Whitlam announced that the ALP withdrew its motion. But immediately after the Speaker, Sir William Aston, had received petitions, Whitlam gave notice of a motion for the following day's sitting. That motion read "That this House no longer has confidence in the government."[34] It was a censure motion in its most classic and simple form.

But the drama was not wholly confined to the chamber of the House of Representatives. Outside the Chamber, the Chief Government Whip, Max Fox, and the assistant Government Whip, Geoff Giles, and others were taking a count of heads to see if Gorton "still had the numbers." As subsequent events showed, their counting was faulty. The advice Gorton received was that he would "walk it in." One of Gorton's supporters, Robert ("Duke") Bonnett, was in hospital in Queensland. Bonnett had offered to fly down from Queensland to cast his vote in the party room in Gorton's favour, even if he had to be carried into the party room on a stretcher. Bonnett or one of Bonnett's Queensland associates was phoned that night from the Whip's room. Bonnett's vote was not needed, was the advice given. The vote would be heavily in Gorton's favour. Bonnett's vote would only add one to Gorton's assured majority. Bonnett had no reason to leave hospital to fly to Canberra. He could stay where he was, everything was under control.

I still cannot understand this almost amateur approach. In the harsh ALP environment where I received my early training, the axiom always was "Run scared." Even if there .were not the slightest doubt about winning, the winner always ensured that he was backed by the maximum vote. If corpses had been allowed to vote, I have no doubt that the bodies would have been carried in, the cadavers' arms raised at the appropriate moment, and the meeting concluded before burials took place.

However, an unusual happening had taken place, a happening which may have contributed to the Gorton supporters' otherwise inexplicable complacency. On this occasion, Gorton and Dudley Erwin were on opposite sides of the political fence. Erwin who, as government whip, had worked with Fraser and Scott to get Gorton the prime ministership in 1968 and who, later, had first been appointed leader of the House of Representatives and Minister for Air by Gorton and then fired from both positions by Gorton, apparently had some reason to phone Gorton. Though Gorton and Erwin had fallen out, and Erwin had complained bitterly and publicly about the degree of influence exercised over

Gorton by his secretary, Miss Gotto, Gorton seemingly still had respect for Erwin's ability, manifested during Gorton's 1968 and 1969 leadership struggles, to count numbers. At some stage in their conversation the question of "the numbers" arose.

Erwin may have been speaking from genuine conviction. On the other hand, he may have been working on the principle that all is fair in love, war, poker, and politics, or so convinced of the advantage of "running scared" that he was pessimistic even when speaking to an opponent. He told Gorton that it looked on his soundings as though Gorton would "walk it in." Gorton seemed assured of a good majority in any ballot involving his leadership. One of the antiGorton group's major difficulties was Malcolm Fraser's personal unpopularity. Fraser was "lead under the antiGorton forces' saddle," Erwin said. As Gorton had already been assured from other, less hostile sources than Erwin that he would "walk it in" Erwin's pessimistic judgment of the prospects of the side he was openly backing could have been a factor contributing to the decision to leave Bonnett in Queensland.

Other external pressures were being felt. The press generally was critical of Gorton. On Tuesday, March 9, David Solomon wrote in the *Canberra Times* "On Friday, the *Age* spoke of a 'government in decay'. On Sunday, the *Sunday Telegraph* called for the displacement of Mr Gorton as Prime Minister. . . . The *Canberra Times* on Friday complained about the government 'manipulating the news' and yesterday examined the act of self-destruction which the government was engaged in. The *Sydney Morning Herald* warned the government that it must hang together, or hang separately." But the *Sydney Morning Herald* was to go still further. In a leader, the *Sydney Morning Herald* commented "The Prime Minister has shown all too clearly that he cannot manage a team nor hold it together. The confrontation with Mr Fraser is only the latest of a series of crises in which he has been involved—it would be flying in the face of all the evidence to think it will be the last. Mr Gorton has shown that he is crisis-prone. An atmosphere of perennial crisis is conducive neither to good government nor to the retention of public confidence."[35]

The arguments that were dividing the Liberal Parliamentary Party started to divide the Liberal organisation. The Queensland Liberal Party President, Eric Robinson, who had been a persistent Gorton critic in Liberal Party forums but who had maintained a façade of loyalty in public, said "The Liberal Party would be better off with a new leader. The Liberal Party has to put its house in order, or it could be defeated at the next Federal election. The Prime Minister has placed the Liberal Party and the government in a very undesirable situation. I will seek the support of the Queensland Executive to speak up and make our position perfectly clear. Prime ministers and parliamentarians come and go but a great party has to look to the future and plan accordingly. The Liberal Party has to regain electoral support. Since Mr Gorton has been Prime Minister the party seems to have gone from one crisis to another. It had lost valuable and experienced ministers who did not seem able to serve under Mr Gorton, who has not displayed the qualities to keep a team together. If the leadership issue is not settled quickly, it is highly likely the Queensland Liberal organisation will take a strong stand."[36] Queensland Liberal parliamentarians said that they had been assured by members of the Queensland Liberal Executive that they, the parliamentarians, would be protected on their Liberal parliamentary preselections if they voted against Gorton either in the party room or in the Parliament.

The Liberal Federal President, Mr Robert Southey, a Victorian and ardent Gorton follower, sprang to Gorton's defence. "I deplore Mr Robinson's gratuitous intervention in a sphere which is solely the responsibility of the Parliamentary Party," Southey said in a statement which he would probably have rephrased if he had to make it twenty-four hours later. "It should be understood quite clearly that Mr Robinson does not speak for the Liberal Party of Australia . . . Mr Gorton, in common with his predecessors has had the support and loyalty of the (Liberal) Federal Executive. The Federal Executive does not intrude into the province of the Parliamentary Party and I do not believe that Mr Robinson will induce us to alter our traditional procedure."[37]

The Liberal Parliamentary Party met for a second time on Tuesday, March 9, 1971. Originally, the meeting was scheduled to start at 7.45 pm and to last until 8 pm when the House of Representatives sitting was resumed. The meeting was to give Gorton the opportunity to reply to Fraser's charges about the manner in which the call out order for the use, if required, of the Pacific Islands Regiment on the Gazelle Peninsula had been issued and authorised. But the meeting continued on as Gorton and Fraser argued about the propriety of the way in which this issue had been handled. Most of the Liberals stayed in the party room, only one or two appearing in the chamber of the House of Representatives. The meeting again ended inconclusively, but with Gorton supporters convinced that Gorton had "downed" Fraser, and a further meeting called for the next morning, Wednesday, at 10 am.

On Wednesday, March 10, 1971, nearly as many ALP parlia-

437

mentarians and pressmen as Liberal parliamentary participants in the meeting gathered in King's Hall in Parliament House, Canberra, whence opened out the lobby to the government parties' room where the Liberal parliamentarians were assembled in their secret conclave, just a few yards from the Prime Minister's office. There was tension. Everyone was aware that the moment of decision was approaching.

In the privacy of the party room, Gorton said the party was facing the most serious situation it had been called upon to face since it had come into existence. The Opposition had a motion of no-confidence in the Government before the House of Representatives. The Party would have to decide who would be sitting at the centre table in the Prime Minister's chair to handle it. Whoever was sitting at the table would have to deal with the motion. If it were to be he, then a vote of confidence must be passed in him in the room that morning. He was not trying to rush anyone, and did not mind a long debate.

Fairbairn listed what he considered the government's and Mr Gorton's shortcomings. The government was reeling like a punch drunk boxer from one Gorton-induced crisis to another, crises for which Gorton must take responsibility, Fairbairn said. It was obvious a number of members felt that they morally could not vote confidence in the Prime Minister's leadership. Sooner or later, if things went on the way they were going these members would vote for a censure motion in one form or another and that would mean the end of the Liberal government. He was one in this position. He proposed before the meeting closed to move a vote of no confidence in the Prime Minister.[38]

Jess said that he was in the same position as Fairbairn. He could not, with a clear conscience, vote confidence in Gorton's leadership. He had lost confidence. After Fairbairn had made his declaration, and Jess had reiterated his stand, there were then four who would not support Gorton in a vote of confidence in the House of Representatives—Fairbairn, Jess, Howson, and Turner. But it soon became apparent that there were more than this four prepared to take the same attitude. There was more than enough to bring about the government's defeat on the floor of the House of Representatives.

Dr Malcolm Mackay spoke. A Presbyterian divine who had turned businessman and politician, Mackay derided the ["Packer"] "plot" theory being advanced by proGorton Liberals as the reason for the present questioning of Gorton's leadership. Was there a plot? Mackay asked. There had been character assassination of Gorton promoted by the Liberals political enemies. But was the current

438

mess due entirely or even in part to a "plot"? Did Fraser switch suddenly and decide to resign only after seeing Alan Reid on TV? Was Fairbairn just a case of political ambition that had missed the bus? How then did the Party account for McMahon's difficulties with Gorton? For the disappearance from politics of Hasluck and Fairhall?

Take Fraser, Mackay said. Fraser had resigned from one of the most powerful offices in the nation, and he had made some enormous accusations. Did Fraser arrive at these conclusions suddenly? Was he the kind of man to say the things he had because some pressmen had told him to say them? Was Fairbairn that type of man? Or was it that both men after traumatic experiences had found it was the final straw that breaks the camel's back?

Gorton said he was mystified by Fraser's sudden emergence in the role of a relentless opponent, Mackay said. Mackay said he accepted that Gorton was mystified. Gorton was mystified because he did not perceive the other things that were behind all that had happened. He, Mackay, had oscillated between optimism and dismay. He knew of a happening in the Health Department about which the Minister for Health, Jim Forbes was never informed by the Prime Minister. Forbes might well have resigned over that. Was it that the Liberal ministers could all produce many examples of such indifference to the courtesies, indeed to the essential checks and balances, of teamwork?[39]

Mackay asked if Liberal ministers had come to accept erratic individualism as inevitable. He had seen so many glimpses of this pattern of erratic individualism in operation that he was now convinced that Gorton held such things to be of secondary importance to getting the job done as seemed best to him personally at the time. Mackay said he could not believe that the massive electoral movement against the Liberals was due to the success of the ALP. The ALP was, in his view, a dreadful alternative and most people knew this and were prepared to say so. The Liberals had one hope and one hope only. About twenty months remained until the next election, a scant time in which a new leader could rebuild the image of the Liberal Party and swing back the tide of public opinion. The only solution was for a clear and decisive change. The Liberals were past the point of no-return under Gorton. The greatest service Gorton could do the party and the nation would be to resign and for the Liberals to find a new leader.

Les Irwin said that he had a high personal regard for Gorton. Gorton was one of the most maligned men in Australian political history. He had been more maligned than even the ALP Premier of NSW during the depression years, Jack Lang. But the sad fact had to be faced up to that under Gorton the Liberal Party had no electoral future. Irwin appealed to Gorton to step down voluntarily from the prime ministership and prove that he was an even greater Australian than Irwin had given him credit for being. Gorton treated the request from Irwin with great courtesy. Himself a fighter pilot in World War II, Gorton had a high regard and great respect for Irwin, who had flown in World War I the fragile aircraft of that era when flying was barely out of its infancy. "I would willingly stand down, Les, if I felt it were for the good of Australia," Gorton told Irwin. "But I feel it is not."

As though confirming Gorton's later self-judgment that he "probably wasn't a good politician"[40] Alan Jarman, a young Victorian and devoted Gorton follower, came in and formally moved a vote of confidence in Gorton, reserving his right to speak later. Jarman's motion was seconded by Len Reid, also from Victoria. Though both estimable men, neither could be described as yet having established themselves as significant figures in the Liberal Party. Jarman had entered the Parliament only in 1966. Reid's period in the Parliament had been even briefer. He had entered the Parliament at the 1969 elections.

Gorton's tactics throughout this and the earlier Liberal meetings were puzzling. He did not want to quit the Prime Ministership. His reply to Irwin proved that. But he acted throughout as though the death wish were upon him. It is a golden rule of politics that a parliamentary leader does not seek a vote of confidence from his party. The very seeking suggests that he needs a vote of confidence. The attitude he takes is that he has the confidence of the party. He takes it for granted. It is for others to prove the opposite. The only time when a shrewd leader who wanted to survive would even consider a vote of confidence in a difficult situation would be if he could persuade, or intimidate, the main beneficiary from a vote of "no confidence" into moving the vote of confidence. McMahon would, obviously, be the main beneficiary from a "no confidence" motion. Backed by a Ministry which was supporting him almost as a block, Gorton had already intimidated McMahon into giving a pledge that he would not contest the leadership against Gorton. With McMahon standing aloof from the Gorton-Fraser fracas and still unaware of the depth of backbench feeling about the inadequacy of Gorton's leadership,[41] it was possible that McMahon could be persuaded in the interests of party unity, or intimidated by the sheer weight of proGorton ministerial backing into agreeing to move the vote of confidence in Gorton, if it was felt that such a vote of confidence had to be secured. But no attempt was made by Gorton supporters to persuade McMahon to play any kind of role designed to secure Gorton's survival. It was left to Jarman and Reid to move the confidence motion. A sigh of relief went up from Gorton's critics.

From Gorton's viewpoint, it was also a mistake to have a confidence motion moved instead of allowing his opponents to move a no confidence motion. It left him one vote down. In the event of a tied vote—and however unlikely the Gorton supporters may have viewed this it was a contingency that had to be provided against—the vote would be resolved in the negative. If it were a vote of confidence in Gorton it would be defeated. If it had been a vote of no confidence in Gorton it would also in such circumstances have been declared defeated. The antiGorton Liberal parliamentarians were presented with an advantage.

There was another puzzling aspect of the Gorton tactics. Possibly from overconfidence, an overconfidence stimulated by Erwin's self-pitying estimate that Gorton would "walk it in," Gorton agreed, without argument, to a secret ballot. Gorton would probably not have lost in a vote taken on a show of hands. Men are always more courageous in a secret ballot than when they have to demonstrate publicly, under the eyes of a man who still has the potential to survive and shape their future, where they stand. There was no obligation upon Gorton to agree to a secret ballot. Neither the Liberal Parliamentary Party's rules or traditions provided for a secret ballot. As the meeting's chairman, Gorton could have ruled that the vote be decided by a show of hands. He could probably have got away with this ruling without challenge, after a bold speech asserting his belief in the courage of Liberals and their willingness to stand up and be counted publicly on a matter in which their consciences were deeply involved. If there had been a motion of dissent from this ruling, he would probably have won that motion for it would have had to be decided on a show of hands.

With Jarman moving, and Reid seconding, the motion of confidence, Gorton's position weakened. Jarman said that for the past five weeks there had been moves by a section of the Liberal Party to get the Prime Minister out of office. He said that the situation had resembled that when Menzies was deposed from the prime ministership in 1941. Jarman said he was loyal and he considered those who were threatening to cross the floor of the Parliament to vote with the Opposition disloyal to the Liberal Party. It was the Press seeking to depose Gorton. The Press had taken the place of the Parliamentary Opposition because there was no viable opposition.

Sir John Cramer, a Liberal Party veteran who had been one of the party's founders, said that what he was interested in was the future of the party, not personalities. He thought there should be a vote. He was surprised by the way in which Fraser had announced his resignation to the Parliament and not to the party. Jess said that Fraser was not the issue. The issue was Gorton. Turning to Gorton, Jess said "I like and respect you as a man, but not as a Prime Minister. The party needs and must have a new leader."[42]

Kevin Cairns asked what advice would Gorton give the Governor-General if he were defeated in the confidence motion. Senator Sir Magnus Cormack, from Victoria, a Gorton supporter, protested. Such a question was improper. Cairns said that there was nothing improper about the question. A straight answer would release many of the people in the room—enable them to vote on the merits of the issue. Everybody in the room knew his circumstances. He had a large family and no resources. He had been phoned by a minister, not a Queenslander, and threatened that if he voted against Gorton and Gorton was defeated Gorton would advise the Governor-General to have a general election which would mean almost certainly the return of an ALP government and that he, Cairns, would be out of Parliament and without an income within six weeks. He was entitled to know where he stood. So were others in a position similar to himself.

Gorton said that the question was hypothetical. But he said that he would take no action that would have the effect of installing an ALP government. Those present at the meeting interpreted this as meaning that if the vote went against him, Gorton would recommend to the Governor-General that his replacement be sworn in as Prime Minister and not seek a general election. Howson said the Prime Minister lacked integrity. It was plain he had lost the nation's confidence. Senator George Branson, from Western Australia, said that there had been enough talk but Irwin argued that the Liberal Party was democratic and everyone should have his or her say. The debate dragged on. Bate was the last speaker.

Bate said that his first loyalty was to Australia, his second to the Liberal Party. When those two loyalties came into conflict, he must adhere to his first loyalty. It had emerged from Fraser's resignation that there had been difficulties in getting Cabinet meetings. This had happened when Fraser had refused to sign the order to call out the Pacific Islands Regiment and possibly an Australian battalion in the Mantaungan crisis, Bate said. The troops were not trained as riot police but to shoot down and destroy an enemy. He believed many decisions had been made by Gorton outside the Cabinet meetings. The government had been unconstitutional and illegal. One-man government left wide blanks in administration. One could not blame the newspapers for intruding on government when there were actually few Cabinet meetings and no constitutional government at all. Under those conditions, he could not accept being bound by any Party majority. Unless Gorton was replaced, he would go into the House of Representatives and vote the Prime Minister out "for ever."[43]

Gorton proposed that the vote be taken in the party room. It was taken. The result was a 33/all tie. Gorton ruled that he had a casting vote as chairman. He cast it in favour of "no confidence" thereby voting himself out of office in unique circumstances. He declared that the office of Liberal Leader—the office which would confer the prime ministership upon his successor—was vacant. Cramer nominated McMahon for the vacant position. Party members argued that intending candidates should nominate themselves. Gorton asked "Will you stand, Billy?" McMahon said "Yes." Snedden nominated himself. McMahon won the ballot and was declared Liberal leader. Hulme asked Gorton if he would stand for the deputy leadership of the Liberal Party, vacated by McMahon's elevation. "Yes," said Gorton. Fairbairn and Fraser nominated themselves. Gorton's vote exceeded the combined Fairbairn-Fraser vote. Gorton was declared elected as Liberal Party Deputy leader.

Meantime, while this was going on in the privacy of the Liberal Party room, excitement was mounting in King's Hall, still crowded with ALP parliamentarians, and pressmen. Eggleton emerged from the government lobby and announced that McMahon had replaced Gorton as Liberal Party leader. He disappeared back into the Government lobby. He reappeared. He announced that Gorton had been elected deputy leader. "You must be joking," a pressman said, unbelievingly. For once Eggleton's urbanity slipped. "I don't joke on such matters," he said tersely.

A count of heads immediately started to work out who comprised the thirty-three who had voted against Gorton. These counts are always subject to minor error. On my count, three House of Representatives' Ministers, and twenty-two back bench Liberal MHRs had voted "no confidence" in Gorton. Gorton's Senate strength had also eroded. Eight of the twenty Liberal senators had voted against him.

At 2.32 pm on the same day, Wednesday, March 10, 1971,

443

after the Speaker, Sir William Aston, had recited the daily prayers, Gorton announced formally to the House of Representatives that a change had taken place in the Leadership of the Liberal Parliamentary Party. "I shall be in touch with his Excellency the Governor-General to tender my resignation as Prime Minister and to offer him certain advice as to whom he should give the commission to form a new government," Gorton said. "In the meantime in these circumstances, I suggest that the House should adjourn until next Monday. I therefore move that the House at its rising adjourn until Monday, March 15, 1971, at 2.30 pm."[44] The House duly adjourned.

On March 15, 1971, when the House reassembled at 2.30 in the afternoon, McMahon, the durable little man who in 1968 had failed to reach the prime ministership which he had striven desperately but forlornly to achieve but who in 1971 had had the office virtually handed to him without him lifting a finger, was in the Prime Minister's chair at the centre table in the green curtained, green cushioned House of Representatives, a seat in which no man, whatever previously his reputation, can be sure of performing adequately until he has been through a testing period. McMahon announced his elevation to the high office of Prime Minister and that Gorton had been sworn in as Defence Minister[45], replacing the elongated, elegant Malcolm Fraser now lolling back, with an air of detachment and disinterest, on a back bench.

One phase of the Gorton experiment, the experiment of a man of action who believed in being himself, in mistaking stubbornness for strength, in insisting upon his own capricious way, and upon the substitution of personal rule for the time-tested method in a parliamentary democracy of team work and cooperation, was over. But the experiment was still not completely over, as Disraeli told the House of Commons on February 28, 1859, "Finality is not the language of politics." Gorton was still there, still with a following which was dwindling because politicians, like courtiers, must live on the basis "The King is dead—Long live the King", but still a force to be reckoned with as Deputy Leader of the Liberal Party and while holding the powerful office of a senior Minister of State. But it was only one phase of the Gorton experiment that was over. There will always be Gorton-type experiments. For ever since men came down out of the trees to live in settled communities, men who wish to rule or who enjoy ruling—the political animals of the human species—have been experimenting in styles of ruling and methods of ruling.

That is what makes politics at once changeless and infinitely varied and gives them their eternal fascination.

NOTES

1 Fraser later revealed that the Army wanted the base on Mornington Peninsula, in Victoria—Representatives, Daily Hansard, March 9, 1971, p 681.

2 This is the explanation for Fraser's comment "One odd thing about the *Telegraph* report is that the journalist who wrote it at no time sought to check its accuracy with me, although a copy was shown to the Prime Minister (Mr Gorton), who told me that in its original form General Daly's name had featured"—Fraser, Commonwealth Representatives' Daily Hansard, March 9, 1971, p 679/680.

3 Peter Samuel justifiably commented on the "Meet the Press" programme of March 7, 1971, that the newspaper stories themselves were not the type of stories that should have "rocked the government". It was the reaction of ministers to those stories that had "rocked the government".

4 Transcript of "Meet the Press" TV programme, Channel Nine, Sydney, Sunday, March 7, 1971.

5 By sheer coincidence, Max Hawkins, of the *Brisbane Telegraph,* had had an appointment with Sir Thomas Daly on the Monday evening. Hawkins was told that Sir Thomas would be a bit late because he had "been summoned to see the PM".

6 The three service Ministers—Killen, Navy, Peacock, Army, and Senator Tom Drake-Brockman, Air—had ministerial responsibility for their Departments but functioned under the general supervision of the Minister for Defence.

7 With Sir Rohan Delacombe, governor of Victoria, acting as Commonwealth administrator during the absence overseas of the Governor-General, Sir Paul Hasluck, a military guard of honor had been flown to Canberra on chartered aircraft. As the government's economy drive had been announced, with considerable publicity, this had aroused extensive criticism.

8 *The Australian,* March 5, 1971.

9 Official statement issued by Gorton's Canberra office, March 5, 1971.

10 Official statement, issued by Gorton's Canberra office, March 5, 1971.

11 Official statement, issued by Gorton's Canberra office, March 4, 1971.

12 "The purpose of this (visit by Daly to the PM's office) . . . was to make it clear that I knew that the allegations against the Army were false, that I had the utmost confidence in the army and its commanders, and that I wanted Sir Thomas Daly and the army to know this"—Gorton, official statement, issued by Gorton's Canberra office. March 4, 1971.

13 "We think he (Gorton) is our best asset"—Chief ALP whip, Gil Duthie on ABC programme, "This Day Tonight", March 9, 1971.

14 Official statement issued by Gorton's Canberra office, March 5, 1971.

15 *Sun-Pictorial,* Melbourne, March 13, 1971.

16 "Packer" was Sir Frank Packer, the managing director of Australian Consolidated Press Ltd., by which I was employed.

17 Gorton described me as "the hatchet man" in his interview with Trengrove—*Sun-Pictorial,* Melbourne, March 13, 1971.

18 Transcript of "Meet the Press" programme, Channel Nine, Sydney, March 7, 1971.

19 My belief was that Fraser for all practical purposes had made up his mind to resign on Saturday, March 6, 1971.

20 Fraser made this charge in an official statement, issued on March 8, 1971. I was one of the pressmen who got "premature" access to the

contents of the letter. In my case at least I got it from elsewhere than the Prime Minister's office.

21 Commonwealth Representatives' Daily Hansard, March 9, 1971, pp 679/684.
22 Commonwealth Representatives' Daily Hansard, March 9, 1971, pp 679/684.
23 There had been some turbulence on the Gazelle Peninsula because of a dispute between the administration and the Mantaungan Association, representing a section of the Tolai people, on land rights.
24 The Lodge is the Prime Minister's official residence in Canberra.
25 Commonwealth Representatives' Daily Hansard, March 9, 1971, pp 679/684.
26 Commonwealth Representatives' Daily Hansard, March 9, 1971, p 684.
27 Ibid., p 284.
28 The call to Fraser's home was made at about 8 pm, some three hours after Gorton had seen Daly.
29 Commonwealth Representatives' Daily Hansard, March 9, 1971, pp 684/687.
30 Commonwealth Representatives' Daily Hansard, March 9, 1971, p 687.
31 Broadcasting of Parliament that day on the ABC National network was from the House of Representatives.
32 Commonwealth Representatives' Daily Hansard, March 9, 1971, p 689.
33 Commonwealth Representatives' Daily Hansard, March 9, 1971, p 692.
34 Ibid., p 693.
35 *Sydney Morning Herald,* March 10, 1971.
36 Issued by Robinson, in Brisbane, March 9, 1971.
37 Official statement, issued by Liberal headquarters, Canberra, March 9, 1971.
38 From the author's notes, compiled on March 10 and March 11, 1971.
39 From the author's notes compiled on March 10 and March 11, 1971.
40 Gorton, interviewed by Alan Trengrove, *Sun-Pictorial,* March 13, 1971.
41 As late as Tuesday night, McMahon's advice to such of his friends among the antiGorton group as approached him was that Gorton "had the numbers" and that they should not push ahead with any antiGorton move because they would be unsuccessful and longterm would destroy themselves politically. The irony was that the man who was shortly to have the prime ministership virtually thrust upon him did not realise how close was his appointment with destiny.
42 From the author's notes compiled on March 10 and March 11, 1971.
43 From the author's notes, compiled on March 10 and March 11, 1971.
44 Commonwealth Representatives' Daily Hansard, March 10, 1971, p 759.
45 Gorton had asked for the Defence portfolio and had been given it by McMahon who believed that unless there were very serious factors acting to the contrary the Liberal Deputy Leader was entitled to the portfolio of his choice.

80, 412, 426; Australia-UK shipping, 174; appointed treasurer, 380-81, 394.

Butler, Clyde: 271.

Butler, Dr. David: 338.

Button, John: 251, 278n13.

Byrne, Con: 145, 161, 317n66.

C

Cairns, Dr. J. F.: Background and character, 98, 251; Defence attitudes, 98-9, 142, 154n29, 205, 246-8; relations with Whitlam, 105, 108-9, 247-8, 251-2; Immigration, 256; Finance, 339-40.

Cairns, Kevin: Clashes with Gorton, 198, 309-10, 364, 379, 397, 399, 442; background, 309; election campaign, 310, 336, 344, 349.

Calder, S. E.: 223, 346n25.

Calwell, Arthur Augustus: Resigns ALP leadership, 87, 99; Defence attitudes, 88, 97-8, 99, 142, 246, 341-2; background and character, 92-3; Leadership of ALP, 92-99, 161, 269; relations with Whitlam, 95-100; 112n41, 246-248, 249-51, 254, 341-2; Immigration, 255.

Cameron, Clyde: Background and character, 92, 246, 252; relations with Calwell, 92, 251; State-aid, 102, 249, 252, 260, 272-3; relations with Whitlam, 112n43, 252, 260, 387; A.W.U., 205-6, 252; theory on '69 elections, 324-5, 334, 346n14.

Cameron, Donald: 223, 344, 349, 364, 410.

Campbell, Enid: 210n57.

Carmody, —: 200.

Carrick, John: 72, 73, 75, 76, 230, 243n41, 345n2.

Casey, Lord: 71, 72, 82, 141.

Cathie, I.: 275.

Cavanagh, —: 203, 209n38.

Chalk, Gordon: 363.

Chalmers, Rob: 403.

Chamberlain, F. E. ("Joe"): Background and character, 95-6; relations with Whitlam, 95, 101, 107, 255, 276-7; Role of Labor, 96; Federal Executive, 98, 100; relations with Wyndham, 100, 258; State-aid, 249, 273-4; Federal Secretaryship election, 261-2.

Chaney, Fred: 41, 49n42, 50n47, 198, 223, 229.

Chifley, Joseph Benedict: 29, 39, 47n4, 85n25, 86, 90, 91, 133, 260, 281.

Chipp, Don: 31, 36-7, 49n35, 381.

Cohen, Sam (Q.C.): 101, 104-7, 259, 260, 269, 280n51.

Colbourne, W. R.: 260, 262.

Cole, George: 136, 137, 154n24.

Coppin, Ray: 211, 225.

Cormack, Sir Magnus: 172, 189, 198, 208n12, 354-5, 359, 366n12, 442.

Cotton, Robert: 228-9, 359, 366n22, 376, 381.

Courtnay, Frank: 107.

Cramer, Sir John: 311, 375-6, 442-43.

Crawford, George: 275, 387.

Crean, Frank: 99, 100.

Cremean, J. L.: 136.

Crisp, Professor L. F.: 63n6, 110n12, 111n18, 154n22, 331.

Crook, Mrs.: 214, 218, 225.

Crook, William: 211, 218, 219, 225, 234.

Cullen, Peter: 209n44.

Curtin, John: 86, 90, 97, 196, 260.

D

Daly, Fred: 82, 83, 99, 222-24, 254-5.

Daly, General Sir Thomas: 416, 418-25, 430-33.

Dalziel, Allan: 135.

Darling, Dr. Sir James: 48n30.

Darman, Jeffrey: 218, 234.

D'Avagour, George: 322.

Davidson, Kenneth: 183n20, 394, 415n1.

Davis, Kevin: 331.

Davison, Frank: 130n30.

Debre, —: 235.

Deer, A. F.: 122, 123.

Delacombe, Sir Rohan: 445n7.

Delamothe, Dr. Peter: 395.

Downer, Sir Alexander: 79, 166, 295, 317n45.

449

background and character, 71-2, 81, 84n13; Singapore-Malaysia, 144-5, 188, 290.
Hawke, R. J.: 266.
Hawkins, Max: 445n5.
Hayden, William: 274, 275.
Haylen, Les: 110n16.
Healy, D. W.: 289.
Henderson, Rupert: 237.
Henty, Denham: 37.
Hewitt, Sir Lennox: Background and character, 45-6, 119, 128n7; relations with Gorton, 45, 47, 50n54, 119, 226; Head of P.M.'s Department, 46-7, 230, 295, 382; Washington visit, 55-6; Esso-BHP agreement, 165, 356, 384-5; Australia-U.K. shipping, 173.
Hickling, Vice-Admiral Harold: 242n10.
Hills, Pat: 414.
Hoffmann, Gerard Charles: 200, 202, 203.
Hoffmann, Mary: 201, 202, 203.
Holding, Clyde: 271.
Holloway, Edward: 207n1.
Holt, Harold: Death, 9-10, 24, 27, 69; style of Government, 10, 12-13, 35, 42, 46, 69, 119, 125-6, 137, 170, 187, 196, 216, 296; Commonwealth-State relations, 13, 29-30, 77-8, 178; relations with DLP, 13, 65, 137, 140-41, 143; electoral style, 14, 31, 131-2, 137; political career, 17, 20, 44, 65, 119, 170-1; health, 24-6; discontent in Party, 25-6; Defence, 31-2, 137, 188, 283, 310; Parliamentary performance, 134, 187.
Holten, R. N.: 381.
Holyoake, Keith: 290.
Howson, Peter: Background and character, 35; VIP flights issue, 35, 44, 162; dropped from Ministry, 36, 49n31; Freeth speech, 311; criticism of Gorton, 386, 409, 411, 442; offshore legislation, 395-7; opposition within party, 399; Gorton-Fraser dispute, 429, 438, 442.

Hughes, Alan: 320, 345n3.
Hughes, Tom: 221, 222, 224, 242n23, 242n26, 242n29, 378, 381, 431.
Hughes, W. M.: 186, 212.
Hulme, Alan: 80, 352, 362-4, 427, 443.
Hunt, Ralph: 246, 336.

I

Ingleton, G. C.: 110n6, 110n8.
Irwin, Les: 26, 47n9, 200, 308-10, 378, 439, 440.

J

Jack, William: 85n25.
James, Bert: 206, 220-22, 253, 260.
James, Francis: 75.
Jarman, Alan: 440, 441.
Jefferson, Thomas: 353.
Jennings, F. W.: 55, 231.
Jess, John: Background and character, 36, 189; "Voyager" inquiry, 36, 216, 405; relations with Gorton, 189, 203-5, 378, 408-9, 442; "Hoffmann Affair", 204; preselection threat, 399; Gorton-Fraser dispute, 429, 438, 442.
Jessop, D. S.: 223.
Johnson, Frank: 110n6.
Johnson, Lyndon B.: 32, 36, 53, 56, 142, 211, 218.
Johnson, Percy: 250.
Jones, Andrew: 333-4, 346n38, 347n42.
Josey, Alex: 144.
Joshua, Robert: 135, 136, 154n21.

K

Kailis, Michael: 315.
Kane, John: 401.
Keefe, J. B. ("Jim"): 104-107, 260, 270, 274.
Kelly, C. R. ("Bert"): 381.
Kelly, Ned: 110n7.
Kennedy, Andrew David: 245.
Kennelly, P. T. ("Pat"): 107, 206, 251, 253, 260.
Keon, S. M.: 136.
Killen, D. J.: Background and character, 41, 49n46, 215; St John, 215-6; relations with Gorton, 221, 363-4, 381, 403.

451

452

454